Unit 9

Drug Prevention and Treatment

Four selections in this section discuss drug dependence and treatment. Topics covered include educational programs, live-in therapeutic communities, and integrating former drug abusers back into the community.

The concepts in bold italics are developed in the article. For further expansion please refer to the Topic Guide, the Index, and the Glossary.

Topic Guide

This topic guide suggests how the selections in this book relate to topics of traditional concern to students and professionals involved with the study of drugs, society, and behavior. It is useful for locating articles that relate to each other for reading and research. The guide is arranged alphabetically according to topic. Articles may, of course, treat topics that do not appear in the topic guide. In turn, entries in the topic guide do not necessarily constitute a comprehensive listing of all the contents of each selection.

TOPIC AREA	TREATED IN:	TOPIC AREA	TREATED IN:
Addiction	2. Getting Real About Getting High 3. Opium, Cocaine, and Marijuana 7. Addiction and Dependence 8. Hooked/Not Hooked 9. Drugs of Choice 10. Dirty Drug Secret 11. Nicotine Becomes Addictive 12. 'Monkey Model' of Addiction 14. Drugs and Free Will 15. Intoxicating Habits 16. Pleasurable Chemistry 17. Lure of Drugs 18. Complex Genetics of Alcoholism 21. Old, Weak, and a Loser 23. How and Why of a Cocaine High 29. Opiates 32. Innocent Victims 33. Alcohol and the Family 36. Advertising Addiction 49. Out in the Open 50. Changing World of Alcoholics Anonymous 51. R$_x$ for Addiction	Children/Teenagers	19. Temperance 20. Costly and Scarce, Marijuana Is a High More Are Rejecting 21. Old, Weak, and a Loser 22. "1990 National Household Survey on Drug Abuse" 27. Steroids and Sports 32. Innocent Victims 33. Alcohol and the Family 39. Crack Dealers' Rotten Lives
		Cigarettes	See Nicotine
		Cocaine	2. Getting Real About Getting High 3. Opium, Cocaine, and Marijuana 4. Coke Inc. 7. Addiction and Dependence 8. Hooked/Not Hooked 9. Drugs of Choice 10. Dirty Drug Secret 12. 'Monkey Model' of Addiction 22. "1990 National Household Survey on Drug Abuse" 23. How and Why of a Cocaine High 38. Men Who Created Crack 39. Crack Dealers' Rotten Lives
Advertising	36. Advertising Addiction 37. Teflon Coating of Cigarette Smoking 38. Men Who Created Crack		
		Crack	4. Coke Inc. 7. Addiction and Dependence 9. Drugs of Choice 10. Dirty Drug Secret 21. Old, Weak, and a Loser 23. How and Why of a Cocaine High 38. Men Who Created Crack 39. Crack Dealers' Rotten Lives
Alcohol	1. Drugs 'R' Us 5. Interview With James Schaefer 6. War on (Some) Drugs 15. Intoxicating Habits 18. Complex Genetics of Alcoholism 19. Temperance 22. "1990 National Household Survey on Drug Abuse" 30. Alcohol 33. Alcohol and the Family 36. Advertising Addiction 49. Out in the Open 50. Changing World of Alcoholics Anonymous		
		Decriminalization	See Legalization
		Epidemiology	3. Opium, Cocaine, and Marijuana 10. Dirty Drug Secret 19. Temperance 20. Costly and Scarce, Marijuana Is a High More Are Rejecting 21. Old, Weak, and a Loser 22. "1990 National Household Survey on Drug Abuse"
Amphetamine	22. "1990 National Household Survey on Drug Abuse" 26. Zing! Speed		
Biological Factors	7. Addiction and Dependence 8. Hooked/Not Hooked 9. Drugs of Choice 11. Nicotine Becomes Addictive 12. 'Monkey Model' of Addiction 13. High Times in the Wild Kingdom 14. Drugs and Free Will 15. Intoxicating Habits 16. Pleasurable Chemistry 18. Complex Genetics of Alcoholism 23. How and Why of a Cocaine High 29. Opiates 30. Alcohol 32. Innocent Victims	Etiology	8. Hooked/Not Hooked 9. Drugs of Choice 11. Nicotine Becomes Addictive 12. 'Monkey Model' of Addiction 13. High Times in the Wild Kingdom 14. Drugs and Free Will 15. Intoxicating Habits 16. Pleasurable Chemistry 17. Lure of Drugs 18. Complex Genetics of Alcoholism 23. How and Why of a Cocaine High
		Family	32. Innocent Victims 33. Alcohol and the Family
Caffeine	35. Is Coffee Harmful?		

TOPIC AREA	TREATED IN:	TOPIC AREA	TREATED IN:
Fighting the Drug War	1. Drugs 'R' Us 2. Getting Real About Getting High 3. Opium, Cocaine, and Marijuana 4. Coke Inc. 6. War on (Some) Drugs 39. Crack Dealers' Rotten Lives 42. How to Win the War Against Drugs 43. Drug War Is Killing Us 44. Just Say Whoa! 45. Legally Bombed 46. Drug Policy 47. Dutch Model	**Marijuana (cont'd)**	20. Costly and Scarce, Marijuana Is a High More Are Rejecting 22. "1990 National Household Survey on Drug Abuse" 25. Marijuana
		Nicotine	1. Drugs 'R' Us 2. Getting Real About Getting High 9. Drugs of Choice 11. Nicotine Becomes Addictive 22. "1990 National Household Survey on Drug Abuse" 34. How Smoking Kills You 37. Teflon Coating of Cigarette Smoking
Heroin	2. Getting Real About Getting High 3. Opium, Cocaine, and Marijuana 4. Coke Inc. 6. War on (Some) Drugs 7. Addiction and Dependence 8. Hooked/Not Hooked 9. Drugs of Choice 12. 'Monkey Model' of Addiction 14. Drugs and Free Will 16. Pleasurable Chemistry 22. "1990 National Household Survey on Drug Abuse" 40. Perilous Swim in Heroin's Stream	**Race, Drug Use and**	3. Opium, Cocaine, and Marijuana 5. Interview With James Schaefer 21. Old, Weak, and a Loser 22. "1990 National Household Survey on Drug Abuse" 38. Men Who Created Crack 39. Crack Dealer's Rotten Lives
		Research, Drug	5. Interview With James Schaefer 7. Addiction and Dependence 8. Hooked/Not Hooked 9. Drugs of Choice 11. Nicotine Becomes Addictive 12. 'Monkey Model' of Addiction 13. High in the Wild Kingdom 14. Drugs and Free Will 15. Intoxicating Habits 18. Complex Genetics of Alcoholism 22. "1990 National Household Survey on Drug Abuse" 23. How and Why of a Cocaine High 25. Marijuana 28. Good Drugs, Bad Effects 33. Alcohol and the Family
History of Drug Use	1. Drugs 'R' Us 2. Getting Real About Getting High 3. Opium, Cocaine, and Marijuana 6. War on (Some) Drugs 11. Nicotine Becomes Addictive 19. Temperance 20. Costly and Scarce, Marijuana Is a High More Are Rejecting 21. Old, Weak, and a Loser 22. "1990 National Household Survey on Drug Abuse" 38. Men Who Created Crack		
Law Enforcement	1. Drugs 'R' Us 2. Getting Real About Getting High 3. Opium, Cocaine, and Marijuana 4. Coke Inc. 5. Interview With James Schaefer 6. War on (Some) Drugs 20. Costly and Scarce, Marijuana Is a High More Are Rejecting 21. Old, Weak, and a Loser 38. Men Who Created Crack 39. Crack Dealers' Rotten Lives 40. Perilous Swim in Heroin's Stream 42. How to Win the War Against Drugs 43. Drug War Is Killing Us 44. Just Say Whoa! 45. Legally Bombed 46. Drug Policy 47. Dutch Model	**Socioeconomic Issues**	1. Drugs 'R' Us 2. Getting Real About Getting High 3. Opium, Cocaine, and Marijuana 21. Old, Weak and a Loser 22. "1990 National Household Survey on Drug Abuse" 32. Innocent Victims 36. Advertising Addiction 37. Teflon Coating of Cigarette Smoking 38. Men Who Created Crack 39. Crack Dealers' Rotten Lives 41. Why Drugs Cost More in U.S.
		Treatment, Drug	5. Interview With James Schaefer 8. Hooked/Not Hooked 12. 'Monkey Model' of Addiction 14. Drugs and Free Will 15. Intoxicating Habits 17. Lure of Drugs 24. Prozac Backlash 28. Good Drugs, Bad Effects 32. Innocent Victims 33. Alcohol and the Family 41. Why Drugs Cost More in U.S. 48. In Making Drug Strategy, No Accord on Treatment 49. Out in the Open 50. Changing World of Alcoholics Anonymous 51. Rx for Addiction
Legalization	43. Drug War Is Killing Us 44. Just Say Whoa! 45. Legally Bombed 47. Dutch Model		
Marijuana	1. Drugs 'R' Us 3. Opium, Cocaine, and Marijuana 7. Addiction and Dependence 19. Temperance		

Thinking About Drugs

Everything that exists can be looked at or thought about in a variety of ways, through the lens of different perspectives. Although each perspective tells us something different about what we are looking at, some are more relevant and insightful than others. The phenomena of drug use and abuse follow this rule. Some perspectives toward drugs tell us a great deal about their reality; others tell us little beyond the biases of the observers using them.

How should we think about drug use? What perspectives tell us about the reality of drugs? The first thing we should know about drugs is that they encompass an extremely wide range of substances. Ask the man and woman in the street what "drugs" are and, in all likelihood, most of the answers you get will include illegal substances—crack, cocaine, heroin, perhaps LSD, marijuana, and PCP or "angel dust." Answers you will be less likely to receive will be the legal drugs—alcohol, tobacco, our morning cup of coffee, prescription drugs, and routinely available over-the-counter (OTC) medications, such as aspirin. But in at least two respects, legal substances such as alcohol, Valium, and aspirin are drugs in the same way as illegal substance such as LSD, heroin, and crack are. First, all but the OTC drugs are *psychoactive*, that is, mind-active; they influence the workings of the human mind—how we think, feel, and even act; and even the over-the-counter drugs are active in some other way—at the very least, they influence the workings of the human body. A second parallel is that both legal and illegal drugs are often overused, misused, and abused, thereby causing a great deal of damage to human life and to society generally. In fact, legal drugs—cigarettes and alcohol specifically—kill 20 to 30 times as many people as illegal drugs. Clearly, the distinction between legal and illegal drugs is an artificial, humanly created one, not extremely crucial in most respects to the student of drug use. "Drugs 'R' Us" and "The War on (Some) Drugs" emphasize the fuzziness of the line between legal and illegal drugs and the damage that the use and abuse of legal drugs cause to our society.

The second lesson any meaningful approach imparts to us is that there is a great deal of widely disseminated misinformation about drug use; much of what most of the public believes about the subject is wrong. We tend to exaggerate the dangers of illegal drug use and minimize the dangers of legal drug use. In "Getting Real About Getting High," physician and author Andrew Weil argues that drugs per se are not the problem—it is the way in which they are used. Drugs should be taken responsibly, in their natural forms, in moderation, for the purpose of conscious expansion. Regardless of whether or not you agree with this thesis, it is provocative and controversial.

The third important conclusion we have to draw from a careful look at the phenomenon is that drug use and abuse are not confined to the twentieth century. Drug abuse is an ancient problem; humans have been ingesting psychoactive substances since the Stone Age—and possibly longer—over 10,000 or 12,000 years ago, when alcohol was first discovered. In the United States, alcohol was consumed in vastly greater quantities in the late 1700s and early 1800s than it is today, and in the second half of the nineteenth century, addiction to narcotics, such as morphine and opium, was far more common, on a per-population basis, than heroin addiction is today. Problems associated with drug abuse and abuse have always, and, in all likelihood, will always, be with us. "Opium, Cocaine and Marijuana in American History" provides a detailed discussion of late nineteenth century and early twentieth century drug use—quite a different picture than what most of us think.

The fourth lesson we learn from looking at drugs is that illegal drug use generates an immense network of social relations that exert a powerful influence worldwide. The base on which this network rests is the purchase and use of illegal substances by the consumer. The drug problem will not go away until people stop using drugs; it is futile to denounce drug dealers when the demand—and the profits—are so huge. "Coke Inc." discusses the size,

appeal, and the impact of the global drug trade for powdered cocaine, crack, and heroin.

The fifth lesson any meaningful approach imparts to us is that drug use is a sociological, psychological, and even anthropological phenomenon; that is, it is generated and sustained by the people interacting in a specific setting and their customs and social networks. While drug use may be universal, or nearly so, the specific qualities it possesses in a particular community or society are dependent on the characteristics of the users themselves, that community, and that society. Too often, drug use and abuse are looked upon as a simple pathology—a sickness—in need of removal. Given this limited perspective, we will never be able to understand what sustains them, what they grow from. When we begin asking who uses drugs and in what social situations and contexts, we begin to understand why they are so difficult to eradicate and what part they play to users and abusers. The interview with James Schaefer stresses this sociological and anthropological side of the use of one drug, alcohol.

Looking Ahead: Challenge Questions

What is a drug? How are psychoactive drugs different from drugs that only influence the workings of the human body? From the point of view of a drug's effects, is it meaningful to distinguish between legal and illegal drugs? Why are certain legal psychoactive substances not widely regarded as drugs?

Why is a study of drug use and law enforcement in the past important? Does it tell us something important about the current drug scene? Why have the lessons of history been lost on the present generation?

How would you go about studying drug use? What issues and questions are important to you?

Why do drugs, drug use, and drug sales make such a powerful impact on our society?

Is it possible to use drugs reasonably and sensibly, in moderation, as Dr. Andrew Weil suggests?

DRUGS 'R' US

Daniel Lazare

Judging from what one hears in Washington these days, there are two theories as to why people use drugs. One is the Republican theory, advanced most vehemently by drug czar William Bennett, that people indulge in heroin, cocaine and the like because law and order has broken down, and families, churches and schools are disintegrating. The other is the Democratic theory, which holds that people do drugs because they're poor, downtrodden and longing for escape. "Up with hope, down with dope," says Jesse Jackson, appearing to imply that once social conditions are ameliorated, the drug problem will vanish like a puff of smoke.

But rarely are things so simple. While racism and poverty help explain why some Americans resort to ultra-potent substances like crack, they're hardly the whole story. Throughout history people have resorted to various mind-altering substances, from beer to peyote, for reasons that are as varied as human experience itself. They've taken drugs to get closer to God or to heighten their experiences here on Earth; to sharpen their senses or anesthetize their brains; to blend in with the crowd or to distinguish themselves from the pack.

During the '20s, middle-class kids drank bathtub gin to show their contempt for the repressive, puritanical America of Calvin Coolidge. Forty years later, they demonstrated revulsion for American consumerism by turning their nose up at booze and puffing away happily on pot. In the '70s, yuppies snorted coke because it seemed to go with the quickening pace on Wall Street, while, more recently, aspiring arbitrageurs have downed gallons of black coffee in imitation of caffeine-junkie Ivan Boesky.

Thus, the question of intoxication turns out to be as complex as sex, death, money or other fundamental aspects of the human condition. One generation's meat quite frequently turns out to be another's poison. The only constant is that most people do something to alter their conscious state. While Mormons eschew all mind-altering substances right down to coffee, tea and chocolate, they and people like them are a distinct minority.

What's your drug? In fact, all of us may be hooked in one way or another, teetotalers included, whether we know it or not. Since the '70s, medical researchers have zeroed in on a group of internally generated mood-control agents known as endogenous morphines, or endorphins, that are believed to play a key role in determining whether we're anxious or relaxed, unable to concentrate or immersed in thought.

Ironically, endorphins are chemically related to forbidden exogenous opiates such as opium, morphine and heroin, and produce a similar psychological state—a sense of bliss, floating and transcendence of ego.

For centuries, people who have spoken of "losing" themselves in their work, of shutting out the world while they concentrate on an intellectual problem, may actually have describing a heightened mental state brought on by an internally generated drug. They may not be so much devoted to their profession as devoted to a chemical high that scientists now believe may be brought on by hard work or vigorous physical exercise.

Committed joggers, of course, are so devoted to their daily "runner's high" that many injure themselves through over-training. When ordered by a doctor to stop, they may often display such classic symptoms of withdrawal as irritability, nervousness and loss of concentration.

When doctors speak of being addicted to their work, according to *Messengers of Paradise: Opiates and the Brain,* an interesting new book by Charles F. Levinthal, they may mean it quite literally. One surgeon interviewed as part of a 1975 study said operating was "like taking narcotics." Another compared it to heroin. A third confessed that he never felt under more stress than when he was vacationing with his family in the Bahamas. A fourth said he was so nervous after two days of sight-seeing in Mexico—the first vacation for him and his wife in years—that he volunteered his services to a local hospital and spent the rest of his vacation in surgery.

Surgeons are not the only ones who describe work in such terms. A world-class chess master quoted by Levinthal said that whenever he sits down to a game, "Time passes a hundred times faster . . . it resembles a dream state. A whole story can unfold in seconds, it seems." In his 1934 novel, *The Search,* C. P. Snow described the ecstasy of scientific discovery in terms bordering on the hallucinatory: "It was as though I had looked for a truth outside myself, and finding it had become for a moment a part of the truth I sought; as though all the world, the atoms and the stars, were wonderfully clear and close to me, and I to them. . . ." This may have been literary hyperbole—or an accurate description of a scientist who has made the breakthrough of a lifetime and is soaring on opiates as a result.

Whatever their political or moral value, hard work and self-discipline may also be routes to self-medication. Similarly, those dependent on outside sources to satisfy their

opiate craving may never have learned to generate their own. Conventional solutions to the "problem" of addiction frequently make it worse. By throwing exogenous-opiate junkies in jail or depriving them of employment—one goal of militant organizations like Partnership for a Drug-Free America—they likely will remain locked in their exogenous addiction and will never be able to produce their own drugs in ways that society deems legitimate.

Alcohol—the legal high: If opiates, internal or external, are the most common mind-altering substances, then alcohol is a close second. We celebrate anniversaries with champagne, the end of the work day with beer and a good meal with wine. In 1954, the French government estimated that a third of the electorate derived all or part of its income from the production or sale of alcoholic beverages, while in Italy a few years later an estimated 10 percent of arable land was said to be given over to viticulture.

According to archaeologists, beer-making is as old as agriculture; in neolithic times, it was probably the only method of preserving the nutritive value of grain. Since then, alcohol has been brewed from just about every conceivable fruit or vegetable—mead from honey, sake from rice, wine from palm, mezcal and Central American pulque from agave and cactus. North American Indians even made a liquor from maple syrup, while South American Indians made one from various jungle fruits.

According to the Book of Genesis, grape wine was discovered by Noah, who promptly got drunk and threw off all his clothes, presumably in celebration. Approximately 1,000 years later, the Book of Proverbs advised: "Give strong drink to him who is perishing, and wine to those in bitter distress; let them drink and forget their poverty, and remember their misery no more"—a reminder that seeking escape from oppressive social conditions through intoxication is not necessarily a cardinal sin.

Why is alcohol so popular? For one thing, users have learned to savor the taste of beer, wine, cognac, eau de vie and so on that goes with inebriation. For another, it is a source of nutrients, goes well with food and, as a common agricultural byproduct, is all but unavoidable in a wide range of cultures. It is also a highly sociable drug that a vast range of societies have used to bring people together to laugh, talk, sing, dance and worship (e.g. the Passover seder, in which inebriation is a *mitzvah* or commandment).

Finally, alcohol has the advantage of being highly modulatory. Whether at a party or dinner, experienced users know how much to drink in order to attain an appropriate level of intoxication. They may happily gulp down one and another, but then wait until their mind has settled a bit before venturing on to a third. At a business gathering, they may decide not to drink at all.

Of course, alcohol has its dark side—18 million problem drinkers in the U.S. alone, 23,000 alcohol-related traffic deaths per year, tens of thousands of work-related injuries—but it also has benefits that are frequently overlooked. While everyone knows of marriages destroyed by alcohol, how about the marriages it helps save? Who speaks up for the worker who, after a hard day, fortifies him or herself with a drink or two before facing up to the rigors at home?

Whereas feudal peasants worked to exhaustion and then, on feast days, drank to collapse, industrial man uses alcohol in smaller amounts to fine-tune the means of production—himself. After working eight hours, he uses it as a reward and relaxant. Would the same worker be more productive if he didn't settle himself down with a beer, but instead fidgeted nervously in front of the TV or yelled at the kids? Perhaps. But considering that periods of peak economic growth have sometimes coincided with periods of peak alcohol consumption (e.g. the U.S. in the '50s), the answer, very possibly, is that productivity would not be enhanced.

By the same token, despite a pronounced shift since the '70s from hard liquor to white wine, low-alcohol beer and the ubiquitous Perrier-with-a-twist, industrial productivity has been stagnant. Americans are drinking less, but not working better as a result.

Dying for a smoke: Then there is nicotine, a mood-control agent whose popularity worldwide is only slightly less than that of alcohol. Beginning in 1493, when Columbus returned from the New World with an interesting new plant called tobacco, nicotine's progress has, until recent years, been unchecked. Users were executed in 17th-Century Russia, while Bavaria, Saxony and Zurich decreed bans. Whenever Sultan Murad IV traveled around the Ottoman Empire during this period, he delighted in executing his subjects for the heinous offense of lighting up. "Even on the battlefield . . . he would punish them by beheading, hanging, quartering or crushing their hands or feet," according to one account.

Nevertheless, the popular will has prevailed. When the director general of New Amsterdam tried to impose a smoking ban in 1639, virtually the entire male population camped outside his office in protest. While fond of wine, Thomas Jefferson inveighed against tobacco (which he called "productive of infinite wretchedness"), yet after the revolution it emerged as a major cash crop.

Besides being useful as a fumigant, nicotine has a mild calming effect that can be used to promote sociability, which is why it quickly became a fixture in coffee houses and taverns. Rip Van Winkle, everybody's favorite peaceful layabout, was, according to his creator, Washington Irving, never to be seen without his hunting rifle, his dog and his pipe. Gen. Douglas MacArthur smoked a corncob pipe, a homely touch that was immediately picked up by the press, while college men in the '50s favored briars because it gave them the firm-jawed look appropriate to the American Century.

Since then, however, nicotine in general, and cigarettes in particular, have been under sustained assault. Smokers nowadays are segregated in restaurants, barred from lighting up on airplanes, shunned by co-workers and harassed by friends. Yuppies pollute the air with their BMWs, but nonetheless are aghast at the thought of soiling their lungs with so much as a whiff of someone else's "sidestream" smoke. Yet, in a certain roundabout sense, we owe a debt of

For centuries, people who have spoken of losing themselves in their work or shutting out the world may have been describing an elevated state brought on by an internally generated drug.

gratitude to nicotine for helping to show how to run a proper anti-drug campaign. Smokers are encouraged by an array of government subsidies, but millions of nicotine addicts have been persuaded to quit through means that stop somewhat short of driving them into the arms of Uzi-toting drug dealers.

Rather than driving users underground, the anti-smoking forces have mounted a nonstop propaganda campaign that has proved devastatingly effective simply because it is true. Outside the tobacco lobby, few people doubt that cigarettes cause lung cancer and are a prime contributor to heart and respiratory diseases causing hundreds of thousands of deaths in the U.S. each year. The credible campaign appeals to people's self-interest, rather than bludgeoning them into obedience.

Meanwhile, amid all the hysteria over crack, no one seems to notice the growing amount of tobacco advertising pitched directly at the inner-urban market. Faced with declining sales, cigarette manufacturers have tried to recoup by appealing to blacks and Hispanics, a strategy as devastating in terms of health and mortality as the efforts of the Medellin and Cali cartels. Yet, if affluence and education rise, it seems reasonable to presume that nicotine addiction will decline in these areas as well.

Reefer madness: On the other hand, probably no drug has been the subject of more lies than marijuana. The 1936 propaganda film *Reefer Madness* is valuable both as a camp classic and a window onto the obsessions of a middle-class society then terrified of sex, jazz and "letting go." Although American society seemed to be coming to its senses in the '70s, when marijuana came within a hair's breadth of decriminalization, it has since beaten a hasty retreat behind a curtain of disinformation and lies.

Due to the war on drugs, marijuana is back as an official "gateway" drug leading inexorably, according to official dogma, to cocaine, heroin and a lifetime of addiction. Yet millions of students have used marijuana since the '60s with no noticeable ill-effect. Millions of adults with kids, jobs and mortgages relax occasionally with a joint without winding up in the gutter. But simple facts like these mean little to a Republican-Democratic establishment hopelessly hooked on rhetoric and revenge.

The curious thing about marijuana, though, is that just as its evils have been vastly inflated by the government, its virtues have probably been exaggerated by supporters as well. In Holland, where marijuana is decriminalized, surveys indicate that a smaller percentage of people smoke than in the U.S. In India and the Caribbean, where marijuana is ubiquitous, those with the economic means prefer booze. Steve Hagar, editor of *High Times* magazine, the pot-smoker's bible, tells of an American traveler who, when offered palm wine in an African village, asked for some potent local herb instead. The villagers were puzzled: why would anyone prefer something as lowly as marijuana to a delicacy like palm wine?

Why indeed? If drug prohibition were lifted, marijuana would undoubtedly find a niche in American society, but probably not much more. Laborers, taxi drivers and construction workers might find it useful in relieving boredom, but others might find that its hypnotic quality makes them feel groggy. Some might prefer it on weekends, while others might find that its effects are not very sociable. It makes many people quiet and withdrawn, which is why the noise level at a party usually drops whenever joints begin circulating. People opposed to noisy parties on principle might appreciate marijuana for precisely that reason. But judging from the experience in Holland, where marijuana is neither stigmatized by the government nor glamorized by the underground, a majority, arguably, would not.

Just say yes: Given the multiplicity of drugs and uses, what is one to make of a slogan like "Just Say No," endorsed by nearly the entire political spectrum, from Jesse Jackson to Jesse Helms? What's most apparent about the slogan is its arbitrariness. It does not ask Americans to forgo all mind-altering substances, obviously, since drugs like caffeine, nicotine or highly addictive Valium are still freely available.

It does not ask them to steer clear of only the most dangerous since, in terms of sheer bodies, alcohol and nicotine kill approximately 150 Americans for every one who succumbs to the effects of heroin, coke or other prohibited substances. (According to the National Council on Alcoholism, alcohol and tobacco were implicated in more than half a million deaths in 1985, while illicit substances were found to be factors in only 3,562.) Banning one without the other is like banning deer rifles while permitting sales of automatic weapons to go forward unimpeded.

Rather, the purpose of the "Just Say No" campaign is to shore up political authority. Using the circular logic favored by authoritarian governments, the campaign asks Americans to forgo those substances that have been prohibited not for reasons of health but for reasons of custom and politics. It urges them to just say no for no other reason than that their leaders have just said no.

The results may be unreasonable, but that's exactly the point. Right-wing authoritarianism is, in the final analysis, irrationality by decree. Those on top seek to limit debate not because it's disruptive but because it may lead to something more intelligent and democratic, and thereby upset their rule. Similarly, if drug czar William Bennett succeeds in enforcing unthinking drug obedience, he and other conservative hardliners no doubt will try to achieve it in other areas as well, such as abortion rights, collective bargaining, race relations and foreign policy.

The goal is mass cerebral anesthetization, more complete than that achieved by any drug.

GETTING REAL ABOUT GETTING HIGH

An Interview with Andrew Weil, M.D.

BY RICHARD GOLDSTEIN

The current war on drugs is taking its toll on knowledge about drugs. There has been no debate about the assumptions that underlie our laws, or about the reasons so many people—young and old, rich and poor—choose to break them. If anything, the antidrug crusade has had, as its aim, the elimination of discussion and dissent.

In 1983, Andrew Weil, a drug researcher, and Winifred Rosen, a writer of books for young people, published *Chocolate to Morphine: Understanding Mind-Active Drugs* (Houghton Mifflin). It is a remarkably revealing book, even for adults; but its language and contention that "drugs are here to stay" are clearly aimed at teenagers. Teaching adolescents who want to use drugs how to do so with the least damage to self and society is controversial in liberal times, but in the current climate, that idea seems, to some, impermissible.

Paula Hawkins (Republican, Florida), who faces a tough battle for her Senate seat, recently read selections from Weil's book into the Congressional Record. "With drug abuse running rampant," she proclaimed, "we may well ask ourselves why it is that our children are being exposed to such garbage. . . . I would recommend that all curricula be redirected to teach our children to say no to drugs. No more teaching about responsible use." As a result of Hawkins's objections, the Tampa school board voted to remove *From Chocolate to Morphine* from school library shelves. Does the senator support that decision? "Her statement speaks to the point," an aide replied—and declined to say more.

Andrew Weil is a lecturer at the University of Arizona College of Medicine. He has written several books on drugs and consciousness, including *The Natural Mind* (Houghton Miflin). "The truth about drugs cannot do harm," Weil writes. "It may offend sensibilities and disturb those who do not want to hear it, but it cannot hurt people. On the other hand, false information can and does lead people to hurt themselves and others. . . . People make decisions on the basis of the information available to them. The more accurate the information, the better their decisions will be."

What's going on now?

Well, I think there's a politically motivated drug panic which is more severe than anything I've seen in the 20 years I've been involved in this issue. Some of it is because the elections are approaching. Some of it is to divert people's attention from issues that are more serious. Some of it is generated by the news media, which have learned that fearmongering sells programs and papers.

But the media are always titillating, and there are always serious problems that people are trying to hide. Why didn't this happen 10 years ago?

It *was* happening 10 years ago, but not in as extreme a form. I think it is the same stuff that's gone on for most of the century. There was an anti-opium paranoia in this culture 80 years ago, a lot of it motivated by racial prejudice against the Chinese. There was an anticocaine hysteria around the time of the First World War, which was motivated by racial prejudice against blacks. There was marijuana stuff going on in the '20s and '30s, and all the '60s stuff around psychedelics, which produced tremendous polarization of society. Whenever a new intoxicant comes into a culture, it invokes this kind of response. Usually, the people who take up a new intoxicant are going to be the deviants—the subcultures and ethnic minorities and outsiders; they're perceived with suspicion already and their drug use is colored by that. There was an antitobacco hysteria in Europe and Asia in the 16th and 17th centuries, when some countries tried to prohibit its use by the death penalty. That didn't work; in fact, if anything, it hastened the spread of it.

Are drugs more prevalent in America today?

Well, no, I think we've always been a drug-ridden society. There probably were as many psychoactive drugs in use 100 years ago. But there was no crime associated with drugs. There was no use of these things by very young children. There was no use of them to drop out of society or act out anger or aggression against authority. I think all of those features of the drug problem are creations of our policies. The more we create stiffer penalities and so forth, the more we produce the very thing we want to change. As I say, the policies that we've followed have created the phenomena that we're afraid of. The reason we have kids using crack today is because of the approach we've taken in trying to deal with this through criminal law. It has made drugs attractive and it has made worse forms of drugs come into existence.

Do you anticipate that the result of this hysteria will be that drugs become more prevalent?

Yeah, I think that they will continue to be prevalent and to be used in worse and worse ways. By more and more people. Wars on drugs never work. The end result of them is to stimulate interest and curiosity on the part of people who other-

From *The Village Voice*, September 30, 1986, pp. 21-22, 24. Reprinted by permission of the author and *The Village Voice*.

1. THINKING ABOUT DRUGS

wise wouldn't be interested in them. It also, I think, encourages the drug taking in negative ways: To act out anger and resentment against authority. Especially when information is presented in a hypocritical manner as this society is now doing. In other words, we have this bill called the Drug Free America Act, but there's no intention to include alcohol and tobacco. The government continues to subsidize tobacco addiction, and cigarettes are the worst form of drug abuse in this culture, the greatest public health problem that we have, and the most flagrant example of drug pushing, since most of it is pushed on teenagers, who are lured by advertising into thinking it's cool to smoke. If you want to talk about death penalties for drug pushers start with the executives of tobacco companies.

But the argument against illegal drugs is that they produce violent, antisocial behavior.

Look, maybe there's, at the outside, something like 300 deaths from crack a year. That's not good, but how many deaths are there from cigarettes a year? Something like 300,000. How many instances are there where somebody on crack has committed an act of violence? I don't know. But compared to the number of acts of violence committed under the influence of alcohol, it's insignificant.

Are you suggesting that consumption of alcohol is more dangerous than consumption of crack?

In terms of its pharmacological power, the behavior it produces, and the numbers of people involved in its use.

Would that be true of angel dust?

It's true of all of them. I think there is no illegal drug that comes near alcohol in dangerousness. All you have to do is ask law enforcement agencies about the association of alcohol and violent crime.

What is the pharmacology of crack? How dangerous is it?

I think its dangers are exaggerated. I don't think it's a good drug; I don't think it's wise to smoke cocaine, first of all. If you want to explore its effects, you should chew coca leaves; I think that's a safe way to do it. It's not good to take cocaine out of coca leaves and it's especially not good to put it into your brain by smoking.

Why is it relatively safe to take coca leaves?

Because the content of cocaine is very low, so you're taking it in a highly dilute form, combined with other substances that moderate its effects, and when you chew coca leaves the cocaine that's there

gets into your bloodstream and brain very slowly. So it's not just what the drug is, or the dose, but the manner in which you introduce it into the body. There's an enormous difference between chewing a coca leaf and letting a small amount of cocaine diffuse slowly into the bloodstream, and smoking cocaine and having it rapidly rise in concentration and enter into the brain. That's why tobacco—cigarettes—is the most addictive drug known: Because nicotine is a very strong drug, stronger than cocaine in terms of its effects. And that manner of introducing it into the brain enhances addictiveness. So when you smoke cocaine, that's the most extreme way to experience its pharmacological effects; that's a stupid way to take it. But our policies have made coca leaves disappear from the market, because they're bulky and nobody wants to smuggle them, and we have created a situation in which it's profitable to smuggle this isolated, refined drug. And also to find ways of using a drug to get the maximum pharmacological power out of it.

What you're suggesting is that if there were a more open environment for drug use, people would, as a consequence of having more choice, choose substances that are better for them.

Might. Especially if they were educated. I'm not just arguing for a more open situation; I think it has to go hand in hand with real drug education. What passes for that today seems like thinly disguised attempts to steer people away from the drugs we don't like by exaggerating their dangers, while not paying attention to the drugs that we do like. And I think that leaves our culture very uneducated about the benefits and risks of psychoactive substances.

So let's talk about an alternative way of educating young people about drugs.

I think the alternative is first of all to be objective about all drugs. I mean, there's nothing that sets alcohol, tobacco, and caffeine apart from crack, marijuana, and PCP. I think grade school students should start to learn about the nature of addiction. It's not just a drug problem: people get addicted to sex, food, athletics. Most people get caught up in addictive behavior. And you need teaching about that as well. I think there are two basic strategies: one is to teach people to satisfy their needs without using drugs at all. I'm very much in favor of that, and it's something I try to practice in my own life. But realistically a lot of people are going to use drugs because they take you where you want to go with no work. And I think it is important to encourage those people to use drugs sensibly. And that's the issue that just drives these Reaganites up the wall. You're talking about responsible drug use.

Why is there such a consensus on this issue, as opposed to, say, pornography—another form of pleasure-taking that's said to produce antisocial behavior.

All I can say is that if you look around the world at different societies, you see the need to divide behavior in this area into good and evil. In every society you see the same pattern: A small number of drugs are encouraged and defined as being good, and the rest are banned as being evil.

What is it about drugs that distinguish them from other forms of pleasure? Is it their capacity to alter consciousness?

I think that's the root of it, and I think it's that they are so powerful.

Does what's really going on have to do with the desire to regulate consciousness?

That's possible. I have written in other books that nondrug methods of altering consciousness often bring on the same kind of response.

There seems to be a desire to track transcendence toward the religious passions. Even toward militaristic ones. And there are more and more ceremonies that have to do with patriotism, sports—ceremonies of muscularity—but these are public highs. Maybe there's a connection between this tendency and the repression of drugs, which are, in this society anyway, a private and individual experience.

That is possible.

How does it feel to be singled out by a U.S. senator? Are you apprehensive about articulating your ideas in public now?

Well, I think that the hysterical mood that I've seen, this kind of legislative-feeding frenzy, and the fact that I don't see people standing up to be counted on the other side, makes me feel that this is really not the time to debate the Reaganites in public. I just don't want to draw that kind of heat.

Are you in a tenured position?

No, I'm not, and obviously, life can be made difficult in that area. The thing is that this is all past work of mine. My current work is in alternative medicine; I have a medical practice, my research on medicinal plants. I'm not actively doing this drug stuff any more.

So you're tempted to retreat.

Yeah, but I've put it all out there. Over the past few weeks, when I've been asked to be on TV and radio shows, I've turned them down and told them that they can go read the book.

How do you know that your information about the effects of drugs is accurate? You yourself talk about the highly subjective nature of these substances.

I know it both, first of all, from my own experience with them and, secondly, from having studied them from many different perspectives. I've studied drugs from the point of view of botany and medicine and psychology and psychiatry and sociology and politics, as well as having worked and lived in many different countries around the world, looking at these same issues. So I think that, more than most people, I don't adhere to any one frame of reference.

Let's define the terms set and setting.

Set is expectation of what a drug will do, both conscious and unconscious, and *setting* is the environment in which the drug is used, both the physical environment and cultural environment. And those factors are major determinants of drug effect, at least as important as pharmacology. So I don't see anything intrinsic about, say, PCP that makes people violent. I think it is likely to do that in certain sets and settings. The majority of people who use PCP are prone to violence and often take that drug out of anger and frustration—to get messed up. In that context, it's very likely to cause violent behavior.

Let's design a curriculum for high school students that would be realistic about drugs. How would you approach that?

First, so that people have a sense of how set and setting modify the effects of drugs. And then you could talk about problem sets and settings: The idea of taking drugs to get out of bad moods, for example, or taking drugs when you're bored, as opposed to using them for positive reasons. For example, many people use drugs as an excuse for social interaction, as we do with coffee. Many people have used drugs for religious experience. I would look at traditional people who use hallucinogenic plants in that way. And I would try to encourage people to find nondrug methods of satisfying their needs. I think that's very legitimate.

In your book you talk about forming a relationship with a drug. How would you define a bad relationship?

Addiction is one example. Unconscious use of a drug—that is, not knowing what

> *I don't think it's wise to smoke cocaine. If you want to explore its effects, you should chew coca leaves.*

it is or not knowing that you're using a drug. Using it so frequently that you're impairing your health or your social or economic functioning. Using it so frequently that it's lost a desired effect.

So, for example, you would encourage people to use marijuana less frequently because being sparing about it enhances the effect.

Right. And losing the effect is a step on the way to using it addictively.

To enhance the effects of drugs, what general suggestions do you have?

I think, first, a very important one: that less is more.

What would be a good relationship with heroin, if it's possible?

I think probably it would be best to use it in the form of opium and to take opium by mouth rather than to smoke it or inject one of its derivatives.

What would you teach a teenager about heroin?

That the addictive potential of it is very great, that the physical harmfulness is not, that the addictive potential of it is increased by putting it into the body in very direct ways, that the consequences of addiction to heroin are not terrific in terms of limitation of freedom—and that's a serious issue—and that all addicts think they can avoid addiction at the beginning.

Is it true, though, that heroin is not more addictive than cigarettes?

I think cigarettes are more addictive than heroin.

So in effect when you teach young people about cigarettes you would be very severe.

I would say that you should never smoke a cigarette. I think if you want to experiment with tobacco, you should put some in your mouth and chew it to see what its effects are and then you can decide if you want to use it or not; but it is not reasonable to smoke a cigarette to see if you like it or not, because the risk of addiction is too great.

What about coffee?

The thing to emphasize is that it's a very strong drug, with addictive potential and also the potential to alter behavior significantly and affect the body. It should not be thought of as a beverage, and it should be used only occasionally, not regularly.

How would you reduce the incidence of drug-related crime?

If drugs were legalized there would be no drug-related crime.

How do you know that?

Most of the crime associated with drugs has to do with their enormously inflated price, which is a direct consequence of their illegalization, so that people have to get the money to afford them, which often involves committing crimes. But the pharmacological effects of many drugs are against violence— that's certainly true with heroin, and probably with marijuana.

One thing we haven't talked about is the demographics of drug use. If you were looking at this from the perspective of a black woman living in Bed-Stuy who was in great danger of being mugged by almost exclusively male drug users, wouldn't you feel differently?

Probably.

You see these faces at the anticrack rallies, a lot of them are poor people who are just fed up with living in fear.

Right.

What would you say to those people?

That governmental policies—not crack or heroin or any other substance—have put you in danger. And that, as result of these policies, everything associated with this problem has gotten bigger and worse.

Research: Robert Marchant

Opium, Cocaine and Marijuana in American History

Over the past 200 years, Americans have twice accepted and then vehemently rejected drugs. Understanding these dramatic historical swings provides perspective on our current reaction to drug use

David F. Musto

DAVID F. MUSTO is professor of psychiatry at the Child Study Center and professor of the history of medicine at Yale University. He earned his medical degree at the University of Washington and received his master's in the history of science and medicine from Yale. Musto began studying the history of drug and alcohol use in the U.S. when he worked at the National Institute of Mental Health in the 1960s. He has served as a consultant for several national organizations, including the Presidential Commission on the HIV epidemic. From 1981 until 1990, Musto was a member of the Smithsonian Institution's National Council.

Dramatic shifts in attitude have characterized America's relation to drugs. During the 19th century, certain mood-altering substances, such as opiates and cocaine, were often regarded as compounds helpful in everyday life. Gradually this perception of drugs changed. By the early 1900s, and until the 1940s, the country viewed these and some other psychoactive drugs as dangerous, addictive compounds that needed to be severely controlled. Today, after a resurgence of a tolerant attitude toward drugs during the 1960s and 1970s, we find ourselves, again, in a period of drug intolerance.

America's recurrent enthusiasm for recreational drugs and subsequent campaigns for abstinence present a problem to policymakers and to the public. Since the peaks of these episodes are about a lifetime apart, citizens rarely have an accurate or even a vivid recollection of the last wave of cocaine or opiate use.

Phases of intolerance have been fueled by such fear and anger that the record of times favorable toward drug taking has been either erased from public memory or so distorted that it becomes useless as a point of reference for policy formation. During each attack on drug taking, total denigration of the preceding, contrary mood has seemed necessary for public welfare. Although such vigorous rejection may have value in further reducing demand, the long-term effect is to destroy a realistic perception of the past and of the conflicting attitudes toward mood-altering substances that have characterized our national history.

The absence of knowledge concerning our earlier and formative encounters with drugs unnecessarily impedes the already difficult task of establishing a workable and sustainable drug policy. An examination of the period of drug use that peaked around 1900 and the decline that followed it may enable us to approach the current drug problem with more confidence and reduce the likelihood that we will repeat past errors.

Until the 19th century, drugs had been used for millennia in their natural form. Cocaine and morphine, for example, were available only in coca leaves or poppy plants that were chewed, dissolved in alcoholic beverages or taken in some way that diluted the impact of the active agent. The ad-vent of organic chemistry in the 1800s changed the available forms of these drugs. Morphine was isolated in the first decade and cocaine by 1860; in 1874 diacetylmorphine was synthesized from morphine (although it became better known as heroin when the Bayer Company introduced it in 1898).

By mid-century the hypodermic syringe was perfected, and by 1870 it had become a familiar instrument to American physicians and patients [see "The Origins of Hypodermic Medication," by Norman Howard-Jones; SCIENTIFIC AMERICAN, January 1971]. At the same time, the astounding growth of the pharmaceutical industry intensified the ramifications of these accomplishments. As the century wore on, manufacturers grew increasingly adept at exploiting a marketable innovation and moving it into mass production, as well as advertising and distributing it throughout the world.

During this time, because of a peculiarity of the U.S. Constitution, the powerful new forms of opium and cocaine were more readily available in America than in most nations. Under the Constitution, individual states assumed responsibility for health issues, such as regulation of medical practice and the availability of pharmacological products. In fact, America had as many laws regarding health professions as it had states. For much of the 19th century, many states chose to have no controls at all; their legislatures reacted to the claims of contradictory health care

philosophies by allowing free enterprise for all practitioners. The federal government limited its concern to communicable diseases and the provision of health care to the merchant marine and to government dependents.

Nations with a less restricted central government, such as Britain and Prussia, had a single, preeminent pharmacy law that controlled availability of dangerous drugs. In those countries, physicians had their right to practice similarly granted by a central authority. Therefore, when we consider consumption of opium, opiates, coca and cocaine in 19th-century America, we are looking at an era of wide availability and unrestrained advertising. The initial enthusiasm for the purified substances was only slightly affected by any substantial doubts or fear about safety, longterm health injuries or psychological dependence.

History encouraged such attitudes. Crude opium, alone or dissolved in some liquid such as alcohol, was brought by European explorers and settlers to North America. Colonists regarded opium as a familiar resource for pain relief. Benjamin Franklin regularly took laudanum—opium in alcohol extract—to alleviate the pain of kidney stones during the last few years of his life. The poet Samuel Taylor Coleridge, while a student at Cambridge in 1791, began using laudanum for pain and developed a lifelong addiction to the drug. Opium use in those early decades constituted an "experiment in nature" that has been largely forgotten, even repressed, as a result of the extremely negative reaction that followed.

Americans had recognized, however, the potential danger of continually using opium long before the availability of morphine and the hypodermic's popularity. The American Dispensatory of 1818 noted that the habitual use of opium could lead to "tremors, paralysis, stupidity and general emaciation." Balancing this danger, the text proclaimed the extraordinary value of opium in a multitude of ailments ranging from cholera to asthma. (Considering the treatments then in vogue—blistering, vomiting and bleeding—we can understand why opium was as cherished by patients as by their physicians.)

Opium's rise and fall can be tracked through U.S. import-consumption statistics compiled while importation of the drug and its derivative, morphine, was unrestricted and carried moderate tariffs. The per capita consumption of crude opium rose gradually during the

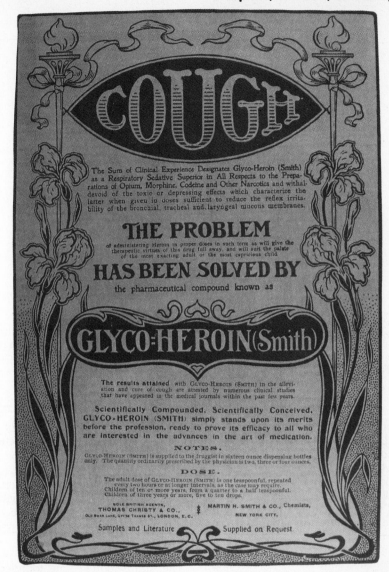

COUGH

The Sum of Clinical Experience Designates Glyco-Heroin (Smith) as a Respiratory Sedative Superior in All Respects to the Preparations of Opium, Morphine, Codeine and Other Narcotics and withal devoid of the toxic or depressing effects which characterize the latter when given in doses sufficient to reduce the reflex irritability of the bronchial, tracheal and laryngeal mucous membranes.

THE PROBLEM

of administering Heroin in proper doses in such form as will give the therapeutic virtues of this drug full sway, and will suit the palate of the most exacting adult or the most capricious child

HAS BEEN SOLVED BY

the pharmaceutical compound known as

GLYCO=HEROIN (Smith)

The results attained with GLYCO-HEROIN (SMITH) in the alleviation and cure of cough are attested by numerous clinical studies that have appeared in the medical journals within the past few years.

Scientifically Compounded, Scientifically Conceived, GLYCO-HEROIN (SMITH) simply stands upon its merits before the profession, ready to prove its efficacy to all who are interested in the advances in the art of medication.

NOTES.

GLYCO-HEROIN (SMITH) is supplied to the druggist in sixteen ounce dispensing bottles only. The quantity ordinarily prescribed by the physician is two, three or four ounces.

DOSE.

The adult dose of GLYCO-HEROIN (SMITH) is one teaspoonful, repeated every two hours or at longer intervals, as the case may require. Children of ten or more years, from a quarter to a half teaspoonful. Children of three years or more, five to ten drops.

SOLE BRITISH AGENTS,
THOMAS CHRISTY & CO.,
OLD SWAN LANE, UPPER THAMES ST., LONDON, E.C.

MARTIN H. SMITH & CO., Chemists,
NEW YORK CITY.

Samples and Literature Supplied on Request.

1800s, reaching a peak in the last decade of the century. It then declined, but after 1915 the data no longer reflect trends in drug use, because that year new federal laws severely restricted legal imports. In contrast, per capita consumption of smoking opium rose until a 1909 act outlawed its importation.

Americans had quickly associated smoking opium with Chinese immigrants who arrived after the Civil War to work on railroad construction. This association was one of the earliest examples of a powerful theme in the American perception of drugs: linkage between a drug and a feared or rejected group within society. Cocaine would be similarly linked with blacks and marijuana with Mexicans in the first third of the 20th century. The association of a drug with a racial group or a political cause, however, is not unique to America. In the 19th century, for instance, the Chinese came to regard opium as

HEROIN COUGH SYRUP was one of many pharmaceuticals at the turn of the century that contained mood-altering substances. The name "heroin" was coined by Bayer in 1898, a year before the company introduced aspirin.

a tool and symbol of Western domination. That perception helped to fuel a vigorous antiopium campaign in China early in the 20th century.

During the 1800s, increasing numbers of people fell under the influence of opiates—substances that demanded regular consumption or the penalty of withdrawal, a painful but rarely life-threatening experience. Whatever the cause—overprescribing by physicians, over-the-counter medicines, self-indulgence or "weak will"—opium addiction brought shame. As consumption increased, so did the frequency of addiction.

At first, neither physicians nor their patients thought that the introduction of the hypodermic syringe or pure

1. THINKING ABOUT DRUGS

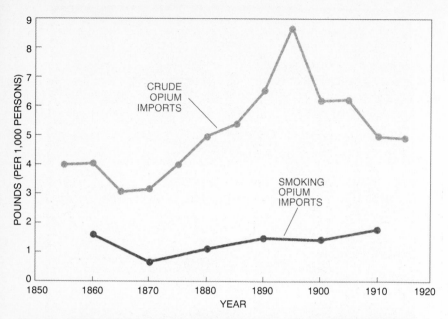

OPIATE CONSUMPTION was documented by the Treasury and the Commerce Departments, starting in the mid-19th century. The importation of smoking opium became illegal in 1909, and crude opium and its derivatives were severely restricted in 1915. After 1915, the data reflected medicinal use.

morphine contributed to the danger of addiction. On the contrary, because pain could be controlled with less morphine when injected, the presumption was made that the procedure was less likely to foster addiction.

Late in the century some states and localities enacted laws limiting morphine to a physician's prescription, and some laws even forbade refilling these prescriptions. But the absence of any federal control over interstate commerce in habit-forming drugs, of uniformity among the state laws and of effective enforcement meant that the rising tide of legislation directed at opiates—and later cocaine—was more a reflection of changing public attitude toward these drugs than an effective reduction of supplies to users. Indeed, the decline noted after the mid-1890s was probably related mostly to the public's growing fear of addiction and of the casual social use of habit-forming substances rather than to any successful campaign to reduce supplies.

At the same time, health professionals were developing more specific treatments for painful diseases, finding less dangerous analgesics (such as aspirin) and beginning to appreciate the addictive power of the hypodermic syringe. By now the public had learned to fear the careless, and possibly addicted, physician. In *A Long Day's Journey into Night*, Eugene O'Neill dramatized the

painful and shameful impact of his mother's physician-induced addiction.

In a spirit not unlike that of our times, Americans in the last decade of the 19th century grew increasingly concerned about the environment, adulterated foods, destruction of the forests and the widespread use of mood-altering drugs. The concern embraced alcohol as well. The Anti-Saloon League, founded in 1893, led a temperance movement toward prohibition, which later was achieved in 1919 and became law in January 1920.

After overcoming years of resistance by over-the-counter, or patent, medicine manufacturers, the federal government enacted the Pure Food and Drug Act in 1906. This act did not prevent sales of addictive drugs like opiates and cocaine, but it did require accurate labeling of contents for all patent remedies sold in interstate commerce. Still, no national restriction existed on the availability of opiates or cocaine. The solution to this problem would emerge from growing concern, legal ingenuity and the unexpected involvement of the federal government with the international trade in narcotics.

Responsibility for the Philippines in 1898 added an international dimension to the

growing domestic alarm about drug abuse. It also revealed that Congress, if given the opportunity, would prohibit nonmedicinal uses of opium among its new dependents. Civil Governor William Howard Taft proposed reinstituting an opium monopoly—through which the previous Spanish colonial government had obtained revenue from sales to opium merchants—and using those profits to help pay for a massive public education campaign. President Theodore Roosevelt vetoed this plan, and in 1905 Congress mandated an absolute prohibition of opium for any purpose other than medicinal use.

To deal efficiently with the antidrug policy established for the Philippines, a committee from the Islands visited various territories in the area to see how others dealt with the opium problem. The benefit of controlling narcotics internationally became apparent.

In early 1906 China had instituted a campaign against opium, especially smoking opium, in an attempt to modernize and to make the Empire better able to cope with continued Western encroachments on its sovereignty. At about the same time, Chinese anger at maltreatment of their nationals in the U.S. seethed into a voluntary boycott of American goods. Partly to appease the Chinese by aiding their antiopium efforts and partly to deal with uncontrollable smuggling within the Philippine Archipelago, the U.S. convened a meeting of regional powers. In this way, the U.S. launched a campaign for worldwide narcotics traffic control that would extend through the years in an unbroken diplomatic sequence from the League of Nations to the present efforts of the United Nations.

The International Opium Commission, a gathering of 13 nations, met in Shanghai in February 1909. The Protestant Episcopal bishop of the Philippines, Charles Henry Brent, who had been instrumental in organizing the meeting, was chosen to preside. Resolutions noting problems with opium and opiates were adopted, but they did not constitute a treaty, and no decisions bound the nations attending the commission. In diplomatic parlance, what was needed now was a conference not a commission. The U.S. began to pursue this goal with determination.

The antinarcotics campaign in America had several motivations. Appeasement of China was certainly one factor for officials of the State Depart-

ment. The department's opium commissioner, Hamilton Wright, thought the whole matter could be "used as oil to smooth the troubled water of our aggressive commercial policy there." Another reason was the belief, strongly held by the federal government today, that controlling crops and traffic in producing countries could most efficiently stop U.S. nonmedical consumption of drugs.

To restrict opium and coca production required worldwide agreement and, thus, an international conference. After intense diplomatic activity, one was convened in the Hague in December 1911. Brent again presided, and on January 23, 1912, the 12 nations represented signed a convention. Provision was made for the other countries to comply before the treaty was brought into force. After all, no producing or manufacturing nation wanted to leave the market open to nonratifying nations.

The convention required each country to enact domestic legislation controlling narcotics trade. The goal was a world in which narcotics were restricted to medicinal use. Both the producing and consuming nations would have control over their boundaries.

After his return from Shanghai, Wright labored to craft a comprehensive federal antinarcotics law. In his path loomed the problem of states' rights. The health professions were considered a major cause of patient addiction. Yet how could federal law interfere with the prescribing practices of physicians or require that pharmacists keep records? Wright settled on the federal government's power to tax; the result, after prolonged bargaining with pharmaceutical, import, export and medical interests, was the Harrison Act of December 1914.

Representative Francis Burton Harrison's association with the act was an accidental one, the consequence of his introduction of the administration's bill. If the chief proponent and negotiator were to be given eponymic credit, it should have been called the Wright Act. It could even have been called a second Mann Act, after Representative James Mann, who saw the bill through to passage in the House of Representatives, for by that time Harrison had become governor-general of the Philippines.

The act required a strict accounting of opium and coca and their derivatives from entry into the U.S. to dispensing to a patient. To accom-

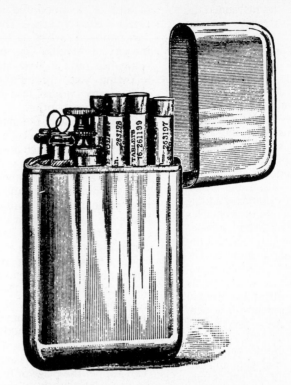

1894 EMERGENCY KIT by the Parke-Davis Company carried cocaine, morphine, atropine and strychnine as well as a hypodermic syringe.

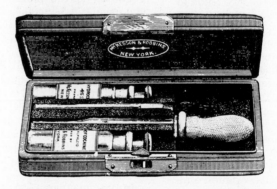

POCKET COCAINE CASE manufactured by pharmacists McKesson & Robbins was one of many drug kits on the market in the late 1800s.

plish this control, a small tax had to be paid at each transfer, and permits had to be obtained by applying to the Treasury Department. Only the patient paid no tax, needed no permit and, in fact, was not allowed to obtain one.

Initially Wright and the Department of Justice argued that the Harrison Act forbade indefinite maintenance of addiction unless there was a specific medical reason such as cancer or tuberculosis. This interpretation was rejected in 1916 by the Supreme Court—even though the Justice Department argued that the Harrison Act was the domestic implementation of

the Hague Opium Convention and therefore took precedence over states' rights. Maintenance was to be allowed.

That decision was short-lived. In 1919 the Supreme Court, led by Oliver Wendell Holmes and Louis Brandeis, changed its mind by a 5-4 vote. The court declared that indefinite maintenance for "mere addiction" was outside legitimate medical practice and that, consequently, prohibiting it did not constitute interference with a state's right to regulate physicians. Second, because the person receiving the drugs for maintenance was not a bona fide patient but just a recipient of drugs,

the transfer of narcotics defrauded the government of taxes required under the Harrison Act.

During the 1920s and 1930s, the opiate problem, chiefly morphine and heroin, declined in the U.S., until much of the problem was confined to the periphery of society and the outcasts of urban areas. There were exceptions: some health professionals and a few others of middle class or higher status continued to take opiates.

America's international efforts continued. After World War I, the British and U.S. governments proposed adding the Hague Convention to the Versailles Treaty. As a result, ratifying the peace treaty meant ratifying the Hague Convention and enacting a domestic law controlling narcotics. This incorporation led to the British Dangerous Drugs Act of 1920, an act often misattributed to a raging heroin epidemic in Britain. In the 1940s some Americans argued that the British system provided heroin to addicts and, by not relying on law enforcement, had almost eradicated the opiate problem. In fact, Britain had no problem to begin with. This argument serves as an interesting example of how the desperate need to solve the drug problem in the U.S. tends to create misperceptions of a foreign drug situation.

The story of cocaine use in America is somewhat shorter than that of opium, but it follows a similar plot. In 1884 purified cocaine became commercially available in the U.S. At first the wholesale cost was very high—$5 to $10 a gram—but it soon fell to 25 cents a gram and remained there until the price inflation of World War I. Problems with cocaine were evident almost from the beginning, but popular opinion and the voices of leading medical experts depicted cocaine as a remarkable, harmless stimulant.

William A. Hammond, one of America's most prominent neurologists, extolled cocaine in print and lectures. By 1887 Hammond was assuring audiences that cocaine was no more habit-forming than coffee or tea. He also told them of the "cocaine wine" he had perfected with the help of a New York druggist: two grains of cocaine to a pint of wine. Hammond claimed that this tonic was far more effective than the popular French coca wine, probably a reference to Vin Mariani, which he complained had only half a grain of cocaine to the pint.

Coca-Cola was also introduced in 1886 as a drink offering the advantages of coca but lacking the danger of alcohol. It amounted to a temperance coca beverage. The cocaine was removed in 1900, a year before the city of Atlanta, Ga., passed an ordinance (and a state statute the following year) prohibiting provision of any cocaine to a consumer without a prescription.

Cocaine is one of the most powerful of the central nervous system euphoriants. This fact underlay cocaine's quickly growing consumption and the ineffectiveness of the early warnings. How could anything that made users so confident and happy be bad? Within a year of cocaine's introduction, the Parke-Davis Company provided coca and cocaine in 15 forms, including coca cigarettes, cocaine for injection and cocaine for sniffing. Parke-Davis and at least one other company also offered consumers a handy cocaine kit. (The Parke-Davis kit contained a hypodermic syringe.) The firm proudly supplied a drug that, it announced, "can supply the place of food, make the coward brave, the silent eloquent and . . . render the sufferer insensitive to pain."

Cocaine spread rapidly throughout the nation. In September 1886 a physician in Puyallup, Washington Territory, reported an adverse reaction to cocaine during an operation. Eventually reports of overdoses and idiosyncratic reactions shifted to accounts of the social and behavioral effects of long-term cocaine use. The ease with which experimenters became regular users and the increasing instances of cocaine being linked with violence and paranoia gradually took hold in popular and medical thought.

In 1907 an attempt was made in New York State to shift the responsibility for cocaine's availability from the open market to medical control. Assemblyman Alfred E. Smith, later the governor of New York and in 1928 the Democratic party's presidential candidate, sponsored such a bill. The cost of cocaine on New York City streets, as revealed by newspaper and police accounts after the law's enactment, was typically 25 cents a packet, or "deck."

Although 25 cents may seem cheap, it was actually slightly higher than the average industrial wage at that time, which was about 20 cents an hour. Packets, commonly glycine envelopes, usually contained one to two grains (65 to 130 milligrams), or about a tenth of a gram. The going rate was roughly 10 times that of the wholesale price, a ratio not unlike recent cocaine street prices, although in the past few years the street price has actually been lower in real value than what it was in 1910.

Several similar reports from the years before the Harrison Act of 1914 suggest that both the profit margin and the street price of cocaine were unaffected by the legal availability of cocaine from a physician. Perhaps the formality of medical consultation and the growing antagonism among physicians and the public toward cocaine helped to sustain the illicit market.

In 1910 William Howard Taft, then president of the U.S., sent to Congress a report that cocaine posed the most serious drug problem America had ever faced. Four years later President Woodrow Wilson signed into law the Harrison Act, which, in addition to its opiate provisions, permitted the sale of cocaine only through prescriptions. It also forbade any trace of cocaine in patent remedies, the most severe restriction on any habit-forming drug to that date. (Opiates, including heroin, could still be present in small amounts in nonprescription remedies, such as cough medicines.)

Although the press continued to reveal Hollywood scandals and underworld cocaine practices during the 1920s, cocaine use gradually declined as a societal problem. The laws probably hastened the trend, and certainly the tremendous public fear reduced demand. By 1930 the New York City Mayor's Committee on Drug Addiction was reporting that "during the last 20 years cocaine as an addiction has ceased to be a problem."

Unlike opiates and cocaine, marijuana was introduced during a period of drug intolerance. Consequently, it was not until the 1960s, 40 years after marijuana cigarettes had arrived in America, that it was widely used. The practice of smoking cannabis leaves came to the U.S. with Mexican immigrants, who had come North during the 1920s to work in agriculture, and it soon extended to white and black jazz musicians.

As the Great Depression of the 1930s settled over America, the immigrants became an unwelcome minority linked with violence and with growing and smoking marijuana. Western states pressured the federal government to control marijuana use. The first official response was to urge adoption of a uniform state antinarcotics law. Then a new approach became feasible in 1937, when the Supreme Court upheld the National Firearms Act. This act prohibited the transfer of machine guns be-

tween private citizens without purchase of a transfer tax stamp—and the government would not issue the necessary stamp. Prohibition was implemented through the taxing power of the federal government.

Within a month of the Supreme Court's decision, the Treasury Department testified before Congress for a bill to establish a marijuana transfer tax. The bill became law, and until the Comprehensive Drug Abuse Act of 1970, marijuana was legally controlled through a transfer tax for which no stamps or licenses were available to private citizens. Certainly some people were smoking marijuana in the 1930s, but not until the 1960s was its use widespread.

Around the time of the Marihuana Tax Act of 1937, the federal government released dramatic and exaggerated portrayals of marijuana's effects. Scientific publications during the 1930s also fearfully described marijuana's dangers. Even Walter Bromberg, who thought that marijuana made only a small contribution to major crimes, nevertheless reported the drug was "a primary stimulus to the impulsive life with direct expression in the motor field."

Marijuana's image shifted during the 1960s, when it was said that its use at the gigantic Woodstock gathering kept peace—as opposed to what might have happened if alcohol had been the drug of choice. In the shift to drug toleration in the late 1960s and early 1970s, investigators found it difficult to associate health problems with marijuana use. The 1930s and 1940s had marked the nadir of drug toleration in the U.S., and possibly the mood of both times affected professional perception of this controversial plant.

After the Harrison Act, the severity of federal laws concerning the sale and possession of opiates and cocaine gradually rose. As drug use declined, penalties increased until 1956, when the death penalty was introduced as an option by the federal government for anyone older than 18 providing heroin to anyone younger than 18 (apparently no one was ever executed under this statute). At the same time, mandatory minimum prison sentences were extended to 10 years.

After the youthful counterculture discovered marijuana in the 1960s, demand for the substance grew until about 1978, when the favorable attitude toward it reached a peak. In 1972 the Presidential Commission on Marihuana and Drug Abuse recommended "decriminalization" of marijuana, that is, legal possession of a small amount

for personal use. In 1977 the Carter administration formally advocated legalizing marijuana in amounts up to an ounce.

The Gallup Poll on relaxation of laws against marijuana is instructive. In 1980, 53 percent of Americans favored legalization of small amounts of marijuana; by 1986 only 27 percent supported that view. At the same time, those favoring penalties for marijuana use rose from 43 to 67 percent. This reversal parallels the changes in attitude among high school students revealed by the Institute of Social Research at the University of Michigan.

The decline in favorable attitudes toward marijuana that began in the late 1970s continues. In the past few years we have seen penalties rise again against users and dealers. The recriminalization of marijuana possession by popular vote in Alaska in 1990 is one example of such a striking reversal.

In addition to stricter penalties, two

MARIHUANA TAX STAMP of 1937 established governmental control over the transfer and sale of the plant. The stamp was never available for private use.

other strategies, silence and exaggeration, were implemented in the 1930s to keep drug use low and prevent a recurrence of the decades-long, frustrating and fearful antidrug battle of the late 19th and early 20th centuries. Primary and secondary schools instituted educational programs against drugs. Then policies shifted amid fears that talking about cocaine or heroin to young people, who now had less exposure to drugs, would arouse their curiosity. This concern led to a decline in drug-related information given during school instruc-

tion as well as to the censorship of motion pictures.

The Motion Picture Association of America, under strong public and religious pressure, decided in 1934 to refuse a seal of approval for any film that showed narcotics. This prohibition was enforced with one exception—*To the Ends of the Earth,* a 1948 film that lauded the Federal Bureau of Narcotics—until *Man with a Golden Arm* was successfully exhibited in 1956 without a seal.

Associated with a decline in drug information was a second, apparently paradoxical strategy: exaggerating the effects of drugs. The middle ground was abandoned. In 1924 Richmond P. Hobson, a nationally prominent campaigner against drugs, declared that one ounce of heroin could addict 2,000 persons. In 1936 an article in the *American Journal of Nursing* warned that a marijuana user "will suddenly turn with murderous violence upon whomever is nearest to him. He will run amuck with knife, axe, gun, or anything else that is close at hand, and will kill or maim without any reason."

A goal of this well-meaning exaggeration was to describe drugs so repulsively that anyone reading or hearing of them would not be tempted to experiment with the substances. One contributing factor to such a publicity campaign, especially regarding marijuana, was that the Depression permitted little money for any other course of action.

Severe penalties, silence and, if silence was not possible, exaggeration became the basic strategies against drugs after the decline of their first wave of use. But the effect of these tactics was to create ignorance and false images and present no real obstacle to a renewed enthusiasm for drugs in the 1960s. At the time, enforcing draconian and mandatory penalties would have filled to overflowing all jails and prisons with the users of marijuana alone.

Exaggeration fell in the face of the realities of drug use and led to a loss of credibility regarding any government pronouncement on drugs. The lack of information erased any awareness of the first epidemic, including the gradually obtained and hard-won public insight into the hazards of cocaine and opiates. Public memory, which would have provided some context for the antidrug laws, was a casualty of the antidrug strategies.

The earlier and present waves of drug use have much in common, but there is at least one major difference. During the first wave of drug use, anti-

1. THINKING ABOUT DRUGS

drug laws were not enacted until the public demanded them. In contrast, today's most severe antidrug laws were on the books from the outset; this gap between law and public opinion made the controls appear ridiculous and bizarre. Our current frustration over the laws' ineffectiveness has been greater and more lengthy than before because we have lived through many years in which antidrug laws lacked substantial public support. Those laws appeared powerless to curb the rise in drug use during the 1960s and 1970s.

The first wave of drug use involved primarily opiates and cocaine. The nation's full experience with marijuana is now under way (marijuana's tax regulation in 1937 was not the result of any lengthy or broad experience with the plant). The popularity and growth in demand for opiates and cocaine in mainstream society derived from a simple factor: the effect on most people's physiology and emotions was enjoyable. Moreover, Americans have recurrently hoped that the technology of drugs would maximize their personal potential. That opiates could relax and cocaine energize seemed wonderful opportunities for fine-tuning such efforts.

Two other factors allowed a long and substantial rise in consumption during the 1800s. First, casualties accumulate gradually; not everyone taking cocaine or opiates becomes hooked on the drug. In the case of opiates, some users have become addicted for a lifetime and have still been productive.

Yet casualties have mounted as those who could not handle occasional use have succumbed to domination by drugs and by drug-seeking behavior. These addicts become not only miserable themselves but also frightening to their families and friends. Such cases are legion today in our larger cities, but the percentage of those who try a substance and acquire a dependence or get into serious legal trouble is not 100 percent. For cocaine, the estimate varies from 3 to 20 percent, or even higher, and so it is a matter of time before cocaine is recognized as a likely danger.

Early in the cycle, when social tolerance prevails, the explanation for casualties is that those who succumb to addiction are seen as having a physiological idiosyncrasy or "foolish trait." Personal disaster is thus viewed as an

 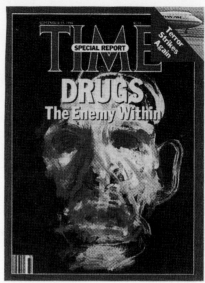

TIME MAGAZINE COVERS from 1981 and from 1986 reflect a clear change in American views toward mood-altering drugs, specifically cocaine.

exception to the rule. Another factor minimizing the sense of risk is our belief in our own invulnerability—that general warnings do not include us. Such faith reigns in the years of greatest exposure to drug use, ages 15 to 25. Resistance to a drug that makes a user feel confident and exuberant takes many years to permeate a society as large and complex as the U.S.

The interesting question is not why people take drugs, but rather why they stop taking them. We perceive risk differently as we begin to reject drugs. One can perceive a hypothetical 3 percent risk from taking cocaine as an assurance of 97 percent safety, or one can react as if told that 3 percent of New York/Washington shuttle flights crash. Our exposure to drug problems at work, in our neighborhood and within our families shifts our perception, gradually shaking our sense of invulnerability.

Cocaine has caused the most dramatic change in estimating risk. From a grand image as the ideal tonic, cocaine's reputation degenerated into that of the most dangerous of drugs, linked in our minds with stereotypes of mad, violent behavior. Opiates have never fallen so far in esteem, nor were they repressed to the extent cocaine had been between 1930 and 1970.

Today we are experiencing the reverse of recent decades, when the technology of drug use promised an extension of our natural potential. Increasingly we see drug consumption as re-

ducing what we could achieve on our own with healthy food and exercise. Our change of attitude about drugs is connected to our concern over air pollution, food adulteration and fears for the stability of the environment.

Ours is an era not unlike that early in this century, when Americans made similar efforts at self-improvement accompanied by an assault on habit-forming drugs. Americans seem to be the least likely of any people to accept the inevitability of historical cycles. Yet if we do not appreciate our history, we may again become captive to the powerful emotions that led to draconian penalties, exaggeration or silence.

FURTHER READING

AMERICAN DIPLOMACY AND THE NARCOTICS TRAFFIC, 1900-1939. Arnold H. Taylor. Duke University Press, 1969.

DRUGS IN AMERICA: A SOCIAL HISTORY, 1800-1980. H. Wayne Morgan. Syracuse University Press, 1981.

DARK PARADISE: OPIATE ADDICTION IN AMERICA BEFORE 1940. David T. Courtwright. Harvard University Press, 1982.

THE AMERICAN DISEASE: ORIGINS OF NARCOTIC CONTROL. Expanded Edition. David F. Musto. Oxford University Press, 1987.

AMERICA'S FIRST COCAINE EPIDEMIC. David F. Musto in *Wilson Quarterly*, pages 59-65; Summer 1989.

ILLICIT PRICE OF COCAINE IN TWO ERAS: 1908-14 AND 1982-89. David F. Musto in *Connecticut Medicine*, Vol. 54, No. 6, pages 321-326; June 1990.

COKE INC.

INSIDE THE BIG BUSINESS OF DRUGS

MICHAEL STONE

Acting on a tip from the Brooklyn district attorney, federal Customs agents raided a warehouse on 44th Drive in Long Island City early last November. They were looking for cocaine, and they found it—400 pounds stuffed in cardboard boxes lying in plain view. But that was only the start. Against a wall, the agents found hundreds of twenty-gallon cans filled with bricks of cocaine packed in lye so corrosive it had begun to eat through the metal containers. It took a police unit seven days to move out the drugs. By then, the agents had uncovered nearly 5,000 bricks: 4,840 kilograms—5.3 tons—of cocaine.

Richard Mercier, the agent in charge of the operation, says that in 1973, he put a dealer away for 34 years for possession of three ounces of cocaine. In those days, the seizure of a kilogram of drugs—2.2 pounds—was a major bust. After the Long Island City raid, Mercier recalls, he surveyed a 24-foot truck piled four feet high with cocaine. "How much more is out there?" he wondered.

Three months after that bust, in the early-morning hours of February 3, a police anti-crime unit rounded the corner at Lenox Avenue and 128th Street in Harlem and saw a young man we'll call Willie waving a .357 Magnum at a group of youths across the street. Someone yelled, "Yo, burgundy!"—the code name for the officers' red Chevy—and Willie darted into a nearby tenement. The cops cornered him in a second-floor apartment, and Willie dropped a brown bag containing almost 300 vials of crack. On a bench next to him, police found a plastic bag containing 2,900 more vials of crack. In a wastebasket they discovered more than $12,000 in small bills. It was Willie's second arrest. He was fifteen.

These events evoke the images New Yorkers most commonly associate with the city's drug trade: mountains of white powder smuggled by a faceless international cartel, and the dead-end kid hawking crack in the ghetto. But the smuggler and the street dealer are only the most obvious players in the city's bustling drug business. Between them, an army of unseen workers—middlemen, money counters, couriers, chemists, money launderers, labelers, and arm-breakers—tend the vast machinery of New York's dope trade. Seven days a week, 24 hours a day, they process, package, and distribute the hundreds of kilos of heroin and cocaine required to feed the city's habit.

A legion of entrepreneurs also supply New Yorkers with tons of marijuana, as well as a dazzling assortment of pharmaceuticals: barbiturates, amphetamines, LSD, ecstasy. You can still buy PCP on West 127th Street, and officials have run across "ice," a potent new methamphetamine derivative, in East New York. But today, the huge heroin and cocaine/crack markets are the focus of law-enforcement efforts, for these are the drugs that are corroding city life.

During the past decade, New York's drug business has undergone a revolution. Ten years ago, cocaine was still exotic, a drug popular with celebrities and people trying to be hip. Crack wasn't even an idea. Though heroin was plentiful, users tended to be older and more discreet about their habits. A *Times* survey in December 1981 asked New Yorkers to rate the most important problems facing the city, and drugs didn't make the top ten. The appetite for drugs that's since sprung up has developed together with a business that aggressively marketed its products and worked feverishly to keep pace with the demand it was creating. At times, dealer and user seemed locked in a fatal embrace, each egging the other on to new and dangerous highs.

The breakneck expansion in sales and revenues destabilized New York's entrenched distribution networks, ushered in an era of intense competition, and sparked episodes of unprecedented violence. Thousands of organizations—from mom-and-pop candy-store operations to vast criminal conspiracies—sprouted to meet the demand. The drug trade also became an equal-opportunity employer: As the Mafia pulled back from—or was muscled out of—the business, blacks and other minority-group members who'd previously been relegated to the lower levels of distribution were drafted into key roles. And with cocaine and heroin selling at several times the price of gold, street-smart young men suddenly found themselves awash in cash.

At the same time, these dealers influenced the type, price, availability, and quality of drugs in the city. Crack was an immediate success here, though in Boston and Chicago the drug is relatively rare. The taboo on selling dangerous drugs to minors, observed a generation ago, was breached, and now teenagers and even younger children play important roles in the trade.

Despite the efforts of the authorities and the opposition of community groups, the city's drug lords—many of them unedu-

The city's drug lords—many of them uneducated and seemingly unemployable—have built and managed amazingly efficient markets.

cated and seemingly unemployable—have developed and managed remarkably efficient markets. Gone are the periodic shortages that hit the city when organized crime ran the drug supply. The new traffickers not only increased profits but lowered prices and raised product quality. One wonders what might have been accomplished if all that energy, innovation, and daring had been harnessed to a worthy enterprise.

VERYONE AGREES THAT THE DRUG BUSINESS IS BIG BUSIness, but there's wide disagreement over its exact size. The most quoted estimate—which comes from the House Narcotics Committee—is that retail drug sales nationally for 1987 amounted to $150 billion, a figure that one committee aide claims has grown substantially since then. There are no official figures for New York, but Sterling Johnson Jr., the city's special narcotics prosecutor, thinks the city's share may be as much as $80 billion.

Other experts argue that these numbers are grossly inflated. "If New Yorkers were spending $80 billion a year on drugs," says Peter Reuter, a researcher at the Rand Corporation, "then every man, woman, and child in the city would have a habit." Reuter calls the government's estimates "mythical numbers," created by agencies whose budgets and influence grow with the perceived size of the problem.

In fact, there simply isn't enough information to get an accurate reading of the size of the drug trade, although there are ways to make rough guesses. The most common method estimates the amount of drugs smuggled into the area and then multiplies that figure by the street value of the drugs to get a total price. For example, on the basis of figures from several law-enforcement agencies, it's estimated that officials intercepted around 14,000 kilograms of cocaine in the metropolitan area in the past twelve months, an amount experts assume to be around 10 percent of all the cocaine shipped here. Since the street value of a kilogram of cocaine runs from $80,000 to $190,000, cocaine sales in the city, according to the formula, ranged between $11.2 billion and $26.6 billion.

There are several problems with this method, however. For one thing, different government agencies often take credit for the same bust, thus inflating the overall figure for the amount seized. What's more, recent studies indicate that a substantial portion—perhaps 40 percent—of the cocaine and heroin brought into the country never reaches the street. Instead, it's consumed by dealers and their cronies or used as payments for services like prostitution. Finally, there's no good reason to believe that there's a fixed ratio between seizures and imports.

A second method for computing the size of the drug business focuses on heroin and is based on the number of users and the average cost of their daily habit. The state Division of Substance Abuse Services estimates that there are 200,000 heroin addicts (as opposed to recreational users) living in the city. If they spend an average of $50 a day to satisfy their habits, then addicts alone account for $3.6 billion in heroin sales each year.

Once again, however, the experts disagree on the data. Working from studies of the criminal activities of narcotics addicts, Reuter calculates that the common estimate of the number of heroin addicts and the cost of their addiction is far too high. "If there were 200,000 addicts in New York, each spending $50 a day, the city would have ceased to exist," he says. "The junkies would have stolen it long ago."

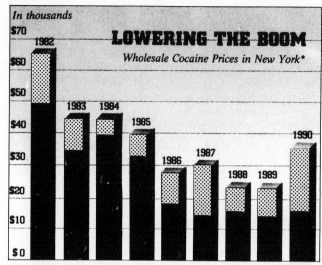

* Per kilogram. Prices vary depending on the location of the deal and the status of the buyer. The annual range is indicated in dots. By way of comparison, the consumer price index has risen 58 percent in the past decade.

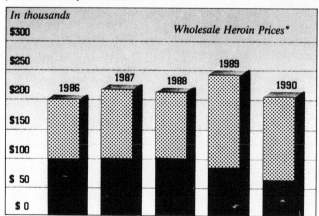

The average cost of a heroin habit is anybody's guess. "It might be $150 to $200 per day," says Paul Dinella, a former addict who until recently worked for the Division of Substance Abuse. "All I know is that a junkie will spend whatever he can get." Dinella also points out that most addicts vary their drug use over time. Some "dry out" periodically; around 40,000 heroin users entered treatment facilities around the state last year. Thousands more were jailed. When surveyed, though, addicts tend to exaggerate their habits, citing what they spend when they're binging. One study found that a group of addicts overstated the amount they spent on drugs by a factor of four.

A third approach attempts to place drug sales within the context of the economy as a whole. New York's gross economic product is about $180 billion. Given Sterling Johnson's drug-trade figure—$80 billion—that would mean that New Yorkers spend nearly half of what they produce on drugs. Many experts think that's impossible. Rather, they estimate that the city's underground economy is around $18 billion and that drug revenues are some fraction of that.

The wild card here is out-of-town sales. New York is a shipping point for many drugs, one of three or four main distribution centers in the United States. Revenues from these wholesale deals add billions to the total drug trade here and go some ways toward reconciling the difference between estimates based on interception and consumption.

Inevitably, the experts view the size of the drug problem through their personal lenses. The cop and the prosecutor see the crack crews on every corner and think the world has gone crazy. The economists and academicians look for the paper trail that tens of billions of dollars should leave and can't find it. Still, even moderate estimates place drug sales in New York at around $12 billion; by contrast, restaurant and bar revenues in the metropolitan area total around $7 billion.

In any case, the business has grown explosively in the past decade. Even heroin use is on the rise after declining for years. There are a few small positive signs: a recent reduction in casual cocaine use among high-school seniors, a decline in cocaine-related emergency-room visits after a dramatic rise, and a flattening out of the growth rate of crack consumption. But these developments may simply show that the market is saturated. "So we've stabilized crack use at record levels of consumption," says a House Narcotics Committee aide. "Is that something to be proud of?"

ALMOST EVERY COCAINE DEAL THAT takes place in New York begins in Colombia. Although the coca plant grows mainly in Peru and Bolivia, Colombians process about 80 percent of the region's crop and export it around the world. Of the estimated 450 tons of cocaine produced last year, as much as 75 tons may have passed through New York, says Arthur Stiffel, top Customs agent at Kennedy airport.

The Colombians smuggle cocaine in ways limited only by the imagination. Government agents have found the drug concealed in the cages of poisonous snakes and in blocks of chocolate. Every year, they intercept hundreds of human "mules" who swallow cocaine-filled condoms to sneak the stuff past Customs. Typically, Colombia's cartels smuggle boat- or planeloads of cocaine into a southern border state, then truck the drug up to New York. Recently, according to Stiffel, the smugglers have also been flying shipments directly into local airports. In June 1988, a Customs unit in Miami seized 1,200 kilos of cocaine that were en route to Suffolk County Airport in Westhampton, the first installment of a 15-ton load targeted for Long Island's East End summer population. The huge cargo ships that visit New York-area ports are another favorite vehicle for traffickers. "Not even counting what's hidden in the merchandise, a one-inch dropped ceiling in a standard container could hold thousands of pounds of cocaine," says Customs agent Richard Mercier. "But we only have the resources to inspect 3 percent of the containers that come in."

ON THE TRAIL

Kilograms of Cocaine Seized by the DEA in New York State.

Fiscal Year		Fiscal Year	
1990	8,715*	1985	332
1989	4,468	1984	1,119
1988	8,817	1983	229
1987	1,430	1982	335
1986	1,960	1981	149
	* To date	1980	160

Mercier's arithmetic explains the government's dilemma. Because the markup on cocaine is so high—a kilo that costs $4,000 to produce in Colombia sells in New York at wholesale for $14,000 to $23,000 and recently even as high as $35,000—the cartels would make a hefty profit even if Mercier's colleagues beat the odds and intercepted half the illegal drugs entering the city. The Colombians, of course, aren't indifferent to government seizures, but it costs them more to lose customers and sales to competitors than to lose an occasional shipment.

Some officials attribute a recent rise in the wholesale price of cocaine to the effectiveness of the war on drugs here and in Latin America. Others say it's too soon to tell if the war is helping, and in any case, drug prices vary widely depending on the location of the deal and the status of the buyer.

OST OF THE COCAINE BROUGHT INTO NEW YORK—80 to 90 percent, says the DEA—is imported by the Cali cartel, an association of traffickers from Colombia's third-largest city. Headed by the two Rodriguez-Orjuela brothers and José Santa Cruz–Londoño, the group was formed in the early eighties to set drug policy and coordinate smuggling.

Before the cartel took over, most traffickers shipped their drugs to Miami, then sold them to middlemen with connections around the country. This arrangement worked fine as long as the market remained small and import prices stayed high. But as more and more traffickers got into the act and production levels jumped, import prices in Miami plummeted. As a result, the demand for cocaine rocketed, and local distributors racked up huge profits.

Today, the DEA maintains that the Cali cartel controls the first line of distribution in New York. Operating through teams, or "cells," of salaried employees, the cartel sells to the legions of mid-level dealers who ultimately supply the city's street dealers and retail organizations. Kenneth Robinson, one of the DEA's Cali experts, says that each cell typically includes a supervisor, or underboss, six to eight managers, and assorted workers. The supervisor takes possession of the drug shipments and stores them in safe houses—generally, private homes or warehouses. The managers place their orders through coded phone calls directly to the cartel in Colombia, which relays them to the supervisor. The supervisor then contacts the managers and arranges delivery at a safe house or at some public place, such as a mall, where the proliferation of shopping bags can help hide the transfer of drugs and money.

The cartel managers are the bureaucrats of the drug business. Contrary to the popular image of cocaine cowboys with flashy life-styles and flamboyant personalities, typical managers live modestly, blending into the suburbs where they often live. Overall, the cartel's operations are disciplined and difficult to trace. Money and drugs are kept separately, beepers are leased from legitimate businesses, written records are limited, and workers are trained in countersurveillance. When FBI undercover agents posing as money launderers recently met with cartel members, the Colombians brought along their lawyers.

But beneath the corporate veneer, the Colombians operate according to a code of violence and intimidation. Stiffel speculates that many of the cartel leaders came of age during Colombia's civil wars, when killing was a way of life. "They're not like the Mafia," says Robinson. "The Mafia isn't going to touch your family. But the Colombians will kill you, your wife, your children, and your dog. They're not going to leave anyone to take revenge later on."

Their methods are effective. Robinson points out that of the 400 or so cartel members arrested in the United States, only a handful have cooperated with the police. And in a business often disrupted by ripoffs and blunders, the Colombian operation seems to run smoothly. "I've busted dozens of Colombians over

the years—peasants guarding rooms with tens, twenties, fifties piled floor to ceiling," Stiffel says. "But I've never yet found one of them with more than a few dollars in his pocket."

Government officials don't know how much money the cartel actually makes from its New York operations. DEA agents busted a Cali money-laundering outfit in Great Neck and found records that indicated revenues of $44 million in less than two months. The 5.3-ton load in Long Island City—also identified as part of a Cali operation, though no one has been arrested in connection with the raid—would have brought around $200-million at wholesale prices. Robinson thinks that the Cali cartel has three or four cells operating independently of one another in the New York area and that, on average, it takes two or three months to distribute a major delivery.

One drug ring busted in Manorville,

Long Island, is thought to have generated

revenues of $200 million to $250 million a year.

New York's huge market has attracted other importers as well. In fact, Stiffel disputes the view that the Cali cartel controls New York's cocaine hierarchy. Rather, he argues that New York's traffickers are caught up in a kind of feeding frenzy, with all of Colombia's major cartels, as well as other groups and individual importers, competing for coca dollars. Two years ago, an apparent turf dispute between Cali and the Medellín cartel, the world's largest cocaine producer, sparked a rash of murders in Queens.

Last May, FBI agents busted a Medellín-operated ring based in Manorville, Long Island, that supplied cocaine to Jackson Heights, Flushing, and Jamaica, Queens. Agents say the group handled 6,400 kilos of cocaine during one five-month period in 1988. Jules Bonavolonta, the agent in charge of the investigation, estimates conservatively that the ring was generating revenues of $200 million to $250 million a year.

The Mafia has also continued to bring cocaine into the city. Law-enforcement officials speculate that at the time former Bonanno-family soldier Costabile "Gus" Farace murdered DEA undercover agent Everett Hatcher in February 1989 ("Death of a Hood," *New York*, January 29, 1990), he was building a cocaine-distribution ring in South Brooklyn and Staten Island. Farace was allegedly supplied from Miami by Gerard Chilli, his former prison mate and a reputed capo in the Bonanno family. Farace was gunned down last November because his actions had brought too much heat on the mob, investigators say.

After cocaine leaves the cartel's cell, it generally passes through a series of middlemen before reaching the street. Along the way, a dealer—who generally works on consignment—has three ways to make money. He can broker his supply intact and tack on a commission. He can divide it into smaller units and mark up the price. Or he can "cut" (dilute) the cocaine with harmless adulterants like milk sugar—in effect, increasing the amount of cocaine he has to sell.

In one typical sequence, using low-end prices, a high-level broker buys 100 kilos of pure cocaine at $17,000 per kilo and sells them in ten-kilo lots at an average price of $19,000 per kilo, earning $200,000. The second dealer sells the ten kilos for $23,000 a kilo, earning $40,000. His customers cut the cocaine by a third, producing, in all, 133 kilos, which they break into around 4,700 one-ounce units and sell to dealers for $800 each, for a total profit of about $1,460,000. Finally, these dealers add another one-half cut, creating in all 200 kilos, or about 7,050 ounces, of adulterated cocaine. That cocaine is converted into

crack at a rate of about 350 vials per ounce of cocaine. The crack vials are sold on the street for, say, $5 each, earning the dealers $8,577,500, of which around 20 percent goes to the street sellers.

This pyramid form of distribution has two main virtues: It maximizes the dealer's access to his market while minimizing his involvement in potentially dangerous transactions. No one at an intermediate level deals with more than a handful of contacts. Yet, after just five transfers, the system has supplied hundreds of street sellers who are reaching tens of thousands of customers. And the original 100 kilos of cocaine valued at $1.7-million have produced more than $12 million in revenues—a markup of around 700 percent.

SHARING IN THESE PROFITS ARE LITERALLY THOUSANDS of new, ethnically diverse mid-level dealers. Until the cartels arrived, cocaine distribution had been a closed shop, largely controlled by Cubans. But when the Colombians opened up the market in the early eighties, they created what one dealer at the time called the "ethnicization" of cocaine. Saddled with an oversupply of drugs, the cartels fronted "trusted friends" and associates, who sold to anyone—Latinos, blacks, Italians, even cops—who could deliver the cash. "Our undercover guys were always being told by dealers, 'I think you're "the man," ' " says Joseph Lisi, a New York police captain. "They'd say, 'Right, I'm the man. But I've got $80,000 in this briefcase, and if you don't want to deal with me, I'm out of here right now.' They'd never make it to the door."

Meanwhile, as prices began to fall, demand surged, and small-time street sellers suddenly found business soaring. If the Colombians were looking for dealers who could move "weight"—large quantities—those dealers were looking for high-level suppliers who could help them expand. All over the city, small cocaine retail outfits began cropping up—Dominicans in Washington Heights, blacks in Harlem and South Jamaica, Jamaicans in Brownsville, Bedford-Stuyvesant, and East New York.

The appearance of crack in late 1984 accelerated the process. No one group could control its spread. An ounce of cocaine that could be bought on the street for $1,000 yielded 320 to 360 vials of crack—more if cut—that sold for $10 each in hot locations. (The price is lower in poor neighborhoods that don't get suburban traffic.) Anyone with a few hundred dollars and a hot plate could go into business and triple his money overnight. Thousands of people did, and the old order—already shaken—crumbled completely. Crack turned the lower level of the cocaine trade into a freewheeling, decentralized business, with new outfits springing up and established groups growing into multi-million-dollar, citywide organizations.

DEA agents discovered just how sophisticated some of these groups had become when they started investigating the Basedballs organization in 1985. The brainchild of Santiago Polanco, now 29, Basedballs started out in 1982 as an outfit selling grams and half-grams of cocaine along Audubon Avenue, east of the George Washington Bridge—a prime drug location because of its suburban traffic from New Jersey. The operation was small, but profitable enough to enable Polanco to walk into an Englewood Cliffs car dealership in 1984 and plunk down $43,000 in cash for a Mercedes-Benz.

When crack appeared on the scene, Polanco was one of the first dealers to recognize its potential and aggressively market the drug. He packaged his product in red-topped vials, calling the stuff Basedballs—a play on the term "free-basing"—and took pains to ensure brand quality. He hired "cooks" to process the cocaine, and when one dealer was caught tampering with the product, Polanco had him beaten with a baseball bat. Among the customers driving over from New Jersey, Basedballs quickly became one of the most sought-after brands.

Though they often handle substantial sums, most street

dealers make only modest profits for the roughest work in the business.

Basedballs employees were the only dealers on Audubon Avenue around 173rd, 174th, and 175th Streets. Organization members later told DEA agents that they had bought the territory from its former owners, but, just in case, Polanco imported a team of hit men from his family's village in the Dominican Republic to protect Basedballs's turf and ease its expansion. By 1986, the organization had wrested control of the intersection of Edgecombe Avenue and 145th Street—a prime spot, easily accessible to the Bronx across the 145th Street Bridge—from a group of black dealers and opened a string of new spots in Harlem and the South Bronx.

As Basedballs's business expanded, so did its organization. Polanco secured a major supplier, a Dominican who dealt directly with the cartels in Colombia. Polanco also centralized Basedballs's operations in a headquarters at 2400 Webb Avenue in the Bronx. There, his workers cooked, packaged, and stockpiled crack in separate apartments. And he arranged with one of the dozens of money-changing companies along upper Broadway to launder Basedballs's revenues through an investment company he set up in the Dominican Republic.

Meanwhile, Polanco began distancing himself from Basedballs's day-to-day operations, adding layers of bureaucracy and spending more and more time in the Dominican Republic. By the summer of 1986, Basedballs employed as many as nine mid-level managers to deal with street-level managers at a score of locations around the city. Each location manager, in turn, supervised teams of dealers, none of whom were supposed to know the people more than one level above them.

It took law-enforcement agents and their informants nearly two years to penetrate the highest levels of Basedballs's organization. They can only guess how much money the operation made, but by one estimate, Polanco may have been clearing $20-million a year. One DEA agent saw the fruits of Polanco's activities in the Dominican Republic: two nightclubs, a jeans company, a 30-unit condominium complex, an office building, a palatial home, and a gold-plated gull-wing Mercedes. Today, Polanco is believed to be serving a 30-year sentence in a Dominican prison for homicide, and U.S. law-enforcement officials have dismantled his organization and locked up more than 30 of his associates. But agents estimate that there may be dozens of organizations as large as, or larger than, Basedballs operating in New York.

A T THE BOTTOM OF THE distribution pyramid stands the street seller, subject to arrest, to ripoffs, to calculated violence by competitors. This is especially true for crack dealers. Over the past five years, law enforcement has focused on the cocaine trade, with street dealers the most visible target. They are also the first to get shot when a fight breaks out over turf, which is far more common in the cocaine trade than in the older, more established heroin business. Even the crack dealer's clients present special risks. "I wouldn't deal that crack s—-," says Reuben, a former heroin dealer in the South Bronx. "Once a [heroin addict] gets his fix, he's cool. But when those crackheads start bugging out, you don't know what they're going to do."

In contrast to the myth, most street dealers make only modest profits. The stories about their vast incomes probably arise in part because they generally don't point out the distinction between the large sums of cash they handle and the relatively small commissions they earn. "After factoring in the long hours, they

may come out a couple of dollars an hour ahead of the minimum wage," says Philippe Bourgois, an anthropologist studying East Harlem's drug culture.

Willie, the fifteen-year-old caught on gun- and drug-possession charges in Harlem last February, was probably earning about $300 to $350 per week, according to his arresting officer, Terry McGhee. "We see these kids out there in the cold, not moving from one spot, selling for ten hours at a stretch with nothing but a space heater. Maybe at the end of the night, they'll get paid $50," McGhee says. "I'll tell you one thing: You couldn't get a cop to do that."

But to compare dealing to a mainstream job may miss the point. Many youngsters drift in and out of the drug trade as a way of making pocket money or supporting their own drug habits. Part-time work is hard to find in the slum neighborhoods where most dealers live, and a full-time job often means a long commute and menial work. What's more, though a dealer's hours are long, they are often spent with friends on the streets. Willie, for example, belonged to a group called Boogie-Down Productions—the BDP—a gang of up to twenty teenagers that still pushes drugs on 128th Street and Lenox Avenue. "A lot of these young kids who become dealers are joining a crew," says McGhee. "It gives them access to power. Access to guns. It means no one can push them around anymore."

Crews like these are not simple throwbacks to the gangs of the fifties. They're richer and far better armed, and they're manipulated by adult criminals for profit. But their gang structure ensures discipline and loyalty. The graffiti on the walls of an abandoned BDP hangout—THIS BLOCK BELONGS TO THE BDP—indicate that Willie and his pals were protecting their turf, not just a business enterprise.

In even the poorest markets, however, some dealers make out well. "Everyone who goes into the crack business perceives that he's going to get rich," Bourgois says. "And some of them will. Kids who are responsible or street-smart or especially tough can still get promoted very quickly to manager and get a cut of the profits." Also, street dealing is the entry point into the trade, a way to make contacts or amass enough capital to go into business for oneself. Some street dealers get regular salaries or per diems, but many work on commission—usually between 10 and 20 percent. One of Basedballs's dealers boasted to DEA agents that he cleared $1,4000 in commissions during one eight-hour shift on Audubon Avenue.

B EFORE CRACK, HEROIN WAS THE DRUG OF CHOICE IN THE slums, and its popularity is said to be rebounding. According to Division of Substance Abuse data, roughly one in every sixteen working-age men in New York is a heroin addict. The ratio has remained constant over the past five years, but the high mortality rate associated with heroin—especially since the outbreak of AIDS among IV-drug users—may conceal an increase in new addicts. Meanwhile, heroin use among twenty-year-olds—a better indicator of trends in demand—has been rising.

Some experts think the change comes as a reaction to crack, as former crack users switch to a relatively milder drug. Others attribute the comeback to an improvement in the quality of heroin. Greater purity not only gives users a better high but enables them to snort the drug instead of shooting it. At least two factors account for heroin's better quality. For one, Southeast Asia—noted for its pure heroin—now supplies about 70 percent

of the New York market. For another, the recent decentralization of heroin distribution in the city has increased the supply and fostered competition among dealers.

THROUGHOUT THE SIXTIES AND SEVENTIES, THE MAFIA dominated the heroin market as the major importer and distributor. In the early eighties, however, the so-called Pizza Connection prosecutions weakened the mob's hold and cut the flow of heroin from Sicily into the United States. Law-enforcement officials say that the ethnic Chinese took over as the industry's new leaders.

In fact, New York's Chinese have been smuggling heroin into the city for years, but until recently, they distrusted the distributors—most of them black—who supplied the street networks; as a result, Chinese smugglers delegated a few of their elders to broker the drug through the Mafia. But around the time that the Mafia began pulling out of the trade, Chinatown began to change.

"Thirty to 40 years ago, Chinatown was very provincial," says Michael Shum, an agent in the DEA's New York Southeast Asian Heroin Task Force. "People from different regions spoke different dialects. In my grandmother's day, if you were Fukienese and you went into a store owned by Toy Shanese, they wouldn't sell you groceries. Forget about drugs—if you didn't speak their language, you couldn't buy a tomato."

Today, Shum says, the old rivalries have broken down and cash has become a universal language. In one recent case, DEA agents turned up a connection between Puerto Rican heroin dealers and members of a Chinese youth gang; the young men had met in school and later "married up" in jail.

The big Chinese move into heroin has had two profound effects on the market. By stepping up their smuggling activities, the Chinese have flooded the city with Southeast Asian heroin. And by dealing directly with minority distributors, they have bypassed the Mafia middlemen who were notorious for heavily cutting their product. As a result, the average drug sold on the street has gone from being as low as 2 percent pure heroin in the early eighties to around 40 percent today.

Still, the heroin trade remains highly profitable. A kilo of pure heroin that costs around $11,000 in Bangkok can be sold for between $85,000 and $125,000 to an Asian broker in the United States or for $150,000 to $240,000 to a mid-level dealer acting as an intermediary between the importer and the street. Markups like these have attracted a grab bag of international trafficking organizations in addition to the Chinese, and even diplomats and businessmen have joined the trade. "We map out ten to twenty major trafficking routes and find out there are ten to twenty more," says DEA agent Dwight Rabb. "We're being inundated with dope."

Because of the huge markup, the drug cartels can afford to lose an occasional shipment to a bust.

Government agents have seized heroin hidden in imported cars, wheelbarrow tires, and the caskets of servicemen killed overseas. The "condom eaters" have also been busy. "Last year, we arrested 123 Nigerians alone at JFK, most of them carrying internally," says Arthur Stiffel, whose Customs agents use X-ray machines to search suspects. "This year, they're running at double the rate."

Though the Chinese dominate the heroin trade in the city, no single group controls the supply. Various foreign nationals—including Nigerians, Ghanaians, Pakistanis, Indians, Thais, and Vietnamese—and assorted American organized-crime groups all smuggle heroin independently of one another. What's more, the Chinese in the trade often operate separately. Unlike the Mafia, Chinatown's criminal organizations—descended from Hong Kong's ruthless triads—do not require their members to pay tribute or even, in many cases, to get permission to deal. Indeed, the new generation of Chinese traffickers may have broken into the violent American market at the expense of their ties to traditional criminal hierarchies. "When the young American Chinese go to Hong Kong now, the guys over there don't want to have anything to do with them," says Dwight Rabb. "The Hong Kong Chinese call them 'bananas'—yellow on the outside, white on the inside."

From the mid-level to the street, heroin distribution has mainly been controlled by black organizations. However, law-enforcement officials report that lately Chinese gangs have been selling in northern Queens and that Hispanic groups—often backed by cocaine money—have broken into the business. But the big heroin markets are found in the predominantly black slums, and dealers from outside are unwelcome.

Older and more established than their crack counterparts, these networks give the heroin business a stability unique in the drug trade. Many of them were Mafia franchises and developed along the same organizational lines as the mob. Until their recent bust, a handful of powerful dealers in southeastern Queens divided the lucrative market there into territories. In Harlem where several groups often run outlets on the same street or even in the same building, agreements over turf are strictly regulated.

WHAT'S MORE, HEROIN'S HIGH PRICE AND NARROW DIStribution make the business easier to control than the crack trade. For one thing, there's simply less heroin around. For another, top distributors are especially guarded about the people with whom they deal. Even if an enterprising young street dealer could find a connection, a kilo of heroin might cost him $200,000 or more wholesale—about six times as much as a similar amount of cocaine.

Heroin's high prices are reflected in the dealer's huge profit margins. While cocaine is rarely cut more than once, heroin can be "stepped on" two or three times. Mid-level transactions are based entirely on relationships; a trusted broker need never touch the product and only rarely the cash. From 1985 until recently, Lorenzo "Fat Cat" Nichols, the legendary Queens drug trafficker, ran a multi-million-dollar operation from prison. In 1988, according to the FBI, he was moving an average of 25 kilos of cocaine and 3 kilos of heroin a month. He bought the heroin from Chinese broker "John" Man Sing Eng—whom he'd met in prison—and, using two lieutenants as go-betweens, sold them to more than a dozen customers.

The big heroin money, however, is made by the dealers who process the drug and market it through networks of street sellers. Take the case of Earl Gibson, a veteran black dealer whose operation included a heroin mill in Queens and selling locations in Brooklyn, in the Bronx, and on the Lower East Side. Before his conviction on drug charges two years ago, Gibson cut, packaged, and sold about a kilo of heroin every four days, earning $150,000 to $200,000 a week. Gibson's occasional partner, Raymond Sanchez "Shorty" Rivera, a Puerto Rican dealer based on the Lower East Side, generated that kind of revenue every day. Based on the testimony of workers for Rivera—who has also been convicted—the FBI estimates that he was grossing more than $60 million a year.

WITH MONEY LIKE THAT TO BE MADE, THE DRUG BUSIness is a powerful lure. In 1987, when he was seventeen, a young Dominican we'll call Pedro had already tried several times to get into the drug business, passing his requests through an acquaintance who worked as a courier for one of the leading distributors in the Bushwick–East New York section of Brooklyn. The distributor, a fellow Dominican in his mid-twenties who knew Pedro and his family, eventually agreed to front him a small supply of heroin.

Pedro took in a partner who knew a location for selling—a spot on his East New York block that had opened up when the previous dealer was nabbed by police. Since neither youth had any extensive experience, they hired a seller recently out of jail. In those days, two distributors in the area were selling different brands, one called Goodyear and the other Airborne; Pedro handled Airborne.

The distributor supplied Pedro with heroin already cut and packaged in units called packs, each of which contained 100 $10 bags. Pedro took the packs on consignment and eventually returned 80 percent of the proceeds to the wholesaler. He paid a further 10 percent to his seller and split the remaining 10 percent with his partner—leaving him just $50 profit per pack sold.

Nevertheless, business was solid—on a good day, he could sell fifteen packs. Most clients were local addicts who could afford only a bag or two at a time, but, Pedro recalls, some were middle-class men in business suits. Others were out-of-town dealers who bought in bulk and who got discounts from Pedro.

Over the next two years, Pedro was able to open five locations, including spots on Knickerbocker Avenue and in Bushwick Park—prime areas that are restricted to well-connected dealers. At the height of his operation, he was personally clearing $600 a day.

Over time, though, competition picked up and cut into Pedro's revenues. By the time he got out last year, he was making $200 a day; now, he says, most dealers are just trying to survive.

"They're making $1,000 a week, if they're lucky," he says. "That may seem like a lot, but to a dealer, that's nothing." In Pedro's world, a successful dealer must project a certain image: He's got to be tough and free-spending. Fancy cars, gold jewelry, and designer warm-up gear are only the most obvious marks of his position. He's also got to pay for trips to Florida (stressed-out street dealers like to relax at theme parks) and pick up the tab at restaurants and clubs.

Beyond all that, a high-flying life-style can be especially expensive in the slums. Pedro's Cutlass Supreme was stolen right after he'd sunk $3,000 into customizing the tires and sound system. At a party, his $1,500 gold chain and medallion were lifted at gunpoint. And several times, he says, he was ripped off for the drugs he was carrying.

Meanwhile, Pedro's risks were high. Once, early on, some competing dealers tried to move in on one of his locations. Under the terms of their agreement, Pedro's wholesaler was supposed to provide him with protection. Instead, he supplied him with guns—expecting Pedro and his cronies to take care of themselves.

"Like most young guys from the neighborhood, carrying a gun made me feel power," he recalls. "At the time, I only thought about shooting other people. I never thought about getting shot myself."

Over time, twelve of the young men he worked with were arrested and jailed. He says that since their release, two have been killed trying to re-enter the drug trade and another was killed because he owed money to Pedro's former supplier. In fact, the police have determined that more than quarter of New York City's record 1,905 homicides last year were drug related.

The demise of his associates and the decline of his business finally led Pedro to give up dealing. But he still recalls the many times he rebuffed his mother's tearful pleas to stop. "That really made me sad, to see my mother cry," he says. "But not my mother or any job was ever going to give me the money that drugs was bringing to me."

*The Indiana Jones of the tavern scene,
this anthropologist studies the
American drinker like a lost tribe of the
Amazon. In documenting the rituals
of the bar, he's discovered how and why
we booze it up the way we do*

INTERVIEW
JAMES SCHAEFER

A. J. S. Rayl

The rain drizzles down on the car windows as Jim Schaefer pulls off the main road and into a packed parking lot. "Most anthropologists spend a lifetime trying to find a tribe that will accept them," Schaefer says as we approach a building pulsing with light and music. Nailed to the door is a big sign that reads: ANYONE WHO IS NOT OF LEGAL AGE WILL BE ARRESTED ON THE SPOT AND ESCORTED FROM THE PREMISES. "But my tribe," he continues, "is here and now. And they accept me." Schaefer is an anthropologist whose tribe is American drinkers. Associated professor and director of the Office of Alcohol and Drug Abuse Prevention at the School of Public Health at the University of Minnesota, he has spent almost 20 years studying American drinkers, the bars they patronize, and the role of alcohol in society.

We enter the Hoggsbreath, a bar on the outskirts of St. Paul. Clearly this is Schaefer's territory. Like some kind of Indiana Jones of the tavern scene, he swashbuckles a path through the mass of humanity to the watering hole and orders drinks. The Hoggsbreath is a theme bar and thus features a different sort of ambience every night. Monday nights the theme is country and west-

ern, and that means there'll be a tight-jeans contest, complete with free shots for the contestants, and all the bumping and grinding it takes to win, "And things," Schaefer warned earlier, "can get down and dirty."

"Hey, there's the professor!" shouts the bar's cowboy DJ. "And he says if you listen to slow country music you're gonna drink more. Whaddya thinka that!" The tribe responds with boos and hisses. Then these urban cowboys break into a chant: "Bullshit! Bullshit! Bullshit!"

Born in Schenectady, New York, in 1942, Schaefer is the son of a General Electric scientist who discovered the principle of cloud seeding. As a young child Schaefer showed an interest in anthropology, archaeology, and hunting for arrowheads and other buried relics in upstate New York. The West always held an allure, and in 1960 Schaefer enrolled in the University of Montana as a forestry major. But with most of his time spent in Missoula's heavy party scene at the local bars, he was on the verge of flunking out. To pick up his grade point average, he was advised to go into anthropology, a subject that had a reputation for being easy at Montana. In those courses Schaefer found direc-

tion, however unintentionally. He earned a degree in anthropology in 1966 and "made it into graduate school" at the State University of New York at Buffalo.

When Schaefer couldn't come up with a topic for his doctoral thesis, his adviser asked what it was that Schaefer felt he knew a lot about. In a moment of unadulterated honesty, he replied, "Drinking." His life's work began that day. Schaefer completed his dissertation, a cross-cultural study of family structures, supernatural belief systems, and drunkenness in 57 tribal societies worldwide. In 1973 he earned his Ph.D. with distinction.

Schaefer returned to the University of Montana as an assistant professor. And with newfound awareness and self-control, he returned to the Missoula bar scene—this time to study the whys and wherefores. He also spent a year as the Fulbright Visiting Lecturer at Sri Venkateswara University in India and a year as a National Institute of Alcohol Abuse and Alcoholism Research Fellow at the Center for Alcohol Studies of the University of North Carolina. But mainly, during the next decade Schaefer, along with research assistants and students, hung out at local bars, investigating patron behavior and environmental influences. Conducting their research in an unobtrusive, par-

ticipant-observation style, Schaefer and colleagues discovered that the jukebox served as a mood-selection device. He realized further that by studying the impact of music, decor, lighting, and other factors on customers, he could draw up an environmental-risk profile with regard to overindulgence for almost any bar.

And on this particular night at the Hoggsbreath? "It's definitely high-risk," Schaefer says. "The bar is crowded. The dance floor is crowded. People can't really move. They'll get frustrated and start drinking more. And check out the lighting. It's what I call twilight lighting: It's light enough to see but dark enough to cover the faults."

In 1978 Schaefer moved to Minneapolis, to the University of Minnesota, where he has since taken part in several research and development projects. In 1979 he and University of Montana graduate student Paul Bach published a paper on slow country music and drinking. It put Schaefer on the map in many circles, both scientific and lay. In 1985 he was enlisted as a coproject investigator with sociologist Richard Sykes, also of the University of Minnesota, for a long-term study on self-regulation of alcohol abuse among tavern patrons in the Midwest. He is currently participating in an investigation of biological markers for alcohol consumption and a study of environmental influences on gambling and drinking.

Alcohol remains the United States' number one recreational drug. Schaefer has crossed detached scientific lines and become something of an activist in community education, outreach, and intervention programs geared toward reducing alcohol abuse. In 1982 he organized Anthropologists Concerned for Anthropologists, a support group for those professionals struggling with alcohol and drug abuse. The same year he was awarded a grant to head the Grand Rapids, Minnesota, Drinking and Driving Project. It gained nationwide attention when Schaefer replanted old Burma Shave signs along Minnesota highways (IT'S BEST FOR/ ONE WHO HITS/ THE BOTTLE/ TO LET ANOTHER/ USE THE THROTTLE). And in 1988 he was appointed to the science advisory board of the American Council on Alcoholism.

Schaefer is frequently hired as an expert witness for both plaintiffs and defendants in drunk driving cases. He has served as a consultant to major law firms around the country and to the Federal Trade Commission on product liability and fraudulent advertising practices.

Schaefer is also an entrepreneur of sorts. In recent years he has helped design bars and has lent his expertise to the development of Alcosorb, an anti-intoxicant and hangover remedy, for 21st Century Pharmaceuticals.

A.J.S. Rayl spent an extended weekend with Schaefer, barhopping throughout the Twin Cities—from cowboy night at the Hoggsbreath to the upscale Rupert's to small neighborhood bars.

Omni: How did your bar research begin?
Schaefer: I took a job at the University of Montana and while visiting some of the old places ten years after, I thought about applying ideas I'd gleaned from theoretical work. What could I observe in an actual place where people drank? I started hanging out all over again, only this time as an anthropologist.

Sammy Thompson, owner of the Trail's End in Missoula, was by far the best bartender I'd ever seen. A maestro, he orchestrated the scene. One day, about five P.M., the jukebox ran out of plays and suddenly I saw the place die. While people weren't verbalizing it, their eyes were saying, "What's wrong here?" Sammy picked up on it right away and brought out this bean game, a long-necked jug with maybe fifteen beans in it, one of which was red. The one who winds up with the red bean loses and forks out the money to play the jukebox.

As the guy with the red bean headed toward the jukebox, regulars started shouting out the songs people wanted to hear. I suddenly realized that here was a microcosm of bar culture and that the jukebox was a mood-selection device. That was really neat—something I could systematically investigate. My graduate student Paul Bach came up with an ingenious way to measure the relationship between mood, music, environment, and drinking. We'd put a tape recorder on the table in front of the jukebox and tape the ten- to twelve-o'clock set of songs on consecutive Friday nights. We observed patrons drinking in different areas of the bar. We'd also tap our table with a pen or glass every time someone in our sample areas sipped a drink.

Back at the office, Paul converted the music into beats per minute and correlated it with the number of sips per minute. We assumed that as the tempo went up, the drinking would, too, but it didn't turn out that way. Slower songs went with faster sipping.

Next we looked at lyric content and tried to figure out whether country-western [CW] songs tended to portray images of self-controlling the world—internal locus of control—or external. Slower songs tended to be sad—"your lyin' cheatin' heart" or "cryin' in the beer" type songs. Country music is not like the "I Want Your Sex" stuff of modern rock and roll. Country is more of a working-class blues—'I'm sufferin' and hurtin' since you been gone' variety. It's the stuff of the work-hard, play-hard folks who are the hard core of this country, whether they live in Detroit, Los Angeles, or the Rocky Mountain west. I don't know if you need to put warning labels on CW songs, but the surgeon general might be interested!
Omni: Have you gone into a bar and challenged the norms, say, punched numbers for certain kinds of songs on the jukebox at the wrong time?
Schaefer: Yeah, and do they give you stares! There is a recognition of normative sounds in a bar, and when that norm is being broken or challenged, people will leave or let their preferences be known. At the Trail's End, we did things like playing a sequence of slow songs and took a baseline count of the number of times the cash register rang at twenty-minute intervals. I did that a couple of times, and once the sales quadrupled.
Omni: You also began to establish a risk profile with regard to overdrinking. What did you find?
Schaefer: There's a greater likelihood in a "high-risk" environment. For instance, moderately lit bars with a twilight kind of darkness—bright enough for effective cruising, but dark enough to cover up faults—are high-risk.

Heavy drinking also occurs when the ratio of men to women is high, like five to one. The men get very frustrated because they have a limited capacity for expressing themselves. There's also a premium on being able to get to a table and, you know, "cut out a heifer"—take her out to the dance floor and she's yours. A small, crowded dance floor is high-risk. You can't do your thing. You're bumping into people, so you tend to drink more. I've looked at the artwork, too. High-risk bars often show images of action: In a cowboy bar you'll see a picture of a cowboy bustin' a bull. Or, in other bars, sports pictures: Somebody is about to make a touchdown or is skiing off a cliff. This can be an affirmation of risky or highly competitive behavior and tends to encourage a bragging, storytelling bravado, and there's more drinking.
Omni: What about low-risk drinking environments?
Schaefer: Bright and very dark bars are relatively low-risk. Casino bars, in particular, are on the bright side because the premium is not on drinking but gambling. Darker bars tend to be more of a romantic setting for couples or lonesome singles. In yuppie bars, where you dress up and eat food, there's a premium on not spilling, not getting messy, and that sets a certain decorum for the group. If there's a big dance floor and lots of space to move around, then there's a premium on struttin' your stuff: You're out there swinging, gliding, or stomping—or you're Cotton-Eyed Joe. In bars where there's moderate drinking, I found landscape artwork or just wallpaper. And there are family-type bars, usually restaurants with a sec-

tion where the kids play video games and the women can eat and socialize. These tend to be low-risk because the premium isn't on drinking. These places aren't real common in the United States.

Omni: How does behavior differ in certain types of bars?

Schaefer: Observation—not testing—tells me the drinking in the rock scene—disco, rock, or live-band pop—is more controlled. A slightly different game's being played. In the country-western bar there's more male acting out and rowdy behavior: "Let's get drunk and *be* somebody." In the rock and pop scenes there's a premium on meeting someone, impressing them with your good taste in drink, clothing, and maybe dancing.

Omni: What about the *Cheers* kind of bars, the neighborhood bars?

Schaefer: If we are talking about reinforcing a core value system, a shared system of values that is anchored in a community, then *Cheers* bars act as places where everybody knows your name, there's a place for you to be someone, and they know what you drink. It's a home away from home that provides you with the security of peer group protection. If Norm has a drinking problem, someone will see him about it. If Sam Malone is a teetotaler, they respect it. They'll joke about his fake male prowess, lack of intellect, but they don't joke about his drinking. It might be interesting to see some real intoxication on *Cheers,* see them cut somebody off and perhaps go through treatment. There are possibilities on that show that aren't being explored.

Omni: According to your studies, how often do people who go to bars actually become intoxicated?

Schaefer: The bad news is that more than fifty percent of the people in a bar at a given time in the area we sampled were intoxicated, twelve percent seriously. By intoxication we mean drinking at a rate of three or more drinks an hour and actually consuming three or more drinks an hour. If you drink at that rate for two hours, you're well over the legal limit [.10 milligram] for blood alcohol.

Surprisingly, Richard Sykes's study showed that the vast majority of bar staff are pretty darn accurate in gauging just how intoxicated their patrons are. Our objective observers' estimates of slightly and seriously intoxicated patrons almost perfectly matched the perceptions of the bartenders and cocktail waitresses interviewed. We originally thought that they would substantially underestimate the number of intoxicated people.

But while bartenders are accurate, they frequently are overserving. In most jurisdictions, overserving is against the law, though it's a law that's not enforced. The feds aren't out there trying to monitor that,

In small-town America, the bar is the gossip center— the center of social activity. Without that corner bar to go to, there would be more homicides, violence, and trouble.

but overserving makes for drunk driving and is the stuff of alcohol abuse.

Omni: Have you found regional differences in drinking patterns?

Schaefer: Lots. The Southeast generally has very low consumption rates, yet every third generation has serious drinking problems. There is strict adherence to the Bible, and Fundamentalists often teach that one must abstain entirely from alcohol. This is overdone in many households, and as a result, the next generation reject the values and become alcohol abusers. Yet the societal effects [job impairment, drunk driving, familial breakup, and so forth] of problem drinking in the Southeast are the lowest in the country. The vast middle of the United States tends to be the beer-consuming part of the country. In the upper Midwest we have moderate drinking, and that part of the country is also right in the middle in terms of social problems related to drinking. New York City and Washington, DC, are extremely heavy drinking areas. Texas, Nevada, California, Oregon, and Washington—wine states—show heavy drinking and high rates of alcohol abuse. And the indexes of alcohol problems in the New England states are very high. It's thought that where wine is inexpensive, there's a pump-priming effect: Wine consumption leads to consumption of spirits and beer.

Omni: What about gender differences?

Schaefer: Men drink more than women. That hasn't changed. Older men drink earlier in the day. Women drink about half as much as men and tend to drink later in the day, as well as later in the week. Perhaps women feel that later is safer because more people are around. If a lady were to go into a bar alone early in the week, she might be perceived as not meeting the cultural norm. Now Tuesday night is ladies' night, and that's a widespread phenomenon. Women do come out, at least for the first shift, to drink the free champagne. Usually they leave then,

unless they meet someone who's worth staying around for. There's still a stigma against a woman being intoxicated in public. Women pay attention to making sure they don't show signs of it.

Omni: But certainly you've seen women who've had a little too much, and men responding to it with a sort of endeared amusement?

Schaefer: You mean when they become foulmouthed, telling jokes, and being more like a guy? Sure, but when it goes beyond the cultural norms, then she becomes the subject of exploitation. There are a good number of predators looking for women who've had a little too much. They follow an agenda of buying her a good stiff drink to make sure she's over the edge, presumably not caring what happens to her. It works differently in other parts of the world. When I was in India, it was taboo for a woman to drink in public, but alcohol is available everywhere. I saw partying college women who would go up to men and feign drunkenness, feign passing out, so they could have sex. The women wanted it, so they played the same game the other way around.

Omni: Are there racial differences in drinking patterns?

Schaefer: You'd find about the same rate of alcoholism among whites, blacks, Hispanics, Latinos, and Chicanos. There is, however, more excessive drinking among American Indians than any other group. Their unique tribal traditions have now become essentially welfare-state traditions, a culture of poverty. There are some proudly held core traditions, but the majority are losing that core value system. There's tragedy on every reservation. There's no history of moderate drinking among Native Americans, although there's now an attempt to increase a culture of sobriety. Biological or genetic factors may also play against them with regard to metabolizing alcohol.

Some evidence suggests that genetic factors play a role for Orientals as well. But the consequences differ from those for the Native Americans. The vast majority of Japanese and Chinese people have an enzyme system that is slow to break down acetaldehyde, the first metabolite of alcohol, which is probably more intoxicating and damaging to the system than ethanol. This enzyme defect translates to a flushing response, dizziness, pounding of the heart, sweating, and general dysphoria. This unpleasantness may be protective against alcohol abuse. The abuse problem is at a low percentage in first-generation Orientals.

Omni: Is the same metabolic factor present in the American Indian?

Schaefer: Possibly. American Indians are part of the Asiatic gene pool. Although, having migrated millennia ago, they must

be considered very diluted Asians. There is a strong theoretical argument, supported by animal studies, that if one persists in drinking heavily in the face of this enzyme defect, that person will quickly become addicted to alcohol. It may be that persistent heavy drinking under those circumstances causes a biological adaptation similar to tolerance buildup in normal people—only much faster. Lab rats with this deficiency that are exposed to alcohol quickly develop another enzyme, THP [tetrahydropapaveraline], a by-product of acetaldehyde. THP seems to enhance the animals' craving for ethanol, and they go after it until they convulse or die. It may be that due to the extreme stress caused by their cultural disenfranchisement, the American Indians continue to drink in spite of the protection conferred by the enzyme defect. So this devastating mechanism of addiction has taken hold.

Omni: What's the role of the local bar?

Schaefer: If any society chose to reject alcohol, it would probably have other, more serious problems. There's the workplace, the homeplace, and this third place, where we talk, drink, and release ourselves from our everyday worries and troubles. A little bit of drinking goes a long way in terms of the health of the community. Without that outlet we'd have more fighting, violence, and civil strife. In Minnesota we recently passed stricter drunk driving laws that upshifted the penalties for drunken driving. Shortly thereafter, when the cops started busting people, domestic violence increased. The heavy drinkers were staying at home. Bar sales went down, but package store sales went up, as did spouse and child abuse.

It's an age-old explanation, but I am more and more convinced that drinking alcohol in a relatively controlled public environment, where professionals are trained to recognize the intoxicated and immature drinkers, is the context in which our society can blow off steam. In small-town America the bar *is* the gossip center, the center of social activity. Without that corner bar to go to, there would be more homicides and violence.

Omni: But can't we learn to release tension without alcohol?

Schaefer: With milk and cookies? It's been tried and it's not nearly as successful as with alcohol.

Omni: So the release lies in the high?

Schaefer: Right. Some psychopharmacologists say altered states may be another human drive. I'm not necessarily buying into that, but there are people who believe that the occasional search for an altered state of consciousness is a healthy way of adjusting to life.

Omni: In your opinion, what is a safe level of alcohol consumption?

Schaefer: If you're downing more than thirty-five drinks a week, or five drinks a day, you're risking chemical dependency and medical consequences like cirrhosis, pancreatitis, cancer, and stroke. A person weighing more than one hundred thirty pounds should stick to about eight to ten drinks a week, with no more than five in one sitting. More than five per sitting could cause long-term problems. For someone weighing less than one hundred thirty pounds, we recommend seven to eight drinks a week, with no more than four at one sitting. We also recommend that people stand when drinking, because people feel their intoxication more rapidly if they only have two-point support. If you know your weight, you should have your blood alcohol chart memorized. God, I can't believe I said that, but it's the truth. Know just how many drinks you can drink. Stick to your limit. If you can't, get help.

Omni: You mentioned that at one time you had a drinking problem.

Schaefer: In the early Sixties a lot of events brought me to that realization. I was really kind of out of control, and a lot of my buddies knew it.

Omni: How did you deal with it?

Schaefer: I never did anything official. I slowed down, got into a relationship with the woman I ended up marrying, and stayed married for a considerable period of time. If I had been living in Minnesota, for example, I would have been confronted and counseled into a treatment program. But back then in Montana—and still in Montana—the value system was one where people took care of their own problems. The opinion of my alcohol-recovering friends to the contrary, I can now drink and then leave it alone. I don't drink the bottle dry. I intersperse nonalcoholic drinks with my alcohol. What I did was mature out of my drinking problem from a hell-raiser to a family man.

Of course, by choosing my career in the alcohol abuse prevention field, I was helping myself. I exposed myself to all the reasons why people drink, biological as well as sociocultural. I continue to be in contact with treatment people and work extensively in developing programs that educate and train people in abuse prevention. I guess my work and life are a kind of therapy. Having been there—literally having gone to skid row and back, getting into fights, getting arrested and thrown in the drunk tank, and then getting bailed out by my favorite bartender at the Trail's End—gives me a unique kind of credibility.

I can now get into the scenes quickly. That's very subjective, and from a scientist's point of view, that subjectivity is often questionable. But the typical anthropological scheme is to use your intuitive and deductive powers by going into a scene, coming back with preliminary data, then systematically replicating them. The original insights usually come from a subjective, involved participant frame of reference. There's trial and error in understanding cultural patterns.

Omni: Why is alcohol abuse the country's number one drug problem?

Schaefer: American society is very immature. We're on this treadmill of "Gotta go! Gotta get the bucks!" It may be endemic in a capitalist system that we tend to overdo in our lives and sometimes burn out. Our self-imposed, highly competitive system puts us all under a great deal of risk for outlets such as excessive drinking or bouts of depression. Our biochemical, neurochemical wiring hasn't been prepared for these kinds of stresses. Self-medicating is a pattern of culturally approved behavior.

Per capita consumption of alcohol is, on average, declining, indicating that by the mid-Seventies, community tolerance for alcohol abuse had reached its peak. A number of things occurred, the most recent being housewife Candy Lightner forming the group Mothers Against Drunk Driving [in 1981]. People resolved that driving while drunk is a totally inappropriate social behavior. But the reality is a lot of people still drink and drive.

You change behavior in a Judeo-Christian society by deglamorization and mild repression. Look at cigarette smoking. That's what our drunk driving laws do. The recognition of alcoholism as a disease was a major step in the direction of helping people with problems. People arrested today have a slightly lower blood alcohol level than they did in the early Eighties. Yet I do foresee alcoholism continuing to be the number one drug problem in the coming millennium.

Omni: What about Alcoholics Anonymous [AA] or the Betty Ford Clinic or the many other treatment centers? How well do they work?

Schaefer: The twelve-step program of AA is a blueprint for living that has helped a huge number of people recover from very serious problems with alcohol. It's a wonderful and effective fellowship. At Betty Ford you enroll full-time as an inpatient for a month, then return on an outpatient basis or, in some cases, not until you relapse. There is a good likelihood of a slip, maybe a full-blown relapse, with any of these treatment programs. Statistics are hard to come by, but I've heard that about one in four slips. And of those, one in four has a full-blown relapse [within four years] and will need to get back into a program.

Omni: Philosopher Herbert Fingarette created a stir two years ago by hypothesizing that alcoholism is really just a bad drinking habit.

1. THINKING ABOUT DRUGS

Schaefer: There have been few governing ideas about alcohol. There's the "Colonial" view: Alcoholism is a moral wrong. That eventually led to Prohibition: demon rum wrapped up in temperance. Then came the idea, surfacing about thirty years ago, that people who become chemically dependent suffer from an illness. The majority position is that of Fingarette's philosophy. Although in the United States its greatest expression has been found in behavioral psychology, it dominates European thinking about drinking. Alcohol, the argument goes, is a beverage that we learn to use. Some people get into trouble; some don't. The problem is behavioral, not genetic.

If you buy into the other, disease model—which, quite frankly, has been primarily conceived as a particular kind of alcoholism—then your only choice in correcting the problem is complete abstinence. Yet I accept the idea that some people change their alcoholiclike behavior and control their intake or spontaneously stop without help. I think Fingarette makes a good case for behavior modification as a possibility for some people with drinking problems. Such programs work best with persons who have a stable social and spiritual framework with which to rebuild their lives.

But I believe that up to twenty-five percent of all alcohol problems may someday be explained by genetic factors. Many families have gone from generation to generation inheriting the biological baggage of addiction. But the legacy doesn't necessarily have to be genetic. It can be passed on through poor family patterning in a disruptive atmosphere, a weakened moral network.

Omni: Will it ever be possible to eradicate alcoholism?

Schaefer: Yes and no. Remember that with alcoholism we're only talking about seven percent of the population. The biggest societal cost is not from alcoholism but *periodic* abuse of alcohol and other drugs. Treating the psychosocial part of alcoholism is our best chance for eradicating the problem in the short run. We can reduce the risk by building a culture with a better sense of individual responsibility about alcohol use. We can also build stronger families, neighborhoods, and communities with more awareness about appropriate use of alcohol among adults. That is what prevention's all about.

Now, the biological part may be more difficult. First we have to elucidate the precise addictive pathways. In the future we may understand the chemical structure of the chromosomes and where the genetic markers for the addictive potential lie. Then with gene therapy, say, we could adjust a person's genetic makeup prior to the reproductive years. That way he would not pass on the addictive genetic material to his children, and then eventually we might be able to eradicate the defect from the gene pool. Maybe we could give the person a choice of having the adjustment done or not. If not, then he could pay a large fine or something. [He laughs.] Alternatively, we could transplant a lot of livers and related body parts in addicts and abusers. Any biological tinkering might be too Draconian for our libertarian tastes. Yet another way of dealing with these problems is to create a novel family of drugs of anti-intoxicants that enable you to experience better living through chemistry, so you could drink, enjoy it, and not suffer the medical consequences.

Omni: Haven't you been consulting on the development of such a product?

Schaefer: I'm a scientific consultant with 21st Century Pharmaceuticals, a company here in Minneapolis. It has a patent on a product called Alcosorb that is much like what I've described. It's not a drug; it's a microversion of the charcoal slurry used in acute poisonings. Alcosorb is an activated carbon caplet that acts as a superfilter in the intestine. After the first stage of clinical tests, it looks promising. It appears to alter dramatically the blood alcohol level. Alcosorb will be controversial because it won't completely block the intoxicating effects of alcohol.

We are talking an *Alice in Wonderland* view now, but I think we can get close to blocking the physical consequences of alcohol abuse with a product that would absorb the toxic substances created by ethanol. It would save your liver and pancreas but still allow you to enjoy the intoxicating effects. It would require, of course, that we develop a whole cultural value system around it.

Omni: But wouldn't that open a Pandora's box of trouble? Without the threat of a hangover, what's to stop a person from getting drunk every night? Doesn't this encourage addiction to alcohol?

Schaefer: Not necessarily. In the short run it causes an ethical dilemma for people promoting the use of such a product. Should people always have to suffer the natural consequences of overconsumption: pounding heart, sweats, waking up in a pool of urine, the foul odor? If this product kept you from receiving those messages, it would not be a good idea. But again, this is a futuristic idea, and we need revolutionary changes in how we deal with the problems of addiction. I envision sophisticated chemistry enabling us to block or reduce some of the effects that are very costly to individuals, communities, and society as a whole.

The dog tests on Alcosorb are under way now in Texas, and they're looking good. We need to test humans at relatively high blood alcohol levels. So our next big hurdle will be the current federal guidelines that prohibit us from taking humans up to very high alcohol levels.

Omni: Tell us about the search for the biological marker of alcohol *consumption*, rather than alcoholism.

Schaefer: We're interested in detecting in simple blood samples whether an individual has been drinking during the prior week, month, three or four months, or year. Based on the ratio of certain blood chemistry structures, we should be able to see a person's drinking history and advise the individual or family about the relative risk of developing problems related to alcohol abuse or potential addiction.

We are not trying to develop a marker for alcoholism per se. There are numerous gross blood-based measurements available, and although perhaps useful for verifying alcoholism in some people who already have a problem, they have what we think are some fatal flaws: They depend on liver damage, for one thing, and that's already looking at the problem after the fact. They don't take into account, nor do they reflect, alcohol intake or dose-related responses, so they put the cart before the horse. We are looking for a marker covering the continuum, from abstinence to heavy abuse. We are investigating people with different levels of consumption: those who don't drink, those who drink moderately, social drinkers who overdo it from time to time, and heavy drinkers who do *not* develop full-blown chemical dependency problems.

The principal investigator, biochemist John Belcher, also at the University of Minnesota, has studied ways of detecting risks in both smokers and people in passive or secondary smoke situations such as airplanes. With alcohol we're looking at two different metabolic pathways. One is the oxidative pathway, where we're following the breakdown of the ethanol molecule into its various metabolites, particularly acetaldehyde.

In the other, nonoxidative pathway we're following the fatty acid ethyl esters and studying disruptions in chemical structure as a result of varying doses of alcohol. Using mass spectrometry and novel gas chromatography techniques, we're analyzing the sequences of certain amino acid chains and long-chain peptides for minute differences. On a preliminary basis we've found remarkable differences between people who drink and those who don't. That was our first clue that we were on to something. Now we're sorting through our data to make sure we are not creating our own monster through var-

ious detection methods: fusions, dilutions, saturations, and so forth.

We have examined a couple dozen nondrinkers and about a dozen drinkers and are comparing their blood samples under different doses. My role is recruiting the subjects. I'm out there beating the bushes for drinkers, abstainers, and recovering alcoholics, those who have abstained for five, ten, and seventeen years. We want to see if their hemoglobin structures are any different from people who have never been exposed to alcohol. We'll give some subjects doses of alcohol; then we'll take blood samples over various periods of time. We have them come back the next day, three days, then a week later, and months later. They'll keep a diary, too, of any drinks they have. We hope to correlate blood structures we've analyzed with their self-reports. What got us very excited about this was that we were able to isolate a particular point in a hemoglobin molecule, the first line on the chart we think will eventually be able to delineate the light, moderate, and heavy drinker. And we found it in a place we never thought we'd find it: in the abstainer.

Omni: Grants for alcohol-related studies are plentiful. Have times changed?

Schaefer: Yes. The National Institute of Alcohol Abuse and Alcoholism is now very interested in research on drinking environments. And I've seen a number of proposals for investigating such things as what happens when you deregulate a state with liquor controls or begin to train bar staffs in a specific community. Ten years ago people were skeptical of the relevance of my work. It was pretty lonesome out there. Now there's lots of attention. Richard Sykes and I put in a proposal to recruit a hundred groups of drinkers to essentially go out and drink in bars, wearing body-packed microcassette recorders. We'll transcribe their conversations in time-sync so we can analyze how bar customers make decisions about drinks, reorders, and driving.

Omni: What do you hope to achieve by your work?

Schaefer: I like my idea of the hospitality covenant where a community gets the retail liquor businesses together and they promulgate their own set of voluntary standards. A number of communities are employing my idea. Also, I hope more social scientists will now be willing to get out to do work in the establishments, the grocery and liquor stores, and not rely on proxy studies. Unless you've done your share of hanging out, you can't ask the right questions.

Omni: Do you think the role of alcohol will change in the next few years?

Schaefer: Right now we're headed for a continuation of neo-Prohibition. I think we're going to continue to swing to the right regarding alcohol controls, because the governing image is still of alcoholism as a disease whose spread must be curbed. In the long run, though, there'll be a rebound, and we'll see per capita consumption go back up. But what our children's children will do with alcohol is anybody's guess. I also expect we'll legalize marijuana. All the cigarette companies are patiently waiting. They've already trademarked names.

Omni: Bar owners have consulted you about the design of their establishments.

What ideas do you have for future bars?
Schaefer: I would have exits that mimic the field sobriety tests. The exit itself would resemble a fun house. You'd go into a tunnel with a floor that's not quite level. To get out you'd have to navigate a maze. Maybe the sides would be electronic so if you hit them, there'd be a light show—and then a cab would be waiting for you when you finally made it out. If you did. Or you might automatically be given a breath test. Instead of waiting for the sobriety test from Smokey, why not have the bars provide it?

Omni: Will we always have bars?
Schaefer: In the late Seventies I was giving a paper in Norway on alcohol abuse. On a day off, I headed for a bar, where I met two guys who said they had a film showing at a local film festival. They were George Lucas and Mark Hamill, and they asked me if I wanted to come to their screening. I did, and *Star Wars* came on, and it was fantastic. One scene that bothered me a bit, though, was the cantina scene, with the pulling down of hookahs by all those weird creatures. I asked Lucas, who is anthropologically trained, about it. He said he believed there's always going to be a place where ideas are brokered. And it's more likely going to be in a situation where people can have unlimited access to whatever chemical they want. Although I argued with him on details, Lucas is basically right. There's always going to be a place to go to achieve altered states—the third place. And in the future we'll have much more open minds about the benefits of achieving altered states now and then.

The War on (Some) Drugs

Stephen Jay Gould

Gould teaches paleontology at Harvard University. His most recent book is Wonderful Life: The Burgess Shale and the Nature of History, *published by Norton.*

Categories often exert a tyranny over our perceptions and judgments. An old joke—perhaps it even happened—from the bad old days of McCarthyism tells of a leftist rally in Philadelphia, viciously broken up by the police. A passerby gets caught in the melee and, as the cops are beating him, he pleads, "Stop, stop, I'm an anticommunist." "I don't care what kind of communist you are," says the cop, as he continues pummeling.

We seem driven to think in dichotomies. Protagoras, according to Diogenes, asserted that "there are two sides to every question, exactly opposite to each other." We set up our categories, often by arbitrary division based on tiny differences; then, mistaking names for moral principles, and using banners and slogans as substitutes for reason, we vow to live or die for one or the other side of a false dichotomy. The situation is lamentable enough when the boundaries are profound and natural; if cows declared war on chickens, we might deplore the barnyard carnage, but at least the divisions would be deep, and membership by birth could not be disputed. But when humans struggle with other humans, the boundaries are almost always fluid and largely arbitrary (or at least a curious result of very recent historical contingencies).

Our current drug crisis is a tragedy born of a phony system of classification. For reasons that are little more than accidents of history, we have divided a group of nonfood substances into two categories: items purchasable for supposed pleasure (such as alcohol) and illicit drugs. The categories were once reversed. Opiates were legal in America before the Harrison Narcotics Act of 1914; and members of the Women's Christian Temperance Union, who campaigned against alcohol during the day, drank their valued "women's tonics" at night, products laced with laudanum (tincture of opium).

I could abide—though I would still oppose—our current intransigence if we applied the principle of total interdiction to all harmful drugs. But how can we possibly defend our current policy based on a dichotomy that encourages us to view one class of substances as a preeminent scourge while the two most dangerous and life-destroying substances by far, alcohol and tobacco, form a second class advertised in neon on every street corner of urban America? And why, moreover, should heroin be viewed with horror while chemical cognates that are no different from heroin than lemonade is from iced tea perform work of enormous compassion by relieving the pain of terminal cancer patients in their last days?

Consider just a few recent items rooted in our false classification.

1. A *New York Times* editorial describes methadone as a drug that "blocks the craving for heroin." You might as well say that a Coke blocks the craving for a Pepsi. Methadone and heroin are both opiates, but methadone is legal as a controlled substitute for heroin (fine by me; I think they both should be controlled and decriminalized). We permit methadone because some favorable features lead to easier control (oral administration, longer action, and a less intense high), but methadone is a chemical cousin to heroin.

2. Representative Charles Rangel (Dem., N.Y.), implacable foe of legalization, spurns all talk about this subject as the chatter of eggheads. In 1988, in a *New York Times* op-ed piece, he wrote, "Let's take this legalization issue and put it where it belongs—amid idle chitchat as cocktail glasses knock together at social events." Don't you get it, Mr. Rangel? The stuff in the glasses is as bad as the stuff on the streets. But our classifications permit a majority of Americans to live well enough with one while forcing a minority to murder and die for the other.

3. Former surgeon general C. Everett Koop, who was hired by Reagan to be an ideologue and decided to be a doctor instead, accurately branded nicotine as no less addictive than heroin and cocaine. Representative Terry Bruce (Dem., Ill.) challenged this assertion by arguing

that smokers are not "breaking into liquor stores late at night to get money to buy a pack of cigarettes." Koop properly replied that the only difference resides in social definition as legal or illegal: "You take cigarettes off the streets and people will be breaking into liquor stores. I think one of the things that many people confuse is the behavior of cocaine and heroin addicts when they are deprived of these drugs. That's the difference between a licit and an illicit drug. Tobacco is perfectly legal. You can get it whenever you want to satisfy the craving."

We do not ponder our methods of classification with sufficient scrutiny—and have never done so. Taxonomy, or the study of classification, occupies a low status among the sciences because most people view the activity as a kind of glorified bookkeeping dedicated to pasting objects into preassigned spaces in nature's stamp album. This judgment rests on the false premise that our categories are given by nature and ascertained by simple, direct observation. Nature is full of facts—and they are not distributed isotropically, so nature does provide some hints about divisions.

But our classifications are human impositions, or at least culturally based decisions on what to stress among a plethora of viable alternatives. Classifications are therefore theories of order, not simple records of nature. More important, since classifications are actively imposed, not passively imbibed, they shape our thoughts and deeds in ways that we scarcely perceive because we view our categories as "obvious" and "natural."

Some classifications channel our thinking into fruitful directions because they properly capture the causes of order; others lead us to tragic and vicious errors (the older taxonomies of human races, for example) because they sink their roots in prejudice and mayhem. Too rarely, in our political criticism, do we look to false taxonomies, particularly to improper dichotomies, as the basis for inadequate analysis.

Our drug crisis is largely the product of such a false dichotomy. At the moment, hundreds of thousands of drug users live in tortured limbo, driven to crime, exposed to AIDS, and doomed (at least statistically speaking) to early death. Millions of others suffer palpably from the deeds of the addicted—experiencing violence, robbery, or simple urban fear that steals the joy from life. Billions of dollars go down the rathole to enrich the entrepreneurs or to try to stem the plague by necessarily ineffective interdiction. The politics of several nations in our hemisphere are corrupted, the cultures of whole peoples severely compromised.

William Jennings Bryan once argued that we were about to crucify mankind on a cross of gold. Are we not now significantly lowering the quality of American life for everyone, and causing thousands of deaths directly, by basing our drug policy on something even worse—a false and senseless classification?

Use, Addiction, and Dependence

Of all approaches to drug use and abuse, perhaps the least fruitful and most fallacious is what might be called the *either-or* perspective, that is, the view that one is either a complete abstainer *or* an addict, that there is no in-between territory; as soon as one "fools around" with drugs, one becomes "hooked for life." The reality is quite otherwise. In fact, drug use is a continuum, not an either-or proposition. Experimentation does not necessarily lead to regular use, and regular use does not necessarily lead to compulsive use or addiction. For every drug, it is possible to find users at every point along the spectrum—from experimentation to occasional use to regular use to

outright addiction. There is no inevitable "slide" from less to more involved levels of use.

At the same time, there is a biological and biochemical *basis* for physical dependence, or addiction. Certain drugs possess properties unique to themselves that influence how—and how often—they are used. Most researchers today believe that addiction, or physical dependence, is strongly linked to how *reinforcing* drugs are. Some drugs are highly reinforcing, which means that it is extremely pleasurable to take them; these drugs are more likely to generate a physical dependence in the user. With other drugs, the pleasure is less immediate, more diluted, less sensuous and more of an acquired taste; these drugs are less likely to generate a physical dependence.

Physical dependence can be demonstrated even in laboratory animals in experiments. If certain drugs are self-administered, these animals will take them again and again if they are available, and they will undergo a great deal of pain and deprivation to do so; on the other hand, certain other drugs are difficult for researchers to get animals to self-administer, and animals will discontinue them fairly readily when they can. Drugs that animals will self-administer extremely readily and which, it can be inferred, are highly reinforcing, are: heroin, amphetamines, and cocaine (including, presumably, crack); drugs that animals have relatively little interest in taking in the laboratory setting and which, it may be inferred, are far less reinforcing, are: alcohol, marijuana, and the hallucinogens. In biological terms, then, looking at the factor of reinforcement alone, it can be said that heroin, amphetamines, and cocaine possess a high addiction potential, while that of alcohol, marijuana, and the hallucinogens is fairly low.

Another factor has to be emphasized: *route of administration*, that is, *how* a drug is taken. Certain methods of use are highly reinforcing, that is, the drug's effects are immediate and highly sensuous; other methods are less so, that is, the drug's effects are slower, more muted, less immediately sensuous. Intravenous injection and smoking are more immediate, more highly reinforcing methods of use; oral (swallowing a pill, for instance, or drinking alcohol) and nasal (sniffing or "snorting" cocaine or heroin) ingestion are slower, less reinforcing techniques. When a highly reinforcing drug is taken in a highly reinforcing

fashion, its addiction potential is large; when a less immediately pleasurable drug is taken in a less reinforcing fashion, its addiction potential is far smaller.

These two factors—the characteristics of the drug and the mechanism of use—help explain why heroin, crack, and injected cocaine are likely to generate a high proportion of drug-dependent users. However, there are many features of the drug scene that are not fully explained by the biological model: Why, for instance, are there so many alcoholics, given that the drug is not especially reinforcing and it is nearly always taken in a nonespecially reinforcing fashion? Why does nicotine, a psychoactive chemical found in tobacco, generate so many addicts when laboratory animals avoid taking it altogether? Why is marijuana, taken via a highly reinforcing technique, likely to generate users dependent on the drug? Clearly, sociological and cultural factors come into play here, and determine how, and how often, certain drugs are taken.

Each of our readings emphasizes the complexity of use, addiction, and dependence. On the one hand, drugs are chemical substances with pharmacological properties; they have the *potential* to do things to the human body, as "Addiction and Dependence" and "Nicotine Becomes Addictive" emphasize. On the other hand, "Hooked/Not Hooked," "Drugs of Choice," "A Dirty Drug Secret," and "The 'Monkey Model' of Addiction" emphasize that biological explanations can take the observer only so far in understanding drug use; after all, immense variation can be seen among different drug users—and even from one laboratory animal to another. Clearly, to understand use and dependence, we need a broad, eclectic approach.

Looking Ahead: Challenge Questions

What is the difference between dependence on a legal drug and dependence on an illegal drug?

What is the difference between dependence and addiction?

What is the most addicting drug known?

Is alcohol addicting? Are cigarettes?

Is it possible to use drugs on a recreational, sporadic, once-in-a-while basis?

What is the difference between the user and the addict?

Why is the degree of immediate pleasure generated by different drugs so strongly related to a drug's potential for chemical dependence?

ADDICTION AND DEPENDENCE

Erich Goode

Although it has been known for at least 2,000 years that certain drugs "have the power to enslave men's minds," it was not until the nineteenth century that the nature of physical addiction began to be clearly understood. At that time, a "classic" conception of addiction was formed, based on the opiates—at first, opium and morphine, then, after the turn of the century, heroin as well. Much later, it was recognized that alcohol, sedatives, such as barbiturates, and "minor" tranquilizers also produced most of the symptoms of "classic" addiction.

What is "classic" addiction? If a person takes certain drugs in sufficient quantity over a sufficiently long period of time, and stops taking it abruptly, the user will experience a set of physical symptoms known as *withdrawal.* These symptoms—depending on the dose and the duration—include chills, fever, diarrhea, muscular twitching, nausea, vomiting, cramps, and general bodily aches and pains, especially in the bones and the joints. It does not much matter what one thinks or how one feels about the drug, or even whether one knows one has been taking an addicting drug. (One may not attribute one's discomfort to the drug, but these physical symptoms will occur nonetheless.) These symptoms are not psychological—that is, "all in the mind." They are physiological, and most of them can be replicated in laboratory animals. The withdrawal syndrome is the nervous system's way of "compensating" for the removal of the drug after the body has become acclimatized to its presence and effects.

Although the label "addicting" has been pinned at some time or another on practically every drug ever ingested, it began to be recognized that certain drugs simply do not have physically addicting properties. Regardless of the dose administered or the length of time the drug is ingested, the same sort of withdrawal symptoms exhibited with heroin, alcohol, or the barbiturates cannot be induced in humans or animals taking LSD, marijuana, or cocaine. Users will not become physically sick upon the discontinuation of the use or administration of these drugs. In a word, these substances are not addicting in the "classic" sense of the word. If we mean by "addicting" the appearance of "classic" withdrawal symptoms after prolonged use

and abrupt discontinuation, then certain drugs are addicting and others are not.

This bothered a number of officials and experts a great deal. Saying that a drug is not addicting seemed to border perilously close on stating that it is not very dangerous. Something had to be done. Some new concept or terminology had to be devised to make nonaddicting drugs sound as if they were in fact addicting. In the early 1950s, the World Health Organization, in an effort to devise a new terminology that would apply to the "abuse" of all drugs, and not simply those that are physically addicting, adopted the term "drug dependence." As it appeared in its final form in a later statement, drug dependence was defined as:

> . . . a state of psychic dependence or physical dependence, or both, on a drug, arising in a person following administration of that drug on a periodic or continued basis. The characteristics of such a state will vary with the agent involved, and these characteristics must always be made clear by designating the particular type of drug dependence in each specific case. . . . All of these drugs have one effect in common: they are capable of creating, in certain individuals, a particular state of mind that is termed "psychic dependence." In this situation, there is a feeling of satisfaction and psychic drive that require periodic or continuous administration of the drug to produce pleasure or to avoid discomfort (Eddy et al., 1965, p. 723).

Under the new terminology, each drug has its own characteristic type of dependence: There is a "drug dependence of the morphine type," a "drug dependence of the cannabis [marijuana] type," a "drug dependence of the alcohol type," and so on. In other words, the new terminology is a definition, or a series of definitions, by enumeration, for it was felt that no single term could possibly cover the diverse actions of the many drugs in use (or "abuse").

The new terminology was extremely imprecise and clearly biased. The intent of the drug experts who devised this terminology was ideological: To make sure that a discrediting label was attached to as many widely used drugs as possible. Under the old terminology of "classic" addiction, it was not possible to label a wide range of drugs as "addicting." It thus became necessary to stigmatize substances such as marijuana

and LSD with a new term that resembled "addicting." In other words, the scientists and physicians who devised the new terminology of "dependence" were in effect disseminating propaganda to convince the public that nonaddicting substances were just as "bad" for them, that they could be just as dependent on them as on the truly "addicting" drugs. Medical authorities labeled the continued (or even the sporadic) use of nonaddicting drugs as "dependence" in large part because they were unable to understand why anyone would want to take them in the first place.

Physical dependence is a powerful concept. With a great deal of accuracy, it predicts what will happen physiologically to an organism that takes enough of a certain drug for a long enough period of time. Can psychological dependence be an equally useful concept? Does the fact that it was devised for propagandistic purposes mean that it is automatically meaningless?

During the 1970s and 1980s, researchers began to see some strong parallels between physical and psychological dependence. To put it another way, the fact that one drug is physically addicting and another is not does not seem to predict the patterns of their use very well. Some crucial facts and findings have emerged in the past generation—since the World Health Organization's notion of psychological dependence was formulated—to suggest that perhaps the concept of psychological dependence may not be meaningless.

First, . . . *most* regular users of heroin are not physically addicted in the classic sense. They take wildly varying amounts of heroin on a day-by-day basis, often go a day or two without the drug and do not suffer powerful withdrawal symptoms, take several doses a day for the next several days, and so on (Johnson et al., 1984; Johnson, 1984; Zinberg, 1984). If physical addiction were so crucial in determining use, this pattern would be unlikely, perhaps even impossible.

Second, even the heroin users who are physically addicted and withdraw—whether because of imprisonment, the intervention of a treatment program, or self-imposed withdrawal—usually go back to using heroin; roughly nine addicts in ten who withdraw become readdicted within two years. If physical dependence were the major factor in continued use, we would predict a much lower relapse rate than this. If the physical compulsion or craving is absent, why return to a life of addiction?

Third, many of the drugs that are not physically addicting are often used in much the same way that the addicting drugs are—that is, frequently, compulsively, in large doses, at an enormous personal and physical toll on the user. How could an addicting drug like heroin and a nonaddicting drug like amphetamine or cocaine produce similar use patterns? If addiction—the product of a biochemically induced craving—is the

principal explanation for compulsive use, then how is this possible?

Fourth, and perhaps most crucial, was the hold that cocaine, a supposedly nonaddicting drug, was found to have on laboratory animals. The researchers who conducted these experiments wanted to answer several basic questions: How reinforcing is cocaine? How dependent do animals become on the drug? How much will they go through or put up with to continue receiving it? They discovered that animals will go through practically anything to continue receiving their "coke."

Three key sets of experiments establishing cocaine's dependence potential were conducted. In all three, a catheter was inserted into the vein of a laboratory animal (rats, monkeys, and dogs were used). A mechanism, usually a lever, was rigged up so that animals could self-regulate intravenous (IV) administration of the drug. In one set of experiments, animals were given a choice between cocaine and food; they could have one or the other, but not both. Consistently, laboratory animals chose to continue receiving cocaine instead of food, to the point where they literally died of starvation.

In a second set of experiments, the cocaine was abruptly withdrawn; pressing a bar no longer produced any cocaine. The researchers reasoned that the longer that unreinforced bar-pressing behavior continued, the more dependency-producing a drug is: The more frequently that animals press the bar before they give up—before bar-pressing is "extinguished"—the greater the dependence potential of the drug. Not only did animals that had taken cocaine over a period of time continue to press the bar many times after the drug was withdrawn, but, even more remarkable, they did so far longer than did those animals that had taken heroin—a clearly addicting drug! (A summary of the experiments conducted on the dependence potential of cocaine in animals may be found in Johanson, 1984.)

In a third experiment, one set of laboratory rats was allowed to self-administer cocaine; and a second set, heroin. Both groups could do this continuously and ad libitum—that is, at will, as much or as little as they chose. Those rats that self-administered heroin developed a stable pattern of use, maintained their pretest weight, continued good grooming behavior, and tended to be in good health. Their mortality rate was 36 percent after thirty days. Those self-administering cocaine ad libitum exhibited an extremely erratic pattern of use, with "binges" of heavy use alternating with brief periods of abstinence. They lost 47 percent of their body weight, ceased grooming behavior, and maintained extremely poor physical health. After thirty days, 90 percent were dead (Bozarth and Wise, 1985).

It is absolutely crucial to emphasize that humans are not rats, and experimental conditions are not the same

2. USE, ADDICTION, AND DEPENDENCE

as everyday life. What animals do in the laboratory may not tell us even in a rough way what humans do in real life. At the same time, laboratory experiments give us the framework within which drug effects can be understood. They establish the inherent pharmacological properties of drugs. Just *how* people take them is another matter; for that we have to examine drug use in naturalistic settings. Laboratory experiments give us an important *clue* as to how drugs might be taken in real life; they do not provide the whole story.

The facts and findings that these experiments brought to light point to the inescapable conclusion that the concept of psychological, or psychic, dependence is a meaningful, powerful mechanism. In fact, the results of the many studies conducted on the subject "indicate that psychological dependence might be more important than physical dependence" in much drug use, including narcotic addiction. "Psychological dependence, based on reinforcement is apparently the real driving force behind even narcotic addiction, and tolerance and physical dependence are less important contributors to the problem" (Ray and Ksir, 1987, p. 26). Taking a highly reinforcing or intensely pleasurable drug over a period of time does not necessarily lead to physical addiction, but it does lead to a powerful desire to repeat the experience, and to make enormous sacrifices in order to do so. The more intensely pleasurable or reinforcing the experience is, the more psychologically dependency-producing it is.

But aren't many activities or substances pleasurable? In a letter to the editor of *Trans-action* magazine, one observer (Freidson, 1968, p. 75) commented on the assertion that marijuana produces a "psychic dependence" by saying: "What does this phrase mean? It means that the drug is pleasurable, as is wine, smoked sturgeon, poetry, comfortable chairs, and *Trans-action*. Once people use it, and like it, they will tend to continue to do so *if they can*. But they can get along without it if they must, which is why it cannot be called physically addicting."

Clearly, we run into a conceptual dilemma here. On the one hand, many activities or substances are pleasurable; does it make any sense to dub all of them psychologically dependency-producing? To do so is to be guilty of using a concept that is so broad as to be all but meaningless. On the other hand, certain drugs do produce a syndrome that is clearly distinct from, but as powerful as—indeed, in some ways, even more powerful than—physical dependence. Unlike several of the activities or substances mentioned above, such as comfortable chairs, poetry, and smoked sturgeon, an alarmingly high proportion of users *cannot* get along without certain drugs—cocaine being the outstanding example. We are led to the following inescapable conclusions with respect to drugs and dependence.

First, psychic and physical dependence are two separate and to some degree independent phenomena. That is, someone, or an organism of any species, can be psychologically dependent on a given drug without being physically dependent. Likewise, the reverse is also true: it is possible to be physically dependent on a drug without being psychologically dependent—for instance, as a result of having been administered that drug without realizing it (in an experiment, for instance, or in the form of a medicine or painkiller in a hospital).

Second, substances vary in their potential for causing psychological dependence—with cocaine ranking highest, heroin next, possibly the amphetamines after that, and the other drugs trailing considerably behind these three. It is highly likely that this potential is closely related to how reinforcing each drug is—that is, the intensity of the pleasure that each delivers to the user. The more reinforcing the drug, the higher its potential for psychic dependency.

Third, psychological dependence is a continuum, with gradations between substances, whereas physical dependence is probably more of an all-or-nothing affair. The potential for psychological dependence is a matter of degree. Heroin, barbiturates, and alcohol are clearly dependency-producing drugs; this property can be demonstrated in laboratory animals. Drugs either *are* or *are not* physically addicting. In contrast, drugs can be arranged along a continuum of psychic dependency—with cocaine ranking high on this dimension, and marijuana ranking considerably lower on it.

Fourth, substances vary in their "immediate sensuous appeal" (Lasagna et al., 1955; Grinspoon and Bakalar, 1976, pp. 191–194). This is not quite the same thing as the capacity to generate pleasure. It is, more precisely, *the capacity to generate intense pleasure without the intervention of learning or other cognitive processes*. For the most part, one has to learn to enjoy marijuana (Becker, 1953; Goode, 1970, pp. 132ff.) The same is true of alcohol. It has been asserted for heroin, but it may be less true than has been previously assumed (McAuliffe and Gordon, 1974). Certainly it is true of many pleasurable activities and substances—including eating smoked sturgeon, reading certain books and magazines, and appreciating fine art. Here, the pleasure is great but cultivated. In any case, it is not true of cocaine and, to a lesser degree, amphetamines. Subjects who take these substances without knowing what they are taking tend to enjoy them the very first time and want to take them again. In short, they have an immediate sensuous appeal (Lasagna et al., 1955).

Fifth, different routes of administration are differentially capable of generating intense and immediate pleasure in individuals who take drugs by these means. As we've seen, intravenous injection is one of the fastest ways to deliver a drug to the brain; smoking—especially of cocaine—is also an extremely rapid

and efficient means of drug-taking and is therefore highly reinforcing and likely to cause psychological dependence. Injecting and smoking cocaine have been described as being like "a jolt of electricity to the brain." On the other hand, chewing coca leaves, which contain less than 1 percent cocaine, is far less instantly reinforcing and is far less likely to lead to dependency (Weil and Rosen, 1983, p. 46).

And sixth, individuals vary with regard to their degree of susceptibility or vulnerability to becoming psychologically dependent on varying substances or activities. Clearly, the variation from one person to another in this respect is vastly greater than from one animal to another of the same species, or even from representatives of some animal species as compared with those of others.

The term "behavioral dependence" is sometimes used as a synonym for psychological dependence (Ray and Ksir, 1987, p. 25). This is not entirely accurate. Psychological dependence can refer to both a potentiality and an actuality: We can say that cocaine has a high potential for psychological dependence, and we can say that a specific individual, John Doe, is psychologically dependent on cocaine. On the other hand, the concept of behavioral dependence always refers to an actuality. It makes no sense to refer to a drug having a high potential for behavioral dependence; we can only say that John Doe is behaviorally dependent on a particular drug.

Behavioral dependence refers to actual, concrete behavior enacted by an actual, concrete person taking an actual, concrete drug. What has John Doe gone through or given up in order to take or continue taking a specific drug? What is John Doe now going through to do so? What will John Doe go through? To continue taking their drug of choice, some individuals have lost their jobs, destroyed their marriages, given up all their material possessions, gone into enormous debt, ruined their health, threatened their very lives. They exhibit behavioral dependence. While psychological dependence can be inferred from someone's behavior, behavioral dependence is what we see concretely—an actual person sabotaging or giving up concrete values and possessions previously held in esteem to take a specific drug. We recognize behavioral dependence by the sacrifices a particular user makes to get high. Behavioral dependence has been known for some time to be common among alcoholics and heroin addicts. It is now known that cocaine causes similar manifestations in users as well.

In short, although physical dependence (or "classic" addiction) is a very real and very concrete phenomenon, behavioral dependence does not depend on physical addiction alone. In many ways, the distinction between physical dependence and true psychological dependence—for the drugs that are powerfully reinforcing—is largely irrelevant. Chronic users of drugs that produce "only" psychological dependence behave in much the same way (that is, are *behaviorally dependent*) that addicts of physically dependency-producing drugs do. On the other hand, to throw drugs that produce a weak psychological dependence (such as marijuana) into the same category as drugs that produce a powerful one (such as cocaine) is misleading. Many experts "now regret" the distinction they once drew between cocaine as a "psychologically addictive" drug and narcotics like heroin that are "physiologically addictive." Heroin is "addictive" in a different way—it is both physically and psychologically dependency-producing. But both drugs activate pleasure centers in the brain in such a way that users feel impelled to take them again and again. Some users can overcome this message, but it is a factor that all users have to contend with. "We should define addiction in terms of the compulsion to take the drug rather than whether it causes withdrawal," says Michael A. Bozarth, an addiction specialist (Eckholm, 1986a).

REFERENCES

Becker, Howard S. 1953. "Becoming a Marijuana User." *American Journal of Sociology*, 59 (November): 235–242.

Bozarth, Michael A., and Roy A. Wise. 1985. "Toxicity Associated with Long-Term Intravenous Heroin and Cocaine Self-Administration in the Rat." *Journal of the American Medical Association*, 254 (July 5): 81–83.

Eckholm, Erik. 1986a. "Cocaine's Vicious Spirals: Highs, Lows, Desperation." *The New York Times* August 17, p. 2E.

Eddy, Nathan B., H. Halbach, Harris Isbell, and Maurice H. Seevers. 1965. "Drug Dependence: Its Significance and Characteristics." *Bulletin of the World Health Organization*, 32: 721–733.

Freidson, Eliot. 1968. "Ending Campus Drug Incidents." *Transaction*, 5 (July-August): 75, 81.

Goode, Erich. 1970. *The Marijuana Smokers*. New York: Basic Books.

Grinspoon, Lester, and James B. Bakalar. 1976. *Cocaine: A Drug and Social Evolution*. New York: Basic Books.

Johanson, Chris E. 1984. "Assessment of the Abuse Potential of Cocaine in Animals." In John Grabowski (ed.), *Cocaine: Pharmacology, Effects, and Treatment of Abuse*. Rockville, Md.: National Institute on Drug Abuse, pp. 110–119.

Johnson, Bruce D. 1984. "Empirical Patterns of Heroin Consumption Among Selected Street Heroin Users." In G. Serban (ed.), *The Social and Medical Aspects of Drug Abuse*. New York: Spectrum Publications, pp. 101–122.

Johnson, Bruce D., et al. 1985. *Taking Care of Business: The Economics of Crime by Heroin Abusers*. Lexington, Mass.: Lexington Books.

Lasagna, Louis, J. M. von Felsinger, and H. K. Beecher. 1955. "Drug-Induced Changes in Man." *Journal of the American Medical Association*, 157 (March 19): 1006–1020.

McAuliffe, William E., and Robert A. Gordon. 1974. "A Test of Lindesmith's Theory of Addiction: The Frequency of Euphoria Among Long-Term Addicts." *American Journal of Sociology*, 79 (January): 795–840.

Ray, Oakley, and Charles Ksir. 1987. *Drugs, Society, and Human Behavior* (4th ed.). St. Louis: Times-Mirror/Mosby.

Weil, Andrew, and Winifred Rosen. 1983. *Chocolate to Morphine: Understanding Mind-Active Drugs*. Boston: Houghton Mifflin.

Zinberg, Norman E. 1984. *Drug, Set, and Setting: The Basis for Controlled Intoxicant Use*. New Haven, Conn.: Yale University Press.

Hooked

Why Isn't Everyone an Addict?
Not Hooked

Deborah Franklin

Deborah Franklin is a staff writer.

In 1974, cocaine was making a splash among the American middle class, and Craig Reinarman was a graduate student in sociology casting about for thesis ideas. Academic journals were rife with papers on the seductive horrors of cocaine; a leading drug researcher writing in the *Journal of the American Medical Association* called cocaine "the highest high of all," and warned that where cocaine went, depraved addiction and rampant violence were sure to follow. But Reinarman noticed that when he shelved the journals and went home to the potlucks and parties of his San Francisco neighborhood, where some of his peers were beginning to dabble in cocaine, he saw a different picture.

"I was an ethnographer, accustomed to looking at a little social world and describing what I saw," says Reinarman, now a sociologist with the University of California at Santa Cruz. "And in this case, what I *didn't* see was moral depravity, decomposing lives, physical ill health, or anything remotely resembling the classic definition of addiction.

"I figured I might be on to something."

What he was on to was moderate, measured use of a drug that most people assumed could never be used in a moderate, measured way. There was a precedent. The late Norman Zinberg, a Harvard University psychiatrist, had described "weekend warriors"—people who restricted their heroin use to a Friday night pop without becoming addicted. They could walk away from heroin, and did every now and then, without undergoing the withdrawal pangs that junkies suffer. They never increased the amounts they used, and they never stole nor otherwise compromised their values to get more heroin. Most were successful, middle-class students and businesspeople who, when they wanted to relax, happened to snort or shoot heroin instead of drinking martinis. To understand why these people didn't become addicted, Zinberg said, it was necessary to look beyond biochemistry, to the motivations and environment of the drug user.

The idea that "hard" drugs can be used moderately is as surprising today as it was two decades ago. The $10-billion-a-year federal drug war has taken wide aim, and in its wartime vernacular, every drug user is an abuser, and every drug abuser a budding addict.

Certainly, the oft-told tales of alcoholics or crack addicts whose lives have crumbled under the weight of a habit are tragic and true. But press a knowledgeable drug warrior, and he or she will agree that there is another side to the story. In every survey and study ever commissioned to gauge the scope of America's drug problem, one result has held constant: Most of the people who use alcohol, heroin, cocaine, or any other recreational drug never develop the life-warping, bottomless craving known as addiction.

How come? At a time when the War Against Drugs is siphoning twice as much from the national coffers as the combined wars against cancer, AIDS, and heart disease, it is prudent to pause, and to ask how so many are able to avoid chemical bondage. It may be impossible to imprison

 From *In Health*, November/December 1990, pp. 39-52. Copyright © 1990 by Hippocrates Partners. Reprinted by permission.

every user and dealer; worse, it may be irrelevant. Better, say many researchers, to tease apart the reasons why some become addicted and others don't.

SURVEYING THE DRUG SCENE in 1974, sociologist Reinarman figured that the conventional line on cocaine was pure bunk. There have been drug scares as long as there have been moralists, he reasoned; before cocaine, it was reefer madness or demon rum that was to blame for society's decline. So Reinarman proposed a small study. He called the San Francisco–based Institute for Scientific Analysis, a nonprofit think tank noted for sponsoring social science studies too small or too controversial to gain mainstream attention, and convinced sociologists Sheigla Murphy and Dan Waldorf to join him in a little cultural spying. As Margaret Mead had hunkered down with a village of Samoans 50 years earlier to learn the daily rituals and values of that culture, Reinarman and his crew would eat, party, and otherwise hang out with a network of cocaine snorters and sellers.

The network consisted of ten members of two extended families—the Joyces and the Austens*— and 22 of their assorted spouses, lovers, friends, and acquaintances. The group was linked by the four Austen and three Joyce sisters, who ranged in age at the start of the study from 19 to 30. Mostly native San Franciscans born to educated, white, middle-class parents, the young women and their friends were taking college classes and working part-time as they mosied toward careers. Nearly all were single and childless, with few responsibilities.

"It was a very social time in all our lives, and drugs were just a part of that," says Dede, the youngest Joyce sister. In 1990, she is the only member of the group willing to discuss her drug use with a reporter, and then only by phone. "Today if college kids hear that you do drugs, they look at you like you're some kind of monster," she says. "But at that time people were still lighting up joints in movie theaters."

The group's emotional heart in 1974, and chief conduit for family gossip as well as drugs, was Dede's eldest sister, 27-year-old graduate student and cocktail waitress Bridget Joyce. She had lived with a couple of small-time drug dealers over the years, and periodically sold cocaine and marijuana herself. Her apartment served as the group's chief meeting place; on weekends members would gather there to study, shoot the bull, work on each other's cars. In the evenings, visitors would be offered beer, wine, or marijuana—"as routinely as any suburbanite would be offered cocktails or mixed drinks," Reinarman says. Drugs were never

_____

*The names and other identifying characteristics of this group have been changed.

the focus, they simply greased the social wheels.

"Most members were seasoned drug users who had experimented with hallucinogens and a variety of other illicit drugs in the late 1960s and early 1970s," Murphy says. About half had experimented with injecting cocaine, but all said they preferred snorting. Injecting or smoking a purified version of cocaine, they said, seemed to produce a rush too intense and fleeting to be safely worked into a well-rounded life.

_____

MOST MADE SNORTING TOO MUCH COKE SOUND LIKE EATING TOO MUCH PIZZA OR WATCHING TOO MANY DOUBLE FEATURES. YOU JUST STOP. NO BIG DEAL.

_____

Cocaine was considered a luxury, restricted to special occasions and close friends. Typically, once every few weeks or so, someone would buy one or two grams for the group—about 50 or 100 lines— to be snorted over the course of a weekend. (For most casual users, one matchstick-sized "line" of snorted cocaine hydrochloride produces a general alertness and sense of well-being that lasts about 20 or 30 minutes.)

Most agreed that there was a downside to using too much cocaine, and they regulated their use to minimize it. A weekend binge could irritate the throat and nasal passages, leaving users with what felt like a bad head cold. The drug also seemed to act as a sensual intensifier, which was great if you were already feeling lively and energetic, but wearing if you were tired or depressed. According to group wisdom, taking cocaine when you had a headache only intensified the pain.

They also discovered that continual cocaine use over a 10- or 12-hour period (snorting every 20 or 30 minutes) led to short-term tolerance, which meant that users stopped feeling as high from the drug. And after that came the inevitable crash, a landing that could be soft or could be hard.

"Instead of going full tilt—sharp, clear, everything all together, incredible thinking power—it starts dwindling away and eventually dissipates into a shitty feeling mentally, a very depressed state and physically run-down," a heavy user told one of the researchers in describing the landings that weren't soft. To help ease the crash, users would sometimes take one or two quaaludes or other sedatives toward the end of a coke binge.

Most had neither the time, money, nor inclination to experience such crashes frequently, any more than they were willing to suffer frequent

hangovers. For many, simply the need to be at work early Monday morning kept both cocaine and alcohol binges in check. But a few others, with more flexible schedules, periodically used coke every day for months. After a month or more of such steady use, the snorter would begin to feel chronically tense, restless, and irritable—"coked out"—to a degree as obvious to him or her as to the rest of the group. The few who snorted that much cocaine learned to recognize such symptoms, and alleviated them by abstaining for a week or so, and after that cutting back to less regular use.

The group was concerned about one member in 1974. Nineteen-year-old Lisa Austen, a charming party girl, was admired and valued by friends and family both for her social stamina and her ability to organize "boogies" for herself and everyone else. But her sisters worried that her alcohol-fueled party binges were at times excessive. The Austens' parents had died in an accident in 1971, leaving each daughter with a substantial inheritance. The three older women had used their money to buy houses; Lisa was using hers to finance month-long ski trips and Hawaiian vacations. Still, it was primarily her heavy drinking, not her moderate cocaine habit, that concerned her friends and family.

Even the four or five heaviest users of cocaine, defined by the researchers as anyone who said they used at least two grams a week for six months or more, or who used any amount daily, didn't fit the classic definition of chemical dependency. But all agreed that the drug did sometimes wield considerable power, as a user sought to maintain the high and avoid the crash.

"It's psychologically addicting, I think," one heavy user named Leo told the sociologists. "You continue to use so you don't have to go through the space of coming down, you know, just to keep from coming down."

Most group members made snorting too much coke sound like eating too much pizza or having too much sex or watching too many double features. You spend too much time doing one thing and you feel sick, and need a break. But you can always walk away. No harrowing withdrawals, no life of decrepitude, no confessing to strangers at a Cokenders' meeting. You just stop. No big deal.

At the end of six months, Reinarman, Murphy, and Waldorf put away the notebooks and wound up their study. Cocaine's reputation as a violent seductress was groundless, they decided—a conclusion they would, however, feel compelled to amend 11 years later. In 1975 they confidently reported in a published summary: "Cocaine is much more mild and subtle in its effects than its legal or mythological status would indicate."

IN HIS BASEMENT LABORATORY in San Diego, George Koob is conducting a few drug experiments of his own. A leading neurobiologist at the Research Institute of Scripps Clinic, Koob is studying the ways cocaine and heroin alter the inner work-

Easy to Get Hooked On, Hard to Get Off

TO RANK today's commonly used drugs by their addictiveness, we asked experts to consider two questions: How easy is it to get hooked on these substances and how hard is it to stop using them? Although a person's vulnerability to a drug also depends on individual traits—physiology, psychology, and social and economic pressures—these rankings reflect only the addictive potential inherent in the drug. The numbers below are relative rankings, based on the experts' scores for each substance.

	10	20	30	40	50	60	70	80	90	100

NICOTINE

ICE, GLASS (METHAMPHETAMINE SMOKED)

CRACK

CRYSTAL METH (METHAMPHETAMINE INJECTED)

VALIUM (DIAZEPAM)

QUAALUDE (METHAQUALONE)

SECONAL (SECOBARBITAL)

ALCOHOL

HEROIN

CRANK (AMPHETAMINE TAKEN NASALLY)

COCAINE

CAFFEINE

PCP (PHENCYCLIDINE)

MARIJUANA

ECSTASY (MDMA)

PSILOCYBIN MUSHROOMS

LSD

MESCALINE

Research by John Hastings

ings of brain cells. His laboratory is lined with what look like hotel-room refrigerators. Except that these boxes aren't refrigerated, and instead of cold drinks each houses a rat high on cocaine.

Each rat wears a metal skullcap anchoring an electrode, through which Koob and his colleagues can both stimulate and record the activity of a middling section of the animal's brain. A clear plastic catheter also tethers each rat to its own bottle of cocaine-laced salt water. Every time the rat presses a lever, a drop of the liquid flows down the tube and directly into the upper left chamber of the animal's heart.

There's something funny—funny strange—about these rats. Theirs isn't a druggy contentment; remove the box lid and they want to look around. But neither do they exhibit the feverish darting of an escaped hostage or speed-crazed hysteric. When graduate student Athina Markou picks one up, holding it gently in the crook of her arm as she uses both hands to tweak the catheter, the rat stands as comfortably still as a horse being groomed.

"Our rats are all chippers," Koob says, using the street term coined years ago to describe people who take opiates every now and then. "They can start and stop taking cocaine without any ill effects, as long as they're only exposed to it for a few hours a day."

Brain researchers realized four decades ago that if they electrically stimulated a stirrup-shaped stretch of neurons slightly off center in a rat's brain, the animal seemed enthralled; it would traverse a maze, run a treadmill, or perform any other task the inventive researchers set before it, simply to get more stimulation. That section of the brain came to be called the "reward system." Most drug researchers now believe that the reward system at least partly underlies drug intoxication and, perhaps, addiction.

For instance, when all wired up and left to their own devices, Koob's rats will press a lever to electrically stimulate the reward system at an even, predictable rate of once or twice a second. If he then adds cocaine, putting them on a steady, metered drip, they'll press the electrical lever more often, as though the cocaine enhances the pleasure. Stop the cocaine drip, and they'll immediately return to the slower, steady pressing.

That pattern holds true as long as the rats' access to cocaine is limited to about three hours a day. But if, instead, Koob and Markou give the rats cocaine for 24 hours straight and then take it away, mimicking a cocaine binge, the animals respond quite differently. After a moment of frantic pressing, they'll stop completely, as though somehow the longer-term drug use has damped their ability to feel pleasure. Koob and Markou believe the rats' response mimics the coke-outs experienced by cocaine bingers.

Scientists don't know exactly how cocaine affects the brain's reward circuitry. They do know

that many of the neural "wires" in the circuit rely on the chemical dopamine to transmit messages from cell to cell. The brain cell that's sending a message squirts out its chemical signal—dopamine. The dopamine is detected by the next cell in line, and the message—in this case, pleasure—is passed along. Almost immediately the dopamine molecules floating around between the cells are taken up again by the transmitting cell and repackaged in a neat bit of biological recycling.

Cocaine seems to block the removal of dopamine from between the cells. As a result, or so goes one theory, the receiving cell is overstimulated, producing the cocaine high. The transmitting cell depletes its dopamine stores and temporarily loses its ability to send messages. This dearth of dopamine, say researchers, might be at the root of the cocaine crash: No dopamine, no pleasure.

NINE OF EVERY TEN PEOPLE WHO LIGHT UP A CIGARETTE WILL HAVE TROUBLE QUITTING, COMPARED WITH TWO OF TEN FIRST-TIME COCAINE USERS.

That's a nice, understandable model of how the biology might work, Koob says, but it's a little too pat. There is every indication from behavioral studies that even among lab rats, better known for their overbred sameness than their idiosyncratic flair, individual differences abound.

For example, Koob currently has about a hundred rats in training for his lever-pressing cocaine experiments, and their enthusiasm for the procedure—and the drug—varies widely. "At least thirty to forty percent of the rats will not take cocaine, or at least not readily," he says. "On the other hand, sixty to seventy percent will take it immediately, without training. How come?"

The variation in response is not unique to cocaine. In a test a couple of years ago, Koob came across a rat with an inordinate affection for heroin. The test regimen was similar to the cocaine experiment: three hours of unlimited access to the drug. "I'll never forget it," he says. "Back then, we had to put the levers in and take them out at the beginning and end of each session. Normally that wasn't a problem, you'd just open the cage door, stick the lever in, and the rats wouldn't bother you. But this one particular rat wouldn't let us do that. You'd open the door and he'd grab the lever out of your hand, run to the back of the cage and frenetically gnaw on the lever." Unlike the rest of the rats who merely pressed often enough to keep a steady level of the drug circulating through their blood, this

Is There an Addictive Personality?

IT'S TEMPTING TO THINK you can spot the vulnerable ones—the lonely and needy types or the hyper thrill-seekers—those friends and acquaintances whose behavior makes them most likely to become dependent on drugs. In fact, there's no such thing as an addictive personality. Most researchers now studying drug use believe that it takes a combination of factors—not only psychological influences, but also biological and social forces—to push drug users to addiction. And the particular mix varies from person to person.

Some of the major factors are described below. A single isolated characteristic means nothing; having an alcoholic parent, for instance, doesn't preordain alcoholism in a child any more than snorting a line of coke leads inevitably to cocaine addiction. But the more of these characteristics a person has, and the stronger each trait or condition is, the more vulnerable that person is to addiction.　　　　　　　　　　—D.F.

THE DRUG

A Fast, Big Bang

The more intense the euphoria produced by a substance, and the quicker it's over, the more likely it is that a user will take large amounts of the drug often. That's why crack cocaine is more likely to produce dependency than subtler, slower-acting powder cocaine, and why both drugs are much more likely to lead to addiction than a hallucinogen such as LSD.

▼

A Painful Crash

If a drug creates painful withdrawal symptoms, psychological or physical, a heavy user is more likely to continue using it just to avoid that pain. Withdrawal from alcohol, barbiturates (prescription sedatives), and narcotics is particularly difficult. Many researchers also believe that the sudden depression that follows withdrawal from a cocaine binge helps fuel the addiction.

THE BODY

An Addict in the Family

Having an alcoholic parent increases the risk of having a drinking problem, partly because of inherited body chemistry; abuse of other drugs may also have a genetic component, but that's less well established.

▼

Chronic Pain

Narcotics are often the most effective treatment for the pain of cancer and surgery, and there is a lot of evidence that the drugs *do not* lead to addiction in these patients. But other kinds of chronic pain—back pain, migraines, or the pain of arthritis, for example—don't usually respond to narcotics such as morphine, Percodan, or Demerol, and can foster dependence in people who take increasing doses hoping for relief.

▼

Drug Sensitivities

Some people feel the exhilaration of a drug's high and the pangs of its withdrawal more acutely than others—perhaps because of slight genetic differences that lead to differences in the way their bodies react to or metabolize the drug.

THE MIND

Brash, Lacks Self-Control

Uninhibited people who rarely put the brakes on in their lives are more likely to lack restraint in their drug use as well.

▼

Lacks Values
That Constrain Drug Use

Certain religious tenets, a strong health ethic, or any core beliefs that value sobriety can all limit drug use. Without them a person is more vulnerable to addiction.

▼

Has Low Self-Esteem,
Feels Powerless

Drugs can grant a feeling of power, so heavy use may be more tempting for people who feel frustrated and defeated.

▼

Depressed

According to one theory, some depressed and anxious people may be susceptible to uncontrolled drug use because they have an underlying neurochemical imbalance that the drugs temporarily correct.

THE SETTING

Barren Environment

War zones, urban slums, and prisons are all more likely to foster heavy drug use than places that offer alternative adventures, pleasures, and opportunities.

▼

No Supportive Social Group

Isolation or alienation from friends and family can encourage uncontrolled drug use.

▼

Drug-Rich Environment

Whether a drug user is rich or poor, if most of his or her friends and mentors are compulsive, out-of-control drug users, he or she is more likely than the average person to use drugs that way, too. Conversely, being surrounded by people who use drugs moderately is a tempering influence. Having easy access to a plentiful, cheap drug supply also tends to increase use.

▼

Few Social Guidelines
for Acceptable Use of a Drug

In the United States, it's generally acceptable to drink alcohol in the early evening, but not before noon. As long as the drinker's not driving, most people believe it's okay to get tipsy or even drunk on a Friday night with friends, but not on a Tuesday night alone. Such rules and rituals—different for every culture and every drug—help moderate use. Illegal substances, pushed outside the circle of social respectability, aren't as bound up in social constraints, and may be more likely to be used to excess.

particular animal took more and more heroin each day, at the expense of eating and drinking.

"He effectively became hugely dependent on heroin in just his three-hour sessions until he eventually overdosed and died," Koob says. "Now where did *he* come from?"

Even in animals, let alone people, it's neither easy nor cheap to study variation; just for starters, you need a lot more subjects to turn up subtle differences than you need to hunt for broad similarities. But in the last five years, a few researchers have noticed that if you focus on the trees instead of the forest, you get a different—and in many ways more informative—picture. Some of the most interesting clues so far have emerged from alcohol research.

T. K. Li, for example, a geneticist at Indiana University in Indianapolis, noticed in the mid 1970s that while almost all rats dislike the taste of alcohol, it is easier to get some—about two in a hundred—to drink than others. The characteristic, he learned, seems to be inherited. By breeding about 20 generations, each time mating only those animals that somewhat liked alcohol, he eventually developed a strain in which nearly every member of every litter preferred an unflavored, 10 percent solution of ethanol to water. (That's about the same concentration of alcohol as is found in most wines.) The animals not only found pleasure in alcohol, they also had a high, long-lasting tolerance to its negative effects. Genetically endowed with the two distinct characteristics, Li's rats were much more likely than most to become chemically dependent, he says.

In the last few years, researchers have also selectively bred lines of rats and mice that, because of differences in their genetic makeup, either strongly prefer or strictly avoid opiates, cocaine, and some tranquilizers. Another strain of rats is more sensitive to the stimulant effects of cocaine, still another more sensitive to the drug's tendency to cause seizures at high doses. Some animals metabolize alcohol faster, and so can drink more without getting intoxicated. Others get intoxicated with very low blood levels of alcohol. The point to be taken from all this research, Li says, is that there are a number of distinct ways that individuals can differ in their biological response to drugs.

And if rats can vary, how much more so people, whose neural wiring has a few extra miles of loops and cross-connections. In fact, the animal work dovetails nicely with the findings of researchers studying children of alcoholics. Marc Schuckit, of the University of California at San Diego, found in several studies that sons of alcoholics are less sensitive than men with no family history of alcoholism to the drug's effects: They can drink others under the table, achieve a high level of alcohol in their blood, and still perform mental and physical gymnastics. Because they could drink more alcohol before feeling its effects, Schuckit argues, they might be more likely to drink enough to develop dependency.

Studies of identical twins and adopted children convincingly show that a vulnerability to alcoholism is partly inherited. But the important flip side of such results is that genes don't *determine* alcoholism; the vast majority of the children of alcoholics, and of identical twin siblings of alcoholics, do not develop the disorder.

It's highly unlikely that specific "addiction" genes exist, researchers say. Instead, a few hundred genes may work together to coordinate the metabolism of alcohol or other drugs, and perhaps several dozen others control the release and recycling of a neurotransmitter at a synapse. It probably takes major inherited flaws in several genes to gum up the works of even one such process, and a number of such fractured processes to lay the biological groundwork for addiction.

THE LIKELIHOOD OF ADDICTION IS DETERMINED IN PART BY HOW FAST THE DRUG GETS INTO THE BRAIN, HOW BIG THE BANG IS, AND HOW LONG THE BANG LASTS.

There is also no guarantee that just because you aren't biologically vulnerable, you won't become addicted to a particular drug if you take enough of it. Some drugs, by the nature of their chemistry, seem intrinsically more habit-forming than others.

"There's some abuse potential with marijuana," Koob says. "For example, it's probably at least as dangerous for someone to drive while high on marijuana as to drive while drunk. But on my list of drugs likely to produce dependency—people who are out of control of their use and want to quit, but can't—it's pretty far down the line."

By the same token, LSD may be dangerous if it makes you think you can fly and you dive out a window, but it's unlikely to produce addiction. "It is just not a drug that people take in a compulsive way," Koob says. Some people scoffed when the Surgeon General four years ago called nicotine the most addictive drug known. But survey figures indicate that nine of every ten people who light up a cigarette will one day have trouble quitting, compared with perhaps two of ten first-time cocaine users. It is important to remember, says Koob, that not all dangerous drugs are equally addictive, and not all addictive drugs are equally dangerous.

You can also change a hard drug into a soft one, and vice versa, by changing the way you take it into your body. For example, periodically chewing a wad of lime-treated coca leaves, as many native

Peruvians still do their entire lives, may never produce addiction because the cocaine that reaches the brain that way is released slowly and in small quantities. Alternatively, snorting powder cocaine delivers more of the refined drug to the brain faster, and smoking crack—a concentrated form of cocaine—delivers the drug even more efficiently. From coca leaves to crack, there is a progression in the likelihood of producing addiction that is largely determined, Koob says, by "how fast the drug gets into the brain, how big the bang is, and how long the bang lasts." Even Reinarman, who thinks that at least some of crack's devil-drug reputation is hype, calls smoking crack cocaine "using an already powerful drug in the most dangerous way possible."

"I think the suspicion of many people working in the field," says Koob, "is that if you make the route of administration strong enough, and the access to the drug continuous and unlimited, you could turn any chipper into an addict."

Of course, people are more than the sum of their biological parts, and many drug users choose to limit their own access to a drug. Norman Zinberg was one of the first to point out that while drugs are indeed chemically powerful, that chemistry is

---

Are Teenagers Saying No?

The young are permanently in a state resembling intoxication;
for youth is sweet and they are growing.—ARISTOTLE, *Nicomachean Ethics*

BY THE TIME THEY REACH their teen years, today's young people are looking for something stronger than the sweetness of youth to induce intoxication. Yet for all their wild hair, their nose studs, and their jaded-rebel posturing, teenagers are almost as conventional as adults when it comes to using drugs: They're much more likely to drink or smoke than take illegal substances, and they view drugs in general with increasing disfavor.

"In fact," says Lloyd Johnston of the University of Michigan's Institute for Social Research, "the likelihood of a young person in high school actively using illicit drugs is only about half what it was a decade ago." The institute annually surveys students in 135 high schools across the country, from big-city public schools to small, exclusive academies in ritzy suburbs. According to its findings, in just the past five years marijuana smoking has gone down about 35 percent, the use of stimulants such as amphetamines has fallen off more than 45 percent, and the number of teens who regularly take cocaine has dropped by almost 50 percent.

Johnston says this decline is in part a result of teenagers' growing perception that drugs can be harmful: Eight in ten teenagers concede that regular marijuana use is unhealthy, he says, and six in ten think even trying cocaine is risky. Both of these numbers have been on the rise since before 1986.

Not that your average high schooler isn't curious. According to a recent institute survey, nine out of ten kids try alcohol during their teens, and two out of three experiment with cigarettes. About 60 percent of the drinkers become social users, who drink at least once a month, whereas just 5 percent develop daily habits. A third of those who try cigarettes become daily smokers.

Nor is everyone's curiosity satisfied by booze and cigarettes. For example, 44 percent of teenagers try marijuana, 38 percent of them going on to smoke at least once a month and 7 percent to smoke daily. Twenty percent try stimulants; between 10 and 15 percent sample depressants. But the number of high schoolers who actually go on to use these drugs regularly is minuscule—around one percent for each.

Cocaine appears to attract more hype than it does teenage users. Just 10 percent of teens have tried the drug, according to the institute's figures, and fewer than 5 percent have tried crack—about one-third of each group going on to use the drug at least monthly. Experimenting with more exotic substances—LSD, PCP, heroin—is even less common, and regular use of these drugs during the teen years is almost unheard of.

The University of Michigan surveys don't include high school dropouts, who are more likely than regular students to use drugs, and who are more

numerous in impoverished school districts than in middle-class or affluent regions. "But we're seeing some of the same antidrug attitudes in poorer areas as well," says Johnston, "such as the backlash against crack users recently reported in poor sections of Brooklyn."

Simply experimenting with drugs—sampling, without regular use—causes teenagers no apparent harm, at least while they're still teenagers, according to the most recent evidence. Researchers led by psychologist Jack Block of the University of California at Berkeley followed 101 Oakland-area young people from age 3 through age 18, exhaustively tracking the boys' and girls' psychological development and drug use, among other things. By their senior year in high school, most fell into one of three groups: those who were smoking marijuana at least weekly, some of them sampling stronger drugs; those who smoked pot only occasionally; and those who abstained from drugs altogether.

Both before and after they started taking drugs, the frequent users tended to be impulsive, insecure, and alienated from their peers and families—significantly more so than the young people who didn't develop regular drug habits. But the middle group, the experimenters, were at least as well developed psychologically as youngsters who shunned drugs altogether, even slightly less anxious and socially inhibited.
                                                —*Benedict Carey*

Ice, LSD, Chocolate, TV: Is Everything Addictive?

ACCORDING TO THE STANDARD psychiatric definition, any drug user who passes three of the nine tests below is hooked. We asked several researchers to apply the tests not only to drugs but also to other substances and activities—chocolate, sex, shopping. Their responses show it's possible to become addicted to all sorts of things. For example, serious runners could pass three of the tests by spending more time running than originally intended, covering increasing distances, and experiencing withdrawal symptoms (a devoted runner forced to stop because of an injury, say, might become anxious and irritable.) Of course, that sort of dependency isn't necessarily destructive. Conversely, a drug that fails the addictiveness test—LSD, for instance—may be harmful just the same. That so many things are potentially addictive suggests the addiction's cause is not confined to the substance or activity—our culture may play a large role, too.

	Nicotine	Alcohol	Caffeine	Cocaine	Crack	Heroin	Ice*	LSD	Marijuana	PCP	Valium, Xanax, etc.**	Steroids	Chocolate	Running	Gambling	Shopping	Sex	Work	Driving	Television	Mountain Climbing
TAKES substance or does activity more than originally intended	✔	✔	✔	✔	✔	✔	✔		✔	✔	✔	✔	✔	✔	✔	✔	✔	✔		✔	✔
WANTS to cut back or has tried to cut back but failed	✔	✔	✔	✔	✔	✔	✔		✔	✔	✔	✔	✔	✔	✔	✔	✔	✔		✔	✔
SPENDS lots of time trying to get substance or set up activity, taking substance or doing activity, or recovering	✔	✔		✔	✔	✔	✔	✔	✔	✔	✔		✔	✔	✔	✔	✔	✔		✔	✔
IS OFTEN intoxicated or suffers withdrawal symptoms when expected to fulfill obligations at work, school, or home		✔		✔	✔	✔	✔		✔	✔	✔										
CURTAILS or gives up important social, occupational, or recreational activities because of substance or activity		✔		✔	✔	✔	✔		✔	✔	✔		✔	✔	✔	✔	✔	✔		✔	✔
USES substance or does activity despite persistent social, psychological, or physical problems caused by substance or activity	✔	✔	✔	✔	✔	✔	✔	✔	✔	✔	✔	✔	✔	✔	✔	✔	✔	✔		✔	✔
NEEDS more and more of substance or activity to achieve the same effect (tolerance)	✔	✔	✔	✔	✔	✔	✔				✔										
SUFFERS characteristic withdrawal symptoms when activity or substance is discontinued (cravings, anxiety, depression, jitters)	✔	✔	✔	✔	✔	✔	✔				✔		✔	✔	✔	✔	✔	✔		✔	✔
TAKES substance or does activity to relieve or avoid withdrawal symptoms	✔	✔	✔	✔	✔	✔	✔				✔										

*Methamphetamine smoked
**Benzodiazepines

Research by Valerie Fahey

played out in a person who has specific values and a wide range of competing motivations. In a refrain that would be picked up by those who came after, Zinberg argued that a stake in the conventional world—a rewarding job, or healthy relationships, or goals and dreams that seem within grasp—are motivators as powerful as any chemical. Many people who might be biologically vulnerable to drug addiction, or who sample a particularly potent form of the drug, escape addiction because they have goals and values that aren't compatible with heavy drug or alcohol use.

Conversely, there are people who may be more vulnerable for social reasons: those at the bottom-most rung of the socioeconomic ladder who can't see their way clear to climb up, for example, or those at the top of the ladder who no longer recognize the possibility that they could fall. Like the caged rats who have nothing to do all day but press a lever for cocaine, such people have few competing motivations to constrain their drug use.

IN 1986, 11 YEARS AFTER they had closed the books on the Joyce and Austen clan, Murphy, Reinarman, and Waldorf looked up the group members again.

"They called me the Rambo of interviewers," Murphy says. "They'd put me off and put me off, and I'd go to their houses and wake them up, and say 'Here are the bagels and the coffee, let's talk.' I'd pound on the door, and yell, 'It's Sunday, I *know* you're still asleep. Come *on.*' "

Dede, now 37 and finishing the last few courses of an undergraduate business degree, explains the reluctance: "It's not like that was a bad part of our lives, but it's behind us now, just not something we want to dwell on. We've moved on."

And so they have. The intervening years have brought seven marriages and five divorces, 12 academic degrees, nine children, and ten houses. Two are artists, and one is a poet, but most are mid-career lawyers, teachers, or businesspeople. The two members who did the most cocaine over the longest period (13 years) are well ensconced in profitable careers as an attorney and the owner of a small art business. "We're talking Middle America here," Dede says, and laughs.

Most members of the group still do some drugs, but in a less concerted way than in 1974. Dede and her husband—she met him at a party in 1973—will still have a beer, or smoke a joint to relax at the end of a long day, but no longer have time for the late-night-bull-session-party-till-you-drop weekends that they both enjoyed ten years ago. "When you're young you do stupid stuff," she says. "I used to routinely take a quaalude and snort a line, and you know that that sort of slowing your heart down and then jolting it can't be good for you." She says the words with the matter-of-fact reluctance of a middle-aged runner who gave up jogging because it was too hard on the knees.

She and her husband save cocaine for birthdays, anniversaries, or other special occasions, and never use more than a quarter gram in a month. "We bought a gram almost a year ago and still have it," she says. "People who use more regularly hear that and say, 'How can you keep from going through the drawers for it?' But who has time? Between going to work and school and keeping a relationship solid, there's very little time left."

If all, instead of merely most, group members had gone on to have a drug career like Dede's, Murphy, Waldorf, and Reinarman might not have felt the need to amend their early report. But there were a few troubling cases that led them to note in their published follow-up in 1986, "From our current perspective we realize that our description [in 1974] probably would have been less sanguine had we studied the group longer."

REINARMAN CALLS THE DRUG WAR AN IDEOLOGICAL FIG LEAF. "UNFORTUNATELY, THESE KIDS CANNOT 'JUST SAY NO' TO POVERTY AND UNEMPLOYMENT."

For example, there's Maria. In 1974, the second eldest Joyce sister was a 24-year-old single college student working part-time as a telephone operator. The most conservative member of a flamboyant family, she was, for the first five years, the most moderate in her cocaine use. As Maria remembers it, she sometimes felt "the urge to do more" even during those first years, and might have acted on the urge if she'd had a bigger budget or a cheaper supply. In 1980, that abundance arrived. Her older sister Bridget and a few friends began selling cocaine to supplement their own incomes and were generous with the family. Daily access to the drug did not increase Bridget's use, but marked the beginning of problems for Maria.

Maria stepped up her daily consumption, staying up late at night to do cocaine by herself long after everyone else had gone to bed. Increasingly worried, her friends and family stopped giving or selling it to her; in reaction, the formerly responsible, straitlaced Maria began to steal the drug from them. "I handled the guilt by just doing more cocaine," she told Murphy. The heavy, uncontrolled use lasted 18 months, including one harrowing night of hallucinations and convulsions, until the day she learned she was pregnant. Immediately, with the support of her family, but without professional help, she quit.

"Everybody comes to a decision point with their drug use," says Dede. "For me it was getting married and buying a house, for Maria it was getting

pregnant. When she found something she wanted more than sitting around the house and getting high, she stopped."

But Murphy, Reinarman, and Waldorf aren't so sure that everybody gets an equal chance to decide. Despite the tightly knit safety net of family support, education, and relative wealth, a few members of the group fell through. For example, Bridget and her husband, Sebastian, both blame his escalated cocaine and heroin use for the disintegration of their marriage; it also derailed his career and, despite great desire, he has struggled unsuccessfully to pull away from drugs. Today he is an on-again, off-

again methadone maintenance patient working as a limousine driver in New York City.

And then there's Lisa. She continued to live with cocaine dealers, and would often put up the money for large cocaine buys that her lovers would sell. She and five others once snorted an ounce of cocaine in two days—more than 500 liberal lines—and at her peak she regularly used five or six ounces a month. By 1978, she had depleted her inheritance on drugs and travel, and began working as a cocktail waitress and bartender in a San Francisco nightclub. Cocaine was integral to back-

---

The Rise and Fall of a Street Drug

DURING THE JAZZ AGE, cocaine kept people dancing. A decade later, barbiturates greeted the Great Depression. And when the sixties rolled around, the counterculture got high on LSD. Almost all drugs go in and out of fashion, their popularity riding the ups and downs of economic and social change.

A good recent example is the animal tranquilizer phencyclidine. Like other abused drugs, it was once a promising medicine. But its development as a human anesthetic came to an abrupt halt in 1965 when researchers discovered it provoked nightmares and delusions in many patients.

Phencyclidine made its first illicit appearance in the summer of 1967 at a free rock concert in the Panhandle of San Francisco's Golden Gate Park. The amateur chemists who passed it out called it the PeaCePill, or PCP. In small to moderate doses, PCP can be either a stimulant or a depressant. But because paranoia and frightening hallucinations often accompany large amounts, it quickly earned a reputation as a bummer drug. By 1969, after a brief appearance on the East Coast, PCP had all but vanished from the drug scene.

In 1970, the federal government cracked down on illegal drugs and imposed strict penalties on people caught making or importing them. As a result, speed, quaaludes, and LSD became harder to find. The price of cocaine soared. With the competition under fire, the underdog moved in.

PCP had two of the most important traits a street drug needs. It was easy

to make: Even a layman could get his hands on the necessary chemicals, retire to his kitchen, and turn a $100 investment into $100,000 worth of drugs. And it was cheap: A cigarette of mint or parsley leaves laced with PCP cost only a couple of dollars. By the early seventies, PCP's star was rising.

Along with its new popularity came a new type of user—the kind typically attracted to drugs on the fast track. Instead of big-city hippies, they were white, middle-class teenagers, who could get their hands on a PCP joint more easily than they could a six-pack of beer. And by smoking the drug instead of swallowing it, they could control the dose and avoid some of the unpredictable side effects that had frightened users in the sixties. Almost 750,000 kids aged 12 to 17 had tried PCP by 1976. A year later, that figure had nearly doubled.

As PCP spread from the big coastal cities inland, a drug's usual migration, disturbing news reports began to surface, stories of people committing violent crimes while high on the drug. "Sixty Minutes" aired interviews with two PCP users: one who had stabbed a pregnant woman and murdered her child, and another who had shot and killed his parents.

The government reacted; it stiffened jail sentences for individuals convicted of making or selling the drug, kept a watchful eye on people who purchased its key ingredients, and launched anti-PCP programs. California, for example, spent $600,000 teaching educators

how to prevent PCP abuse.

More importantly, street experience backed up the media scares and official warnings. Between 1976 and 1979, the number of hospital emergency room visits involving PCP almost quadrupled, totaling an estimated 10,000 in 1979. The government's education efforts, coupled with a public panic, seemed to turn the tide: A year later, the number of PCP emergencies fell by a third, and the figure continued to drop through the early eighties. PCP finally appeared to be falling out of fashion.

But not for everyone. In 1983, PCP abuse was on the upswing again, mainly among the inner-city poor, who often adopt drugs that the middle class deems dangerous and discards. By the mid-eighties, more than half the hospital patients with PCP-related emergencies were black, and almost two-thirds were in their twenties, mostly men. As abuse approached its 1979 levels, a new and cheaper version of another middle-class drug appeared—crack cocaine. Unlike PCP, its high was predictable. As crack's popularity soared, PCP's declined. By 1989, PCP use was concentrated in only a few urban areas, including parts of San Jose, California, and Washington, D.C.

Will PCP just fade away? A recent survey of high school seniors showed a slight increase in its use, but not enough to mark a trend. If the main supplies of imported drugs ever dry up, though, America's homemade high could quite possibly make a comeback.

—Mary Hossfeld

stage life at the club, and she continued to use more and more, drinking alcohol to counteract the wired feeling. Today both her drinking and cocaine use are out of control and her family is worried. "She is the one person in the group of thirty-two who has come closest to the stereotypical image of an addict—one who loses it all because of their drug use," Murphy says.

What went wrong? Reinarman is willing to hazard a guess. "She was the youngest—sixteen when her parents died—and losing them was hardest on her. She was least prepared to take that kind of tragedy, and then suddenly, boom—she's

handed a big chunk of change. She's moving in circles where drug use is everywhere, so she kind of went off the deep end." She may also have been particularly vulnerable to alcoholism.

"She always drank too much. Before she could drink legally, she was guzzling down beers with the best of the boys," Reinarman says. "Then she started cocaine, and when you titrate cocaine and alcohol, you've got an upper and a downer, which means you can drink more and not feel it—though it's definitely having an effect on your body—and you can snort more cocaine and not feel over-amped. Lisa often did that. It's a nice high, but you don't recognize the toll it's taking." Eventually, like

Why Do People Take Drugs?

THERE ARE WAYS to ask the question that make the answer seem self-evident. What's so seductive about the mellow, golden languor that slides out of a bottle of whiskey? Where's the charm in coffee's edgy omnipotence? Why the allure of psychedelics' existential ecstasy, the meaning of the universe in a warped and vibrating flower?

The quick answer, the obvious one, is that people take drugs because they like what drugs do to them. Right or wrong, that's nothing new. By 2500 B.C., the Sumerians had a symbol for opium that archeologists translate as "joy" or "rejoicing." Nor is drug use unusual. According to addiction expert Andrew Weil, every culture but the ice-dwelling Inuit has fashioned some kind of drug from available plants—and if ice could intoxicate, the Inuit probably would have had themselves a drug as well. It's enough to make some researchers talk about a human "drive" for intoxication.

Nevertheless, the very word *intoxication* makes it clear that whether casual or compulsive, drug use is a form of self-poisoning. Such loopy human behavior begs for a psychological explanation, and experts, largely focusing on addicts, have come up with many. Self-destructiveness, for instance. Peer pressure. More recently, Harvard psychiatrist Edward Khantzian has suggested that some addicts use drugs to self-medicate—that they're not after a high so much as just trying to reach ground level. When he asked addicts what drugs did for them, he says, they'd tell him, "Well, they made me feel normal."

According to Khantzian, such drug users choose their drug with almost a physician's attention to specific symptoms. For instance, many people who gravitate to cocaine do so because they suffer from depression; typically, the drug energizes and at least temporarily boosts self-esteem. Drug users whose history of family violence has left them with an overwhelming sense of rage may be drawn to a narcotic like heroin, which dampens fear and aggression.

Khantzian's theory segues nicely into another explanation for the drug use of addicts and non-addicts alike: the "Life is nasty, brutish, and short" theory posited by, among others, writer Aldous Huxley. In *The Doors of Perception*, an essay prompted by his experience with mescaline, he predicted that people would always need what he called artificial paradises: "Most men and women lead lives at the worst so painful, at the best so monotonous, poor and limited that the urge to escape, the longing to transcend themselves if only for a few moments, is and has always been one of the principal appetites of the soul."

In other words, drug-taking as escapism. Yet it's evident that Huxley believed he found a different sort of transcendence through mescaline. Elsewhere in his essay, he describes looking at a bouquet of flowers and understanding grace, "the miracle, moment by moment, of naked existence." That's the standard sixties rationale for drug-taking: to rise above normal limits to perception. The idea still has currency.

According to Harvard drug researcher Lester Grinspoon, the desire to take drugs springs from the same roots as creativity and intuition. "There are many people who use cannabis for very serious reasons," Grinspoon says. "They say that alteration of consciousness allows them to see around corners they otherwise can't see around."

Can't—or, more precisely, don't, says Grinspoon. There *are* other doors to this kind of perception. Sensory deprivation, sufi dancing, or long-distance running; breathing exercises, fasting, or religious experiences: All can make you high. In fact, any child who's ever spun round and round into a dizzy stupor knows a drug-free high. So do the children who hold their breath or take turns choking each other into near-unconsciousness for the sheer head-changing thrill of it. Such behavior reflects the human desire for mental as well as physical variety, and it makes Weil put an asterisk next to the universal "human urge to take drugs." Really, he says, it's a more general drive to experience altered states of consciousness.

Ultimately, perhaps, drug-taking reflects *two* basic human characteristics. The desire to alter one's consciousness is the first. The second might be called, for lack of a better term, laziness. "There are many ways to alter consciousness that don't involve a molecule introduced into your body," Grinspoon says. "But many take discipline and training. And Americans are impatient."

—*Lisa Davis*

Li's two-in-a-hundred rats that enjoy the buzz of alcohol and are also immune to its negative effects, Lisa drank enough booze and snorted enough coke to become physically and psychologically dependent on both drugs.

SHEIGLA MURPHY IS NOW in the midst of another ethnographic study, this time of inner-city women who use powder cocaine and crack. The world she's profiling this time, though only a few miles from where the Joyces and Austens grew up, is bleak. "For impoverished people, life on the streets has gotten very hard and mean in the last decade," she says. She tells of driving to interview one subject in the study, a black woman who lives in a neighborhood of boarded-up buildings and broken glass. In front of one house—a known crack house, Murphy says—an angry man guarded the doorway. Across the face of the building, F . . . THE BITCHES had been spray-painted in foot-high black letters. Behind the locked door of her nearby two-room apartment, the single, working mother struggles to raise two small children. The woman also, every now and then, smokes crack.

Is *she* likely to be a lifelong moderate user, or is she merely in the early stages of addiction? "It's too soon to tell," Murphy says, but the fact that the woman is able to hold together a job, a place to live, and a family life are good indicators that her two-year-old drug habit hasn't overwhelmed her.

There is, as yet, no good way of estimating how typical such "controlled use" of crack is, but in Murphy's study—she's logged about 200 hours of interviews with 63 of the 125 women she eventually hopes to talk to—it seems to be rare. "We see a few," says coworker Jeanette Irwin, "and there are similarities among them. They are the ones who tend to have real conventional ideas about how they should live. They say things like, 'My parents always told me I should stay in school and get a good job.' They place restrictions on their lives, and those restrictions carry over to their drug use." The self-imposed restrictions, Murphy says, are the same sorts of social rules that the Joyces and Austens used to circumscribe their drug use.

For those who would argue that addiction, not controlled use, is a more typical outcome of drug use in the inner city, Murphy whole-heartedly agrees. Recreational drugs clearly do their worst damage among the nation's poor. But by focusing on the chemicals to the exclusion of the powerful social forces that push casual drug use out of control, drug warriors miss the point, Murphy says.

Reinarman goes further, calling the drug war "an ideological fig leaf" that politicians have used to hide the true urban ills that their fiscal policies have aggravated: urban ills that foster addiction.

"For the New Right," he says, "people don't abuse drugs because they are jobless, or poor, or depressed, or alienated; they are jobless, poor, depressed, or alienated because they use drugs."

"It kills me to read in the paper about someone who 'spent all their money on crack,' as though that's a sign of ultimate decadence," Murphy says. "If you're on General Assistance, getting two hundred dollars every two weeks, all your money won't buy you much of a drug or anything else. Crack has come along and made those people's lives worse—but not that much worse."

Still, even if a drug war doesn't solve societal ills, can it hurt? Reinarman says yes, for at least two reasons. First, it diverts resources from other programs that might be more useful in moderating drug use. "The 'Just Say No' administration has just said no to virtually every social program aimed at creating alternatives for inner-city young people," he says. "Unfortunately, these kids cannot 'Just Say No' to poverty and unemployment."

Secondly, and this affects the drug-naive teen as surely as his streetwise counterpart, people who exaggerate the dangers of drugs inadvertently romanticize them as well. Reinarman likes to cite the words, taken down by a colleague, of a 1987 college student who had just read a *Newsweek* editorial likening crack to medieval plagues and the attack on Pearl Harbor.

"I had never heard of it until then," the student said, "but when I read that it was better than sex and that it was cheaper than cocaine and that it was an epidemic, I wondered what I was missing. The next day I asked some friends if they knew where to get some."

"There's no reason to lie to kids," Murphy says. "The truth is bad enough. Cocaine is not a benign drug but then neither is alcohol. As I tell my own kids and their friends, any youngster who takes a drink doesn't know whether they'll be among the twelve percent of people who will become alcoholic. And in the same way, a certain percentage of people may be especially vulnerable to cocaine dependence." Youngsters should also recognize, says Murphy, that illegal drug use is more dangerous today. For example, the risk of arrest is higher than it was 20 years ago, and because drug use is more covert, teens are less likely to learn rules for moderate use. "But ultimately," she says, "parents have only so much influence over their children. Taking drugs is a personal decision."

Craig Reinarman spends much of his time these days giving lectures on the sociology of deviance to college students. His office at UC Santa Cruz carries the flavor of the old days—antiwar posters and labor-union placards wedged between walls lined with books. Over his door, plainly read from his desk, is a bold banner from Nancy Reagan's campaign to warn children away from drugs. JUST SAY NO it screams in bright red letters, except that Reinarman has used a blue ballpoint pen to change the "NO" to a quieter "be careful."

Drugs of Choice

Drug users who never suffer addiction attract scientific interest

BRUCE BOWER

Nancy Reagan's battle cry in her war on drugs was "Just say no" — a simple phrase that carries the implicit message that once you say "yes" and take a snort of cocaine or a swig of whiskey, or taste any intoxicating substance, you risk falling into dangerous, uncontrolled drug use.

Many recent theories reflect this notion in suggesting that repeated exposure to an addictive substance inevitably saps the human will and segues into unrestrained drug consumption.

But what those theories ignore, and what some people forget amid alarming stories of crack cocaine deaths and other drug-induced tragedies, is that many people "just say yes" to over-the-counter or under-the-table substances and use them moderately without getting hooked.

Although most drug researchers concentrate on abusers, some focus on people who manage to control their ingestion of mood-altering drugs. In fact, some investigators maintain that occasional users may help clarify the nature of drug addiction and present new approaches to preventing or curing it.

"The occasional user of narcotics and other drugs is more common than most people realize," says psychopharmacologist Ronald K. Siegel of the University of California, Los Angeles. "These users are difficult to study because they do not regularly appear in hospitals, clinics, coroners' offices, courts or other places where abusers surface."

On the other hand, researchers cannot point to a typical "addictive personality" or predict who will and who will not become addicted to a particular drug.

One attempt to illuminate the nature of controlled drug use focuses on people who ingest a highly toxic, extremely habit-forming and entirely legal substance — nicotine. Psychologist Saul Shiffman of the University of Pittsburgh and his colleagues study "tobacco chippers" — light smokers who regularly use tobacco without developing symptoms of physical or psychological dependence.

"Chipping" is a street term originally used to describe the occasional use of opiates such as heroin.

Tobacco chippers are not easily found. Federal statistics indicate one-quarter to one-third of U.S. adults smoke cigarettes. Recent studies of smokers find that more than 90 percent experience intense cravings for cigarettes and other withdrawal symptoms typical of nicotine dependence.

Shiffman and his co-workers compared 18 tobacco chippers who regularly smoke five or fewer cigarettes per day with 29 dependent smokers who consume 20 to 40 cigarettes daily.

Chippers differed from dependent smokers in a number of ways, Shiffman reports in the April PSYCHOPHARMACOLOGY. Dependent smokers reported numerous signs of withdrawal, such as irritability and cigarette craving, after an enforced overnight abstinence; chippers appeared unaffected by the deprivation and reported regularly abstaining from smoking for days at a time. Thus, chippers continue to smoke without any of the withdrawal symptoms that reinforce the addiction in other smokers, Shiffman asserts.

Chippers appear psychologically distinct from dependent smokers, he adds. They report less stress in their daily lives and more effective methods of coping with stress, perhaps lessening their need to smoke.

Tobacco chippers also tend to smoke while drinking a cup of coffee or in response to other external cues, Shiffman says, whereas dependent smokers "basically smoke when they're awake." His research team confirmed this observation with reports from 25 chippers and 25 dependent smokers who carried hand-held computers for several days, on which they recorded their moods and activities just before lighting up a cigarette.

Chippers smoke as often when they are alone as when they are with others who are smoking, Shiffman says, dampening suspicions that occasional smoking is primarily a social behavior.

Further findings suggest tobacco chippers and dependent smokers may differ biologically, he notes. Surprisingly, chippers report fewer uncomfortable reactions to their first cigarette, such as dizziness, coughing and nausea, than do heavy smokers. Also, fewer of the chippers' relatives ever smoked, and more of their smoking relatives successfully gave up cigarettes.

Despite the contrasts between the two groups of smokers, chippers fully inhale tobacco smoke and absorb the same amount of nicotine from each cigarette as do heavy smokers, Shiffman and his co-workers found in a study to appear in the ARCHIVES OF GENERAL PSYCHIATRY. After smoking one cigarette, chippers' blood nicotine levels increase in amounts equal to those of dependent smokers, as do

their blood levels of a long-lasting nicotine metabolite.

The researchers also found that heavy smokers who agreed to reduce their consumption to five cigarettes per day compensated by inhaling more deeply and tripling their per-cigarette nicotine intake. Chippers, however, do not compensate for their limited use with deeper inhalation.

"I don't claim to understand how chippers do what they do," Shiffman says. But long-term observations of their smoking behavior and physiological responses will illuminate individual differences in tobacco use and perhaps help clarify the nature of dependent smoking, he contends.

Shiffman's work follows in the footsteps of research on heroin chippers directed by the late Norman E. Zinberg, a psychiatrist at Harvard Medical School in Boston. Zinberg held that three major forces mold a person's use of and experience with heroin or any other substance: the pharmacology of the drug, the personality of the user and the physical and social setting in which use takes place.

Zinberg saw the social setting as an especially powerful influence on heroin use. In 1972, he observed two types of heroin addicts in England, where these users obtained the opiate legally through public clinics. The first type used heroin in a controlled fashion and functioned adequately or even quite successfully, while the second took heroin constantly and lived desperate, self-destructive lives. But the latter group was not a cause of societal unrest, crime or public hysteria, Zinberg writes in *Drug, Set, and Setting* (1984, Yale University Press), because British social and legal sanctions allowed them to live as addicts.

Zinberg then studied small groups of heroin chippers and addicts in the United States. He found that occasional users did not experience the distressing withdrawal symptoms of hard-core addicts and tended to use heroin at specific times when it would not disrupt their jobs or other responsibilities.

The Vietnam War also provided a natural laboratory for studying controlled heroin use. Southeast Asian heroin was cheap, plentiful and delivered in an easy-to-use smokable form. About one out of three U.S. soldiers tried heroin while in Vietnam and half of them became addicted, according to surveys conducted in the early 1970s by psychologist Lee N. Robins of Washington University in St. Louis and her colleagues.

Yet when these veterans came home and left the bleak social setting of the war behind, their craving for heroin largely diminished. In one study, Robins and her co-workers interviewed 617 enlisted men before their return from Vietnam in 1971 and again three years later. Half the veterans addicted in Vietnam had used heroin since their return home, but only 12 percent of those became readdicted.

As early as 1947, heroin chippers were recognized as "joy poppers" who used the drug occasionally without signs of addiction, Siegel points out.

"Even if most heroin addicts had once been chippers," he asks, "why didn't all chippers become addicts? Is there a secret to controlled intoxicant use?"

No one offers a simple answer to this question, but in Siegel's opinion, the drug dose taken by an individual and its frequency are critical.

Consider crack, a smokable form of cocaine produced from cocaine hydrochloride powder through a chemical process known as freebasing. Smoking crack leads to a much faster and more intense intoxication than sniffing cocaine hydrochloride. In the early 1980s, Siegel studied about 200 arthritis sufferers under treatment at a desert clinic in California, where they regularly received Esterene — the pharmaceutical trade name for an experimental form of crack. Not one case of abuse surfaced in Siegel's investigation.

Esterene proved nonaddictive because doses were fixed by physicians and the drug was sniffed through the nostrils and absorbed slowly through the nasal membranes, he contends. Esterene did not cure arthritis, but many patients — who did not know they were using a form of cocaine — reported less pain and greater freedom of movement after the treatments.

Esterene remains nonaddictive when used outside a medical setting, Siegel says. The Esterene program in California is now banned, but Siegel located 175 people in the Los Angeles area who concocted crack at home for a variety of reasons. Some were cocaine users attracted to reports that snorting crack was safer than snorting cocaine hydrochloride powder, while others were elderly people seeking relief from arthritis or depression.

Again, these crack users — including those with a history of cocaine consumption — experienced few problems. They reported more energy and less physical pain but did not experience the rapid and reinforcing euphoria that helps give cocaine its addictive punch. While daily cocaine hydrochloride users snort the white powder around the clock, the 175 people sniffing their homemade crack took the drug infrequently and displayed no physical side effects or signs of dependency.

In contrast, street users of crack repeatedly smoke large doses of the drug, which rapidly enters the brain. Taken in this way, crack produces an almost instantaneous "rush" of intoxication, promoting rapid addiction as well as toxic physiological effects.

Nonetheless, Esterene users, crack addicts and other consumers of both legal and banned drugs share a common motivation, Siegel argues in *Intoxication: Life in Pursuit of Artificial Paradise* (1989, E.P. Dutton). "People use intoxicants to change the way they feel and satisfy their needs for psychological or physical stimulation," he says. "Intoxicating drugs are medications for the human condition."

Siegel, hardly in the mainstream of drug research, draws harsh criticism from those who believe abstinence is essential in the prevention of drug addiction. But his book has been read widely in scientific circles, as well as by at least one official in the White House Office of Drug Control Policy.

The pursuit of substances that alter mood and consciousness has evolved into a "fourth drive," on a par with sex, thirst and hunger, Siegel contends. Not only is intoxicant use a characteristic of people in virtually all societies, but evidence of the fourth drive turns up throughout the animal kingdom, he says. Siegel and his colleagues have observed the self-administration of naturally occurring drugs among mammals, birds, insects, reptiles and fish (SN: 11/5/83, p.300). Bees, for instance, taste the nectar of opium flowers and drop to the ground in a stupor, then go back for more; elephants seek out fermented fruits and proceed to get drunk; and monkeys munch hallucinogenic mushrooms and then assume a reflective pose, sitting with their heads on their hands.

Yet animals do not have significant problems with uncontrolled drug use in the wild, Siegel says. They consume infrequent, relatively small drug doses in the natural plant form, a pattern not likely to produce addiction.

Humans are another story. "We take benign intoxicants out of their natural packages, purify them and turn them into poisons," Siegel says.

Efforts to stem the ravages of addiction by cutting off drug supplies wither before the power of the fourth drive, and legalizing currently outlawed drugs will not make them safe, he argues. Moreover, it seems unrealistic to expect that drug addiction will disappear if people are taught about controlled "chipping" techniques or exposed to educational messages through the media, he says.

2. USE, ADDICTION, AND DEPENDENCE

If society acknowledges both controlled and excessive drug use as efforts to meet the needs of the fourth drive for a change in mental state or mood, the next step is a scientific search for safe intoxicants, or "utopiants," Siegel contends. These designer drugs would balance pleasurable effects with minimal or no toxic consequences, have fixed durations of action and contain built-in chemical antagonists to prevent addiction or overdose.

In one possibility Siegel cites, future molecular chemists may combine Esterene preparations with nitrenidipene — a chemical that reverses cocaine overdoses — to create a controllable form of cocaine.

In the meantime, Siegel supports efforts to prevent and treat drug abuse, including plans by the National Institute on Drug Abuse to spend nearly $100 million annually in search of medications that block the effects of cocaine and other illicit drugs.

But the fight against dangerous drugs must also embrace the scientific pursuit of safe intoxicants, he maintains. "Just saying 'no' often does not work, because the fourth drive is too strong," Siegal says. "This is not moral surrender [in] the war on drugs. The development of safe, man-made intoxicants is an affirmation of one of our most human drives and a challenge for our finest talents."

A Dirty Drug Secret

Hyping instant addiction doesn't help

LARRY MARTZ

How could Marion Barry be on crack?" demanded a skeptical New York editor, debating the Washington mayor's recent arrest in a sting operation. "If you're on that stuff, I thought you go out of your mind. You forget your kids' names, sell your wife, do nothing but smoke crack. So how could he run a city?"

Don't tell the kids, but there's a dirty little secret about crack: as with most other drugs, a lot of people use it without getting addicted. In their zeal to shield young people from the plague of drugs, the media and many drug educators have hyped the very real dangers of crack into a myth of instant and total addiction. It has yet to be proved that Marion Barry was using crack or any other drug, but his semblance of control doesn't prove he wasn't. By the best estimate, at least 2.4 million Americans have tried crack, but contrary to the myth, less than half a million now use it once a month or more. And even among the current users, there are almost surely more occasional smokers than chronic abusers. As children in drug-using communities can see for themselves, the users show a wide range of drug symptoms, from total impairment to almost none.

That doesn't mean it's safe to play with crack, or with most other drugs, legal or illegal. Addiction is a slippery slope. But what worries a growing number of drug experts is that the cry of wolf about instant addiction may backfire. "It's a dangerous myth," says Herbert Kleber, the demand-reduction deputy to federal drug czar William Bennett. "If the kids find out you're lying, they'll think you're lying about other things too." The pattern is an old one. Exaggerated warnings about demon rum at the turn of the century sparked derision; the 1936 scare movie, "Reefer Madness," became a cult film for jeering potheads in the '60s and early '70s. And that in turn, as Kleber says, helped foster the delusion that cocaine itself was safe.

"We're seeing a whole lot of scare tactics," says Sheigla Murphy, codirector of a National Institute on Drug Abuse study of cocaine use among San Francisco-area women. "The truth is bad enough. We don't have to exaggerate it." But the scare tactics have triggered a wider skepticism about the whole drug issue. A New York Times op-ed piece recently denounced "Bennett's Sham Epidemic," accusing him of manipulating figures to create a false sense of emergency. Some experts call for legalizing drugs on grounds that the war is hopeless, the cure worse than the disease. How bad is the truth? Three key questions:

■ **Is there an epidemic?** The latest NIDA study of national drug use found mostly good news: nobody knows precisely why, but people are using fewer drugs. Taken in 1988 and released last summer, the survey found that use of all illicit drugs had fallen by 37 percent since the 1985 study. NIDA officials estimate that the heroin-addict population is steady at 500,000 or more. Marijuana users who said they had smoked in the past month fell from 18 million in 1985 to 11.6 million, a drop of 33 percent. And cocaine use showed the steepest decline of all: monthly users fell by 50 percent, from 5.8 million to 2.9 million.

The big, new problem was crack, a form of cocaine too rare to measure in 1985. The NIDA survey estimated that there were 484,000 regular crack users. And including crack, the survey found an increase in the number using cocaine weekly or oftener, from 647,000 to 862,000. This seemingly precise statistic was projected from just 44 users in the sampling of 8,814 households, but Bennett said it was "terrible proof that our current drug epidemic has far from run its course."

The survey itself is problematical. To begin with, it reaches only households and thus ignores the homeless, prisoners and people in barracks and dormitories. Then, too, it expects honest answers to a question that one researcher neatly mocks: "Hi, I'm from the government. How often do you use illegal drugs?" But whatever its flaws, most researchers accept the survey as a valid indicator of trends. In any case, Bennett argues, the good news proves that defeatists in the drug war are wrong, while the growing crack problem shows that it's not time to ease up.

■ **How addictive is crack?** One answer is another question: compared to what? Among widely used drugs, nicotine is by far the most addictive. According to Jack Henningfield, NIDA's chief clinical pharmacologist, fully 90 percent of casual cigarette smokers escalate to the point of addiction. The nation has 106 million users of alcohol, and one of every eight is a problem drinker. But there are no precise lines separating casual users, abusers and addicts, and in any case addiction differs widely from one drug to another. Stressing that it's a rough estimate, Kleber says that perhaps one cocaine user out of four or five will become a chronic abuser or addict. With crack cocaine, he says, the figure may be one in three.

For at least a few crack smokers, addiction can indeed seem nearly instantaneous. The chemistry of cocaine in the brain seems to be the same in any form, but the drug reaches its target much more efficiently through the lungs than by any other means. The tiny dose of crack provides a fast, intense high, followed by a quick depression encouraging the user to repeat the experience. This can lead to binges lasting for hours or days, sometimes starting with the first pipeful. Some users smoke just a few crack pellets; some spend the weekend smoking and return to their jobs; a few lose all control. But the mothers who sell their babies for crack are a tiny minority.

Any addiction is hard to break, but some users find crack surprisingly easy to drop. In her San Francisco study, Murphy has

found at least two women who went cold turkey from full-scale addiction. "They were just sick to death of it," she says, "tired of the high, didn't want it anymore." But people can also walk away from other drugs. Sociologist Lee Robins of Washington University in St. Louis found that 90 percent of a sampling of Vietnam veterans simply gave up drugs including heroin, morphine and amphetamines after coming home in 1971. In general, says neuroscience professor Michael Gazzaniga of Dartmouth Medical School, drug abuse of all kinds dwindles as users grow older: "After 35, it just drops off precipitously."

■ **So it's safe to take drugs?** No. Especially with any form of cocaine, the passage from casual use through abuse to addiction is perilously easy. As UCLA criminologist James Q. Wilson puts it, cocaine is unlike other drugs: tobacco may shorten life, but cocaine debases it. The user feels talkative, affable, brilliant and confident, no matter how far along the slippery slope he or she may be. In reality, however, the high becomes the main goal in life, and the user will rationalize doing almost anything to get the drug. "The loss of control involves the delusion that you are still in control," says Marian Fischman, a biologist at Johns Hopkins Medical School. It may be telling that shortly before his arrest, Mayor Barry was referring to himself as "invincible."

Nevertheless, some experts argue that some or all illicit drugs should be legalized. The key question here is how much added drug use legalization would promote. Some researchers, like Dartmouth's Gazzaniga, maintain that every society has a natural level of substance abuse that won't vary much in any case: as cocaine rises, heroin and alcohol wane. But the evidence for this beguiling theory is thin, and the risks are high. As Wilson argues, it boggles the mind to imagine that making drugs safer and cheaper wouldn't lead to more use. If a legalization experiment fails, he warns, "There is no way to put the genie back in the bottle, and it is not a kindly genie."

That argument will continue: in the end, the war on drugs is a commitment the whole society has to make. But whether we fight or surrender, it's crucial to see the enemy clearly. The truth is bad enough; there's nothing to be gained, and a lot to be lost, by hyping the dangers of drugs.

NICOTINE BECOMES ADDICTIVE

It has taken more than half a century to prove finally and indisputably that the colorless, oily liquid in tobacco hooks smokers just as surely as heroin does junkies.

ROBERT KANIGEL

Robert Kanigel, author of Apprentice to Genius, *is working on a biography of the Indian math prodigy Ramanujan.*

1942. British tanks battled Rommel's Panzers in North Africa. The pages of *The Lancet*, Britain's leading medical journal, told of physicians killed in battle and tuberculosis patients denied extra rations at home. Meanwhile, Glasgow physician Lennox Johnston was shooting up with nicotine.

Three or four times a day he'd inject himself with a hypodermic syringe of nicotine, the colorless oily liquid that, on exposure to air, gives tobacco its pungent smell and brownish color. After eighty shots, he found that he liked them better than cigarettes and felt deprived without them. He observed a similar pattern among 35 volunteers to whom he also gave nicotine shots. "Smoking tobacco," he'd assumed from the start, "is essentially a means of administering nicotine, just as smoking opium is a means of administering morphine." And nothing in the course of his study led him to change his mind.

Later, critics objected to Johnston's lack of scientific controls. "And they were right," says Jack Henningfield, a smoking researcher at the Addiction Research Center in Baltimore. "But Johnston was right, too": nicotine was why people smoked—a judgment embodied in the very title of the Surgeon General's latest report on smoking, *Nicotine Addiction*, issued last spring.

The 618-page report drew sneers from the tobacco industry, but no full-dress rebuttal. "We haven't had to," insists Tobacco Institute spokesman Gary Miller, pointing to newspaper editorials that damned the report as the work of zealots and painted its conclusions as ill-founded. "Smokers and non-smokers are just not buying it." But if anything, Surgeon General Everett Koop's report—which summarized the work of hundreds of scientists in thousands of studies, and was itself reviewed by dozens of outside experts—granted scientific legitimacy to folk wisdom and anecdotal evidence of centuries' standing.

The phrase, *tobacco addict*, goes back at least to the eighteenth century, when Samuel Johnson used the expression. *Dope fiend*'s entry into the language during the 1870s was followed by *cigarette fiend* just a few years later; today *nicotine fit* is in common usage. More than half a century before the Surgeon General's report, John L. Dorsey, a Baltimore physician writing in *The Practitioner*, took as a given "that the use of tobacco in its various preparations is a form of drug addiction. . . . The real addict, the smoker of 20 to 50 cigarettes a day, cannot lay aside the habits of years with an easy nonchalance. He has ahead of him wretched days of withdrawal symptoms

which will usually end with surrender to the habit." In the devastated cities of Europe after World War II, people cheated, stole, and prostituted themselves for a smoke, and German prisoners of war on diets of 900 calories a day would sometimes swap food for cigarettes.

Indeed, midst today's climate of inhospitability to smoking, and confronted with a thick, citation-studded government report fairly bursting with proof that smoking is addictive and nicotine is its agent, it can be hard to recall that anyone ever thought otherwise. Yet for all those, like Dr. Dorsey, who deemed tobacco addictive,

*"The cloud of white smoke
rising before the smoker
is soothing and companionable.
The gradual ascent of the completed rings,
their changing forms
and their picturesque movements
disappearing into thin air
all tend to rouse the imagination."*

others had insisted its hold on the smoker was weak. "Smoking," pharmacologist W.E. Dixon had written in the same journal just a few years before, "does not lead to addiction comparable with that of morphine or cocaine. . . . The loss of one's smokes is an annoyance, but not a tragedy."

Why, then, *did* smokers reach for their cigarettes 20 or 30 or 40 times a day—or as was more common in Dixon's day, their pipes and cigars? "The cloud of white smoke rising before the smoker is soothing and companionable," noted British pharmacologist Sir Robert Armstrong-Jones in the 1920s. "The circular shape of the completed rings are attractive. Their gradual ascent unaided and without apparent effort from the 'gurgling briar,' their changing forms and their picturesque movements disappearing into thin air, all tend to rouse the imagination." Smoking, then, granted pleasure—even, as Armstrong-Jones would have it, aesthetic pleasure. Indulging in it hardly made you a drug addict. Oral gratification, "pulmonary eroticism," and all manner of other psychological explanations were trotted out over the years, too. Was it not these that held the smoker in thrall, and not anything so insidious as an addictive drug?

Until recently, of course, the issue wasn't really thrashed about much. After all, smoking, in the view of most scientists, physicians, and smokers, was harmless. So whether or not it was addictive didn't *matter*.

And then, almost all of a sudden, it did.

First came the early studies, in the 1950s, linking smoking to lung cancer and other health problems. Then, the Surgeon General's landmark 1964 report saying as much. Then, over the next 15 years, the steady drumbeat of data buttressing that conclusion: Smoking *was* dangerous to your health. It gave you lung cancer. It contributed to heart disease. It was responsible, yearly, for 300,000 people dying before their time . . .

Mort Levin, a retired Johns Hopkins School of Medicine epidemiologist who established some of the earliest

ties between smoking and lung cancer, still remembers the press conference, at the Hotel de la Paix in Paris in the early 1950s, at which he first presented his findings to the world. Afterwards, some in the audience came up and told him they planned to sell their cigarette company stock. When Levin's evidence became known, they said, people would simply give up smoking and the tobacco companies would go under.

Well, people *didn't* stop smoking. The tobacco companies *didn't* go under. All during the 1950s, the prevalence of smoking among adult males barely budged from its long-steady figure of just over fifty percent. The 1964 report brought it down to the mid-40s, but meanwhile more women were smoking—from less than 20 percent of them in the 1930s to about 30 percent in the 1960s. All told, cigarette sales rose.

Nor was it that people hadn't gotten the message. A 1969 poll found that 81 percent of Americans in their twenties, and 71 percent of all Americans, thought smoking caused cancer. Every magazine ad, every billboard, every cigarette packet carried the word. People apparently wanted to give it up; one recent Gallup Poll, for example, found that 77 percent did. But they didn't, or wouldn't, or couldn't. Why? A question previously accorded scant attention now beginning in the 1960s and then more insistently during the 1970s became one of consuming interest: Was smoking, in some meaningful sense of the word, "addictive"? And if so, was nicotine responsible?

* * *

Of the 4,000 chemical constituents of tobacco, nicotine, which takes its name from Jean Nicot, the sixteenth century French ambassador to Portugal who introduced tobacco to the French court, constitutes 1.5 percent of it by weight and has long been known to have powerful pharmacological effects. Indeed, its use to study transmission of nerve impulses even before 1900 left a whole branch of the cholinergic nervous system forever dubbed "nicotinic."

In his 1931 study, *Phantastica: Narcotic and Stimulating Drugs*, L. Lewin asserted that "the decisive factor in the effects of tobacco, desired or undesired, is nicotine and it matters little whether it passes directly into the organism or is smoked." In 1961, F. S. Larson and two other Medical College of Virginia pharmacologists came out with their classic, encyclopedic survey of the tobacco literature. That nicotine played a role in maintaining tobacco use was to them abundantly clear; but as to how central a role, or whether smoking was a habit, or an addiction, or something else altogether, they reached no consensus. Meanwhile, when it came to hard data, Lennox Johnston's war-time experiment remained largely alone.

And that's how matters stood for a quarter century, until 1967. In that year, B. R. Lucchesi and his colleagues at the University of Michigan Medical School,

took another swipe at the question. It was Johnston's work all over again, but this time *with* the controls.

Experimental subjects would arrive at the lab in the morning, having gone without food, drink, or cigarettes since midnight. After blood pressure and heart rate tests, they would enter sound-proofed air-conditioned isolation booths, get hooked up to instruments, and have 23-gauge hypodermic needles inserted in their forearms. To each needle was attached a Y-shaped extension, one arm of which dispensed salt solution, the other nicotine. During some six-hour sessions they got nicotine equivalent to one or two cigarettes an hour. During others they'd get only saline solution. They never knew which. Throughout each session, while kept busy with tests of reaction time, hand steadiness and the like, the volunteers could smoke whenever they wished.

Would they smoke less when they were getting nicotine fed into their veins?

They did. Subject No. 4 consistently smoked about 11 cigarettes per session when he wasn't getting IV nicotine, eight when he did. For Subject No. 2, it was seven and four. Moreover, subjects tended to smoke less of the cigarettes they did consume. "Small but significant," the authors labeled nicotine's effect. There were plainly other factors in their smoking. But just as plainly, the nicotine they got through the needle was nicotine they didn't have to get from their smokes.

*During the 1970s the evidence mounted.
And yet none of it
made smoking an addiction.
Because for many people, even today,
addiction meant only one thing.
It meant morphine or heroin. It meant* bad.

In 1971 came evidence of quite a different sort. Sponsored by the American Cancer Society, William A. Hunt and two colleagues at Loyola University of Chicago compared relapse rates of smokers trying to give up smoking, as reported in dozens of earlier studies, with those of alcoholics trying to give up alcohol and heroin addicts trying to give up heroin. The studies had been performed under vastly different circumstances and so the results of the comparison, the authors apologized, were merely "illustrative."

But *illustrate* they did, in the form of a memorable graph. The horizontal axis represented time since going off heroin, alcohol, or tobacco. Plotted on the vertical axis was the percentage of those still off—100 percent at first, then a fall-off over subsequent weeks and months. And the thing you could never get out of your mind once you'd seen it was that laying the curves for any of the three atop the others, you could scarcely distinguish one from the other: Smokers, the graph said, had as much trouble staying off cigarettes as alcoholics did in staying off drink—and as heroin addicts did in staying off junk.

During the early and mid-1970s, a series of seemingly small, methodological improvements helped give re-

searchers a clearer sense of how nicotine exerted its addictive spell. Puff on a cigarette and nicotine reaches its primary site of action, the brain, within seven seconds, being taken up by the circulatory system through capillaries in the lungs. Nicotine levels in the blood, then, give a measure of how much has reached the brain. And now, more reliable methods for measuring blood levels began to be reported in the literature.

When they were applied, the same figure would crop up with uncanny regularity in experiment after experiment. For some smokers it was 20, for others 50, but on average 35 nanograms per milliliter was how much nicotine, in billionths of a gram per milliliter of blood, smokers seemed to "want." When his blood level fell substantially below it, the smoker lit up—whereupon the figure would shoot up to perhaps fifty. Then, over the next half hour or hour, it would decline, to perhaps 20 or 25. Which meant it was time for another cigarette. And so on during the smoker's waking hours. Plot blood concentration over the course of a day and you'd wind up with a saw tooth marching across the paper.

The "titration hypothesis," researchers called it, using lab terminology for the precise adjustment of a chemical's concentration to some particular value. And while the data never made for so tidy a picture as the model implied, a wide variety of evidence supported its general outlines: smokers manipulated their smoking pattern to get the desired blood levels of nicotine, inhaling more or less deeply, or more or less often. When smoking a low-nicotine cigarette, they might cover up the air vents designed to dilute the smoke—and wind up with blood levels far higher than otherwise. It was as if smokers could "read" their own blood. Thirty-five nanograms per milliliter? They were happy. Twenty? They'd want a cigarette, but could manage without one. Five? They were climbing the walls.

During the early and mid-1970s, the evidence mounted. And yet to most lay people, most physicians, and even most smoking researchers, none of it made smoking an addiction, and none of it made nicotine an addictive drug. Because then—and for many people even today—"addiction" meant one thing. It meant addiction to the opium poppy. It mean morphine or heroin. It meant *bad*.

* * *

Before World War I, the line separating "good" drugs from "bad" was hazier than it is today. Anyone could go out and buy McMunn's Elixir of Opium or any of at least 600 such "soothing syrups," "pain killers" and "cough medicines," all containing opiates. According to E. M. Brecher in *Licit and Illicit Drugs*, it wasn't unknown for a prominent physician to take morphine every day for 30 or 40 years and never lose a day of work because of it. Sigmund Freud used cocaine for years.

"An opium den at the beginning of the century was a social club. When you say 'opium den,' think 'bar,' " says Neal Grunberg, a psychologist at the Uniformed Services University of the

2. USE, ADDICTION, AND DEPENDENCE

Health Sciences in Bethesda, Maryland who helped write some of *Nicotine Addiction's* key sections. Being addicted carried few of the connotations—evil, crazed, criminal—it does now. Etymologically, to be addicted means to be *bound over* against one's will like a prisoner or a slave—whether to a drug or anything else. That older, broader, more innocent sense of the word lingers today in such expressions as being addicted to chocolates, or addicted to love.

*By the 1980s, it had become clear that
while abstaining from tobacco
did not induce a withdrawal syndrome like
that seen among heroin users,
the symptoms were just as distinct,
just as specific, and just as measurable.*

Then, in 1914, came the Harrison Narcotics Act which, aimed at regulating the drug trade, came to be interpreted as a ban on narcotics use for all but the most narrowly medical purposes. For the first time, morphine and its opiate cousins were illegal. The nation's estimated 200,000 addicts turned to illicit drug dealers—and became criminals.

During the 1940s, classic studies with narcotics addicts imprisoned at the federal facility in Lexington, Kentucky, began to lay the groundwork for an understanding of addiction. But in the process, addiction began to lose its earlier, broader meaning and to ever more intimately fuse with heroin abusers in the public mind. Between about 1940 and 1965, as Jack Henningfield reckons it, addiction came to *mean* opiate addiction, with all its intimations of back alley drug deals and junk-crazed muggers.

So that when, in 1957, the World Health Organization established its definition of addiction, the opiates model was about the only model around. To be addictive, WHO said, a drug had to cause physical dependence, pronounced changes in behavior, and withdrawal symptoms. Cocaine and amphetamines, both today universally regarded as addictive, were excluded, being classed as merely "habituating."

In 1964, WHO discarded the distinction between habituating and addictive. "It was refuted, disowned, by the very committee that put the old definition together," says Jerome Jaffe, director of the Addiction Research Center. But the change came too late to influence the Surgeon General's landmark study appearing that same year. Applying the old definition, the Surgeon General ruled that nicotine was not addictive. Because, says Jaffe, evidence for withdrawal symptoms and behavioral changes among tobacco users was, at the time, still scanty. Yes, nicotine was so potent that barely one smoker in ten could keep to fewer than five cigarettes a day. Yes, it might be "habituating," to use the discarded WHO definition. Yes, it might be "dependence-producing," to use jargon that came into use later.

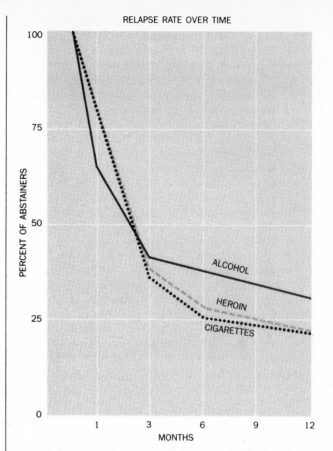

Smokers trying to give up the weed backslide about as frequently as alcoholics and heroin addicts trying to give up their favorite drugs.

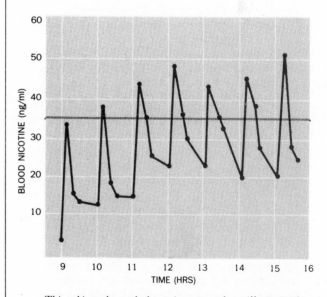

This subject who smoked one cigarette an hour illustrates the titration hypothesis—how smokers manipulate their smoking pattern, inhaling more or less deeply or more or less often, to get the desired blood levels of nicotine—on average 35 nanograms per milliliter.

But no, it wasn't addictive. *Heroin* was addictive.

"We tend not to believe that the things we do routinely and normally are bad," observes Neil Grunberg. So it was with smoking. All through the 1930s, 40s, and 50s cigarette smoking had been advertised as a symbol of success, of healthy sexuality, of the American way of life. It was socially acceptable. It didn't make you crazy. It wasn't heroin. And so, as evidence mounted through the early 1970s that smokers were—to again invoke addiction's etymological roots—*bound over* to the drug, resistance to the idea lingered.

You could see it at a conference, "Smoking As a Dependence Process," held by the National Institute of Drug Abuse in 1978. At it, many of the presentations given were fairly riddled with ambivalence. On the one hand, *of course* smoking was addictive, and *of course* nicotine was responsible. On the other hand, there was reluctance, reaching even beyond normal scientific caution, to say so as long as any gaps remained in the scientific record.

M.A.H. Russell of Maudsley Hospital in England, for example, reviewed the evidence for nicotine's role—how it affected behavior and performance in ways that might be reinforcing, how it induced tolerance in animals, and so on—only to add a cautionary note: "If we could prove that nicotine is what smokers seek, we could be confident that the puzzle was virtually completed. Unfortunately this is not the case and we cannot escape the nagging fact that powerful addictive syndromes occur where pharmacological factors clearly play no part." How did we know, in other words, that smoking, with its comforting little rituals, wasn't more like such persistent habits as gambling, say, or nail biting?

Jerome Jaffe, then at Columbia University's College of Physicians and Surgeons, also expressed doubt. In a paper with Maureen Kanzler, he noted that, while nicotine *seemed* responsible for smoking's hold on the smoker, "reliable laboratory evidence that nicotine is a reinforcer of drug-taking behavior has been more difficult to develop than comparable evidence for drugs like morphine, amphetamine or cocaine." It was hard to get animals to give it to themselves. And when they did, they did so less compulsively than they did other drugs.

"We believe that most drinkers of gin and tonic want the gin more than the fizz or the quinine, that people who drink paregoric want the morphine and not the camphor," wrote he and Kanzler. But their personal convictions aside, they weren't *quite* ready to say it was nicotine that smokers craved more than the flare of the match, the lung-filling pull of the inhalation, or the leisurely rise of smoke rings into the air.

* * *

How did we know that smoking,
with its comforting little rituals,
wasn't more like such persistent habits
as gambling, say, or nail biting?

The doubts, though, were soon to be dismissed once and for all. Just as a generation earlier hundreds of millions of dollars had poured out of the National Cancer Institute to pin down smoking's effects on health, now NIDA sank resources into the study of tobacco addiction. "This is a psychoactive drug with effects that fit the most stringent definitions of addiction," Jack Henningfield remembers NIDA director William Polling pronouncing with certainty; now it was time to make the case airtight. "All of a sudden," recalls Henningfield, "this behavior-controlling drug was being studied by people trained to study behavior controlling drugs." And within a few years beginning in the late 1970s, the remaining doors through which nicotine might escape the label of addictive were slammed shut.

One measure of addictive potential can be gained by simply asking human subjects how much they like whatever they're being fed through an intravenous needle, comparing the drug at various dosages to a placebo. Give a small dose of morphine and people like it significantly more, on a standard five-point scale, than a placebo. Up the dose and they prefer it still more. Do the same for a drug like chlorpromazine, known not to encourage compulsive use, and subjects like it no more than a placebo; a higher dose changes matters not at all. Give them nicotine, as Jack Henningfield reported in a key experiment, and the scores climb with higher dosages just the way they do for morphine.

Around this time came a series of studies by the Addiction Research Center's Steven Goldberg and colleagues at Harvard. One anomaly long nagging at the composure of smoking researchers had been nicotine's apparent failure to satisfy the self-administration test. If a drug is addictive, you'd expect people and animals to fairly lap it up—or, the way such experiments are done, to eagerly press a lever that metered it out to them. At the 1978 conference, there'd been reports of self-administration in rats, but at unimpressively low levels. And other researchers had been unable to demonstrate it at all.

What Goldberg and his colleagues did was to mimic human smoking behavior in monkeys. When people smoke, any effects of the nicotine become intimately linked to—and amplified by—environmental cues: *Dinner's over. Time for a smoke.* So with the nicotine they delivered intravenously, the experimenters periodically flashed an amber light. Sure enough, the monkeys would press away, usually about once or twice a second, self-administering the drug. When the nicotine, unbeknownst to the animals, was replaced by saline, lever pressing fell off dramatically. When the monkeys were given mecamylamine, a drug known to block nicotine's pharmacological actions, pressing likewise fell. The results were clear. "In one fell swoop," says Henningfield, "all the equivocal studies were out."

2. USE, ADDICTION, AND DEPENDENCE

During the same period came key work on nicotine's withdrawal effects. Three hundred years before, following tobacco's introduction to England, King James I observed that smokers "are not able to forebear the same, no more than an old drunkard can abide to be long sober, without falling into an uncurable weakness and evil constitution." But difficulty in giving up smoking is one thing, withdrawal effects quite another. "You feed a vending machine that doesn't deliver, and you start beating on the machine," offers Jerome Jaffe, playing attorney for the defense. His point? "*Any* time you interrupt a habit, you can get irritable. Now if I give up smoking, do I vomit? Do I have seizures? Do I fall down on the floor, have hallucinations?" Junkies and alkies do. Smokers don't. Q.E.D., tobacco was not addictive, Jaffe portrays the skeptics insisting.

But by the early 1980s it had become clear that while abstaining from tobacco did not induce a withdrawal syndrome like that seen among heroin users, the symptoms were just as distinct, just as specific and just as measurable. Retrospective studies consistently showed signs of irritability, restlessness, difficulty concentrating, and weight gain. Now, the same symptoms showed up in more reliable prospective studies. Why, you could give smokers a battery of psychological and cognitive tests, watch their performance deteriorate within eight hours after their last smoke, then watch it return to normal once they started smoking again—or even, for that matter, when you fed them nicotine-laced chewing gum.

There had been other arguments long raised against calling nicotine addictive. Smoking, some said, doesn't exhibit tolerance; you don't require ever-increasing doses to achieve the desired effect. Sure it does, Henningfield points out. You don't *start out* smoking two packs a day. "And there are *no* drugs that people escalate their use of forever."

But wasn't it so, insisted critics like Gary Miller of the Tobacco Institute, that most ex-smokers gave it up on their own without outside help, or drugs, or treatment programs? What kind of an addiction is that? An addiction like any other, says Henningfield. Of alcohol users, for example, only 15 per cent are alcoholics. And nine in ten servicemen addicted to heroin in Vietnam got off once they got home. Because a drug exerts a powerful hold, doesn't mean it exerts an absolute hold.

Proponents of nicotine's central role in keeping smokers smoking don't say, and never said, that nicotine was the whole story. Give nicotine intravenously and smoking drops—but does not stop. Give nicotine chewing gum to would-be quitters and, without counseling and support, their relapse rate is almost as high as if you just let them go cold turkey. As Jerome Jaffe points out, "there's a lot of conditioning that goes with the inhalation of cigarette smoke. You have thousands of couplings" between the pleasure you get from smoking and the rituals surrounding it. To give up smoking means giving up nicotine—but also much more.

Later in the 1980s would come studies holding up whole new areas of nicotine's workings to the scientist's searchlight. Kenneth Kellar and his colleagues at Georgetown Medical Center, for example, discovered binding sites in the brain at which nicotine presumably acts. Other researchers experimented with nicotine gum, introduced in 1984 as a means of supplying smokers with a more benign source of nicotine while weaning them off cigarettes. Still others explored nicotine's role as a mood regulator and its ability to improve scores on cognitive tests through subtle nervous system effects.

But in essence, by the early 1980s, the case was already made; smoking was addictive—not just by the new, 1964 WHO definition but by the earlier, more rigid 1957 one—and nicotine was what made it so. So it was just a matter of time before the full force of the federal government lined up behind that determination.

In 1982, NIDA director William Pollin formally testified before Congress that nicotine was an addictive drug.

Later that year, summarizing Pollin's testimony and bearing the imprint of the U.S. Department of Health and Human Services, appeared a Public Health Service pamphlet, *Why People Smoke*. Placing tobacco right beside heroin, alcohol, and marijuana among drugs of abuse, the pamphlet reckoned it "the most widespread example of drug dependence in our country," one that drew its power and compulsion from nicotine.

In 1987, the American Psychiatric Association, which seven years before had included tobacco dependence within its Diagnostic and Statistical Manual of Mental Disorders, established "nicotine withdrawal" as an organic mental disorder.

Then, finally, on May 16, 1988, Surgeon General Koop stood before the cameras and microphones....

* * *

About ten years earlier, in a hospital in Jaipur, India, a three-year-old Hindu child from a rural family was admitted to the pediatrics ward for malnutrition, anemia, and acute bronchitis. Two days later, the child was given a transfusion. During it, despite two shots of tranquilizer, he could not be stilled. Later, "the child was unable to sleep," the doctors who wrote up the case in *Clinical Pediatrics* reported, "crying and fretting through much of the night, begging for bidis."

A bidi is a crude, indigenous form of cigar popular in India, typically a three inch-long wad of sun-cured tobacco wrapped in Tendu leaf. It turned out that the boy's grandmother had surreptitiously supplied them to him for the past six months, and that he now smoked, inhaling deeply, eight to ten of them daily. When denied the bidis at the time of the transfusion, he became cranky and irritable and could neither eat nor sleep comfortably.

The three Indian physicians had little doubt about what they were seeing. They entitled their case study, "Probable Tobacco Addiction in a Three-Year-Old Child."

THE 'MONKEY MODEL' OF ADDICTION: A DANGEROUS MYTH

Dr. William Wilbanks

Professor, Dept. of Criminal Justice, Florida International University, N. Miami, FL 33181

THE MONKEY MODEL OF ADDICTION

Many drug treatment specialists and most of those (especially politicians) who seek to educate our youth about the dangers of drugs appear to endorse what I term the "monkey model" of drug addiction. The monkey model asserts that those who take such drugs as heroin and cocaine will inevitably increase their intake until they reach a point where the craving for the drug high and the fear of withdrawal causes them to "lose control". The loss of control is evidenced by the willingness to sacrifice all—to the point of self-destruction—to ingest the drug.

This popular belief in the inevitable loss of control with continued experimentation with drugs is buttressed by animal research that allegedly shows that monkeys will press a lever to get more cocaine until they kill themselves. The monkeys cannot help themselves because the addictive power of cocaine is so great. Television has helped popularize the "monkey model" of addiction in that many TV documentaries have presented the animal research as proof of this rather mechanistic view of the nature of addiction.

A paper presented at the International Conference on Drug Policy Reform, Oct. 22, 1988, Washington, D.C. at Workshop #17, "Theories of Addiction and Their Relationship to National Drug Control Policies." Sponsored by the Drug Policy Foundation, 4801 Mass. Ave., N.W., Suite 400, Washington, D.C. 20026-2087

This paper is intended only to serve as an outline for oral remarks by Dr. Wilbanks at the panel described above. A more detailed article ("The New Obscenity: 'I Can't Help Myself' ") includes a bibliography of 30 sources and reference citations in the text and is available upon request from Dr. Wilbanks at the above address. The complete speech/article (minus the bibliography) was published by Vital Speeches of the Day *in its Aug. 15, 1988, issue. A Condensed version was published by* The Readers Digest *in its December, 1988 issue.*

The monkey model of addiction is perhaps best illustrated by the statement of a cocaine addict who said that while he was addicted his greatest fear was that he would win the million dollar state lottery. He knew that if he had a million dollars he would buy and consume cocaine continuously until he died. The monkey model presents the image of a helpless "addict" overwhelmed by the power of drugs. We are told that the addict "can't help himself" and that he has "lost control."

The belief in and presentation of the monkey model of addiction is not limited to TV reporters. It is apparently endorsed by many leading authorities on addiction. On September 21, 1988, ABC devoted a Nightline program to addiction. Dr. Timothy Johnson, ABC's medical expert, hosted the program and interviewed two leading authorities on addiction, Dr. Jerome Jaffe of the National Institute on Drug Abuse, and Dr. Anna Rose Childress of the U. of Penn. School of Medicine. These three authorities presented a mechanistic view of addiction in that they spoke of the psychological and physiological causes of addiction without once mentioning the role of personal values and self-discipline.

One person on the Nightline program, John Pierce, an ex-addict, did speak of the importance of values and self-discipline but his comments were completely ignored by Dr. Johnson and his two guests. Dr. Johnson asked the ex-addict if all the scientific talk he had heard thus far on the program "rang true" to his experience. After Pierce talked about the importance of self-esteem, personal values, his relationship to significant others and the importance of learning to resist the craving for drugs, one would have thought that Dr. Johnson as host would have asked his two experts to comment on this layman's view of the cause of addiction. Instead Dr. Johnson went back to his focus on the psychological and physiological causes of addiction. Those watching the program could only assume that Dr. Johnson, Dr. Jaffe and Dr. Childress all believed that Pierce's focus on values and self-disci-

From a paper presented at the *International Conference on Drug Policy Reform* by William Wilbanks, October 22, 1988, pp. 1-4.

63

pline was naive and incorrect. In my view, the experts on Nightline left the impression with the TV audience that they endorsed the monkey model of addiction.

The monkey model of addiction is part of an emerging philosophy that I call "The New Obscenity". This philosophy strikes at the very core of the concepts of the human will and personal responsibility. The philosophy is obscene in that it offends and denies the quality that makes us human—our capacity to make moral choices. Those who endorse the New Obscenity view the human mind in mechanistic terms as the simple arbiter of competing psychological and physiological forces. In this mechanistic view the stronger force wins the battle and thus there is little room for choice.

There is certainly no room for the belief that certain of these alternative choices or forces are "temptations" and that they can and should be resisted. In the words of Dr. Thomas Szasz: "Temptation—resisted or indulged—has been supplanted by drives, instincts and impulses—satisfied or frustrated. Virtue and vice have been transformed into health and illness." (*Ceremonial Chemistry*, p. 149).

The medicalization of deviance has no place for the concept of moral choice and temptation. Solutions to human problems are not seen as moral but as technical and medical. This "scientific" philosophy sees man as a responsive organism being acted upon by biological and social forces rather than as a responsible agent acting in and on the world. Man is seen as "progressing" historically from the medieval belief that addicts were sinful to the enlightenment notion that they were evil or criminal to the "modern" belief that addicts are sick. Clearly the monkey model of addiction sees addicts as persons being acted upon by forces beyond their control rather than as actors who have the capacity to control their behavior.

CRITICISMS OF THE MONKEY MODEL OF ADDICTION

But there are many critics of the monkey model of addiction. Stanton Peele and his co-authors in *The Meaning of Addiction* summarize the animal research allegedly proving the validity of the monkey model and suggest that the available research does not support the mechanistic view that animals when presented with cocaine will choose that drug over food, water, sex, etc. The monkey model is based on research with rats in cages but when rats in more natural settings are utilized the research does not support the theory that drugs are so powerful that rats will forego food, water and sex for the drug.

And even if the animal research did suggest a mechanistic theory of addiction one could not jump to the conclusion that man behaves like monkeys when confronted with drugs. To suggest that man and monkeys behave in a similar fashion is, in my view, obscene since such a view denies the basic dignity and freedom of man. The monkey model suggests that man has no more power over his own behavior than animals even though man does have the power of choice and reason.

I find it curious that some of the most outspoken advocates of the monkey model of addiction are conservative Christians and Evangelicals who supposedly are adamant in viewing man as being on a different plane than the animals. The Evangelicals (and A.A.) appear to believe that the addict faces forces beyond his control but can overcome those forces with the help of God.

Also, the existence of many controlled users contradicts the monkey model of addiction. If addiction is inevitable once experimentation with drugs begins how does one explain the large number of persons who use drugs in a controlled fashion. Peele (*The Meaning of Addiction*, p. 28) cites several authorities to support his contention that there are approximately 6 controlled users for every "addict" for such drugs as alcohol and heroin. Norman Zinberg's book, *Drug, Set, and Setting: The Basis for Controlled Intoxicant Use*, documents the rather widespread existence of controlled drug use.

And a paper by Patricia Erickson and Bruce Alexander raises doubt about the "addictive liability" of cocaine and suggests that most people who continue to use cocaine do not use it frequently and very few become compulsive users. Further, it would appear from national survey data that there are approximately 24 Americans who have tried cocaine for every one American who has become an addict. A 24:1 ratio of experimenters to addicts and a 6:1 ratio of controlled users to addicts would appear to contradict the monkey model of addiction.

IMPLICATIONS OF THE MONKEY MODEL FOR DRUG POLICY

The monkey model of addiction has several implications for national drug control policies:

First, those who propose the monkey model apparently see this model of addiction as being an *effective deterrent to experimentation with drugs*. The monkey model is presented to youth as a "scare story" as to what will happen if they touch drugs. The suggestion is that if one experiments with drugs one will inevitably consume more and more drugs until one is addicted. The message is that we are all like monkeys and that we will be overpowered by drugs if we dare to try drugs since we can no more overcome the power of drugs than can the monkey in the cage who presses the lever for more and more cocaine until it kills itself via an overdose.

Second, the monkey model of addiction apparently *sees any less mechanistic theory of addiction as being an ineffective deterrent*. When I debate the monkey model the most common reaction to my position is something like, "But if people listen to you they might be encouraged to experiment with drugs since you are suggesting that some people can be 'controlled users'." I am told that the best policy is to simply tell people that no matter who they are—no matter what their values are and no matter how disciplined they are—they will become addicted if they experiment with drugs. The notion of controlled drug use is seen as heresy that will encourage those who listen to that heresy to experiment with drugs and to attempt to be controlled users and will inevitably result in more people winding up in the Hell of addiction.

One gets the impression in debate on this issue that the advocates of the monkey model are suggesting that model is true because it is the most effective deterrent and any theory that deviates from that model is wrong because alternative models of addiction do not discourage drug experimentation and thus are ineffective deterrents. It is heresy to question the monkey model of addiction because that model is an effective foundation for the holy war on the evils of drug abuse.

Third, since the monkey model has no room for the notion of personal control over drug intake this model is quite ineffective in designing strategies to prevent addiction once an individual begins to experiment with drugs. Thus *the monkey model has led to the focus on TREATMENT and DETERRENCE programs so that PREVENTION programs have been ignored*. In other words, our nation has developed a model of addiction that lends itself well to DETERRENCE (scare stories) and TREATMENT (the treatment specialist will cure the 'medical problem' of the addict) but that is incompatible with PREVENTION programs that attempt to help the person struggling with the craving for drugs to control that craving before he reaches the point of addiction.

The monkey model would appear to assume that addiction is inevitable once an individual experiments with drugs such as cocaine (especially "crack" cocaine) or heroin. The person experimenting with drugs is told, "you can't help yourself," and thus any efforts at self-control are seen as futile in face of the overpowering force of the drug. In short, the monkey model appears to see the only effective prevention strategy as "don't touch drugs or you'll become an addict" and has no prevention (of addiction) strategy once experimentation with drugs occurs.

Fourth, the belief in the monkey model *may lead to greater levels of addiction if those who hear and believe in this theory of addiction believe that their efforts at self-control are futile in the face of the overpowering nature of drugs*. Once a person experiments with drugs and finds that he likes the effect he may believe that he is now addicted and give up any efforts at self-control since the monkey model tells him such effort is doomed to failure.

In fact, the monkey model of addiction contributes to what psychologists call "learned helplessness" or a sense of impotence in face of the overwhelming power of drugs. The person experimenting with drugs faces the growing intensity of craving for the drugs at the same time he is exposed to the monkey model of addiction. It is easy for him to believe that he has reached the point where he has lost control and to cease his efforts to resist the temptation to continue drug use. In short, the person struggling with the temptations of drugs is told (brainwashed?) that he is helpless against the power of drugs and that belief or prediction becomes a self-fulfilling prophecy. Some research does support the idea that "addicts" have an external rather than an internal locus of control that is consistent with the concept of learned helplessness. Thus the monkey model of addiction perpetuates the "great tautology"—that any behavior that is uncontrolled is uncontrollable.

Fifth, I am opposed to the legalization of "hard" drugs as long as the monkey model of addiction is the dominant model used in drug education programs. It seems clear to me that more people would try hard drugs such as cocaine if these drugs were legal. And if those who experiment with drugs continue to believe in the monkey model of addiction they would likely quickly come to the view that their desire and even craving for the drug meant that they were addicted and had "lost control". If we ever seriously propose that drugs be legalized we need to revamp our education programs so that those experimenting with drugs are helped to avoid addiction by prevention programs that recognize that only a small minority of frequent users become addicts.

Prevention programs will have to "market" the techniques used by controlled users to avoid the greater number of addicts that would result from the greater number of drug experimenters. I am afraid that such prevention programs would be viewed as endorsing or encouraging the recreational use of drugs and thus that they would not be politically feasible. The American public may be willing to legalize drugs to take the profit motive out of the drug problem. The public, by agreeing to legalization, may simply be resigned to the fact that there are a lot of addicts who steal if they can't afford their drugs. But would the public accept legalization if they believed drug education programs associated with legalization would "promote" the "recreational use of drugs"? I think not. In short, I think the prevention programs that would be required for any effective legalization program would be tougher to sell the public than legalization itself.

Why Drugs?

Why do people use and abuse drugs? And why do some people use, abuse, and become dependent on, certain psychoactive substances while others do not? What explanations account for drug use? The medical profession calls explanations that attempt to answer the "why" question, *etiology*; what is the etiology or cause of drug use and abuse? In short, *Why drugs*?

A variety of perspectives attempt to answer the "why" question. In the early 1980s, a federal agency, the National Institute on Drug Abuse, published a nearly 500-page monograph entitled *Theories of Drug Abuse*, which described some 40 different explanations of why people abuse drugs. Clearly, a definitive explanation of drug use and abuse—one on which nearly all informed observers will agree—has not yet been devised. This issue is still fraught with controversy.

Some experts believe that drug use is a universal human need—indeed, an instinct that is characteristic of all, or most, members of the animal kingdom. "High Times in the Wild Kingdom" summarizes this perspective, originally put forth by Andrew Weil in his book, *The Natural Mind* in 1972, and recently expanded by Ronald Siegel in *Intoxication: Life in Pursuit of Artificial Paradise*. Siegel's conclusion is that, since humans have a universal need to get high, and since all currently known intoxicating substances have dangerous side-effects, scientists ought to search for one that is completely safe. While most experts do not agree with this theory, it is worthy of attention.

The "animal instinct" theory, however, does not address the question of the *variability* of drug use among humans. After all, instinct or not, some of us are lifetime abstainers, others use drugs (alcohol and coffee, for instance) safely, moderately, and without untoward effect, and still others are compulsive, drug-dependent abusers. How do we account for the difference? For an answer to this type of question, we have to look at explanations that seek differences among individuals.

Some experts believe that there is a genetic basis to dependence and addiction—that, for example, some people are born with a genetic propensity to abuse and become dependent on addictive drugs such as alcohol. What exactly does this "genetic propensity" consist of? With respect to alcohol, some observers believe that an unusual insensitivity to the effects of alcohol causes some people who drink to drink to excess; this insensitivity causes them to feel only slightly drunk when they are very drunk, which influences them to drink more than others do. The same could be true of drugs generally, some argue. "Probing the Complex Genetics of Alcoholism" explores the difficulties in drawing conclusions in this controversial area.

The genetic theory is controversial and is not accepted by all, or even most, drug abuse experts. Some observers argue that there is a syndrome known as the "addictive personality." Those individuals who become chemically dependent did so because they are, to quote Benjamin Stein, author of "The Lure of Drugs," "lonely, sad, frightened people" who have a basic personality flaw for which drugs offer a crutch that "organizes" their lives. Still other experts argue that alcohol and other chemical dependencies are "intoxicating habits," that the chemically dependent have simply learned to do the wrong things with the substances they use and abuse. Just as Pavlov's dogs learned to salivate at the sound of a bell, the stimuli in the addict's environment serve as cues that generate a drug craving. Addicts associate these cues with pleasure because they have been associated with reinforcement in the past; such associations can be unlearned as readily as they were learned. Still other experts point to more natural causes. The brain produces a set of morphine-like chemicals called endorphins (or "endogenous morphines") which, under certain circumstances, give us a "natural high." When endorphins are released, the body feels pleasure and wants to repeat what caused it; could these endorphins be a clue to the etiology of drug use and abuse?

Sociological perspectives stress the influence of the society, the culture, social contexts or settings, and subcultures within a given society on drug dependence. Certain categories in the population are more likely to use and abuse drugs than others; certain drugs penetrate poorer neighborhoods more readily than more affluent ones; men learn that it is acceptable and normative to drink at higher levels than women do; drinking in some societies takes place in family settings, and tends to be moderate, whereas in other societies, drinking typically takes place among single men in a bar setting, and tends to be more excessive; and so on. In any explanation of drug and alcohol abuse, it is incomplete and misleading to leave sociological factors out of the picture.

Recently, many observers have concluded that several explanations are necessary for a complete understanding of the "why" question. Perhaps, one day, an integrated theory may emerge.

Looking Ahead: Challenge Questions
Why do people use drugs? Why do some people use certain drugs? Why do some people who use drugs

abuse and become dependent on them—while others do not? Why do so many drug users not become drug abusers? Where does use end and abuse begin?

Is abuse a chemical, a genetic, a psychological, or a sociological phenomenon? Is it a combination of all of these factors? In what way? Is it a different combination for different individuals?

Is drug abuse rational or irrational behavior? Why?

If drug abuse can be explained by factors beyond the individual's control, are we, therefore, not responsible for our abuse of drugs?

If the supply of a certain drug suddenly dried up, would

the users and abusers of that drug simply stop taking drugs altogether—or turn to another chemical substance?

Do we need a different explanation for use than we do for abuse? Abuse than for addiction and dependence? Do we need a different explanation for the abuse of each drug separately?

If alcoholism is genetically caused, how can one member of the same family become an alcoholic, one an abstainer, and the third a moderate drinker? If drug abuse is hereditary, what about other factors?

Why can some people handle alcohol while others cannot?

High Times in the Wild Kingdom

Is drug abuse natural?

One of the surest ways to kill a rat is to let it shoot cocaine. Teach a rat, or a dog or a monkey, to dose itself at will, and it typically becomes just as helpless as any urban junkie. Addicted animals will give up food or companionship, even endure electrical shocks, to get another fix. And they'll continue to dose themselves as their lungs and nervous systems start to fail.

This is in the lab, of course. Such depravity would never occur in nature, right? Wrong, says Ronald Siegel, a psychopharmacologist at UCLA. In a recent book titled "Intoxication: Life in Pursuit of Artificial Paradise,"* Siegel argues that the urge to get high is as basic and universal as the desire for food or sex—and that it has some of the same consequences in the wild as it has in urban America. "The entire animal kingdom is driven by the same pursuit," he says. "It is part of our nature."

Siegel traces the roots of today's drug problem back 135 million years to the Cretaceous Period, when angiosperm plants started manufacturing toxic chemicals as a defense against herbivores. By the time humans discovered the pleasing effects of certain plant toxics, some 5,000 years ago, other animals were already forging "the new chemical bond we call addiction." Humans have recently carried the relationship to new extremes, of course, by extracting and refining the poisons of choice. But modern drug taking remains part of a "long natural tradition." Siegel doesn't always back his assertions with data, and his prose style is a bizarre amalgam of Scientific American and the New York Post. Yet despite its flaws, his treatise offers a refreshing perspective on the drug problem, and it's full of amusing yarns.

Addiction, as Siegel makes clear, is not always a bad thing. Australian koalas spend their lives feeding exclusively on eucalyptus leaves, not just for nutrition but to alter their body temperatures and make themselves unpalatable to parasites and predators. The leaves are bitter medicine: infants have to start out on a predigested pulp excreted by their mothers. But once they learn the habit, there's no giving it up. They die when deprived of eucalyptus, because their addicted bodies have no other way to get nutrients.

Other animals use drugs for sheer pleasure. In the Canadian Rockies, bighorn sheep grind their teeth to the gums nibbling at a narcotic lichen that grows on bare rocks. And various creatures eat the hallucinogenic mescal beans that grow in the Texas desert, even though the beans lack usable nutrients. When Siegel led a group of goats to a patch of shrubs to gauge the veracity of this rumor, several munched themselves into a daylong delirium. So did one of his pack horses (he had to restrain the others). Small wonder that the Wichita Indians, who developed an entire pharmacology by observing animals, became mescal eaters themselves.

Drunk elephants: Psychedelics don't have a broad animal following, but drunkenness seems ubiquitous. It often results from a chance encounter with fermented fruit or grain, yet many creatures actively lust after alcohol. Farm animals are notorious for breaking into vats of moonshine mash. So are elephants. Siegel recounts how a herd of 150 once raided an illegal still in West Bengal, drank liberally, then "rampaged across the land, killing five people, injuring a dozen, demolishing seven concrete buildings and trampling twenty village huts." Baboons can get carried away, too. In "The Descent of Man," Darwin recounts how a troupe in North Africa "held their aching heads with both hands and wore a pitiable expression" a day after gulping down bowls of strong beer. "When beer or wine was offered them, they turned away with disgust."

Luckily, natural forces usually converge to keep animals from wasting their lives, even when they lack a sense of restraint. When flocks of migrating robins arrive in southern California each February, they gorge themselves on ripening firethorn and toyon berries. For a few weeks the birds go utterly berserk, and many die in high-speed flying accidents. But because the berries are seasonal, sobriety prevails the rest of the year. In the Andes, llamas, birds, snails, insects and people all consume cocaine by eating leaves or seeds from the coca plant. But the drug's natural packaging effectively prohibits harmful doses.

Insect anarchy: There are exceptions to this pattern, however—instances in which drug use tears at the fabric of animal society. Ranchers have known since the 19th century that locoweed, a flowering plant native to the American Southwest, can turn cattle and horses into crazed, hopeless junkies. Many addicts die of starvation or thirst, as they give up food and water in favor of the drug. And their offspring tend to perpetuate the cycle of dependency. *Lasius flavus,* or yellow ant, suffers similarly from its appetite for beetle juice. Colonies of yellow ants typically feed and care for *Lomechusa* beetles in exchange for the chance to lick an intoxicating goo from their abdomens. If the worker ants drink too much, they get careless and damage the ant larvae in their care. The workers' addiction also compromises their loyalties: in a crisis, they tend to safeguard the beetles' larvae instead of their own kin's. Entire societies can collapse as a result.

The fact that drug use is natural doesn't mean it's good, then, just that chanting "no" isn't likely to rid us of it anytime soon. The most controversial alternative—to haul off and legalize currently controlled substances—could prove disastrous, given the deadly pharmacopia we've amassed. The obvious solution, in Siegel's view, is to restructure our chemical environment—to fabricate drugs that "balance optimal positive effects, such as stimulation or pleasure, with minimal . . . toxic consequences." If medical science could perform that feat, he reasons, everyone could have a good time and no one would get hurt. It's a fanciful notion, a bit like that of erecting a high-tech global missile shield. The difference is that, in this case, a partial success would represent progress.

GEOFFREY COWLEY

Drugs and Free Will

Jeffrey A. Schaler

Jeffrey A. Schaler is a psychotherapist in Silver Spring, Maryland. He is a doctoral candidate in human development at the University of Maryland. He lectures on drugs, alcoholism, and society in the department of justice, law, and society at American University, Washington, D. C.

That was the disease talking. . .I was a victim." So declared Marion Barry, 54, mayor of the District of Columbia. Drug addiction is the disease. Fourteen charges were lodged against him by the U.S. attorney's office, including three counts of perjury, a felony offense for lying about drug use before a grand jury; ten counts of cocaine possession, a misdemeanor; and one count of conspiracy to possess cocaine.

Barry considered legal but settled for moral sanctuary in what has come to be known as the disease-model defense. He maintained that he "was addicted to alcohol and had a chemical dependency on Valium and Xanax." These are diseases, he asserted, "similar to cancer, heart disease and diabetes." The implication: It is as unfair to hold him responsible for drug-related criminal behavior as it is to hold a diabetic responsible for diabetes.

The suggestion was that his disease of addiction forced him to use drugs, which in turn eroded his volition and judgment. He did not voluntarily break the law. According to Barry, "the best defense to a lie is truth," and the truth, he contended, is that he was powerless in relation to drugs, his life unmanageable and "out of control." His behaviors or acts were purportedly the result, that is, symptomatic, of his disease. And jail, say those who agree with him, is not the answer to the "product of an illness."

This disease alibi has become a popular defense. Baseball's Pete Rose broke through his "denial" to admit he has a "gambling disease." Football's Dexter Manley claimed his drug use was caused by addiction disease. Addiction treatment professionals diagnosed televangelist Jimmy Swaggart as having "lost control"

of his behavior and as being "addicted to the chemical released in his brain from orgasm." They assert that Barry, Rose, Manley and Swaggart all need "twelve-step treatment" for addiction, the putative disease that, claims the multimillion-dollar addiction treatment industry, is reaching epidemic proportions and requires medical treatment. To view addiction-related behaviors as a function of free will, they often say, is cruel, stigmatizing and moralistic, an indication that one does not really understand the disease.

Others are more reluctant to swallow the disease model. After testing positive for cocaine in 1987, Mets pitcher Dwight Gooden said he could moderate his use of the drug and was not addicted. This is heresy according to disease-model proponents, a sign of denial, the salient symptom of the disease of addiction and considered by some to be a disease itself. There is no such thing as responsible drug taking or controlled drinking for an addict or an alcoholic, they assert.

The tendency to view unusual or questionable behavior as part of a disease process is now being extended, along with the characteristic theory of "loss of control," to include all sorts of "addictive" behaviors. We are currently experiencing the "diseasing of America," as social-clinical psychologist Stanton Peele describes it in his recent book of the same name (1989). The disease model is being applied to any socially unacceptable behavior as a means of absolving people of responsibility for their actions, criminal or otherwise. The practice is justified on this basis: Drug use constitutes an addiction. Addiction is a disease. Acts stemming from the disease are called symptoms. Since the symptoms of a disease are involuntary, the symptoms of drug addiction disease are likewise involuntary. Addicts are thus not responsible for their actions.

Is this analogizing of drug addiction to real diseases like diabetes, heart disease and cancer scientifically valid? Or is the word "disease" simply a misused metaphor? Does drug use truly equal addiction? Are

the symptoms of drug addiction really involuntary?

Loss of Control

At the heart of the idea that drug use equals addiction is a theory known as "loss of control." This theory may have originated among members of Alcoholics Anonymous "to denote," as described by researcher E.M. Jellinek in his book The Disease Concept of Alcoholism (1960), "that stage in the development of [alcoholics'] drinking history when the ingestion of one alcoholic drink sets up a chain reaction so that they are unable to adhere to their intention to 'have one or two drinks only' but continue to ingest more and more—often with quite some difficulty and disgust—contrary to their volition."

Loss of control also suggests that addictive drugs can start a biochemical chain reaction experienced by an addict as an uncontrollable physical demand for more drugs. Drug addicts are people who have allegedly lost their ability to control their ingestion of drugs.

In a speech in San Diego two years ago, National Drug Policy Director William Bennett explained that a drug "addict is a man or woman whose power to exercise. . .rational volition has. . .been seriously eroded by drugs, and whose life is instead organized largel—even exclusively—around the pursuit and satisfaction of his addiction."

Yet, there is a contradiction in Bennett's point of view. If an addict's power to exercise rational volition is seriously eroded, on what basis does the addict organize life "largely even exclusively around the pursuit and satisfaction of his addiction"? An act of organizing is clearly a volitional act, an act of will.

Three Models of Drug Use

Etiological paradigms for understanding drug use can be distilled into three models. Aside from the disease model, there are two other ways of looking at drug addiction: the free-will model and the moralistic model.In the free-will model drug use is envisioned as a means of coping with environmental experience, a behavioral choice and a function of psychological and environmental factors combined. The nervous system of the body is conceived of as a lens, modulating experience as self and environment interact. The self is like the film in a camera, where experience is organized and meaning is created. The self is not the brain.

Individual physiological differences affect the experience of self. They do not create it. The quality of a camera lens affects the image of the environment transposed to the film. When the image is unpleasant, drugs are used to modify the lens.

The self is the executor of experience in this model, not the nervous system. Drug use may or may not be an effective means of lens modification. The assessment of drug effectiveness and the price of drug use are viewed as moral, not medical, judgments.

The recommended therapy for the drug user is: 1) a matter of choice; 2) concerned with awareness and responsibility; 3) a process of values clarification; 4) a means of support to achieve specific behavior goals; and 5) an educational process that involves the learning of coping strategies.

The moralistic model harkens back to the days of the temperance movement and is often erroneously equated with the free-will model. Here, addiction is considered to be the result of low moral standards, bad character and weak will. Treatment consists of punishment for drug-using behavior. The punitive nature of America's current war on drugs with its call for "user accountability" is typical of the moralistic perspective.

Addicts are viewed as bad people who need to be rehabilitated in "boot camps." They are said to be lacking in values. President Bush gave a clear example of this during the televised debates of the 1988 presidential campaign. When asked how to solve the drug problem, he answered, "by instilling values."

The drug user's loss of values is often attributed to the presence of a disease. A "plague" and "epidemic" of drug use are said to be spreading across the land. Since users are sick and supposedly unaware of their disease, many people feel justified in coercing them into treatment, treatment that is primarily religious in nature. Thus, the moralistic model is paternalistic.

In the disease or medical model, addicts are considered to have physiological differences from normal people, differences based in a genetic source or created through the chemical effects of drugs. Instead of focusing on the interaction between the self and the environment, advocates of the disease model view the interaction between physiology and the chemicals in drugs as both the disease and the executor of behavior and experience. In this sense the model is mechanistic. The person is viewed as a machine, a highly complex machine, but a machine nevertheless. The disease of addiction is considered to be incurable. People in treatment can only reach a state of perpetual recovery. Treatment of symptoms involves admitting that one is ill by breaking through denial of the disease and turning over one's life to a "higher power" in a spiritual sense and psychological support to achieve sobriety. Addicts are not bad but sick people. Intervention is required because the machine has broken. Thus, the disease model is both paternalistic and mechanistic.

Addiction Redefined

Proponents of the will and the disease models dis-

agree with the moralistic perspective, but for different reasons. The former believe addicts should not be punished for having unconventional values. They believe treatment should focus on changing the psychological and environmental conditions conducive to drug use. Coping skills should be taught along with the building of self-esteem and self-efficacy. The latter believe that addicts should not be punished for being sick and that treatment should focus on the biological factors that cause and reinforce drug use.

James R. Milam and Katherine Ketcham, authors of *Under the Influence* (1981), are popular spokespersons for the disease-model camp. They argue that alcoholics should not be held accountable for their actions because these are the "outpourings of a sick brain. . .They are sick, unable to think rationally, and incapable of giving up alcohol by themselves."

Similarly, physician Mark S. Gold, an expert on cocaine use and treatment, says in his book *800-CO-CAINE* (1984) that cocaine should not be regarded as a benign recreational drug because it can cause addiction. As with alcoholism, says Gold, there is no cure for cocaine addiction except permanent and total abstention from its use. Cocaine produces "an irresistible compulsion to use the drug at increasing doses and frequency in the face of serious physical and/or psychological side effects and the extreme disruption of the user's personal relationships and system of values." According to Gold "if you feel addicted, you are addicted." Addiction, be it to alcohol or cocaine, is, as far as Milam, Ketcham and Gold are concerned, identical to loss of control. The drug itself and physiological changes in the addict's body are said to control further ingestion of drugs in what is viewed as an involuntary process.

It may be helpful to look at how the term "addiction" has developed. Its use in conjunction with drugs, disease, loss of control, withdrawal and tolerance developed out of the moralistic rhetoric of the temperance and anti-opium movements of the nineteenth century, not through scientific inquiry. Such a restrictive use of the word served multiple purposes according to psychologist Bruce Alexander of Simon Fraser University in British Columbia, lead author of an article on the subject. Linking addiction to drugs and illness suggested it was a medical problem. It also helped to scare people away from drug use, a tactic that became increasingly important with anti-opium reformers. Etymologically, the word "addiction" comes from the Latin "dicere" (infinitive form) and, combined with the preposition "ad," means "to say yes to," "consent." Consent implies voluntary acceptance.

The idea of choice, volition or voluntariness inherent in the meaning of the word "addiction" is significant to will-model proponents because the concept of addiction as a disease depends so much on the loss-of-control theory. Most people think of addiction with the element of volition decidedly absent. Studies of alcoholics and cocaine and heroin addicts conducted over the past twenty-six years appear to refute this claim, however.

The Myth of Loss of Control

In 1962 British physician and alcohol researcher D.L. Davies rocked the alcoholism field by publishing the results of a long-term follow-up study of patients treated for alcoholism at the Maudsley Hospital in London. Abstinence, long considered the only cure for alcoholism, was seriously questioned as the only form of treatment when seven out of ninety-three male alcoholics studied exhibited a pattern of normal drinking. Physiological differences purportedly present in alcoholics did not seem to affect their ability to control drinking.

Four years later, *The Lancet* published an important study by British psychiatrist Julius Merry that supported Davies's findings. Alcoholics who were unaware they were drinking alcohol did not develop an uncontrollable desire to drink more, undermining the assertion by supporters of the disease model that a small amount of alcohol triggers uncontrollable craving. If alcoholics truly experience loss of control, then the subjects of the study should have reported higher craving whether they believed their beverages contained alcohol or not.

According to the loss-of-control theory, those with the disease of alcoholism cannot plan their drinking especially when going through a period of excessive craving. Yet, psychologist Nancy Mello and physician Jack Mendelson, leading alcoholism researchers and editors of the *Journal of Studies on Alcohol,* reported in 1972 that he found alcoholics bought and stockpiled alcohol to be able to get as drunk as they wanted even while undergoing withdrawal from previous binges. In other words, they could control their drinking for psychological reasons; their drinking behavior was not determined by a physiologically uncontrollable force, sparked by use of alcohol.

As Mello and Mendelson wrote in summary of their study of twenty-three alcoholics published in *Psychosomatic Medicine:* "It is important to emphasize that even in the unrestricted alcohol-access situation, no subject drank all the alcohol available or tried to 'drink to oblivion.' These data are inconsistent with predictions from the craving hypothesis so often invoked to account for an alcoholic's perpetuation of drinking. No

empirical support has been provided for the notion of craving by directly observing alcoholic subjects in a situation where they can choose to drink alcohol in any volume at any time by working at a simple task. There has been no confirmation of the notion that once drinking starts, it proceeds autonomously."

A significant experiment conducted by Alan Marlatt of the University of Washington in Seattle and his colleagues in 1973 supported these findings by showing that alcoholics' drinking is correlated with their beliefs about alcohol and drinking. Marlatt successfully disguised beverages containing and not containing alcohol among a randomly assigned group of sixty-four alcoholic and social drinkers (the control group) asked to participate in a "taste-rating task." One group of subjects was given a beverage with alcohol but was told that although it tasted like alcohol it actually contained none. Subjects in another group were given a beverage with no alcohol (tonic) but were told that it did contain alcohol.

As Marlatt and co-authors reported in the *Journal of Abnormal Psychology*, they found "the consumption rates were higher in those conditions in which subjects were led to believe that they would consume alcohol, regardless of the actual beverage administered." The finding was obtained among both alcoholic and social drinker subjects. Marlatt's experiment suggests that according to their findings the ability of alcoholics to stop drinking alcohol is not determined by a physiological reaction to alcohol. A psychological fact—the belief that they were drinking alcohol—was operationally significant, not alcohol itself.

Similar findings have been reported in studies of cocaine addiction. Patricia G. Erickson and her colleagues at the Addiction Research Foundation in Ontario concluded, in their book *The Steel Drug* (1987), after reviewing many studies on cocaine that most social-recreational users are able to maintain a low-to-moderate use pattern without escalating to dependency and that users can essentially "treat themselves." They state, "Many users particularly appreciated that they could benefit from the various appealing effects of cocaine without a feeling of loss of control."

Erickson and co-authors cite in support a study by Spotts and Shontz (1980) that provides "the most in-depth profile of intravenous cocaine users to date." They state: "Most users felt a powerful attachment to cocaine, but not to the extent of absolute necessity. [A]ll agreed that cocaine is not physically addicting. . .[and] many reported temporary tolerance."

In a study by Siegel (1984) of 118 users, 99 of whom were social-recreational users, described by Erickson et al. as the only longitudinal study of cocaine users in

North America, "all users reported episodes of cocaine abstinence."

These results thus further support the hypothesis that drug use is a function of psychological, not physiological, variables. Even the use of heroin, long considered "the hardest drug," can be controlled for psychological and environmental reasons that are important to heroin addicts. A notable study of 943 randomly selected Vietnam veterans, 495 of whom "represented a 'drug-positive' sample whose urine samples had been positive for opiates at the time of departure" from Vietnam, was commissioned by the U.S. Department of Defense and led by epidemiologist Lee N. Robins. The study shows that only 14 percent of those who used heroin in Vietnam became re-addicted after returning to the United States. Her findings, reported in 1975, support the theory that drug use is a function of environmental stress, which in this example ceased when the veterans left Vietnam. Veterans said they used heroin to cope with the harrowing experience of war. As Robins and co-authors wrote in *Archives of General Psychiatry*:

. . .[I]t does seem clear that the opiates are not so addictive that use is necessarily followed by addiction nor that once addicted, an individual is necessarily addicted permanently. At least in certain circumstances, individuals can use narcotics regularly and even become addicted to them but yet be able to avoid use in other social circumstances. . .How generalizable these results are is currently unknown. No previous study has had so large and so unbiased a sample of heroin users.

The cocaine and heroin studies are important for several reasons. They challenge the contention that drug addiction is primarily characterized by loss of control. Moreover, these and similar studies support the idea that what goes on outside of a person's body is more significant in understanding drug use, including alcoholism, than what goes on inside the body.

Consider for a moment how a person enters and exits drug use. While disease-model proponents such as Milam, Ketcham and Gold, claim that abstinence is the only cure for this "special disease," implying that strength of will is irrelevant, we must recognize drug use, and abstinence from it, for what they really are —volitional acts.

Addiction and the Law

This is a markedly different process from that in real diseases. A person cannot will the onset of cancer, diabetes or epilepsy. Nor can these diseases be willed away. While people may exercise responsibility in

relation to their diseases, they cannot be held responsible for actually creating them. Research supports the idea that drug use does not automatically lead to loss of control—a drug-ingestion frenzy devoid of any volitional component. Unfortunately, viewing addiction as a disease has often led to attempts to absolve drug users of their responsibility for criminal actions.

The extent of an addict's responsibility for criminal behavior has been debated in the courts for more than twenty-five years. Recently, in *Traynor v. Turnage* (1988), the Supreme Court upheld the right of the Veterans Administration (VA) to define alcoholism to be the result of willful misconduct. The petitioner in this case asserted he was unable to claim VA education benefits because he was an alcoholic; he further claimed that he suffered from a disease called alcoholism and that the law prohibits discrimination on the basis of a disease. The VA called his alcoholism "willful misconduct." Soon thereafter, however, Congress passed a law for veterans that expressly forbids considering the disabling effects of chronic alcoholism to be the result of willful misconduct. However, this law does not define alcoholism as a disease, nor does it prohibit drug addiction from being regarded as "willful misconduct."

According to Herbert Fingarette, a professor of philosophy at the University of California in Santa Barbara and an expert on addiction and criminal responsibility, much of the controversy arising from *Traynor* and similar cases—such as *Powell v. Texas* (1968), a case involving the disease-model defense of a man convicted for public intoxication—stemmed from a Supreme Court ruling in *Robinson v. California* (1962).

In this case the Court decided that narcotics addiction is a disease and held that criminal punishment of a person thus afflicted violates the Eighth Amendment's prohibition against cruel and unusual punishment. As Justice William O. Douglas concurred, "The addict is a sick person." But the Court ruled only insofar as Robinson's status as a drug addict was concerned. Its decision had nothing to do with any acts stemming from that status.

In *Powell* the Court held against the use of status as an alcoholic as exculpatory. Powell, an alcoholic, was held to be responsible for his criminal actions. In *Traynor,* the Court upheld the decision made in *Powell.* Traynor and Powell were not absolved of responsibility for their actions because of their alcoholism disease. Robinson, however, was absolved of criminal responsibility because of his status as a drug addict. In *Robinson,* the Court equated punishment for the status of narcotics addiction with punishment for disease afflic-

tion. From this viewpoint, an addict's acts are considered to be inseparable from his status as an addict because they are a symptom of the disease and thus an involuntary result of status.

The critical point here is the inseparability of status and act. Certain acts are considered to be part of disease status. Disease is involuntary. Therefore, acts stemming from the disease are exculpable. Are the acts that stem from status really involuntary? This belief is the legal corollary to Jellinek's notion of loss of control.

Disease vs. Behavior

According to professor of psychiatry Thomas Szasz at the State University of New York in Syracuse, a disease, as textbooks on pathology state, is a phenomenon limited to the body. It has no relationship to a behavior such as drug addiction, except as a metaphor. Szasz argues against the disease model of addiction on the basis of the following distinction between disease and behavior. In *Insanity: The Idea and Its Consequences* (1987) he writes:

> [B]y behavior we mean the person's 'mode of conducting himself' or his 'deportment'. . .the name we attach to a living being's conduct in the daily pursuit of life. . . [B]odily movements that are the products of neurophysiological discharges or reflexes are not behavior. . . The point is that behavior implies action, and action implies conduct pursued by an agent seeking to attain a goal.

The products of neurophysiological discharges or reflexes become behavior when they are organized through intent, a willful act. Drug-taking behavior is not like epilepsy. The former involves intentional, goal-seeking behavior. An epileptic convulsion is an unconscious, unorganized neurophysiological discharge or reflex, not a behavior.

In another example, smoking cigarettes and drinking alcohol are behaviors that can lead to the diseases we call cancer of the lungs and cirrhosis of the liver. Smoking and drinking are behaviors. Cancer and cirrhosis are diseases. Smoking and drinking are not cancer and cirrhosis.

The alleged absence of voluntariness or willfulness forms the basis of legal rulings that extend beyond the minimalist interpretation of *Robinson,* exculpating criminal behavior on the basis of a person's supposed disease status. Yet because behavior such as drug use involves voluntariness it seems an individual who uses drugs should not be absolved of responsibility for criminal behavior on the grounds that his actions are

involuntary symptoms of drug addiction disease.

Many advocates of the disease model cite as further evidence for their view the results of genetic studies involving the heritability of alcoholism. Recently, the dopamine D2 receptor gene was found to be associated with alcoholism. A study by Kenneth Blum and co-authors, published in the Journal of the American Medical Association, suggests that this gene confers susceptibility to at least one form of alcoholism. The goal of this and similar studies is to identify the at-risk population in order to prevent people from becoming alcoholics and drug addicts.

What such studies do not tell us is why people who are not predisposed become alcoholics and why those who are predisposed do not. It seems more than reasonable to attribute this variance to psychological factors such as will, volition and choice, as well as to environmental variables such as economic opportunity, racism and family settings, to name just a few. Experimental controls accounting for genetic versus environmental influences on alcoholic behavior are sorely lacking in these studies.

The basis upon which people with alleged alcoholism disease are distinguished from mere heavy drinkers is arbitrary. No reliable explanation has yet been put forth of how the biological mechanisms theoretically associated with alcoholism and other forms of drug addiction translate into drug-taking behavior. Moreover, Annabel M. Bolos and co-authors, in a rigorous attempt to replicate the Blum findings, reported higher frequencies of the D_2 receptor gene found in their control population than in the alcoholic population in the same journal seven months later.

Treatment

Finally, the contribution of treatment to exposing the myth of addiction disease warrants mention. Since his arrest at the Vista Hotel in Washington, D.C., Marion Barry has undergone treatment for alcohol addiction and chemical dependency at the Hanley-Hazelden clinic in West Palm Beach, Florida, and at the Fenwick Hall facility near Charleston, South Carolina. Barry said he needs treatment because he has "not been spiritual enough." His plan is to turn his "entire will and life over to the care of God . . . using the twelve-step method and consulting with treatment specialists." He said he will then "become more balanced and a better person."

The twelve-step program Barry is attempting to follow is the one developed by Alcoholics Anonymous (AA), a spiritual self-help fellowship. AA is the major method dealing with alcoholism today. All good addiction treatment facilities and treatment programs aim at getting the patient into AA and similar programs such as Narcotics Anonymous. Yet several courts throughout the United States have determined that AA is a religion and not a form of medicine, in cases involving First Amendment violations, most recently in *Maryland v. Norfolk* (1989). Anthropologist Paul Antze at York University in Ontario has written extensively on AA and describes the "point-by-point homology between AA's dramatic model of the alcoholic's predicament and the venerable Protestant drama of sin and salvation."

Successful treatment from this perspective is dependent upon a religious conversion experience. In addition, patients are required to adopt a disease identity. If they do not, they are said to be in denial. But such an approach is a psychologically coercive remedy for a moral problem, not a medical one. And here—in their concepts of treatment —is where the disease model and moralistic model of addiction seem to merge.

With so much evidence to refute it, why is the view of drug addiction as a disease so prevalent? Incredible as it may seem, because doctors say so. One leading alcoholism researcher asserts that alcoholism is a disease simply because people go to doctors for it.Undoubtedly, addicts seek help from doctors for two reasons. Addicts have a significant psychological investment in maintaining this view, having learned that their sobriety depends on believing they have a disease. And treatment professionals have a significant economic investment at stake. The more behaviors are diagnosed as diseases, the more they will be paid by health insurance companies for treating these diseases.

Most people say we need more treatment for drug addiction. But few people realize how ineffective treatment programs really are. Treatment professionals know this all too well. In fact, the best predictor of treatment success, says Charles Schuster, director of the National Institute on Drug Abuse, is whether the addict has a job or not.

George Vaillant, professor of psychiatry at Dartmouth Medical School, describes his first experience , using the disease model and its effectiveness in diagnosing alcoholism, in *The Natural History of Alcoholism* (1983):

> ". . . I learned for the first time how to diagnose alcoholism as an illness. . . Instead of pondering the sociological and psychodynamic complexities of alcoholism. . . [A]lcoholism became a fascinating disease. . . [B]y inexorably moving patients into the treatment system of AA, I was working for the most exciting alcohol program in the world . . . After initial discharge, only five patients in the Clinic sample never relapsed to alcoholic drinking, and

there is compelling evidence that the results of our treatment were no better than the natural history of the disease."

This is important information because the definition of who an alcoholic or drug addict is and what constitutes treatment as well as treatment success can affect the lives of people who choose not to use drugs as well as those who choose to. For example, Stanton Peele has written extensively on how studies show that most people arrested for drinking and driving are directed into treatment for alcoholism disease, yet the majority are not alcoholics. Those receiving treatment demonstrate higher recidivism rates, including accidents, driving violations, and arrests, than those who are prosecuted and receive ordinary legal sanctions.

Furthermore, in a careful review of studies on treatment success and follow-up studies of heroin addicts at the United States Public Health Service hospital for narcotics addicts at Lexington, Kentucky, where "tens of thousands of addicts have been treated," the late Edward M. Brecher concluded in Licit & Illicit Drugs (1972) that "[a]lmost all [addicts] became readdicted and reimprisoned . . . for most the process is repeated over and over again . . . [and] no cure for narcotics addiction, and no effective deterrent, was found there—or anywhere else."

Brecher explained the failure of treatment in terms of the addictive property of heroin. Vaillant suggested that tuberculosis be considered as an analogy. Treatment, he said, rests entirely on recognition of the factors contributing to the "resistance" of the patient. And here is the "catch-22" of the disease model. Addiction is a disease beyond volitional control except when it comes to treatment failure, wherein "resistance" comes into play.

Neither Brecher nor Vaillant recognized that treatment does not work because there is nothing to treat. There is no medicine and there is no disease. The notions that heroin as an addictive drug causes addicts not to be treated successfully, or that "resistance" causes alcoholics to be incurable, are mythical notions that only serve to reinforce an avoidance of the facts: Addicts and alcoholics do not "get better" because they do not want to. Their self-destructive behaviors are not disturbed. They are disturbing.

All of this is not to suggest that the people we call addicts are bad, suffering from moral weakness and lack of willpower, character or values. Drug addicts simply have different values from the norm and often refuse to take responsibility for their actions. Public policy based on the disease model of addiction enables this avoidance to continue by sanctioning it in the name of helping people. As a result, criminals are absolved of responsibility for their actions, drug prevention and treatment programs end up decreasing feelings of personal self-worth and power instead of increasing them, and people who choose not to use drugs pay higher taxes and health insurance premiums to deal with the consequences of those who do.

Drug use is a choice, not a disease. Still, our current drug policies give the drug user only two options: treatment or jail. But if the drug user is sick, that is, is not responsible for his behavior, why should he go to jail for his illness? And if the drug user is someone who chooses to use drugs because he finds meaning in doing so, why should he be forced into treatment for having unconventional values? "Unconventional values" is not a disease.

"Treatment" for drug addiction is a misnomer. Education is a more appropriate term. In this modality a drug addict is given psychological and environmental support to achieve goals based on an identification of values and behavior-value dissonance. Behavioral accountability is stressed insofar as people learn about the consequences of their actions.

The legal arguments set forth to exculpate criminals because of addiction disease do not seem to be supported by scientific findings. Quite to the contrary, research suggests that drug addiction is far from a real disease. And as long as drug addiction can be blamed on a mythical disease, the real reasons why people use drugs—those related to socioeconomic, existential and psychological conditions including low self-esteem, self-worth and self-efficacy—can be ignored.

Readings Suggested by the Author:

Alexander, B.K. *Peaceful Measures: Canada's Way Out of the "War on Drugs."* Toronto: University of Toronto Press, 1990.

Douglas, M. (ed.). *Constructive Drinking: Perspectives on Drink from Anthropology.* New York: Cambridge University Press, 1987.

Fingarette, H. *Heavy Drinking: The Myth of Alcoholism as a Disease.* Berkeley, Calif.: University of California Press, 1988.

Institute of Medicine. *Broadening the Base of Treatment for Alcohol Problems.* Washington, D. C.: National Academy Press, 1990.

Peele, S., Brodsky, A. and Arnold, M. *The Truth about Addiction and Recovery.* New York: Simon and Schuster, 1991.

Szasz, T. S. *Ceremonial Chemistry: The Ritual Persecution of Drugs, Addicts, and Pushers.* Holmes Beach, Fla.: Learning Publications, 1985.

Intoxicating Habits

Some alcoholism researchers say they are studying a learned behavior, not a disease

BRUCE BOWER

Most alcoholism treatment programs in the United States operate on the assumption that people seeking their help have a disease characterized by physical dependency and a strong genetic predisposition. The goal of treatment, therefore, is total abstinence.

Herbert Fingarette, a philosophy professor at the University of California, Santa Barbara, pored over alcoholism and addiction research and came up with a suggestion for the many proponents of this approach: Forget it.

In a controversial new book (*Heavy Drinking: The Myth of Alcoholism as a Disease*, University of California Press, 1988), Fingarette says alcoholism has no single cause and no medical cure, and is the result of a range of physical, personal and social characteristics that predispose a person to drink excessively.

"Let's view the persistent heavy drinking of the alcoholic not as a sin or disease but as a central activity of the individual's way of life," he contends. Seen in this context, alcoholism treatment must focus not just on the drinking problem, but on developing a satisfying way of life that does not revolve around heavy drinking. Total abstinence — the goal of medical treatment centers as well as Alcoholics Anonymous — is unrealistic for many heavy drinkers, holds Fingarette.

Disputes over the nature of alcoholism have a long and vitriolic history. But Fingarette's arguments reflect a growing field of research, populated mainly by psychologists, in which alcoholism and other addictions — including those that do not involve drugs, such as compulsive gambling — are viewed more as habits than as diseases. Addictive behavior, in this scheme, typically revolves around an immediate gratification followed by delayed, harmful effects. The habitual behavior nevertheless continues and is often experienced by the addict as uncontrollable.

"Addiction occurs in the environment, not in the liver, genes or synapses," says psychologist Timothy B. Baker of the University of Wisconsin in Madison. Biology may, in some cases, increase a person's risk of developing a dependency, but "an individual chooses to take drugs in the world. The likelihood of a person trying a drug or eventually becoming addicted is influenced by his or her friends, marital happiness, the variety and richness of alternatives to drug use and so on," Baker contends.

Expectations and beliefs about alcohol's power to make one feel better shape the choices leading to alcohol addiction, according to one line of investigation. The most notable of these beliefs, says psychologist G. Alan Marlatt of the University of Washington in Seattle, is that alcohol acts as a magical elixir that enhances social and physical pleasure, increases sexual responsiveness and assertiveness, and reduces tension (SN: 10/3/87, p.218).

The initial physical arousal stimulated by low doses of alcohol pumps up positive expectations, explains Marlatt. But higher alcohol doses dampen arousal, sap energy and result in hangovers that, in turn, lead to a craving for alcohol's stimulating effects. As tolerance to the drug develops, a person requires more and more alcohol to get a short-term "lift" and a vicious cycle of abuse picks up speed.

Despite falling into this addictive trap, Marlatt says, some people drastically cut back their drinking or stop imbibing altogether without the help of formal treatment. In these cases, he maintains, external events often conspire to change an individual's attitude toward alcohol. Examples include an alcohol-related injury, the departure of a spouse, financial and legal problems stemming from drinking or the alcohol-related death of another person.

When treatment is sought out, Marlatt advises, the focus should be on teaching ways to handle stress without drinking and developing realistic expectations about alcohol's effects. Marlatt and his co-workers are now developing an "alcohol skills-training program" for college students, described more fully in *Issues in Alcohol Use and Misuse by Young Adults* (G. Howard, editor, Notre Dame University Press, 1988). Preliminary results indicate many students who consume large amounts of alcohol every week cut down considerably after completing the eight-session course. In fact, says Marlatt, children of alcoholics show some of the best responses to the program and are highly motivated to learn how to drink in moderation.

Psychologists teach the students how to set drinking limits and cope with peer pressure at parties and social events. Realistic expectations about alcohol's mood-enhancing powers are developed, and participants learn alternative methods of stress reduction, such as meditation and aerobic exercise.

The program does not promote drinking, says Marlatt, and students showing signs of hard-core alcohol dependency are referred for treatment that stresses abstinence. "But it's inappropriate to insist that all students abusing alcohol are in the early stages of a progressive disease," he contends. "Our approach acknowledges that drinking occurs regularly and gives students more options and choices for safer drinking."

A similar approach to helping adult alcoholics has been developed by psychologists W. Miles Cox of the Veterans Administration Medical Center in Indianapolis and Eric Klinger of the University of Minnesota in Morris. Their model, described in the May JOURNAL OF ABNORMAL PSYCHOLOGY, holds that although a number of biological and social

factors influence alcohol abuse, the final decision to drink is motivated by conscious or unconscious expectations that alcohol will brighten one's emotional state and wipe away stress. An alcoholic's expected pleasure or relief from a drinking binge, for example, may outweigh fears that it eventually will lead to getting fired or divorced.

Cox and Klinger's technique aims at providing alternative sources of emotional satisfaction. They have developed a questionnaire to assess an alcoholic's major life goals and concerns. A counselor then helps the alcoholic formulate weekly goals based on his or her responses. Counseling also attempts to reduce the tendency to use alcohol as a crutch when faced with frustration. "Alcoholics often have unrealistically high standards and lack the capacity to forgive themselves for not meeting these standards," Cox says.

The focus on an alcoholic's concerns and motivation is intended to complement other treatments, say the researchers. It is consistent, they note, with the efforts of Alcoholics Anonymous to drive home the negative side of drinking and the benefits of not drinking.

The context in which people consume alcohol is another part of the addictive process under study. Any combination of drinking and mildly pleasant activity, such as television viewing, conversation or card games, appears to provide the best protection against anxiety and stress, report psychologists Claude M. Steele and Robert A. Josephs of the University of Michigan's Institute of Social Research in Ann Arbor. Alcohol's ability to draw attention away from stressful thoughts and onto immediate activity may play a key role in its addictive power, they suggest.

Steele and Joseph tested this theory in their laboratory. They gave enough vodka and tonic to adult subjects to induce mild intoxication. Another group expected to receive vodka and tonic, but was given tonic in glasses rubbed with alcohol to create the odor of a real drink. Everyone was told that in 15 minutes they would have to give a speech on "What I dislike about my body and physical appearance." Researchers asked some from each group to sit quietly before making the speech, while others were asked to rate a series of art slides before speaking.

Those subjects who drank alcohol and rated slides reported significantly less anxiety over the speech than the other participants. Viewing the slides when sober had no anxiety-reducing effects.

According to the researchers, this supports the notion that alcohol's reduction of psychological stress has less to do with its direct pharmacological effects than with its knack for shifting attention with the aid of distractions.

On the other hand, being intoxicated and doing nothing before the speech significantly increased subjects' anxiety, note the investigators in the May JOURNAL OF ABNORMAL PSYCHOLOGY. Without any distraction, alcohol appears to narrow attention to the upcoming situation.

Recent investigations also suggest alcohol users are motivated by alcohol's ability to reduce psychological stress among people who are highly self-conscious and constantly evaluating themselves. Steele and Josephs did not, however, evaluate the "self-awareness" of their subjects.

A different approach to unraveling drinking behavior involves the search for cues that set off an alcoholic's craving or irresistible urge to drink. Just as Pavlov's dogs were conditioned to salivate after hearing a bell that previously had preceded the appearance of food, there are internal and external "bells" that provoke craving in many alcoholics, explains psychiatrist Arnold M. Ludwig of the University of Kentucky Medical Center in Lexington.

These cues are often quite specific, he says. For instance, recovered alcoholic and major league baseball pitcher Bob Welch has reported experiencing a craving to drink during airplane flights, after a game of golf and after pitching.

In a survey of 150 abstinent alcoholics reported in the fall 1986 ALCOHOL HEALTH & RESEARCH WORLD, Ludwig finds nearly all of them can identify one or more "bells" that trigger craving. With the exception of "internal tension," mentioned as a cue by more than half the subjects, there was considerable individual difference in reported drinking "bells." These included going to a dance, feeling lonely, having a barbecue, seeing a drink in an advertisement and driving past former drinking hangouts.

Alcoholics Anonymous, notes Ludwig, teaches that four general conditions — hunger, anger, loneliness and tiredness — make recovered alcoholics more vulnerable to drinking urges, an observation supported by research on craving.

Other evidence, Ludwig says, suggests that the more times uncomfortable withdrawal symptoms — shakiness, agitation, hallucinations or confusion — have been relieved by drinking in the past, the greater the likelihood that familiar drinking cues will elicit craving in alcoholics.

Many alcoholics feel helpless and bewildered when craving strikes, seemingly out of the blue. "But craving is not the elusive, mysterious force many believe it to be," says Ludwig. To successfully recover, he contends, alcoholics must become aware of the emotional and situational cues that trigger drinking urges.

The first drink in the right setting, he adds, often whets the appetite for more. Alcoholics should seek out "safe havens" where drinking is discouraged, he suggests, such as workplaces, Alcoholics Anonymous and outdoor activities.

Whereas Ludwig sees drinking cues as stoking the internal embers of craving, other researchers focus solely on external "reinforcers" that affect an alcoholic's drinking behavior. When important reinforcers outside the realm of drinking, such as a job or marriage, are lost, say psychologists Rudy E. Vuchinich and Jalie A. Tucker of Wayne State University in Detroit, a recovered alcoholic becomes more likely to resume drinking.

"The growing consensus from clinical studies [points to] the important role of environmental variables and changes in life circumstances in influencing the drinking behavior of alcoholics," they write in the May JOURNAL OF ABNORMAL PSYCHOLOGY. But the development of appropriate environmental measures to study drinking is still in the early stages, the investigators add.

While research into the psychology of alcohol addiction is beginning to mature, it remains largely ignored by the biologically oriented advocates of alcoholism-as-disease, says Marlatt. The research and clinical communities are especially polarized over suggestions from addiction studies that some alcoholics — about 15 to 20 percent, according to Marlatt — can safely engage in moderate or social drinking.

The characteristics of alcohol abusers who can handle controlled drinking are not clear, but Marlatt and other researchers see milder alcoholics as prime candidates for this treatment approach.

Given that most current alcoholism treatment is based on the disease model of total abstinence, which has been endorsed by the American Medical Association and the American Psychiatric Association for many years, reconciliation between opposing theoretical camps is not imminent.

"But biological and genetic approaches to alcoholism need to be integrated with psychological and social approaches," Marlatt says. "This really hasn't been done yet."

A Pleasurable Chemistry

Endorphins, the body's natural narcotics, aren't something we have to run after. They're everywhere.

Janet L. Hopson

Janet L. Hopson, who lives in Oakland, California, gets endorphin highs by contributing to Psychology Today.

Welcome aboard the biochemical bandwagon of the 1980s. The magical, morphine-like brain chemicals called endorphins are getting a lot of play. First we heard they were responsible for runner's high and several other cheap thrills. Now we're hearing that they play a role in almost every human experience from birth to death, including much that is pleasurable, painful and lusty along the way.

Consider the following: crying, laughing, thrills from music, acupuncture, placebos, stress, depression, chili peppers, compulsive gambling, aerobics, trauma, masochism, massage, labor and delivery, appetite, immunity, near-death experiences, playing with pets. Each, it is claimed, is somehow involved with endorphins. Serious endorphin researchers pooh-pooh many or most of these claims but, skeptics notwithstanding, the field has clearly sprinted a long way past runner's high.

Endorphin research had its start in the early 1970s with the unexpected discovery of opiate receptors in the brain. If we have these receptors, researchers reasoned, then it is likely that the body produces some sort of opiate- or morphine-like chemicals. And that's exactly what was found, a set of relatively small biochemicals dubbed "opioid peptides" or "endorphins" (short for "endogenous morphines") that plug into the receptors. In other words, these palliative peptides are sloshing around in our brains, spines and bloodstreams, apparently acting just like morphine. In fact, morphine's long list of narcotic effects was used as a treasure map for where scientists might hunt out natural opiates in the body. Morphine slows the pulse and depresses breathing, so they searched in the heart and lungs. Morphine deadens pain, so they looked in the central and peripheral nervous systems. It disturbs digestion and elimination, so they explored the gut. It savages the sex drive, so they probed the reproductive and endocrine systems. It triggers euphoria, so they scrutinized mood.

Nearly everywhere researchers looked, endorphins or their receptors were present. But what were they doing: transmitting nerve impulses, alleviating pain, triggering hormone release, doing several of these things simultaneously or disintegrating at high speed and doing nothing at all? In the past decade, a trickle of scientific papers has become a tidal wave, but still no one seems entirely certain of what, collectively, the endorphins are doing to us or for us at any given time.

Researchers do have modern-day sextants for their search, including drugs such as naloxone and naltrexone. These drugs, known as opiate blockers, pop into the endorphin receptors and block the peptides' normal activity, giving researchers some idea of what their natural roles might be. Whatever endorphins are doing, however, it must be fairly subtle. As one researcher points out, people injected with opiate blockers may feel a little more pain or a little less "high," but no one gasps for breath, suffers a seizure or collapses in a coma.

Subtle or not, endorphins are there, and researchers are beginning to get answers to questions about how they touch our daily lives—pain, exercise, appetite, reproduction and emotions.

•ANSWERS ON ANALGESIA: A man falls off a ladder, takes one look at his right hand—now cantilevered at a sickening angle—and knows he has a broken bone. Surprisingly, he feels little pain or anxiety until hours later, when he's home from the emergency room. This physiological grace period, which closely resembles a sojourn on morphine, is a common survival mechanism in the animal world, and researchers are confident that brain opiates are responsible for such cases of natural pain relief. The question is how do they work and, more to the point, how can we make them work for us?

The answers aren't in, but researchers have located a pain control system in the periaquaductal gray (PAG), a tiny region in the center of the brain, and interestingly, it produces opioid peptides. While no one fully understands how this center operates, physicians can now jolt it with electric current to lessen chronic pain.

One day in 1976, as Navy veteran Dennis Hough was working at a hospital's psychiatric unit, a disturbed patient snapped Hough's back and ruptured three of his vertebral discs. Five years later, after two failed back operations, Hough was bedridden with constant shooting pains in his legs, back and shoulders

From *Psychology Today*, July/August 1988, pp. 29-30, 32-33. Copyright © 1988 by Sussex Publishers, Inc. Reprinted by permission.

and was depressed to the point of suicide. Doctors were just then pioneering a technique of implanting platinum electrodes in the PAG, and Hough soon underwent the skull drilling and emplacement. He remembers it as "the most barbaric thing I've ever experienced, including my tour of duty in Vietnam," but the results were worth the ordeal; For the past seven years, Hough has been able to stimulate his brain's own endorphins four times a day by producing a radio signal from a transmitter on his belt. The procedure is delicate—too much current and his eyes flutter, too little and the pain returns in less than six hours. But it works dependably, and Hough not only holds down an office job now but is engaged to be married.

Researchers would obviously like to find an easier way to stimulate the brain's own painkillers, and while they have yet to find it, workers in many labs are actively developing new drugs and treatments. Some physicians have tried direct spinal injections of endorphins to alleviate postoperative pain. And even the most cynical now seem to agree that acupuncture works its magic by somehow triggering the release of endorphins. There may, however, be an even easier path to pain relief: the power of the mind.

Several years ago, neurobiologist Jon Levine, at the University of California, San Francisco, discovered that the placebo effect (relief) based on no known action other than the patient's belief in a treatment) can itself be blocked by naloxone and must therefore be based on endorphins. Just last year Levine was able to quantify the effects: One shot of placebo can equal the relief of 6 to 8 milligrams of morphine, a low but fairly typical dose.

Another line of research suggests that endorphins may be involved in self-inflicted injury—a surprisingly common veterinary and medical complaint and one that, in many cases, can also be prevented with naloxone. Paul Millard Hardy, a behavioral neurologist at Boston's New England Medical Center, believes that animals may boost endorphin levels through self-inflicted pain and then "get caught in a self-reinforcing positive feedback loop." He thinks something similar may occur in compulsive daredevils and in some cases of deliberate self-injury. One young woman he studied had injected pesticide into her own veins by spraying Raid into an intravenous needle. This appalling act, she told Hardy, "made her feel better, calmer and almost high."

Hardy also thinks endorphin release might explain why some autistic children constantly injure themselves by banging their heads. Because exercise is believed to be an alternate route to endorphin release, Hardy and physician Kiyo Kitahara set up a twice-a-day exercise program for a group of autistic children. He qualifies the evidence as "very anecdotal at this point" but calls the results "phenomenal."

•RUNNER'S HIGH, RUNNER'S CALM: For most people, "endorphins" are synonymous with "runner's high," a feeling of well-being that comes after an aerobic workout. Many people claim to have experienced this "high," and remarkable incidents are legion. Take, for example, San Francisco runner Don Paul, who placed 10th in the 1979 San Francisco Marathon and wound up with his ankle in a cast the next day. Paul had run the 26 miles only vaguely aware of what turned out to be a serious stress fracture. Observers on the sidelines had to tell him he was "listing badly to one side for the last six miles." He now runs 90 miles per week in preparation for the U.S. men's Olympic marathon trial and says that when he trains at the level, he feels "constantly great. Wonderful."

Is runner's high a real phenomenon based on endorphins? And can those brain opiates result in "exercise addiction"? Or, as many skeptics hold, are the effects on mood largely psychological? Most studies with humans have found rising levels of endorphins in the blood during exercise.

However, says exercise physiologist Peter Farrell of Pennsylvania State University, "when we look at animal studies, we don't see a concurrent increase in the brain." Most circulating peptides fail to cross into the brain, he explains, so explaining moods like runner's high based on endorphin levels in the blood is questionable. Adds placebo expert Jon Levine, "Looking for mood changes based on the circulating blood is like putting a voltmeter to the outside of a computer and saying 'Now I know how it works.'" Nevertheless, Farrell exercises religiously: "I'm not going to waste my lifetime sitting around getting sclerotic just because something's not proven yet."

Murray Allen, a physician and kinesiologist at Canada's Simon Fraser University, is far more convinced about the endorphin connection. He recently conducted his own study correlating positive moods and exercise—moods that could be blocked by infusing the runner with naloxone. Allen thinks these moods are "Mother Nature's way of rewarding us for staying fit" but insists that aerobic exercisers don't get "high." Opioid peptides "slow down and inhibit excess activity in the brain," he says. "Many researchers have been chasing after psychedelic, excitable responses." The actual effect, he says, is "runner's calm" and extremes leading to exhaustion usually negate it.

In a very similar experiment last year, a research team at Georgia State University found the mood-endorphin link more elusive. Team member and psychologist Wade Silverman of Atlanta explains that only those people who experience "runner's high" on the track also noticed it in the lab. Older people and those who ran fewer, not more, miles per week were also more likely to show a "high" on the test. "People who run a lot—50 miles per week or more—are often drudges, masochists, running junkies," says Silver-

man. "They don't really enjoy it. It hurts." For optimum benefits. Silverman recommends running no more than three miles per day four times a week.

Silverman and Lewis Maharam, a sports medicine internist at Manhattan's New York Infirmary/Beekman Downtown Hospital, both agree that powerful psychological factors—including heightened sense of self-esteem and self-discipline—contribute to the "high" in those who exercise moderately. Maharam would still like to isolate and quantify the role of endorphins, however, so he could help patients "harness the high." He would like to give people "proper exercise prescriptions," he says, "to stimulate the greatest enjoyment and benefit from exercise. If we could encourage the 'high' early on, maybe we could get people to want to keep exercising from the start."

The questions surrounding exercise, mood and circulating endorphins remain. But even if opioids released into the bloodstream from, say, the adrenal glands don't enter the brain and give a "high" or a "calm," several studies show that endorphins in the blood do bolster the immune system's activity. One way or the other, regular moderate exercise seems destined to make us happy.

•APPETITE CLOCKS AND BLOCKS: Few things in life are more basic to survival and yet more pleasurable than eating good food—and where survival and pleasure intersect, can the endorphins be far behind? To keep from starving, an animal needs to know when, what and how much to eat, and researchers immediately suspected that opioid peptides might help control appetite and satiety. People, after all, have long claimed that specific foods such as chili peppers or sweets give them a "high." And those unmistakably "high" on morphine or heroin experience constipation, cravings and other gastrointestinal glitches.

Indeed, investigators quickly located opiate receptors in the alimentary tract and found a region of the rat's hypothalamus that—when injected with tiny amounts of beta endorphin—will trigger noshing of particular nutrients. Even a satiated rat will dig heartily into fats, proteins or sweets when injected with the peptide. Neurobiologist Sarah Leibowitz and her colleagues at Rockefeller University produced this result and also found that opiate blockers would prevent the snack attack—strong evidence that endorphins help regulate appetite. The opiates "probably enhance the hedonic, pleasurable, rewarding properties" of fats, proteins and sweets—foods that can help satiate an animal far longer than carbohydrates so it can survive extended periods without eating.

Intriguingly, rats crave carbohydrates at the beginning of their 12-hour activity cycles, but they like fats, proteins or sweets before retiring—a hint that endorphins control not just the nature but the timing of appetites. Leibowitz suspects that endorphins also help control cravings in response to stress and starvation, and that disturbed endorphin systems may, in part, underlie obesity and eating disorders. Obese people given opiate blockers, for example, tend to eat less; bulimics often gorge on fat-rich foods; both bulimics and anorexics often have abnormal levels of endorphins; and in anorexics, food deprivation enhances the release of opiates in the brain. This brain opiate reward, some speculate, may reinforce the anorexic's self-starvation much as self-injury seems to be rewarding to an autistic child.

Researchers such as Leibowitz are hoping to learn enough about the chemistry of appetite to fashion a binge-blocking drug as well as more effective behavioral approaches to over- or undereating. In the meantime, people who try boosting their own endorphins through exercise, mirth or music may notice a vexing increase in their taste for fattening treats.

•PUBERTY, PREGNANCY AND PEPTIDES: Evolution has equipped animals with two great appetites—the hunger for food to prevent short-term disintegration and the hunger for sex and reproduction to prevent longer-term genetic oblivion. While some endorphin researchers were studying opioids and food hunger, others began searching for a sex role—and they found it.

Once again, drug addiction pointed the way: Users of morphine and heroin often complain of impotence and frigidity that fade when they kick their habits. Could natural opioids have some biochemical dampening effect on reproduction? Yes, says Theodore Cicero of Washington University Medical School. Endorphins, he says, "play an integral role—probably the dominant role—in regulating reproductive hormone cycles."

This formerly small corner of endorphin research has "exploded into a huge area of neurobiology," Cicero says, and researchers now think the opioid peptides help fine-tune many—perhaps all—of the nervous and hormonal pathways that together keep the body operating normally.

Cicero and his colleagues have tracked the byzantine biochemical loops through which endorphins, the brain, the body's master gland (the pituitary), the master's master (the hypothalamus) and the gonads exchange signals to ensure that an adult animal can reproduce when times are good but not when the environment is hostile. Cicero's work helped show that beta endorphin rules the hypothalamus and thus, indirectly, the pituitary and gonads.

The Washington University group also sees "a perfect parallel" between the brain's ability to produce endorphins and the onset of puberty: As the opioid system matures, so does the body sexually. A juvenile rat with endorphins blocked by naloxone undergoes puberty earlier; a young rat given opiates matures far later than normal and its offspring can have disturbed hormonal systems. Cicero calls the results "frighten-

ing" and adds, "there couldn't possibly be a worse time for a person to take drugs than during late childhood or adolescence."

Endorphins play a critical role in a later reproductive phase, as well: pregnancy and labor. Women in their third trimester sometimes notice that the pain and pressure of, say, a blood pressure cuff, is far less pronounced than before or after pregnancy. Alan Gintzler and his colleagues at the State University of New York Health Science Center in Brooklyn found that opioid peptides produced inside the spinal cord probably muffle pain and perhaps elevate mood to help a woman deal with the increasing physical stress of pregnancy. Endorphin activity builds throughout pregnancy and reaches a peak just before and during labor. Some have speculated that the tenfold drop from peak endorphin levels within 24 hours of delivery may greatly contribute to postpartum depression.

•CHILLS, THRILLS, LAUGHTER AND TEARS: Just as the effects of morphine go beyond the physical, claims for the opioid peptides extend to purely esthetic and emotional, with speculation falling on everything from the pleasure of playing with pets and the transcendence of near-death experiences to shivers over sonatas and the feeling of well-being that comes with a rousing laugh or a good cry.

Avram Goldstein of Stanford University, a pioneer in peptide research, recently collected a group of volunteers who get a spine-tingling thrill from their favorite music and gave them either a placebo or an opiate blocker during a listening session. Their shivers declined with the blocker—tantalizing evidence that endorphins mediate rapture, even though the mechanics are anyone's guess.

Former *Saturday Review* editor Norman Cousins may have spawned a different supposition about endorphins and emotion when he literally laughed himself out of the sometimes fatal disease ankylosing spondylitis. He found that 10 minutes of belly laughing before bed gave him two hours of painfree sleep. Before long, someone credited endorphins with the effect, and by now the claim is commonplace. For example, Matt Weinstein, a humor consultant from Berkeley, California, frequently mentions a possible link between endorphins, laughter and health in his lectures on humor in the workplace. His company's motto: If you take yourself too seriously, there's an excellent chance you may end up seriously ill.

Weinstein agrees with laughter researcher William Fry, a psychiatrist at Stanford's medical school, that evidence is currently circumstantial. Fry tried to confirm the laughter-endorphin link experimentally, but the most accurate way to assess it would be to tap the cerebrospinal fluid. That, Fry says, "is not only a difficult procedure but it's not conducive to laughter" and could result in a fountain of spinal fluid gushing out with the first good guffaw. Confirmation clearly awaits a less ghoulish methodology. But in the meantime, Fry is convinced that mirth and playfulness can diminish fear, anger and depression. At the very least, he says, laughter is a good aerobic exercise that ventilates the lungs and leaves the muscles relaxed. Fry advises patients to take their own humor inventory, then amass a library of books, tapes and gags that dependably trigger hilarity.

Another William Frey, this one at the University of Minnesota, studies the role of tears in emotion, stress and health. "The physiology of the brain when we experience a change in emotional state from sad to angry to happy or vice versa is an absolutely unexplored frontier," Frey says. And emotional tears are a fascinating guidepost because "they are unique to human beings and are our natural excretory response to strong emotion." Since all other bodily fluids are involved in removing something, he reasons, logic dictates that tears wash something away, too. Frey correctly predicted that tears would contain the three biochemicals that build up during stress: leucine-enkephalin, an endorphin, and the hormones prolactin and ACTH. These biochemicals are found in both emotional tears and tears from chopping onions, a different sort of stress.

Frey is uncertain whether tears simply carry off excess endorphins that collect in the stressed brain or whether those peptides have some activity in the tear ducts, eyes, nose or throat. Regardless, he cites evidence that people with ulcers and colitis tend to cry less than the average, and he concludes that a person who feels like crying "should go ahead and do it! I can't think of any other physical excretory process that humans alone can do, so why suppress it and its possibly healthful effects?"

All in all, the accumulated evidence suggests that if you want to use your endorphins, you should live the unfettered natural life. Laugh! Cry! Thrill to music! Reach puberty. Get pregnant. Get aerobic. Get hungry. Eat! Lest this sound like a song from *Fiddler on the Roof*, however, remember that stress or injury may be even quicker ways to pump out home-brew opioids. The bottom line is this: Endorphins are so fundamental to normal physiological functioning that we don't have to seek them out at all. We probably surf life's pleasures and pains on a wave of endorphins already.

Test yourself by imagining the following: the sound of chalk squeaking across a blackboard; a pink rose sparkling with dew; embracing your favorite movie star; chocolate-mocha mousse cake; smashing your thumb with a hammer. If any of these thoughts sent the tiniest tingle down your spine, then you have have just proved the point.

The Lure of Drugs:

They 'Organize' An Addict's Life

Benjamin Stein

Benjamin Stein, an aide in the Nixon-Ford White Houses, is a lawyer and free-lance writer in Los Angeles. His latest book is "Hollywood Days, Hollywood Nights" (Bantam).

AND NOW for a few words about drugs . . .
Everyone in America talks on television and at political gatherings about drugs — politicians, preachers, teachers, lawyers, law enforcement officials, even parents. Everyone talks about drugs, that is, except for the one group most directly affected by drugs: drug addicts and users. It might make sense for the nation to listen to what they think.

Now, I am not exactly a drug addict. But I do take a variety of tranquilizing and sleeping pills, and in my past life, when I was a '60s kind of guy, I used my share of what was hip. That was a while ago, but for whatever reasons since the days of law school, through the days in Washington, in the bureaucracy, in the White House, at a university, and the days in New York, at a great newspaper, and in Los Angeles, around the studios, and the cars and the bars and the flash and the cash and the trash, I have spent much time with drug users. Even now, I am involved in a number of self-help programs for major, heavy-duty drug abusers. These are not people I am studying. These are my friends, and this is a big part of my life.

In a word, I know something about drugs and drug users from the inside out.

I'd like to share a little bit of what I know, and correct a few wrong impressions. Some of these have public policy implications, and some of them are just interesting in the way learning about any new kind of people is interesting.

First, drug addicts do not become drug addicts by mistake, by accident or because someone lurks on a corner offering reefers. Drug addicts do not get high just because they have nothing else to do and getting high would be a cool way of spitting on the bourgeoisie.

Drug addicts (and by that is meant, without any doubt, alcohol addicts) get that way because drugs have a way of, temporarily, organizing an otherwise disordered life. I have heard hundreds, maybe thousands of drug addicts talk about how they got into drugs so heavily that drugs ruled their lives.

Every single one of them wanted

some outside power to take over his life. Each man or woman felt that his or her life was grossly defective, that he or she was severely lacking the basic equipment needed to cope with existence. "I feel like I was dropped here from another planet without any travel brochure," one particularly articulate young man once said. "I have felt like a lonely, heartbroken child my whole life," said another man, who spoke for every addict I have ever known. "I never felt like I even belonged in my own skin, let alone in my family or in my high school," said another young woman. I defy anyone to find a drug addict who had a happy childhood or who emerged from childhood with a well-integrated personality.

Drugs — and again, this includes alcohol in a big way — made the psychically split feel whole again. "When I first started to use coke, I felt six-feet tall and bulletproof," said one diminutive man. "I used blow (cocaine) in eighth grade, and I wondered where it had been all my life," said another man. "For the first time, I felt like I belonged, like I could talk to people, like I was going somewhere," is a sort of synthesis of hundreds of comments by addicts about how the felt when they got onto drugs. In other words, drugs that are illegal do exactly what prescription psychoactive drugs do.

Drugs are not like going to a dance or having a vacation or getting a great stereo or even like having sex. They are not interludes in otherwise different lives. For the drug addict, the effect of the drug, the knowledge that a drink or a shot or a snort or a pill can change their relation to the universe is the overwhelming fact of their lives for the time they are allowing drugs to organize their lives. They genuinely believe that their lives would be unbearable without drugs.

In other words, you will not stop drug addiction by nuclear bombing Peru. The drug addict will find something legal, something by prescription, something that will organize his life again and take his shattered self and make it real.

That is, drug addiction is not a problem made by smugglers. It is a problem of lonely, sad, frightened people — some of them truly wonderful people — who want something to help, and if they can't get it from Colombia, they will get it from the corner liquor store or from a doctor, and they will be addicts all the same.

The problem in America is not the importation of illegal drugs. The problem is the minds and hearts and

bodies of broken people who need to be made whole by something, and drugs come easily to hand.

Second, and this is crucial, drug addiction in each case is usually self-limiting in either tragic or miraculous ways. The tragic way in which drugs are self-limiting is obvious: People die from them sooner or later.

The miraculous way comes from the fact that drugs simply do not keep on succesfully organizing addicts' lives. Addicts come to know that. At some point, early or late, the drug addict sees that the negative effects of the habit are far more dangerous than whatever life he had before he took up drugs. He finds that sleepless nights, car crashes, nights in jail, loss of family, loss of job, loss of self-respect, loss of home are worse than what he had before. In other words, the drug has lost its ability to put the addict back into one piece again. The drug addiction has made him far more shattered than he ever was before he began to get high.

Drug addicts get saved by having something to organize themselves without drugs. This can be religion, self-help groups, new friends, a new environment, new creative challenges or some combination. Those who felt themselves psychically crippled before they used drugs or alcohol will still feel incomplete when they stop using or drinking. They need something to fill up the empty spaces inside.

To an astonishingly impressive extent, Alcoholics Anonymous (by far the largest active multi-faith non-profit organization in Southern California) gives men and women a reason to live, and organizing principles (their famous and inspiring 12-step program) to glue splintered egos together. (Every drug addict and alcoholic knows of at least one person whose life has been saved by AA, and knows that the opportunity is out there.) I have no doubt that there are religious organizations outside AA that do excellent work as well.

The point is that drug addiction is something that comes from inside

millions of individuals. It will never be stopped by speedboats and helicopters and search dogs, nor by defoliating marijuana acreage in Humboldt County, California. It will be slowed down (not stopped, because realistically it is never going to be stopped altogether) when millions of individuals realize that there are alternatives to drugs for binding up wounds, alternatives that do not cut still deeper lacerations, alternatives that build lives.

It's a happy sign that the Congress has realized this, in an election year, and has increased funding for drug treatment centers. But the continuing illusion that pouring money into high-tech search gear for border patrols — the path Washington took in earlier legislation — will stop drug abuse when drugs are available freely inside the stores of America is a joke.

The idea that drug addicts will stop booting up because of appeals by movie stars or politicians' wives simply bears no relation to the reality of the problem. Drug addicts need to be brought back to sanity one by one, from the inside out. To the extent that the government can help addicts by helping hospitals, drug treatment centers and self-help groups make their services more widely available, then it can help the addicts I know. (It is deeply instructive to know, however, that AA, which has probably saved more addicts than every other public or private program put together, proudly will not accept any outside contributions, and is entirely self-supporting from the dollars and quarters placed onto plates at the meetings.)

There are more truths that can be learned by listening to the people most directly affected by addiction — the addicts. I have only touched on a few. But it is clear that the huge volume of knowledge of what drug addiction is and how it can be stopped lies mainly in the experience of drug addicts, present and recovering, grateful or still suffering. It might make sense to listen to them.

> '*The point is that drug addiction is something that comes from inside individuals. It will never be stopped by speedboats, helicopters or search dogs.*'

Probing the Complex Genetics of Alcoholism

Recent findings of an "alcoholism gene" haven't held up—but a huge new study funded by NIH may help to nail down the basis of this costly condition

LAST APRIL, RESEARCHERS CAUSED A FLURRY in the media when they announced in the *Journal of the American Medical Association* that they had for the first time identified a gene—an allele of the D2 dopamine receptor—that they believed to be implicated in severe cases of alcoholism. But the first test of the finding, reported last month by researchers at the National Institute on Alcohol Abuse and Alcoholism (NIAAA), has failed to confirm it.*

Frustrating findings are common in the world of alcoholism research, where for the past two decades researchers have been trying, so far without success, to identify biological markers—and more recently, actual genes—signaling a predisposition to alcoholism. Indeed, some scientists are beginning to suspect that there may be no genes for alcoholism per se, but rather for a general susceptibility to compulsive behaviors whose specific expression is shaped by environmental and temperamental factors.

Definitive answers may be on the horizon: The NIAAA, in an attempt to crack the biological riddles of the disease, has launched a massive study—massive for the behavioral sciences anyway—a kind of Manhattan Project on the genetics of alcoholism. Budgeted at $25 million for the first 5 years, it's a multisite, multilevel study including everything from psychological tests to DNA probes that will involve 600 alcoholics and potentially thousands of their family members.

The study will take off from the fragments of knowledge scientists now have about society's most costly disease. For example, it

is now widely accepted that a vulnerability to the disorder can be partly inherited. (This certainty is based on results of adoption, twin, and family studies that have been rolling in since the mid-1970s, as well as by success in breeding strains of rats that prefer alcohol over water in their drinks.) Scientists are also now certain that many genes are involved, and that they are different for different groups of individuals.

But the tremendous variability shown in alcoholism has prevented researchers from pinning those genes down more specifically.

For many alcoholics, the disease is associated with psychiatric problems: childhood conduct disorder, for example, which is marked by aggression and other antisocial activities, has emerged as one behavioral predictor for alcoholism. But there are also many alcoholics who apparently function normally until they end up in the hospital with cirrhosis. Other mysteries: why alcoholism can set in either early and fast, or gradually develop over decades; and why some alcoholics are binge drinkers, and others "maintenance" drinkers. And the epidemiology is actually changing: the average age of onset has moved from the mid-

20's to under 20, and although some alcoholics stick to alcohol, more and more are taking advantage of the availability of illicit drugs.

What kinds of genes can account for even a part of this variability? Are the functions they mediate metabolic or behavioral? The principal investigator of the NIAAA study,† neuroscientist Henri Begleiter of the State University of New York's Health Science Center at Brooklyn, says he has come to the conclusion that no genes specific to alcoholism exist. Noting that it is getting harder and harder to find a "pure" alcoholic, he suspects that the disorder results from an underlying "behavioral disregulation that is not specific to alcoholism...a set of biological factors which are heavily influenced by environmental events and can lead to very different adverse outcomes." These outcomes include problems that look like addictions, such as gambling and eating disorders, as well as other compulsions and disorders of impulse control.

There is no evidence to contradict this

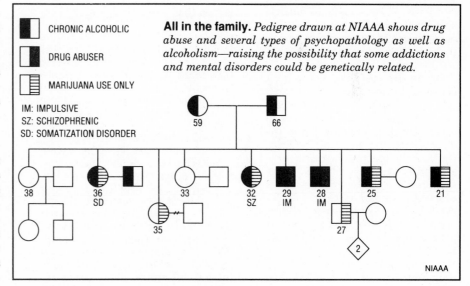

All in the family. *Pedigree drawn at NIAAA shows drug abuse and several types of psychopathology as well as alcoholism—raising the possibility that some addictions and mental disorders could be genetically related.*

idea, says Begleiter: For example, low levels of platelet monoamine oxidase (MAO) have long been suspected to be related to alcoholism, but now it seems they may correspond better to compulsive disorders in general. Furthermore, although he has

*The study, "Allelic Association of Human Dopamine D2 Receptor Gene in Alcoholism," was reported in the 18 April 1990 *JAMA* by a team headed by Kenneth Blum of the University of Texas Health Science Center and Ernest Noble of the University of California at Los Angeles. The NIAAA study, "Population and Pedigree Studies Reveal a Lack of Association Between the Dopamine D2 Receptor Gene and Alcoholism," by Annabel M. Bolos et al., appeared in the 26 December 1990 *JAMA*. Two other research teams, at Washington University and McGill University, are also testing the Blum-Noble finding with family studies of alcoholics.

†Principal investigators at the six sites in the National Collaborative Studies on the Genetics of Alcoholism are neuroscientist Bernice Porjesz at SUNY; psychiatric geneticist Theodore Reich at Washington University in St. Louis; psychologist Victor Hesselbrock at the University of Connecticut; psychiatrist Marc Schuckit of the University of California at San Diego; neuroscientist Floyd Bloom of Scripps Clinic and Research Foundation; geneticist Michael Conneally and psychiatrist John Nurnberger at Indiana University, and psychiatrist Raymond Crowe, University of Iowa.

identified anomalies in the brain waves of young sons of alcoholics, Begleiter doesn't think the phenomenon is specific to alcoholics, pointing to the fact that similar results have been found with cocaine abusers.

Psychologist Victor Hesselbrock of the University of Connecticut, one study investigator who agrees with Begleiter, says he thinks a number of scientists are "privately" leaning to the same view. But other researchers, while open to the idea of a generalized susceptibility, continue to place emphasis on the possibility that there are genes specific to alcoholism. Kenneth Blum of the University of Texas Health Science Center, for example, believes there may be genes for "compulsive disease" (he and his colleagues suspect their dopamine gene is one), but also "subgenes"—what biologists call modifier genes—that dictate susceptibilities to particular substances. The NIAAA study's co-principal investigator Theodore Reich, psychiatric geneticist at Washington University, is even more emphatic: He contradicts study leader Begleiter by saying, "I am convinced there is a pharmacogenetics of alcoholism." He predicts, "We'll begin to see the [reemergence] of primary alcoholics" as the crack epidemic wanes.

Psychiatrist Marc Schuckit of the University of California at San Diego is also in this camp, based on his research with high-risk sons of alcoholics. Many subjects, he says, experience a "decreased intensity" of response to alcohol, suggesting that people drink too much because they are getting "less feedback." Since a recent study using Valium with the same subjects failed to show these decreased responses, Schuckit believes they are specific to alcohol.

The genetic picture is enormously complicated by the fact that mental disorders, particularly anxiety, depression, manic depression, and personality disorders are seen in close to half of alcoholics, according to the National Institute of Mental Health's epidemiologic Catchment Area Study. But which conditions precede alcoholic drinking, and the circumstances under which they lead to alcoholism, are not understood. Possible genetic linkages with alcoholism cannot be ruled out in some cases—most notably with antisocial personality disorder, which by definition begins in adolescence and which often includes criminal activity and substance abuse.

Schuckit, for one, says most alcoholics do not have mental disorders and that the search for a genetic predisposition should focus on this group. But other researchers disagree, in large part because so many alcoholics have antisocial personality characteristics—about one-quarter, according to the NIAAA (only 1.5% of the general population qualifies for the diagnosis). Many scientists, therefore, view the disorder as part and parcel of the puzzle of alcoholism.

Enter the NIAAA collaborative study which was started a year ago in hopes of fitting together all the disparate pieces. Principal investigator Begleiter characterizes it as part of a "new era of research on the genetics of predisposition" that is "much more complex, challenging, and interesting" than the search for "typical Mendelian disorders."

Indeed, the study involves an elaborate design in which state-of-the-art behavioral and biological assessments will be applied to an unprecedentedly large population. All six sites will follow the same research protocols, and technical people have been trained to carry out all tests in an identical manner. The first phase has involved the development of several new assessment instruments, including a 71-page diagnostic questionnaire covering drinking and drug habits, medical history, and psychiatric problems. These, along with tests of cognitive and motor skills, electrophysiological measurements, and biochemical assays, will be administered to the 600 alcoholics and their immediate families as well as to members of 200 control families where no addictions (as far as can be ascertained) exist. One-third of the subjects will be women, who have hitherto received short shrift in genetics studies. Says Reich: "We'll be trying to put together the whole phenotype" of alcoholism.

The next phase will involve segregation analysis to model potential mechanisms of inheritance and to characterize the effect of genes suspected to be involved in alcoholism and other familial disorders. Finally, there will be formal linkage studies, involving dozens of members each from between 100 and 200 families of alcoholics, for an in-depth look at candidate genes and their association with diagnoses and with possible biological markers. These include blood platelet enzymes such as adenylate cyclase and monoamine oxidase, neurotransmitters, and brain waves. Perhaps the most promising candidate as marker at the moment, according to several investigators, is a decrement in a certain brain wave, called the P3 wave, that Begleiter has identified in studies of young sons of alcoholics. The anomaly, which is linked to the processing of significant sensory stimuli, is also evident in alcoholics.

Ultimately, the study will result in the creation of a tissue bank of blood cells from alcoholics and family members that will "capture the full range of variation" in alcoholism, says Reich. That will enable the products of the study to be used for many years, to be available for the rapid testing of new hypotheses as they come along. Psychiatrist Robert Cloninger of Washington University says the study design "has a lot of information." For example, "If we find a linkage in St. Louis, we can tell Indiana and New York to check it." So, although baseline data will be collected for prospective research, "We'll be able to replicate within the study without doing follow-up."

The field of behavioral genetics, says NIAAA director Enoch Gordis, "is ripe for this attack" because of advances in computerized pedigree analysis and biotechnology. Cloninger points out that such a study wouldn't have flown 10 years ago because not enough of the human genome had been explored; but now, he says, "There are markers spanning 95% of the human genome. If there are major susceptibility genes, the probability of finding them approaches one." Whether that will happen in 5 years depends on luck, but "it really is a matter of time."

In any case, investigators say the study will help researchers agree on a typology for alcoholics that will sort out which cases are strongly genetically influenced. It may lead to new pharmacological treatments, and to the development of tests combining biological and psychological indicators to predict individuals at risk for alcoholism and other addictions. Another likely outcome, says Cloninger, will be closer coordination between what have been the separate domains of alcoholism and drug abuse research.

Begleiter says he will be "overjoyed" if, as he suspects, it turns out that all addictions stem from "the same biological core of anomalies." In that case, he says, the study "will tell us a hell of a lot more than just about alcoholism." It would imply the same research model could be extended to "many other disorders," and would justify a much broader application of the basic model of alcoholism treatment. Indeed, it could mean nothing less than a major reconceptualization of the disease.

CONSTANCE HOLDEN

Patterns and Trends in Drug Use

Drug use is socially patterned; different drugs are used in different frequencies by different social categories in the population. In addition, drug use displays a trend: It varies over time. Consequently, in order to understand the phenomenon of drug use, we must examine its pattern and trends. Who uses drugs? How frequently? And how does this change from year to year?

More basically, how do we study drug use? Won't people simply lie about their use that, with respect to illegal drugs, is a criminal act? With the legal drugs, our job is relatively easy. All officially tabulated sales are taxable, which means that there are detailed and precise records on how many purchases of what quantities of which legal drugs available for inspection. Legal drug sales are a matter of public record, so, in order to know how much alcohol, tobacco, prescription drugs, and over-the-counter drugs are used, we look at their official sales.

The matter is not *quite* this easy, of course. There are unofficial sales of legal drugs—moonshine whiskey, cigarettes and cigars smuggled into the United States from abroad, legal drug use by American tourists on vacation in other countries, and so on—that do not get recorded anywhere. And someone may purchase a bottle of liquor, put it on the shelf, and never drink it at all; this represents a sale, but no use. Because of these and other complexities, scientists refer to sales as "apparent" consumption; sales are not *exactly* consumption, but they are very close to it. Sales per year represent a very rough, but fairly accurate, reflection of levels of actual use of legal drugs.

With respect to alcohol specifically, there is another complexity: Different alcoholic beverages contain different percentages of alcohol, which scientists call *ethanol* or ethyl alcohol. In the United States, for distilled beverages, the "proof" of a type of drink designates the percentage of ethanol it contains; to get that percentage, simply divided the proof by a factor of two. So, 100–proof vodka is 50 percent ethanol; 80–proof whiskey is 40 percent alcohol. Each type of drink contains its own specific percentage of ethanol. Beer is 4–5 percent alcohol; wine is 12–13 percent; "fortified" wines, such as sherry and port, are nearly 20 percent; distilled beverages, such as vodka, gin, rum, Scotch, and tequila, are 40–50 percent ethanol. Thus, for the many types of alcoholic drinks it is necessary to apply a "conversion factor": For beer, to determine the consumption of alcohol or ethanol itself, one must divide the total quantity of beer sold by 20 or 25; for wine, one must divide by 8; for whiskey, divide by 2 or 2.5, depending on the proof; and so on. Though these tabulations are complicated, they can be done.

With illegal drugs, the matter is more difficult. Here, we have no official record of sales. How do we know who uses and who does not? Whether use changes over time? Many social scientists believe that, to answer these questions, we can conduct surveys. How do we know about drug use? Simply ask a sample consisting of an accurate cross-section of Americans about their own use, some experts believe. Would people lie about their own drug use? The evidence suggests that most people tell the truth about matters like that—to the best of their ability, of course. It is important that we sample a fairly large number of respondents, and that they reflect the composition of the population at large. But study after study has shown that the answers people give in a survey tell us a great deal about their drug use patterns.

What patterns do we see in drug use, judging from the many currently-available surveys on the subject? Many of the findings of these studies are fairly commonsensical. Men tend to use illegal drugs—and alcohol as well—more than women. The young use more than the old, urban residents more than rural dwellers, residents of the East and the West coasts more than those living in the South and the Midwest, high school and college drop-outs more than those who graduate, and—especially very recently—the poor more than the affluent.

With respect to trends, one dramatic change took place in the 1980s that is still ongoing: Drug use, both legal and illegal, is declining significantly and dramatically. The peak for illegal drug use was the late 1970s; not only are Americans using less, they also disapprove of drug use more, they are more likely to believe that it is harmful, and less likely to favor legalization, even of marijuana. Alcohol and, somewhat less so, tobacco use also declined during the 1980s and into the 1990s, although far less sharply than was true for the illegal drugs.

But in addition to this downhill overall trend, we also notice a less heartening one. One of the most remarkable changes in the area of drug use and abuse in recent years is the growing *divergence* in drug use patterns between

the poor and the affluent, between middle and lower class Americans. While drug use declined among the members of the middle classes, among the lower and working classes, it increased, remained stable, or declined much more slowly. Thus, the people with the most resources to deal with the problem of drug use are giving it up, while those with the fewest resources are most likely to continue. It is painful paradoxes such as these that we must grapple with in this extremely difficult area of study.

Looking Ahead: Challenge Questions

What changes have taken place in the drug use and abuse patterns in the United States during the past generation or so? Why do certain drugs experience ups and downs in popularity over time? Do you think that these variations are a matter of availability, cultural preference, stresses and strains—or what?

Why are certain categories in the population more likely to use and abuse certain drugs? Why are others less likely to do so?

How accurate are surveys on drug use?

Why do you think that members of the middle and the lower classes are diverging in their drug use patterns over time?

What do you foresee as the "drug of the future"? What will the drug use patterns be in the near future? Will drug use and abuse remain high in the United States a decade from now? Or do you foresee a decline? Why?

Temperance: An Old Cycle Repeats Itself

Drinking and drug use fall, a trend experts say may intensify.

Gina Kolata

Today is the day after the biggest drinking holiday of the year. Although many Americans presumably overindulged, more and more are looking with disdain on the rite of getting drunk.

At the same time, the nation's tolerance for cigarette smoking is growing thin, and the use of drugs like marijuana and cocaine has gone from glamorous to despicable in a few short years, social scientists have found.

In fact, experts say, America is in the midst of a major new temperance movement, the third in its history.

"There has been a significant shift away from accepting drugs as being normal, as being with it, as being chic," said Dr. Mitchell S. Rosenthal, president of Phoenix House Foundation, a drug treatment and education center in New York, and chairman of the Governor's Advisory Council on Drug Abuse.

"Ten years ago, there was still a belief that one could be smarter, sexier and work better if one used drugs," he said. But now "there is a considerable awareness at all levels of society, both rich and poor, that drug use is dangerous and that one will pay personal as well as social dues for using drugs."

Dr. Herbert Kleber, deputy director of the office of demand reduction in the Office of National Drug Control Policy, agreed. "In the 1960's and 1970's, drug use became what I and others call normalized," he said. "The non-user was the loner. But over the past 5 to 10 years, that attitude has begun to shift."

The National Household Survey on Drug Abuse, conducted each year by the National Institute of Drug Abuse, shows a steady decline over the past decade in the use of alcohol, cigarettes and illicit drugs. The survey, conducted from March through June, used personal interviews combined with questionnaires and involved 9,259 Americans, aged 12 and over, who are representative of the population.

For example, according to the 1990 data, released at the end of December, the percentage of young adults aged 18 to 25 who said they used alcohol in the past month fell to 63 in 1990 from a peak of 76 percent in 1979. The percentage of those who said they had smoked cigarettes in the past month dropped to 32 percent from a peak of 50 percent in 1976. The percentage who said they had used cocaine in the past month plunged to 2 percent from 9 percent in its peak year, 1979. And the percentage using an illicit drug in the past month plummeted to 15 percent from 37 percent in 1982, the first time the question was asked.

Gallup polls conducted by telephone in July and December found fewer Americans are drinking and smoking. The December poll, which involved a national sample of 1,007 adults aged 18 or older, found that 57 percent said they sometimes drank alcoholic beverages. In 1978, 71 percent said they did. In the July Gallup poll, based on 1,240 adults, 27 percent said they had smoked cigarettes in the past week. In 1954, the smoking high point, 45 percent said they had smoked in the week before the poll was taken.

The Gordon S. Black Corporation, a polling company in Rochester that has tracked American attitudes about drugs and alcohol since 1987, found that even in the past three years it has seen marked shifts. For example, in 1987, 66 percent of teenagers said that taking drugs frightened them. In 1990, 74 percent were afraid of taking drugs. In 1987, 32 percent of adults said that people who had one or two drinks a day were at great risk. In 1990, that percentage increased to 39 percent. The company polls a national sample of 7,000 to 8,500 people, Mr. Black said.

An Intensifying Trend

Dr. Rosenthal, Dr. Kleber and others predicted that the trend against drinking, smoking and drug use would intensify in the next decade. One expert, Dr.

'People don't realize how much their attitudes have shifted.'

David F. Musto, a historian of medicine at Yale University School of Medicine, even predicted that alcohol would meet with the kind of social disapproval now reserved for cigarettes.

If such temperance takes hold and drug use falls to very low levels in the middle class, some experts fear politicians will turn their backs on poor people who may still desperately need publicly financed drug treatment services.

"The danger is that we will have a shrinking political interest in the problem and the most vulnerable and high

risk populations will not get the kind of services they need," Dr. Rosenthal said.

Shift in Attitudes

But Dr. Ansley Hamid, an anthropologist at John Jay College of Criminal Justice in New York who studies drug use in the inner city, said there was less tolerance for drugs there too. Drug use "is definitely starting to wane," he said. "People are using much less cocaine. They have cut back on marijuana and alcohol as well. All the assumptions we had about the drug world are being shook up a little bit."

Dr. Musto noted that the change in attitudes toward drinking and drugs was so profound that many people had disowned notions they held not too long ago.

"People don't realize how much their attitudes have shifted," Dr. Musto said, adding that the change occurred gradually but steadily over the past decade. People often are only aware of how profound the social movement has been when they look at movies from the 1970's, when scenes of drinking and drug use were common or when they look back at incidents that seemed perfectly normal in the not so distant past.

Dr. Charles Blitzer, director of the Woodrow Wilson International Center for Scholars in Washington, recalled his first day on a job in the 1960's when he was taken to lunch by his new colleagues. He was the only person at the table who did not order an alcoholic beverage. A colleague turned to him, he recalled, "with a look of horror on her face and said, 'You *do* drink, don't you?'"

Dr. Musto said that although he never enjoyed smoking, the social pressure to smoke when he was in college in the 1950's was so great that "I felt it was my duty to find my brand."

A Backlash May be Next

He explained that this was the third temperance movement in American history. Both previous movements lasted 20 to 30 years, both were accompanied by a health consciousness like the one gripping Americans today, and both, at their peaks, took on a moralistic tone that led to a backlash, a new age when drinking and drugs were encouraged.

The first temperance movement began around 1820 and peaked around 1850, Dr. Musto said. At that time, all of New England as well as many other states prohibited the sale of alcoholic beverages. This was followed by an upsurge in drinking, which peaked in 1890. Then Americans began to turn against alcohol, cigarettes and drugs. In 1920, the nation prohibited the sale of alcohol. Prohibition ended in 1933 in

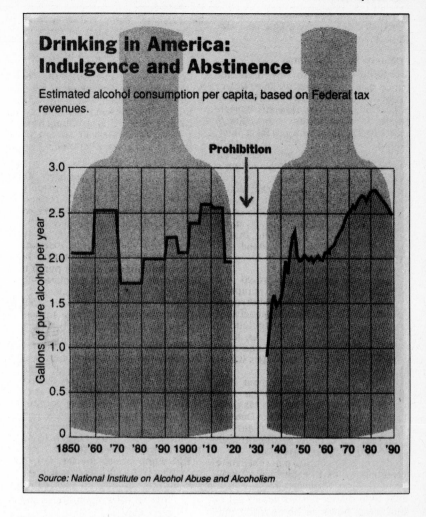

Drinking in America: Indulgence and Abstinence

Estimated alcohol consumption per capita, based on Federal tax revenues.

Source: National Institute on Alcohol Abuse and Alcoholism

part, Dr. Musto said, because the Federal Government wanted the revenue it could raise by taxing alcoholic beverages. A new era of tolerance for drugs and alcohol began, which peaked around 1979.

The turning point for every tolerance movement came when more and more

---

One expert predicts that those who drink will meet with the disdain now reserved for smokers.

Americans began to see for themselves the ravages of drug use, Dr. Musto said. Dr. Kleber stressed that the turn away from drugs and alcohol was given impetus by movements like the parents' movement, Mothers Against Drunk Driving and National Families in Action, a group that fights the availability of drugs to teen-agers.

Penalties for Marijuana

Sue Rusche, a founder of National Families in Action, said she began the

group in 1977 when she and other parents were appalled by statements from national leaders that advocated teaching teen-agers to learn to use drugs responsibly and by the proliferation of stores selling drug paraphernalia. Eleven states lifted criminal penalties against marijuana use in the 1970's. "Professionals were telling us not to worry if our kids used marijuana," Ms. Rusche said.

But two of the states, Alaska and Oregon, have recently voted to recriminalize marijuana, she said.

Ms. Rusche and others began to speak out vociferously against drugs. Now, she said, "there has been a big attitudinal change."

Dr. Musto added that if the current temperance movement followed the patterns of the past two movements, it would last another 10 or 20 years, getting more and more severe and moralistic in tone, before ending with a wild backlash, a sort of counterrevolution that is manifest in widespread acceptance of drugs and alcohol and an age of excess.

And that is what frightens Ms. Rusche. "It could happen all over again," she said.

Costly and Scarce, Marijuana Is a High More Are Rejecting

Joseph B. Treaster

Not long ago, hosts at some Upper East Side dinner parties would set out little silver bowls of home-rolled marijuana cigarettes along with the after-dinner drinks. Rock concerts unfolded under canopies of marijuana smoke, and the drug's syrupy aroma drifted across schoolyards and campuses, construction sites and corporate offices, public parks and private patios.

But as quietly and gradually as the widening of a waistline, America's infatuation with the herb of many names—grass, pot, dope, weed, ganja, sess, sens, smoke, skunk and, quaintly, in the long ago, Mary Jane—has been fading.

In New York and throughout the country, lighting up is no longer hip, not in high school, not at college, not at most social events and, with the advent of widespread random drug testing, certainly not on the job.

Marijuana has become a scarce commodity selling for as much as $800 an ounce

The great marijuana cloud has grown wispy as rebellion and the quest for nirvana have yielded to conformity and the struggle for survival, as health concerns and a vague fear of getting into trouble have risen above the desire to get giddy.

Part of the shift, undoubtedly, has also been because of relentless police pressure that has transformed an abundant drug once available for $20 or $30 an ounce into a scarce commodity selling in some quarters of New York for $800 an ounce, more than twice the price of gold.

"It's not cool anymore," said a high school senior in Manhattan, capturing the mood of the 90's with the language of the 60's.

Although the glory days of the Beatles are generally remembered as the peak of the marijuana craze, the popularity of the drug gathered momentum through the 70's and stayed relatively strong until the late 80's.

Advocates insist that marijuana—the mildest and by far the most widely tried illegal drug in America—is no more harmful than alcohol, not even the latest strains, which are 10 times more potent than the grass of the flower children. Still, it has been as much a target of the national antidrug campaign as cocaine, heroin, LSD and barbiturates, and many people have clearly taken the prohibitions to heart.

No conclusive medical evidence on the long-term effects of marijuana has been developed. But Federal officials contend it is a steppingstone to other drugs. Many addicts do report that marijuana was their first drug. But legions of former smokers say they never went on to anything stronger. "Most of us," said one professional woman in her mid-40's, "just dropped out of drugs and called it a day."

Using pot does not fit the personal vision of today's American youth

Ultimately, it seems, marijuana just does not fit the personal visions of growing numbers of New Yorkers and other Americans. Nor do most other drugs, including cocaine, alcohol and nicotine, all of which are being increasingly rejected.

Some of those most militantly opposed to marijuana and other drugs are schoolchildren who for several years now have been attending antidrug classes and watching antidrug messages on television.

One junior high school student in Queens said she had no interest in experimenting with marijuana. "It just

doesn't seem like it would be fun or anything," she said. "We've heard so much about it, that it's horrible and stuff."

And the Manhattan high school senior said that although marijuana was widely accepted as recently as her freshman and sophomore years, she now finds that "everyone is really scared about getting into college and getting good jobs and doing drugs doesn't help."

The two young women, like many other people interviewed for this article, spoke on the condition that they not be identified because they were socially uncomfortable about being associated with drugs in any way.

"Using pot," the high school senior said, "is like dropping out of the race"; which, of course, was precisely the attraction for many in her father's generation.

Former pot smokers—or almost-former pot smokers—are everywhere.

Nathan J., a 20-year-old college sophomore, rarely smokes now because he found he was losing his edge in volleyball and Frisbee games. A 28-year-old dancer who said she smoked heavily in high school takes a drag every couple of years and finds to her disappointment that she becomes paranoid and self-conscious and ends up wondering why she tried it again. Her friend, a graphic artist, said she decided she could not tolerate the loss of hand-eye coordination. A lawyer in her 40's said that while she didn't believe smoking was bad, it began to seem "foolhardy" to risk an arrest that "could wreck your career."

Marijuana use has, by all estimates, significantly decreased in recently years.

Marijuana smoking reached its peak in 1979, when the National Institute on Drug Abuse estimated, based on its survey, that more than 31.5 million Americans had used the drug at least once during that year. By 1990, when the most recent statistics were compiled, the marijuana-smoking crowd had diminished by more than a third, to 20.5 million.

With the nation's population steadily rising, those smoking marijuana in 1990 represented 10.2 percent of all Americans over the age of 12, compared with 17.8 percent in 1979.

More than 66 million people have tried marijuana at least once, compared with 22.7 million who have sampled cocaine, the National Institute on Drug

Abuse says. In 1990, the institute estimated that 10.2 million Americans had used marijuana within the last month, compared with 1.6 million who had used cocaine.

These estimates may understate total marijuana use, many drug experts say, but probably accurately reflect a pronounced decline. Even organizations that advocate making marijuana legal and regulating it like alcohol say there has been a significant decrease.

People still smoke marijuana at rock concerts. But they look around before they pull out a joint and they hold off if they see an usher coming. A New York woman studying at the University of Rhode Island said most of her circle of friends smoked marijuana. "But," she added, "it's become much more of a taboo topic, much less socially acceptable. It's gone under the rug."

Back in 1979, almost all the marijuana smoked in the United States was grown in other countries and it all seemed to have romantic names. There were Thai Sticks, Cambodian Red, Colombian Gold, Panama Red and some from Mexico known simply by place names, Oaxaca and Michoacán. The United States Customs Service seized more than 3.5 million pounds of marijuana in 1979. Last year, Federal agents intercepted 222,274 pounds, or one-sixteenth as much.

Marijuana smuggling is difficult due to the bulk and the problems faced with concealing it; as a result, much more marijuana is grown domestically

The great wall of boats, planes and radar thrown up by the Federal Government may not have dented the cocaine trade, but it nearly killed marijuana smuggling. Marijuana is much bulkier and harder to conceal than cocaine and, until recently, it sold for much less.

"We used to call it the Big Green Elephant," said a charter boat captain in Miami. "You could smell it a quarter of a mile away." He, like others with intimate knowledge of the trade, agreed to speak only with the promise of anonymity.

Unable to get through the barriers or unwilling to risk jail for the lower profits from marijuana, some smugglers dropped out; others shifted to cocaine.

"For a lot of guys, bringing in a load of marijuana was a form of high adventure," the Miami skipper said. "But it

became very dangerous and guys said, 'This is ridiculous.' "

As recently as 1984, the biggest percentage of America's marijuana was from Colombia. Now Mexico is the main foreign supplier and the most sought-after marijuana is grown in California, Oregon and Hawaii.

The war against domestically grown marijuana accelerated in early 1990, after President Bush was embarrassed at a conference on drugs in Colombia at which Alan García, then President of Peru, suggested that Washington could hardly expect Latin America to stop growing the raw material for cocaine when marijuana farmers flourished in the United States.

Government spray planes wiped out 85 to 90 percent of Hawaii's marijuana, administration officials say. Millions of other marijuana plants were destroyed in national parks and on other public lands that farmers had begun cultivating to avoid the Government's seizing private property used for illegal crops. Scores of greenhouses, each containing hundreds of plants, were raided and Federal agents began tracking marijuana farmers through the records of companies that sell nursery supplies.

"You can't wink at marijuana," said Robert C. Bonner, the chief of the Drug Enforcement Administration. "It is not a benign drug. It affects productivity and general alertness. It has a corruptive influence on law enforcement and public officials. And if we want other countries to control cocaine production, we have to lead by example."

Federal spending to fight marijuana at home nearly doubled in the 1991 fiscal year, to $35 million, and the administration requested $87 million for 1992.

After the air raids in Hawaii, the retail price of marijuana there leaped from $2,000 a pound to $6,000, which is $375 an ounce, or $16 more than an ounce of gold.

Prices fluctuate around the country, but in the Northeast these days it is not unusual to pay $280 an ounce. Most sales, the dealers say, are of quarter-ounce packets. Street hustlers still offer plastic sandwich bags of what looks like marijuana for $10. But quite often, experienced smokers say, the hustlers are peddling diluted marijuana or a jumble of nonintoxicating herbs.

After the federal government made massive raids on marijuana growing areas, the price of the drug on the street tripled

4. PATTERNS AND TRENDS IN DRUG USE

As a hedge against being conned, many buyers get friends to refer them to reputable dealers. The New York police devote little energy to catching marijuana dealers. But even so, to protect themselves, many dealers refuse to sell to strangers.

One New York dealer wears a beeper and promises delivery in midtown within half an hour of receiving a telephone order. Another works out of his tasteful apartment on the Upper West Side of Manhattan, offering three grades of marijuana for as much as $800 an ounce.

Cocaine is currently selling in New York for $800 to $1,200 an ounce. The same amount of heroin is fetching more than $5,000.

The Upper West Side dealer's customers are lawyers, doctors, stockbrokers and other well-paid professionals. To them, price is of little consequence. But it does matter to many people.

"If it goes up anymore, I'm going to stop smoking," said an art major at one Northeastern college.

Some marijuana users have turned to growing their own. One professional, for example, has a small garden in a closet of his home on Staten Island. Hundreds if not thousands of other New Yorkers are growing a few marijuana plants on windowsills.

But the best quality comes from plants that require more attention than most people want to give. So a legion of outlaw horticulturists are developing throughout the country. One of them, a young man who lives in Maryland, told of setting up nurseries in the recreation room and basements of three houses not far from Washington, and of tending marijuana bushes on small plots of Government land in the capital.

"D.C. is an excellent growing environment for marijuana," he said. "With all that concrete, it retains about five degrees more heat than the outlying areas and you get approximately one to two weeks more growing time."

Old, Weak and a Loser: Crack User's Image Falls

Gina Kolata

Crack has begun to get a bad name among a growing number of young people in New York City's poorest neighborhoods, according to some teenagers, police officers and researchers who work on the streets. Rather than a challenge, something to test a teenager's mettle, they say, the smokable form of cocaine is gaining a reputation as a drug "for losers."

These young people tell how their families, friends and neighbors have been broken by the drug, and, along with several crack addicts and police officers, they tell of a violent backlash, in which groups of teen-agers and even younger children have set upon crack addicts and beaten them up or pelted them with sticks or stones.

One teen-ager who says he has turned to violence is 18-year-old Luis Solla, who lives in the Williamsburg section of Brooklyn and works as a lifeguard at a fitness center. His 21-year-old brother, he says, is a crack addict and dealer who was thrown out of the house at 17 and into prison at 19. His sister, who is 19, was also a crack addict. She abandoned her baby, and ran off to live with her crack-dealing boyfriend in Connecticut.

'We Don't Do Crack'

"I don't want to be like some people out here," Mr. Solla said. "They lose their homes because they're on it. I don't want to get involved with that."

Every day, he says, he is reminded of crack's toll. "All my friends, we don't do crack because we look at the older guys on the block," he said. "They're all bad crackheads. I look at them and I see what they're doing, and I don't want to be like that." He and his friends, he added, "fight with crackheads. We beat them up. We're trying to get them out of the neighborhood."

These reports of changing attitudes are largely anecdotal, and law-enforcement officials say they have no hard evidence of major changes in patterns of drug use. But for researchers who work on the streets of New York, they offer hope that five years after the arrival of crack, social pressures and the daily sights of devastation are turning some young people away from the drug. Along with experts at drug-treatment centers, they say that the addict population seems to be getting older, a sign, they say, that the epidemic may be starting to wane.

"I'm seeing that there is a movement away from crack," said Dr. Terry Williams, a sociologist at the City University of New York who lives in East Harlem and has been studying the epidemic there, "Right now, it's certainly clear that that's happening at the street level."

Dr. Ansley Hamid, a researcher at the John Jay College of Criminal Justice who works in Williamsburg and other areas of Brooklyn, agrees. "Young people are ridiculing crackheads in their neighborhoods, even beating them up, and are abstaining from drugs themselves, other than a little marijuana and beer," he said.

'They're Like Fiends'

On the streets of Williamsburg, one of Mr. Solla's friends, 16-year-old Joseph Drexler, looks around and sees two uncles and an aunt who are homeless crack addicts. "I don't even consider them family," he said.

Mr. Drexler has also seen friends and acquaintances ruined by the drug. "I have a few friends; they're older than me but I grew up with them all my life," he said. "They started using crack a long time ago. They're crackheads. They live on my block and they rob all the time; they rob off their best friends, their families. They're like fiends. They'll do anything to get the money. We don't want them on our block."

On a recent afternoon, a skeletal young woman in a red tank top and dirty white pants huddled on a rubble-strewn crack corner in the Bushwick section of Brooklyn and told of a harrowing experience at the hands of a gang of children.

The woman—who, fearing reprisal, spoke on the condition that her name not be used—said she was 25 and began smoking cocaine eight years ago, when it was sold as a powder and she had to cook it up into a smokable form. Now she prostitutes herself and sells crack to support her habit.

Children's Taunts, and Sticks

She is humiliated, she says, by the children's taunts—"crackhead," "thirsty crackhead." "Do you know how much that hurts?" she asked, "to have to hear that from a little 7-year-old, 12-year-old kid?"

Several months ago, a gang of boys armed with sticks took her by surprise while she was smoking crack.

"Me and my friend, we're smoking, you know," she said. "They came up on me, about six, seven of them. Someone smashed me from the back and I turned around. There was a little kid on me. He just started hitting me. I'm on the ground."

The boys backed her up against a

garage door. "They cracked my head. They wanted to burn my pants—on me. I had pants on and they wanted to burn them." Her neighbors turned away. "That block was full of more people— dealers, crackheads, even the ones that just hang around. My people. My so-called people. Nobody did nothing. Ev-

---

'People say they don't want those scaly crackheads on the block.'

---

erybody just walked away. I was the only one there, with the little kids beating up on me."

Vickie R., a 25-year-old prostitute and crack addict, has also been attacked by the gangs.

"A month ago, I was coming down the block and I was going to cop and my stem fell out of my purse," she said. "I picked it up and put it in my purse because I didn't want the kids to see it, but one of the little kids, he seen it. So he come up and he says, 'Ah, look, there goes a crackhead.' Then another one come by on a bike and throws a bottle at me. He tells me. 'You crack-heads watch. I'm going to get rid of you.' "

Eventually, a group of her friends chased the boys away. "But it was at that point, you know the tension. If these people wouldn't be there, they would have beat me."

Not only are crack addicts fair game, Vickie said; anyone who looks like an addict is at risk.

"Them kids are disgusted with people that do crack," she said. "Anybody that's skinny and look like a crackhead, they go off. They don't want no crack-heads around them. Instead of the parents being the ones to tell the crackheads, 'We don't want you smok-ing on the block,' it's the little kids."

Officer Sees Attitudes Change

Police Officer C. Bullock, a fresh-faced 25-year-old who works on the streets of Washington Heights, said he had seen women who are crack addicts and, usu-ally, prostitutes, beaten up by young people. "They're easy prey," he ex-plained, and because of their own crimi-nal activity, are unlikely to report the attacks.

But Officer Bullock said he had defi-nitely seen a change in attitudes about crack, at least in Washington Heights.

"Most kids are against it," he said, explaining that they had become only too aware of how dangerous the drug is. "In this neighborhood, they see it, they hear it, they live it. A lot of people say they don't want those scaly crackheads on the block. They feel they're an eye-sore."

Lieut. Joseph McNulty, who coordi-nates a police program to teach about drugs in the schools, said the officers who conducted the eight-week courses were also seeing young people turning away from crack. "We notice that there is a changing attitude," Lieutenant McNulty said. Not only are the users older, he said, but fewer teen-agers seem to be starting to use drugs. "We haven't had an up-to-date survey to ver-ify this, but we feel it anyway," he added.

Crack Addicts Are Older

"There is most definitely a strong awareness in the youngest generation that crack is a loser's drug," said Dr. Philippe Bourgois, an ethnographer from San Francisco State University who lives in East Harlem and works in its neighborhoods. "Now, 'thirsty crack-head' is the ultimate insult," referring to crack users' insatiable appetite for the drug.

Social scientists and drug-treatment experts say they, too, are seeing an aging of the addict population. And while that is partly because those who became addicted at the start of the epidemic are getting older, they believe that it also suggests that fewer young people are starting to use crack.

Dr. Williams has been studying the

cocaine epidemic since the early 1980's, before crack came on the scene, and he routinely asks addicts how old they are. "The average crack addict is now in the mid- to late 20's," Dr. Williams said. "At the beginning of the epidemic, the average age was 18."

Dr. Hamid and Dr. Richard Curtis, a colleague at the John Jay College of Criminal Justice, said they had not star-ted using crack in the last year; the vast majority of addicts they meet began using crack several years ago.

Recently, Dr. Hamid said, he visited a Bushwick crack house where pros-titutes went to exchange sex for the drug. "All these girls were coming out of the woodwork, looking like the brides of Dracula," he said. "Not a single one of them had started using crack later than 1984 or 1985."

At Phoenix House, not only has the average age of crack addicts seeking treatment risen; there has been a pro-portionate decrease in teen-age appli-cants. This year [1990], 20 percent of the addicts applying for treatment are age 16 to 19, said Stephen Dnistrian, a spokesman. Last year [1989], 33 per-cent were in that age group.

Jose R., a stocky 21-year-old heroin addict whose track marks are partly hidden by the ears of a Playboy bunny tattooed on his arm, says he can mea-sure the two years he just spent in prison by the changes he now sees in his Bushwick neighborhood.

Jose sells heroin, a drug that is being used by crack addicts to ameliorate their high.

"I came back and I said, 'Wow, what happened here?' " said Jose, who was released in February after serving a sentence for a drug-related crime. "I'm not seeing new people starting with crack. People that have never done it, they're really afraid. The AIDS virus, the way they see people becoming. It de-stroys you, you know. So people are afraid. People who have never done it are afraid to.

"A few years ago, every teen-ager would try crack. But most of the teen-agers nowadays, once they come around here and see this, they don't want none of it."

"Overview of the 1990 National Household Survey on Drug Abuse"

The 1990 National Household Survey on Drug Abuse is the tenth in a series that began in 1971 under the auspices of the National Commission on Marijuana and Drug Abuse and has been sponsored by the National Institute on Drug Abuse [NIDA is a division of the Department of Health and Human Services (HHS)] since 1974.

The survey covers the population age 12 and older living in households in the contiguous United States. The results are based on personal interviews combined with self-administered answer sheets from 9,259 respondents, randomly selected from the household population. This is the largest sample ever used in this survey and includes an over-sampling of Blacks, Hispanics, young people, and the Washington, D.C. metropolitan area, enabling us to make reliable estimates about the levels of drug use among these populations. Not included in the survey are the homeless, persons living in military installations, dormitories, and other group quarters, and institutions such as hospitals and jails.

Three major age groups are covered in this survey: youth age 12 to 17; young adults age 18 to 25; and older adults age 26 and over. The survey data provide the basis for prevalence estimates and other statistics which contribute to an understanding of the extent of drug use in the United States in 1990.

As with any sample survey, the results of this survey are estimates of the values that would be obtained if the data were collected from all members of the population from which the sample was drawn.

HHS Secretary Louis W. Sullivan, M.D., today released results of the department's 1990 National Household Survey on Drug Abuse, which continues to show declining use of most illicit drugs by Americans, including a dramatic 45 percent drop in "current" cocaine use (use at least once in the past month) since the last survey in 1988.

"We are seeing the fruits of our long-standing efforts to rid this country of the devastating hold of illicit drugs," Secretary Sullivan said. Dr. James O. Mason, assistant secretary for health said, "The news is encouraging and will most certainly provide reinforcement to the millions of people who have been working so diligently to eliminate the drug abuse problems that have affected so many of us."

During the past five years, current cocaine use has decreased a total of 72 percent. The number of current cocaine users dropped from 5.8 million (2.9 percent of the population age 12 and older) in 1985 to 2.9 million (1.5 percent) in 1988, to 1.6 million (0.8 percent) in 1990.

The 1990 survey also found a 44 percent reduction in current use of any illicit drug in the past five years, down from 23 million in 1985, to 14.5 million in 1988, to 12.9 million in 1990. The overall rate for current use was 6.4 percent, down from 7.3 percent in 1988.

Youth are one of the major concerns, and the number of adolescents using drugs fell by 13 percent from 1.8 million in 1988 to 1.6 million in 1990. In addition, adolescents currently using cocaine fell by 49 percent from 225,000 in 1988 to 115,000 in 1990.

"Despite this impressive good news about our progress in reversing our nation's drug using habits, however, many pockets of serious drug problems remain," Secretary Sullivan said.

Among the continuing severe problems, Dr. Sullivan cited the fact that among the 6.2 million past-year cocaine users in 1990, 662,000 (10.6 percent) used the drug once a week or more. However, even the 662,000 represented a decline in the total number from 862,000 in 1988. In addition, 336,000 (5.4 percent) used cocaine daily or almost daily throughout the year, compared with 292,000 in 1988.

The survey also found that while the number of current cocaine users decreased in 1990, the number of current crack users remained stable. There were nearly half a million current crack users among the 1.6 million current cocaine users.

"We must reach out more vigorously to this core of persons who are heavy drug users. They no doubt account for a significant portion of the violence, crime, child abuse and other destructive behaviors associated with drug use," Secretary Sullivan said.

Reprinted from *National Institute on Drug Abuse (NIDA)*, December 1990, pp. 1-13.

95

4. PATTERNS AND TRENDS IN DRUG USE

The secretary also noted that in spite of the overall decline to 6.4 percent in any current illicit drug use, demographic subgroups with higher rates included young adults age 18–25 years old (14.9 percent); blacks (8.6 percent); individuals in large metropolitan areas (7.3 percent); those living in the West region (7.3 percent); and the unemployed population (14.0 percent).

Marijuana remains the most commonly used illicit drug in the United States. Approximately 66.5 million Americans (33.1 percent) have tried marijuana at least once in their lifetime, and 20.5 million people had used marijuana at least once in the past year. Of these past-years users, 5.5 million used marijuana once a week or more and 3.3 million used the drug daily or almost daily. "Current" use of marijuana has been decreasing since 1979, when there were 22.5 million (12.7 percent) users. In 1990, there were 10.2 million (5.1 percent) current users.

Current alcohol and cigarette use continued to decline in 1990 as it did from 1985 to 1988. There were 102.9 million current drinkers of alcoholic beverages in 1990 compared with 113.1 million in 1985 and 105.8 million in 1988. Weekly alcohol drinkers decreased from 54.6 million in 1985, to 47.3 million in 1988, to 41.7 million in 1990.

Current cigarette use during this period dropped from 60.3 million (32 percent) in 1985, to 57.1 million (29 percent) in 1988, to 53.6 million (27 percent) in 1990. Secretary Sullivan said, "This represents a decrease of 6.7 million persons smoking cigarettes in the past five years. I view this as a remarkable achievement as more and more people start taking responsibility for their own health."

Other survey findings include:

- Over 4.8 million (8 percent) of the 60.1 million women 15–44 years of age (the childbearing years), have used an illicit drug in the past month. Slightly over 500,000 (0.9 percent) used cocaine and 3.9 million (6.5 percent) used marijuana in the past month.
- Among 18–34-year-old full-time employed Americans, 24.4 percent used an illicit drug in the past year, and 10.5 percent used an illicit drug in the past month. Of these full-time workers, 9.2 percent used marijuana, and 2.1 percent used cocaine in the past month.
- Among 20–34-year-olds who have not completed high school, 15.6 percent were current marijuana users and 2.9 percent were current cocaine users. The rates are higher than rates for high school graduates of the same age (9.3 percent and 1.8 percent).

The National Household Survey is a probability-based sample of 9,259 people representative of the U.S. household population age 12 and over. Not included in the survey are those who live in military installations, nursing homes, dormitories, hospitals, jails, prisons, or the homeless. The 1990 survey, conducted in March-June this year, represents the 10th in a series of surveys conducted every two to three years since 1972 by the National Institute on Drug Abuse. In order to monitor changes in drug use closely, data collection will now be conducted every year in response to the National Drug Control Strategy.

TREND ANALYSIS

- Current prevalence rates for use of any illicit drug among persons 12 years of age and older continued to decrease from 23 million drug users (12.1%) in 1985, to 14.5 million users (7.3%) in 1988 to 13 million users (6.4%) in 1990.
- The number of current cocaine users decreased significantly from 2.9 million (1.5%) in 1988 to 1.6 million (0.8%) in 1990, continuing a previous decline. This represents a 72% decrease in the number of current cocaine users since 1985, when there were an estimated 5.8 million (2.9%) current cocaine users.
- Current cigarette use dropped from 32% in 1985 to 29% in 1988, and presently stands at 27%, representing a significant decrease from 1988. This represents a 3.5 million decrease in the number of cigarette smokers in the last two years. The previous three-year period, 1985–88, experienced a 3.2 million decrease, for a total decrease of 6.7 million persons since 1985.
- There were 102.9 million current drinkers of alcoholic beverages in 1990 compared with 105.8 million in 1988, and 113.1 million in 1985. The alcohol use rates in 1985, 1988, and 1990, for those aged 12 and over, are 59%, 53%, and 51%, respectively.

1990 ANALYSIS

- Overall in 1990, 74.4 million Americans age 12 or older (37 percent of the population) had tried marijuana, cocaine or other illicit drugs at least once in their lifetime.
- Almost twenty-seven million Americans (13.3%) used marijuana, cocaine or other illicit drugs at least once in the past year.
- Among youth (12 to 17 years old), 15.9% used an illicit drug in the past year and 8.1% used an illicit drug at least once in the past month. Comparable rates for young adults (18–25 years old) are 28.7% and 14.9% respectively; and for adults 26 years old and over the rates are 10.0% and 4.6% respectively.
- The overall current (past month) prevalence rate for any illicit drug use (12 years old and over) was 6.4%. Rates for males and females are 7.9% and 5.1%, respectively. In addition to males, other demographic subgroups with rates in excess of the overall rate are those for blacks (8.6%), large metro areas (7.3%), those living in the West region (7.3%), and the unemployed population (14.0%).
- Over 4.8 million or 8 percent of the 60.1 million women 15–44 years of age (the height of childbearing years) have used an illicit drug in the past month. Slightly over one-half million or 0.9% used cocaine and 3.9 million (6.5%) used marijuana in the past month.
- Among 18–34-year-old full-time employed Americans, 24.4% used an illicit drug in the past year, and 10.5% used an illicit drug in the past month. Of these full-time workers, 9.2 percent used marijuana, and 2.1% used cocaine in the past month.

Lifetime Prevalence of Drug Use: 1972 to 1990

Youth age 12–17

	1972	1974	1976	1977	1979	1982	1985	1988	1990
Marijuana	14.0%	23.0%	22.4%	28.0%	30.9%	26.7%	23.6%	17.4%	14.8%
Hallucinogens	4.8	6.0	5.1	4.6	7.1	5.2	3.3	3.5	3.3
Cocaine	1.5	3.6	3.4	4.0	5.4	6.5	4.9	3.4	2.6
Heroin	0.6	1.0	0.5	1.1	0.5	*	*	0.6	0.7
Nonmedical Use of:									
Stimulants	4.0	5.0	4.4	5.2	3.4	6.7	5.6	4.2	4.5
Sedatives	3.0	5.0	2.8	3.1	3.2	5.8	4.1	2.4	3.3
Tranquilizers	3.0	3.0	3.3	3.8	4.1	4.9	4.8	2.0	2.7
Analgesics	-	-	-	-	3.2	4.2	5.8	4.2	6.5
Alcohol	-	54.0	53.6	52.6	70.3	65.2	55.5	50.2	48.2
Cigarettes	-	52.0	45.5	47.3	54.1	49.5	45.2	42.3	40.2
Any Illicit Use	-	-	-	-	34.3	27.6	29.5	24.7	22.7

Young Adults age 18–25

	1972	1974	1976	1977	1979	1982	1985	1988	1990
Marijuana	47.9%	52.7%	52.9%	59.9%	68.2%	64.1%	60.3%	56.4%	52.2%
Hallucinogens	-	16.6	17.3	19.8	25.1	21.1	11.3	13.8	12.0
Cocaine	9.1	12.7	13.4	19.1	27.5	28.3	25.2	19.7	19.4
Heroin	4.6	4.5	3.9	3.6	3.5	1.2	1.2	0.4	0.6
Nonmedical Use of:									
Stimulants	12.0	17.0	16.6	21.2	18.2	18.0	17.1	11.3	9.0
Sedatives	10.0	15.0	11.9	18.4	17.0	18.7	11.0	5.5	4.0
Tranquilizers	7.0	10.0	9.1	13.4	15.8	15.1	12.0	7.8	5.9
Analgesics	-	-	-	-	11.8	12.1	11.3	9.4	8.1
Alcohol	-	81.6	83.6	84.2	95.3	94.6	92.6	90.3	88.2
Cigarettes	-	68.8	70.1	67.6	82.8	76.9	75.6	75.0	70.5
Any Illicit Use	-	-	-	-	69.9	65.3	64.3	58.9	55.8

Older Adults age 26+

	1972	1974	1976	1977	1979	1982	1985	1988	1990
Marijuana	7.4%	9.9%	12.9%	15.3%	19.6%	23.0%	27.2%	30.7%	31.8%
Hallucinogens	-	1.3	1.6	2.6	4.5	6.4	6.2	6.6	7.4
Cocaine	1.6	0.9	1.6	2.6	4.3	8.5	9.5	9.9	10.9
Heroin	*	0.5	0.5	0.8	1.0	1.1	1.1	1.1	0.9
Nonmedical Use of:									
Stimulants	3.0	3.0	5.6	4.7	5.8	6.2	7.9	6.6	6.9
Sedatives	2.0	2.0	2.4	2.8	3.5	4.8	5.2	3.3	3.7
Tranquilizers	5.0	2.0	2.7	2.6	3.1	3.6	7.2	4.6	4.2
Analgesics	-	-	-	-	2.7	3.2	5.6	4.5	5.1
Alcohol	-	73.2	74.7	77.9	91.5	88.2	89.4	88.6	86.8
Cigarettes	-	65.4	64.5	67.0	83.0	78.7	80.5	79.6	78.0
Any Illicit Use	-	-	-	-	23.0	24.7	31.5	33.7	35.3

- Estimate Not Available
* Low precision--no estimate shown

Annual Drug Use: 1972 to 1990

Youth age 12-17

	1972	1974	1976	1977	1979	1982	1985	1988	1990
Marijuana	-	18.5%	18.4%	22.3%	24.1%	20.6%	19.7%	12.6%	11.3%
Hallucinogens	3.6	4.3	2.8	3.1	4.7	3.6	2.7	2.8	2.4
Cocaine	1.5	2.7	2.3	2.6	4.2	4.1	4.0	2.9	2.2
Heroin	*	*	*	0.6	*	*	*	0.4	0.6
Nonmedical Use of:									
Stimulants	-	3.0	2.2	3.7	2.9	5.6	4.3	2.8	3.0
Sedatives	-	2.0	1.2	2.0	2.2	3.7	2.9	1.7	2.2
Tranquilizers	-	2.0	1.8	2.9	2.7	3.3	3.4	1.6	1.5
Analgesics	-	-	-	-	2.2	3.7	3.8	3.0	4.8
Alcohol	-	51.0	49.3	47.5	53.6	52.4	51.7	44.6	41.0
Cigarettes	-	-	-	-	13.3**	24.8	25.8	22.8	22.2
Any Illicit Use	-	-	-	-	26.0	22.0	23.7	16.8	15.9

Young Adults age 18-25

	1972	1974	1976	1977	1979	1982	1985	1988	1990
Marijuana	-	34.2%	35.0%	38.7%	46.9%	40.4%	36.9%	27.9%	24.6%
Hallucinogens	-	6.1	6.0	6.4	9.9	6.9	4.0	5.6	3.9
Cocaine	-	8.1	7.0	10.2	19.6	18.8	16.3	12.1	7.5
Heroin	-	0.8	0.6	1.2	0.8	*	0.6	0.3	0.5
Nonmedical Use of:									
Stimulants	-	8.0	8.8	10.4	10.1	10.8	9.9	6.4	3.4
Sedatives	-	4.2	5.7	8.2	7.3	8.7	5.0	3.3	2.0
Tranquilizers	-	4.6	6.2	7.8	7.1	5.9	6.4	4.6	2.4
Analgesics	-	-	-	-	5.2	4.4	6.6	5.5	4.1
Alcohol	-	77.1	77.9	79.8	86.6	87.1	87.2	81.7	80.2
Cigarettes	-	-	-	-	46.7**	47.2	44.3	44.7	39.7
Any Illicit Use	-	-	-	-	49.4	43.4	42.6	32.0	28.7

Older Adults age 26+

	1972	1974	1976	1977	1979	1982	1985	1988	1990
Marijuana	-	3.8%	5.4%	6.4%	9.0%	10.6%	9.5%	6.9%	7.3%
Hallucinogens	-	*	*	*	0.5	0.8	1.0	0.6	0.4
Cocaine	-	*	0.6	0.9	2.0	3.8	4.2	2.7	2.4
Heroin	-	*	*	*	*	*	*	0.3	0.1
Nonmedical Use of:									
Stimulants	-	*	0.8	0.8	1.3	1.7	2.6	1.7	1.0
Sedatives	-	*	0.6	*	0.8	1.4	2.0	1.2	0.8
Tranquilizers	-	*	1.2	1.1	0.9	1.1	2.8	1.8	1.0
Analgesics	-	-	-	-	0.5	1.0	2.9	2.1	1.9
Alcohol	-	62.7	64.2	65.8	72.4	72.0	73.6	68.6	66.6
Cigarettes	-	-	-	-	39.7**	38.2	36.0	33.7	31.9
Any Illicit Use	-	-	-	-	10.0	11.8	13.3	10.2	10.0

- Estimate Not Available
* Low precision--no estimate shown
** Includes only persons who ever smoked at least 5 packs

Current (Past Month) Drug Use: 1972 to 1990

Youth age 12–17

	1972	1974	1976	1977	1979	1982	1985	1988	1990
Marijuana	7.0%	12.0%	12.3%	16.6%	16.7%	11.5%	12.0%	6.4%	5.2%
Hallucinogens	1.4	1.3	0.9	1.6	2.2	1.4	1.2	0.8	0.9
Cocaine	0.6	1.0	1.0	0.8	1.4	1.6	1.5	1.1	0.6
Heroin	*	*	*	*	*	*	*	*	*
Nonmedical Use of:									
Stimulants	-	1.0	1.2	1.3	1.2	2.6	1.6	1.2	1.0
Sedatives	-	1.0	*	0.8	1.1	1.3	1.0	0.6	0.9
Tranquilizers	-	1.0	1.1	0.7	0.6	0.9	0.6	0.2	0.5
Analgesics	-	-	-	-	0.6	0.7	1.6	0.9	1.4
Alcohol	-	34.0	32.4	31.2	37.2	30.2	31.0	25.2	24.5
Cigarettes	-	25.0	23.4	22.3	12.1**	14.7	15.3	11.8	11.6
Any Illicit Use	-	-	-	-	17.6	12.7	14.9	9.2	8.1

Young Adults age 18–25

	1972	1974	1976	1977	1979	1982	1985	1988	1990
Marijuana	27.8%	25.2%	25.0%	27.4%	35.4%	27.4%	21.8%	15.5%	12.7%
Hallucinogens	-	2.5	1.1	2.0	4.4	1.7	1.9	1.9	0.8
Cocaine	-	3.1	2.0	3.7	9.3	6.8	7.6	4.5	2.2
Heroin	-	*	*	*	*	*	*	*	*
Nonmedical Use of:									
Stimulants	-	3.7	4.7	2.5	3.5	4.7	3.7	2.4	1.2
Sedatives	-	1.6	2.3	2.8	2.8	2.6	1.6	0.9	0.7
Tranquilizers	-	1.2	2.6	2.4	2.1	1.6	1.6	1.0	0.5
Analgesics	-	-	-	-	1.0	1.0	1.8	1.5	1.2
Alcohol	-	69.3	69.0	70.0	75.9	70.9	71.4	65.3	63.3
Cigarettes	-	48.4	49.4	47.3	42.6**	39.5	36.8	35.2	31.5
Any Illicit Use	-	-	-	-	37.1	30.4	25.7	17.8	14.9

Older Adults age 26+

	1972	1974	1976	1977	1979	1982	1985	1988	1990
Marijuana	2.5%	2.0%	3.5%	3.3%	6.0%	6.6%	6.1%	3.9%	3.6%
Hallucinogens	-	*	*	*	*	*	*	*	0.1
Cocaine	-	*	*	*	0.9	1.2	2.0	0.9	0.6
Heroin	-	*	*	*	*	*	*	*	*
Nonmedical Use of:									
Stimulants	-	*	*	0.6	0.5	0.6	0.7	0.5	0.3
Sedatives	-	*	0.5	*	*	*	0.6	0.3	0.1
Tranquilizers	-	*	*	*	*	*	1.0	0.6	0.2
Analgesics	-	-	-	-	*	*	0.9	0.4	0.6
Alcohol	-	54.5	56.0	54.9	61.3	59.8	60.6	54.8	52.3
Cigarettes	-	39.1	38.4	38.7	36.9**	34.6	32.8	29.8	27.7
Any Illicit Use	-	-	-	-	6.5	7.5	8.5	4.9	4.6

- Estimate Not Available
* Low precision--no estimate shown
** Includes only persons who ever smoked at least 5 packs

4. PATTERNS AND TRENDS IN DRUG USE

ANALYSIS BY DRUG

Cocaine

- Among the 6.2 million people who used cocaine in the past year, 662,000 (10.6%) used the drug once a week or more and 336,000 (5.4%) used the drug daily or almost daily throughout the year. While the number of past year and past month cocaine users has decreased significantly since the peak year 1985, frequent or more intense use has not decreased. Of the 12.2 million past year cocaine users in 1985, an estimated 647,000 used the drug weekly and 246,000 used it daily or almost daily.

- Rates for use of cocaine in the past year declined for youth (12–17 years old) from 4.0% in 1985 to 2.9% in 1988 to 2.2% in 1990. For young adults (aged 18–25), the rates for 1985, 1988, and 1990, are 16.3%, 12.1% and 7.5%, respectively. These decreases between 1985 and 1990 were statistically significant for both age groups.

- The rate of current (past month) cocaine use was 0.8% overall, a significant decrease from the 1988 rate of 1.5%. The rate of current cocaine use for males (1.1%) was over twice as high as that for females (0.5%). Other demographic subgroups for which the rates of current cocaine use are the highest were the unemployed (2.7%), blacks (1.7%) and Hispanics (1.9%).

- Approximately 1.4% of the population 12 years old and over have used crack at some time in their lives, and one-half of one percent used crack during the past year. These rates changed very little from those in 1988. This translates to about one million past year crack users for each year, 1988 and 1990. Past year use in 1990 is highest among males (0.8%), blacks (1.7%) and the unemployed (1.3%). By age group, the highest rate is for young adults 18–25 years old (1.4%).

Marijuana

- Marijuana remains the most commonly used illicit drug in the United States. Approximately 66.5 million Americans (33.1%) have tried marijuana at least once in their lives. Nearly three million youth, over 15 million young adults, and in excess of 48 million adults aged 26 and older have tried marijuana.

- In 1990, the lifetime rate of marijuana use for youth was 14.8%, while the rate for young adults was 52.2%. These rates have been steadily decreasingly since 1979, when they were 31% and 68%, respectively.

- Rates of past month use of marijuana did not change significantly between 1988 and 1990, decreasing slightly from 5.9% to 5.1%. Rates were highest for males (6.4%), blacks (6.7%), and the unemployed (12.3%).

- Of the 20.5 million people who used marijuana (at least once) in the past year in 1990, over one-quarter, or 5.5 million, used the drug once a week or more.

Alcohol and Tobacco Products

- The decline in the rates of lifetime alcohol use seen between 1985 and 1988 (from 56% to 50%) for youth continued in 1990 to 48%. Past year use was 41% in 1990, and has experienced a steady decline since 1979. In 1990, less than 25% of youth have had at least one drink during the past month. This is similar to 1988 survey results.

- For young adults, the prevalence of alcoholic beverage use is substantially higher than for youth: 88% have tried alcohol, 80% have used alcohol in the past year, and 63% have used alcohol during the preceding month. Although this represents little change from 1988, drinking alcohol has steadily declined since 1985. The 1990 rates for drinking among young adults in the past year and past month are significantly lower than those reported in 1985 (87% and 71%, respectively in 1985).

- Of the 133 million people age 12 and older (66% of the population) who drank (alcohol) in the past year, nearly one-third, or 42 million, drank at least once a week.

- Nearly three-quarters of the American population (73.2%) have tried cigarettes, and slightly over a quarter (26.7%) are past month (current) smokers—a decrease from 28.8 percent in 1988. Current use of cigarettes among youth is almost 12%; 32% among young adults; and 28% among adults 26 and over.

- Four percent of youth and 6% of young adults used smokeless tobacco during the past month. These data indicate little change from 1988.

- Of the 7.1 million current users of smokeless tobacco, over 91% are males. In contrast with patterns of illicit drug use, rates of use of smokeless tobacco are highest for whites, those living in non-metropolitan areas, and those living in the South.

Other Drugs

- Hallucinogens, which first gained prominence during the mid-sixties, include such drugs as LSD, PCP, mescaline, and peyote. Past year prevalence rates for hallucinogens decreased significantly between 1988 and 1990 (1.6% vs. 1.1%). Males (1.7%) exhibit the highest prevalence rates. Although past year prevalence is highest among the two age groups, 12–17 (2.4%) and 18–25 (3.9%), lifetime prevalence is highest among the 26–34-year-old population (15.7%).

- While many youth (7.8%) and young adults (10.4%) have experimented with inhalants, past month use is only 2.2% for youth and 1.2% for young adults. There were no significant changes in inhalant prevalence between 1988 and 1990.

- Past month nonmedical use of psychotherapeutic drugs, i.e., sedatives, tranquilizers, stimulants, and analgesics, have stabilized at the 1988 rate of under 2% from the higher (3.2%) rate in 1985. A significant decrease was noted for past year use for the age groups 18–25 and 26–34. In 1988, the rates were 11% and 10%, respectively. For 1990, they decreased to 7% and less than 6%. This dramatic reduction translates to nearly 3 million less past year users in these two age groups.

Population Estimates of Lifetime and Current Drug Use, 1990

The following are estimates of the number of people 12 years of age and older who report they have used drugs nonmedically. Drugs used under a physician's care are not included. The estimates were developed from the 1990 National Household Survey on Drug Abuse.

	12–17 yrs. (pop. 19,977,918)				18–25 yrs. (pop. 29,020,582)				26+ years (pop. 152,189,483)				TOTAL (pop. 201,187,983			
	%	Ever Used	%	Current User	%	Ever Used	%	Current User	%	Ever Used	%	Current User	%	Ever Used	%	Current User
Marijuana & Hashish	15	2,954,000	5	1,030,000	52	15,140,000	13	3,692,000	32	48,413,000	4	5,483,000	33	66,507,000	6	10,206,000
Hallu-cinogens	3	652,000	1	186,000	12	3,485,000	1	243,000	7	11,203,000	*	*	8	15,339,000	*	553,000
Inhalants	8	1,548,000	2	441,000	10	3,019,000	1	344,000	4	5,729,000	*	*	5	10,296,000	1	1,188,000
Cocaine	3	518,000	1	115,000	19	5,620,000	2	630,000	11	16,601,000	1	856,000	11	22,739,000	1	1,601,000
Crack	1	201,000	*	45,000	3	802,000	1	192,000	1	1,755,000	*	*	1	2,757,000	*	494,000
Heroin	1	145,000	*	7,000	1	166,000	*	25,000	1	1,343,000	*	*	1	1,654,000	*	48,000
Stimulants	5	898,000	1	191,000	9	2,621,000	1	350,000	7	10,444,000	*	*	7	13,963,000	1	957,000
Sedatives	3	658,000	1	182,000	4	1,157,000	1	215,000	4	5,700,000	*	*	4	7,515,000	*	568,000
Tranquilizers	3	533,000	1	110,000	6	1,702,000	1	151,000	4	6,433,000	*	*	4	8,668,000	*	568,000
Analgesics	7	1,292,000	1	274,000	8	2,349,000	1	340,000	5	7,766,000	1	923,000	6	11,408,000	1	1,536,000
Alcohol	48	9,636,000	25	4,895,000	88	25,599,000	63	18,368,000	87	132,145,000	52	79,656,000	83	167,380,000	51	102,919,000
Cigarettes	40	8,041,000	12	2,327,000	71	20,468,000	32	9,143,000	78	118,733,000	28	42,162,000	73	147,241,000	27	53,633,000
Smokeless Tobacco	12	2,356,000	4	775,000	22	6,306,000	6	1,734,000	13	19,710,000	3	4,602,000	14	28,372,000	4	7,111,000

*Amounts of less than 5% are not listed.

Terms:
Ever Used: used at least once in a person's lifetime.
Current User: used at least once in the 30 days prior to the survey.

The Major Drugs of Use and Abuse

Perhaps the most important lesson we can learn in any realistic study of drug use is that different drugs have different effects. Smoking marijuana does not feel the same, or do the same things to the human mind and body, as injecting heroin; snorting cocaine is very different in most respects from swallowing a tab of LSD or drinking a gin and tonic. In order to know what drugs do—and are—it is absolutely essential to examine each drug or drug type individually.

Pharmacologists—scientists who study the effect that drugs have on humans and animals—classify drugs into categories. To begin with, some drugs are *psychoactive*, that is, they influence the workings of the mind; others are strictly medicinal, they influence the body but not the mind. Although some drugs that are not psychoactive, such as certain over-the-counter medications, are improperly used, psychoactive drugs are far more likely to be misused, abused, and over-used; clearly, they are more interesting to us here.

Psychoactive drugs are generally classified into the following types:

General depressants depress, inhibit, or slow down a wide range of organs and functions of the body and retard signals passing through the central nervous system, that is, the brain and spinal cord—in most cases, they slow down, relax us, make us drowsier, less alert, less anxious. In most cases, they facilitate sleep. Examples include alcohol, tranquilizers, and sedatives. In sufficiently large doses, depressants can produce intoxication and, if taken over a long enough period of time, physical dependence. If too large a dose is taken at one time, it is possible to die of an overdose of a depressant drug—alcohol included.

Narcotics, or *narcotic analgesics* dull the perception of pain, produce an intense "high" upon administration—and are highly addicting. They include heroin, morphine, opium, codeine, and the synthetic narcotics. Like general depressants, overdosing is a strong possibility with a large dose of a narcotic drug. There are some other analgesics or painkillers that are not as effective as the narcotics that do not produce an intoxication (such as aspirin).

Stimulants speed up signals passing through the central nervous system; they inhibit fatigue, and produce arousal, alertness, even excitation. Animals—and humans—find stimulants extremely reinforcing, that is, they will repeat self-administered doses, even when it interferes with other things they want, such as food, water, and sex. Cocaine and the cocaine derivative, crack, are the most well-known of the stimulants; they also include the amphetamines, or "speed," and an amphetamine cousin, methamphetamine ("crank" or "ice"), as well as caffeine and nicotine.

Hallucinogens, or "psychedelics," produce extreme mood, sensory, and perceptual changes; examples include LSD, mescaline, and psilocybin. The term "hallucinogen" implies that users always or typically experience hallucinations when they take drugs of this type; that is, in fact, rarely the case. Most of the time when users under the influence "see" things that do not concretely exist, they are aware that it is the drug and not the real world that is causing the vision. The term "psychedelic," a word taken from the ancient Greek, implies that the mind is "made manifest"—that is, it works best—under the influence, another extremely misleading notion. In some classifications, PCP or "angel dust," originally an animal tranquilizer, is regarded as an hallucinogen. In addition, "ecstasy," or MDMA, chemically related to the amphetamines, is also thought of as an hallucinogen. Marijuana, once thought to be an example of a hallucinogen, does not quite fit into this category, and must be regarded as a separate type of drug altogether.

Over-the-counter (OTC) medications are not psychoactive and do not produce a high or intoxication; in order to become dependent on one or another OTC remedy, or overdose on one, it is necessary to take extremely large doses. They are not entirely "safe"—no drug is—but relative to the psychoactive drugs, they are relatively so. Aspirin and other analgesics or painkillers cause hundreds of deaths by overdose (nearly all of them suicides) each year in the United States, an indication that there is some measure of danger in any substance that causes bodily changes.

As we saw in the introduction to unit 2, in addition to the impact of the specific drugs or drug type used, there is the factor of *route of administration*—that is, *how* a drug is used. Some drugs, used via certain routes or methods of use, generate an immediate, powerful, sensuous sensation; other routes of administration produce a slower, less

intense, less immediate or "mellower" feeling. Smoking and intravenous (IV) administration produce the quickest and most intense high; oral (swallowing) and intranasal (sniffing or "snorting") ingestion produce a slower, less intense high. Of course, some drugs cannot be taken certain ways; marijuana is not water-soluable, and, therefore, cannot be injected, and does not get absorbed by the nasal membranes, and cannot be snorted. Alcohol—obviously—cannot be smoked. Still, for a number of drugs, what a drug can do to the human mind and body is partly dependent on the way it is taken.

Looking Ahead: Challenge Questions

Which of the major drugs of use is most dangerous?

What is it about each drug or drug type that some users find appealing? How can two drugs with very different effects become equally popular in a given society at a given time? Why are some drugs more popular during one decade and a very different one at another time?

Given the fact that cocaine, and its derivative, crack, is so pleasurable and reinforcing, how is it possible to stop its spread?

What is it that drug users and abusers are seeking when they take certain drugs? What is the appeal of each one? What is so bad about certain drugs—marijuana and "ecstasy," for instance—if used in moderation?

Why should users take a drug that is clearly dangerous to their health and their very lives?

The How and Why of a Cocaine High

Advancing methods for treating addiction

William Booth
Washington Post Staff Writer

BALTIMORE—No one knows exactly what a squirrel monkey feels when it does cocaine. But government scientists at the Addiction Research Center here know this: A monkey will flip a switch for hours just to get another dose of cocaine. And just as some humans will go on a reckless binge of abuse, so too will a monkey hit the switch for more and more cocaine until researchers stop the experiment.

But scientists caution that just because they can get a monkey to feed its addiction so voraciously, it does not necessarily support the popular belief that cocaine is the most addictive of abused drugs.

Indeed, they say, the reason the animal keeps hitting the lever may just be because cocaine makes the monkey superalert and hyperactive.

A monkey might be just as addicted to alcohol, but after a few drinks, in contrast to cocaine's effect, the monkey might stop hitting the lever because it feels sleepy or dazed.

In the last few years, drug researchers have learned an enormous amount about cocaine. Not only do they know more about its true addictive properties, they now at last have a rough idea of how cocaine produces its high.

Addiction scientists have learned, for example, that the drug stimulates a still-mysterious pathway in the brain that is involved in feelings of pleasure and reward.

Indeed, some scientists think they now know at least one region of the brain where cocaine does its work, a structure called the nucleus accumbens, which is responsible for helping humans orient and move toward things they find pleasurable, whether the object of their desire is a member of the opposite sex, a fine wine or a rock of crack cocaine.

In addition, researchers know the exact molecular site in the nucleus accumbens where the cocaine molecule binds to its special receptor.

This in turn has led to a better understanding of how cocaine acts to overstimulate certain nerve cells in the brain, a phenomenon that makes users feel good.

Armed with this knowledge, new drugs are being developed to treat the worst symptoms of withdrawal, to suppress cocaine craving and to reduce cocaine-associated depression.

When a user smokes crack in a pipe, researchers believe, he is employing one of the most efficient drug delivery systems known.

In both animals and humans, scientists say, smoked cocaine reaches the brain so quickly that it is almost impossible to distinguish a dose delivered by intravenous injection from a dose delivered by a glass pipe.

"How fast does it get to the brain? We're not sure. It's too fast to measure in the lab," says Jonathan Katz, a behavioral pharmacologist at the Addiction Research Center, a branch of the National Institute on Drug Abuse.

Katz says he assumes crack cocaine reaches the brain in seconds.

Unlike snorting cocaine powder, a relatively slow and inefficient route, smoking crack delivers the drug directly to the lungs, where it is readily absorbed by the blood, pumped once through the heart and then up to the brain.

One researcher compared smoking crack to driving a nail of cocaine directly into one's forehead.

A "single significant dose" of cocaine—in other words, enough to get a person with a history of cocaine use high—increases breathing, boosts blood pressure and may double heart rate. Hunger, fatigue and depression fade. A subject feels vigorous, happy, hypersexual, friendly and alert. Some scientists describe this collection of sensations as euphoria.

Although a full explanation of how cocaine produces euphoria remains elusive, researchers do know that the drug appears to affect the limbic system, the part of the brain involved in the powerful emotional responses, of which the best-known are those important to human survival, such as the primal urges to feed, fight, flee and reproduce.

THE ANATOMY OF A HIGH

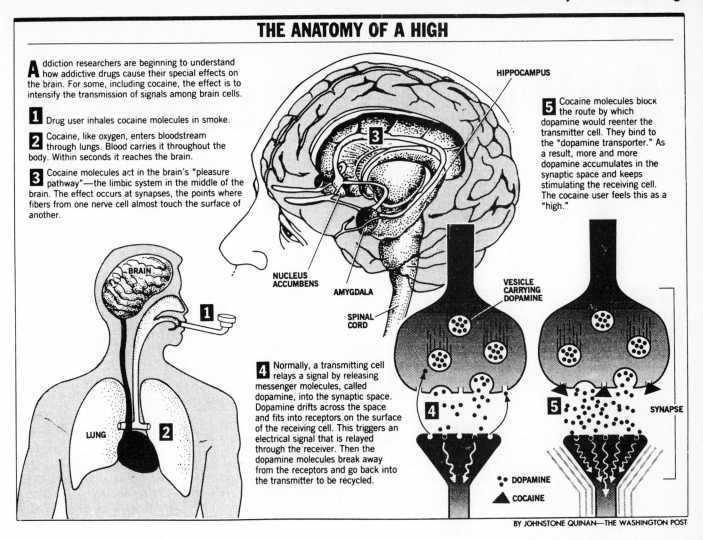

Addiction researchers are beginning to understand how addictive drugs cause their special effects on the brain. For some, including cocaine, the effect is to intensify the transmission of signals among brain cells.

1 Drug user inhales cocaine molecules in smoke.

2 Cocaine, like oxygen, enters bloodstream through lungs. Blood carries it throughout the body. Within seconds it reaches the brain.

3 Cocaine molecules act in the brain's "pleasure pathway"—the limbic system in the middle of the brain. The effect occurs at synapses, the points where fibers from one nerve cell almost touch the surface of another.

5 Cocaine molecules block the route by which dopamine would reenter the transmitter cell. They bind to the "dopamine transporter." As a result, more and more dopamine accumulates in the synaptic space and keeps stimulating the receiving cell. The cocaine user feels this as a "high."

HIPPOCAMPUS

NUCLEUS ACCUMBENS

AMYGDALA

SPINAL CORD

BRAIN

LUNG

VESICLE CARRYING DOPAMINE

SYNAPSE

4 Normally, a transmitting cell relays a signal by releasing messenger molecules, called dopamine, into the synaptic space. Dopamine drifts across the space and fits into receptors on the surface of the receiving cell. This triggers an electrical signal that is relayed through the receiver. Then the dopamine molecules break away from the receptors and go back into the transmitter to be recycled.

•• DOPAMINE

▲ COCAINE

BY JOHNSTONE QUINAN—THE WASHINGTON POST

Although several components of the limbic system are under study, the one area that appears to get the most action is the nucleus accumbens. The nucleus accumbens is uniquely situated to communicate between the limbic system and the part of the brain called the motor cortex, which directs movement.

"When you see a pretty girl and alert to her presence and orient toward her, or when you smell a good bordeaux wine sauce and move toward the smell, it is the nucleus accumbens that is helping you orient and move toward those things you perceive as pleasurable," says George Koob, a psychopharmacologist at the Research Institute of the Scripps Clinic in San Diego.

Scientists believe that cocaine stimulates the nucleus accumbens by meddling with a special chemical messenger called dopamine. In the nucleus accumbens, cocaine enters the tiny space where one nerve cell almost touches another, a sort of no man's land called the synaptic space.

For one nerve cell to transmit a signal to another, it must make the signal cross the synaptic space. To do this a neuron releases a load of dopamine molecules. Each dopamine molecule travels across the space, briefly attaches itself to a receptor on the receiving cell and then heads back into the neuron from which it was released.

Cocaine, however, stops the dopamine from returning to the neuron that released it, according to Michael Kuhar of the Addiction Research Center. It forces the dopamine to remain in the synaptic space, where it keeps stimulating the receiving neuron over and over again.

In a sense, it is not the cocaine that makes a user high, it is the dopamine that lingers in the synaptic space, overstimulating the nucleus accumbens.

"It jazzes it up," says Koob.

In a normal person, Koob says, the nucleus accumbens may be activated from time to time. But under the influence of cocaine a person is feeling full-blown pleasure almost non-stop, wallowing in a kind of "brain hedonism."

In fact, a common complaint among former cocaine addicts is that they have difficulty getting enjoyment from life's simple, undrugged pleasures, such as sex and eating.

Indeed, Koob believes that one reason cocaine may be so addictive is that it not only makes users feel good, but it also makes them more active, enabling them and motivating them to take more and more of the drug—just like the laboratory animal in the experimental chamber that keeps hitting the lever for more cocaine—until overdose and death overtake them.

"That's what makes cocaine so powerful," says Koob.

A Prozac Backlash

Does America's favorite antidepressant make sane people crazy?
Despite a string of dramatic accusations, the jury is still out.

Miracles are hard to come by, but to many Americans Prozac looked just like one. Introduced in 1987, the new antidepressant took the market, and the public imagination, by storm. Not only was it easier to prescribe than the other available treatments, but it seemed to alleviate a wider range of afflictions, from depression and anxiety to bulimia and obsessive-compulsive disorder. Best of all, it didn't cause the weight gain, low blood pressure or irregular heart rhythms common to many treatments. In just three years, Prozac became the nation's top-selling antidepressant (a title it still holds, with nearly a million prescriptions being filled every month). Instead of complaining about its price—20 times that of older drugs—happy customers lined up to bear their testimonials. "Prozac has made us a celebrity," says Eugene L. Step of the Indianapolis-based Eli Lilly & Co., which makes the drug. "I have become a far more avid viewer of talk shows." But the talk-show chatter has lately taken a radical new turn.

Self-described "Prozac survivors" now appear on "Donahue" to accuse the drug of turning sane people into murderers and self-mutilators. Scores of unhappy customers are filing lawsuits against Lilly, seeking huge awards for misfortunes they blame on Prozac (box). Some are using the drug as a criminal defense, saying they shouldn't be held accountable for crimes they committed while taking it. One activist group, an offshoot of the Church of Scientology, is even demanding that the Food and Drug Administration remove Prozac from the market. Lilly, meanwhile, is standing staunchly by its product, and psychiatrists have lost little of their initial enthusiasm. Many fear the current uproar will scare patients away from a potentially lifesaving treatment. "This drug is transporting a lot of people from misery to well-being," says Dr. Jerrold Rosenbaum of Harvard Medical School and Massachusetts General Hospital. "A flurry of sensational anecdotes shouldn't stop that."

The horror stories vary in texture, but they share a common theme. Joseph Charles Gardner Jr. started taking the drug in December 1988 to ease the depression that had settled over him after his father died of a heart attack. The 32-year-old resident of St. George, Utah, had always been quiet and conservative, serving as a Mormon missionary, attending Brigham Young University, holding jobs as a schoolteacher, a sheriff's deputy and a medical worker. Everything changed during 1989. Acquaintances say Gardner became restless and irritable after he started taking Prozac, and took to hanging out in bars. In April of that year, he married a Nevada casino worker named Nancy Snow, but she left him after three weeks. By the end of the year, he had twice tried to kill himself with overdoses of barbiturates. "People thought something was wrong," says his lawyer, Alan Boyack, "but nobody ever associated it with Prozac. He just kept taking this drug on the advice of his physician, and he starts going dingy."

Nancy Snow's divorce became final in September 1989, but Gardner didn't want to let go. The following July he approached her in a St. George bar and her best friend, a 32-year-old nurse named Janice Fondren, told him to leave her alone. Gardner was enraged. Later the same week, according to police, he showed up armed at Fondren's apartment. After a brief argument, he allegedly shot her through the heart, drove 22 miles to a remote section of the Shivwit Indian Reservation and left her naked body in the dirt. Gardner is now in a state hospital, where court-appointed psychiatrists have found him temporarily incompetent to stand trial. If he is finally arraigned, his lawyer says he will admit killing her, but will attribute his behavior to Prozac.

Rhonda Hala didn't kill anyone during the 18 months she took Prozac, but she blames the drug for nearly killing her. The 41-year-old Long Island secretary says she had never had any serious problems until late 1988, when a hospital psychiatrist prescribed Prozac (along with a muscle relaxant and later a tranquilizer) to alleviate the aftereffects of major back surgery. After 10 days on the drug, Hala says she became unbearably restless. "You sit down and every nerve in your body has to move," she recalls. "You feel like you're going to jump right out of your skin."

Then came an unaccountable longing for pain, which she satisfied by tearing at the flesh on her thighs, arms and torso. Over the next year she gouged herself with anything she could lay her hands on—screws, bottle caps, shower hooks, tacks, pens, razors. She had a dozen scenarios for suicide, but death was never the main objective. "I had to hurt," she says. "I never thought of taking an overdose of drugs. That would have been too painless." Last year, after her doctor took her off Prozac, Hala says she promptly stopped mutilating herself.

Kentucky massacre: Today she is one of roughly 60 clients from around the country for whom Leonard Finz, a New York personal-injury lawyer, is filing separate suits against Lilly. Finz's Prozac plaintiffs include everyone from the widow of rock star Del Shannon, who killed himself while taking Prozac in February 1990, to the families of several men killed by Joseph Wesbecker of Louisville, Ky. Wesbecker, a 47-year-old pressman with a history of psychiatric problems, was taking Prozac and several other medications in September 1989 when he stormed through the Standard Gravure printing plant with an AK-47. He shot 20 co-workers, eight of them fatally, before taking his own life. That Prozac caused the massacre is, to Finz, self-evident. "Lilly," he claims, "had its finger around the trigger of Joe Wesbecker's rifle."

Juries will have to decide whether Lilly is legally to blame for this carnival of mis-

fortune. Scientists, meanwhile, are grappling with the more important question of whether Prozac can actually make people suicidal and violent. The evidence is still open to different interpretations. On at least two points, though, there is no debate.

The first is that depression itself can cause suicide and violence, even in people receiving treatment. Fully 15 percent of all clinically depressed patients end up taking their own lives. Since no antidepressant—neither Prozac nor any of the alternatives—has more than an 80 percent success rate, it stands to reason that some users will continue to think and act erratically. "Prozac tends to be used by people with psychiatric problems," says Dr. W. Leigh Thompson of Lilly Research Laboratories. "Some people with psychiatric problems happen to be violent."

Experts also agree that virtually any antidepressant could prompt a depressed person to act on impulses he already harbored, simply by making him restless. Roughly a quarter of all antidepressant users experience jitteriness and agitation as side effects. Various antidepressants can also cause an unbearable muscle restlessness called akathisia. Most people don't become violent or suicidal just because they feel restless. But the sensation can be too much for a mentally ill person to bear.

The question is whether Prozac, unlike other antidepressants, can directly induce violent or suicidal thoughts—thoughts that don't stem from an underlying illness. Dr. Martin Teicher, of Harvard Medical School and McClean Hospital, believes that it can. Teicher became something of a celebrity last year after he published a paper in the American Journal of Psychiatry, describing a strange thing that happened in his clinic. Six patients, depressed but not suicidal, had suddenly developed an "intense, violent suicidal preoccupation" after taking Prozac for two to seven weeks. Teicher couldn't rule out depression as the source of their self-destructive impulses—all six patients had considered killing themselves in the past. But their suicidal thoughts came on so suddenly during treatment that Teicher suspected Prozac had actually caused them.

Other researchers have since reported a handful of similar cases. In a recent letter to The New England Journal of Medicine, doctors in Syracuse, N.Y., described two previously nonsuicidal patients—a depressed man and a depressed, bulimic woman—who became suicidal within weeks of starting Prozac. According to the letter, the obsessions receded after they stopped taking the drug. And last month psychiatrists at the Yale Medical School's Child Study Center reported the emergence of intense self-destructive thoughts in several adolescents receiving Prozac for obsessive-compulsive disorder. The Yale researchers, led by Drs. Robert King and Mark Riddle, speculate

that by disrupting production of the chemical messenger serotonin, Prozac may directly affect the brain's ability to regulate aggression. But they couldn't be sure that the patients' underlying conditions weren't the real culprit. Besides suffering from obsessions and compulsions, the report said four of the six children had been depressed or suicidal in the past.

Dark thoughts: Do these case reports reflect a unique, Prozac-related syndrome? Should violent thoughts be counted among the drug's direct side effects? The obvious way to find out is to study large groups of patients. But when researchers have gone looking for the "Teicher syndrome," they haven't found it. In one of Lilly's clinical trials, researchers randomly assigned 3,065 depressed patients to Prozac, a placebo or one of five other antidepressants. At the beginning of the six-week treatment period, all seven groups were equally prone to suicidal thoughts. By the end of the trial, the Prozac group was the least suicidal of the seven. More recently, in a one-year study, researchers at Rush-Presbyterian-St. Luke's Medical Center in Chicago monitored 100 Prozac users and found no increase in the risk of suicide or violence. And two Boston psychiatrists have just published results from a survey intended to gauge suicidal thinking among 1,017 patients treated with various antidepressants during 1989. Drs. Maurizio Fava and Jer-

'The Drug Did It': A Tough Sell in Court

Joseph Wesbecker gained a kind of immortality in death. After his 1989 rampage in Louisville, Ky., he became a symbol: the best-known violent Prozac user. Widows of three of Wesbecker's victims and his son are suing Eli Lilly & Co., Prozac's maker—just a few of about 60 pending civil suits. Prozac has made its way into criminal court, too. More than 20 defendants claim a "Prozac defense": the drug, they say, made them do it.

Most of the cases are a long shot, legal experts agree. Civil plaintiffs and criminal defendants alike have to prove that Prozac caused the violent behavior—a hard sell when the patients had histories of illness. In other cases against big pharmaceutical companies over such products as the Dalkon Shield and thalido-

mide, the damage was physical—more obvious than a psychological shift.

Civil plaintiffs have other hurdles to jump. Those suing doctors for malpractice must show the physicians didn't follow Lilly's prescription guidelines. Those suing Lilly must prove the company was reckless or negligent to let the drug out on the market, a difficult argument that will focus on the reliability of the drug's prerelease testing. Leonard Finz, the lead lawyer in many Prozac suits, says that Lilly's tests were inadequate and excluded patients with suicidal tendencies—the very users who appear most affected by the drug.

Deep pockets: Lilly says it is so confident of its testing that it will not settle any civil cases. Its tests of the drug go back to 1976, and Lilly can

prove that it included suicidal patients. Says Eugene L. Step, executive vice president at Lilly: "The message is really simple: depressed people commit suicide." And Lilly spokesman Edward West says the "Prozac defense" hasn't produced a single "not guilty" verdict. Yet three criminal defendants received reduced penalties with the Prozac defense, claims the Citizens Commission on Human Rights, an interest group linked to the Church of Scientology. The group often speaks out against psychiatry, and collects horror stories about psychiatric drugs.

Though Lilly's position seems strong, juries have a way of evening the odds. In the battle of expert witnesses and technical testimony, issues can become clouded. And juries often show sympathy

for the little guy—especially against a big corporation with deep pockets. "You take these cases before a jury and who the hell knows what might happen," says Robert Litan of the Brookings Institution, a legal liability expert. "It's a lottery." And while the Prozac defense is creative, it's not unique. Criminal conduct is being blamed on everything from drugs to junk food. Prozac parties are watching one case especially closely: in 1989 a Utah judge freed Ilo Grundberg, who killed her mother while under the influence of the insomnia drug Halcion. Now Grundberg is pursuing a $21 million civil suit against Halcion's maker, Upjohn. Upjohn denies that its drug is responsible—but if the company loses in court, the case could make the going tougher for Lilly.

JOHN SCHWARTZ *and* BOB COHN *with bureau reports*

rold Rosenbaum, both of Harvard Medical School and Massachusetts General Hospital, found that no drug was associated with significantly more suicidal thinking than any other. A number of patients became suicidal while receiving treatment, but never in the sudden, inexplicable manner Teicher described.

Maybe Prozac does make some people crazy; the available evidence doesn't settle the question. But if the Teicher syndrome is real, it is exceedingly rare—too rare to show up in studies designed to detect it, and too rare in the view of most psychiatrists to warrant big changes in prescribing practices. Teicher hopes that future research will enable doctors to predict how individual patients will react to the drug. But even he has no plans to stop prescribing it in the meantime. Antidepressants are not cough drops. Dr. Joseph Lipinski of Harvard Medical School and McLean Hospital likens them to loaded pistols. They all pose hazards. But until better treatments come along, Prozac remains a vital weapon against a formidable illness.

GEOFFREY COWLEY *with* KAREN SPRINGEN *in Indianapolis,* JEANNE GORDON *in St. George and* CARLA KOEHL *on Long Island*

MARIJUANA

Is there new reason to worry?

Winifred Gallagher *is a Senior Editor of* American Health.

America just can't decide what to do about marijuana. Some people equate smoking pot with sipping wine, others with abusing hard drugs. Most rank it somewhere in between. The confusion is awkward but understandable: Marijuana is the nation's most popular but perhaps least understood illegal psychoactive substance.

So far, studies of pot's health effects suggest what many who've smoked it would predict: For most people, occasional use probably isn't particularly harmful. Heavy use over long periods is likelier to be dangerous, although the kind of expensive, long-term studies that proved the destructive effects of tobacco and alcohol remain to be done. At present, those who seem most at risk include young people, pregnant and nursing women, heart patients and the emotionally unstable. Harvard psychiatrist and drug researcher Norman Zinberg summarizes the inadequate and conflicting data this way: "Nothing's been proved, but there's reason to worry."

There's a pressing reason to learn more about marijuana's effects: The pot on the street has increased in strength and potential harmfulness. Thousands of professional growers, many of them in Northern California,

have transformed American homegrown from a cottage industry into a multibillion-dollar-a-year agribusiness. These knowledgeable farmers use sophisticated technologies like hydroponics to cultivate pot powerful enough to command astronomical prices—more than $100 an ounce in big cities.

Recent studies show there are plenty of customers, though not quite as many as there used to be. Pot smoking peaked in 1978, and has declined since, especially among teenagers. The number of highschool seniors who smoke it daily fell by over half from 1978 to 1986. However, the drug remains enormously popular: Some 62 million Americans have tried it, and 18 million smoke it regularly. Many of today's smokers are the babyboomers who first lit up in the '60s and '70s. But some have found that the drug that mellowed them as hippies can make them uptight as yuppies.

One reason that pot smoking makes many graying members of the Woodstock generation anxious these days is that even occasional use can jeopardize their livelihoods; Many face tests to detect traces of the drug in their urine as a condition of employment. Even long-ago indulgence

can damage reputations, as Judge Douglas Ginsburg learned when he was forced to withdraw himself from consideration for the U.S. Supreme Court.

The uncertainty over almost every aspect of marijuana has created confusing, contradictory policies. At the same time that the practice of urine testing spreads, laws in many states increasingly treat users with leniency. Although smokers can still be jailed in some states, they are now merely fined in others where the drug has been "decriminalized." In Alaska they can even legally grow their own. Smoking marijuana continues to become more socially acceptable, but the question remains: Is it safe?

What Pot Is, How It Works

Marijuana is not a simple—or even a single—drug. Its wide range of effects on body and mind is caused by the more than 400 chemicals of the Cannabis sativa plant especially the 60 or so that are unique to it—the cannabinoids (see "Medical Benefits?"). Some of these may contribute only minimally to the "high," but THC (delta-9-tetrahydrocannabinol) produces most of the psychoactive effects. While the potency of street

Signs of Trouble

"There are no simple signs that a person has a serious problem with marijuana, but there are some common patterns," says Dr. Robert Millman, of the New York Hospital-Payne Whitney Clinic. "An interaction of the drug, the person and the environment is usually involved." According to the American Psychiatric Association, 4% of adults in this country suffer from "cannabis dependence" at some time in their lives.

Doctors stress that it can be very difficult to distinguish whether a pot problem is a symptom or a cause. The problem is that users in trouble often have pre-existing personality or mood disorders, which are aggravated by the drug. However, indications of a dependence on marijuana include:

■ A pattern of daily or almost daily use, usually developed over a long period. Chronic heavy users generally increase the frequency of smoking over time, rather than the dose. But they also find, with long-term use, that they eventually get less pleasure from smoking.

■ Impaired ability to function socially or on the job.

■ Use of other drugs together with marijuana.

■ Lethargy.

■ Anhedonia—the inability to feel pleasure.

■ Attention and memory problems.

Pot mellowed the hippies, but can make yuppies uptight.

drugs varies greatly, the average concentration of THC by weight has increased from about 1% or less in the '60s and '70s to anywhere from 4% to 10% in the '80s.

When marijuana is smoked, THC enters the lungs, passes into the blood stream and is carried to the brain in minutes. Both THC and its chemical by-products dissolve in fatty tissue—such as the brain, the adrenals, the gonads and the placenta—and remain there for three or more days. (These chemicals can be detected in the urine of frequent smokers for four weeks or more.) It's worrisome that these compounds linger in the body and accumulate with repeated smoking, but there's no evidence yet that they cause harm.

In the brain itself, according to Dr. Billy Martin, a professor of pharmacology at the Medical College of Virginia in Richmond, THC seems to turn on a number of biochemical systems. In low concentrations it may cause two or three changes; in stronger doses, 10 or 12. Says Martin: "The high is probably a combination of effects—sedation, euphoria and perceptual alterations—each caused by a separate mechanism." He thinks that molecules of THC produce their effects by fitting into special receptor cells in the

brain, like keys in locks. If Martin and his colleagues could prove the existence of the receptors, their discovery would suggest that a THC-like biochemical occurs naturally—the body's own version of marijuana. "Such a substance could serve in the maintenance of mental health," Martin says, "perhaps by helping the individual to calm down or protect himself against stress."

High Anxiety

During the marijuana high, which lasts for two to four hours after smoking, users often experience relaxation and altered perception of sights, sounds and tastes. One of pot's commonest side effects is the "munchies"—a craving for snacks, especially sugary ones. Participants in a study at Johns Hopkins ate more snacks—and consumed more calories per day—while they had access to marijuana in a social situation.

The high can be subtle and somewhat controllable, and intoxicated users can seem sober to themselves and

others. But this *feeling* of sobriety is one of pot's greatest risks to well-being. Hours after the sensation of being stoned is over, the drug can still impair psychomotor performance.

The user's coordination, visual perceptions, reaction time and vigilance are reduced, which can make it dangerous to drive, fly or operate machinery. In a study done at Stanford University, simulated tests of pilots' skills showed they were affected for up to 24 hours after smoking, although they felt sober and competent. Another California study showed that a third of the drivers in fatal car crashes had been smoking marijuana. Driving under the influence of pot may be especially dangerous, because the driver may not know when his ability to function is askew.

Short-term memory and learning ability are also curtailed for hours after smoking. This delayed effect could be a serious problem for students, especially frequent smokers. Because the duration and extent of marijuana's psychomotor effects are not known for sure, the practice of testing urine to determine workers' competence is very controversial. "For the first two to four hours, say, on a Saturday night, the drug decreases one's ability to think, drive and work," says Dr. Reese Jones, a drug researcher and professor of psychiatry at the University of California, San Francisco. "But it's yet to be determined if those effects are still present on Monday morning."

Dr. Robert Millman, director of the alcohol and drug abuse service of the New York Hospital-Payne Whitney Clinic, agrees. "Most of the urine screenings that test positive for drugs

Medical Benefits?

Marijuana may have some medical uses, but it's no wonder drug.

Marijuana can be a useful medicine, but it's no wonder drug. People have used it for 5,000 years to assuage a variety of complaints, most recently in the effort to help treat glaucoma, asthma, spasticity, seizures and certain other nervous system irregularities, as well as the nausea that accompanies chemotherapy. In fact, doctors can now legally prescribe THC, pot's most active ingredient—usually in a capsule marketed as Marinol—for chemo patients.

However, marijuana has not proved itself to be superior to other drugs for most patients. So far, it's just an alternative that may work better for certain people. Many scientists doubt it will ever be a truly significant addition to the pharmacopeia. Its action is neither potent nor focused enough to produce the predictable, clear, isolated effects of first-class drugs. Moreover, the intoxication it causes often makes THC medication undesirable.

On the other hand, marijuana does have limited but documented medical potential. With further research, its components could be teased apart. Those that produce the desired effects—say, the suppression of vomiting or relaxation of muscles—could be isolated, and the rest, causing euphoria and sedation, could be eliminated. Its remedial action is sometimes different from that of standard drugs, which could point pharmacologists to new research directions—one reason scientists are dismayed over the reduction of research funds.

man Zinberg, author of *Drug, Set, and Setting* (Yale University Press, $10.95), studied a group of marijuana smokers, he concluded that "essentially, marijuana doesn't cause psychological problems for the occasional user." Many of his colleagues agree. Most of Zinberg's subjects described the drug as not particularly deleterious to normal functioning, and difficult (though not impossible) to abuse; they tended to restrict smoking to leisure time and special occasions, often planned around food.

Deadheads & Other Potheads

The researchers' consensus on long-term heavy marijuana smokers is bleaker, although hard data are more elusive than those on the drug's acute effects. For the vast majority of users, pot isn't physically addictive. It ranks far below drugs such as cocaine and heroin—or alcohol and tobacco—in inviting compulsive use. Nonetheless, a significant number of smokers use the drug frequently, often daily. Such regular use is one of the most obvious signs of a serious marijuana problem; heavy daily smokers are usually at least a bit out of it (see "Signs of Trouble").

Being out of it is less noticeable in the countries where the three large field studies of chronic users were conducted than in the fast-paced United States. Marijuana is widely accepted in Jamaica and Costa Rica, and within certain subcultures in Greece. These studies found that pot smokers were by and large as healthy—and functioned as well—as nonsmokers. However, although these surveys didn't prove any major, permanent health consequences of long-term pot use, that doesn't mean there aren't any. Researchers caution that the subjects of these studies were mostly poorly educated, working-class adults who have lower standards for produc-

pick up signs of pot—a very widely used drug," he says. "Companies are confused about what to do—should they fire everybody?"

Evaluating marijuana's impact on mental ability is difficult, but gauging its effects on emotional health is even more so. Responses are subjective and unpredictable. Marijuana is often associated with a feeling of mellowness, but it causes anxiety as well. It might make one user drowsy, and another—or the same user on a different occasion—hyperactive. One smoker becomes chatty, another withdrawn.

The strength of the drug, frequency of use, and physiological differences among users—for example, in body size and neural sensitivity to the drug—help account for the wide range of reactions. "About a third of people who smoke it feel no effects, a third feel ill and a third feel high," says Dr. Renaud Trouvé, a drug researcher and assistant professor of anesthesiology at Columbia-Presbyterian Medical School in New York.

What Timothy Leary and others called "set and setting"—the mental state of the user and the environment in which the drug is taken—also plays a part in emotional reactions to marijuana. According to Millman, many people now in middle age found smoking pot relaxing as youths within the laid-back '60s counterculture. As they've increased in age, power and responsibility, they've tuned out, turned off and dropped in.

"There's a natural history to marijuana use," he says. "The baby boomers have acquired a sense of their vulnerability and of the finiteness of time—'This is my life we're talking about!'" he says. "Feeling lethargic and giving up control make them anxious now."

That fear of losing control, or even one's mind, can induce paranoia and anxiety—pot's commonest unpleasant side effects—in people who would not have had these problems if they hadn't taken the drug, according to Millman. Moreover, he says, "marijuana can open a door to psychosis in predisposed persons similar to the action of many hallucinogens like LSD." Many doctors suspect that in these rare instances of users losing touch with reality, the drug has simply activated a latent psychiatric problem. Because of marijuana's potential for stirring up the psyche, psychiatrists say those with pre-existing disorders should stay away from it.

However, after Harvard's Dr. Nor-

tivity and health than middle-class Americans. And it took decades, not years, to determine the serious risks now known to be associated with alcohol and tobacco.

For those who look on pot as a buffer against stress, so-called "self-medication" can be dangerous: The person who smokes in an effort to "treat" his depression, anxiety or personality quirks may only add to his trouble. The psychological problem most often associated with chronic marijuana smoking is the "amotivational syndrome." Those thought to have it—many of them teens and young adults—show diminished goal-orientation, passivity and an inability to master new problems. However, the syndrome poses a chicken-or-egg question: Does heavy pot use cause poor motivation, or vice versa?

New York Hospital's Millman prefers the term "aberrant motivation" to describe the inert attitude of some heavy smokers. "When parents arrive at my office with a son in a ponytail and a tie-dyed shirt, they don't have to say a word. The kid is abusing drugs and doing badly in school and at home—but somehow he can get himself to a Grateful Dead concert in Ohio with $7 in his pocket. He doesn't lack motivation, he's just focusing it in the wrong direction."

Millman, who thinks such flawed motivation is caused by the combination of pot and pre-existing psychological problems, has found that some adolescents smoke grass not only to escape from their troubles, but to explain them. Such self-handicapping protects their egos against feelings of failure. "Many of the kids I see have made pot smoking the rationalization for psychopathology—they and their peers can say they act weird because of dope, rather than because they have an untreated learning disability or an emotional disorder," he says.

Some teens smoke to give themselves an excuse for failure.

Children and teenagers are endangered by any drug, because their bodies and minds—especially their judgment—are immature. A study of middle-class adolescents dependent on marijuana, reported in the May 1987 issue of the journal *Clinical Pediatrics*, helped identify those who may be at highest risk from the drug. Many were learning-disabled, had family histories of alcoholism, and personal and academic problems. Their parents and in some cases therapists hadn't suspected their pot smoking for a year after they started, perhaps because other problems may have disguised the drug use.

The connection between pot, poor motivation and learning disabilities is particularly troubling in an era when 28% of students drop out of high school. The sedation, skewed psychomotor functioning and involvement with other drugs and drug-abusing peers associated with marijuana make any use by teens unwise. A kid who tries pot also has an estimated 10% risk of becoming a daily smoker—and frequent use, at this age, can become truly disastrous.

Revving Up the Heart

Proof of the physical risks of marijuana is as elusive as proof of its dangers to the mind. The lack of comprehensive long-term human studies and the limits of animal research frustrate scientists like Renaud Trouvé. He's convinced that marijuana stresses the heart, lungs and immune and endocrine systems, particularly when it's used frequently. "As for the short-term physiological effects of marijuana, one can believe what is written," he says. "As for the long-term effects, we just don't know."

For example, it seems reasonable that pot smoking would be bad for the lungs. Marijuana contains more tar and carcinogens than tobacco and is inhaled longer and harder. But while heavy users do show a measurable airway obstruction and seem more prone to bronchitis and sinusitis, no links to serious lung diseases like cancer or emphysema have been established. In

Marijuana has more carcinogens than tobacco does.

fact, perhaps the worst threat to the lungs of pot smokers is the herbicide paraquat, which was sprayed widely on marijuana fields, especially in Mexico. The use of the chemical, which can cause severe lung damage, has been discontinued, although it's being considered as a way to deter growers in California and Hawaii.

The effects of marijuana on the reproductive system also seem ominous, but remain unproved. The drug temporarily lowers the level of the sex hormone testosterone in men, and decreases the number, quality and motility of sperm, but the impact on fertility is unknown. However, testosterone also helps govern puberty's changes in boys. Some researchers think that low levels of the hormone could impair adolescent development.

Women who smoke heavily may experience menstrual irregularities, including a failure to ovulate. When pregnant monkeys, rats or mice are exposed to heavy doses of pot, their offspring are more likely to have a low birth weight or to be stillborn. There's no clear proof that marijuana causes birth defects, but doctors urge pregnant and nursing women to treat pot with the same caution they give to alcohol and tobacco.

Similarly grim but inconclusive observations suggest that marijuana use can adversely affect other organs and systems in the body. Some researchers have found that marijuana can cause microscopic brain-cell damage in monkeys—but human brain damage hasn't been shown. Some studies suggest that marijuana can suppress immune function to some extent, but scientists don't yet know whether that degree of dysfunction affects health. What's more, marijuana increases the heart rate by as much as 90 beats per minute. This added workload could be very dangerous for those with cardiovascular disorders such as angina, but

Pot can change sex hormone levels, for men and for women both.

▬▬▬▬▬▬

there's no evidence that it causes any permanent harm to healthy hearts.

Toward a Sound Pot Policy

What state-of-the-art marijuana research tells experts is that we need to know more. In 1982, the Institute of Medicine published "Marijuana and Health," a 188-page report based on solid research and compiled by a committee of 21 scientists. Its conclusion, echoed by many marijuana researchers today: "Marijuana has a broad range of psychological and biological effects, some of which, at least under certain conditions, are harmful to human health. Unfortunately, the available information does not tell us how serious this risk may be."

The uncertainty that surrounds marijuana use is compounded when it's compared to the nation's other drugs—both legal and illegal. Despite increasing decriminalization and public tolerance of pot, half of all drug arrests made by local police in 1985—almost 500,000—involved marijuana, according to *The New York Times*. Many citizens consider this police enforcement an inappropriate use of resources that could be used to fight the greater menace of deadly drugs like heroin and cocaine—or, for that matter, tobacco and alcohol, which cause hundreds of thousands of deaths each year.

It's unlikely that either of these two legal, lethal drugs would be lawful if they were discovered today. "The light use of marijuana is certainly not as bad for you physically as alcohol or tobacco," says Harvard's Zinberg. "Our drug policy is based on morals, not on health considerations. The person with a drink in his hand says to himself, 'I'm bad enough, but that guy smoking pot over there is worse.'"

Zinberg says the best approach toward a sound policy on marijuana would be continued decriminalization accompanied by 15 years of serious long-term research. By then, the public would have enough information to make personal choices and public policy decisions. Reese Jones believes

We need more money for basic research, not for drug testing.

▬▬▬▬▬▬

that, regardless of policy changes, marijuana's popularity may gradually die out as the group of heavy users ages.

The one point on which all those concerned with marijuana agree is that having so little knowledge of the drug is a dangerous thing. Despite its prevalence and the unanswered questions about its use, federal support for marijuana research, still in its infancy, has decreased— diverted to less-used but "hotter" drugs like cocaine. "I'm a researcher with conservative views on drug use who hasn't found the hard data on the health effects of marijuana," says Jones. "There's a lot of uncertainty about it—you can't say it's unsafe, but there's no proof it's benign, either. We should be studying it to find out, but all the research money is going to help figure out how to detect it in people's urine instead."

SPEED: THE CHOICE OF A NEW GENERATION

Stanley Young

When the phone rings in the middle of the night, you just answer it.

"I heard you wanted to talk about speed and stuff . . . " In the background a talk-fest party is going full-bore.

"Sure." I reply. "But couldn't you phone back in the daytime? After all—it's 3:30 in the morning."

"Sure it's 3:30 in the morning. That's the whole *point* of it, isn't it?"

Party hearty America. Speed is back. Taste it again for the very first time. These days in selected areas of the country—mostly the West Coast, Hawaii and Texas—methamphetamine or "crystal," "crank," "zip," "chris" or "meth," or "crystal meth" as it's known on the street—is the definite choice of a new generation. Catch the wave, but as always, watch out for that rip tide. The stuff still kills.

To those who went through the drugged-out 60s, the notion that speed is coming back always brings a wry smile, as if bell-bottoms and beads were right around the corner. In fact, speed has never gone out of fashion. A national opinion poll last summer indicated that of all drugs ever used recreationally, speed is second only to pot, a few points ahead of cocaine. But coke got the media coverage, and speed didn't. Speed isn't collected by barefoot peasants on Andean mountainsides, nor has it been used by Gucci-garbed dudes in high rise condos. Speed is snorted and popped mostly by white working-class guys and gals to help them get through a day of manual or boring labor. Then they use it on weekends to rock and roll. The people using it were just never glamorous or exciting enough to make speed news.

Now it is. Students at USC cramming for finals use it, high-desert cowboys mixing crank with beer and booze use it, and jaded Hollywood teens use it, adding a quarter-tab of LSD to their drug cocktail.

"I started out at 8 o'clock on Friday night," said a 21-year-old user after a weekend binge. Miss X, as she likes to be called, holds a steady job as a secretary. She is bright, well-read, and has been using speed since she was 13. "I did some crystal, around $10 worth, then a friend came over and we did four more lines of speed. I topped that with a quarter-hit of LSD. When we got back to my house about 2:00 in the morning, we did another quarter-hit of acid, then a big line of crystal, and of course, some beer. We were hoping to have some pot, but it never showed. We were having a really fun time, but I think we were majorly more affected by the LSD. We stayed up until about 3:00 in the afternoon the next day. I would have been able to stay up longer, but my jaw was starting to get very tight, my nerves were on fire. It was the GRIND, you know."

"In the last nine months, I started to use it again," says Lucy, another 21-year-old from the San Fernando Valley. "It used to be just me and a friend doing it. But now, there's a whole world of people out there that do this drug. A WHOLE WORLD!"

The statistics bear her out. Even though the numbers tend to lag behind what is really going on in the streets, there is more than a trend going on. Surge is more like it. Last year 810 clandestine labs that "cook" meth were seized nationwide, an increase of almost 100 percent over the previous year. In Los Angeles county, drug seizures of crystal meth in the last three years were up 131 percent over the previous three years. Emergency room cases in 1987 were up 100 percent over 1985: In Dallas, the numbers went from 69 to 492, and in San Diego, from 85 to over 800—a 10-fold increase.

If the use of meth in San Diego is a sign of things to come across the country, be prepared to see crank replace crack as the drug problem of the 1990s. Half of those currently in San Diego County drug rehab facilities were strung out on meth, and one out of every three prisoners booked into the county's

ling of the drug industry. Ephedrine, the naturally-occurring base of speed, had been used medicinally by the Chinese for centuries to help lung congestion and lower fever. When supplies of ephedrine dwindled in the 1920s, Gordon Alles, a young research chemist in Los Angeles, recreated a forgotten synthetic reproduction of ephedrine from 1887. Alles, who tried the new drug on himself, realized that it did a lot more than open up congested bronchial passages: it had the power to alleviate fatigue and create euphoric confidence and alertness.

Biochemically, speed mimics the effects of adrenaline on the body, which sets the brain and the whole body humming, ready for action. Amphetamines produce the same result by inhibiting the "reuptake" of the brain's hormones across the junctions of the nerve endings and the brain cells. As a result, the receptor cells in the brain continue to fire randomly, somewhat like a flash bulb that can't turn itself off. This constant stimulation allows the body to release stored energy.

"We would snort, have a cocktail with friends, go to a party, cop a half a gram and drink some more booze. Then, you know, you're happening. You're cruising."

prisons have methamphetamine "on board" (in their urine samples) when they're booked, the highest percentage in the country. Four out of 10 homicides in the county and almost half of the crisis intervention calls are meth-related. "In San Diego County methamphetamine use is just so pervasive, epidemic doesn't quite go far enough to tell you the dimensions of the problem," says Ron d'Ulisse, who works with the DEA in San Diego County. "It's borderline horrible. There isn't an economic group that is not impacted by this drug. We've seen it distributed down into the elementary schools, K through 6, among affluent people, poor people, in the inland desert and along the beach."

These new populations now using crank are unusual. Previously speed was always known as the poor man's cocaine. "If you want to have a good time on speed, then a quarter [gram] will last you a whole weekend," says Lucy. "That's about 25 bucks. Cocaine, man, for that money, it wouldn't last you two hours, and you'll be dying for more. One line of crystal keep you up all night. It's very potent shit." And if there's long, hard or boring work to do, speed, again, is the choice over coke. Says one recovering addict: "On coke you can slam every 30 to 40 minutes. But on good crystal, you do it once and you're good for a day and a half. Everybody I worked with carried little vials of crystal about with them, although they weren't shooting it like me. With them it was more a snorting trip." Speed is the Ollie North of drugs, a pure "can-do" substance, even if it, like the good Marine, had to go beyond the law to do it.

Amphetamines were not always illegal (now they're classified as "dangerous drugs" along with PCP, LSD and synthetic heroin). When they first came out in the early 1930s, amphetamines were the dar-

Speed produces none of its own energy. That's why people "crash" on speed, sometimes sleeping for days on end recovering from a lengthy binge. That's why they feel tapped-out when they wake up after crashing: they've been running on fumes for days.

Back in the 30s, the inner workings of amphetamines were not understood. What was understood was the commercial applications of this new zippy drug. At first, amphetamine was only available in a volatile form, so a device for breathing the stuff was created, and by 1932, Smith Kline and French laboratories had scooped up Alles's patent and was producing the Benzedrine Inhaler. (As late as 1966 Dristan contained 250 mg. of mephentermine, a relative of methamphetamine but only about one-third as potent.) Within a few years, Benzedrine was available in a solid pill form, and amphetamines (Alpha-Methyl-beta-PHenyl-EThyl-AMINE) were a part of American culture.

Even now, the Army is reported to be searching for a viable form of amphetamine to give its ground troops in the event of extended maneuvers, so the lure for speed remains, even among official circles. To this day, the drug is still prescribed legally, mostly for obesity.

The drug company convinced the medical establishment that this new wonder pick-me-up drug had all sorts of useful applications, and got the immediate and official O.K. of the AMA. Studies were conducted, but they all ignored or denied the possibility of adverse effects. Ironically, this was the depths of the Depression years, and the country needed any kind of pick-me-up available. Within months, "purple hearts" were available on the black market and people were stuffing them down by the handful if they wanted to stay up all night and dance. Speed was the

perfect drug for doing boring repetitive tasks for long periods of time—a perfect description of life in the Army.

When World War II broke out, amphetamines were willingly handed out to soldiers and airmen who needed to stay up for long periods of time. Meanwhile, the Germans were using an even more potent isomer of speed—methamphetamine—and we now know that all the Panzer Divisions of the Wehrmacht were constantly stoked on the drug. Hitler got intravenous injections of methamphetamine, and his later paranoid delusions and bizarre conduct are now considered to be a direct consequence of the drug, making der Führer one of the first speed freaks.

After the war, enormous surplus amounts previously earmarked for the military flooded the civilian markets. Japan's postwar reconstruction was fueled by speed, until they realized that too much of the drug turned people weird and regulated amphetamine use in the early 1950s. (To this day, the Japanese have a major amphetamine abuse problem.) Scandinavia was a hotbed of its abuse, and in America speed simply became a part of the normal psychopharmacological landscape.

Truck drivers popped "bennies" to stay awake; millions of housewives lined up at their doctors to get new prescriptions for their "diet pills." There was some concern about odd side effects, such as paranoia and violent behavior, but they were discounted. The drug companies were making a fortune, churning out amphetamines under dozens of different names (Dietamine, Racephen, Ritalin) but the nation that was diddy-bopping along on speed at the time knew them by their street names: Black Beauties, Big Cross-Tops and Little Whites. The drug was everywhere. Rumor has it that JFK got intravenous shots of methamphetamine right in the Oval Office when he had to stay up and perform at peak levels for long periods of time.

Then came the 60s. A subculture of drug users who used speed almost exclusively—popping it or shooting it—developed, and began to evince all the symptoms we now associate with classic amphetamine abuse. These wild-eyed, manic burnout cases would blither on endlessly, rip off anything not welded in place, then go into fits of erratic and violent behavior. Welcome the speed freak. They were shunned by other sorts of drug users, and ended up congregating with the only segment of the population who could stomach their company—other speed freaks.

Speed literally spelled the end of the age of Flower Power. Speed and love, it seems, are absolutely incompatible, and when the bohunk amphetamine freaks invaded the Haight, the Summer of Love turned into the long and discontented Winter of Speed. Among the baby-boomers who came of age during the Sixties and watched the destructive effects of amphetamines, speed has never lost its opprobrium. Nevertheless there was still a large and willing population pool for its use. Speed settled into its low-media profile and continued to be used regularly, mostly by lower-class whites.

That might explain why Hell's Angels and other outlaw biker clubs have always been intimately entwined in the illegal production and distribution of speed. "I was already doing speed when I hooked up with a guy from Hell's Angels," says Marki, now off crank for good. "They have factories all over the place. They drink all the time, and they snort speed, but never fix it. That's 'cause bikers never put needles in their bodies; it's like a law of the land." Marki remembers how there was never a lot of dealing out of the house. "Nobody sat around dealing small amounts, or selling it off the corners or around schools. They had a very business-like approach, and they had it well set up. They'd just go off to other places and come back with it. They never, never took the women along." Once the shipment was moved, they'd keep only as much as they needed for their personal use—a quantity that could be flushed down the toilet in case of a bust.

Some say that the outlaw biker gangs held a franchise on the drug: others prefer the term "stranglehold." "There was a case down in Victorville," recalls Ralph Lochridge, a DEA agent in Los Angeles. "Hell's Angels had fronted a guy about a quarter-pound of crank which he was supposed to take down to San Diego." The runner and his girlfriend used all the drug themselves. "The Hell's Angels hunted him down and shot him to death in his pickup truck. That's not untypical: they're pretty ruthless. And they have to be: speeders are dangerous types."

The FBI has been targeting outlaw biker gangs up and down the West Coast with some success, as part of their organized-crime-busting unit. One recent bust, "Operation *Cacus*," resulted in the arrest of 38 Hell's Angels, seizures of $3.5 million in cash, 25 pounds of gold and 40 pounds of methamphetamine. Other clubs have been implicated in the trade as well: the Ghost Riders, the Bandidos and the Gypsy Jokers.

When the Hell's Angels controlled things, the traffic in crystal was steady and predictable: there was some order to the operation. "The upside of having the Hell's Angels controlling the market is that their product was relatively safe," says Lochridge. "They pretty much kept the supply and demand in tune."

But the FBI's intrusion into the biker's distribution system may actually have helped produce the recent rise in the quantity of speed available on the West Coast. With the bikers' stranglehold loosened there was an explosion of Mom and Pop labs. Everybody with a stove, a pot and more than a little larceny in their heart started cranking out crank.

San Diego, the worst hit by this methamphetamine amateur hour, plays an important role in its genesis. In 1981, California regulated the sale of phenyl acetic acid, one of methamphetamine's precursor chemicals. As a consequence, producers rediscovered a long-forgotten method of making methamphetamine—the ephedrine reduction process. Previously, cooking up the crank had required a modicum of chemistry expertise: measuring, distilling and reducing in a multi-stage operation. The new process was made for bone heads. "All it requires is a few ingredients thrown together for any period of time, cooked at any temperature and the end result is methamphetamine," says d'Ulisse. "At the same time, a number of companies established themselves in the San Diego area and sold everything necessary to manufacture the drug." Clandestine labs bloomed everywhere under the clear San Diego skies and meth flooded the streets. "They had no sophisticated distribution system. They just dumped everything into the county."

At present there's enough crank produced every month in San Diego to keep every man, woman and child in the county fried from now to Christmas.

Elsewhere up and down the West Coast, and in Texas, amateur production continues to grow. Crank has become the moonshine of the Information Age, and there's always another, newer process just around the corner. "The underground chemists are always ahead of us. Always," says Robert Sager, in charge of the DEA labs in San Francisco. "They've got the motivation and the time. And the money."

Money makes the drug world go 'round, and is the major reason for the sudden popularity of speed. Whereas a pound of cocaine now costs about eight grand, for a simple five grand you can set up a clandestine lab and turn out a few pounds of meth on your own. Even if you only produce a few pounds, at $8,000 to $10,000 a pound, you're getting a good return on your five-grand investment. That means that even if the new Drug Czar, and the entire constellation of Customs, Treasury, DEA, FDA, FBI, Army and the Coast Guard are able to seal off every inch of the border and coastline as tight as a tamperproof seal, there would *still* be a massive drug problem in America. And no foreign government to blame, either.

"With crank you can make $50,000 in no time at all," says Lochridge of the DEA, "and you don't have to deal with Colombians. You don't have to deal with anyone, except the law. And the Hell's Angels." At least the Angels are American. In fact this whole underground crank industry is 100-percent American.

Most of the labs these days are set in remote areas to hide the smell. The acrid and pungent odor of a crank lab is noticeable even at a distance from the lab, and the chemicals used permeate fabrics and skin. "That's the main thing that gives them up, the smell, the neighbors," says DEA Agent J.

A lot of times, especially in the Northwest, "cooks" will make the stuff around a barn full of cows or pigs to try to mask the stench. Out in the high desert area preferred by the LA cooks, elaborate setups will filter the gases through cat litter, or send it through underground pipes away from the lab. While they may be easy to sniff out, staking out a crank lab has a distinct disadvantage: most of the cooks use the product they're making.

"A lot of the cooks are junkies," says J. "They do the speed themselves. That's the problem with doing surveillance on these guys. They're all wired up so they can stay awake for two or three days without being bothered, and we're out there just trying to keep our eyes open, drinking coffee." Having to spend days on a stakeout in a cold car in some god-forsaken part of the high desert might explain why a heavy growth of beard, a T-shirt and jeans is acceptable dress for members of the Clandestine Lab Unit. In fact, except for the two government-issue .38s strapped to his side in well-burnished leather holsters, Agent J looks a little like a biker-type himself.

Last year on the West Coast, clandestine labs were being busted at the rate of about 40 a month, and 96 percent of them were manufacturing crank. Some of the operations were industrial in size—one lab caught *in flagrante delicto* last year was producing 150 pounds in a SINGLE REACTION. The average lab, however, produces 23 pounds a week. Even at low street values for single pounds, this is about $25,000 of product a day.

The methamphetamine that these crank labs produce varies widely in quality. "I've seen stuff that was as gooey as peanut butter," says Sager. "That's what they called it up in Oregon: peanut butter crank." If the cooks are using the older amalgam process, the meth can be laced with mercury. Sometimes lead acetate can be left in the speed as a residue. In short, users can't really be one-hundred-percent sure of the street product. "They're really up against it," notes Sager. "A lab will only tell them they've got meth; it won't tell them if there is a also a small amount of deadly contaminants." Sager has also been getting reports from Colorado and Hawaii about users smoking crystal meth, and there is talk on the street about the latest twist, "croak," a mixture of crank and coke, also smoked.

Sometimes the low-end of these amateur cooks will only produce a few grams for personal use, usually out of rented motel rooms. Since the 'cleaning,' or final finishing of crank uses benzene, a highly explosive (and carcinogenic) product, it is not rare for these would-be chemists to blow up their rented accommodations. Things got so bad in the Northwest last year that the Oregon Lodging Association and the Portland area motel managers met last February for the sole purpose of discussing how to deal with methamphetamine labs in motel rooms.

Meanwhile, busting the larger labs has its own dangers. "A lot of times we'll be going into an explosive

Hitler's paranoid delusions and bizarre conduct are now considered to be a direct consequence of meth, making der Führer one of the first speed freaks.

situation. Literally," says J. Combine the sort of paranoia that extended speed use engenders, the constant pressure to remain secret, and the presence of millions of dollars worth of illegal drugs, and many of the labs resemble armed camps. "We're finding that about half of them are booby-trapped one way or another; either explosives—time bombs—or two chemicals set behind the door which make cyanide gas when mixed." Sometimes a cook will kick over a flask of ether going out of a window. When the fumes hit a naked flame, the whole operation blows sky high. Then federal agents garbed in white hazardous material suits have to come in to put together the evidence. Given the setting and the danger, lab busting is sometimes straight out of the movies: plastic explosives going off, arrays of AK-47s, Uzis and sawed-off shotguns, agents dropping out of the desert sky.

Despite the success the lab busters are having, the fact still remains that, at best, for every crank lab that's toppled at least five go undetected. That's a lot of crank.

Most of it is used in conjunction with other drugs. "In the beginning it was just more social," says Diane, a recovering crystal addict in her late 20s who comes from a well-to-do family in Los Angeles. "We would snort, have a cocktail with friends, go to a party, cop a half a gram and drink some more booze. Then, you know, you're happening. You're cruising." That's how most people start up. In the social scene, the cool setting, the clubs. "As time goes on, you're cruising a little more. And then—we don't go *anywhere*. We just stay at home. It progresses into that state where you don't want to share, where you don't want to do anything and you're totally living for the drug."

Not everybody gets to that stage, but the steps along the way are insidious. "You build a tolerance to it," says Derek, who works as a carpenter in the Hollywood studios, and now a recovering addict. "You get up in the morning, you take a couple of whites, throw 'em in your coffee. That goes on for a month of two, and pretty soon, it's not the same 'oomph.' So you put four in, then five, then 10. Then someone says, 'Why are you taking all those pills, man? Why don't you just do a couple of lines of this?' You do a couple of lines, and your nose is bleeding, and you say, 'I'm snorting this shit but it's just not working.' Then someone comes up and says, 'Hey, I got an outfit right here, buddy. This'll fix it all. . . .' And it does."

Shooting crystal is a completely different high from snorting it. "You want to shoot up as much as you can," says Ellen, who's has since cleaned up her act. "It's a mental rush, your head starts tingling. You feel like you're on another planet, and for those few minutes you feel like there's nothing happening, like there's nothing going on. It's four or five minutes before you actually get into the grit-your-teeth, bite-your-cheek speed feeling." Then you're up for days. "It just gets worse and worse. You need sleep and you can't. You don't eat 'cause you can't."

Speed makes you active. You want to do something, anything. But after days without sleep, you start "tweaking." "I'd start by cleaning my house, then I'd find something, pull it out, and figure I'd clean it up later," says Betty, a recovering crystal user. "By the end of the night the place was a disaster area." Obsessive behavior is typical of speeders. Diane, an LA artist, remembers coming home to discover her roommate had pulled out every hair of her eyebrows with a pair of tweezers. "You do shit that you just do when you're tweaking," says Derek. "One time I smoked a pencil and thought it was a cigarette."

After continuous lack of sleep, the drug's psychosis-forming powers come alive and present you with panoply of paranoid hallucinations straight out of Elm Street: spiders on the wall, bugs crawling under your skin which you dig at with a knife. And then there's the constant companion of paranoia—the ever-present knowledge that *everyone* is out to get you. "No matter where I looked, someone was there," wrote William Burroughs Jr. in his 1974 autobiographical novel *Speed*. "Tiny people slept in my ashtray and a giant slouched, sulking, against the Chrysler building. The trees in Washington Square were filled with faces from the past that blew in the breeze. In the mirror my own face crawled with a dozen others. I myself labored under the illusion that I had died weeks ago at 1,000 mph ta ra! ta ra! and was running headlong on accumulating momentum into the approaching Fall." Burroughs Jr. died at 33, in 1981.

Not everybody who uses speed gets to the inner circle of hell. Obviously. Some people can handle it. Others can't. Most users are able to maintain a sporadic intake of the drug, going on occasional binges, then sleeping it off. The problem is, even for those who think they can handle it, using speed is like sucking on a candy bar with razor blades inside. The drug gives you energy by borrowing off your future reserves. Pretty soon, that future arrives, you're running on a deficit, so you go to the energy bank and borrow from speed again.

Like America going begging to foreign lenders for hard cash, speed-freaks hit the sidewalk to cop some crank to help them get through their own energy-debt crisis. Pretty soon, you're under foreign ownership, and the drug is telling you what to do. "If you're with some guy who has a bag, believe me, you're going to do what you have to do to get some," says Diane. "You'll just do it."

"Speed is the perfect drug for people who feel dumb and inadequate," says psychologist Bill Cloke. "It replaces feeling of anxiety or fear or boredom with elements of excitement and drama. It takes care of performance anxiety, and covers a whole range of self-doubt and inadequacy." Users agree. "You feel like you're on top of it, like you're better," says Jane. "I like crystal. It just gives you a feeling that you're IT."

Speed is the product of the technological society and fits perfectly into its ethos. It's the Protestant work ethic in crystal form. Speed just says "Go!" When you're on it you feel good, you feel like doing, creating, working. Time flies and soul-numbing repetitive activities—working on assembly lines, checking out groceries—become bearable.

The new generation that is turning to speed lives in an America which has lost its dream: they can't afford the houses they grew up in; they live in a world of increasing environmental despair; and watch a government totally lacking in wisdom or ethical leadership. The whole country feels dumb and inadequate, so why shouldn't some poor soul who's struggling to make the rent and the payments on his 4x4 use? Speed makes you feel good about yourself, makes you feel in control, even if those feelings are ephemeral and ultimately false. Speed is the drug that helps you move faster, running not so much to a better future as away from a dreary present. The same society that produced the drug in the first place now also creates the conditions that engender its use. And yet another generation will reap the bitter chemical harvest of those amphetamine seeds.

Steroids and Sports
Are a Losing Proposition

Raja Mishra

Raja Mishra is a sophomore at the University of Maryland at College Park. He wrote this during a summer internship with FDA's Office of Public Affairs.

Ben Johnson, the Canadian sprinter, expected the 1988 Summer Olympics in Seoul, South Korea, to be the zenith of his track and field career. He would compete against his arch-rival, American sprinter Carl Lewis, in the event that was his specialty: the 100-meter dash. When the starting pistol sounded, Johnson was off like a man possessed. He crossed the finish line victorious and became the toast of the athletic world, as well as a hero to his fellow Canadians. The next morning, however, events took a 180-degree turn. Johnson became the shame of his country, and his cherished gold medal was stripped. Tests revealed that he used steroids.

* * * * *

A 23-year-old bodybuilder, complaining of severe groin pains, was taken to the hospital. Doctors found his liver and kidneys had stopped working. He was immediately rushed to the intensive-care unit. Four days later, he died when his heart stopped. His autopsy revealed that he was a steroid abuser.

* * * * *

While preparing for his prom night, a high school senior drank a "health formula," which he had been taking for some time to increase muscle and reduce fat. His evening of romance was never to be. Twenty minutes after drinking the formula, which contained GHB (an illegal drug promoted as an anabolic steroid alternative), he lapsed into a coma. His parents found him sprawled on the floor and rushed him to the hospital. Doctors said if he had been found half an hour later, he probably would have died.

* * * * *

These three cases, though different, all involve the illegal use of anabolic steroids or similar "performance-enhancing" drugs.

What exactly are these drugs that have damaged so many lives?

Steroids are a synthetic version of the human hormone called testosterone. Testosterone stimulates and maintains the male sexual organs. It also stimulates development of bones and muscle, promotes skin and hair growth, and can influence emotions. In males, testosterone is produced by the testes and the adrenal gland. Women have only the amount of testosterone produced by the adrenal gland—much less than men have. This is why testosterone is often called a "male" hormone.

The average adult male naturally produces 2.5 to 11 milligrams of testosterone daily. The average steroid abuser often takes more than 100 mg a day, through "stacking" or combining several different brands of steroids.

Researchers first developed steroids in the 1930s to rebuild and prevent the breakdown of body tissues from disease.

The controversy surrounding steroids began in the 1950s during the Olympic Games when the athletic community discovered that athletes from Russia and some East European nations, which had dominated the games, had taken large doses of steroids. Many of the male athletes developed such large prostate glands (a gland located near the bladder and urethra that aids in semen production) that they needed a tube inserted in order to urinate. Some of the female athletes developed so many male characteristics, chromosome tests were necessary to prove that they were still women.

Even though the side effects of steroid abuse had become known, the demand for them increased in the athletic community. Since then, the sale of steroids has ballooned into a $100-million-a-year black market.

Dangers Abound

Steroids fool the body into thinking that testosterone is being produced. The body, sensing an excess of testosterone, shuts down bodily functions involving testosterone, such as bone growth. The ends of long bones fuse together and stop growing, resulting in stunted growth. Steroid abuse has many dangerous side effects (see box).

Adding to the danger is the way some steroids are manufactured and distributed. The drugs are often made in motel rooms and warehouses in Mexico, Europe, and other countries and then smuggled into the United States. The potency, purity and strength of the steroids produced this way are not regulated, and therefore it is almost impossible for users to know how much they are taking. Counterfeit steroids are also sold as the real thing. So it's often impossible to tell exactly what some products contain.

New Trends

A new, alarming trend, is the use of other drugs to achieve the "performance-enhancing" effects of steroids. These steroid "alternatives" are sought in order to avoid the stiff penalties now in effect against those who possess anabolic steroids without a valid prescription. The two most common are gamma hydroxybutyrate (GHB) and clenbuterol.

GHB is a deadly, illegal drug that is a primary ingredient in many of these "performance-enhancing" formulas. The GHB that caused the prom night tragedy was marketed under the name "Somatomax PM." Rumors among teens that it caused a "high" increased the public health problems with GHB. In fact, the drug does not produce a high. It does, however, cause headaches, nausea, vomiting, diarrhea, seizures, and other central nervous system disorders, and, possibly, death.

Clenbuterol, another steroid "alternative," has become an extremely popular item on the black market. The drug is used in some countries for certain veterinary treatments, but is *not* approved for any use—in animals or humans—in the United States. In Spain, 135 people became ill with muscle tremors, fast heart rates, headaches, dizziness, nausea, fever, and chills after eating beef liver that contained residues of the drug.

"The lack of information about clenbuterol is its greatest hazard. Most of the research we do have is from humans who ingested the drug by eating meat from animals who had been administered it, but as far as ingestion straight into humans, much work needs to be done," says Donald Legget, a compliance officer with FDA's Center for Drug Evaluation and Research who deals with enforcement of laws against steroid distribution.

Why Does Anyone Use Them?

With so many harmful effects from steroids and similar illegal drugs, why do so many young people continue to use them?

One answer is social pressures. Many young men feel they need to look "masculine," that is, strong and muscular. Bodybuilding stresses such muscularity, and some men—and women—abuse anabolic steroids to increase muscle mass and definition.

And then there's the "winning isn't everything, it's the only thing" philosophy common in so many school athletic pro-

grams. Some student athletes feel so pressured to succeed in their respective sports that they resort to steroids for help.

Another reason, say many experts, lies in the basic nature of young people not

---

Steroids May Give You More Than You Bargained For

Established side effects and adverse reactions:

acne
genital changes
water retention in tissue
yellowing of eyes and skin
oily skin
stunted growth
fetal damage
coronary artery disease
sterility
liver tumors and disease
death
In women: male-pattern baldness, hairiness, voice deepening, decreased breast size, increased body hair, and menstrual irregularities

Other possible side effects and adverse reactions:

abdominal pains
hives
chills
euphoria
diarrhea
fatigue
fever
muscle cramps
headache
unexplained weight loss/gain
nausea and vomiting
vomiting blood
bone pains
depression
impotence
breast development in men
aggressive behavior
urination problems
sexual problems
gallstones
high blood pressure
kidney disease

to concern themselves with long-term effects. The desire to make the football team or to impress peers is much more immediate than the future prospect of possible damage to the liver, heart, and other vital organs.

In its effort to alert teenagers to the dangers of steroid abuse, FDA has developed a series of pamphlets, posters, and public service announcements. Recently, anabolic steroids were placed in the same regulatory category as cocaine, heroin, LSD, and other habit-forming drugs. This means that, in addition to FDA, the Drug Enforcement Agency helps to enforce laws relating to their abuse.

Celebrities like bodybuilding champs Arnold Schwarzenegger and Lee Haney and professional wrestler Jesse Ventura have spoken out against steroid use. Major magazines, ranging from *Newsweek* to *Muscle and Fitness*, have published articles warning of the dangers of steroid abuse.

The courts are handing down stiff sentences for people dealing in illegal steroids and similar drugs. Distributors have been sentenced to three to six years in jail and fined up to six figures. FDA, working with other law enforcement agencies, has made hundreds of arrests and broken up several large distribution and manufacturing rings.

Athletic organizations have joined the fight. The Olympic Games are now closely monitored to prevent athletes who use steroids from participating, as Ben Johnson found out. The National Football League has a strict testing policy in its training camps and hands down fines and suspensions for those who test positive, and bans for repeat offenders. The National Collegiate Athletic Association, too, has established stricter measures for testing and disciplining steroid users.

Although it may be true that in combination with intensive weight training and a high-calorie, high-protein diet, steroids can augment short-term muscle gain, teens need to ask themselves: Is it worth all the short-term health effects and the possibility of long-term, permanent damage? Is it worth the disgrace of being eliminated from competition, or even of being arrested?

After taking a long, hard look at the facts, most teens will realize that using drugs to boost athletic performance is a no-win situation.

Good drugs, bad effects

A prescription should not cause hallucinations, anxiety or fear. But many drugs do just that

Julie Radman of Chicago had been taking her prescription drugs for just a few weeks when her mother found her staring at the kitchen carving knives, hallucinating. A figure stood on one side, Radman recalls, urging her to kill herself; a second figure on the other side whispered reassurances that soon she would be all right.

Radman was taking neither Prozac nor Halcion, drugs that have made front page news recently for allegedly having driven some users to violence. (Halcion was banned in Great Britain earlier this month [October 1991].) Radman was on prednisone, a frequently prescribed steroid, to quiet the symptoms of inflammatory bowel disease, or Crohn's, along with a second drug to keep intestinal spasms at bay and a third to quench the inflammation in her colon. It was mainly the prednisone, doctors at Lutheran General Hospital later told Radman, that caused her hallucinations and suicidal thoughts six years ago. A synthetic version of the corticosteroid hormones produced by the body's adrenal glands, the drug had triggered steroid psychosis.

Radman injured no one and has long since recovered, and corticosteroids are still a first-line treatment for Crohn's because they are excellent anti-inflammatory drugs. But experts say that many doctors still do not warn patients about possible side effects, even though prednisone's psychotic episodes, mood-swing reactions and hallucinations are well documented and, to varying degrees, affect from 5 percent to 30 percent of adults taking the drug. Joan Telley of the Greater New York chapter of the Crohn's and Colitis Foundation of America, who has led support groups for six years, says many people who first learn about the problem at group meetings find that changing the dose or switching to another drug after consulting with a doctor often takes care of it.

Prednisone is hardly the only prescription drug that can cloud the mind unexpectedly. Drugs prescribed for heart disease, asthma, parkinsonism, arthritis and ulcers also can cause emotional problems. But rare is the doctor who raises the possibility before the prescription is filled. Many physicians worry that their patients may be too suggestible to hints of psychiatric side effects, and they may have a point. In one recent study in which patients unknowingly received a sugar placebo instead of a real medication, 14.1 percent said the sugar pill made them fatigued and 12.6 percent said it made them dizzy.

Blues aplenty. But cases like Radman's are not unique. Dizziness, for example, is a potential side effect of more than 1,000 prescription drugs, many of them quite common. It also is a symptom for which you would want to be alert—at least as much as, say, for the possibility of a drug-induced rash. Depression, a second example, is a recognized side effect of more than 300 drugs. Unless you know that, however, it is easy to blame your blues on

The drugs with the strongest punch

The drugs below produce psychiatric reactions ranging from anxiety to hallucinations in at least 3 percent of patients in one or more studies, as reported by the manufacturer. Tranquilizers and antidepressants were not considered, since their side effects are predictable. The list is alphabetical.

Drug *(manufacturer)*	Use	Side effects	Frequency/comments
Adrenalin Chloride Solution *(Parke-Davis)*	Respiratory distress, acute hay fever	Anxiety, fear	Common but transient
Duragesic Transdermal System *(Janssen Pharmaceutica)*	Skin patch for pain	Hallucinations	3%-10% of patients
Hylorel *(Fisons Corp.)*	Hypertension	Unspecified psychological problems	3.8%
Intron A *(Schering Corp.)*	Cancer, genital warts	Amnesia, depression	Up to 14% and 28% respectively
Lopressor tablets *(Geigy Pharmaceuticals)*	Heart, hypertension	Depression	5%
Lupron *(TAP Pharmaceuticals)*	Cancer	Memory disorder	Fewer than 5%
Octamide PFS *(Adria Laboratories)*	Diabetic gastrointestinal symptoms	Restlessness, fatigue, lassitude	10%
Permax tablets *(Lilly)*	Parkinson's disease	Hallucinations	13.8% of patients in controlled trials
Phenurone *(Abbott Laboratories)*	Epilepsy	Unspecified psychiatric disturbances	17%
Reglan *(A. H. Robins Co.)*	Acute heartburn	Restlessness, fatigue, lassitude	10%
Roferon-A *(Roche Labs)*	Cancer	Depression	16%
Tonocard tablets *(Merck Sharp & Dohme)*	Heart	Confusion, disorientation, hallucinations	2.1%-2.7% generally; 11.2% in a study of seriously ill patients

USN&WR—Basic data: Physicians' Desk Reference

your illness rather than consider the possibility that they could be drug related.

Mental side effects, in fact, are listed in the Physicians' Desk Reference, the 2,497-page bible of prescribers and dispensers, for well over 1,000 of the nearly 3,000 prescription and over-the-counter drugs included. Not all of the problems are worrisome. By law, drug makers must note every suspected side effect, even if it is based on a single case report. Such full disclosure also limits drug makers' liability when untoward events do happen.

But with so many drugs posing potential problems, large numbers of Americans could find themselves in trouble. A computer search of the new compact-disc version of the PDR found, for instance, that Halcion is among 310 drugs for which depression is listed as a possible side effect. Halcion is also one of 26 drugs linked to amnesia. The search revealed that psychotic episodes may be symptoms of 112 drugs and hallucinations symptoms of 257 medications. Nine drugs on the market in the United States list hostility, 28 list suicidal thoughts and 52 list fear.

Reporting gap. And those are just the drugs for which evidence has accumulated. Doctors report new cases in medical journals with astounding frequency — sometimes involving only a single patient — to put fellow physicians on notice to watch for often unverified problems. In the July issue of *Neurology,* researchers reported that a man of 43 who received cyclosporine to suppress his immune system after a kidney transplant hallucinated that he saw brightly colored road maps lining the walls of his hospital room. Recently, a physician at Long Island Jewish Medical Center wrote the *New England Journal of Medicine* about five dialysis patients who thought they saw cartoon figures and animals after being given recombinant human erythropoietin to correct their anemia. In May's *Annals of Pharmacology,* a West Virginia cardiologist wrote about a 41-year-old man who became panicky and depressed four weeks after starting treatment with enalapril maleate for hypertension. The symptoms vanished when he stopped taking the drug.

Doctors are supposed to report such observations to the Food and Drug Administration. Few do so. In one national study of 1,121 physicians, 37 percent said they had detected serious drug side effects, but only 5 percent had told the FDA, and 43 percent said they didn't even know how to report problems.

Physician vigilance is vital because laboratory studies and premarketing trials are severely limited. Studies for new drugs usually last no more than three years and seldom involve more than 3,000 patients — and few of them have

Common drugs that bend the mind

Of the 100 most prescribed brand-name prescription drugs, about 1 in 4 poses some risk of an unwelcome effect on the mind. To be listed here, the incidence of side effects, as reported by the manufacturer, must be 1 percent or greater. As with the listing on the preceding page, tranquilizers and antianxiety and antidepressant drugs were dropped. "Rank" reflects the drug's position on the list of the 100 most prescribed drugs.

Rank	Drug (manufacturer)	Use	Side effects	Frequency/comments
2	Lanoxin (Burroughs Wellcome)	Heart	Blurred vision, dizziness, apathy, psychosis	Fewer than 5% of patients
7	Cardizem (Marion Merrell Dow)	Hypertension	Dizziness	1.5%
11	Vasotec (Merck Sharp & Dohme)	Heart, hypertension	Dizziness, vertigo	7.9% and 1.6% respectively
12	Tenormin (ICI Pharma)	Heart, hypertension	Dizziness, vertigo	4% and 2% respectively
13	Procardia (Pfizer Labs)	Heart	Nervousness, jitteriness, disturbed sleep, blurred vision, disturbed balance, dizziness	2% or fewer; 10% for dizziness
16	Naprosyn (Syntex Laboratories)	Anti-inflammatory	Dizziness, vertigo, tinnitus	More than 1%
17	Tagamet (Smith Kline & French)	Ulcers	Somnolence, dizziness	1%, usually mild
18	Calan (G. D. Searle)	Heart, hypertension	Dizziness	3.3%
22	Proventil (Schering Corp.)	Bronchial spasm	Dizziness, nervousness	5% and 10% respectively
23	Lopressor (Geigy Pharmaceuticals)	Heart, hypertension	Dizziness, depression	10% and 5% respectively
26	Voltaren (Geigy Pharmaceuticals)	Anti-inflammatory	Dizziness	3%
31	Ventolin (Allen & Hanburys)	Bronchial spasm	Tremors, dizziness, nervousness, insomnia	20%, 7%, 4% and 1% respectively
33	Halcion (Upjohn)	Sleep	Dizziness, nervousness	7.8% and 5.2% respectively
35	Cipro (Miles Inc. Pharmaceutical Division)	Antibiotic	Restlessness	1.1%
41	Feldene (Pfizer Labs)	Arthritis	Dizziness, somnolence, vertigo	More than 1%
49	Motrin (Upjohn)	Pain, anti-inflammatory	Dizziness, nervousness	1% to 3%
57	Pepcid (Merck Sharp & Dohme)	Ulcer	Dizziness	1.3%
63	Hismanal (Janssen Pharmaceutica)	Allergies	Nervousness, dizziness	2%
69	Zestril (Stuart Pharmaceuticals)	Hypertension	Dizziness	6.3%
74	Corgard (Bristol Laboratories)	Heart, hypertension	Dizziness	2%
82	Clinoril (Merck Sharp & Dohme)	Anti-inflammatory	Dizziness, nervousness, tinnitus	More than 1%
87	Lozol (Rhône-Poulenc Rorer Pharmaceuticals)	Heart, hypertension	Dizziness, lethargy, malaise, nervousness, tension, anxiety, irritability, agitation (all greater than 5%); vertigo, insomnia, depression, blurred vision (fewer than 5%)	See percentages at left; manufacturer suspects many of the effects are due to causes other than the drug
91	Anaprox DS (Syntex Laboratories)	Pain, anti-inflammatory	Dizziness, vertigo	3%-9% and more than 1% respectively
93	Flexeril (Merck Sharp & Dohme)	Muscle spasms	Dizziness, blurred vision, nervousness, confusion	Fewer than 3%; 11% for dizziness
94	Isoptin (Knoll Pharmaceuticals)	Heart	Dizziness	3.3%
97	Persantine (Boehringer Ingelheim Pharmaceuticals)	Anticoagulant	Dizziness	13.6%

USN&WR – Basic data: *American Druggist* (February 1991); Physicians' Desk Reference

complicated medical conditions, are already taking other drugs or are particularly susceptible because they are young or old. An audit last year by the General Accounting Office found that the manufacturers of more than half of 218 new drugs introduced between 1976 and 1985 were ordered to overhaul the information that appears in the PDR and on package inserts. Serious risks that cropped up after the approval of bromocriptine, a Parkinson's drug, for instance, forced the maker to add psychosis, hallucinations, paranoid reactions and depression to the list of potential problems.

The distribution of the hazards is decidedly unequal. Pregnant women, children and the elderly run the most risk of unexpected psychiatric side effects because of their general exclusion from preclinical drug trials and because their systems metabolize medications differently than do those of relatively young healthy men. People over 80 face three times the chance of adverse drug reactions—including those that target the mind—than people under 50. Older people also are much likelier to be taking more than one medication, multiplying the possibility of drug interactions.

Watching the kids. Prednisone can cheat death for children with asthma, cancer and rheumatoid arthritis. It can also alter their behavior, thinking and mood, says Sally Satel, a doctor at the West Haven Medical Center in Connecticut, who found no mention of prednisone's mental effects in 11 gener-

'Pregnant women, children and the elderly run the most risk.'

———

al pediatric texts and nine comprehensive child-psychiatry texts. Yet several studies suggest that between 25 percent and 50 percent of children on corticosteroids experience serious mood and behavior disturbances.

Moreover, anyone who runs to the library to get the word on prednisone in the latest PDR may search in vain for the version he is taking. Manufacturers have to pay for space in the PDR and can opt for a mere listing that describes none of

the side effects. Prednisone is made by several different companies, and only Upjohn, which markets the steroid as Deltasone, gives it more than a brief mention. Fortunately, the PDR is not the only resource. The Complete Drug Reference by the U.S. Pharmacopeial Convention (Consumer Reports Books, 1991, $39.95) was the No. 1 choice in a recent *U.S. News* ranking by experts of the top 10 drug books. Compiled by an independent, not-for-profit corporation, the book offers complete information on over 5,500 prescription and nonprescription medications.

Frank discussions with your doctor and pharmacist about possible side effects and any mood reactions you subsequently experience are obviously best. But you may have to broach the subject forcefully. Especially if you're old, physicians are likely to overlook a drug's potential adverse effect on your emotional state. If a pill is healing your body, it might be hard for some doctors to consider that it could be hurting your mind.

BY DOUG PODOLSKY WITH
RICHARD J. NEWMAN

Facts About . . .

Opiates

Addiction Research Foundation

Synopsis

The opioids include both natural opiates—that is, drugs from the opium poppy—and opiate-related synthetic drugs such as meperidine and methadone.

The opiates are found in a gummy substance extracted from the seed pod of the Asian poppy, *Papaver somniferum*. Opium is produced from this substance, and codeine and morphine are derived from opium. Other drugs, such as heroin, are processed from morphine or codeine.

Opiates have been used both medically and non-medically for centuries. A tincture of opium called laudanum has been widely used since the 16th century as a remedy for "nerves" or to stop coughing or diarrhea.

By the early 19th century, morphine had been extracted in a pure form suitable for solution. With the introduction of the hypodermic needle in the mid-19th century, injection of the solution became the common method of administration.

Heroin (diacetylmorphine) was introduced in 1898 and was heralded as a remedy for morphine addiction. Although heroin proved to be a more potent painkiller (analgesic) and cough suppressant than morphine, it was also more likely to produce dependence.

Of the 20 alkaloids contained in opium, only codeine and morphine are still in widespread clinical use today. In this century, many synthetic drugs have been developed with essentially the same effects as the natural opium alkaloids.

Opiate-related synthetic drugs, such as meperidine (Demerol) and methadone, were first developed to provide an analgesic that would not produce drug dependence. Unfortunately, all opioids (including naturally occurring opiate derivatives and synthetic opiate-related drugs), while effective as analgesics, can also produce dependence. (Note that where a drug name is capitalized, it is a registered trade name of the manufacturer.)

Modern research has led, however, to the development of other families of drugs. The narcotic antagonists (e.g., naloxone hydrochloride)—one of these groups—are used not as painkillers but to reverse the effects of opiate overdose. Another group of drugs possess both morphine-like and naloxone-like properties (e.g., pentazocine, or Talwin) and are sometimes used for pain relief because they are less likely to be abused and to cause addiction. Nevertheless, abuse of pentazocine in combination with the antihistamine tripelennamine (Pyribenzamine) was widely reported in the 1980s, particularly in several large cities in the United States. This combination became known on the street as "Ts and blues." The reformulation of Talwin, however, with the narcotic antagonist naloxone has reportedly reduced the incidence of Ts and blues use.

Appearance

Opium appears either as dark brown chunks or in powder form, and is generally eaten or smoked. Heroin usually appears as a white or brownish powder, which is dissolved in water for injection. Most street preparations of heroin contain only a small percentage of the drug, as they are diluted with sugar, quinine, or other drugs and substances. Other opiate analgesics appear in a variety of forms, such as capsules, tablets, syrups, elixirs, solutions, and suppositories. Street users usually inject opiate solutions under the skin ("skin popping") or directly into a vein or muscle, but the drugs may also be "snorted" into the nose or taken orally or rectally.

Effects

The effects of *any* drug depend on several factors:

- the amount taken at one time
- the user's past drug experience
- the manner in which the drug is taken
- the circumstances under which the drug is taken (the place, the user's psychological and emotional stability, the presence of other people, simultaneous use of alcohol or other drugs, etc.).

Short-term effects appear soon after a single dose and disappear in a few hours or days. Opioids briefly stimulate the higher centres of the brain but then depress activity of the central nervous system. Immediately after injection of an opioid into a vein, the user feels a surge of pleasure or a "rush." This gives way to a state of gratification; hunger, pain, and sexual urges rarely intrude.

The dose required to produce this effect may at first cause restlessness, nausea, and vomiting. With moderately high doses, however, the body feels warm, the extremities heavy, and the mouth dry. Soon, the user goes "on the nod," an alternately wakeful and drowsy state during which the world is forgotten.

Reprinted by permission from *Addiction Research Foundation*, January 1991.

5. MAJOR DRUGS OF USE AND ABUSE

As the dose is increased, breathing becomes gradually slower. With very large doses, the user cannot be roused; the pupils contract to pinpoints; the skin is cold, moist, and bluish; and profound respiratory depression resulting in death may occur.

Overdose is a particular risk on the street, where the amount of drug contained in a "hit" cannot be accurately gauged.

In a treatment setting, the effects of a usual dose of morphine last three to four hours. Although pain may still be felt, the reaction to it is reduced, and the patient feels content because of the emotional detachment induced by the drug.

Long-term effects appear after repeated use over a long period. Chronic opiate users may develop endocarditis, an infection of the heart lining and valves as a result of unsterile injection techniques.

Drug users who share needles are also at a high risk of acquiring AIDS (acquired immune deficiency syndrome) and HIV infection (human immunodeficiency virus). Unsterile injection techniques can also cause abscesses, cellulitis, liver disease, and even brain damage. Among users with a long history of subcutaneous injection, tetanus is common. Pulmonary complications, including various types of pneumonia, may also result from the unhealthy lifestyle of the user, as well as from the depressant effect of opiates on respiration.

Tolerance and Dependence

With regular use, *tolerance* develops to many of the desired effects of the opioids. This means the user must use more of the drug to achieve the same intensity of effect.

Chronic users may also become psychologically and physically dependent on opioids.

Psychological dependence exists when a drug is so central to a person's thoughts, emotions, and activities that the need to continue its use becomes a craving or compulsion.

With *physical dependence*, the body has adapted to the presence of the drug, and withdrawal symptoms occur if use of the drug is reduced or stopped abruptly. Some users take heroin on an occasional basis, thus avoiding physical dependence.

Withdrawal from opioids, which in regular users may occur as early as a few hours after the last administration, produces uneasiness, yawning, tears, diarrhea, abdominal cramps, goose bumps, and runny nose. These symptoms are accompanied by a craving for the drug. Major withdrawal symptoms peak between 48 and 72 hours after the last dose and subside after a week. Some bodily functions, however, do not return to normal levels for as long as six months. Sudden withdrawal by heavily dependent users who are in poor health has occasionally been fatal. Opioid withdrawal, however, is much less dangerous to life than alcohol and barbiturate withdrawal.

Opioids and Pregnancy

Opioid-dependent women are likely to experience complications during pregnancy and childbirth. Among their most common medical problems are anemia, cardiac disease, diabetes, pneumonia, and hepatitis. They also have an abnormally high rate of spontaneous abortion, breech delivery, caesarian section, and premature birth. Opioid withdrawal has also been linked to a high incidence of stillbirths.

Infants born to heroin-dependent mothers are smaller than average and frequently show evidence of acute infection. Most exhibit withdrawal symptoms of varying degrees and duration. The mortality rate among these infants is higher than normal.

Who Uses Opioids

Opiates and their synthetic counterparts are used in modern medicine to relieve acute pain suffered as a result of disease, surgery, or injury; in the treatment of some forms of acute heart failure; and in the control of moderate to severe coughs or diarrhea. They are not the desired treatment for the relief of chronic pain, because their long-term and repeated use can result in drug dependence and side effects (such as constipation and mood swings). They are, however, of particular value in control of pain in the later stages of terminal illness, where the possibility of dependence is not a significant issue.

A small proportion of people for whom opioids have been medically prescribed become dependent; they are referred to as "medical addicts." Even use of non-prescription codeine products, if continued inappropriately, may get out of control. Medical advice should be sought, since withdrawal symptoms

Opiates* *Do You Know . . .*

Opiates are very strong painkillers (much stronger than the Aspirin and Tylenol that people take for minor pain). The name "opiates" comes from opium, a gummy substance collected from the seed pod of the opium poppy.

Morphine and codeine are drugs made from opium.

Heroin is made by adding a chemical to morphine.

Although a large number of other strong painkillers are made wholly from chemicals (e.g. Demerol, Percodan, Dilaudid, and methadone), they are all called opiates because they are chemically similar and have many similar uses.

What do opiates look like?

Opium comes in dark brown chunks or powder, and is usually eaten or smoked.

Heroin on the street is usually a white or brownish powder. It is usually dissolved in water and injected under the skin or into a vein or muscle, but it can also be sniffed into the nostrils or smoked ("chasing the dragon").

Other opiates come in a variety of forms – tablets, capsules, syrups, solutions, and suppositories.

Who uses opiates?

Doctors and dentists prescribe opiates for patients who are in severe pain. Because these painkillers are

*Street Names: junk, H, horse, smack, shit, skag (for heroin); M, morph, Miss Emma (for morphine); meth (for methadone); percs (for Percodan, Percocet); juice (for Dilaudid)

may result from abrupt cessation of use after physical dependence has been established. Because members of the medical and allied health professions have ready access to opioids, some become dependent.

The largest proportion of non-medical use, however, falls into the street-use category. Currently, heroin is the most popular opiate among street users; these users are also prone to heavy use of other psychoactive drugs, such as cocaine, alcohol, certain sedative/hypnotics, and tranquillizers.

During the past few years, synthetic opioids such as hydrocodone, hydromorphone, oxycodone, and meperidine have gained prominence as drugs of dependence. Users sometimes urge physicians to write them prescriptions for the opioid of preference. These opioids are also frequently stolen from pharmacies and sold on the street. Today, illicit use of such opioid-based medicines as Percodan, Dilaudid, and Novahistex DH is common.

Opioids and the Law

The federal Narcotic Control Act regulates the possession and distribution of all opioids. The act permits individual physicians, dentists, pharmacists, and veterinarians, as well as hospitals, to keep supplies of certain opioids. Members of the general public must obtain these drugs from such authorized sources. Although the act also permits the prescribing of methadone in the treatment of opioid dependence, permission is given only to specially licensed physicians, and use is governed by specific guidelines.

If tried by summary conviction, a first offence for opioid possession carries a maximum penalty of a $1,000 fine and six months imprisonment. For subsequent offences, the maximum penalty is a $2,000 fine and 12 months imprisonment. If tried by indictment, opioid possession carries a maximum penalty of seven years imprisonment. Importing, exporting, trafficking, and possession for the purposes of trafficking are all indictable offences and carry a maximum penalty of life imprisonment. Cultivation of opium is also an indictable offence and carries a maximum penalty of seven years imprisonment.

It is illegal to obtain a prescription for opioids or any other "narcotic" from health care professionals without notifying them that you have obtained a similar prescription through another practitioner within the preceding 30 days.

---

addictive, they shouldn't be taken steadily for a long time. But they are safe in the short term – for example, if you have had surgery or have an abscessed tooth. When someone is dying from a painful disease, the risk of addiction is not important, and opiates are given for as long as needed to keep the person in comfort.

Certain kinds help people who are addicted to illegal opiates such as heroin; they are given a safer, legal drug (usually methadone) so that they can live a more normal life off the "street" and, in many cases, finally become drug-free.

Other medical uses of opiates are to control bad coughs or diarrhea. Some non-prescription products contain a small amount of codeine.

People who use opiates illegally are looking for a different effect – a "high" and a mellow, relaxed feeling. Although heroin gets the most publicity, many users take illegally obtained prescription drugs.

Are these drugs dangerous?

Yes. Opiates can be dangerous if they are used without medical supervision. Here are some of the reasons.

- These drugs (especially heroin) can kill you if you seek the "high" by taking larger doses than your body is used to. And with street heroin, it is easy to overdose accidentally, because the purity of the drug varies so much – anywhere from zero percent on the low end to an occasional 30 percent on the high end. The purer the heroin, the more likely an overdose.

- Many people inject opiates because the effect (called the "rush") is faster and stronger. But they run extra risks: tetanus, other infections, liver disease, and even brain damage from dirty needles and impurities in the drug, and AIDS or hepatitis from needles shared with others.

- Many heroin users also abuse other drugs, such as barbiturates, alcohol, cocaine, and amphetamines, with the risk of becoming hooked on these drugs as well.

- Pregnant women who take these drugs risk problems during pregnancy and childbirth. Their babies suffer from withdrawal symptoms and can die if not treated.

How addictive are opiates?

You can – quite quickly – become physically and psychologically dependent on opiates.

If you use them steadily, you become *tolerant* to the desired effect. That is, you must take more and more of the drug to get a "high" or even to control pain. If it's the high you're after, however, at a certain point no amount of the drug will work unless you stop taking it for a few weeks.

Once you become *physically dependent* on opiates, stopping use abruptly will make you sick. Although people rarely die from *withdrawal*, it can be miserable (much like a bad case of flu). People often also feel very depressed and anxious, are unable to sleep or eat, and desperately want more of the drug (*psychological dependence*). This craving is especially great for heroin, and heroin is therefore one of the hardest drugs for an addicted person to quit.

Facts About . . .

Alcohol

Addiction Research Foundation

Drug Class: Sedative/Hypnotic

Synopsis

Alcohol is often not thought of as a drug—largely because its use is common for both religious and social purposes in most parts of the world. It *is* a drug, however, and compulsive drinking in excess has become one of modern society's most serious problems.

Beverage alcohol (scientifically known as ethyl alcohol, or ethanol) is produced by fermenting or distilling various fruits, vegetables, or grains. Ethyl alcohol itself is a clear, colorless liquid. Alcoholic beverages get their distinctive colors from the diluents, additives, and by-products of fermentation.

In Ontario, beer is fermented to contain about 5% alcohol by volume (or 3.5% in light beer). Most wine is fermented to have between 10% and 14% alcohol content; however, such fortified wines as sherry, port, and vermouth contain between 14% and 20%. Distilled spirits (whisky, vodka, rum, gin) are first fermented, then distilled to raise the alcohol content. In Canada, the concentration of alcohol in spirits is 40% by volume. Some liqueurs may be stronger.

The effects of drinking do not depend on the *type* of alcoholic beverage—but rather on the *amount* of alcohol consumed on a specific occasion. The following table outlines the alcohol content of various beverages. The right-hand column shows the amount of alcohol consumed in each drink.

How Alcohol Works

Alcohol is rapidly absorbed into the bloodstream from the small intestine, and less rapidly from the stomach and colon. In proportion to its concentration in the bloodstream, alcohol decreases activity in parts of the brain and spinal cord. The drinker's blood alcohol concentration depends on:

- the amount consumed in a given time
- the drinker's size, sex, body build, and metabolism
- the type and amount of food in the stomach.

Once the alcohol has passed into the blood, however, no food or beverage can retard or interfere with its effects. Fruit sugar, however, in some cases can shorten the duration of alcohol's effect by speeding up its elimination from the blood.

In the average adult, the rate of metabolism is about 8.5 g of alcohol per hour (i.e. about two-thirds of a regular beer or about 30 mL of spirits an hour). This rate can vary dramatically among individuals, however, depending on such diverse factors as usual amount of drinking, physique, sex, liver size, and genetic factors.

Effects

The effects of *any* drug depend on several factors:

- the amount taken at one time
- the user's past drug experience
- the manner in which the drug is taken

Beverage	% alcohol by volume	Size of drink		Grams of alcohol
		mL	oz	
Beer (bottle)	5	341	12	13.4
Beer (can)	5	355	12.5	14.0
Light beer (bottle)	3.5	341	12	9.4
Light beer (can)	3.5	355	12.5	9.8
Wine	12	142	5	13.4
	12	170	6	16.1
Fortified wine	20	56.8	2	8.9
Spirits	40	28.4	1	8.9
	40	35.5	1.25	11.2
	40	42.6	1.5	13.4

Reprinted by permission from *Addiction Research Foundation*, January 1991.

- the circumstances under which the drug is taken (the place, the user's psychological and emotional stability, the presence of other people, the concurrent use of other drugs, etc.).

It is the amount of alcohol in the blood that causes the effects. In the following table, the left-hand column lists the number of milligrams of alcohol in each decilitre of blood – that is, the blood alcohol concentration, or BAC. (For example, an average person may get a blood alcohol concentration of 50 mg/dL after two drinks consumed quickly.) The right-hand column describes the usual effects of these amounts on normal people – those who haven't developed a tolerance to alcohol.

BAC (mg/dL)	Effect
50	*Mild intoxication* Feeling of warmth, skin flushed; impaired judgment; decreased inhibitions
100	*Obvious intoxication in most people* Increased impairment of judgment, inhibition, attention, and control; Some impairment of muscular performance; slowing of reflexes
150	*Obvious intoxication in all normal people* Staggering gait and other muscular incoordination; slurred speech; double vision; memory and comprehension loss
250	*Extreme intoxication or stupor* Reduced response to stimuli; inability to stand; vomiting; incontinence; sleepiness
350	*Coma* Unconsciousness; little response to stimuli; incontinence; low body temperature; poor respiration; fall in blood pressure; clammy skin
500	*Death likely*

Drinking heavily over a short period of time usually results in a "hangover" – headache, nausea, shakiness, and sometimes vomiting, beginning from 8 to 12 hours later. A hangover is due partly to poisoning by alcohol and other components of the drink, and partly to the body's reaction to withdrawal from alcohol. Although there are dozens of home remedies suggested for hangovers, there is currently no known effective cure.

Combining alcohol with other drugs can make the effects of these other drugs much stronger and more dangerous. Many accidental deaths have occurred after people have used alcohol combined with other drugs. Cannabis, tranquillizers, barbiturates and other sleeping pills, or antihistamines (in cold, cough, and allergy remedies) should not be taken with alcohol. Even a small amount of alcohol with any of these drugs can seriously impair a person's ability to drive a car, for example.

Long-term effects of alcohol appear after repeated use over a period of many months or years. The negative physical and psychological effects of chronic abuse are numerous; some are potentially life-threatening.

Some of these harmful consequences are primary – that is, they result directly from prolonged exposure to alcohol's toxic effects (such as heart and liver disease or inflammation of the stomach).

Others are secondary; indirectly related to chronic alcohol abuse, they include loss of appetite, vitamin deficiencies, infections, and sexual impotence or menstrual irregularities. The risk of serious disease increases with the amount of alcohol consumed.

Early death rates are much higher for heavy drinkers than for light drinkers or abstainers, particularly from heart and liver disease, pneumonia, some types of cancer, acute alcohol poisoning, accident, homicide, and suicide. No precise limits of safe drinking can be recommended.

According to 1988 figures from Statistics Canada, 2,828 deaths were directly attributable to alcohol in that year. There were, however, an estimated 13,870 more deaths – five times as many – indirectly caused by alcohol.

Tolerance and Dependence

People who drink on a regular basis become *tolerant* to many of the unpleasant effects of alcohol, and thus are able to drink more before suffering these effects. Yet even with increased consumption, many such drinkers don't appear intoxicated. Because they continue to work and socialize reasonably well, their deteriorating physical condition may go unrecognized by others until severe damage develops – or until they are hospitalized for other reasons and suddenly experience alcohol withdrawal symptoms.

Psychological dependence on alcohol may occur with regular use of even relatively moderate daily amounts. It may also occur in people who consume alcohol only under certain conditions, such as before and during social occasions. This form of dependence refers to a craving for alcohol's psychological effects, although not necessarily in amounts that produce serious intoxication. For psychologically dependent drinkers, the lack of alcohol tends to make them anxious and, in some cases, panicky.

Physical dependence occurs in consistently heavy drinkers. Since their bodies have adapted to the presence of alcohol, they suffer withdrawal symptoms if they suddenly stop drinking. Withdrawal symptoms range from jumpiness, sleeplessness, sweating, and poor appetite, to tremors (the "shakes"), convulsions, hallucinations, and sometimes death.

Alcohol and Pregnancy

Pregnant women who drink risk having babies with fetal alcohol effects (known as fetal alcohol syndrome or FAS). The most serious of these effects include mental retardation, growth deficiency, head and facial deformities, joint and limb abnormalities, and heart defects. While it is known that the risk of bearing an FAS-afflicted child increases with the amount of alcohol consumed, a safe level of consumption has not been determined.

Who Uses Alcohol

In a 1990 nation-wide Gallup poll, 79% of adults reported they had at some point drunk alcohol. A 1989 survey of adults in Ontario found that 83% reported ever having used alcohol, with 55% saying they have five drinks or more at a single sitting and 10% reporting daily drinking.

Among young people between 12 and 19 years, a 1985 national survey recorded 73% using alcohol at least once in the past year.

5. MAJOR DRUGS OF USE AND ABUSE

Of Ontario students in grades 7, 9, 11, and 13 polled in 1989, 66% admitted to alcohol use, with more than 80% of the grade 11 and 13 students saying they drank. More than one in five of all those who drank said they did so more than once a week. Since the legal drinking age in Ontario is 19, it appears that alcohol has a high degree of social acceptance, whether legal or not.

Total alcohol consumption in Canada during 1988/89 reached 202.9 million litres. This corresponds to an average annual consumption of 9.9 L of alcohol for each Canadian over the age of 15 – that is to say, about 11 drinks per week or a little under two drinks a day. Beer, making up 52% of the total volume, was the most popular drink, with spirits in second place at 31%, and wine a distant third at 17%.

In recent years, Canadians have spent about $9.6 billion a year for alcohol in retail stores and another estimated $2.6 billion for alcohol consumed in taverns and restaurants.

There is a direct relationship between the overall level of consumption within a population and the number of alcohol-dependent people. A nation with a low per capita consumption rate has a lower number of heavy users, whereas one with widespread use and high per capita consumption has a proportionately higher rate of alcohol-related diseases and deaths.

Most researchers agree that one in 20 drinkers in North America has an alcohol dependency problem.

Alcohol and the Law

Alcohol legislation is a joint responsibility of the federal and provincial governments, and many laws regulate its manufacture, distribution, advertising, possession, and consumption.

In Ontario, marketing and consumption of alcohol is primarily governed by the provincial Liquor Licence Act. It is an offence for anyone under 19 years to possess, consume, or purchase alcohol. It is also illegal to sell or supply alcohol to anyone known to be or appearing to be (unless that person has proof otherwise) under the age of 19. It is not illegal, though, for parents or guardians to give an under-age child a drink at home. Provisions similar to Ontario's apply in most other Canadian provinces and in the Yukon and Northwest Territories, as well as in many states in the United States.

The act also makes it illegal to sell or supply alcohol to a person who appears to be intoxicated.

As well, anyone who sells or supplies alcohol to others –

whether these are patrons of a tavern or restaurant or guests in a private home – may be held civilly liable if intoxicated patrons or guests injure themselves or others.

The federal criminal law sets out a range of drinking and driving offences. It is illegal, for example, to operate a motor vehicle, boat, or aircraft while impaired by any amount of alcohol or other drugs. The manner in which one drives, slurred speech or physical incoordination, and the smell of alcohol may all be used as evidence of a person's impairment.

It is also a criminal offence to drive with a blood alcohol concentration (BAC) above .08% (which means with more than 80 mg of alcohol in each 100 mL of blood in one's bloodstream).

The Criminal Code sets out complex provisions authorizing police to demand breath samples or, in limited circumstances, blood samples, from suspected drinking drivers. Those refusing to comply can be convicted unless they have a reasonable excuse.

The Ontario Highway Traffic Act gives police broad powers to stop drivers to determine if they have been drinking and to issue a 12-hour licence suspension if their BAC is above .05% (i.e. higher than 50 mg of alcohol per 100 mL of blood).

Drinking and driving is by far the largest criminal cause of death and injury in Canada. In 1988, there were 121,307 Canadians charged with federal drinking and driving offences: 110,773 for impaired operation of a motor vehicle; 1,194 for impaired operation causing bodily harm; and 158 for causing death. Another 8,786 people were charged for failure or refusal to provide a breath sample for testing. In all, 19,808 Canadians were jailed for drinking and driving offences in 1988/89.

Alcohol*

Do You Know . . .

Is alcohol a drug?

Yes. Alcohol is called a depressant drug because it *slows down* your brain's ability to think and to make decisions and judgments. Whether the alcohol comes in beer, wine, or liquor doesn't matter. It's the *amount of alcohol* in your drink, not the *type* of drink, that affects you.

*Street Names: booze, brew, hooch, grog

What is problem drinking?

If drinking seriously interferes with your life, you have a drinking problem.

If drinking, to you, means getting drunk, not remembering what you did, passing out, or feeling embarrassed about the night before, these are signs of a problem. Other signs are:

- getting into fights when you drink,

- having sex, when you drink, with someone you don't particularly like,

- being frequently hung over or late for work or school,

- being charged with impaired driving.

And if drinking is your major way of coping with

stress, or if you cannot control how much you drink at any one time, you have a problem.

What is sensible drinking?

Sensible drinking does not interfere with:

- your health
- your job or your studies
- your relationships
- your safety
- the safety of others

A pattern of sensible drinking means days of not drinking mixed with days of light drinking.

Can drinking hurt me physically?

Drinking a lot of alcohol over a long time can do serious damage to your body.

- Brain damage, ulcers, liver disease, malnutrition, heart disease, and various cancers are more common among heavy drinkers.
- People who drink heavily are likely to die younger than people who drink lightly or not at all.
- Pregnant women who drink risk having babies with birth defects, sometimes very serious ones. It is known that the more a pregnant woman drinks, the higher the risk; but it is not known whether just one or two drinks are really "safe."

How dangerous is mixing alcohol with other drugs?

It can be very dangerous.

- Especially risky is taking a few drinks with other depressant (or "downer") drugs, such as tranquillizers and sleeping pills. The alcohol and the other drug boost the effect of each other, and a person unexpectedly may seem very drunk, pass out, go into a coma, or even die. Even common non-prescription drugs such as antihistamines (for colds and allergies) can make you dopey and clumsy when you take alcohol at the same time.

- Taking stimulant drugs such as caffeine, cocaine, or amphetamines after drinking a lot of alcohol isn't a good idea either. These drugs can trick you into thinking you are sober, but you're really not – you are just wider awake and more hyper.

- Researchers now believe that alcohol makes the body absorb the cancer-causing chemicals in tobacco and cannabis more quickly. If you drink *and* smoke, you may be more likely to get cancer of the mouth, neck, or throat.

- Some medicines can't do their job as well if they are mixed with alcohol. Other medicines can interact violently with alcohol, causing side effects such as cramps, vomiting, and headaches.

When it comes to alcohol and other drugs, the best advice is: Don't mix.

The Impact of Drug Use on Society

Illegal drug users will often argue that society has no right to concern itself with their drug taking. "I'm only harming myself," they will insist, "society has no right to interfere with my private life." Legal and moral arguments aside, the fact is, users do more than increase the likelihood of harming themselves when they take drugs. They can harm others as well, both directly and indirectly—directly, by upping the odds of accidents, crime, and violence, and indirectly, as a result of increasing the cost of caring for them and their offspring, lowering productivity, and stimulating the underground economy, thereby undermining the viability of certain neighborhoods. In short, drugs can have a number of undesirable long-term consequences.

Of all drugs, experts agree, cigarettes cause the greatest loss of life over the long run. The surgeon general of the United States estimates that over 400,000 Americans die prematurely every year as a consequence of cigarette smoking. The increased cost of medical care for those who have contracted diseases as a consequence of smoking is incalculable, running at the very least into the tens of billions of dollars per year—considerably more than the government earns in taxes from tobacco products. Smokers have three times the chance of dying before the age of 65 as nonsmokers, and twice the chance of dying before the age of 75; a nonsmoker has about the same chance of living to the age of 75 as a smoker does of living to 65! Smokers of more than 2 packs a day have 23 times the chance of dying of lung cancer as nonsmokers. But since tobacco is legal, and the deaths it causes are slow and long-term and likely to strike only the middle-aged and the elderly, most of us do not become overly distressed about its use.

Alcohol causes some 150,000 premature deaths a year, perhaps half from the increased likelihood of accident and violence and the other half from the various diseases the drug causes. One estimate links 3 out of every 100 deaths directly to the consumption of alcohol—and admits that this is probably a gross underestimation. Estimates of the dollar cost of alcohol consumption to American society, which include medical care and loss of productivity, range between $100 and $200 billion per year. Just the deaths from the increased likelihood of automobile crashes—over 20,000 per year—far outweigh the number of premature deaths caused by all the illegal drugs combined. Of all the long-term impacts of heavy alcohol consumption, perhaps the most poignant and painful is that on the family of the heavy drinker. The children of alcoholics are victims who have to spend their entire adulthood struggling with the pain of the childhood they spent with an alcohol-dependent parent.

Illegal drug use has a serious impact on the user and on society generally, but it is likely to be very different from that of the legal drugs. Most users of heroin and cocaine die not of the chronic, long-term effects of their drugs of choice, but from overdoses. Through a program called DAWN (the Drug Awareness Warning Network), the federal government collects and complies drug overdose data, which are divided into *emergency room episodes* and *medical examiners reports* (or lethal overdoses). In 1990, DAWN estimated that there were roughly 370,000 drug episodes in the United States that required some hospital or clinic care. The drug mentioned the most in causing these nonlethal overdoses was *alcohol* (and alcohol was mentioned only if taken in conjunction or in combination with another drug), with 115,000 mentions. After that, cocaine, with 80,000 mentions, and the narcotics, with close to 60,000 mentions, most often caused acute, hospital and clinic emergencies. The drugs that caused the greatest number of deaths by overdose were the same three that caused hospital emergencies—alcohol (in combination), in third place, cocaine, in second place, and narcotics, still the champion death-dealing drug used in the United States today. All drugs do not necessarily kill in the same way. Cigarettes never appear in DAWN's data because it kills over the long run; its effects are *chronic* and not *acute*. Alcohol's effects are both chronic and acute—that is, one can die as a consequence of long-term use or as a result of a single episode of use. The lethal effects of illegal drugs such as heroin and cocaine are acute; they usually kill during a single episode of use, which means it is the young rather than the old who die from heroin and crack use.

The children born to mothers dependent on crack are themselves physically dependent. Such newborns are more likely to suffer from a variety of medical problems, and to become behavioral problems when they grow

older. Again, society foots the bill in paying for their care. Entire neighborhoods have been undermined by the sale and use of illegal drugs, most recently, crack, tearing families apart, skyrocketing the homicide rate, alienating children from school, and generating a climate of fear and paranoia. It is difficult to imagine that such an impact would not generate widespread concern and efforts to deal with these problems. But are they a consequence of drug abuse itself, or do they occur because society has criminalized certain drugs? We will find out in unit 8, "Fighting the Drug War."

Looking Ahead: Challenge Questions

Is the overall impact on society of the legal drugs—tobacco, alcohol, prescription and over-the-counter drugs—more positive or negative? Are the troublesome effects of the legal drugs (including medical problems and violence) simply the price we have to pay for tolerating substances whose use is too firmly entrenched to eliminate? If the impact of tobacco and alcohol has been as disastrous as experts claim in the societies in which they are used, why is their use tolerated?

Does drug abuse contribute to the "downfall of civilization," as some observers have argued?

If legal drugs contribute to far more premature deaths than illegal drugs, why do the latter receive so much more media attention than the former? Why are most people so much more interested in the use of cocaine, crack, and heroin than in cigarettes and alcohol?

If alcohol abuse causes such pain to those the alcoholic loves most, why can't he or she simply given up drinking?

Faced with overwhelming evidence that cigarettes kill, why do some people continue to smoke? How can cigarette companies continue to claim, as they do, that no conclusive proof exists that cigarettes cause disease or death?

If a pregnant woman becomes a crack addict, and endangers the life of her child, should she be criminally liable for her behavior? Is she committing a crime?

What can neighborhoods do to protect themselves against the impact the abuse of a drug has on them?

Can a common household beverage such as coffee really be as harmful as some experts claim?

The Cost of Drug Abuse: $60 Billion a Year

Stephen Labaton

Economists say the cost of illicit drugs to American society has risen substantially in the last few years, to far more than $60 billion annually. At the same time they are discovering vast new areas of additional economic impact that they are only now beginning to understand.

The new estimate for the annual total cost is based on the first major Federal study since 1984 of the adverse economic effects of drug addiction, and according to the researchers it represents an increase since 1985 of more than $10 billion, even after discounting for inflation. Increased medical costs for crack addicts and drug-addicted AIDS patients represent a significant portion of the rising expense.

"It's clear that for 1989, the cost of drugs on society is tremendous, far more than $60 billion," said Dorothy Rice, a former director of national health statistics at the Federal Department of Health and Human Services and a medical economist who was commissioned by the Government to conduct the study. . . .

New Areas Affected

The newly detected areas of economic impact—unexpectedly large cash surpluses that have appeared in some Federal Reserve Banks and artificially altered real estate values—are being explored on campuses and at government agencies that are trying to set drug, health, economic and foreign policies and enforcing existing laws against money laundering.

The medical bills for drug abusers and victims of drug-related crimes, along with the expenses incurred in expanding law enforcement systems, are other important factors adding to the increased costs.

Economists say the current estimates do in fact amount to a staggering price tag. Medical experts compare the drug cost to the enormous economic effects of the nation's battle against cancer, which the American Cancer Society estimates at about $70 billion annually. A recent Rand Corporation study pointed out that the price paid by society for cigarette smoking is completely offset by Federal and state taxes on cigarette sales, but there are no similar revenues generated by illegal drugs.

The costs to some extent are offset at least in the short term by large amounts of cash accumulated by the illegal drug industry, which invests much of that money in legitimate enterprises. But no one knows how to assess that effect, and it is believed to be short-lived.

Considered a Major Industry

"The study means that narcotics is one of America's major industries, right up there with consumer electronics, automobiles and steelmaking," said Robert B. Reich, a political economist at the John F. Kennedy School of Government at Harvard University. "Unlike our other major industries, however, the narcotics industry doesn't have a net effect of creating wealth. It makes us all substantially poorer. In fact, it is like a reverse industry, tearing things down rather than producing anything."

Economists readily acknowledge that figures in economic research on drugs are always difficult to obtain. "It's a very, very tough area to work in because of the assumptions that have to be made and the available data," said Al Harwood, an official at the National Institute on Drug Abuse in Rockville, Md., who has been overseeing the latest study. But he said the recent analyses were more accurate because of advances in gathering basic data and computerizing statistics. More specific costs of drug-related treatment are now available, for example, as well as better information on worker absenteeism and drug-related budgets for local, state and Federal criminal enforcement programs.

The Cost for Addicted Infants

One cost growing at an alarming rate is treatment for infants addicted to drugs, said Senator Lloyd Bentsen, Democrat of Texas, who notes that intensive-care costs alone last year reached $2.5 billion. He said Federal and local governments would soon be spending $15 billion annually to prepare addicted children to enter kindergarten and at least $6 billion more a year to get them through high school.

It is in the broader areas of international and local economies that experts are seeing effects they had not been fully aware of or studied before.

The sudden flow of large amounts of cash in and out of the banking centers of some urban areas is believed to be related to illegal drug profits that are ultimately draining money out of local economies, though where and how is not known.

According to a report by the Federal Reserve, for the first six months of 1989, the Miami Federal Reserve branch reported a cash surplus of $2.8 billion, Los Angeles $2.7 billion, Jacksonville $1.5 billion and San Antonio $1.2 billion. Houston, El Paso and New Orleans all experienced large increases of cash surpluses as well, from 219 percent to 56 percent. Surpluses in Miami and Los Angeles are growing by 10 percent annually.

The Federal Reserve says it believes that these surpluses are drug related, especially since the increases coincide with record-breaking drug seizures in these cities.

Hard Cash Disappears

A more direct effect is the disappearance of hard cash. Over all, the drug industry is contributing to the unaccounted loss of billions in currency from the economy. Experts estimate that perhaps $125 billion in American currency is "missing." Much of it is said to be used in illegal drug and arms transactions, often winding up in foreign banks and markets. It forms the basis for an enormous tax-free underground economy.

According to a study by the Treasury Department, the preferred denominations for drug transactions are $10 and $20 bills. The study, which examined the possibility of withdrawing $100 notes from the economy, says law enforcement agencies around the nation say that $100 notes account for 25 to 30 percent of the currency seized in drug raids and arrests.

New patterns of flight capital, particularly from Peru, Colombia and Bolivia, are also being perceived by economists. Most of the cocaine smuggled into the United States and Europe is processed from coca plants grown in the Andes.

Drug Profits Invested

The Latin drug dealers have traditionally moved a substantial share of their profits out of their relatively poor and unstable countries, adding to economic and political difficulties there, and reinvested the money in apparently legitimate enterprises in North America and Europe. A major share now, however, is going to Hong Kong, where the money is said to be easier to conceal. Indeed, officials say, Hong Kong has become an international center for drug-money laundering.

Experts estimate that as much as $250 billion in assets owned by Latin Americans is invested abroad. A recent report by the House Select Committee on Narcotics Abuse and Control concludes that most of the world's cocaine profits do not return to producer countries but are invested in tax havens, offshore bank accounts and real estate abroad.

In those instances where some money does remain in these drug producing nations, it is not used to help build a solid economy. "Cocaine traffickers are not captains of industry like the Harrimans, Rockefellers and Carnegies of yore," said Rensselaer W. Lee 3d, a consultant who is teaching at George Washington University. The way the narcotics traders "invest" their money locally, he said, is in bribing law enforcement officials, operating assassination squads and buying arms.

A Lift for Peasants

Nevertheless, the report by the House Select Committee notes, the cocaine industry has "revolutionized expectations and aspirations within Andean societies, for peasants especially." It added, "Television sets, videocassette recorders, stereos and cars have become attainable."

Thus the cocaine trade has spawned new constituencies that place new demands on Andean political systems. And, as Mr. Lee put it, entire regions of South America have come to depend economically on coca cultivation.

In Bolivia alone, where the export of legal goods is about $800 million each year, illegal cocaine exports may exceed that amount. As a result, the drug industry has become an institutionalized source of many jobs. It is estimated that 1.5 million people are employed in Andean production of cocaine and as many as 50,000 work in marijuana production in Colombia alone.

'A Safety Valve'

So for the short term at least, the drug industry clearly has some value, both economically and as a temporary relief from political tensions. "Cocaine has acted as a safety valve for the Andean countries where the economy fails to deliver," Mr. Lee said. "This substitution is most advanced in Peru and Bolivia, which have performed poorly on nearly every economic front in this decade."

The broad effect of drug-money laundering on local economies in the United States is being seen by bank regulators who have discovered unusually large numbers of cash sales of real estate, automobiles and boats evidently financed with drug money. In Dade County, Fla., economists have estimated that as much as 2 to 10 percent of the area's business boom has been driven by drug profits, often transacted by cash.

"Either there's a lot of tourists not using credit cards or there's lots of drug money," said Dexter Lehtinen, the United States Attorney in Miami. Mr. Lehtinen said that in Miami, some $220 million in cash has been spent on automobiles in the last three years, while Jacksonville and Tampa had about $24 million in cash sales of cars in the same period. And in parts of southern Florida as much as 20 percent of the transactions for real estate are in cash.

Inflated Prices Seen

Some local officials and prosecutors say that while these sales may prove lucrative to sellers, they have the effect of inflating the price of real estate and causing property taxes to increase as assessments go up. Of course, values of many inner-city properties are also seriously deflated because of the drug business.

Real estate transactions represent only a small piece of drug investments. As regulatory barriers that had limited international investments are being removed, and as stock and currency markets become global, narcotics profiteers are finding it easier to conceal their illegally earned wealth.

"The transferring of profits to avoid tax liability, and hedge and insurance trading are becoming commonplace," said R. Thomas Naylor, a professor at McGill University in Montreal who specializes in the underground economy. "There has become a blurring of the line between the behavior of legal and illegal money."

Innocent Victims

Damaged by the drugs their mothers took, crack kids will face social and educational hurdles and must count on society's compassion

ANASTASIA TOUFEXIS

AT A HOSPITAL IN BOSTON lies a baby girl who was born before her time—three months early, weighing less than 3 lbs. Her tiny body is entangled in a maze of wires and tubes that monitor her vital signs and bring her food and medicine. Every so often she shakes uncontrollably for a few moments—a legacy of the nerve-system damage that occurred when she suffered a shortfall of blood and oxygen just before birth. Between these seizures, she is unusually quiet and lethargic, lying on her side with one arm draped across her chest and the other bent to touch her face, sleeping day and night in the comfort of her cushioned warming table. At best, it will be three or four months before she is well enough to leave the hospital, and even then she may continue to shake from time to time.

AT A THERAPY CENTER IN NEW YORK CITY, the saddest child brought in one morning is three-year-old Felicia, a small bundle of bones in a pink dress, whose plastic hearing aids keep falling off, tangling with her gold earrings. She is deaf, and doctors are not sure how much she can see. She functions at the capacity of a four-month-old. Like a rag doll, she can neither sit nor stand by herself: her trunk is too weak and her legs are too stiff. A therapist massages and bends the little girl's legs, trying to make her relax. Next year her foster mother will put Felicia in a special school full time in hopes that the child can at least learn how to feed herself.

AT A SPECIAL KINDERGARTEN CLASS IN THE LOS ANGELES AREA, a five-year-old named Billie seems the picture of perfect health and disposition. As a tape recorder plays soothing music in the background, he and the teacher read alphabet cards. Suddenly Billie's face clouds over. For no apparent reason, he throws the cards down on the floor and shuts off the tape recorder. He sits in the chair, stony faced. "Was the music going too fast?" the teacher asks. Billie starts to say something, but then looks away, frowning. The teacher tries to get the lesson back on track, but Billie is quickly distracted by another child's antics. Within seconds, he is off his chair and running around.

These children have very different problems and prospects, but they all have one thing in common: their mothers repeatedly took crack cocaine, often in combination with other drugs, during pregnancy. That makes them part of a tragic generation of American youngsters—a generation unfairly branded by some as "children of the damned" or a "biologic underclass." More often, they are simply called crack kids. A few have severe physical deformities from which they will never recover. In others the damage can be more subtle, showing up as behavioral aberrations that may sabotage their schooling and social development. Many of these children look and act like other kids, but their early exposure to cocaine makes them less able to overcome negative influences like a disruptive family life.

The first large group of these children was born in the mid-1980s, when hundreds of thousands of women began to get hooked on the cheap, smokable form of cocaine known as crack. The youngsters have run up huge bills for medical treatment and other care. Now the oldest are reaching school age, and they are sure to put enormous strain on an educational system that is already overburdened and underachieving.

Their plight inspires both pity and fear. Pity that they are the innocent victims of society's ills. Pity that the odds will be stacked against them at home, on the playground and in school. Fear that they will grow into an unmanageable multitude of disturbed and disruptive youth. Fear that they will be a lost generation.

The dimensions of the tragedy are staggering. According to the National Association for Perinatal Addiction Research and Education (NAPARE), about 1 out of every 10 newborns in the U.S.—375,000 a year—is exposed in the womb to one or more illicit drugs. The most frequent ingredient in the mix is cocaine. In major cities such as New York, Los Angeles, Detroit and Washington many hospitals report that the percentage of newborns showing the effects of drugs is 20% or even higher.

The cost of dealing with these children is rapidly escalating. In California drug-exposed babies, many of whom are born prematurely, stay in the hospital almost five times as long as normal newborns (nine days, vs. two days) and their care is 13 times as expensive ($6,900, vs. $522). And that is only the beginning, since many of the crack kids are placed in foster care. In New York City annual placements of drug-affected babies run to 3,500, compared with 750 before the spread of crack. That brings the city's foster-care tab to about $795 million (up from $320 million in 1985). The New York State comptroller's office expects that New York City will spend $765 million over the next 10 years on special education for crack kids.

Among the most visible victims are black and other minority children born into crack-plagued ghettos. It is bad enough that the drug assaults children in the womb, but the injury is too often compounded after birth by an environment of neglect, poverty and violence. "I sometimes believe that babies are better protected before they are born than they are after," says Dr. Barry Zuckerman, head of the division of developmental and behavioral pediatrics at Boston City Hospital.

Even after they give birth to drug-impaired children, many mothers go right on smoking crack. Melinda East, a former crack addict now in treatment in Long Beach, Calif., supported her habit as an often barefoot street prostitute. Her first baby was born with "the shakes," she says, but that did not turn her away from crack. She remembers selling milk and Pampers back to the grocery store for drug money.

Local governments often take crack kids away from still addicted mothers, but that does not guarantee stability for troubled children. Charlie, a five-year-old Los Angeles–area boy with severe behavioral problems, went through three foster homes before an elderly couple became his guardians. He seems to be making progress, but his prospects appear limited. He sometimes erupts into frenzied episodes of thrashing about, pulling his hair, biting and banging his head against a wall.

While poor, black ghetto children have attracted the most attention, they are far from being the only members of the crack generation. Cocaine abuse is common among members of the white upper and middle classes, but it is hidden better. Their babies are usually born at private hospitals that rarely ask mothers about drug use or screen them and their children for illegal chemicals. A 1989 Florida study found similar rates of drug use among pregnant white and black women of equal socioeconomic status, but only 1% of white abusers were reported to authorities, compared with nearly 11% of blacks.

Billie, the kindergartner, is a white child whose mother was addicted to crack, among other drugs. Soon after birth, Billie was whisked away from her and given to wealthy adoptive parents. Growing up in a stable environment, however, has not prevented him from being kicked out of four preschools for disorganized, rowdy behavior. Only when he started at this new school, where his teachers are trained to handle drug-exposed children, did he begin to calm down.

The crack kids are not the first children to be devastated by drugs while their mothers were pregnant. For many years, the unborn have been exposed to opiates, barbiturates, inhaled cocaine and a panoply of other drugs. And fetal alcohol syndrome, brought on by drinking during pregnancy, is believed to be a leading cause of mental retardation in the young.

But the coming of crack made a bad situation worse. This readily available, easily ingested chemical has lured far more women into addiction than any other hard drug has. By the latest estimates, more than 1 million U.S. women use cocaine. Moreover, crack has spurred the use of other drugs. Women who take cocaine are likely to use heroin to prolong a high, then tranquilizers and alcohol to come down. They may indulge in marijuana, PCP and amphetamines. As a result, many crack babies steep in a stew of drugs while in the womb.

AN UNCERTAIN FUTURE

How badly are they damaged? In most cases, no one knows for sure. The question has sparked a fierce debate among doctors, social workers, educators and law-enforcement specialists. On one side are those who fear that most of the children are irredeemably harmed; on the other are those who firmly believe that with enough early treatment for babies and their mothers and special education, the large majority of crack kids can lead normal lives.

Among those who think the damage may be permanent is Kathy Kutschka, a director at the Speech and Language Development Center in Buena Park, Calif. Her department works with 45 crack kids, up to kindergarten age. When she observes them having trouble sitting in a chair or picking up a pencil, she despairs for their future. "Of the children we see," says Kutschka, "none will be able to function in a normal life-style without some kind of sheltered living arrangement."

An increasing number of medical experts, however, vehemently challenge the notion that most crack kids are doomed. In fact, they detest the term crack kids, charging that it unfairly brands the children and puts them all into a single dismal category. From this point of view, crack has become a convenient explanation for problems that are mainly caused by a bad environment. When a kindergartner from a broken home in an impoverished neighborhood misbehaves or seems slow, teachers may wrongly assume that crack is the chief reason, when other factors, like poor nutrition, are far more important.

Even when crack is responsible, the situation is rarely hopeless. "This is not a lost generation," says pediatrician Evelyn Davis of Harlem Hospital in New York City. "These children are not monsters. They are salvageable, capable of loving, of making good attachments. Yes, they present problems that we have not dealt with before, but they can be taught."

THE COST OF COMPASSION

Help is possible if society will pay the price—a very big "if" in these days of tight budgets. Will taxpayers foot the bill to provide the best treatment and schooling to all the crack kids? In Boston a year of special education for a drug-exposed child can cost $13,000, compared with $5,000 spent per youngster at a regular school.

Experts agree that the most vital first step in helping crack kids is to get their mothers off the drug, preferably before birth. Yet only 11% of pregnant addicts get into treatment. Many detox programs do not accept the women because they are not equipped to deal with prenatal medical needs. And very few programs are designed to help drug-dependent women who already have children.

The failure to spend more money for early rehabilitation of crack addicts and their babies may be a social and financial disaster in the long run. Contends T. Berry Brazelton, the noted Harvard pediatrician: "If we worked with these infants from the first, it would cost us one-tenth or one-hundredth as much as it will cost us later. To educate them, to keep them off the streets, to keep them in prisons will cost us billions."

WHAT THE DRUG DOES

Cocaine causes blood vessels to constrict, thus reducing the vital flow of oxygen and other nutrients. Because fetal cells multiply swiftly in the first months, an embryo deprived of a proper blood supply by a mother's early and continuous use of cocaine is "dealt a small deck," says Zuckerman of Boston City Hospital.

Such babies look quite normal but are undersized, and the circumference of their heads tends to be unusually small, a trait associated with lower IQ scores. "Only the most intensive care after birth will give these babies a chance, but many won't receive it," Zuckerman points out.

Occasionally, heavy maternal cocaine use during the later months of pregnancy can lead to an embolism, or clot, that lodges in a fetal vessel and completely disrupts the blood supply to an organ or limb. The result: a shriveled arm or leg, a missing section of intestine or kidney, or other deformities. Such glaring defects, however, are extremely rare.

Cocaine exposure affects brain chemistry as well. The drug alters the action of neurotransmitters, the messengers that travel between nerve cells and help control a person's mood and responsiveness. Such changes may help explain the behavioral aberrations, including impulsiveness and moodiness, seen in some cocaine-exposed children as they mature.

Ultrasound studies of 82 drug-exposed infants by researchers at the University of California at San Diego revealed that about a third have lesions in the brain, usually in the deeper areas that govern learning and thinking. While a similar percentage of babies who are ill but have not been exposed to drugs have such lesions, only 5% of healthy newborns do. The long-term significance of this finding is uncertain, since the brain continues to develop during a baby's first year. If there is damage, it may not surface until a child takes on such complex tasks as learning to talk.

At birth, cocaine babies generally perform poorly on tests measuring their responsiveness. And at one month, some of the infants still do not perform at the level of normal two-day-olds. Cocaine-exposed

babies are easily overstimulated. When that happens, some turn fussy for a while and then doze off; others tense up and squall for hours.

Caring for such infants is frustrating. "You don't do things that come naturally," notes Diane Carleson, a foster mother in San Mateo, Calif. "The more you bounce them and coo at them, the more they arch their backs to get away. Their poor mothers want so badly to make contact, yet they are headed for rejection unless they learn how not to overstimulate them."

Doctors at Harlem Hospital studied 70 such toddlers just under age 2 and found that almost all were slow in learning to talk and that more than half had impaired motor and social skills. An inability to distinguish between mothers and strangers is another hallmark of crack-exposed youngsters.

As the children reach school age, it becomes more difficult to separate the impact of drugs from the effects of upbringing and other influences. Yet many teachers think they can see the lingering legacy of crack. Beverly Beauzethier, a New York City kindergarten teacher, agonizes over some of her pupils. "They have trouble retaining basic things. They are not sure of colors or shapes or their names." Their behavior is also out of the ordinary. "Some are passive and cry a lot; sometimes they just sit in a heap in the corner," says Beauzethier. Even worse, "they can be very aggressive with the other children so that they are hard to stop,

and I have to hold their arms," she says. "This is very scary. We don't know a lot about handling these children."

HELPING HANDS

Doctors and educators are only beginning to design the programs needed to help the crack kids. One notable pilot project is Zuckerman's Women and Infants Clinic at Boston City Hospital, which uses what Zuckerman calls the "one-stop shopping" technique. While pediatricians and child-development experts work with babies, addicted mothers get help in kicking their habits and learn how to care for their children. The first eight babies in the program, tested at age 1, all fell within the normal range on the Bayley scale of infant development; this means they can play pat-a-cake, walk unassisted, jabber expressively and turn pages in a book.

One of the leading organizations working to help older children is the Salvin Special Education Center in Los Angeles, which conducted a three-year pilot program with 50 drug-exposed kids, ages 3 to 5. Salvin's educators cite several elements of a successful school program: small classes (eight pupils to one teacher), fixed seat assignments and a rigid routine, and protection from loud noises and other disturbing stimulation. Activities are emphasized over paper-and-pencil exercises. "We'll read a story and bring it to life

with hand puppets," explains school psychologist Valerie Wallace. Generous warmth and praise help youngsters achieve an emotional equilibrium. Of all Salvin's drug-exposed children, more than half have been able to transfer to regular school classes, with special tutoring and counseling.

Whether such success can be replicated on a large scale is uncertain, but the evidence is encouraging. A study by Dr. Ira Chasnoff and his staff at Chicago-based NAPARE followed 300 cocaine-exposed babies who, along with their mothers, received intensive postnatal intervention. Of 90 children tested at age 3, 90% showed normal intelligence, 70% had no behavioral problems, and 60% did not need speech therapy.

That may be less than complete success, but considering the horrible blow these children suffered before birth, it is remarkable that so many can be helped so much. The studies suggest that early intervention can give the children a fighting chance of leading reasonably normal lives. Such a payback seems more than enough to justify a far greater investment in treatment and rehabilitation. Today's crack kids may be a troubled generation, but they do not have to be a lost generation—unless society abandons them.

—Reported by
Mary Cronin/New York, Melissa Ludtke/Boston
and James Willwerth/Los Angeles

Alcohol and the Family

The children of problem drinkers are coming to grips with their feelings of fear, guilt and rage

Believe it or not, there are still people who think that the worst thing about drinking is a hangover.

Oh, yeah, on New Year's Day I had a hangover that...

No. Forget hangovers.

Huh? So what should we talk about? Cirrhosis?

If you wish, but the liver, with its amazing powers of regeneration, usually lasts longer than the spouse, who tends to fall apart relatively early in the drinker's decline.

You're making it hard for a man to drink in peace.

Sorry, but even if spouses do not abuse alcohol, they can come to resemble drunks, since their anger and fear are enormous: way beyond what you'd find in a truly sober person.

I know, I know, it's terrible what goes on behind closed doors.

You make it sound like there are no witnesses. You're forgetting the children. They grow up watching one out-of-control person trying to control another, and they don't know what "normal" is.

I suppose it's hard for the kids, until they move out.

They may move out, but they never leave their parents behind.

Hmm. Listen, can we talk?

We already are. A lot of people already are.

We are, just now, learning more about heavy drinking, and, simultaneously, putting behind us the notion that what alcoholism amounts to is just odd intervals of strange, and sometimes comic, behavior: W. C. Fields, Dean Martin, Foster Brooks. Since 1935 the members of Alcoholics Anonymous have been telling us, with awesome simplicity, that drinking made their lives unmanageable; Al-Anon brought us the news that relatives and friends of drinkers can suffer in harmony; and then came Alateen and even Alatot, where one picture of a stick person holding a beer can is worth a thousand slurred words. The Children of Alcoholics (COAs)—loosely organized but rapidly growing throughout the United States—reaffirm all of the previous grass-roots movements and bring us new insight into alcoholism's effects on the more than 28 million Americans who have seen at least one parent in the throes of the affliction. The bad news from COAs: alcohol is even more insidious than previously thought.

The good news: with the right kind of help, the terrible damage it does to nonalcoholics need not be permanent.

Imagine a child who lives in a chaotic house, rides around with a drunk driver and has no one to talk to about the terror. Don't think it doesn't happen: more than 10 million people in the United States are addicted to alcohol, and most of them have children. "I grew up in a little Vietnam," says one child of an alcoholic. "I didn't know why I was there; I didn't know who the enemy was." Decades after their parents die, children of alcoholics can find it difficult to have intimate relationships ("You learn to trust no one") or experience joy ("I hid in the closet"). They are haunted—sometimes despite worldwide acclaim, as in the case of

---

There's a Problem in the House

In "Adult Children of Alcoholics," Janet Geringer Woititz discusses 13 traits that most children from alcoholic households experience to some degree. These symptoms, she says, can pose lifelong problems.

Adult children of alcoholics . . .

- guess what normal behavior is.
- have difficulty following a project from beginning to end.
- lie when it would be just as easy to tell the truth.
- judge themselves without mercy.
- have difficulty having fun.
- take themselves very seriously.
- have difficulty with intimate relationships.
- overreact to changes over which they have no control.

- constantly seek approval and affirmation.
- feel that they are different from other people.
- are super-responsible or super-irresponsible.
- are extremely loyal, even in the face of evidence that the loyalty is undeserved.
- tend to lock themselves into a course of action without giving consideration to consequences.

artist Eric Fischl—by a sense of failure for not having saved Mommy or Daddy from drink. And they are prone to marry alcoholics or other severely troubled people because, for one reason, they're willing to accept unacceptable behavior. Many, indeed, have become addicted to domestic turmoil.

'Hurting so bad': Children of alcoholics are people who've been robbed of their childhood—"I've seen five-year-olds running entire families," says Janet Geringer Woititz, one of the movement's founding mothers. Nevertheless, the children of alcoholics often display a kind of childish loyalty even when such loyalty is clearly undeserved. They have a nagging feeling that they are different from other people, Woititz points out, and that may be because, as some recent scientific studies show, they are. Brain scans done by Dr. Henri Begleiter of the State University of New York College of Medicine in Brooklyn reveal that COAs often have deficiencies in the areas of the brain associated with emotion and memory. In this sense and in several other ways—their often obsessive personalities, their tendency to have a poor self-image—the children of alcoholics closely resemble alcoholics. In fact, one in four becomes an alcoholic, as compared with one in 10 out of the general population.

The anger of a COA cannot be seen by brain scans. But at a therapy session at Caron Family Services in Wernersville, Pa., Ken Gill, a 49-year-old IBM salesman, recently took a padded bat and walloped a couch cushion hard enough to wake up sleeping demons. "I came because I was hurting so bad and I didn't know why," he says. "A lot of things were going wrong. I was a workaholic, and I neglected my family." It took Gill only a few hours of exposure to the idea that he might be an "adult child," he says, to realize that his failings as a parent may be if not excused, then at least explained. Like a lot of kids who grew up in an alcoholic household, Gill, who is also a recovering alcoholic, never got what even rats and monkeys get: exposure, at an impressionable age, to the sight and sound of functioning parents. Suzanne Somers, the actress and singer, spent years working out her anger in the form of a just published book called "Keeping Secrets." "I decided that this disease took the first half of my life, and goddam it," she says, "it wasn't going to take the second half of it."

'Control freak': Not every COA has all of the 13 traits (see chart) ascribed to them by Woititz in her landmark work, "Adult Children of Alcoholics" (*1983. Health Communications, Inc.*), and not all have been scarred. (President Reagan, who has written of sometimes finding his father passed out drunk on the front porch, does not appear, from his famous management style, to suffer from any tendency to be a "control freak," a

■ A nine-year-old's nightmare: Living in denial

COURTESY CLAUDIA BLACK

most common COA complaint.) Some children of alcoholics are grossly overweight from compulsive eating while others are as dressed for success as, well, Somers. A few COAs are immobilized by depression. Another runs TV's "Old Time Gospel Hour." What these people *do* have in common is a basic agreement with George Vaillant, a Dartmouth Medical School professor who says that it is important to think of alcoholism not as an illness that affects bodily organs but as "an illness that affects families. Perhaps the worst single feature of alcoholism," Vaillant adds, "is that it causes people to be unreasonably angry at the people that they most love."

The movement is only about six years old, but expanding so rapidly that figures, could they be gathered for such a basically unstructured and anonymous group, would be outdated as soon as they appeared. We do know, though, that five years ago there were 21 people in an organization called the National Association for Children of Alcoholics; today there are more than 7,000. The 14 Al-Anon-affiliated children-of-alcoholics groups meeting in the early '80s have increased to 1,100. With only word-of-mouth advertising, Woititz's book has sold about a million copies; indeed, "Adult Children of Alcoholics" reached the number-three spot on The New York Times paperback best-seller list long before it was available in any bookstore—at a time, in other words, when getting a copy meant

collaring a clerk to put in an order and *saying the title out loud.*

"We turned on the phones in 1982," says Migs Woodside, founder and president of the Children of Alcoholics Foundation in New York, "and the calls are still coming in 24 hours a day." The COAs Foundation sponsors a traveling art show that features the work of young and adult COAs; often, says Woodside, an attendee will stand mesmerized before a crude depiction of domestic violence or parental apathy ("Mom at noon," it says beneath the picture of someone huddling beneath the bedcovers)—and will then go directly to a pay phone to find help. "The newcomers all tend to say the same thing," says Woodside. "'Wait a minute—that's my story, that's *me!'*"

"It's private pain transformed into a public statement," says James Garbarino, president of the Erikson Institute for Advanced Study in Child Development, in Chicago, "a fascinating movement." But when you consider that denial is the primary symptom of alcoholism and that COAs tend by nature to take on more than their share of blame for whatever mess they happen to find themselves in, the rapid growth of the COAs movement seems just short of miraculous—something akin to a drunken stockbroker named Bill Wilson cofounding AA, now *the* model for a vast majority of self-help programs throughout the United States. After all, who would want to spill the family's darkest secret after years of telling teachers, employers and friends that everything was fine? ("A child of an

alcoholic will always say 'Fine'," says Rokelle Lerner, a counselor who specializes in young COAs. "They get punished if they say otherwise.") Who would voluntarily identify themselves with a group whose female members, according to some reports, have an above-average number of gynecological problems, possibly due to stress—and whose men are prone to frequent surgery for problems, doctors say, that may be basically psychosomatic?

The answer is, only someone who had, in some sense, bottomed out, just the way a drinker does before he turns to AA.

The concept of codependency is at the center of the COAs movement. Eleanor Williams, who works with COAs at the Charter Peachford Hospital in Atlanta, defines codependency as "unconscious addiction to another person's dysfunctional behavior." Woititz, in a recent Changes magazine interview, referred to it more simply as a tendency to "put other people's needs before my own." A codependent family member may suspect that he has driven the alcoholic to drink (though that is impossible, according to virtually all experts in the field); he almost certainly thinks that he can cure or at least control the drinker's troublesome behavior. "I actually thought that I could make a difference by cooking my husband better meals and by taking the kids out for drives on weekends [so he could rest]," says Ella S., a Westchester, N.Y., woman. "For all I know, it's a deeply ingrained psychological, and possibly genetic, disease, and here I am going at it with a lamb chop."

Mental movies: Obsessed with her husband's increasingly self-destructive behavior, Ella's next step, in typical codependent fashion, was to hide Bob's six-packs, which made him, to put it mildly, angry. Soon they were fighting almost daily and Ella was running mental movies of their scenes from a marriage all night long. "I was wasting a lot of time and energy trying to change the past, while he kept getting worse," she says. "There was a kind of awkward violence between him and me all the time; our hearts weren't really in it, but it wasn't until he had an affair with an alcoholism counselor *that I got him to* that I left." If you're wondering about children, Ella has a seven-year-old daughter, Ann. Her omission is significant. If life were a horse race, then Ann has been, as they say on the past performance charts, "shuffled back" among the also-rans.

What COAs—all people affected by alcohol—need to learn is that the race is fixed: when there is no program of recovery—either through the support of a group or the self-imposed abstinence of an individual—the abused substance will always win, handily, no matter what the competition. The first step of AA begins, "We admitted we were powerless . . ." But what will become of Ann, who is codependent on *two*

people? Perhaps, sensing that she is not exactly the center of attention, she will reach adulthood with a need for constant approval, a common COA symptom. Or maybe she will, even as a child, react to the chaos by trying to keep everything in her life under control, and thus give the impression that she is, despite everything, quite a trouper, a golden child.

"[Some] don't fall apart until they're in their 20s or 30s," says Woititz, and in some cases, especially those marked by violence or incest and sexual abuse (three times more common in alcoholic households than in the general population), that's the wonder of it all. One eight-year-old patient at Woititz's Verona, N.J., counseling center

woke up in the middle of the night to see her alcoholic mother shoot herself in the head. "The child called the 911 emergency number, got her mother to the hospital and basically saved her mother's life," says Woititz. "When I saw her she was having nightmares—that she wouldn't wake up and witness this suicide attempt. This is not a normal nightmare. The child had become mother to her own mother."

Each unhappy family, as Tolstoy said, is unhappy in its own way. Artist Eric Fischl, 39, in a short videotape he made for the COAs Foundation called "Trying to Find Normal," speaks of stepping over his passed-out mother, in their comfortable-looking (from the outside) Port Washing-

■ The fighting never stops: Living with fear

COURTESY CHILDREN OF ALCOHOLICS FOUNDATION

■ Out of control: Remembering hurts

COURTESY CHILDREN OF ALCOHOLICS FOUNDATION

Heredity and Drinking: How Strong Is the Link?

Research on the genetics of alcoholism took a curious turn a few weeks ago when Lawrence Lumeng analyzed his DNA to demonstrate why he can't tolerate liquor. Lumeng, a biochemist at the Indiana University School of Medicine, is among the 30 to 45 percent of Asians whose response to spirited beverages is a reddened face, headaches or nausea. This "Oriental flush," past studies have shown, arises in those who have an inefficient version of a liver enzyme that is crucial to the body's breakdown of alcohol; this "lazy" enzyme allows the buildup of an alcohol product, acetaldehyde, which is sickening and leads many Asians to shun alcohol. Working with biochemist Ting-Kai Li, Lumeng says that he pinpointed the gene that instructs cells to make the odd enzyme. The experiment offers dramatic evidence that a bodily response to alcohol is genetically dictated—and is thus inherited as surely as eye color.

There is no evidence for the opposite proposition: that a specific gene makes a person *crave* alcohol. Considering the wide variety of reasons why people consume the stuff, it seems unlikely that a "drinking gene" exists. But researchers have firmly established that, compared with other children, an alcoholic's offspring are around four times more likely to develop the problem, even if they were raised by other, nonalcoholic parents. In families with a history of alcoholism, explains C. Robert Cloninger, a psychiatrist and geneticist at Washington University in St. Louis, "what is inherited is not the fact that you are destined to become an alcoholic but varying degrees of susceptibility" to the disorder. So real is the predisposition that many researchers advise adult children of alcoholics (COAs) to drink no alcohol whatsoever.

Even the brains of COAs show faint signs of unusual activity, according to controversial studies by psychiatrist Henri Begleiter of the State University of New York in Brooklyn. Begleiter has found that young boys who have never consumed alcohol produce the slightly distorted brainwave patterns typical of their alcoholic fathers. Such signature brain waves, he says, may mark the son of an alcoholic as likely to develop a drinking problem and perhaps alert him to the risk. However, it remains to be seen whether such brain scans are sufficiently reliable and informative to distinguish potential social drinkers from future alcoholics. The technique, comments psychologist Robert Pandina, scientific director of the Center of Alcohol Studies at Rutgers University, is "at this time not any more valuable" as a predictor of future drinking behavior "than collecting a good family history on an individual."

Other studies show that many COAs respond uniquely to booze. Marc Schuckit, a psychiatrist at the Veterans Administration Hospital in San Diego, has found that college-age sons of alcoholics often react less to a few drinks than other college men; in his studies, the drinkers' sons were generally not as euphoric or tipsy after three to five cocktails. Schuckit believes that this lower sensitivity makes it harder for the alcoholics' sons to know when to stop drinking, starting them down the road to alcohol problems. Preliminary experiments by Barbara Lex of McLean Hospital in Belmont, Mass., confirm that daughters of alcoholics respond similarly. Women from families with a history of alcohol abuse tend to keep their balance better on a wobbly platform after having a drink. Apparently women, too, can inherit traits that might predispose them to addiction, although there are far fewer female than male alcoholics.

Half a beer: The key unresolved issue, of course, is why some individuals from alcohol-scarred families succumb to alcoholism while others don't. Genes play some role in the development, most notably in abstinence. "People say that whether you drink or not has to do only with willpower," explains Indiana's Lumeng, "but the reason I can drink only half a beer is biological."

Yet heredity alone obviously isn't to blame for alcoholism's appalling toll. In fact, about 60 percent of the nation's alcohol abusers are from families with *no* history of the disorder. How much people drink is influenced by factors as prosaic as cost; partly to curb consumption, the National Council on Alcoholism is lobbying to raise federal excise taxes on beer and wine, which haven't changed since 1951. Social influences like cost and peer pressure "are just as important as genes," says Dartmouth psychiatrist George Vaillant. "All the genes do is make it easier for you to become an alcoholic." For now, the value of genetic studies is to warn COAs that they may well have a real handicap in the struggle against the family trouble.

TERENCE MONMANEY *with* KAREN SPRINGEN *in New York and* MARY HAGER *in Washington*

---

ton, N.Y., home and seeing her "lying in her own piss." His work, which has been the subject of a one-man show at the Whitney Museum in New York, is not autobiographical, he says, and yet "the tone [of it] has everything to do with my childhood." His painting "Time for Bed" "relates to my memory of all hell breaking loose," he says. "I guess you could say the boy is me and his shame, embarrassment and sadness is mine as well. The little boy's Superman pajamas are on backwards, so it's like looking in a mirror. I painted the woman standing on a glass table with spiked heels on to give it a sense of fragility and danger. The man only has one arm because I wanted a sense of impotence."

Alcohol leaves every alcoholic and codependent who does not admit his powerlessness over the substance in a constant state of longing. Fischl didn't realize how sad he'd been until his mother died, in an alcohol-related car accident, in 1970. "The thing about having a sick parent is that you think it's your problem," he says. "You feel like a failure because you can't save her." Even when there is no incest, there is seduction. Fischl's mother kept "signaling," he says, "that if you could just come a little bit further with me in this, you can save me."

Some of the other things that alcohol ruins, before it gets to the liver: family meals ("Alcohol fills you up. My father was never interested in eating with us"); gloriously run-of-the-mill evenings around the hearth ("Alcohol makes you tired. My father was in bed most nights at 8"). When enough C_2H_5HO is added to a home, vases may start to fly across the room and crash into walls. All kinds of paper—court-issued Orders of Protection, divorce decrees, bounced checks—come fluttering down. The lights go on and off. Does that mean Daddy's forgotten to pay the bill again, or that the second act is starting?

Every alcoholic household is, in fact, a pathetic little play in which each of the

members takes on a role. This is not an idea that arrived with the COAs movement; a 17-page booklet called "Alcoholism: A Merry-Go-Round Named Denial" has been distributed free of charge by Al-Anon for almost 20 years. Written by the Rev. Joseph L. Kellerman, the former director of the Charlotte, N.C., Council of Alcoholism, "Merry-Go-Round" takes note of the uncanny consistency with which certain characters appear in alcoholic situations. These include the Enabler ("a 'helpful' Mr. Clean . . .[who] conditions [the drinker] to believe there will always be a protector who will come to his rescue"); the Victim ("the person who is responsible for getting the work done if the alcoholic is absent") and the Provoker (usually the spouse or parent of the alcoholic, this is "the key person . . . who is hurt and upset by repeated drinking episodes, but she holds the family together . . . In turn, she feeds back into the marriage her bitterness, resentment, fear and hurt . . . She controls, she tries to force the changes she wants; she sacrifices, adjusts, never gives up, never gives in, but never forgets").

Some of the earliest books in the COAs movement explored the drama metaphor more deeply and defined the roles that children play. Sharon Wegscheider-Cruse, in her 1981 book, "Another Chance" (*Science and Behavior Books, Inc. Palo Alto, Calif.*), wrote about the Family Hero, who is usually the firstborn. A high achiever in school, the Hero always does what's right, often discounting himself by putting others first. The Lost Child, meanwhile, is withdrawn, a loner on his way to a joyless adulthood, and thus, in some ways, very different from the Scapegoat, who appears hostile and defiant but inside feels hurt and angry. (It is the Scapegoat, says Wegscheider-Cruse, who gets attention through "negative behavior" and is likely to be involved in alcohol or other drugs later.) Last and least—in his own mind—is the Mascot, fragile and immature yet charming: the family clown.

'Good-looking' kids: Virtually no one was publishing those kinds of thoughts when Claudia Black, a Laguna Beach, Calif., therapist, began searching for literature on the subject of the alcohol-affected family in the late '70s. "Half of my adult [alcoholic] patients had kids my age and older," she remembers, "but all I found was stuff on fetal alcohol syndrome and kids prone to juvenile delinquency." One thing that fascinated her about young COAs, she says, was that despite their developmental problems "they were all 'good-looking' kids"—presentable and responsible albeit not terribly verbal. "They had friends but weren't honest with them. Everything was 'fine and dandy'."

The title of Black's important 1981 book, "It Will Never Happen to Me" (*M.A.C.

"NOT NOW I'M BUSY"

COURTESY CHILDREN OF ALCOHOLICS FOUNDATION
■ Trauma: Parental neglect

Denver, Colo.), reflects the typical codependent's mix of denial and false bravado. In it, she makes the point that the children in an alcoholic household never have an environment that is consistent and structured, two of the things they need most—and she, too, talks of such stock juvenile "roles" as the Responsible One and the Adjuster. Her unique

warning was that children who survive a parent's alcoholism by displaying unusual coping behavior often experience "emotional and psychological deficits" later on. They are also likely to become alcoholics, says Black, because "alcohol helps these persons become less rigid, loosen up and relax. When they drink they aren't quite so serious." Though those things happen to almost everyone who imbibes, Black says that "for those who are stuck in unhealthy patterns, alcohol may be the *only* thing that can provide relief."

Well, she guessed wrong there: a movement, manifested by often joyous meetings, has come along in the interim. At hundreds of COAs gatherings around the country tonight, people will talk and listen to each other's stories, to cry, to laugh and generally, as Ken Gill says, "recharge their batteries." "This program kept me from being an alcoholic myself," said a woman named Heather at a gathering in an affluent section of San Francisco last week. "Because I was the oldest, everything was always my fault. It's like when you make your parents breakfast and you bring them one scrambled egg and one fried egg—in my house I always scrambled the wrong egg." Heads bobbed in agreement. Who else but COAs could identify with a story about what happens when kids cook for their own mother and father?

Discovering self-esteem: Talking and listening: this is the way we've learned to

It happened once to me; I was but A child happy and Free. Then one day my daddy came Behind me and pushed me Down the stairs. I Just layed there. When I awoke that day was Gone and and I've Been sick For ever long. I was but 3 and daddy always beat on me; He smelt of Beer and wine and the next day he kissed me and said things were Fine.

COURTESY CHILDREN OF ALCOHOLICS FOUNDATION
■ Physical abuse: An adult remembers

deal with problem drinking. And though it sounds wimpy, don't knock it; it's the surest way to alleviate not just the imbibing but the whole range of symptoms we call alcoholism. A woman named Nina stood up at a meeting in Boston last week, practically glossed over the fact that both her parents were alcoholics—and proceeded to speak about how well she was feeling and doing. COAs meetings and literature, she said, had allowed her to discover self-esteem. At another meeting, Carolyn told a story of complaining to her doctor about depression—and hearing the doctor shoot back a question about whether one of her parents was an alcoholic. "I was shocked," she said, and well she might be. Doctors, as a group, have yet to play a major role in helping mitigate the effects of alcohol, perhaps because the average medical-school student spends a grand total of between zero and 10 hours studying the affliction that kills 100,000 people annually.

An avalanche of information is coming, nevertheless, from another kind of M.D.—call them the Masters of Disaster, the people who've lived with alcoholism or worked with alcoholics so closely that they might as well be their kin. Robert Ackerman, a professor of sociology at Indiana University of Pennsylvania, has been studying the children of alcoholics for an exceedingly long time by the standards of the movement—since the early '70s. In his recent book "Let Go and Grow" (Health Communications, Inc.), he reports on a survey he took to test the validity of Woititz's 13 generalizations about COAs, as well as seven more observations of his own. What he found was that "adult children of alcoholics identified about 20 percent more with these characteristics" than did the general population. Other professionals are reporting success with therapies involving hugging, acting out unresolved scenes from long ago and even playing one of several board games for children of alcoholics called Family Happenings and Sobriety. Cathleen Brooks, executive director of a program called Next Step in San Diego, reports that her clients often make life-changing strides after six to 18 months of primary treatment and make the decision never to drink or take drugs.

The 7 million COAs who are under the age of 18 are harder to help, if only because their parents' denial tends to keep them out of treatment. For these children who never know what to expect when they come home from school each day, life, says Woititz, "is a state of constant anxiety."

Some pediatricians think there is a link between such anxiety and childhood ulcers, chronic nausea, sleeping problems, eating disorders and dermatitis. Migs Woodside, from the COAs Foundation, says that the trained teacher can pick the child of an alcoholic out of a crowded classroom. "Sometimes you can tell by the way they are dressed or by the fact that they never have their lunch money," she says. "Sometimes you can tell by the way they suddenly pay attention when the teacher talks about drinking, and sometimes you can tell by their pictures."

Someday, 20 or 30 years from now, those children may feel a vague sense of failure or depression and be hard pressed to explain why. In the meantime, it's their Crayolas that are hard pressed. Beer cans—and not liquor or wine bottles—form a leitmotif in the work of young children of alcoholics. Occasionally, Woodside says, looking a little sad, the big stick figures can be seen tipping the cans into the mouths of the little stick figures.

CHARLES LEERHSEN *with* TESSA NAMUTH
and bureau reports

How Smoking Kills You

Any way you look at it, lighting up is hazardous to your health.

Maureen Callahan

Maureen Callahan is a Boston-based free-lance writer specializing in health and nutrition.

"SURGEON GENERAL'S WARNING: Smoking Causes Lung Cancer, Heart Disease, Emphysema, And May Complicate Pregnancy." These familiar words appear on cigarette advertisements and cigarette packages around the country. Yet, nearly a third of the American adult population still continues the habit, which, says the American Lung Association, prematurely claims more lives than illicit drugs, alcohol abuse, homicide, suicide, and automobile accidents combined.

Why don't people stop? One reason is that cigarettes, or more specifically the nicotine they contain, are addictive. Ninety percent of smokers start smoking before the age of nineteen, and that makes the habit both physically and psychologically hard to shake. In addition, millions of smokers still do not realize (or perhaps don't accept the fact) that smoking is hazardous to health. Even worse, new studies indicate that smokers may be injuring more than themselves when they light up. According to a recent report from the surgeon general of the United States, "involuntary" smoking (inhaling smoke secondhand) may cause disease, such as lung cancer, in healthy nonsmokers.

For people who like to smoke.

Pack-a-day cigarette smokers shave five years off their life expectancy. Heavy smokers, those who smoke two or more packs per day, cut their lives short by as many as eight years. The grim reality, then, is that the health costs of lighting up far outweigh the short-lived euphoric feeling a cigarette provides. Cigarette smoke, with its dozens of toxic gases—including carbon monoxide—and small particles of tar and nicotine, is lethal to the lungs, to the heart, and to the body as a whole. The length of time a person smokes and the degree to which he inhales determine how much toxic gas and how many toxic particles the lungs and body are exposed to. But, in general, smokers are five times more likely to develop chronic bronchitis than nonsmokers because of this exposure to the toxins from cigarettes. Moreover, smoking can cause more serious lung disease in the form of emphysema—a disease in which the natural elasticity of the air sacs in the lungs is lost, causing difficulty in exhaling—and lung cancer. Estimates are that 85 to 90 percent of lung cancer deaths are caused by smoking.

Smoking also increases your risks of developing heart disease and suffering a stroke. Women under the age of 50 who smoke about one and a half packs of cigarettes each day run at least a fivefold greater risk of having a heart attack than their nonsmoking counterparts. The National Heart, Lung and Blood Institute lists smoking among the top major risk factors for heart disease, along with high blood pressure and high levels of blood cholesterol. Giving up cigarettes can reduce the risk for heart disease and, as one study shows, may cut the risk for stroke by more than half. Researchers involved in the Honolulu Heart Program, a major clinical project that studied the risks for stroke among nearly 8,000 men, conclude that smokers have two to three times the risk of stroke as nonsmokers. But when they quit, that risk is cut dramatically.

Who's come a long way, baby?

For women, the risks attached to smoking are much greater than for men. A woman who smokes not only will be more likely to fall victim to heart disease, lung cancer, emphysema, and chronic bronchitis but also puts herself at risk for a multitude of typically female problems ranging from osteoporosis to early menopause. At last count, 28 percent of American women smoke.

Especially alarming is the fact that smoking among teenage girls seems to be on the rise. In the last ten years,

the number of female smokers aged twelve to eighteen has doubled. Twenty-one percent of teenage girls in their senior year of high school smoke daily, an amount that exceeds the numbers of their male counterparts who smoke. If the pace keeps up, the future may see women outsmoking men. That's quite a turnaround when you consider that before World War II, smoking was almost exclusively a male habit.

Thirty-two percent of women between the ages of 20 and 34 smoke. These women, in their childbearing years, are the most susceptible to the hazards of cigarette smoke. For one thing, women who smoke will find it much more difficult to conceive than women who don't smoke. Estimates are that fertility is 25 percent lower in smokers, meaning that on the average it will take much longer to become pregnant. Once pregnant, a woman who continues to smoke has a risk of miscarriage that is three to seven times higher than that of nonsmokers. Her baby runs the risk of being of low birthweight—a condition that has many attendant problems, ranging from mental retardation to chronic infection, all of which can last well into adulthood. A study by Richard Naeye, M.D., chairman of the department of pathology at The Pennsylvania State University College of Medicine, found that babies born to smokers had a 50 percent higher risk of developing Sudden Infant Death Syndrome (SIDS).

At the other end of a woman's reproductive years are some different problems. According to a review study by Donald Mattison, M.D., associate professor of obstetrics and gynecology at the University of Arkansas College of Medicine, women who smoke half a pack a day can bring on early menopause—one to two years ahead of the biological time clock. In addition, women who smoke may actually make themselves more susceptible to the crippling bone disease of old age—osteoporosis. Smoking lowers levels of the female hormone estrogen, a hormone that plays a critical role in keeping bones strong.

Finally, women who take oral contraceptives and smoke put themselves at even greater risk. These women are ten times more likely to suffer myocardial infarction than someone who neither smokes nor takes birth-control pills, according to Gregory Morosco, Ph.D., of the National Heart, Lung and Blood Institute.

Secondhand risks.

When the smoke clears, the evidence may be overwhelming that nonsmokers are at risk from the toxic hazards of cigarettes. A number of recent studies have suggested that nonsmoking wives who have husbands who smoke are much more likely to fall victim to lung cancer and heart disease than those whose husbands don't smoke. Indeed, some researchers have suggested that there is as much as twice the risk for lung cancer in the wives of smokers and three times the risk for heart attack.

The tobacco industry holds the opinion that the hazardous effects of environmental smoke, and even smoking itself, have not been clearly demonstrated. Granted the evidence is still preliminary in many cases, and there are a few studies that have not been able to find a strong connection between secondhand smoke and lung cancer, but most experts agree that passive smoking can be dangerous. The surgeon general, in fact, issued a report last year that called the scientific case proving the dangers of involuntary smoking "more than sufficient." He added that action should be taken in order to protect the nonsmoker from "environmental tobacco smoke," particularly in the workplace.

" . . . Parents may be swayed into kicking the habit when they realize that smoking can lead to problems for their children. . . ."

Companies, government agencies, and restaurateurs have been tightening restrictions on smoking—some are even banning smoking entirely—since the report. Some bans are successful, such as the one that began in 1985 at Pacific Northwest Bell Telephone Company. Others are not. Restaurant owners in Beverly Hills, for example, found they lost customers after the Beverly Hills City Council initiated a total ban on smoking in eating estab-

lishments and in retail stores. The laws were changed after four months because of the restaurant claims of declining sales, and now smoking is allowed only in certain areas of the restaurant that are equipped with special ventilation equipment that meets established health standards.

Parents may be swayed into kicking the habit when they realize that their smoking can lead to problems for their children. Children who have parents that smoke, according to recent research, are more likely to suffer from respiratory infections—colds, bronchitis, pneumonia—than children of nonsmokers. Furthermore, these problems increase as the exposure to smoke increases. For example, the child whose parents both smoke will have more infections than the child with only one parent who smokes. A recent report in the medical journal *Pediatrics* suggests that children exposed to cigarette smoke may experience stunted lung growth. If lungs do not grow to full capacity, these children may be set up for problems with lung disease, including pulmonary failure later in their lives.

Calling it quits.

To date 41 million Americans have kicked the smoking habit. And these numbers may continue to grow. Indeed, one out of every three smokers tries to quit each year. Quitting, in fact, is big business. Last year, Americans spent about $100 million on aids to stop smoking. What do these businesses provide? Help of all different kinds, it appears.

Smokers can choose between programs that focus on hypnosis, acupuncture, or group therapy, or they can simply quit cold turkey. For a more gradual approach, there are chewing gums laced with nicotine and plastic cigarettes with a boost of nicotine but with none of the harmful toxic gases and particles of tar that are found in a regular cigarette. Although these aids may wean people away for the dependency on nicotine, there is a psychological side to cigarette smoking for which many find no substitute. One ex-smoker, Lois Mack, puts it this way: "There isn't a day goes by that I don't want a cigarette, but I won't take one." After 29 years of smoking, the

addiction, she says, is still very much there. But it is controlled.

For many ex-smokers, developing this discipline is the difficult part. The battle to stay smoke-free is a hard one. One of the surest routes to success, according to Tom Ferguson, M.D., author of *The Smokers Book of Health* (G. P. Putman's Sons), is to learn to cope with the urge to smoke. Situations may come up that trigger the desire for a cigarette, but individuals need to find a way to short-circuit that desire. Distractions in the way of a hobby or activity might help. Or it might be wise to avoid situations that make you feel like lighting up. Whatever you do, it must be something that you can stick with. After all, quitting, whether it's cold turkey or gradual, is meant to be a permanent arrangement.

Be smart, don't start.

Still, the best advice is not to start smoking. Not only does smoking speed up the body's metabolic rate 10 percent (which is why many smokers may tend to gain weight once they quit), but it causes a host of serious illnesses ranging from lung cancer to heart disease. Cigarettes, it seems, have nothing to offer but problems. But you can't tell that from the advertisements. Each year, tobacco companies spend $2 billion on advertising that tends to downplay the hazards. Health organizations like the American Medical Association and the American Cancer Society hope to persuade the government to ban the glossy cigarette advertisements. But even if advertisements were banned, here would still be a big task ahead for health professionals. People need to understand fully the dangers of smoking. Until potential smokers realize the risk of their habit, smokers' ranks will continue to swell.

Is Coffee Harmful?

What science says now about caffeine and decaffeination

Corby Kummer

YOU CAN LEARN what fine coffee is and brew it far better than you ever did before. You can really like the taste of the stuff. But the reason most people drink coffee, of course, is the caffeine. Caffeine may do a wonderful job of fortifying you to face the day. You may think you couldn't live without it. But is it bad for you?

Frank evaluation of its hazards is not easy. There is a vast literature on the effects of caffeine on the body, and for every study reaching one conclusion, seemingly there is another that contradicts it. Although most major health risks have been ruled out, research continues at a steady clip. I'll summarize here the work done recently.

The first indictment of caffeine in recent years came in 1972, when a Boston group found an association between heavy coffee drinking (more than six cups a day) and elevated risk of heart attack. The association was never confirmed by other studies, however, and the first studies were shown to have been flawed. In 1974 a twelve-year review by the Framingham Heart Study concluded that there was no association between coffee consumption and heart attacks, coronary heart disease, angina pectoris, or sudden death.

Today the possible link between caffeine and heart disease is still controversial, and remains the most widely studied aspect of caffeine; recent studies have separated out other risk factors, chiefly smoking, that misled researchers in the past. They have so far come up pretty much undecided. Because very high doses of caffeine can provoke arrhythmia (irregular heartbeat), the danger to people who already suffered from arrhythmia was for a while widely researched, but a study reported last year in the *Archives of Internal Medicine* concluded that moderate doses of caffeine did not pose a danger even to people with life-threatening arrhythmia. Last fall a widely publicized study suggested that people who drink decaffeinated coffee experience a rise in serum cholesterol, but the medical community has largely dismissed the study as preliminary and inconclusive, and no supporting studies have appeared. A recent study in the Netherlands, reported last winter in the *New England Journal of Medicine*, found a significant increase in serum cholesterol among drinkers of boiled coffee, still popular there but made very little here; filtered coffee, which is what most Americans drink, had no effect.

A famous health scare associating caffeine with pancreatic cancer turned out to be another case of the missing link: cigarette smoking was the important risk factor, and five years after publication of the study its authors reversed their original findings. Studies associating coffee with bladder, urinary-tract, and kidney cancer have also been inconsistent and inconclusive.

No link to breast cancer has been proved, although whether a link exists between coffee drinking and benign breast disease, or fibrocystic disease, is still controversial. Large and well-controlled studies have virtually ruled out any link between caffeine consumption and the development of fibrocystic disease, but abstaining from caffeine as a way of treating the disease has been less thoroughly studied. Although the studies conducted so far suggest that no significant lessening of fibrocystic disease occurs when women give up caffeine, many women believe that doing so is an effective treatment.

Pregnant women were told in 1980 by the Food and Drug Administration that they should avoid caffeine, on the basis of an FDA experiment in which pregnant rats were force-fed the equivalent of 56 to 87 cups of strong coffee at a time through a stomach tube, and gave birth to offspring with missing toes or parts of toes. A later study giving rats the same exaggerated doses, but orally, in drinking water and at a steadier rate over a day, resulted in none of the birth defects. No later studies on human beings have linked coffee-drinking to any birth defects.

The subject for further study seems to be the connection between heavy consumption—more than six or seven cups a day—and low birth weight or birth defects. The average half-life of caffeine in the body, meaning the time it takes the body to get rid of half the caffeine consumed, is three to six hours. Women in the second and third trimesters of pregnancy clear it half as fast, and caffeine, which passes easily through the placenta, can remain in an unborn child for as long as a hundred hours. (Heavy smokers, in contrast, clear caffeine twice as fast.) Although no dangers to infants have been found when pregnant women or nursing mothers drink moderate amounts of coffee, many doctors recommend on principle that pregnant and nursing women avoid caffeine.

How caffeine works is still incompletely understood, and the prevailing theory took shape only in the early seventies. The theory holds that caffeine acts less by starting than by stopping something, the something being the depressant effects of adenosine, one of the chemicals the body makes to control neural activity. Caffeine blocks the adenosine receptor sites in cells. This theory is not perfect, for reasons including that there are different types of adenosine receptors, but it is widely accepted.

Proponents of caffeine emphasize its ability to increase alertness and enhance performance on various tasks. Its effects are most pronounced, however, on performance levels that are low because of fatigue or boredom. Also, caffeine seems to affect people to a degree that varies according to personality type. For example, it appears to help extroverts keep performing tasks requiring vigilance more than it helps introverts, who are evidently able to plow through such tasks unassisted. Despite the generations of writers who have assumed that coffee helps them think more clearly, caffeine seems to increase only intellectual speed, not intellectual power. Subjects in experiments do things like read and complete crossword puzzles faster but not more accurately.

Some studies reveal a curious fact. One recent study found that people who were given doses of caffeine varying from none to high and at the same time allowed to drink their normal amount of coffee each day had no idea how much caffeine they were consuming overall or whether they were consuming any additional caffeine. Even at the highest additional doses people who ordinarily drank small amounts of coffee reported no irritability, nervousness, or tremors. Numerous other studies reinforce the idea that people respond to caffeine more in relation to how much they think they have consumed than to how much they actually have.

This is not to say that the effects of caffeine are imaginary. Many studies confirm what most people know—coffee keeps you awake. It also often decreases total sleep time and increases the number of times you wake in the night, depending on how much you drink and on how sensitive you are. Variation among people is great. Everyone knows someone like the woman I met in Brazil who told me, "If I'm sleepy, I take a coffee. If I wake up at night, I take a coffee to go back to sleep." Although caffeine does interfere with some phases of sleep, it has in many studies been shown not to decrease rapid-eye-movement sleep, as alcohol and barbiturates do. The sleep disturbance it causes seems to be more severe in older people, which may be one reason why consumption of decaffeinated coffee increases with age.

That caffeine interferes with sleep doesn't mean that it reliably makes you snap to. It doesn't sober you up, black or with milk—your motor functions are just as badly impaired by alcohol as they were before you drank two cups of black coffee, and even if you feel more awake you're just as dangerous a driver. Similarly, caffeine does not counteract phenobarbital or other barbiturates. But it does help reverse the impairment of cognitive activity caused by diazepam, the chemical that is the basis of Valium and many other tranquilizers.

Caffeine speeds up the metabolism and makes you burn calories faster, although not significantly for purposes of weight loss, as amphetamine does. The body metabolizes caffeine almost completely, and it appears in all tissue fluids about five minutes after ingestion, reaching its highest levels after twenty to thirty minutes. Caffeine is a diuretic and thus dehydrating, so don't think that drinking coffee will slake your thirst. Coffee, both regular and decaffeinated, has a laxative effect.

And coffee can cause stomach pain and heartburn. The exact roles played by caffeine and other substances in coffee in stimulating the secretion of gastric acids remains in question, because there has been proof that both caffeinated and decaffeinated coffee can affect the gastrointestinal tract. One study found that regular and decaffeinated coffee each had twice as much effect on the gastrointestinal tract as caffeine alone. Although coffee, with or without caffeine, and caffeine itself are not thought to cause ulcers, their role has been little studied, and both are known to make ulcers worse.

A source of confusion for anyone trying to learn how much caffeine he consumes is the conflicting estimates that appear in studies. Most say that a five-ounce cup of coffee contains from 80 to 100 milligrams of caffeine, although in fact the variation can be much greater, depending on the strength of the coffee. The same amount of tea, brewed for five minutes, has from 20 to 50 milligrams of caffeine; a cup of tea usually contains less caffeine than a cup of coffee because less tea is used per cup. A twelve-ounce serving of cola generally contains 38 (for Pepsi) to 45 (for Coke) milligrams of caffeine. Some studies say that for caffeine to have its effects the minimum oral dose is 85 milligrams, but this too depends on individual sensitivity.

The question of addiction is similarly thorny. According to a review of the literature on caffeine and the central nervous system by Kenneth Hirsh, in *Methylxanthine Beverages and Foods*, recent data show that tolerance to caffeine develops in the central nervous system and in many organ systems. Tolerance has been better studied than its ugly corollary, withdrawal. In sleep studies researchers noticed that heavy coffee drinkers were less disturbed than light or moderate coffee drinkers by drinking coffee before going to sleep and, if they had had no coffee the night before, felt more in need of a cup in the morning. Those little accustomed to caffeine suffer "caffeinism," or coffee nerves, when they have a high dose. Those accustomed to but deprived of it report, and experiments confirm, irritability, inability to work well, nervousness, restlessness, and lethargy.

Worst, and most common, is the headache that comes with giving up caffeine. The headache can be severe and often lasts for one or two days. The adenosine-receptor theory holds that long-term caffeine consumption creates more adenosine receptor sites, and thus sudden abstention from caffeine means unusual sensitivity to adenosine. This could explain withdrawal headache: overreactivity to adenosine in blood vessels in the scalp and cranium can dilate them, and cause a headache. One very effective way to treat the headache, unsurprisingly, is with caffeine, which constricts the blood vessels in the brain; this effect is why caffeine has long been used to treat migraines. (In contrast, caffeine dilates coronary arteries.) The reason so many over-the-counter headache remedies include caffeine,

though, is that it is thought to enhance the effects of the other drugs in them—something that has never been proved. Kenneth Hirsh optimistically thinks that because the body is more sensitive to adenosine after caffeine withdrawal, it will compensate by reducing the number of adenosine receptors to the number that existed before caffeine tolerance developed.

If caffeine is so painful to give up, can caffeine tolerance be compared to addiction to other drugs? Hirsh, like many other scientists, wants to avoid the comparison. "All definitions of addiction . . . eventually boil down to compulsion with and for a drug," he writes. Caffeine, he concludes, just doesn't result in addictive behavior. He points to rat and baboon studies in which animals regularly gave themselves doses of morphine, cocaine, and amphetamine but gave themselves caffeine no more often than saline placebos. Some animals in the experiment seemed more eager for caffeine than others, which supports the idea that individual variation is important. Hirsh, it must be noted, worked for General Foods when he wrote his study, but he is not alone in his conclusions.

However fine one draws the distinction, caffeine use does fit several standards of drug addiction, which include compulsion to continue use, tolerance for the drug, and withdrawal. It is silly to invoke the argument, as caffeine apologists often do, that truly addictive drugs impel their users to commit any act, however violent, to obtain them. You don't have to mug someone in a park at night to get money for a cup of coffee. You can stand on a corner and ask for it.

WHETHER OR NOT caffeine is hazardous or truly addictive, becoming habituated to it and suffering coffee nerves or caffeine withdrawal is no fun, and many people have chosen to drink decaffeinated coffee instead. In 1962, the peak year for American coffee consumption, decaffeinated coffee made up only three percent of coffee sales; today it accounts for more than 20 percent. It's a shame that most decaffeinated coffee is so terrible, because it doesn't have to be. Traditionally, the inferior robusta species of bean has been decaffeinated, not only because it is cheaper but also because it yields more caffeine,

which can be sold to soft-drink and patent-medicine companies, and because it has more body and so can better withstand decaffeination processes. Arabica beans, which are of higher quality, are now being decaffeinated. But the public buys the vastly inferior water-process decaf, because it suffers from an unwarranted fear of chemical decaffeination.

Decaffeination has been practiced since the turn of the century, mostly using chemicals. Every process starts with steaming the beans, to loosen the bond of caffeine to the coffee bean. Then, in the "direct" process, a chemical solvent is circulated through the beans. The beans are again steamed to remove any residual solvent, and dried; the solvent is mixed with water and the caffeine extracted. In the water process, after beans are first steamed they soak in water, which removes not only caffeine but all the other solids that flavor a cup of coffee. Caffeine is removed from the solution, which is reduced to a slurry that is returned to soak with the still-wet beans and give them back some of the lost solids.

The problems of water-process decaffeination are obvious. The water strips out most of the body and the flavoring compounds. What goes back is sometimes from the previous batch of beans, and it won't all go back anyway. Jacobs Suchard, a large Swiss company, has made improvements in the water process that keep more solids intact in the beans. It has mounted a new campaign to promote the Swiss process, in which caffeine is extracted from the water-solids solution with carbon filters rather than with the chemicals that are sometimes used. Specialty coffee decaffeinated at Jacobs Suchard's new factory in Vancouver has made strong showings in taste tests. But most water-process decaffeinated coffee is still a shadow of its former self and must be overroasted, to give the false impression that it has body and flavor.

The most efficient chemical solvent, methylene chloride, is what people think they should avoid. Methylene chloride has been banned for use in hair sprays since it was shown in animal studies to be dangerous when inhaled. But mice fed methylene chloride in drinking water at doses equivalent to 4.4 million cups of decaf a day showed none of the toxicological or carcinogenic response that had occurred when

mice had inhaled it in much smaller quantities. In 1985 the FDA said that the risk from using methylene chloride in decaffeination is so low "as to be essentially non-existent." Methylene chloride evaporates at 100° to 120°F. Beans are usually roasted at a temperature of 350° to 425°, coffee brewed at 190° to 212°. The amount of methylene chloride left in brewed coffee, then, must be measured in parts per billion—comparable to what is in the air of many cities. Even Michael Jacobson, the crusading leader of the consumer-advocacy group Center for Science in the Public Interest, says that caffeine is more dangerous than any chemical residues in decaffeinated coffee. Coffee decaffeinated with methylene chloride certainly tastes better.

A new process, using "supercritical" carbon dioxide, shows great promise. The supercritical fluid, in a state between liquid and gas, is produced under extremely high pressure. It can pass through steamed coffee beans and remove the caffeine without removing other solids, vaporizing when its work is done and leaving not a trace. So far General Foods is the only company using the process, and its production capacity allows it to decaffeinate only its Sanka brand (not its Maxwell House decaf) and Private Collection, a smaller GF venture into specialty coffee. A new processing plant is being built independently in northern California, and when completed (in about two years) it will decaffeinate beans from specialty roasters using supercritical carbon dioxide, which Marc Sims, a consultant in Berkeley, California, who is involved with the plant, prefers to call "natural effervescence."

"Regular, decaf—it's all caf," a woman said dismissively when I recently offered her a choice of coffees after dinner. She was not entirely wrong. Advertisements for coffee that is "97 percent caffeine-free" might as well describe any coffee, since the caffeine content of coffee beans varies from 1.1 to 2.6 percent. It would be better to say "decaffeinated," since the FDA requires that 97 percent of caffeine be removed from unroasted beans. (It has no requirements for brewed coffee.) Coffee decaffeinated by careful firms like Jacobs Suchard and KVW, near Hamburg, which uses methylene chloride, yields 0.03 percent or less caffeine in unroasted

beans. Brewed decaf can thus have one to five milligrams of caffeine per cup, and however little that sounds compared with the supposed minimum 85-milligram dose, it can keep some people—me, for instance—going.

You can rate the processes for yourself. The Coffee Connection (800-284-5282) will send you Jacobs Suchard water decaf. Starbucks, an excellent roaster in Seattle (800-445-3428), and Thanksgiving (800-648-6491) will send you that or KVW chemical decaf. Any of these beans will prove that you don't have to give up what you love about coffee if you give up caffeine.

Not only are people turning away from caffeine, they're turning away from coffee, and in more significant numbers. Since 1962 per capita coffee consumption has fallen by more than a third, from 3.12 to 1.75 cups a day. At the same time, per capita consumption of soft drinks has nearly tripled. The decline can't accurately be attributed to fears about caffeine, because two thirds of it oc-

curred before the first health scare about caffeine, in 1972. The culprit is soft drinks, whose manufacturers spend much more on promotion than coffee companies do. Young people drink cola to wake themselves up, and so do many former coffee drinkers. Pepsi recently test-marketed Pepsi A.M., a cola with more than the usual amount of caffeine.

The coffee trade has naturally been alarmed by this trend, but no one quite knows what to do about it. The big fear is that coffee will go the way of tea—now considered (when served hot, at any rate) to be an old person's drink. Big companies have tried to compete with specialty roasters, as General Foods did when it started its Private Collection line of whole-bean and ground coffee, because the specialty-coffee market has been growing by 15 to 20 percent a year while the mass coffee market has been shrinking.

A recent article in *Tea & Coffee Trade Journal* suggested various ways to combat the decrease: trying to break the coffee-caffeine association, both con-

ceptual and aural, by using brand names to refer to coffee, as with soft drinks; trying to give coffee a youthful image in advertisements, rather than relying on a logo to sell the product; promoting coffee at colleges; dyeing plain old styrofoam cups so they'll look zippy, like soda cans. The Coffee Development Group, an organization dedicated to increasing the consumption of coffee by improving its quality, thinks that one answer is in promoting iced coffee and sweetened coffee drinks, to compete directly with soda. In fact, the fastest-growing part of the specialty-coffee market is coffee mixed with bits of nuts and dried fruit and stirred with flavoring extracts, making really awful combinations that roasters disdain but stock—"those yucky flavors that sell," in the words of Dan Cox, of Green Mountain Coffee, in Vermont, who is the current chairman of the Coffee Development Group.

Yucky they are. Better to drink straight coffee, with or without caffeine, that tastes good.

The Economy of Drug Use

Drugs are not simply used; they are also bought and sold. They are the foundation for a major economic enterprise—or, to be more precise, a number of major economic enterprises. The alcoholic beverage industry earns $50 billion at the retail level in the United States each year; some $30 billion is spent on tobacco products, and $30 billion for pharmaceuticals; and $10 billion is spent for over-the-counter medications. The size of the illegal drug industry is more difficult to determine because, as we saw, its sales are not taxed and, therefore, not officially recorded anywhere. Estimates range from $40 to $100 billion; if we average the various estimates, this would make the illegal drug trade—if combined into a single industry—the most profitable business in the country, with a dollar volume larger than that of General Motors. Several journalists claim that more money is spent on illegal drugs than for any other existing product or service—more than on food, clothes, housing, education, or medical care. This is probably an exaggeration, but no one doubts that the drug trade is huge and extremely profitable.

Each drug is bought and sold in a somewhat different way, by a somewhat different cast of characters. Some drugs are legal, and their manufacturers are seen as

respectable pillars of their communities. Other drugs are illegal, and their sellers are designated as villains, denounced in the media by politicians and other upstanding citizens. Some drugs are produced from plants that grow naturally in the wild or in an agricultural setting: Marijuana is made up of the leaves and flowering tops of the cannabis plant; opium is exuded when the mature pod of a type of poppy is lanced; peyote is the dried, sliced "buttons" of species of desert cactus; psilocybin is the active ingredient in several species of a mushroom, *Psilocybe mexicana* among them, which grow in the southwest. Other drugs are referred to as semisynthetics, and were derived from natural substances that were chemically transformed—cocaine's ultimate origin was the coca plant, heroin's was the opium poppy—while still others are completely synthetic chemicals, manufactured from other chemicals in a laboratory. A particular source will necessitate a particular type of distribution, as well as a distinct economic activity.

Perhaps one of the most painful ironies of the drug scene is the toleration and even encouragement the legal drug trade receives, and the aggressiveness with which they pursue their business. Although some restraints have been placed on the tobacco and alcohol industries—in the United States, cigarettes cannot be advertised on television; warning labels must be placed on all packs of cigarettes sold; advertisements cannot depict alcoholic beverages being drunk on television; still-active athletes cannot advertise alcohol or cigarettes—they are relatively moderate measures. (In some countries, alcohol and tobacco products cannot be advertised at all.) The legal drug industry lobbies forcefully against restrictions of any kind, and is often successful in blocking legislation that would cut into its profits or impede business in any way. For instance, the tobacco industry is waging a (in the long run, losing) campaign to convince the public and legislators that smoking in public is a basic right, comparable to the right of free speech, guaranteed by the Bill of Rights. And so far, the alcoholic beverage industry has been successful in blocking legislation to require that the contents of alcoholic beverages be listed on bottles sold to the public.

The economic activities of the illegal drug trade impact upon society in somewhat different ways. Dealers and smugglers are less likely to attempt to influence legislation or win the hearts and minds of the general public. In contrast, their methods tend to be cruder and more direct. Colombian cocaine kingpins offer the police and judges in their jurisdiction the choice of "plata o plomo"—silver or lead, that is, money or a bullet, a bribe in exchange for not arresting, prosecuting, or convicting them for their crimes, or death for doing so. In the United States, drug dealers have less unopposed powers, but they often dominate certain neighborhoods through intimidation and violence.

In short, those who sell drugs, whether legal or illegal, generally take steps to protect their profits. The economic character of the drug trade translates into power, or, at least, attempts to wield power. While this power is often struggled against and often overcome, it is a fixture of the drug scene and determines many crucial aspects of drug use and abuse specifically, and the structure and dynamics of the society generally. The economic dimension in the world of drug use is so important that it is ignored only at the risk of serious distortion.

Looking Ahead: Challenge Questions

Does the profit earned by the legal drug industry justify its acceptance? Can the same be said of the drug trade? Should drug dealers and smugglers pay taxes? Are the taxes paid by the cigarette and alcohol industries enough to cover the damage their use does to the society?

Should the alcohol and tobacco industries be more tightly regulated than they are? Should alcohol and cigarette ads be banned altogether? Must the contents of alcoholic beverages be listed on bottles sold to the public? Do we have the right to know what we are drinking? Should the tobacco industry be forced to pay for antismoking ads to counter their own commercials?

Is the right to smoke in public a basic right equivalent to free speech, guaranteed by the Bill of Rights? What about the right of the person near the smoker who finds cigarette smoke irritating?

Given the fact that drug dealers enforce their will through violence, how can their activities ever be eliminated?

Does the economic character of the drug trade influence drug use and abuse? How? If there were no profits in drugs, would anyone ever use them?

ADVERTISING ADDICTION: THE ALCOHOL INDUSTRY'S HARD SELL

Jean Kilbourne, Ed. D.

Jean Kilbourne, Ed.D., is the Chair of the Council on Alcohol Policy and is on the Board of Directors of the National Council on Alcoholism. Two award-winning films, "Still Killing Us Softly: Advertising's Image of Women" and "Calling the Shots: The Advertising of Alcohol," are based on her lectures.

Alcohol is the most commonly used drug in the United States. It is also one of the most heavily advertised products in the United States. The alcohol industry generates more than $65 billion a year in revenue and spends more than $1 billion a year on advertising. The advertising budget for one beer — Budweiser — is more than the entire federal budget for research on alcoholism and alcohol abuse. Unfortunately, young people and heavy drinkers are the primary targets of the advertisers.

What does advertising do?

There is no conclusive proof that advertising increases alcohol consumption. Research does indicate, however, that alcohol advertising contributes to increases in consumption by young people and serves as a significant source of negative socialization for young people. Those who argue that peer pressure is the major influence on young people strangely overlook the role of advertising.

The alcoholic beverage companies claim that they are not trying to create more or heavier drinkers. They say that they only want people who already drink to switch to another brand and to drink it in moderation. But this industry-wide claim does not hold up under scrutiny. An editorial in Advertising Age concluded: "A strange world it is, in which people spending millions on advertising must do their best to prove that advertising doesn't do very much!"

About a third of all Americans choose not to drink at all, a third drink moderately, and about a third drink regularly. Ten percent of the drinking-age population consumes over 60 percent of the alcohol. This figure corresponds closely to the percentage of alcoholics in society. If alcoholics were to recover (i.e. to stop drinking entirely), the alcohol industry's gross revenues would be cut in half. Recognizing this important marketing fact, alcohol companies deliberately devise ads designed to appeal to heavy drinkers. Advertising is usually directed toward promoting loyalty and increasing usage, and heavy users of any product are the best customers but, in the case of alcohol, the heavy user is usually an addict.

Another perspective on the industry's claim that it encourages only moderate drinking is provided by Robert Hammond, director of the Alcohol Research Information Service. He estimates that if all 105 million drinkers of legal age consumed the official maximum "moderate" amount of alcohol — .99 ounces per day, the equivalent of about two drinks — the industry would suffer "a whopping 40 percent decrease in the sale of beer, wine and distilled spirits, based on 1981 sales figures."

Such statistics show the role heavy drinkers play in maintaining the large profit margins of the alcohol industry. Modern research techniques allow the producers of print and electronic media to provide advertisers with detailed information about their readers, listeners and viewers. Target audiences are sold to the alcohol industry on a cost per drinker basis.

One example of how magazines sell target audiences appeared recently in Advertising Age: Good Housekeeping advertised itself to the alcohol industry as a good place to reach women drinkers, proclaiming, "You'll catch more women with wine than with vinegar. She's a tougher customer than ever. You never needed Good Housekeeping more."

The young audience is also worth a great deal to the alcohol industry. Sport magazine promoted itself to the alcohol industry as a conduit to young drinkers with an ad in Advertising Age stating, "What young money spends on drinks is a real eye-opener." Budweiser's Spuds MacKenzie campaign is clearly designed to appeal to young people. Miller has a new television commercial featuring animated clay figures of a monkey, an elephant and a lion with a voice that says "three out of four party animals preferred the taste of Miller Lite." Wine coolers are often marketed as soft drinks with ads featuring puppets, animated characters, Santa Claus and other figures that appeal especially to young people. Even in supposedly commercial-free movies, showing in theaters, viewers are targeted. Many films, especially those appealing to young people, include paid placements of cigarettes and alcohol.

The college market is particularly important to the alcohol industry not only because of the money the students will spend on beer today, but because they will develop drinking habits and brand allegiances that may be

From *Multinational Monitor*, June 1989, pp. 13-16. Reprinted with permission of *Multinational Monitor*, P.O. Box 19405, Washington, D.C. 20036, $22/individual.

with them for life. As one marketing executive said, "Let's not forget that getting a freshman to choose a certain brand of beer may mean that he will maintain his brand loyalty for the next 20 to 35 years. If he turns out to be a big drinker, the beer company has bought itself an annuity." This statement undercuts the industry's claim that it does not target advertising campaigns at underage drinkers since today almost every state prohibits the sale of alcohol to people under 21 years old and the vast majority of college freshman are below that age.

The alcohol industry's efforts to promote responsible drinking must also be evaluated carefully. Much of its advertising promotes irresponsible and dangerous drinking. For example, a poster for Pabst Blue Ribbon features a young woman speeding along on a bicycle with a bottle of beer where the water bottle is supposed to be. Obviously biking and drinking beer are not safely complementary activities.

Even some of the programs designed by the alcohol industry to educate students about responsible drinking subtly promote myths and damaging attitudes. Budweiser has a program called "The Buddy System" designed to encourage young people not to let their friends drive drunk. Although this is a laudable goal, it is interesting to note that none of the alcohol industry programs discourage or even question drunkenness per se. The implicit message is that it is alright to get drunk as long as you don't drive; abuse is acceptable, even encouraged.

Myth making

The industry often targets relatively disempowered groups in society, primarily women and minority groups, and associates alcohol with power. For example, a Cutty Sark Whiskey ad features a retired Black baseball player, Curt Flood, promoting its drink. The ad shows Flood holding forth a glass of whiskey with the text "Some people think you can't beat the system. Here's to those who show the way." This ad associates Flood and his successful athletic performance with his drinking Cutty Sark whiskey.

The link between advertising and alcoholism is unproven. Alcoholism is a complex illness and its etiology is uncertain. But alcohol advertising does create a climate in which abusive attitudes toward alcohol are presented as normal, appropriate and innocuous. One of the chief symptoms of alcoholism is denial that there is a problem. It is often not only the alcoholic who denies the illness but also his or her family, employer, doctor, etc. Alcohol advertising often encourages denial be creating a world in which myths about alcohol are presented as true and in which signs of trouble are erased or transformed into positive attributes.

One of the primary means of creating this distortion is through advertising. Most advertising is essentially myth-making. Instead of providing information about a product, such as its taste or quality, advertisements create an image of the product, linking the item with a particular lifestyle which may have little or nothing to do with the product itself. According to an article on beer marketing in Advertising Age, "Advertising is as important to selling beer as the bottle opener is to drinking it. . . . Beer advertising is mainly an exercise in building images." Another article a few months later on liquor marketing stated that "product image is probably the most important element in selling liquor. The trick for marketers is to project the right

message in their advertisements to motivate those motionless consumers to march down to the liquor store or bar and exchange their money for a sip of image."

The links are generally false and arbitrary but we are so surrounded by them that we come to accept them: the jeans will make you look sexy, the car will give you confidence, the detergent will save your marriage. Advertising spuriously links alcohol with precisely those attributes and qualities — happiness, wealth, prestige, sophistication, success, maturity, athletic ability, virility, creativity, sexual satisfaction and others — that the misuse of alcohol destroys. For example, alcohol is often linked with romance and sexual fulfillment, yet it is common knowledge that alcohol misuse often leads to sexual dysfunction. Less well known is the fact that people with drinking problems are seven times more likely than the general population to be separated or divorced.

Image advertising is especially appealing to young people who are more likely than adults to be insecure about the image they are projecting. Sexual and athletic prowess are two of the themes that dominate advertising aimed at young people. A recent television commercial for Miller beer featured Danny Sullivan, the race car driver, speeding around a track with the Miller logo emblazoned everywhere. The ad implies that Miller beer and fast driving go hand in hand. A study of beer commercials funded by the American Automobile Association found that they often linked beer with images of speed, including speeding cars.

The magic transformation

"It separates the exceptional from the merely ordinary." This advertising slogan for Piper champagne illustrates the major premise of the mythology that alcohol is magic. It is a magic potion that can make you successful, sophisticated and sexy; without it, you are dull, mediocre and ordinary. The people who are not drinking champagne are lifeless replicas of the happy couple who are imbibing. The alcohol has rescued the couple, resurrected them, restored them to life. At the heart of the alcoholic's dilemma and denial is this belief, this certainty, that alcohol is essential for life, that without it he or she will literally die — or at best suffer. This ad and many others like it present the nightmare as true, thus affirming and even glorifying one of the symptoms of the illness.

Glorifying alcoholism

Such glorification of the symptoms is common in alcohol advertising. "Your own special island," proclaims an ad for St. Croix rum. Another ad offers Busch beer as "Your mountain hide-a-way." Almost all alcoholics experience intense feelings of isolation, alienation and loneliness. Most make the tragic mistake of believing that the alcohol alleviates these feelings rather than exacerbating them. The two examples above distort reality in much the same way as the alcoholic does. Instead of being isolated and alienated, the people in the ad are in their own special places.

The rum ad also seems to be encouraging solitary drinking, a sign of trouble with alcohol. There is one drink on the tray and no room for another. Although it is unusual for solitary drinking to be shown (most alcohol ads feature groups or happy couples), it is not unusual for unhealthy attitudes toward alcohol to be presented as normal and acceptable.

The most obvious example is obsession with alcohol.

7. ECONOMY OF DRUG USE

Alcohol is at the center of the ads just as it is at the center of the alcoholic's life. The ads imply that alcohol is an appropriate adjunct to almost every activity from lovemaking to white-water canoeing. An ad for Puerto Rican rums says, "You know how to make every day special. You're a white rum drinker." In fact, less than 10 percent of the adult population makes drinking a part of their daily routine.

There is also an emphasis on quantity in the ads. A Johnnie Walker ad features 16 bottles of scotch and the copy, "Bob really knows how to throw a party. He never runs out of Johnnie Walker Red." Light beer has been developed and heavily promoted not for the dieter but for the heavy drinker. The ads imply that because it is less filling, one can drink more of it.

Thus the ads tell the alcoholic and everyone around him that it is all right to consume large quantities of alcohol on a daily basis and to have it be a part of all of one's activities. At the same time, all signs of trouble and any hint of addiction are conspicuously avoided. The daily drinking takes place in glorious and unique settings, such as yachts at sunset, not at the more mundane but realistic kitchen tables in the morning. There is no unpleasant drunkenness, only high spirits. There are never any negative consequences. Of course, one would not expect there to be. The advertisers are selling their product and it is their job to erase any negative aspects as well as to enhance the positive ones. When the product is a drug that is addictive to one out of 10 users, however, there are consequences that go far beyond product sales.

The U.S. culture as a whole, not just the advertising and alcohol industry, tends to glorify alcohol and dismiss the problems associated with it. The "war on drugs," as covered by newspapers and magazines in this country, rarely includes the two major killers, alcohol and nicotine. It is no coincidence that these are two of the most heavily advertised products. In 1987, the use of all illegal drugs combined accounted for about 3,400 deaths. Alcohol is linked with over 100,000 deaths annually. Cigarettes kill a thousand people every day.

A comprehensive effort is needed to prevent alcohol-related problems. Such an effort must include education, media campaigns, increased availability of treatment programs and more effective deterrence policies. It must also include public policy changes that would include raising taxes on alcohol, putting clearly legible warning labels on the bottles and regulating the advertising.

THE TEFLON COATING OF CIGARETTE COMPANIES

Larry C. White

Larry C. White, a lawyer, is the author of Merchants of Death, The American Tobacco Industry, *William Morrow & Co., 1988. Mr. White is a guest columnist invited by Dr. Whelan who regularly writes Top Priority.*

Americans have always loved to hate corporations. From the days of the muckrakers and the great trusts to the consumer movement and the corporate bad guys of the last few decades, it's been great fun and morally uplifting to pillory certain companies. In the 1960s, Dow Chemical was assailed for manufacturing napalm, in the 1970s Nestle was dragged through the mud for aggressively marketing infant formula in the Third World. Then came Johns Manville, the asbestos ogre, and A. H. Robins, whose Dalkon Shield made it the corporate despoiler of women. Some of these companies have undergone the equivalent of capital punishment for their crimes, others have been forced to great lengths to apologize.

The harm that these businesses have inflicted pales when compared to the havoc wreaked by the companies that manufacture cigarettes. Smoking has long been the number one preventable cause of premature death and disease in our society. At least 390,000 Americans die each year of smoking-related illness; and the cigarette companies are unrepentant. Refusing against overwhelming evidence to admit that cigarettes are harmful, cigarette companies gear their advertising towards young people, particularly young blacks, Hispanics and females to encourage smoking.

If the cigarette companies were held to the same standards of conduct as other companies, we would see mass demonstrations in front of the Park Avenue headquarters of Philip Morris, thundering denunciations from media pundits, and heavy pressure for stricter legislation. People who profit from the cigarette trade would be social pariahs.

But none of this has happened. Indeed, cigarette people are quite as respectable as those who don't make a living pushing addictive dangerous drugs. Laurence Tisch, who earns the bulk of his money from Lorillard cigarettes, gave New York University $30 million, in return for which the name of University Hospital was changed to Tisch Hospital. This happened despite the fact that Lorillard's Kents, Newports, and Trues kill about 32,000 Americans each year. When New York's former Speaker of the Assembly Stanley Steingut died in Tisch Hospital of lung cancer recently, the media failed to note the irony. Is it possible to imagine that New York University officials would accept money from a large asbestos manufacturer and rename it, say, the Johns Manville Hospital?

Mr. Tisch's wife Joan sent out a letter soliciting money for the Gay Men's Health Crisis (GMHC) to help in its fight against AIDS. The address on the return envelope was the Loew's Corporation, parent company of Lorillard. Mrs. Tisch's moving description of a man wasting away from AIDS bore an eerie resemblance to death from lung cancer. But GMHC did not notice the irony. Its director said that he was very proud to have Mrs. Tisch associated with GMHC. Would GMHC have been proud to be supported by A. H. Robins?

The nation's leading cigarette company, Philip Morris, which has approximately a 39 percent share of the cigarette market in U.S. sales, is known to many not as a merchant of death, but as a great corporate philanthropist. The company enticed the National Archives to allow it to use the Bill of Rights as part of a sophisticated advertising campaign to burnish the company's reputation. Never mind that its Marlboro cigarette is the number one cigarette brand in the world, or that it is by far the biggest starter brand for young people. The fact that Philip Morris products have killed far more Americans than all the drug dealers of the twentieth century put together will be politely forgotten when the National Archives allows itself to be used for a reception hosted by Philip Morris.

Not only is Philip Morris not in the media doghouse; it is positively adored by some publications. *FORTUNE* magazine recently singled it out as one of the best run companies in the country.

What makes cigarette company respectability all the more surprising is that smoking itself has become very unfashionable. Smoking on flights within the U.S. has been banned, and smoking is now restricted in many public places. We seem to be moving toward widespread acceptance of the idea that people should not smoke in public except in desig-

nated smoking areas. Smoking has lost its glamour; it's become declasse. Most Americans, including smokers, now know that smoking is harmful (although most do not know just how dangerous it is). The increasingly bad image of smoking has not rubbed off on the industry itself, however. The cigarette makers have long been noted for their ability to "make lemonade from lemons." The decline in smoking, instead of hurting the industry's image, has helped defuse criticism. Many opponents of smoking believe that the industry is on its last legs and that cigarettes will go the way of the dodo bird without any further effort. Unfortunately, this is not necessarily true. Cigarette profits are higher than ever and there is no guarantee that the downward trends in smoking prevalence will continue. Cigarettes are still the most heavily advertised product in America.

The news that cigarettes are addictive, announced by Surgeon General C. Everett Koop in 1986, should have shaken the cigarette companies. But, as usual, this teflon industry took the news in stride. After all, smoking has traditionally been seen (by non-smokers who do not know any better) as a matter of free individual choice like choosing to go for a walk or eat an orange. It would take more than an official announcement and a few news stories to change public opinion on this.

The Surgeon General's pronouncements can hardly compete with the more than $2 billion worth of cigarette ads to which Americans are subject. The reason people smoke, the ads say, is really simple—for pleasure, for the sheer fun of it. According to this logic, the cigarette companies have not victimized smokers, but are merely supplying them with what they demand. This contrasts starkly with the victim-perpetrator image of the A. H. Robins and the Johns Manvilles.

Probably the best thing the cigarette makers have going for them is simply that cigarettes and cigarette advertising are ubiquitous—just a normal part of life. Media expert Tony Schwartz points out, "We see the brand logos on door pulls. The ads are everywhere." Cigarettes seem as though they've been around forever (actually they didn't become a mass phenomenon until World War I).

Tragically, cigarette-induced illness and death have become so familiar that we no longer really notice it. Lung cancer, emphysema, and heart attacks are familiar killers and when they appear, seem almost inevitable. One of the greatest ironies of the past several decades is that there are many Americans who will passionately oppose pesticides, which have had no adverse affect on their lives, while patiently tolerating an industry that has literally killed their nearest and dearest.

The lack of media attention to the issue of smoking and cigarettes has two main causes. One is the general feeling among newspeople that these particular stories have been told too many times already. The media in this country are obsessed with novelty. Recently a man in Oregon had brought back from Africa several giant frogs (up to twelve pounds each). This drew coverage on the network news and countless newspaper stories. In terms of what is accepted as "newsworthy," the routine death of hundreds of thousands from a preventable cause doesn't compare with the frogs.

Then there is the effect of cigarette advertising. Cigarette companies do not like anti-smoking stories and they do not hesitate to pull advertising away from media that present it. Now that Philip Morris is highly diversified, it can use its giant food subsidiaries such as Kraft and General Foods to punish publications and broadcast media who dare to publish anti-smoking, or even worse, anti-tobacco company stories. Media self-censorship is rife; most editors and producers think of the potential loss of advertising revenue before they commission a cigarette story.

Unlike other industries which have had very little time to plan strategies to deal with bad news about their products, the tobacco industry has had thirty years to refine its defenses. We are all familiar with denial, but an equally effective defense of the industry's image is through camouflage. Bad news about other products has been turned into protective covering for cigarettes.

A favorite Tobacco Institute defense goes something like this: 'so what if there may be a risk in smoking, there's a risk in driving a car or eating too many eggs.' The unspoken implication is that General Motors and your local butter and egg man are complicit in supplying risky products in exactly the same way as cigarette companies.

It takes some understanding of the risk-benefit balance to unravel this argument. Cars and eggs are very high on the benefit index, and relatively low on the risk index. Thus, the primary function of those who supply them is positive—in general their products are useful and make life better for most people. Cigarettes on the other hand are very high on the risk scale, and are nil on the benefit index. So the primary function of the cigarette makers is negative—to sell a useless risk to their customers.

But the public hears only the tobacco industry point of view. Neither government nor major voluntary health organizations nor consumer education organizations have been able to counter effectively tobacco industry advertising and public relations. The tobacco industry has escaped the public wrath visited on other companies less damaging because the industry itself largely controls what is written and broadcast about it.

THE MEN WHO CREATED CRACK

A shrewd marketing strategy by several groups of drug traffickers flooded the nation with this deadly form of cocaine and left many U.S. cities blighted

GORDON WITKIN WITH MUADI MUKENGE, MONIKA
GUTTMAN IN LOS ANGELES, ANNE MONCREIFF ARRARTE IN MIAMI,
KUKULA GLASTRIS IN CHICAGO, BARBARA BURGOWER IN HOUSTON
AND AIMEE L. STERN IN NEW YORK

The most amazing thing about crack cocaine is that it did not begin rotting America's urban landscape sooner. It has been recognized as a scourge in cities—and none too few suburban and rural areas—for only five years. But the supercharged cocaine, sometimes called "rock," wasn't really new. References to the recipe that used heat and baking soda to turn cocaine hydrochloride, or powder, into the smokable form of freebase called crack appear throughout the 1970s in underground literature, media interviews and congressional testimony. It did not catch on back then, researchers believe, because it was not as pure as other, more processed forms of freebase. Freebasers, who fancied themselves connoisseurs in those bygone days, called it "garbage rock."

What turned crack into a craze was mass marketing that would have made McDonald's proud. Crack was not invented; it was created by a sharp crowd of sinister geniuses who took a simple production technique to make a packaged, ready-to-consume form of the product with a low unit price to entice massive numbers of consumers. Cocaine powder required an investment of at least $75 for a gram, but a hit of crack cost as little as $5. Equally alluring was crack's incredible "high"—an instantaneous euphoria because it was smoked—that could create addicts in weeks.

There were three classes of criminals who created the crack epidemic. The first was composed of anonymous kitchen chemists and drug traffickers in the Caribbean and later in the United States, who used rudimentary science and marketing savvy to help hundreds of small-time criminals set up crack operations. The second was made up of indigenous crime organizations, common in most medium and large American cities, which began to seize local markets from the smaller operators. The third consisted of gangs from both coasts that franchised crack operations into every corner of the country.

The story of how crack infiltrated America is one of daring and enterprise. It also raises distressing questions about the capacity of police agencies to detect and combat massive criminal infiltration into the nation's neighborhoods. It contains lessons for Americans confronting an impending flood of heroin and Europeans tackling a cresting tsunami of cocaine. And it is a cautionary tale about what happens when hopelessness grips whole communities—how it lays them open to the allure of easy money and unspeakable violence.

CHAPTER 1

Early days: smoking coca paste

Two products, coca paste and cocaine freebase made with ether, came before crack—and led indirectly to its debut. Coca paste is an inexpensive, first-stage creation in cocaine processing that sells for as little as $1 a gram. First reports of its use came from Peru in 1971. By 1974, Lima faced a paste-smoking epidemic; by 1980, the practice had spread to

Colombia, Bolivia, Ecuador and Venezuela.

Soon after, Colombia initiated a temporarily successful effort to cut off importation of ether, the primary solvent used to process coca paste into cocaine hydrochloride powder. At the same time, intensified law enforcement efforts began to seal off the Colombia-Florida cocaine pipeline. The result was the widespread transshipment of unrefined coca paste to various Caribbean islands, and then South Florida, for refinement into powder, according to Miami researcher James Hall and University of Delaware criminologist James Inciardi.

Colombian traffickers promoted the idea of cocaine smoking through this new distribution network, hoping to expand sales. Dominican dealers in New York have told sociologist Terry Williams that Colombian wholesalers would include paste in kilo-size shipments of cocaine powder and tell them to give it away free to see how the customers liked it. Paste never did take hold in America, in part because of its harshness. Its future in the Caribbean, though, was bright.

CHAPTER 2

Getting closer: the freebase era

In the early 1970s, American consumers who had seen coca-paste smoking in Latin America apparently came upon the recipe for cocaine freebase through trial and error. Recreational smoking of this type first appeared in 1974 in California. Freebase is created through a chemical process that "frees" base cocaine from the cocaine hydrochloride powder. Crack is a form of freebase, but back in those early days, most freebase was made not from the easy baking-soda recipe but from a more volatile chemical process involving ether and elaborate paraphernalia, such as acetylene or butane torches. This process created freebase purer than crack, and cocaine aficionados mistakenly believed that the purity made it healthier. It was a big hit in Hollywood in the mid-to-late-1970s, helped along by a burgeoning industry that sold pipes, chemicals and extraction kits. By 1980, experts believed between 10 and 20 percent of all cocaine users were doing freebase exclusively, though others resisted it as too complicated and dangerous.

Their fears were confirmed on the night of June 9, 1980, when comedian Richard Pryor set himself on fire while freebasing at his San Fernando Valley home. Pryor suffered third-degree burns over his entire upper torso and parts of his face. It appears likely that the Pryor incident sent many drug users searching for a safer way to freebase, and thus led to wider dissemination of the simpler and safer, though less pure, baking-soda method for making freebase—the recipe that came to be used for crack.

The final and most important force behind the push for crack was the growing street demand for a simple form of smokable cocaine. By 1982, in New York City selling or "copping" zones, as many as 80 percent of the customers wanted "base," according to sociologist Williams, whose book "The Cocaine Kids" provides a riveting window into Gotham's crack culture. That meant the dealers had to cook it up batch by batch for the customers, while they cooled their heels in the dealers' apartments—a level of sustained exposure to outsiders that dealers loathed. One example was Tony, a 29-year-old dealer observed by New York anthropologist Ansley Hamid of the John Jay College of Criminal

HOUSTON. *Johnny Binder and Martha Preston*

■ THE MAN. Prosecutors say he was the "king" of crack in Houston, but he seems to have had more than nine lives. By the time he was 34, Binder had been arrested 34 times but rarely convicted. He even had a government pardon to his credit. Binder had a front tooth with a gold star, and a diamond necklace that hung to his navel. Now 37, he claims to be an honest music promoter and still maintains his innocence. Authorities alleged his partner was Martha Marie Preston, now 42, a charming, well-connected businesswoman. She, too, says she is not guilty and claims to have been railroaded by federal officials.

■ THE OPERATION. Authorities say this pair joined forces in 1983 and parlayed their connections and charisma into a massive crack operation. They say Binder operated crack houses on the southeast side of town and Preston ran the show in the northeast. Together, authorities contend, they controlled 60 to 80 percent of the crack business in Houston, and their operation reaped at least $7,000 a day in profits.

■ STATUS. Binder and Preston were convicted in September 1989 of aiding and abetting in the distribution of cocaine. Both are now serving 40-year sentences.

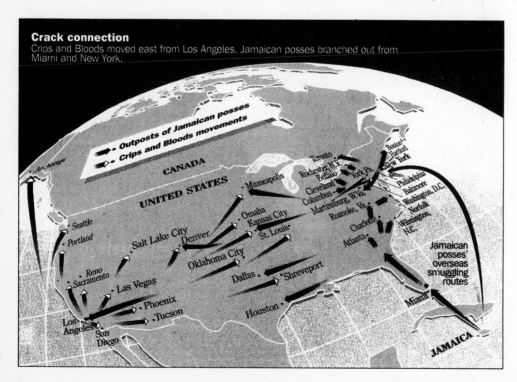

Crack connection
Crips and Bloods moved east from Los Angeles. Jamaican posses branched out from Miami and New York.

➤ = Outposts of Jamaican posses
▷ = Crips and Bloods movements

Justice. "The change in consuming preference placed a fresh burden upon Tony," Hamid wrote in the Spring 1990 issue of *Contemporary Drug Problems*. "Now he was obliged to suffer even larger throngs of customers to remain in his apartment while he, like a crazed apothecary, cooked up their purchases of powder into freebase."

The result of this pressure to handle customers quickly prompted dealers to search for a new product. "They tried to figure out an efficient way to create large batches of cocaine freebase and then package it in such a way that it could be sold at retail in a market they didn't necessarily interact with directly," according to researcher Bruce Johnson of New York-based Narcotic and Drug Research Inc. Crack was the answer.

CHAPTER 3

The Caribbean test market

Offshore, there were other forces driving the development of crack. Researchers believe that residents of the Netherlands Antilles, after experimenting with coca paste, came up with a crack prototype around 1980—a conversion of paste using baking soda, water and rum that came to be known there as "roxanne," "base-rock" or "baking-soda base." In the early 1980s, reports of "rock" began to surface regularly in the southern Caribbean. Dr. Charles Wetli, deputy medical examiner for Dade County, Fla., remembers hearing about it during a trip to the Turks and Caicos Islands as part of a teaching team sponsored by the Drug Enforcement Administration: "A local cop asked about a drug that looked like a pebble, and people would smoke it and go crazy. None of us had ever heard of it."

Meanwhile, rumblings of a similar nature were shaking the Bahamas. By the early 1980s, the vast share of cocaine destined for the United States was being transshipped through the Bahamas' 700 islands and 2,000 cays, with a hefty chunk of it being diverted and consumed by the local population. In 1979, the freebasing of cocaine rock made its debut, and the practice slowly gathered momentum over the next three years.

In the fall of 1983, Bahamian rock abuse surged, especially in the poorer neighborhoods of New Providence and Grand Bahama islands. At Princess Margaret Hospital's community psychiatry department, 35 patients were treated for cocaine addiction in all of 1983; in the first six months of 1984, the total was more than 200. Stumbling addicts, rail thin and malnourished, congregated to smoke rock in tattered abandoned buildings on Grand Bahama, Andros and New Providence islands—in places that came to be known as "base houses," the forerunner of crack houses on the mainland.

Public-health officials groping for answers turned to a burly Bahamian named Chris Finlayson. Dr. David Allen, the islands' leading drug-abuse expert, had met Finlayson

when he came in for treatment after claiming his clothes spoke to him during an acute freebase psychosis. Allen helped the personable and fast-talking Finlayson beat his rock problem temporarily, and then followed as his former patient led him deep into the Bahamas' base house culture.

Finlayson convinced Allen and Dr. James Jekel, a Yale Medical School epidemiologist, that the rock epidemic had been caused by a fundamental switch in marketing strategy by local drug pushers. The doctors already knew that in early 1983, the glut of cocaine powder in the Bahamas had dropped the street price per gram to only one fifth of its previous level. Finlayson told them that at that same time, "the pusher man switched to pushing only rock," relates Dr. Jekel. "You couldn't get powder on the street." Other addicts confirmed Finlayson's story. "The pushers knew that crack addicts keep coming back for more and more, so figured, 'Let's create a demand by getting people to go to crack,'" says Jekel. "How do you get them to go to crack? They figured, 'Let's just sell that and nothing else.' It was a marketing decision."

For Finlayson, that was lethal. He succumbed to drugs on a boat trip and died in 1986. His dying words to Allen in Princess Margaret Hospital were: "When the world tastes this, you're going to have a lot of trouble." Allen and Jekel tried to sound the alarm to a wider audience in the United States, but no one seemed particularly alarmed.

CHAPTER 4

Rock arrives in Los Angeles

While the Caribbean story was unfolding, crack was beginning to show up in California. Addicts reported in Los Angeles that as early as 1978, a process called "smearing" or "pasting" was catching on. It used the baking-soda formula. "Instead of letting it form a rock, you would pour it out on a mirror and take a finger and smear it," recalls one former addict. Then, the dried mound of the drug was smoked. Some contend that this was the transitional product between freebase and crack.

Rock made its L.A. debut around 1980, mostly because it was a faster, easier way for addicts to get their kicks. By 1982, Los Angeles hospital emergency rooms reported the nation's greatest increase in cocaine overdoses, a 90 percent rise over the previous year, according to the National Institute on Drug Abuse, due to "more and more users shifting from snorting to injecting or freebasing." By early 1983, the *Los Angeles Sentinel*, the south central neighborhood's community paper, was reporting a problem with "rock houses"— residences used for dealing crack.

But no one was really prepared for what happened in 1984, when sales of $25 rocks swept south central Los Angeles. Dozens of rock houses "went up overnight," says former LAPD Capt. Noel Cunningham, many of them so fortified that the police for a

DETROIT. *Billy Joe and Larry Chambers*

■ **THE MEN.** The Chambers brothers were originally from Marianna, Ark. They crafted a corporate look-alike organization that dominated the Motor City's crack trade.

■ **THE OPERATION.** Founded in 1983, the Chambers brothers gang just a few years later was running some 200 crack houses that employed up to 500 people, according to police, and was tallying profits of $1 million a week. Many of the workers were teenagers recruited from their native Marianna, a dirt-poor rural hamlet of 7,000 set amid cotton and rice fields 60 miles from Memphis. Twelve-hour shifts and round-the-clock crack sales were the norm. Rules, often posted on crack house walls, were strict: no crack and money to be carried at the same time, no speeding while driving and no lavish automobiles used for business purposes. Quality-control managers posed as crack buyers to keep an eye on the product. Rule breakers were referred to the so-called wrecking crew, which, officials say, exacted discipline by tossing violators out a window.

■ **STATUS.** Billy Joe and Larry were both convicted of running a continuing criminal enterprise. Larry is serving a life sentence; Billy Joe netted 29 years.

while used a 14-foot steel battering ram attached to an armored personnel carrier to break in. Teenagers, many of them gang members working for older, tougher former members, openly dealt rock at dozens of hot spots like 98th Street between Avalon Boulevard and Main Street, making thousands of dollars in the process.

Authorities now believe several below-the-surface developments helped crack's rapid ascent. The big Colombian smugglers were responding to increasing heat in Florida by bringing more and more cocaine over the Mexican border into Los Angeles. They found it convenient to tap into the existing gang structure because gang-ridden areas already had heavy concentrations of drug users and because the gangs had experience manufacturing and selling other drugs like PCP. Finally, the market had been thrown wide open by the December 1983 arrest of Thomas (Tootie) Reese, south central's pre-eminent drug kingpin for the previous two decades.

While all these sands were shifting, law enforcement had something else on its mind: planning for the 1984 Summer Olympics. "There was an awful lot of organizational focus on just keeping the city safe from terrorists," says the DEA's William Coonce. "I think the normal law enforcement took a second seat." Ex-LAPD official Cunningham agrees.

CHAPTER 5
Storming the Miami coast

In the late 1970s and early 1980s, South Florida was already reeling under a deluge of cocaine powder. "Cocaine cowboys" were shooting it out for control of the trade. Hidden behind the mayhem was the conversion of some of the street-level cocaine business from powder to base. The steady flow of Caribbean peoples to Miami, heightened by the early-1980s flood of fleeing Haitians, brought with it the burgeoning knowledge of how to convert paste into "baking-soda base." Crack wasn't far behind.

One early inkling came in November 1982, as researcher Inciardi interviewed a prostitute on a bench near the Miami Marina. "She started talking about something called 'garbage freebase,'" he relates. "Suddenly it clicked. That was an old San Francisco term from the '70s for a rock variety of freebase."

The biggest clue that crack had arrived came around 1982, when a Miami Police Department street narcotics unit busted five drug houses and apartments in the city's Little River and Liberty City neighborhoods, all of them run by a Caribbean-island immigrant who called himself Elijah. He bragged to police that he'd invented rocks, and though the claim is impossible to confirm, former Sgt. Mike Ahearn, who ran the unit, says those were the first rocks he saw. Ahearn recalls the first bust of one of those houses: "I couldn't believe it, there were 30 people in this house, and they didn't look like junkies. These were people with jobs—white, black,

upper class, lower class, young girls. I remember thinking, 'What the hell have we got here?' They said they were doing rocks. They called it a 'rock house.'" By 1984, crack had spread more widely to poor neighborhoods like Overtown and Liberty City, selling for as little as $10, sometimes under brand names like "Rambo" or "Miami Vice." Most of the crack retailers were American blacks, small-scale dealers who bought cocaine powder and picked up the crack recipe from Caribbean wholesalers whom they had first met in the marijuana business. Many Caribbean people were attracted to the illicit economy of the crack trade because their illegal-immigrant status cut them off from legitimate jobs.

CHAPTER 6
The New York flood

Authorities think there was probably a race between Californians and Caribbeans to see who got to introduce crack to the New York market the fastest. The first official to spot its arrival was Bill Hopkins, a former Bronx narcotics cop who headed a state "street research unit" set up to monitor drug trends. As he drove up Arthur Avenue in the Tremont section of the Bronx in December 1983, Hopkins recognized some of the drug abusers in Crotona Park and stopped to hear the men talking about two other abusers who had "freaked out." "You know what that was, don't ya?" asked one man.

"Yeah, that was that crack," said the other.

"My ears perked up, because this was something new, and that's rare," recalls Hopkins. "They said it was 'rock cocaine.'" It was almost another year before Hopkins got a firsthand look at a man who was smoking it. "I learned for the first time it was done with baking soda, not ether," says Hopkins. "And I examined what he had, and it was in vials. I knew we had something new on the market." Within a year, crack had saturated the city.

Nowhere did crack grab hold as tightly as it did in the northern Manhattan area called Washington Heights, a teeming neighborhood with a distinctly Caribbean flavor. When night fell, "copping" zones like West 168th Street or 174th Street and Amsterdam Avenue became choked with traffic. Some 70 to 80 percent of the consumers powering the market were white professionals or middle-class youngsters from Long island, suburban New Jersey or New York's affluent Westchester County— all of whom could easily drive into the community. The neighborhood was diverse enough ethnically, says Hopkins, that "a white guy could come into that neighborhood without standing out like a sore thumb."

Though several groups lived in the Heights, it was Dominicans who came to dominate the crack trade. The drug-dealing Dominicans, like their many legitimate shopkeeping counterparts, proved to be ambitious and well organized. They delivered consistently high-quality crack, and they proved adept at moving easily in both black

NEW YORK. *Santiago Luis Polanco-Rodríguez*

■ THE MAN. Police say Polanco-Rodríguez, a street-savvy Dominican immigrant in his mid-20s, was the marketing genius behind the spread of crack in New York's Washington Heights, the city's first big market.

■ THE OPERATION. In a hotly competitive atmosphere, Polanco-Rodríguez fostered intense customer loyalty by delivering high-quality crack in vials marked "Based Balls," according to authorities. He hatched the idea while selling cocaine powder, which he named "Coke Is It." He switched to crack in the summer of 1985. Over the next two years, the "Based Balls" ring grew, employing up to 100 people and dealing as many as 10,000 red-capped vials each day. Employees even passed out business cards labeled "Based Balls—Cop and Go" that listed retail sales outlets. Police contend that millions in profits were laundered through a full-time accountant and sent back to the Dominican Republic. A finance company was established there to make investments. The take: about $36 million annually.

■ STATUS. Polanco-Rodríguez was among 29 people charged in 1987 in a 57-count federal indictment. He is a fugitive and believed to be in the Dominican Republic.

and white worlds. Most important, perhaps, the cocaine wholesalers—Colombians from Jackson Heights, Queens—preferred doing business with them rather than with American blacks. They had already established links with the Dominicans through earlier marijuana trafficking, and they shared a common language.

The market in 1985 and early 1986 was still in its formative stages, however—marked not by massive organizations but by hundreds of cash-hungry young entrepreneurs. They worked out of apartments, using kitchen utensils. "Anyone could buy the cocaine and make crack," says the city's special narcotics prosecutor, Sterling Johnson. "Back then, there was no General Motors of crack, just a lot of mom and pop operations."

CHAPTER 7

The feds finally catch on

In October 1985, when Robert Stutman took over as the special agent in charge of the federal Drug Enforcement Administration's New York office, one of the first things he heard about was crack. After reading a host of intelligence reports and getting a four-hour briefing from a DEA chemist, he decided to start rattling some cages at headquarters. But Stutman's reputation stood in the way of his cause. DEA Administrator Jack Lawn liked his New York man, but others at headquarters were jealous and suspicious of Stutman's yen for publicity—a trait that earned him nicknames like "Stuntman." As a result, much of what he said about crack in those early days was viewed skeptically in Washington.

Federal officials also had a hard time figuring out how widespread the crack problem had become because they couldn't decode street lingo. Was crack the same as the "rock" the DEA was hearing about in California? Were cocaine rocks the same as "rock cocaine"? The confusion "probably slowed down the law enforcement response," says William Alden, DEA's chief of congressional and public affairs. "It's difficult to establish a strategy when you can't define the target correctly."

Disagreement also raged over whether crack deserved to be treated as something new and different—or simply as a subset of the war on cocaine. "The thing that weighed most heavily against a massive response was the argument that to solve crack, you had to first solve the overall cocaine problem because crack was just a marketing technique," recalls David Westrate, then DEA's assistant administrator for operations. "If this was a completely new drug, we might have had a different response." Others felt crack was an issue better addressed by state and local law enforcement, while the DEA followed its mandate to focus on large traffickers.

Still, Stutman finally prevailed. On June 19, 1986, Lawn and a handful of headquarters brass flew an agency plane to New York for an all-day briefing by DEA agents and chemists, New York police and private treatment providers. As the meeting broke up, news arrived of the sudden death of University of Maryland basketball star Len Bias. Those at the meeting immediately suspected cocaine. "When Jack [Lawn] left," recalls Stutman, "he said, 'You've convinced me we've got to do more.'"

For the next few months, however, the federal effort remained confused. As late as July 15, 1986, Westrate was testifying to Congress that "at this time there is no comprehensive analysis of the crack problem, either from a health or enforcement viewpoint." A DEA intelligence review two months later, while acknowledging crack's availability in 12 cities, nonetheless called it "a secondary rather than primary problem in most areas." Just days later, though, the National Drug Enforcement Policy Board, a multiagency group then directing federal strategy, said the "present crack situation, in short, is bleak."

Lawn himself did follow through. Early that fall, he made an emergency request for $44 million to fund 200 agents who would organize a host of state and local crack task forces nationwide. However, the Justice Department's budget monitors, acting on behalf of Ronald Reagan's budget office, denied the request. "[The budget officials] didn't treat it like a major issue," says Lawn, especially under the tight antideficit strictures of the Gramm-Rudman-Hollings law. Stephen Trott, who chaired the Justice Department's budget board, declined comment.

The DEA's next move was to jury-rig a few special crack programs using its existing budget and some new funds from the Anti-Drug Abuse Act of 1986. In 15 cities across the United States, the agency created two-person crack teams to assist local police. Some feel the effort was inadequate. "Then, as now, there is not the same type of commitment to crack as one would see with cocaine generally," says Democratic Rep. Charles Rangel of New York, chairman of the House Select Committee on Narcotics. "In my opinion, that's because it's in the poorer, minority communities."

CHAPTER 8

Bigger organizations muscle in

By the fall of 1986, the National Cocaine Hotline estimated that 1 million Americans had tried crack, in large part because the drug's marketing structure was changing and distribution was expanding. The outlandish profits and inevitable elbowing over turf led to the creation of larger crack organizations that began to overshadow the small-time operators. Some grew by simply dominating a territory and gradually forcing out competitors, through intimidation if necessary. Others were born of mergers. Either way, organization brought structure—CEOs, lieutenants, distributors, lab operators, runners, enforcers and street dealers. The business even went high tech as telephone beep-

SEATTLE. *Derrick Hargress and the Crips gang's branch operations*

■ **THE MAN.** Now 29, "Vamp" Hargress was a member of a Crips gang "set" known as the Nine-Deuce Hoovers (named after the streets where they hung out). Police think he was the mastermind of the Crips' movement from Los Angeles to Seattle in the late 1980s.

■ **THE OPERATION.** Hargress brought eight cohorts with him from Southern California to Seattle in early 1987. Each week, they transported 15 to 20 ounces of crack from Los Angeles, while running three crack houses that made $6,000 a day. According to Seattle prosecutors, "They also brought with them a level of violence and an element of organization previously lacking in drug distribution in this city." In early 1988, Hargress decided to branch out by sending several of his crew to operate half a dozen crack houses in Oklahoma City. One gang member told Oklahoma City detective Charles McIntyre that they had test-marketed the area first. "He said he used to sell vacuum cleaners door-to-door, and it was very similar," reports McIntyre.

■ **STATUS.** Hargress pleaded guilty in 1988 to selling crack near a school and using a gun to further his drug business. He was sentenced to 25 years in Leavenworth.

ers became tools of the trade. Finding the workers for these groups wasn't difficult. Many inner-city teens felt shut off from legitimate economic opportunity and came to see drug dealing as the only path to prosperity.

Once crack selling became big business, it created operations that finally were sophisticated enough to merit extensive attention from federal law enforcement authorities. Many of these home-grown organizations came to be dominated by charismatic supercriminals who ruled with an iron hand. One city that saw the rise of a highly structured organization was Houston, where prosecutors say Johnny Binder and Martha Marie Preston became the "king" and "queen" of the city's crack business (box, Page 160). In Detroit, brothers Billy Joe and Larry Chambers emerged from humble backgrounds to craft a disciplined empire that grew to dominate Motown's lucrative crack trade (box, Page 161). And in New York, the pre-eminent early figure was a canny street tough named Santiago Luis Polanco-Rodríguez, an immigrant from the Dominican Republic who used marketing savvy to rule Washington Heights (box, Page 162).

CHAPTER 9

Gangs up: Crips and Bloods

As bad as the indigenous organizations were, the spread of gangs was truly disastrous. America was caught in a pincer movement; Los Angeles street gangs moved east and Jamaican posses moved west from the East Coast, and between them, by the end of the decade, they had introduced much of the rest of the country to crack.

The chief Los Angeles gangs were the Crips (approximately 30,000 strong now) and the Bloods (about 9,000). Their expansion took off in 1986. Earlier this year, the Justice Department said that investigative reports had placed Crips and Bloods in 32 states and 113 cities. Their reach extended to places as small as Hobbs, N.M., and Ashton, Idaho. Some experts think the L.A.-based gangs now control up to 30 percent of the crack trade.

While the movement conjures up images of a master plan, authorities say it was really more a matter of happenstance. Neither gang is rigidly hierarchical. Both are broken up into loosely affiliated neighborhood groups called "sets," each with 30 to 100 members. Many gang members initially left Southern California to evade police. Others simply expanded the reach of crack by setting up branch operations in places where they visited friends or family members and discovered that the market was ripe—and the prices they could charge were higher than those in locations where the market was saturated. When authorities unraveled an L.A. ring that introduced crack to York, Pa., they discovered not a grand plan but a lovestruck Crip named Benjamin West, who had followed his L.A.-based girlfriend to York, where she was visiting her mother on a summer vacation. Since crack hadn't yet come to York, authorities say, West stayed to set up his own operation.

Compared with Los Angeles, other cities were easy pickings, especially for "rollers" or "OGs"—older gang members in their 20s—with a thirst for more-serious cash and existing connections to Colombian suppliers. "Gang members candidly concede that they choose their new homes because of market conditions and perceived weakness in the community's ability to deal with them," says a government sentencing memo in one Seattle gang case. "The word that a particular community is an easy mark spreads by word of mouth." Some Los Angeles gang members also struck out for new territory because they had hit the glass ceiling back home. "If you're a third stringer in L.A., you may figure you'll never reach the heights there, but somewhere else you can be the biggest and baddest," says the DEA's James Forget.

Portland and Seattle proved to be two of the most inviting targets. The march from L.A. to Seattle began in early 1987, masterminded by Derrick "Vamp" Hargress, an older member of a Crips set known as the Nine-Deuce Hoovers (box, Page 163). They brought an unprecedented level of violence and a strong criminal infrastructure to Seattle's drug trade, authorities there say. In Portland, police weren't sure what it meant when a Northside apartment raid in December 1987 turned up a man who said he was a Blood from Los Angeles. But they found out soon enough. By mid-1988, some 100 L.A. gang members were in Portland dealing crack, and they attracted at least 230 Portland youths to the gang lifestyle, turning north and northeast Portland into veritable free-fire zones.

CHAPTER 10

Jamaican posses

From the other coast, the great crack sales-branching scheme was put together by transplanted Jamaicans in the mid-1980s. The discovery of it came in one of those classic investigations that begin with a small piece of evidence and grow like kudzu. In the spring of 1984, Agent J. J. Watterson of the Bureau of Alcohol, Tobacco and Firearms was asked to investigate the origins of a dozen smuggled guns found in shipping containers at the port of Kingston, Jamaica. When he began checking gun store records in Dade and Broward counties in Florida, Watterson found the guns were part of a larger purchase; 50 to 75 weapons had been bought by Jamaicans. The few purchasers who could be tracked—many had given false addresses—seemed to live in virtual fortresses, and it wasn't unusual for a Mercedes or BMW to be parked outside. Pretty soon, the guns began turning up in drug and murder cases in Washington, D.C., New York, Detroit, Miami, Chicago and Los Angeles. "It was an amazing scenario," says Watterson. "We had murders everywhere."

What Watterson had discovered were Jamaican "posses": a network of mobile Jamai-

MIAMI. *Jamaicans Vivian Blake and Lester Coke*

■ **THE MEN.** These characters are alleged to be the leaders of the largest Jamaican trafficking group, the Shower posse. Blake operated from Miami; Coke lived in Jamaica but often traveled to the States. Together, they purportedly were major drug and firearms traffickers.

■ **THE OPERATION.** After dealing primarily in marijuana for three years, according to federal authorities, the Shower posse expanded into cocaine around 1985. The posse grew to a membership of about 5,400 in more than a dozen cities. Its primary drug distribution locations included New York City, Rochester, N.Y., Washington, D.C., Detroit and Toronto. The Showers took their name from the fierce gun battles they initiated: They "showered" the area with blood and body parts. In one shootout with a rival posse at a New Jersey picnic, Shower members fired more than 700 rounds.

■ **STATUS.** In September 1988, a federal grand jury indicted 34 members of the Shower posse, including Blake and Coke. The 62-count indictment charged Blake with illegal arms purchases and racketeering that involved nine murders. Blake and Coke are both fugitives, believed to be in either Kingston, Jamaica, or London.

can gangs that came to dominate gun trafficking and crack dealing over wide swaths of the United States, leaving a trail of blood-spattered bodies wherever they turned up. The posses take their name from American Westerns. Today, approximately 40 of the posses, with an estimated membership of 22,000, operate in the United States. ATF officials think they control a third of America's crack trade. The posses are believed to be partly rooted in Jamaican marijuana trafficking groups and were nurtured in the grinding poverty in Kingston and the violence-soaked politics of the island in the period around 1980.

Seeing crack's profit potential, Jamaican traffickers moved quickly. They focused first on the large Caribbean populations in Miami and New York. By mid-1987, at least five groups were operating in South Florida, led by the notorious Shower posse, so named for firefights that showered an area with bullets. The posse was run by a couple of smart but cutthroat gangsters named Vivian Blake and **Lester Coke (box, Page 164). It began by** smuggling marijuana but turned to cocaine in 1985, and, according to authorities, grew to 5,400 members nationwide. In New York, the Jamaican traffickers came to be particularly dominant in Brooklyn. One of the biggest and toughest groups there was the Renkers posse, run by an especially ruthless character named Delroy Edwards, better known as "Uzi" for his taste in weapons (box, Page 166).

Nearly all the posses displayed an extraordinary penchant for violence. On August 4, 1985, a feud between two posses resulted in a frenzied shootout at an Oakland, N.J., picnic attended by some 5,000 Jamaicans. Shower posse members fired well over 700 rounds; three people were killed and 13 wounded. In New York, a man who tried to steal $20 worth of crack from two members of the Spangler posse was kicked unconscious, placed in a bathtub, decapitated and dismembered. The following morning, a street person found the victim's head in the garbage and began kicking it down the street. Since 1985, the ATF has documented more than 3,000 posse-related homicides nationwide. Gun running, meanwhile, has become a lucrative sideline.

Often, the posses were able to establish new beachheads because it took local authorities some time to figure out what was happening. It hardly seemed unusual when Dallas detective P. E. Jones was rousted from a deep sleep at 2:30 a.m. on July 20, 1985, to investigate a murder at the Kool Vibes Club on Second Avenue; it was Saturday night, after all, in a tough neighborhood. But the victim, Howard Gordon, 28, was Jamaican, and the ensuing investigation turned up scores of out-of-town Jamaican drug connections. The homicide probe led to much more. By the time investigators were finished, they had uncovered 500 to 700 Jamaicans—many of them teenagers called "street worms"—involved in 27 Jamaican drug rings

that operated 75 crack houses turning $400,000 in profits a day.

Kansas City was much the same story. In that heartland city, the Jamaicans, with their dreadlocks and accents, stuck out plainly. They were being arrested on drug charges in significant numbers as early as 1983, all of them with phony IDs and passports. But no one knew quite what it meant. By 1986, investigations of a string of 15 murders involving Jamaicans showed police that the posses had brought 450 members into town and were operating at least 50 crack houses. The brains behind the Kansas City invasion were members of the Waterhouse posse (who came from the Waterhouse region of Kingston), which was led by a creative yet vicious thug named Errol "Dogbite" Wilson (box at right).

Other cities showed similar patterns. Prodded by Watterson and his Florida cohorts, ATF launched a national investigation of the posses in January 1987. Since then, the effort has resulted in the prosecution of approximately 1,200 Jamaican defendants. "We made some significant cases, but the fight isn't over," says ATF's Chuck Sarabyn.

By late 1987, two other groups had also gotten involved in interstate trafficking. Dominicans, from their base in New York, moved into New England, dominating the crack trade in places like Providence, R.I., and Stamford, Conn. And migrant farm workers—many of them Haitian—took the crack recipe from Florida into Georgia, North Carolina, southern Delaware, western Michigan and the Dayton, Ohio, area.

Today, though the worst may be over, crack still holds at least half a million people in its grasp. The despair pervading America's inner cities, made worse by the blight caused by crack, continues to provide fertile soil for something similar to grow in its place. Anthropologist Philippe Bourgois, who has been studying East Harlem crack dealers for six years, argues that it is unrealistic to expect a youngster growing up in an environment of evil to develop a healthy concept of equal opportunity and personal responsibility. "The 'common sense' emerging among this newest generation is that 'The System' hates them," writes Bourgois in a recent issue of *The American Enterprise*. That is the reason, he says, that so many inner-city blacks believe there is a secret white conspiracy to destroy them and crack is part of it.

But crack's hold on inner-city kids is logic, not conspiratorial hocus-pocus. High-wage, low-skill manufacturing jobs have disappeared from inner cities. Crack selling became rationalized as the only ticket to prosperity. Those who have studied crack operations uniformly say these kids weren't lazy and drifting; many worked back-breaking hours in the drug trade and yearned to make something of themselves. Given half a chance at productive futures, they just might go for it. If not, some other illicit activity will come along—heroin, ice, gun running, something—and this pathological crime cycle will get another jolt.

KANSAS CITY. *Errol Wilson and the Waterhouse posse*

■ **THE MAN.** Wilson, better known as "Dogbite," rose quickly to become the most powerful of the Waterhouse posse members who controlled crack in Kansas City.

■ **THE OPERATION.** The Waterhousers recruited teenagers in the Jamaican communities of Miami and New York, promising an unheard-of wage of $500 a week. Often that kind of money never really materialized. The youths did get plane tickets and a phone number, and were assigned to crack houses, where they worked like slaves. Jamaican females were used as couriers of cocaine powder from Miami as often as six times a week. Some crack houses took in up to $15,000 a day. The dealers even had a catchy marketing pitch: "Stock Up on Mothers Day." That's the first of the month, when welfare checks are mailed. The crack was always top quality, and the Jamaicans sold bigger pieces for the money than anyone else in town. And always, there were guns—high caliber, top-quality guns.

■ **STATUS.** Wilson was indicted in early 1987 on charges of engaging in a continuing criminal enterprise and distributing cocaine. He was a fugitive until last October, when he died in a car accident in Jamaica.

CHICAGO. *Al Capone and the reason why crack was scarce*

■ THE MYSTERY. While crack raced across the country, infecting communities only a half-hour's drive away, it remained nearly nonexistent in Chicago. As late as 1989, the police seized barely 2 pounds during the whole year. Why didn't crack hit Chicago hard?

■ THE THEORIES. The most convincing explanation is rooted in Chicago's rough-and-tumble criminal tradition. Seventy years ago, Al Capone so dominated the city's bootleg-liquor industry that rivals from other cities never managed to penetrate the market, though many died trying. The same is true of the drug trade today. Jamaican posses and gangs from Los Angeles have hardly set foot in Chicago; much of the reason, authorities say, is that local gangs have been fiercely protective of their already lucrative cocaine and heroin markets. The police, too, have been especially vigilant in attacking crack houses as soon as they have appeared.

■ STATUS. Chicago gangs are now peddling more of the drug, spurred perhaps by some growth in demand or competition from smaller entrepreneurs. In 1990, Chicago police seized three times as much crack as they did in 1989. The city's luck may be running out.

NEW YORK. *Delroy Edwards and the Renkers posse*

■ THE MAN. Edwards, now 31, was reputed to be a former street enforcer for the Jamaican Labor Party. Better known as "Uzi" for his taste in weapons, Edwards arrived in America on a tourist visa in the early 1980s. Police say he began his drug career selling marijuana but moved to crack in 1985.

■ THE OPERATION. Authorities contend Edwards headed an especially ruthless posse known as the Renkers, which ran a huge portion of the crack trade in Brooklyn. In one incident, police say, a teenager suspected of stealing money and drugs from the ring was beaten with a baseball bat, scalded with boiling water and then left hanging from a basement ceiling. He later died. At their peak, the Renkers employed 50 workers and made as much as $100,000 a day selling crack in the Bedford-Stuyvesant, Crown Heights and Flatbush sections of Brooklyn. Later the Renkers branched out to Philadelphia, Baltimore and the District of Columbia. Cops contend that Edwards used a portion of the profits to purchase a house in Amityville, Long Island.

■ STATUS. Edwards was convicted in 1989 on 42 federal charges, including six murders. He is serving a life sentence.

Crack dealers' rotten lives

The rewards for selling drugs are often puny and the dangers severe

Even at their height, crack dealers rarely "live large." For most, the hours are long—up to 14 hours a day—and stressful. The pay is often lousy. Careers are short. Violence, jail time and ripoffs by rivals are common. Chances are better than average that the dealers will end up homeless. Frequently, their pricey sneakers, gold chains and watches are borrowed.

That is the unflattering portrait that is emerging from a series of pathbreaking new studies by social scientists, law-enforcement specialists and other researchers. "The image of great wealth and social standing among crack dealers is a lie," says Philippe Bourgois, an anthropologist from San Francisco State University who is writing a book on crack cocaine in Harlem. "Some make it big, but the reality for most dealers is far more prosaic." Indeed, the new studies paint a tragic picture:

■ A recent study by the Rand Corporation of street-level drug dealers in Washington, D.C., from 1985 to 1987 found that they stood a 1-in-70 chance of getting killed, a rate that was 20 times higher than for a police officer and 100 times larger than for the general work force. Dealers had a 1-in-14 chance of severe injury and a 2-in-9 chance of imprisonment. And the prospects of being jailed have risen dramatically. In New York City, says Richard Curtis, a researcher for the VERA Institute of Justice, most street-level crack dealers have already gone to jail at least once.

■ At the same time, according to Bruce Johnson of Narcotics and Drug Research, Inc., in New York City, the chances of making it into the upper echelon of a drug operation, where salaries can top $100,000, are about 1 in 1,000; the chances of earning a middle-class income of about $30,000 a year are 1 in 200. For the majority, the rewards seem meager, compared with the danger. The Rand study found that the income of 3 out of 8 Washington, D.C., dealers who worked 4 hours every day was less than $24,000 a year. "That's not the kind of income from which Mercedes or great fortunes spring," says Peter Reuter, the principal author of the study. Forty percent of the dealers sold only two days a week, and half of them earned no more than $830 a month. For many, the "earnings" were eaten away by drug use. About half of those surveyed spent an average of about $400 a month on drugs for their own use.

In other cities, the economic prospects for crack dealers are even less promising. In Chicago, according to Felix M. Padilla of De Paul University, drug dealers typically make about $150 a week. John Hagedorn, an anthropologist studying crack dealers in Milwaukee, says it's common there for crack dealers to be earning close to the minimum wage.

One disillusioning story. Harry Rodriguez is one of the many street workers in a crack operation who disputes the hyped image of dealers with "crazy money" pouring out of their pockets. The native of East Harlem, N.Y., says he started selling crack in 1986, when he was 16. He worked about 10 hours a day, six or seven days a week, to sell his quota of 1,000 vials of crack. Each vial cost a customer $5, and, of that, 35 cents belonged to Rodriguez. "In those days, I thought $350 a week was really big money. But when I started to figure how hard I was working to get that, it didn't seem so big, and the real big money never materialized," he says.

Worse, he was squeezed from both ends of his business. His boss rode Rodriguez hard with physical threats to meet his quota. But selling that amount of crack became increasingly difficult because of the wild proliferation of dealers on the street. "It got awful," Rodriguez says. After two years of watching his business erode and seeing his colleagues get arrested or become addicts, Rodriguez decided to get out of crack selling and take a job delivering office supplies. It ended up putting more money in his pocket.

Rodriguez's case illustrates another truth of the streets that has only recently been recognized. The new research shows that street crews are extremely fluid and rarely hierarchical, where intense competition has created a huge market for free-lancers and loosely knit "posses." One of the misconceptions that arose after some spectacular busts of crack operations was that the typical business was a tightly organized hierarchy that offered security—and high pay—to its workers. In fact, the street scene is "hypercapitalism" in an environment of massive violence, according to Ansley Hamid, a professor at the John Jay College of Criminal Justice in New York City.

Even among middle managers, who

rise through the ranks and organize their own crews, making "crazy money" is hard, according to analyst Johnson. Although middlemen can handle large quantities of drugs and a few may gross $5,000 a day, such success over a sustained period is possible only under optimum conditions: No problem employes, which is a rarity; limited police harassment; a complacent community, and limited and nonviolent competition.

Typical of the high rollers who ended up broke and in jail is Leroy Johnson, of Queens, N.Y. He stayed in the business for seven years, outlasting many of his peers. But he was eventually buried by the stress of running his own crew and by his own cocaine addiction. Johnson says competition, combined with keeping reliable workers, was a big problem. "They steal or smoke the work, come up short on the gusto [money] or disappear," he says. And several old friends died that way.

By his own estimation, Johnson, a high-school dropout, was earning $60,000 a year as he imported as much as 40 to 60 kilograms of cocaine a year for a medium-sized New York drug ring. Although he would get a return of double his original investment in each shipment—he paid up to $50,000 per kilogram in some cases—much of the profit was lost. He paid his five workers $300 a week; fed his $3,000-a-week crack habit, and simply lost track of large sums as he renewed his supplies and paid off chemists and other business costs. "You handle huge amounts of money," says Johnson, "but after you've paid off your people, you end up with very little."

Brutality "just business." To maintain his operation, he was brutal. He once disciplined a close friend for stealing a large quantity of cocaine from him by shooting him in his shoulder with a 9-mm handgun. Then he took a shotgun and fired about nine rounds into his friend's legs. Johnson recovered the missing cocaine. "It was just business," says Johnson, now in a drug-rehabilitation program while he serves a sentence of five to 15 years in prison for burglary.

These new findings have important policy implications. The most obvious is that a concerted education campaign on the streets could have a significant payoff. "The Rand study was a useful bit of demythologizing for the kids who think that all lives of drug dealers are candidates for a profile on 'Lifestyles of the Rich and Famous,'" argues federal drug czar William Bennett. Ironically, the new research suggests that one of liberals' favorite solutions to the drug epidemic—a jobs-creation strategy—might not be very helpful because two thirds of the crack dealers included in the Rand study already held full-time jobs.

A portion of the Rand study written by Robert MacCoun concludes that although criminal sanctions alone may soothe the public's political demands, they won't make a dent soon in wiping out crack dealing for several reasons. First, the free-lance nature of street-sales operations is not easily thwarted by law enforcement. Second, the dealers themselves are not easily deterred by the prospect of being arrested, because they see jail as an unavoidable risk and are far more concerned with getting killed or hurt.

A better enforcement strategy in shrinking the crack trade would be imposing stiffer financial and criminal penalties against middle-class buyers—who are still the mainstay of the crack business. That strategy is being seriously studied by Bennett's office. But the drug czar, like others, has become convinced by the new studies that the most potent short-term strategy is getting the word out on the street that crack selling is a ticket to nowhere.

By Scott Minerbrook

The Perilous Swim in Heroin's Stream

SUMMARY: Chinese crime syndicates are getting rich on a river of heroin that flows from the hills of Burma to secret refineries in Thailand and Laos, through shipping points in Bangkok and Hong Kong to thirsting drug markets around the world. Insurgent groups in Asia's Golden Triangle are killing each other for control of the market; in the United States, where the drug, like crack, is available and cheap, some fear that it will set off a similar flood of addiction.

Bangkok, Valentine's Day 1988: The winter rains drenching this sprawling, Southeast Asian city were the worst anyone had seen in years. For more than a week the rain had come down in torrents, flooding Bangkok's twisting, junk-clogged canals and turning its crowded slums into miserable swamps. Traffic in the city, awful at its best, ground to a halt, and the outdoor markets shut down. At least, residents told themselves, the rains were doing one good thing: Layers of grime were washing off the magnificent mirror-clad temples, revealing again just how beautiful they were.

But on the docks at Klong Toey port on the southern edge of the city, the rains were uncovering something else entirely. Workers loading a freighter bound for the United States noticed that, among hundreds of bales of sheet rubber that had been standing in the rain, whitish puddles were starting to form. Dockworkers alerted police, who ripped the bales apart and dug down to the source of the pale ooze: almost 2,400 pounds of pure China White heroin.

What the Thai police stumbled over that afternoon became the largest seizure of heroin yet uncovered anywhere in the world, and it launched investigators on a path that led to the arrests of more than a dozen people and the discovery of a multibillion-dollar syndicate that stretched from the remote hills of northern Thailand to the

money centers of Hong Kong and on to the streets of New York. The deeper investigators dug, the more they found. The smugglers had managed, it was discovered, to bring almost 2 tons of heroin into the United States the year before and had been arranging yet another huge shipment as soon as the Klong Toey delivery reached its New York destination. The network of operatives involved was so vast and so intricate that two years later several of its leaders are still being hunted down; the latest two came into the net in December.

The bust in Bangkok was only one of many signs in the past three years that massive amounts of heroin have been coming into the United States from Southeast Asia, say investigators. As big as the Klong Toey gang was, say investigators, it was only one of dozens of complex, well-organized and hugely profitable heroin syndicates now in operation. Together with thousands of small-time smugglers, they control a river of heroin that runs from the remote opium fields of Burma to secret heroin refineries along the Thai and Laotian borders, down back roads through Thailand to Bangkok, up to Hong Kong by ship and then on to the streets of Australia, Europe and North America.

Huge amounts of highly refined Southeast Asian heroin, of far better quality than the impure, brownish heroin that comes from Mexico, Pakistan and Afghanistan, have been pouring into the drug markets of New York and Los Angeles since 1987, and more crosses the border every day. It arrives

in thousands of ways: hidden in crates of radios and tape recorders from Hong Kong factories; packaged inside lawn mower tires; "body-packed" by couriers who hide it under their clothes; even, in a case now coming to trial, sewn inside dead goldfish. Supply has skyrocketed — heroin seizures have more than tripled since 1985 — and so has quality: What is sold on the street now is more than 40 percent pure, up from only about 8 percent just a few years ago.

So far, Washington's war on drugs has been aimed at the epidemic of crack cocaine that has swept the country since the mid-1980s. But a growing number of doctors, drug officials and politicians warn that an even greater threat from heroin is closing in fast. Significant heroin busts are made almost every week, with little evident effect on either price or supply. Last February, for example, the FBI was shocked to discover that the seizure of a $1 billion, 800-pound shipment — enough to supply every addict in New York for a year — had only a "negligible" effect on prices. "It told us that there's a lot more heroin out there than we know about," said Dave Binney, the head of FBI drug investigations.

What has many drug enforcement and medical authorities worried is that the same factors that fueled the spread of crack — easy availability and low price — could set off a similar explosion in heroin use. And there is another factor: Unlike traditional addicts, few new users inject the drug. Instead they combine heroin with crack and

smoke the mixture to get the effects of both drugs simultaneously, which leads, many fear, to a double addiction.

William Hopkins, director of Street Research in the New York state Division of Substance Abuse Services, has seen the future firsthand, and he's scared. He and his team of researchers go undercover for weeks at a time on the streets of New York, keeping track of which drugs are popular and how they are sold. "We see more people selling heroin than ever before," Hopkins told a hearing of the Senate Judiciary Committee last August. "Smoking heroin with crack has widely spread, and we believe it is growing. And growing rapidly."

Smoking heroin is not a new phenomenon. It has been a favored method in Asia since the 1920s and appears to be coming back in fashion because of the fear of spreading AIDS through shared needles. Instead of injecting the drug, a user simply spoons some onto a piece of tinfoil, holds a lighted match under it, and inhales the upward-curling smoke through a rolled-up bill. It's known as "chasing the dragon."

Mixing heroin with cocaine has been around for a long time, too. Older addicts call it "speedballing" and say it smooths the sometimes edgy cocaine high. A crack high can be more of a roller coaster than highs from most drugs. Smoked in small, hard pellets called rocks, crack produces an intense but short-lived euphoria, followed by a depression so severe that it sometimes leads to suicide.

Therein lies the key to heroin's growing popularity. Sprinkling a bit onto crack can extend its effects for as much as an hour and can soften the crash that follows. Hopkins and others report that dealers, always on the lookout for new products, are now selling souped-up sandwiches of heroin and crack called "moon rock," "parachute rock" or "speedball rock" in small capsules for less than $15 each, a little more than the price of a similar amount of regular crack.

Buying heroin in America's biggest cities is almost as easy as buying aspirin. It is available in glassine envelopes, in short heat-sealed sections of ordinary drinking straws (known as HIS: heroin in a straw) or in vials. Business goes on around the clock, seven days a week, and is often better organized than many legal operations. Some dealers even pass out business cards, printed up with a street corner address and part of a phone number (to be filled in at the last minute). There are sale days and bargains and shopping malls, where a buyer can select whatever drug he wants. If that is too much trouble, home delivery can be arranged, the drugs brought by children on bicycles.

Dealers are said to be targeting users under the age of 22. Already hooked on crack, eager to try something new but unwilling to start using needles, younger users have few compunctions about starting

in on heroin — especially as the price comes down. No studies have been done on how long it takes to become addicted to heroin this way, but addiction appears to be inevitable. And that has enforcement officials concerned that a whole new generation of young, poor, poly-addicted users is emerging.

The people growing rich on this trade belong to international Chinese organized crime syndicates, many based in Hong Kong, which maintain connections in Chinese communities in cities from Bangkok to Los Angeles to Amsterdam. The highly refined heroin they supply, says the Drug Enforcement Administration, now accounts for more than 40 percent of the American market, up from 14 percent in 1985. And the profits they make are huge. In its final form, adulterated and having been passed through many hands, a kilo can bring $1 million to $5 million on the streets of New York. The opium from which it was made, meanwhile, had been bought for just a few hundred dollars from a farmer in the highlands of Southeast Asia.

The emergence of the so-called Chinese connection has been partly due to the prosecutions in recent years of leaders of the big Italian organized crime syndicates, which traditionally ran the heroin trade from Southwest Asia into the United States. Chinese networks, which had previously supplied relatively small amounts of heroin, were quick to step into the void.

But the trade also has blossomed from nearly a full decade of bumper opium crops in the fertile regions of Burma, Laos and Thailand, the countries of Asia's Golden Triangle. Burma has emerged as the world's biggest supplier, and the amounts being grown there are staggering: Drug enforcement experts in Bangkok estimate the 1990 opium poppy crop to be about 2,600 metric tons, up from about 1,300 in 1989. An additional 350 tons are being produced in Laos, and as many as 50 tons will be grown this year in Thailand.

The heroin trail starts in thousands of small fields in the remote mountains where the opium poppy, *Papaver somniferum*, thrives in the alkaline soil. Poppies are by far the largest crop for most of the Burmese hill people. By some estimates, as much as 90 percent of the cultivated land in the northeastern part of the country is given over to them, and some 290,000 acres are thought to be under cultivation.

Tens of thousands of people are involved in growing, refining and transporting the drug, and tens of thousands more profit indirectly from the money that the opium trade brings in. In many areas, it is the only crop that makes economic sense. It takes about 2,000 poppies to produce a kilo of opium, but once grown, the valuable crop is inexpensively

transported by mule through the hills.

The crop is sown in the late fall and is usually harvested about three months later, soon after the plants' white and purple petals have fallen off. The small, green seed capsule that remains is slit several times with a sharp, curved knife, and almost immediately a whitish sap begins to ooze out of the wound. Overnight, the sap dries into a dark brown gum, opium.

Some of the harvest is smoked by the villagers themselves, mostly older people who roll a bit into a small ball and put it on a pin, holding it over a flame until it starts to smoke, then dropping it into an opium pipe. But most of the crop is wrapped in banana leaves and carried by mule to hillside refineries in the border areas, to be turned first into morphine, then into heroin.

The processing is done in small, makeshift labs, often manned just by a chemist, a few assistants and a contingent of guards; all that is really needed is a water source. In some areas, established refineries have been running for years, hidden under a cloak of camouflage netting and often surrounded by mine fields. All are well-protected, both from authorities and from competing traffickers; in Burma, a few are even reputed to have antiaircraft guns.

The initial refining step is quite simple, even crude: The opium is dissolved in hot water and mixed with lime fertilizer, which separates the morphine from the rest of the opium chemicals. Filtered, solidified with ammonia and then dried, the resulting powdered morphine has been reduced to one-tenth the weight of the opium.

But then the process gets much more delicate. Equal portions of morphine and acetic acid must be heated together for six hours at a precise temperature, binding the two chemicals into an impure form of heroin that is more than twice as strong as the original morphine. The brownish powder, when dried, is purified several more times with ether and hydrochloric acid. The final product — a fine, almost fluffy powder known as diacetyl morphine — is China White.

Once dried, the heroin is measured into 700-gram units and wrapped in paper or put into plastic bags, each stamped with an identifying logo. Brand names are important: One of the most famous is called Double UO Globe, made in Laos, which pictures two lions holding a globe in their paws. There are dozens of others, mostly from Burmese refineries; Crouching Lion, Lucky Strike, Panda and Dragon are a few. Each has its own reputation for quality.

With dozens of refineries now in operation, the stream of heroin out of Burma has turned into a flood, and the government in Rangoon appears unable, or unwilling, to do anything about it. That has partly been due to the political instability that has dominated the capital since the riots and subse-

quent military takeover in 1988. With a restless population and some 20 insurgency movements in the border regions, the military has been hard-pressed to devote the few resources it has to fighting a drug war.

For most of the past four decades, in fact, Rangoon has been trying to get full control of the northern and eastern provinces where the traffic flourishes. Ethnic minorities make up about 30 percent of Burma's population, and groups like the Kachin, the Karen, the Arakanese, the Shan and others have long insisted on regional autonomy, even independence. Most of them maintain their own armies, sometimes numbering thousands of troops. Heavily armed and fiercely independent, often under the leadership of a charismatic warlord, groups such as the Kachin Independence Army, the Wa National Army, the Pa-O National Liberation Army, the Karen National Liberation Army and dozens of others roam with little interference from the government.

The funding to keep the regional armies going comes almost entirely from smuggling, say Thai authorities. Teak, gold, jade and antiquities are all taken over the border into Thailand. But the big money-maker for all of them (with the exception of the Karen, a uniquely antidrug group) is heroin. "They all claim they're fighting for their independence," scoffs Lt. Gen. Chavolit Yodmani, head of Thailand's Office of the Narcotics Control Board and the director of his country's war against drugs. "I don't believe it. Many of them are just drug trafficking organizations."

As much as 90 percent of the heroin from Burma is said to be under the control of a single opium warlord: an enigmatic, notorious figure who operates under the nom de guerre of Khun Sa. Born Chang Chi-fu in 1934, Khun Sa heads the Shan United Army, a heavily armed force of 5,000-6,000 that controls a 200-kilometer stretch of the Burmese-Thai border where most of the refineries are located. Kicked out of Thailand in 1982, he now operates out of a fortified headquarters in the Doi Lang mountain range only a few kilometers inside Burma.

While Khun Sa admits to being involved in the drug trade — and has even boasted about it in the Asian press — he insists that he is the leader of a nationalist movement and the recognized chief of the 8 million Shan people. Claiming only to tax the opium that passes through his territory so that he can feed his people, Khun Sa has offered several times to abandon the drug trade if the United States will pay him $100 million a year for six years.

He has found an unusual defender in Abbot Phra Chamrdon Parnchant, a Buddhist who heads a drug rehabilitation program near Bangkok. "Khun Sa does not want to be recognized as a drug dealer," he says. "He says he only collects taxes, and I believe him." A heavyset man with a penetrating stare, tinted glasses and two gold Cross pens tucked into the folds of his brown robes, the abbot was asked by Khun Sa several years ago to serve as his spokesman. After meeting briefly with Henry Kissinger in 1987, he has been trying, without success, to get the White House to discuss a deal with Khun Sa.

For their part, both Washington and Bangkok continue to regard Khun Sa as a criminal and the Shan United Army as his personal bodyguard and trafficking force. "The guy's a drug dealer," says a Western drug official in Bangkok. "And he's stronger now than he's been in a long, long time. He's just sitting up there in his own little fiefdom." The Thai government has put a $25,000 price on his head, but there is little that Bangkok can do as long as he stays in Burma. "If he comes into Thailand," vows Chavolit, "we'll grab him."

Unless, that is, his enemies get him first. Some of the armed groups in northern Burma, such as the Kachin Independence Army and the Shan State Army, are occupied with smuggling heroin north into India and rarely clash with Khun Sa. But there is almost constant skirmishing in the hotly contested areas along the eastern border with Thailand, where a half-dozen groups are vying for the heroin trade. "It's a kaleidoscope up there," says the Western drug official. "Alliances are constantly shifting among the groups. Some that used to fight now are working together. It's a business. And business is business."

Among Khun Sa's most bitter competitors, Thai observers say, is the Wa National Army, another self-styled independence movement heavily involved in drugs. It has become stronger in recent months since teaming up with the Burmese Communist

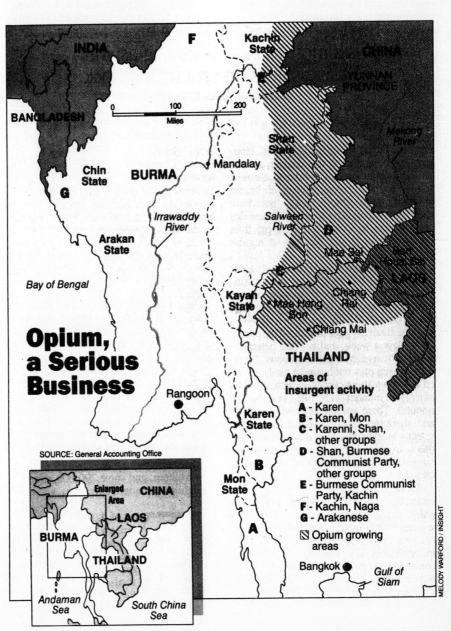

Opium, a Serious Business

SOURCE: General Accounting Office

THAILAND

Areas of insurgent activity

A - Karen
B - Karen, Mon
C - Karenni, Shan, other groups
D - Shan, Burmese Communist Party, other groups
E - Burmese Communist Party, Kachin
F - Kachin, Naga
G - Arakanese

▨ Opium growing areas

MELODY WARFORD / INSIGHT

7. ECONOMY OF DRUG USE

Party, which under the leadership of Taik Aun is thought to control many of the opium growing areas. (The party has also reportedly enjoyed close ties with China, which it has used as a source for heroin-refining chemicals.) Conflicts between the WNA and the Shan United Army have been heating up since fall, often spilling violently over the border into Thailand. (Bangkok sent police reinforcements into the village of Ban Arunothai in early December after fighting broke out between the two groups, each of which accused the townspeople of helping the other.)

While Khun Sa and his army appear to have a firm grip on refining and trafficking opium, Thai authorities say much of the cultivation is under the control of the 3rd and 5th Chinese Irregular Force, headed by Gen. Lee Wan Huan. Numbering fewer than 2,000 troops, the CIF is a descendant of a force of nationalist Kuomintang troops driven out of China and into the Burmese border area after the communist takeover in 1949. Turning to the heroin trade to finance several aborted invasions of China in the early 1950s, the Kuomintang troops gradually degenerated into full-time traffickers. They were the ones who centralized the opium marketing structure (forcing hill tribes to pay an annual opium tax), set up trading routes over the border into northern Thailand and imported chemists from Hong Kong to set up refineries. By the late 1960s, they were producing heroin in the jungle that was almost 99 percent pure.

Perhaps Khun Sa's most dangerous enemy — and a major player in the complex and delicate politics of northeastern Burma — is the 5,000-man Karen National Union, led by Gen. Bo Mya. A genuine independence movement, the KNU is fiercely opposed to drug trafficking — any of its soldiers who get involved with drugs face a death penalty — in part because it depends for much of its funding on outside Christian organizations.

But the group also taxes shipments of jade, tungsten and tin that pass through the 800-kilometer-long region it controls, and its troops are heavily armed. Six Karen were arrested on the Thai border in December with hundreds of AK-47s, M-16s, mortar shells and grenade launchers, as well as more than 20,000 rounds of ammunition.

Unable to deal with both narcotics traffickers and antigovernment insurgents like the Karen and the Burmese Communists, Rangoon has been focusing on the insurgents — to the point that many believe it is now in bed with Khun Sa. In 1988, the Bangkok press reported that Rangoon had cut a deal with the drug lord, giving him free rein along the border in exchange for protection for teak exports (on which the

government depends for foreign currency). Since then, government checkpoints have been relaxed and troops withdrawn from many of the drug trafficking areas. And in March 1984, the Thai press reported that a secret meeting had taken place between Khun Sa and Brig. Gen. Aye San, the head of Burma's Eastern Military Command. The Burmese official agreed to leave Khun Sa alone if he would use his forces against the Karen insurgents and the Burmese Communists. "It's become live and let live with Khun Sa, so the Burmese government can concentrate on the fight with the Karen," says the Western official in Bangkok.

Washington also has long suspected that much of the equipment it has provided to fight opium production, notably helicopters and transport aircraft, has been diverted to the military's anti-insurgency drive. Because of these concerns and in protest against the military's brutal suppression of the 1988 uprising, in which hundreds died, Washington cut $14 million in annual aid last year and refused to recertify Burma as cooperating with antidrug activities. (Decertification means a country is automatically disqualified from receiving direct bilateral aid and requires the United States to vote against it in such multilateral organizations as the World Bank.)

The aid was not doing much good anyway. Many top Burmese police officials, including the head of the narcotics suppression unit, lost their jobs after the military takeover in 1988, and the few antidrug forces left in the country are understaffed, poorly trained and badly equipped. At the height of its efforts a few years ago, the government had five aircraft in its opium eradication squadron: slow, prop-driven Thrushes that could not go into insurgent-controlled areas without risking being shot down. In their best year, the planes sprayed 31,000 acres, about 10 percent of those under cultivation, and there was no eradication effort at all last year. Each year from 1984 to 1987, according to a recent U.S. General Accounting Office report, the Burmese seized an average of 1.5 metric tons of opium, less than 1 percent of the crop. The effect on traffic was "negligible."

Rangoon has tried halfheartedly to defend itself; the state organ Working People's Daily claimed in August that Burma had kept $16.5 billion in heroin from reaching world markets. But the government's usual attitude has been benign neglect; the Working People's Daily observed in 1988 that "opium from the Golden Triangle will spread throughout the world. For Burma, it is not our business what happens once it gets out. We can only look on with folded arms." With that kind of attitude among top brass, the country's opium problem is likely to become increasingly intractable.

Bad as it is there, Burma is not the only source of high-grade heroin. Some 300 metric tons of opium has been coming out of the arid plateaus of northern Laos at least

since 1987, aided, Thai and Western officials say, by top figures in the Marxist government of Prime Minister Kaysone Phomivane. Bangkok officially accused Vientiane of being involved in trafficking in 1987, and the State Department says dryly that the United States "continues to receive reports of the involvement of senior Lao officials in the narcotics trade."

Khun Sa himself is widely reported to enjoy close personal and professional ties with the prime minister and to have moved a number of his refineries into Laos's northern Sayaboury province near some of his Burmese operations. "Two years ago, Khun Sa formed an alliance with Kaysone in Laos," says Francis W. Belanger, the author of "Drugs, the United States, and Khun Sa." Belanger, who met with Khun Sa early in 1989, says flatly that the Burmese drug lord "now has refineries in Laos and can produce his heroin without any outside interference. And if things go to hell in Burma in the next year or two, he can move into Laos and continue his operations there."

Laos would be difficult to patrol even if the government were really trying. Like Burma, vast stretches of it are virtually inaccessible. Narrow mule trails and waterways take the place of roads. The economy is in a semipermanent shambles, making the opium and marijuana trade often the only way for poor villagers to survive. Provincial officials, who rule with a fair degree of autonomy from Vientiane, also depend on the trade: Two Laotian smugglers arrested in Bangkok last May told police they had paid local Lao officials about $2,000 per kilo to ensure safe passage out of the country.

Much of the Laotian heroin is simply ferried across the Mekong River into Thailand late at night at dozens of anonymous crossing points, then funneled into the town of Ban Houai Sai, long notorious to Thai police as a major trading center. But as surveillance has picked up all over Thailand, a new route has reportedly opened up out of central Laos: Multikilo shipments are said to be going east down Highway 13 out the Vietnamese port of Da Nang.

Washington has had little luck enlisting Vientiane in the war on drugs. It offered to fund a crop substitution and narcotics control program in 1987 but was met with mostly blank looks, and Laos was taken off the U.S. aid list last year. Things may or may not be changing: Laos has reportedly started a $5.8 million U.N. plan to eradicate the poppy, though the State Department reports "no known poppy eradication" in the 1988-89 growing season. Vientiane is said by Western officials to be eager to get back on the aid list.

The third corner of the Golden Triangle, Thailand, has been much more successful in attacking trafficking. About 50 tons of opium are still being produced each year in the highlands around Chiang Mai and

172

Chiang Rai, in the remote northern stretches of the country.

Bangkok has been aggressive in trying to wipe out the remaining poppy fields and in getting its hill tribes out of the business. Nine different "crop cultivation control" programs have been started in more than 600 villages, and a slow but apparently steady transition is being made away from the poppy crop and into the less lucrative but much safer ones of coffee, lettuce and kidney beans.

Thai authorities have also been trying to crack down on the refineries still operating along the borders. The surge in opium production in Burma, says the State Department, has led to a corresponding rise in refineries in Thailand. And while Thai authorities have managed to smash dozens in the past decade — nine last year — and claim to have cut production by 70 percent, the country still harbors a substantial refining and smuggling network.

Even if it can wipe out its remaining

Grisly Tonnage in the Triangle

Estimated opium production (in metric tons) in Southeast Asia

- Burma (left)
- Laos (center)
- Thailand (right)

1,400
1,200
1,000
800
600
400
200
0

1985 1986 1987 1988 1989

SOURCE: State Department

poppy fields and refineries, Thailand faces a struggle against smugglers from Burma and Laos. "Thailand is a natural funnel for both heroin and marijuana," says the Western official. "And it's growing. We used to see shipments of 30 or 40 kilos that we thought were big. Now, with the booming economy and the growth in exports, we're seeing shipments of hundreds of kilos."

Getting the heroin into Thailand is no big trick. Most of it is brought over on narrow mule trails at dozens of points in the hills, then gets trucked into small western towns like Mae Hong Son to be sold to middlemen. Some comes over the bridge farther north at Mae Sai, a dusty, beat-up border town that was sacked a decade ago by Khun Sa in one of the city's periodic drug shoot-outs. Mae Sai is the northernmost point of Thailand, and you can pick up Highway 1 there way down to Chiang Mai, Bangkok and the coast. But even here the border barely exists: Thais and Burmese can cross freely 5 kilometers into each other's country to trade (there is a thriving black market in gold and jade, as well), and the bridge is always jammed with trucks, foot traffic, overloaded bicycles and motorcycles. A handful of border guards, machine guns slung casually under their arms, watch the crowd without much interest. After all, anyone with anything to hide would merely wade across the shallow river a mile or two downstream.

There is an array of Thai forces on the border, including the Border Patrol Police, the Thai 3rd Army, the provincial police and agents from the Office of the Narcotics Control Board. They are supplemented by DEA agents, who have three offices in Thailand, and Interpol. "We've got thousands of people up there," says Chavolit.

Nevertheless, the border remains porous, and efforts to control the trade sometimes backfire. A strategic road built by the Thais on the Burmese border near Mae Hong Son in the early 1980s was quickly appropriated by Khun Sa, who established three refineries just over the border and used the road to move heroin into Thailand. When Thai officials responded by destroying a 5-kilometer section of the road, the trafficker brought in tractors and earthmoving machinery and rebuilt it. And when one of his men was killed by a mine planted by the Thai border police last April, Khun Sa reportedly moved in 100 men to guard the road. At last report, they were still in the area.

Once inside Thailand, the heroin usually makes its way to either Chiang Mai or Chiang Rai, where officials say the big deals are made, then down to Bangkok or one of the port cities farther down the coast for shipment out of the country. In these towns, a 700-gram bag of quality heroin will run $3,000 to $4,000, and there are big profits for the middlemen who arrange to transport it to Bangkok, where it will fetch 50 percent more than in the north.

These middlemen tend to be Chinese Haw: Thais of Chinese descent who are known by Thai names but maintain close contacts with other Chinese in Yunnan province in the People's Republic and in Hong Kong. Some are involved in production: Police in Mae Sai reported in October that Haw merchants were known to be running refineries just over the border in Burma. But most are in the transit business, recruiting couriers to move the drugs south.

The couriers could be anyone. Some are Haw themselves, and others are drivers who never know what they are carrying. Some are just people who need a little quick cash: Four women were arrested last June near Chiang Mai when a spot police check uncovered 9.2 kilos of high-grade heroin hidden in girdles designed to make them look pregnant. Profits, in a poor country like Thailand, can be huge. A Haw arrested with 34 kilos as he approached Bangkok in December said he was paid about $8,000 to transport the drug, apparently destined for the Netherlands.

Once in Bangkok, some of the heroin passes into the hands of the city's underworld distribution network. There are about 300,000 addicts in Thailand, more than half of them in the sprawling slums of Bangkok, where heroin is sold a gram at a time in brightly colored paper packages.

But most of what comes into the capital city is quickly exported: mostly to the United States, followed by Hong Kong, Malaysia, the Netherlands and Singapore. Huge amounts leave the country in tiny shipments, either mailed — more than 32 kilos was intercepted in the Bangkok postal system in 1988 — or body-packed out by individual couriers (known to Asians as "ant traffickers") on commercial airlines.

Most large shipments go by freighter. Heroin has been found in plaster Buddhas, in crates of fake jade, even dissolved in fish sauce. While Bangkok's Klong Toey port is still the most important exit point, says the Office of the Narcotics Control Board, increased police surveillance there has pushed some of the smuggling down to little-watched port towns in the southern and eastern provinces. Officials in Bangkok say increasing amounts are being transshipped through Laos to Da Nang, then over to Canada.

As frequently as not, the smugglers are foreigners. About 500 foreigners are in jail in Bangkok on drug charges, most of them Burmese, Chinese, Laotian or Malaysian. Fifteen Hong Kong smugglers were caught in 1988 (with more than half of all the heroin that authorities seized that year), as were 15 Americans and a handful of Middle Easterners and Europeans.

A more recent phenomenon has been the emergence of the so-called African connection. European traffickers have been recruiting couriers in poor Sub-Saharan countries, especially Nigeria, and using them to transport heroin out of both Bang-

kok and the Southwest Asian producing countries, routing them via India, Sri Lanka, Kenya, Nigeria or other countries before going on to New York or European capitals. Some 236 Africans were arrested worldwide in 1988 for heroin smuggling, and Bangkok experienced a miniepidemic this fall: A Nigerian woman was arrested with 58 kilos of heroin at Bangkok's Don Muang International Airport Oct. 16; two were arrested the next week trying to ship out five televisions packed with more than 20 kilos; another was busted Nov. 23 with about 40 kilos.

For those who get caught, the penalties are tough: Anyone convicted of producing or exporting heroin faces a potential death sentence. Thailand seems to be getting increasingly serious about the drug problem. More than 51,000 were arrested in 1988, up from slightly more than 33,000 in 1986, and police crackdowns are ordered periodically; the most recent was in June. But Thailand lacks any kind of conspiracy law, so it can convict only traffickers it catches with drugs. That means that mostly little fish get caught. "We need to go a step beyond getting the couriers, who aren't so important," says Chavolit. "The big guys won't do it themselves."

To close the net around the kingpins, Bangkok is considering a bill that would allow authorities to seize traffickers' assets and to triple penalties if the trafficking is done by government officials. If passed, that provision could make a crucial difference. Corruption is almost a way of life in Thailand, say those who live and work there; it extends from the local cop to the highest levels of the military.

Things are changing, slowly. On Dec. 12, a Thai police investigatory committee accused former police Maj. Gen. Veth Petbarom of being involved in shipping heroin to five countries, including the United States. Veth, indicted in New York on trafficking charges last July, reportedly used his influence to get the drugs through customs checks at Don Muang. "We have to be careful," says Chavolit. "Cases of corruption can take place anywhere."

Much of the heroin leaving the Golden Triangle goes to Hong Kong, which has emerged as a key base of operations for financiers and traffickers. Situated along China's southeastern coast, Hong Kong has the biggest container port in the world and is one of Asia's foremost banking centers, handling some $50 billion a day. Most of the "Chinese Mafia" organized crime groups involved in the drug trade run the actual smuggling networks and launder profits from there, according to the DEA.

The trade has been going on since the 1920s, and the networks have become deeply entrenched. "The proximity to the source countries, the historical connections to Chinese communities elsewhere and the fact that we have very advanced communications and transport links with the rest of the world have given Hong Kong a long history of drug trafficking," says Tsang Yam-pui, chief staff officer of the Royal Hong Kong Police's Narcotics Bureau.

With 200 islands, most of them uninhabited, and hundreds of miles of coastline, it is easy for a trawler to anchor, bury a shipment on the beach and return to Thailand. Sometimes heroin will be dropped off the boat with a floating marker ar a prearranged spot, and another boat will zip out from the shore to pick it up. Others drag it underwater in sealed drums; if intercepted by Hong Kong police, they simply cut the cables and let the evidence sink.

That route is still strong, but Hong Kong police say that an increasing amount is coming in through routes that have opened up in recent years. Opium addiction, once a massive problem in China, was wiped out after the communists took power and began executing traffickers. But as the country's economy opened up to the outside world during the 1980s, the heroin trade came back to life. "All the previously used drug trafficking routes from the Golden Triangle through China to Hong Kong have been reestablished," says Tsang.

From refineries in Burma and Laos, the usual China route extends to K'un-ming, the capital of Yunnan, where a healthy black market exists, then goes overland to coastal cities like Canton (Guangzhou) and Shanghai. "I estimate that between 30 percent and 50 percent of the heroin is coming in from China," says David Tong, director of narcotics investigations for the Hong Kong Customs Service. "Hong Kong traffickers go down to Yunnan to buy the heroin or to the black markets right over the border in Guangzhou or Shenzhen."

They appear to be setting up networks within the People's Republic: Last year a Hong Kong resident was executed after being convicted of recruiting three Chinese couriers.

With the enormous volume of commerce across the border, intercepting the traffic is almost impossible. Some 12,000 vehicles cross every day, and thousands of commercial and fishing boats sail in and out of Hong Kong every day. "Look at this coastline," says Tong, running his hand over the huge, minutely detailed map of the colony that covers an entire wall of his office. "They could come in here or over here or down here. Almost anywhere."

Officials in the colony say the market has been changing as well. Most of the heroin entering the local market for the past few decades has been a rough, brownish, impure form known as No. 3, which Hong Kong addicts smoke. Now, the purer form known as No. 4 or China White, favored by American and European addicts, has apparently taken over, and the price has dropped as well, from $20,000 a kilo in 1987 to about $11,000 today. "In the last 18 months, the market has changed completely," says James Harris, a DEA agent in Hong Kong. "It's all No. 4 heroin now. So everybody who's in the drug business is potentially an exporter. And we're seeing a lot more local dealers crossing over and going into the international market."

Can the heroin tide out of Asia be stopped? So much has been produced that Asian drug officials say huge amounts are now just being warehoused. Even if every poppy plant in the world were chopped down tomorrow, they say, the market could still be fed for more than a year. That kind of oversupply, they say, will inevitably push prices down, and once that happens a real heroin epidemic could spread.

Sometimes even the people fighting the war wonder if it can ever be won. "What are you going to do?" asks Harris, looking out over Hong Kong's teeming streets and the harbor beyond. "Every time you take out somebody big, there's somebody else ready to step right in."

— Stephen Brookes in Thailand, Hong Kong and Washington

Why Drugs Cost More in U.S.

Other Governments Negotiate Prices

Gina Kolata

Americans pay some of the world's highest prices for their prescription drugs. While other governments usually negotiate prices, the United States has traditionally let companies decide for themselves what to charge.

According to one study, Americans paid an average of 54 percent more than Europeans for 25 commonly prescribed drugs. Some essential drugs are especially costly in the United States. A month's supply of Eldepryl, a Parkinson's disease medication from Somerset Labs Inc., costs about $28 in Italy, $48 in Austria and $240 in the United States.

Aerosolized pentamidine, inhaled by people with AIDS to prevent a deadly form of pneumonia, costs $100 wholesale and about $150 retail in the United States, where it is made by the Fujisawa Pharmaceutical Company of Deer Park, Ill. In France, Germany and Britain, Rhône-Poulenc S.A.'s retail price for the identical vial is $26.

Charging for Research

These disparities have become central to a growing debate over how the United States can control its drug costs. Regulators and insurers who have been trying for years to limit hospital costs and doctors' fees are now trying to rein in drug expenses as well.

Drug costs are increasing even faster than other medical expenses. Economists say that drug companies—even foreign ones—are able to charge American patients a disproportionate share of their research costs. Most European governments bargain prices down to levels that cover companies' manufacturing and distribution costs, but much less of their research.

Some of the reasons that drug costs are so high in the United States also have to do with rising medical costs in general. The growing expense of medical technology, the absence of a national health plan and the payment of most medical bills by third parties have confounded most attempts to manage the nation's medical bills.

High drug prices afflict the elderly and chronically ill the most. Americans older than 65 use an average of five prescription drugs, said Ewe Rheinhardt, an economist at Princeton University. Old people are also more likely to have to pay for their prescription drugs themselves because Medicare does not cover drug costs except in hospitals, said Stephen Long, an economist at the Rand Corporation in Washington.

Who Pays the Most for Pills

An index of average drug prices in various countries, with the lowest average equal to 100.

Country	Index
Netherlands	299
United States	279
Germany	269
Denmark	230
Britain	217
Italy	131
France	127
Spain	105
Greece	100

Source: U. S. Senate Special Committee on Aging

The New York Times

7. ECONOMY OF DRUG USE

Many old people are devastated by the prices of their prescriptions. Of their $1,100 monthly income from Social Security, Joseph and Margaret Landin of Dallas spend more than $600 for 10 prescription drugs. Mr. Landin has ailments of the esophagus and prostate gland, and his wife has heart troubles, two slipped disks and arthritis.

"It's terrible," Mr. Landin said, reflecting on the sacrifices necessary to pay for their drugs. "We don't subscribe to the newspaper any more. We don't turn on our air-conditioning," despite summer temperatures that often top 100 degrees. "We used to go out twice a month to eat, but we don't do that any more."

Economists and Federal regulators are concerned that companies are agreeing to sell their drugs cheaply elsewhere, while piling research and development costs onto their prices in the United States. "Obviously, we subsidize the world," said Richard Zeckhauser, an economist at Harvard University.

The costs of producing and distributing most prescription drugs are low, yet the cost of research can be very high. Companies that develop new drugs can negotiate low prices for some buyers and still turn a profit, provided they can charge others enough to pay for their research.

"There is a lot of discretion in how you set prices," the Rand economist, Dr. Long, said. "If you had different markets willing to pay different amounts, then you can produce and sell very cheaply in some of them."

Executives of drug companies attribute the price differences to the workings of the American free market. They warn that attempts to control drug prices in the United States will backfire.

"The U.S. drug industry is one of the strongest in the world," said Gordon Binder, chief executive of Amgen Inc., a biotechnology company. "If the Government meddles with the free market, it could well destroy the industry."

But many large purchasers of drugs say that such high prices in the United States merely guarantee high profits. Lately, drug stocks have been soaring.

"The drug industry has been very successful," said Dr. Norrie Wilkins, president of Clinical Pharmacy Advantage, a Minneapolis company that buys drugs for health maintenance organizations and other cost-containment programs. "Its percent of profits are probably higher than in any other industry. We are in a recession now and a lot of business people and the Government are asking: 'Why has the recession not hit the drug industry? Do they have an unfair advantage?' "

A Federal law passed in December [1990] requires drug makers to cut their prices to the Medicaid program for the poor. Hospitals, insurers and other large purchasers are trying to keep the drug companies from shifting the costs to them.

European Methods Urged

Some authorities say that to receive Europe's prices, the United States should adopt more of Europe's methods. "One of our options is to negotiate prices like they do in Europe, using big buying groups that include public and private purchasers," said David G. Schulke, chief of oversight for the Senate's special committee on aging.

A Federal study has found that state Medicaid agencies paid $474 million more for prescription drugs in 1989 than they would have if they had been bought at the prices negotiated in Canada.

Dr. Zeckhauser of Harvard said that some countries like Australia were particularly adept at negotiating low prices. In a recent study, he and one of his students, Mark Johnston, found that average American prices were more than double the average Australian prices for 80 widely prescribed drugs.

In some European countries, including the Netherlands, Denmark and Germany, drugs cost about as much as in the United States. Guido Adriaenssens, who surveys drug prices for the Belgian Consumers Association, said that none of these countries

The Cost of Drugs, in the United States and Abroad

A sampling of average prices for common brand name drugs in the United States and other countries.

Brand/Drug name	Function	Manufacturer	Average U.S. price	Average price elsewhere
Septra/ Sulfamethoxazole	Antibacterial drug used to treat urinary tract infections	Burroughs Wellcome	$10.90	$7.10
Vibramycin/ Doxycycline	Antibiotic used to treat prostate infections	Pfizer	23.30	15.20
Valium/Diazepam	Mild tranquilizer	Roche Products	9.70	3.60
Xanax/Alprazolam	Mild Tranquilizer	Upjohn	37.50	16.50
Dyazide/Hydro-chlorathiazide	Used to treat high blood pressure	Smithkline Beecham	11.30	8.40

Source: U.S. Senate Select Committee on Aging

Companies are said to add research costs to prices in the U.S.

negotiated their prices. But the Netherlands and Denmark control the amounts of drugs that doctors can prescribe, limiting overall costs, he said. Germany is more like the United States, he said, with high prices and high consumption.

Frustrating Drugstore Visit

Patients' frequent inability to postpone treatment and their dependence on doctors' recommendations contribute to the high costs of drugs. Dr. Reinhardt, the Princeton economist, said that when he recently stopped at a drugstore to pick up a prescription, he felt helpless. "I was madder than hell," he said. "It was my doctor who wrote my prescription. I was never given any option. And when I went to the pharmacy, some gum-chewing clerk threw a bag at me and said '$40.' "

Drug companies are free to set their prices but consumers have little opportunity to comparison-shop, Dr. Rheinhardt said. "We are the world's last free market," he said. "It's not a perfect market, but it is free. A perfect market is one where the customer can really evaluate the product and where it is not an emergency situation." Buying a prescription drug, he said, "is not like buying a pair of socks."

Malpractice Suits Feared

Doctors, assuming that their patients want the best and fearful of malpractice suits if they recommend anything less, may disregard prices when they prescribe drugs, Dr. Long said. Doctors sometimes prescribe an expensive drug when a cheaper one is better. Cardiologists continue to prescribe TPA, a drug that dissolves blood clots, for $2,000 a dose, even though studies have shown that streptokinase, at $200 a dose, serves heart attack patients even better.

Industry representatives agree that Americans are paying a large share of their research costs, but add that the nation enjoys the benefits. Dr. Gerald Mossinghoff, president of the Pharmaceutical Manufacturers Association, said that France's stringent price controls had resulted in a drug industry that he described as "no longer world class," adding, "There really is a cause-and-effect relationship between economic pressure and the amount of research."

Dr. Mossinghoff accused some countries, like Portugal, Greece and Spain, of negotiating "outrageously low" prices for drugs and failing to pay their fair share of research and development costs. "In that context, American consumers are paying for cheaper drugs elsewhere," Dr. Mossinghoff said.

Many older people are devastated by the price of their prescriptions.

But the association says that drug makers can still cover their costs and turn a profit in these other countries—as long as they do not have to extend the same low prices everywhere.

Fighting the Drug War

Everyone agrees that the United States has a drug problem; in fact, until the crisis in the Middle East that began in August 1990 with Iraq's invasion of Kuwait, and the economic recession that has gripped the country with the dawn of the 1990s, more Americans named drugs as the nation's number one problem than any other. But what should be done about drugs? How should we fight the drug war? Is there an answer to these questions—or is it a hopeless, unwinnable battle? Of all drug-related issues, perhaps this one is the most controversial.

There are at least three currently argued perspectives or models on the drug war. The first can be called the *punitive* model. The reason why we are losing the war against drugs, the punitive model argues, is that we are not tough enough on users and dealers. The solution to the drug problem is tougher laws, more arrests, longer jail and prison terms for drug offenders, more police, more lethal police weapons, more interception of drugs smuggled into the country from abroad, more surveillance, fewer constitutional rights for dealers, users, and suspects, more planes, faster boats, more and bigger seizures of drug dealers' assets, more pressure on the governments of countries from which drugs originate, perhaps even the assistance of the armed forces.

The second model might be called the *maintenance* or the *medical* model. Addicts and drug abusers are not criminals, this model argues. Just as alcoholics are not committing any crime when they get drunk in the privacy of their own homes, abusers of the currently illegal drugs should not be arrested or imprisoned for their compulsive, self-destructive behavior. They are sick and in need of medical and psychiatric care, including, as a last resort, maintenance on an addictive drug, such as methadone. Maintenance is typically proposed only for the narcotics; for the other illegal drugs, some alternative form of therapy, which includes, eventually, abstinence, is called for by this model.

The third perspective is the *decriminalization* or *legalization* model. This model proposes that the problem with the use of the currently illegal drugs is the profit motive. Eliminate the laws against the possession, sale, and use of drugs, and they will no longer be profitable to sell, and most of the problems associated with their use—the violence, corruption, and medical problems that sellers and users cause or experience—will disappear. Some proponents of legalization even argue that the use of drugs will actually decline when criminal penalties are removed.

Some proponents of one model argue for that model only for certain drugs and another one for different drugs, while other proponents argue that their model applies to currently illegal drugs across the board. Hardly anyone argues that currently legal drugs, such as tobacco and alcohol, be criminalized. However, some observers do argue that legal penalties against marijuana should be removed, but that they stay in place for drugs such as heroin and cocaine. In fact, in nine U.S. states, making up nearly a third of the country's population, small-quantity marijuana possession has been decriminalized: The possessor cannot be arrested, prosecuted, or jailed, and may receive only a citation equivalent to a traffic ticket. In the 1990s two states recriminalized small quantities of marijuana possession. Nonetheless, most supporters of a strong version of the punitive model favor strictly enforced laws against all currently illegal drugs, and many supporters of legalization favor removing criminal penalties against all currently illegal drugs.

Much of the debate over the question of legalization hinges on whether national alcohol prohibition actually worked. In 1919, legislation banning the sale of all alcoholic beverages in the United States was ratified, and in 1920, the law took effect; it was repealed in 1933, and Prohibition was regarded as a failure. After all, the legalization model argues, if it is not possible to legislate against the sale of alcohol, how can the criminalization of the other drugs work any better? In fact, as historical research shows, Prohibition actually did reduce the consumption of alcohol: Rates of cirrhosis of the liver, traffic accidents, and arrests for drunken driving and public drunkenness all declined sharply. In addition, when alcohol was re-legalized, sales in 1933, the first "wet" year after Prohibition, were far lower than in 1919, the last "wet" year before Prohibition, indicating that many drinkers had given up the alcohol habit during that period. Of course, many other problems accompanied Prohibition, including the rise of organized crime and a number of medical maladies associated with drinking alcohol substitutes—but use did decline.

It is entirely possible that the argument over drug legalization is little more than cocktail party chatter. Very, very few politicians can publicly support legalization and hope to get reelected. Public opinion polls show that 9 out of 10 Americans oppose the legalization of currently illegal drugs, over half believe that legalization would lead to increased use, and, by a margin of 2 to 1, believe that legalization would lead to an increase in the crime rate. Only a quarter support the legalization of marijuana, considered the least dangerous of the illegal drugs; only slightly more than 1 in 20 supports the legalization of heroin and cocaine. Given this sort of opposition, legalization is, for all practical purposes, not a viable political option at this time.

Looking Ahead: Challenge Questions

What is the best way to fight the drug war? Should it be fought at all?

Would legalization take the profit motive out of drug selling? Would it result in diminished use? Or would use increase, as others have argued? Given the fact that decriminalization has not increased the rate of marijuana in the states that have decriminalized small-quantity possession, why shouldn't this also be the case for heroin and cocaine?

If Prohibition actually did decrease the use of alcohol, why was it discontinued? Is Prohibition an acceptable and workable model for the currently illegal drugs? Does arresting the drug user work?

Experts generally agree that interdiction—stopping drugs at the supply side—is not possible, and that demand should be reduced; how can we reduce the demand for drugs?

Is the Dutch model applicable to the United States? Why or why not?

HOW TO WIN THE WAR ON DRUGS

Victory begins and ends at home. Washington should stop focusing on curbing the supply from abroad and put more money into programs that reduce demand in the U.S.

Louis Kraar

AMERICA'S so-called war on drugs is looking more and more like the real thing. Troops invade Panama in part to bring Manuel Noriega to justice for his alleged crimes as a drug trafficker. On the Mexican front, U.S. Marines, deployed for the first time in border patrols, engage marijuana smugglers in a firefight. And in mid-February, President Bush flies to Cartagena, Colombia, for an unprecedented antidrug summit aimed at rallying the governments of Colombia, Bolivia, and Peru to escalate their military struggle with the powerful cocaine cartels.

Will all this saber rattling make much of a difference? Don't bet on it. Despite record seizures, the supply of cocaine on America's mean streets—as well as the many not-so-mean ones—has never been more available or less expensive. In a persuasive study conducted for the Defense Department, Peter Reuter of Rand Corp. concludes that even a vastly more stringent interdiction program would at best reduce U.S. cocaine consumption by a mere 5%. Admits Jack Lawn, chief of the federal government's Drug Enforcement Administration (DEA): "Our enforcement efforts will continue to build statistics and fill prisons, but they won't turn around America's love affair with drugs."

Is the answer, then, to raise the white flag and legalize the stuff? Yes, say a small but influential number of professors and politicians, and at least one big-city judge. They argue that legalization would reduce violent crime and divert money from crooks to the government.

But they're probably wrong. The drugs popular today are so cheap to produce—a vial of crack cocaine selling for as little as $3 costs just 35 cents to import and manufacture—that a black market would continue to thrive alongside the legal one. Nor would legalization stop addicts from stealing to support their habits. What it would surely do is

REPORTER ASSOCIATE *Laurie Kretchmar*

swell the use of substances far more dangerous than alcohol. While 10% of drinkers become alcohol abusers, 20% to 30% of cocaine users wind up addicted. Since 1986 at least 100,000 infants have been born to drug abusers. The intensive care they require is costing several billion dollars a year.

Moreover, not all the battles in the drug war have been losing ones. Heroin use, which in the early 1970s threatened to become epidemic, has stabilized at roughly half a million addicts and attracts relatively few new recruits. Casual use of marijuana and cocaine also seems to be declining. The number of Americans who acknowledge using illicit drugs declined 37% between 1985 and 1988, according to household surveys conducted by the government's National Institute on Drug Abuse. The main reason the U.S. is experiencing what federal drug czar William Bennett describes as "the worst epidemic of illegal drug use in its history" is crack, the new plague.

The U.S. *can* gain further ground in the 1990s—but only by waging a more effective fight against illegal drugs at home. That doesn't mean policymakers ought to abandon longstanding efforts to curb the supply from abroad. But it does mean acknowledging that any new fiscal firepower should be targeted at reducing demand in the U.S.

Under President Bush, annual federal spending on the antidrug fight will have climbed 68%, to $10.6 billion, in two years. In a welcome reversal from the Reagan era cutbacks, Bush is increasing spending on prevention and treatment. But he still devotes only 30% of the budget to attacking the demand side of the problem. Instead, Bush is pouring $2.4 billion—a billion dollars more than Reagan—into the effort to interdict drugs before or as they enter the U.S., mainly by relying more on the armed forces.

FORTUNE would reverse those priorities. We would also invest a few billion dollars more in the struggle than the White House

has proposed, though most of that new money will have to come from states and cities on the front line. Treating every one of the country's drug abusers, for instance, would cost $5.6 billion a year—more than half Washington's total spending on the drug war. Happily, much can also be achieved by simply spending and reacting smarter. Here's what we suggest:

TREATMENT
■ Provide more medical help for addicts.
The toughest challenge is curing the roughly four million Americans who are serious substance abusers. Only about 20% currently get medical help. Many shun it, but most cannot find it. While expensive private treatment centers have plenty of room, public centers—the only ones most addicts can afford—typically have long waiting lists. Says Robert Stutman, a veteran DEA agent in New York: "Imagine if I had cholera and walked into a city hospital and the doctor said, 'Come back in seven months.' It would be a scandal, but that's exactly what happens every day to addicts seeking help."

Though it has increased spending in this area, the Bush Administration is hardly acting like a government faced with an epidemic. Bennett's strategy, shaped more by budgetary constraints than hard evidence, is to focus on the half of the four million addicts whom he deems most capable of being helped. Another million, he argues, can help themselves. The remaining million are "hard-core addicts or career criminals" whom existing methods of treatment can't change much.

Doing better requires new medical techniques as well as more money. Only about half of cocaine addicts stay drug free for up to two years after treatment. Part of the problem is that some 70% of drug users also have an alcohol or mental disorder. Says Dr. Frederick Goodwin, head of the federal government's Alcohol, Drug Abuse, and Mental Health Administration: "We need

more effective matching of individuals with particular treatments." A centralized registry of programs and openings in them would be an inexpensive first step.

Drug addiction can be cured, as successful treatment centers such as Phoenix House demonstrate (see box). Says Frank Gough, a former heroin addict and director of an adult treatment center for Daytop Village in New York State: "We return to society productive, responsible people." The big problem is getting those whose judgment has been spiked by drugs to enter and stay in treatment. Most are pushed into it by their family or the threat of imprisonment.

■ Use local laws to allow courts to commit hard-core addicts to treatment. Few states do this now. But California courts, for instance, can send convicted drug offenders to a special prison that includes a rehabilitation center. This so-called civil commitment program entails frequent drug testing after release and recommitment for those who resume the habit. Says Dr. Mitch Rosenthal of Phoenix House: "If the country wants to get serious, like a good family it has to demand that drug users stay in treatment."

■ Convert surplus military bases to drug treatment sites. As Nancy Reagan learned in trying to set up a rehabilitation center for adolescent drug abusers in Los Angeles, many communities object to having one in their midst. The Pentagon is supposed to identify surplus facilities but has not acted yet. With a glut of unneeded bases about to hit the market, this is an opportunity not to be missed.

■ Expand research on medical treatments for addiction. The idea is to treat brain dysfunctions caused by habitual drug use and, by reducing cravings, make patients more receptive to therapy. Medication is already used to treat many of the nation's 500,000 heroin addicts. Democratic Senator Joseph Biden of Delaware proposes spending $1 billion on research over the next ten years, a realistic target. This is a clear-cut case where Washington must take the lead: Pharmaceutical companies are uncertain whether such products would make money and fret they would hurt the companies' image.

PREVENTION
■ Do more to equip children to resist drugs.
Surprisingly, only about half the nation's public schools provide comprehensive substance-abuse education. Less surprisingly, since the key is building character, it's a struggle to find methods that work. Merely providing information in a classroom does

---

THE TOP DRUG WARRIOR TALKS TOUGH

■ Like the Pope in Stalin's famous put-down, William J. Bennett, the President's designated drug czar, is a general with no divisions at his disposal. Because the war on drugs is run by a host of independent agencies and Cabinet departments, Bennett's primary weapon is thunderous rhetoric.

Since taking office, this Ph.D. in philosophy and former Secretary of Education has commanded headlines with his tough talk. He wishes the military could shoot down small planes carrying narcotics into the U.S. He'd like to execute drug kingpins and once observed that "beheading" them wasn't a bad idea. What about legalizing drugs, at least less dangerous ones like marijuana? "Moral surrender," roars the thunderer. "Why in God's name foster the use of a drug that makes you stupid?"

From his platform at the Office of National Drug Control Policy, Bennett recently outlined his views for FORTUNE:

■ On the legal limits to the drug war: "It's a funny war when the 'enemy' is entitled to due process of law and a fair trial. By the way, I'm in favor of due process. But that kind of slows things down."

■ On destroying the drug cartels: "We would go after them even if it didn't make prudent public-policy sense, because these are the enemies of America and of our children. But it also makes sense."

■ On reducing the supply of drugs: "We grossly underestimated how much is coming in." Still, record seizures and increased interdiction of drugs before they enter the U.S., he claims, "will make a difference in the long run by increasing the price of doing business."

■ On tougher law enforcement: "There's no way to win when the dealer on the streets looks out and says, 'The odds of my going to jail are one in five.' The odds have got to be better."

■ On his claim that one million addicts are beyond treatment: "It's not my triage. They've done it to themselves. You can stand up and say that everybody who has had a serious bout with cocaine is going to recover. But you're lying."

■ On the hazards of drugs: "This stuff does something to the brain, to the mind, to the soul, from which many people cannot recover. If this were something you could get into and get a shot or take a couple of aspirin and be okay, it wouldn't be the calamity it is."

■ On the limits to Washington's role: "There are things the federal government can't do. Restore the moral authority of families, churches, and schools, and you get rid of 85% of this problem. Meanwhile, we have a hell of a short-term problem."

---

little to curb demand and may even stimulate curiosity to try drugs.

Kansas City has proved that mobilizing parents and the community can make drug education more effective. Starting with sixth- and seventh-graders, schools discourage the use of cigarettes, alcohol, and marijuana, widely considered the path to more dangerous substances. Students get classroom training in skills for resisting drug use, involve parents in discussion sessions, and see their efforts covered in the local media. The result: These youngsters show only half the drug use typical among their age group.

Bringing local police into the classroom helps too. The Drug Abuse Resistance Education program that Los Angeles started in 1983 uses specially trained officers as instructors for fifth- and sixth-graders. By appearing in full uniform, the teachers in blue immediately command attention. They

maintain it by dealing with the real world of adolescents, presenting a course that aims at building self-esteem and teaches how to say no without losing friends. The L.A. cops' promising technique has spread to some 2,000 communities in 49 states.

■ Do more to spot drug use early. Many public schools require a health examination for new students, an ideal checkpoint. The Los Angeles County district attorney's office focuses heavily on truancy, an early sign of drug use, and gets families into fighting it.

■ Shout louder from the most bully pulpit around. The nonprofit Partnership for a Drug-Free America has created a starkly emotional series of ads now showing on TV all across the U.S. In one, a young woman snorts cocaine in the privacy of her home, while an offstage voice notes that one out of five users gets hooked, then asks, "But that's

not your problem. Or is it?" In the last scene, she reappears driving a school bus. Space for this $150-million-a-year campaign is donated by newspapers, magazines, and TV. Surveys suggest that the ads do reduce consumption of marijuana and cocaine, particularly in markets that run them frequently. By slightly more than doubling the reach of its ads, the Partnership hopes to expose every American to an antidrug message at least once a day.

■ **Companies should join the drug war.** Already, federal law requires those in fields such as transportation, nuclear power, and defense to maintain a drug-free workplace. With good reason. In 1987 a Conrail train ran through a restricted switch into the path of a high-speed Amtrak train, killing 16 people and injuring 174. The "probable cause," according to the National Transportation Safety Board's report: The Conrail engineer was suffering from marijuana "impairment."

Now other corporations are getting interested in drug testing as a way to cut health insurance costs and productivity losses. According to a study by the Bureau of Labor Statistics, some 9% of corporate America's employees show up for work with illegal substances in their systems. The cost to the economy: an estimated $60 billion a year.

IBM has a model program that protects both the company and its employees from drug abuse. Since 1984 every job applicant has had to undergo a urine test for illegal drugs. Any employee caught bringing drugs into IBM, including its parking lots, gets fired. Employees who act strangely or perform erratically can be referred to the company's medical department, but are not required to take a drug test unless their job is safety sensitive. Those who admit to having a drug problem, however, get counseling and medical attention. Says Dr. Glenn E. Haughie, the company's director of corporate health and safety: "IBM considers drug use a treatable disease." Among his success stories is a manager who ran up big bills on a company credit card before admitting to a decade-long cocaine habit. After treatment the manager is back at work and drug free.

ENFORCEMENT
■ **Unclog the criminal justice system.** Crowded courts have taken much of the risk out of the drug business. Arrestees have a 15% chance of going to jail in New York City and face only slightly worse odds in Washington, D.C. Genuine deterrence requires not only more police but also more prosecutors, judges, and jails. The Administration is expanding the federal prisons, which house over 50,000 people, at a cost of $1.5 billion.

But 85% of drug offenders are in state and local prisons. Many are so jammed that

courts won't allow them to take in newcomers unless someone already there is released. As a result, drug traffickers convicted in state courts serve only 22 months on average, less time than for robbery or aggravated assault. State and local governments will just have to spend more on jails: $5 billion to $10 billion over the next few years. That's about half the costs of the jails they built in the past decade.

■ **Try alternative forms of punishment.** Drug czar Bennett wants swift, sure penalties, but he's willing to see them take forms other than long prison terms. Punishment for recreational drug users, who are more influential than addicts in popularizing drugs, should fit their crime. Says Dr. Herbert Kleber, a Yale psychiatrist who is serving as Bennett's deputy for demand reduction: "The casual user is saying, in effect, that you can enjoy drugs, keep your health and job, have it all."

In Phoenix that kind of attitude can get the casual drug user a heavy fine and a night in jail. In Philadelphia a yuppie shopping at the local cocaine market risks having his BMW auctioned off if he is convicted. Denying teenage offenders a driver's license for a year is another promising deterrent. In Toledo the juvenile court can make parents answer for their children's mistakes by imposing fines or even a few days in jail.

■ **Get communities involved in policing troubled neighborhoods.** Operation Clean in Dallas has enabled residents to regain control of areas once overrun by drug dealers. In a six-week operation, the city first pours in cops to put the heat on dealers. It then brings in the full range of services literally to clean up the neighborhood, and finally stations police foot patrols in the community. So far four such cleanups of inner-city areas have reduced violent crimes significantly. Says assistant police chief Sam Gonzales: "We're displacing drug dealers. We can't allow them to take a foothold in part of the city and say, 'It's mine.'"

In Kansas City, the Ad Hoc Group

UP FROM THE ASHES AT PHOENIX HOUSE

■ New York psychiatrist Mitch Rosenthal, 54, has spent his career disproving what he was taught in medical school about drug abusers: "Once an addict, always an addict." Of the roughly 100 private, nonprofit agencies that offer residential and outpatient treatment programs in the U.S., his Phoenix House is the largest, with six sites in New York and four in California. In the view of many experts, including drug czar William Bennett, it also may be the best.

Rosenthal's guiding principle is that addicts must take responsibility for their actions. In his main program adult abusers voluntarily live together in a drug-free residential community for 18 to 24 months. From 6 A.M. until 10:30 P.M., they are kept on a regimented schedule, ranging from household chores to group therapy sessions. Every privilege, from wearing a tie to making a phone call, must be earned. Punishment for breaking house rules is swift.

Even Phoenix House's biggest fans admit it won't work for everyone. Indeed, half who start quit within the first year. But most of the 30,000 who have stuck with the residential program since its beginning in 1967 have turned their lives around. They remain off drugs, hold down jobs, and stay out of jail.

Salvation doesn't come cheap. Treating adults at Phoenix House costs about

$40 a day; $60 for adolescents. That's considerably more than outpatient programs. But compared with the alternatives—treating an addict in federal prison ($68 a day) or in profit-making clinics ($175 to $1,000 a day for 30 days)—taxpayers, who pick up one-third of the tab, are getting a good deal.

Rosenthal's most innovative venture is Phoenix Academy, a residential high school. Some 225 adolescents have earned diplomas since it opened a New York campus in 1981 and a San Diego site in 1986. The students are the kind of troublemakers most principals brag about expelling. Arturo Wong, 18, an ex–angel dust user who was caught driving a stolen car, came to the academy to beat jail time. Says Wong: "In the long run I know it's helping me out."

Wong is among a privileged lot: New York State has only 500 beds for adolescents needing long-term residential care; San Diego County has just 40. Phoenix Academy accounts for about half the slots in New York—and all of them in San Diego. Before opening, each academy, like other such centers, had to overcome protests from people living nearby. But if Americans are serious about getting kids off drugs, they will have to see such programs not as evidence of the disease but as part of its cure.

– **Laurie Kretchmar**

Against Crime runs a hotline that people can use to report suspected drug dealers to police. The organization also provides $1,000 rewards for information leading to convictions. Says Mary Weathers, director of the citizens' group: "The police cannot always get there, so we try to give visible community support." An offshoot of Ad Hoc called Black Men Together, formed to provide virtuous role models for youth, holds frequent antidrug rallies where citizens (backed by police) use bullhorns to shout suspected dealers off the streets.

Seattle is reclaiming drug-infested neighborhoods with bicycle patrols by pairs of officers who befriend local residents and sneak up on drug dealers. Officer Tony Little, who patrols a low-income housing project, says the technique definitely helps cut down drug trafficking. Riding a 21-speed mountain bike "makes you more approachable than if you're driving a patrol car," he argues. Often acting on tips from residents, the bike cops surprise dealers, put them in handcuffs, and radio for a patrol car. The bikes cost around $500 each.

The Drug Enforcement Administration has 2,800 agents, roughly the number of musicians in the U.S. Army. The Federal Bureau of Investigation has assigned 1,100 agents to drug cases. Given those limits, creative efforts by local police are crucial.

■ **Seize even more drug profits.** The most vulnerable commodity in the narcotics trade is money. Drug sales in the U.S. generate more than $80 billion in tax-free profits a year. But traffickers must find ways to get their proceeds into bank accounts and legitimate businesses to disguise the source. Tracing and confiscating cash and assets deal drugsters a double blow: Money is

much harder for them to replace than drugs, and the government can use it to help pay for the war against them. Says Charles O. Simonsen, chief of the currency investigations branch at U.S. Customs: "We're having a bigger impact taking their money than their drugs. If we can attack the financial infrastructure of a drug organization, we can terminally damage it."

Over the past four years the federal government has seized more than $1 billion in assets. To do more than skim the surface, states should strengthen asset forfeiture laws for drug proceeds. The Treasury, which acquires an enormous amount of data from banks on cash transactions of $10,000 or more, as well as on "suspicious transactions," often still lacks the paper trail needed for convictions. Requiring more information on international wire transfers of money would help. Under prodding from Senator John Kerry of Massachusetts, the Treasury is also negotiating to get key foreign bank centers to maintain their own paper trails—and make them available to criminal investigations.

INTERNATIONAL

■ **Recognize that the long-term solution is to attack the economic roots of the supply problem.** Sure, there's always room for more military cooperation. But remember that farmers in Peru and Bolivia are hooked on coca as a cash crop, while in Colombia, which processes and exports the stuff, cocaine is one of the main earners of foreign exchange. Rensselaer Lee, a business consultant who has studied the South American cocaine trade, warns, "Trying to eradicate the problem quickly may create worse problems by throwing people out of work and destabilizing governments."

To help those economies go straight, the Bush Administration has promised $2.2 billion in military and economic aid over the next five years. That's not a bad start. But Washington could still show more sensitivity to the legitimate economic needs of drug-supplying countries. Recently the U.S. alienated Colombia by allowing the collapse of an international pact for stabilizing coffee prices. The cost to the Bogotá government: several hundred million dollars a year in legal export earnings.

In the struggle against drugs, what can we expect to achieve by the year 2000? Drug czar Bennett's goal is to reduce drug use in the U.S. by 55% in ten years. Sounds terrific, until you realize that's about what the U.S. has done since 1985. And who feels better off today? Moreover, who knows what cheap, new designer drug could come along to fuel the epidemic? Use of a smokable form of methamphetamine called ice, which gets users high for up to eight hours vs. 20 minutes for crack, could spread rapidly. Says Robert W. Burgreen, police chief in San Diego: "Anyone with a chemistry book and the ability to experiment can make meth."

Still, that's no reason to despair, as some do, that this fight is destined to prove another Vietnam. To the extent that it implies the U.S. can win a reasonably swift and clear-cut victory, as it did in World War II, today's drug war rhetoric is misleading. Think instead of another struggle that offered no quick fix but instead required patience, vast resources, bipartisan and international cooperation, but which America saw through successfully—the cold war. Policies based on containment may not stir the blood. Pursued long enough, though, they can ultimately prevail.

THE DRUG WAR IS KILLING US

*Interdiction Has Made Hard Drugs Cheap
and Violence Plentiful.*

There's a Better Way.

Daniel Lazare

After 20 years of troop sweeps, police actions, and military rhetoric, the evidence is all around us. The war on drugs has flopped. It's been more than ineffective—it's actually made things worse. It has caused street crime to mushroom and the murder rate to soar. It has intoxicated ghetto kids with visions of gold chains, black Mercedes, and other fruits of an underground economy. Rather than stopping drugs, it has ensured a flow of harder and harder substances onto the street.

In the 1960s, an estimated 69,000 Americans were addicted to heroin. Today, there may be 250,000 junkies in New York City alone. Meanwhile, the cities are struggling to dig out from under a blizzard of low-priced cocaine. New and far more potent drugs are flooding the ghettos—due largely to interdiction policies that penalize traffickers in soft bulky drugs like marijuana, while actually increasing the supply of coke. In the late 1970s, federal drug prosecutors were congratulating one another over the arrest and conviction of Nicky Barnes, sentenced to life for selling 43 pounds of heroin and coke a month out of a West Harlem garage. Barnes is small potatoes compared to Rayful Edmond, recently convicted of distributing 440 pounds of coke a *week* in Washington, D.C.

This explosion did not occur despite the drug war, but because of it. Putting away drug lords like Barnes backfired by disrupting a stable distribution system, replacing it with something worse, and persuading Barnes's many imitators that they would have to be more aggressive, more ruthless, more sophisticated if they were to take his place. No matter how hard the cops crack down, drug producers, importers, and street dealers manage to keep one step ahead.

"When I first started in the early '80s, a big coke seizure was 70 pounds," muses a former federal prosecutor in Miami. Nowadays, he says, busts that size are so commonplace as to be hardly worth mentioning. In 1981, federal drug agents confiscated 4,263 pounds of cocaine. By late 1989, the haul was approaching 171,000 kilos—40 times as much—not because the Drug Enforcement Administration was getting better at its job, but because smugglers have gotten better at theirs and are pushing so much more stuff through. This is the sort of private sector initiative any free market economist can appreciate. Although the feds have succeeded in pushing marijuana prices up—from $20 an ounce in the 1960s to $200 and up today—coke has plummeted from $50,000 per kilo in the late 1970s to under $10,000 early last year. As a result of this interdiction-driven price structure, marijuana—once a "poor man's drug"—is now a gourmet item; cocaine, once reserved for the media elite, is now the lumpen proletariat's drug of choice.

The cheap, smokeable form of cocaine known as crack—said to have been invented in a Los Angeles kitchen in 1983—is simply the latest product of a process of research and development, along with ever-more sophisticated marketing, that government policies foster. Interdiction places a premium on portability and potency, encouraging dealers to switch to products that give more bang for the buck, while being easier to conceal from the police. The result: hard drugs push out soft drugs, pushers get smarter, and as cops up their firepower, dealers up theirs. Once the crack fad blows over, as undoubtedly it will, other drugs—even cheaper, more mind-blowing and more toxic—will arise to take its place. Who knows what strange fruit the drug war may bear?

This is a record of failure that's hard to beat—not that the government doesn't try. In the late '60s, New York's governor, Nelson Rockefeller, unveiling what he called the toughest drug law in the world, vowed to go after not just drug lords, but users and low-level dealers as well. As a result, the courts ground to a halt as a long line of petty offenders, facing stiff prison sentences, ceased plea bargaining and demanded full-blown trials instead. Last September [1989], drug czar William J. Bennett, unveiling the Bush administration's latest master plan, also vowed to go after . . . petty users and dealers. The consequence, predictably, is that plea bargaining has declined, court dockets are overcrowded, and juries are increasingly reluctant to send people to prison for possession of minuscule amounts of dope. With drug busts running at 750,000 a year nationwide—mostly for pot—prisons are bulging. In New York, where city officials are so desperate for lockup space they've begun housing prisoners on barges, drugs have displaced first-degree robbery as the number one cause of incarceration. In Washington, D.C., they account for more than half of all felony indictments.

So the drug war has led to more drugs, which in turn have led to more arrests and ever more feverish rhetoric out of Washington. "The more it's demonstrated that authoritarian responses don't work," observes ACLU Director Ira Glasser, "the more authoritarian they become. It feeds on itself in a way that is almost classically a form of hysteria."

The self-defeating nature of the drug war is clear from something called Operation Intercept, a massive effort launched by the Nixon administration to stop the flow of marijuana across the Mexican border. Billed as the largest peacetime search-and seizure opera-

Reprinted from *The Village Voice*, January 23, 1990, pp. 22, 24-26, 28-29.

tion in history, Operation Intercept sent customs agents rifling through hundreds of thousands of cars and trucks for nearly three weeks in the fall of 1969. Yet while the campaign snarled traffic and tied up cross-border tourism and commerce, the drug haul turned out to be small. It did succeed, though, in triggering far-reaching changes in the marijuana business.

The cocaine explosion has not occurred despite the drug war—but because of it. No matter how the cops crack down, dealers keep a step ahead.

Stepped-up border controls forced distributors to upgrade their methods. Where previously they had relied on peasants riding public buses, in the aftermath of Operation Intercept they began switching to backcountry routes and eventually to DC-3's. As a U.S. customs agent put it in Elaine Shannon's 1988 best-seller, *Desperados,* Operation Intercept "caused the smugglers to learn to use airplanes. They started hiring pilots. And the loads got bigger." The trade also grew more professional and better capitalized. Paraquat, the herbicide that Mexican officials sprayed on marijuana fields in large quantities at American behest beginning in the late '70s, triggered another commercial revolution. The poison knocked Mexican pot off the market. But instead of stopping the marijuana trade, it caused it to shift south to Guajira Peninsula in northern Colombia, source of the Colombia Gold that would soon become famous among American tokers. Large-scale sweeps by the Colombian military followed, whereupon marijuana cultivation, like the jet stream encountering a local storm center, shifted once again. This time it retreated deeper into the Colombian interior where it came to the attention of drug dealers in the city of Medellin.

Medellin had functioned as a heroin smuggling center in the 1950s. It was also close by the coca fields of Bolivia and Peru. As the U.S. Coast Guard and Customs Service clamped down and smuggling costs rose, it wasn't long before the major marijuana families realized there was more money in the local white powder. Cocaine began finding its way to the U.S. market in increasing quantities. The changing nature of the drug trade is illustrated by a story about Carlos Lehder. In the late '70s, this ambitious young Medellin drug en-

trepreneur arrived at Norman's Cay in the Bahamas to set up a trans-shipment station for drugs bound for Florida. He was irritated to find, however, a small mom-and-pop operation flying planeloads of pot. Lehder and his heavily armed associates permitted the ring to continue, but only if space was cleared on each flight for a shipment of coke. Each planeload of marijuana was worth perhaps $300,000 wholesale; the same weight in cocaine was worth $26 million. Pot was by now small-time. Coke was where the smart money was heading.

In 1982, Ronald Reagan appointed vice-president Bush director of the South Florida Task Force, a super-agency aimed at controlling the flood of hot money and drugs in and around Miami. The task force was highly effective in intercepting rusty freighters loaded with pot, but less effective against smugglers bearing valises full of cocaine. The result was to tip the market more decisively in favor of coke. In 1985, the Reaganites did coke smugglers another favor by launching a massive eradication program, Operation Delta-9, complete with troops and military helicopters, against domestic marijuana growers in all 50 states. Although pot growers tried to recoup by moving their crops indoors to greenhouses and basements, market share was lost. With a major competitor out of the way, the boys from Medellin now had the field to themselves. At some point in the mid-'80s, amid mounting horror stories of broken marriages and ruined careers, cocaine began showing signs of losing favor with the middle class. The results might have been a market glut of disastrous proportions for the cocaine cartel were it not for crack. For a few dollars a vial, it created an intense, short-lived high that proved immensely popular with the ghetto masses.

For cocaine businessmen, the day was saved. For urban blacks and Latinos, the nightmare was just beginning. By embarking on a crusade against pot, federal narcs triggered a series of events that eventually laid the basis for a cocaine catastrophe.

Plus ça change. . . . The great historical precedent for the current impasse is, of course, Prohibition. The war on booze backfired in essentially the same way the war on drugs is boomeranging today. Besides fostering an unprecedented wave of gang violence, prohibition promoted immoderate use by tilting the market away from softer substances to harder ones. A century earlier, Thomas Jefferson had predicted as much, when he observed: "No nation is drunken where wine is cheap, and none sober where the dearness of wine sub-

stitutes ardent spirits as the common beverage."

During Prohibition, beer drinking declined in much the way pot smoking is declining today: The reason wasn't changing taste, but the effect of interdiction on supply and demand. Bootleggers refused to risk their lives for something that was 95 percent water and hops. According to data collected in the late 1920s by Irving Fisher, the famous Yale economist, a glass of beer grew to be twice as expensive as a shot of bathtub gin—meaning, in effect, that Prohibition wound up pushing drinkers toward the hard stuff. The day of having a brew or two with friends was past. The age of getting blind, blotto, buried, canned, etc. had arrived.

The upshot was a wave of drunkenness that left ordinary people aghast. As one witness observed: "Everybody drank as if there would never be another drink. If you opened a bottle, you killed it." With supplies unpredictable, bingeing became the norm. "Eat, drink and be merry," went the doggerel of the day, "for tomorrow, it may be prohibited by law." The columnist Heywood Broun called Prohibition a scheme for replacing good beer with indifferent gin. In Chicago, a Croatian immigrant complained that when working men get their hands on liquor, "they take one drink, then two, then another because they know it will be long before they can have more, and end up by spending their whole pay and then getting very sick." Added another eyewitness: "The raw liquor of those days was not the kind that induced sleep. It made people wild."

Actually, it was the *circumstances* that made people wild—the speakeasies, the illegality, the sexual frisson that comes from rubbing shoulders with gangsters and thumbing one's nose at middle class probity. With repeal, however, the nature of alcohol consumption was transformed. People who would have killed for rotgut whiskey now breezed past liquor stores. In a freer, more tolerant atmosphere, alcohol returned to being ordinary. Drinking increased but there's no evidence that drunkenness did. Some people had difficulty coping with the new freedom—and alcoholism remains a scourge—but taken as a whole, the social cost of drinking—as measured by corruption, enforcement expenditures, and the sheer loss of lives—went down.

Hopefully, legalization would transform the demand for drugs in much the same way. Instead of the desperate desire to get as high as possible in the shortest period of time, people might grow to use drugs more carefully, discriminately, and wisely. Certainly, they

couldn't use them any *less* wisely than under today's overwrought conditions.

Legalization would undercut the drug lords (or at least force them to go legit). By introducing free and open competition, it would bring profits and prices down to normal business levels. Sidewalk dealers, suddenly legitimized, would have no more reason to settle their disputes with Uzis than do liquor salesmen. Whatever reasons black and Latino kids have to quit school, the desire to make big money selling crack would not be among them. And junkies would no more have to rob and steal than would a wino trying to rustle up the fistful of change needed to purchase a bottle of MD 20/20. With drugs subject to pure food and drug laws, overdoses and poisonings would decline.

Instead of expending vast sums for cops, prosecutors, judges, prison guards, etc., society would be able to finance noncoercive drug treatment by taxing hitherto forbidden substances. With the destigmatization of drugs would come a form of junkie liberation—freedom to come out of the shadows, take jobs, demand services, and organize politically against police harassment and the scourge of AIDS.

Legalization is an attempt to rise above the cycle of repression and libertinism that has characterized American culture. Historically, we have spent our off-hours reeling between the temperance hall and the tavern, between the church and the whorehouse, between abstinence and bingeing. The two poles are linked. The preacher needs the local madam to rail against on Sunday mornings, while the madam needs the preacher to insure a steady stream of neurotics in need of release on Saturday nights. Similarly, the cops need the pushers to justify their existence, while the pushers need the cops to maintain what is, in effect, an elaborate price-support system based on government intervention in the marketplace to limit competition and hold down supply.

Legalization would break the cycle by stripping drugs of unnecessary moral baggage, just as decriminalization stripped fornication and booze of theirs. Rather than characterizing drugs as good or evil, legalizers would have them regarded as instruments of pleasure, whose only moral content comes from how they are used. The goal is a society of norms rather than coercion. Society would attempt to set standards, just as the community does now with alcohol and tobacco. But rather than calling in the cops to break down doors, we would recognize that the choice ultimately devolves to the individual.

All of this is deeply threatening to the morality police. Which is why William Bennett, neoconservative cultural warrior, is such a natural for the job of drug czar. As director of the National Endowment for the Humanities beginning in 1981, Bennett attempted to purge the academy of leftists, feminists, black nationalists, and anyone else exhibiting "a strong ideological bias highly critical of the government [or] the economic system." As secretary of education, he campaigned against sex education, abortion, and gay rights, and tried to impose an academic core curriculum based on the received wisdom of certain Western "classics." Now he is out to impose a similar authoritarianism with respect to drugs.

As Bennett declared in a speech in Washington May [1989]: "The drug crisis is a crisis of authority—in every sense of the term 'authority.' . . . What those of us in Washington, in the states, and in the localities can do is exert the political authority necessary to make a sustained commitment to the drug war.

During Prohibition, beer drinking declined as pot smoking has today. The reason wasn't changing taste, but the effect of interdiction.

We must build more prisons. There must be more jails. We must have more judges to hear drug cases and more prosecutors to bring them to trial, including military judges and prosecutors to supplement what we already have." Speaking on a nationwide radio call-in show in June [1989], the drug czar went himself one better by suggesting that the solution to the drug problem might actually be *beheadings*. "Legally, it's difficult," he offered. "But . . . somebody selling drugs to a kid? Morally, I don't have any problem with that at all."

Meanwhile, Bennett & Co. have not been exactly forthcoming with the information that coke and heroin are responsible for an estimated 3–4,000 deaths a year in the U.S. Compare this toll to the 100,000 people who die yearly from alcohol, or the estimated 320,000 who die from diseases related to smoking. Not only are alcohol and tobacco legal, but the latter benefits from a wide array of government price supports and subsidies. The drug war is not directed against drug use per se; merely against the use of certain drugs the culture identifies as beyond the pale. The goal is not to get people to sober up, since certain types of intoxication are still per-

missible but to get them to conform to arbitrary dictates. "Just say no," in this instance, carries a powerful subtext, especially when aimed at young people, minorities, and leftover radicals: Just do as you're told.

"If you want to overthrow the kind of democratic society we have, you need chaos and disorder," observes Eric E. Sterling, counsel to the House Judiciary Committee before joining the ranks of drug-war defectors last January. "If you have enormous disorder and criminality and then adopt tactics to combat them that make them worse, you're playing right into the hands of those who really don't want democratic society and its inconveniences at all."

A social crisis doesn't spring up overnight; it takes years to develop. To the degree that the drug war had a beginning, it is 1875 when San Francisco adopted a ban on opium dens, aimed not so much at the drug as the Chinese immigrants who smoked it. Similar bans spread throughout the West as anti-Chinese agitation rose. In 1883, Congress raised tariffs on imported opium, then, four years later, prohibited imports altogether by Chinese (while allowing the trade to continue in the hands of "Americans"). In 1909, responding to a clamor by American missionaries and merchants opposed to the British opium monopoly in China, Congress banned smoking opium altogether. In 1914, the Harrison Narcotics Act was adopted, limiting the distribution of all opiates, including morphine and heroin, to licensed physicians. By the mid-twenties, opiates were essentially banned.

Nonetheless, as recently as World War I, opiates were favorably regarded. Many physicians viewed them as something of a wonder drug, "God's Own Medicine," as opiates were called, useful in treating everything from menstrual cramps to diarrhea. "If the entire *materia medica* at our disposal was limited to the choice and use of only one drug," observed a writer in the *Journal of the American Medical Association* in 1915, "I am sure that a great many, if not a majority, of us would choose opium." Opium derivatives such as morphine were also used to wean people off alcohol. Opium addiction was considered preferable because opiates, which produce a peaceful, calming effect, didn't interfere with physical coordination, as does alcohol, and did not lead to violent outbursts of temper. Prior to drug prohibition, they also had the advantage of being cheaper. As one medical journal pointed out, 50 cents worth of opium was enough to sustain an addict for 20 days, whereas an alcoholic needed five or 10 times as much.

Cocaine followed a similar pattern. After its introduction in this country in the 1870s and '80s, coke emerged as a popular home remedy. Rolled into small cigars, it seemed to alleviate depression. Vin Mariani, a French wine containing coca leaves, spices, and other flavorings, was world famous as a mild stimulant; the eponymous Angelo Mariani, a chemist, collected 13 volumes of testimonials from, among others, the prince of Wales, the kings of Norway and Sweden, pope Leo XIII, H. G. Wells, Jules Verne, Emile Zola, Sarah Bernhardt, Thomas Edison, and president McKinley. Coca-Cola, one of dozens of coca-based soft drinks on the market at the turn of the century, advertised itself as a temperance drink. Thus, the dominant attitude toward drugs was the opposite of the pro-alcohol, anti-opiate, anti-cocaine policies of today.

Since the Harrison Narcotics Act, the story has been one of spreading crisis, rising alarm, and an increasingly punitive response by the state. In 1918, a Congressional commission found that smuggling was on the upswing while addicts were burrowing deeply underground; yet, rather than reconsidering the logic of Prohibition, they recommended stepped-up enforcement. Reports of cocaine use among blacks triggered hysteria in the South in the 1930s, when many police departments switched from .32 caliber handguns to .38s in the belief that increased firepower was needed to stop coke-crazed Afro-Americans. Following repeal of Prohibition, Harry Anslinger, chief of the Federal Bureau of Narcotics (precursor to today's Drug Enforcement Administration), organized a lurid propaganda campaign to ban marijuana. Newspapers ran stories about mass murderers high on pot, while Hollywood kicked in with the 1936 camp classic, *Reefer Madness,* to the delight of contemporary campus audiences. A year later, Congress obliged by placing marijuana on the list of proscribed substances.

Thereafter, Anslinger continued operating as a one-man ministry of fear. During World War II, he accused the Japanese of spreading opium to demoralize the Chinese. During the Korean War, he accused Chinese Communists of smuggling massive amounts of heroin to "weaken American resistance." As resistance among drug users stiffened, Congress responded by steadily ratcheting up penalties—from two years to a maximum of five for drug law violations in 1914, to 10 years in 1922, to life in the 1950s. In 1966, Nelson Rockefeller, faced with pockets of persistent heroin use amid a general urban crisis, upped the ante to 15 years to life for

possession of two ounces or more of "any narcotic substance," plus stiff penalties for marijuana. *Harper's* magazine predicted that 1970 would go down as "the year of the great drug panic, the year when addiction was a permanent theme in the press and on TV—when government officials and office seekers made instant headlines by pledging a 'massive attack' on the problem." But the magazine was wrong: The best was yet to come.

In the '70s, there was tentative support within the Democratic party for drug law liberalization. A marijuana decriminalization bill sponsored by Jacob Javits and a liberal congressman named Ed Koch (shortly before he ran for mayor) got as far as legislative hear-

ings. Eleven states decriminalized simple possession, while one—Alaska— legalized cultivation for personal use. But then, following Ronald Reagan's triumph in 1980, Democrats began backpedaling furiously. Desperate for a weapon, any weapon, for use against the GOP, they concentrated on outflanking the Republicans on the drug issue on the right.

In 1981, Nancy Reagan embarked on her 'Just Say No' campaign, whereupon Democrats upped the ante by clamoring for a drug czar to coordinate anti-drug operations. Reagan vetoed the idea in early 1983. When David Stockman tried to cut the drug war budget— arguing, as he later put it, that "no matter how many Coast Guard cutters

---

How Many People Does It Take To Convict a Crack Dealer?

It was a stunningly routine "buy-and-bust" case. On September 30, 1988, and again a week later, undercover city police bought crack from dealers hanging out in front of the Modell's sporting goods store at 42nd Street near Eighth Avenue, and then arrested five men. The number of crack vials in the case came to 164, worth $645 (factoring in the discounts offered during the transactions). What follows is a rough breakdown of the number of drug-war soldiers needed to bring a verdict for two of the defendants . . . in federal court, nearly 15 months after the arrests:

• At least 12 police officers.

• Several personnel in central booking to fingerprint and process paperwork. Procedure repeated that day when case is sent to federal court.

• Bail hearing: magistrate, assistant prosecutor, prisoners, U.S. marshals, court-appointed defense attorneys, clerical staff, and an interpreter.

• Assistant prosecutor, calling an undisclosed number of police witnesses, presents case to 23 federal grand jurors.

• Judge presides at arraignment hearing. Defendants plead not guilty. Case assigned to federal court Judge Shirley Wohl Kram. Lawyers meet in court four or five times for scheduling conferences and pretrial motions. Meanwhile, police staff develop and mount photographs, analyze drugs, catalogue evidence. The case is finally ready to go to trial on May 8, 1989. But on that day, the defendants, all out on bail, do not show up.

• U.S. marshals investigate, but cannot locate them. One defendant surrenders, then pleads in June. Another is caught at the Canadian border; a third is arrested on another drug-sales charge. At their respective bail hearings, they are denied bail and incarcerated. Meanwhile, defendants Emengirvo Cosme and Nelson Viscioso remain at large.

• In November 1989, the case is reassigned to its *fourth* assistant prosecutor. In December, the two defendants in custody plead guilty to some of the charges.

• On January 2, 1990, their absence notwithstanding, the trial of Emengirvo Cosme and Nelson Viscioso goes forward before 12 jurors, four alternate jurors, two court-appointed defense attorneys, the prosecutor and a "second-seat" (another prosecutor to supervise him), two court reporters, a courtroom deputy, a law clerk, and Judge Kram.

The prosecution calls eight witnesses, the defense one. Jury deliberations begin on the fifth day of trial, and a U.S. marshal is posted outside their room. The jury takes about 15 minutes to convict Cosme and Viscioso for conspiracy, sales, and possession.

At least 100 drug-war soldiers earned some portion of their salary with this one drug case, which may have cost upwards of $100,000. It is not over yet: Cosme and Viscioso are scheduled to be sentenced on March 14. Their attendance is required, but not guaranteed.

—Jan Hoffman

or AWACs-type planes we deployed, the stuff still kept coming in, by boat, plane, and even parachutist"—congressional Democrats raised a howl, causing the budget director to back off. As the Reagan administration revved up its rhetoric against terrorism, Senator Joseph Biden of Delaware responded with an increasingly popular form of one-upmanship. Yes, he said, terrorism is awful. But the drug menace is even worse. " . . . [W]here are the terrorists getting their money?" he asked in 1984. "They're getting it from drugs. If you want to fight terrorism, you've got to fight drugs." Not altogether displeased at the Democratic turnabout, the Reagan administration accused Moscow not only of fostering terrorism, but, by way of Cuba and Nicaragua, fostering the drug trade as well. A new word, *narco-terrorism,* an '80s update of the old image of heroin-pushing Commies, was born.

The free-floating paranoia of the '80s thus fed on itself as Republicans and Democrats competed to see who could be most hawkish. Democrats mocked Reagan cabinet members for their supposed inaction. Recalls Eric Sterling, whose position on the House Judiciary Committee staff placed him at the center of the storm: "If I heard them say it once, I heard it a thousand times: 'Mr. Secretary, I can't tell you the name of a single one of my constituents who has been killed by the Russians, but I can tell you thousands who have died from cocaine.' " With the death of University of Maryland basketball star Len Bias from a cocaine overdose in June 1986, the frenzy reached new heights. A survey showing that Americans cared more about drugs and health care than Star Wars or contra aid encouraged Democrats to launch new attacks. Republican pollster Richard Wirthlin drafted a lengthy memo to White House chief of staff Donald Regan advising him to consider drugs as the next major presidential initiative after tax reform. Americans were desperate for change, he advised, and would support drastic measures to achieve it. Four weeks after Bias's death, Reagan dispatched troops to Bolivia to assist local police in raids on cocaine laboratories.

With the explosion of crack in the inner cities, the racial nexus, always present in drug politics, underwent a twist. Black Democrats at all levels of government seized on the drug war and made it their own. Although a longtime opponent of the death penalty, Harlem's Charles Rangel, chairman of the powerful House Select Committee on Narcotics, ended up shepherding an omnibus anti-drug bill through Congress in 1988 that contained a provision for capital punish-

ment for drug dealers who kill. He also inserted language barring the use of federal funds to supply addicts with clean needles to prevent the spread of AIDS. In New York, black Democrats who had succeeded in shouting down a Koch proposal for a clean-needles program in 1985 tried again when a scaled-down version was put forward in 1988. This time, they failed. In early 1989, Rangel raised a hue and cry against President Bush for failing to give his new drug czar William Bennett cabinet-level status—a case of a liberal, strangely enough, demanding augmented powers for one of the most rabid conservatives in national government.

At the same time, Jesse Jackson took his "Up with hope, down with dope" message to public high schools, winning praise from, among others, Senator Jesse Helms. For Jackson, who played a crucial role in drumming up liberal support for the drug war, the issue was starkly moral. As he told the Los Angeles-based *New Perspectives Quarterly* recently, "Drugs are poison. Taking drugs is a sin. Drug use is mor-

A rational policy would recognize that not all drugs are dangerous, and that drug use does not necessarily constitute abuse.

ally debased and sick. . . . Since the flow of drugs into the U.S. is an act of terrorism, antiterrorist policies must be applied. . . . If someone is caught transmitting the death agent to Americans, that person should face wartime consequences. The line must be drawn."

Terrorism . . . death agent . . . wartime consequences—this was the language of a political culture that had detached itself from reality and was spinning wildly out of control. Jackson and Rangel notwithstanding, minorities are the greatest victims of the drug war. Military courts such as those sought by Bennett would not be set up in the suburbs, where brokers snort an occasional line of coke and teenagers sneak off to smoke joints. Rather, they'd preside over battle zones like Washington Heights and the South Bronx. That's where the drug trade is concentrated, that's where the cops concentrate their forces, and that's where civil liberties are first to come under assault. It's also where the indirect effects of the drug war—crime, corruption, the displacement of aboveground businesses, and needle-borne diseases such as AIDS—are most intense.

Political pressures are converging on the black community, with polarizing re-

sults. While most leaders demand ever more drastic measures, some have dared to question the cultural orthodoxy. Baltimore's Kurt Schmoke, a former prosecutor, was the first big-city mayor to broach the question of legalization. State senator Joe Galiber has been the first elected official in New York. George Crockett is so far the first member of the U.S. Congress. All three are black.

The alternative to the drug war is a policy based on peaceful persuasion. Instead of ostracizing junkies, throwing dealers in jail, and using the drug trade as a pretext to invade Third World nations, this approach would educate people not to do dangerous drugs, much as a broad-based anti-tobacco campaign has educated millions of Americans over the last 25 years not to smoke cigarettes. Instead of treating drugs as a criminal matter (and now a matter of national security), it would classify them as a public health problem requiring the attention of counselors and medical personnel. Just as cops now realize there is no point to throwing drunks in dry-out tanks, the abuse, harassment, and dehumanization of drug users—what maverick psychiatrist Thomas S. Szasz calls the "verminization" of those who choose to get high outside the officially approved triad of nicotine, caffeine, and alcohol—would cease. A rational policy would recognize that all drugs are not necessarily dangerous, and that drug use does not necessarily constitute abuse. On the other hand, it would recognize that, just as some people persist in smoking, some will persist in doing hard drugs. Rather than punishing those who do, legalization would promote moderation while seeking to minimize the risk to users and the disruption of communities.

Moderation has already asserted itself with regard to legal drugs. Since the health revolution of the 1970s, consumption of alcohol has declined as distilled spirits give way to wine coolers and "lite" beer. With alcohol neither vilified by bluenoses nor celebrated by the underground, it has undergone a process of demystification and deglamorization that allows most people to see booze for what it really is. Americans are drinking more decaffeinated coffee and smoking fewer cigarettes, if they smoke at all. The fact that the '80s are likely to go down in history as the decade of crack *and* the white wine spritzer says volumes about the widening gap between illegal and legal drug use in this society.

Legalization would allow us to look at now-illegal substances more realistically. Heroin, for instance, is highly addictive, although physiologically more benign

when taken over a prolonged period than heavy drinking or cigarettes. It does not cause teeth to rot, appetite to decrease, stomach, intestines, and liver to cease functioning, or any of the other ghoulish effects that have been ascribed to junk by, among others, liberal Supreme Court Justice William O. Douglas. In fact, doctors have found *few* ill effects associated with heroin addiction besides those accruing from criminalization, i.e. the negative health consequence of being thrown in jail, deprived of work, poisoned by impure drugs, and hounded into poverty. For this reason, rather than forcing addicts to use methadone, which, users say, *can* have ill effects, addicts might be better off on a maintenance program of heroin. In Britain, heroin maintenance has been standard medical procedure since 1926. In this country, Dr. William Stewart Halsted (1852–1922) was a pioneer in aseptic surgery even though addicted to daily doses of morphine. Under today's more intolerant conditions he would be condemned to a life in prison or the streets. The loss to the arts—Billie Holiday and Lenny Bruce were banned from performing because of drug addiction—is as absurd as the hipster mystique that surrounds junk as a result of this policy.

Meanwhile, the ban on the use of heroin as a painkiller would cease. According to John Morgan, professor of pharmacology at CUNY Medical School, heroin is medically superior to the widely used Demerol, an artificial opiate whose only advantage lies in its legality. As for marijuana: the DEA recently banned its use as a therapeutic substance, despite the recommendation of its own chief administrative judge, Francis L. Young, who observed in an opinion last year that pot is "one of the safest therapeutically active substances known to man." It's also useful in battling the nausea of chemotherapy, and the effects of glaucoma and epilepsy. According to John Morgan, "there has never been a confirmed overdose due to marijuana alone," while hundreds die each year from internal bleeding brought on by aspirin. Adds Morgan: "The most

effective way to kill yourself with marijuana is by having a bale drop on your head." In Holland, where marijuana has been decriminalized since the '70s, per capita consumption has declined well below U.S. levels.

Finally and most horribly, there are the estimated 100,000 intravenous drug users in New York infected with human immunodeficiency virus (HIV), their 25,000 sexual partners, mainly women, who have caught it as well, and the estimated 4,000 infants and children infected in utero. The HIV epidemic among IV-drug users is a direct consequence of shortsighted criminal penalties that not only outlaw drugs but needles as well. The result is to encourage addicts not to supply their own needles, but to rent used "works" where they shoot up. The state could not have designed a more effective policy for spreading the AIDS virus if it had tried.

Policies like these must end. Addicts must be given access to medical care, encouraged to use condoms, given clean needles and, ideally, high-quality heroin they can vaporize and ingest nasally so they don't have to use needles at all. All of this is as important as supplying gay men with condoms and information about safer sex. Yet virtually none of it's being done. According to public health specialists, junkies with AIDS typically receive no medical attention until they stagger into an emergency room in the final throes of the illness. While the city's needle exchange program was supplying about 300 IV-drug users with sterile hypodermics, an obvious drop in the bucket, David Dinkins has vowed that even this token effort must end.

It is impossible to reach out to addicts amid a real live shooting war aimed equally at drug dealers and drug users. Society cannot drive addicts ever deeper underground while simultaneously urging them to come out in the clean light of day to receive medical help. By verminizing junkies, the drug war encourages them to treat themselves as vermin and infect others through dirty

needles or unsafe sex. The circle of destruction may widen still further as crack takes hold. The reason is a rising incidence of sexually transmitted disease, causing genital lesions that may serve as a "gateway" for the virus, as women exchange sex for crack. From junkies to their sex partners to their partners' partners, rampant drug use and a complete breakdown in medical care are spreading AIDS throughout the ranks of the city's poor.

Legalization would be an improvement, not a panacea. It wouldn't end AIDS, simply slow its spread; it wouldn't wipe out crime, merely eliminate one major cause. People would continue to misuse drugs just as some misuse legal substances today. Addiction might rise; yet at the same time, the overall costs associated with drugs use, direct and indirect, both to the user and to those around him would undoubtedly decrease. Residents of poor neighborhoods would no longer huddle in their apartments while dealers battle with guns out in the street. Ghetto kids would have less reason to look up to dealers as role models. Deprived of a perverse government support system, an overheated trade, which siphons off the ghetto's best and brightest, would disappear.

"I see these dealers standing around with their beepers and gold chains laughing," says Dr. Kildare Clarke, the Jamaican-born chief of emergency services at Kings County Hospital in Brooklyn, who is an outspoken advocate of legalization. "They look at us and say, 'These doctors don't make shit. What they make in a year, we make in a week.' For these people, the money they can make far outweighs the risk of getting shot or killed. There are some days when I have seven gunshot wounds and five stab wounds coming off the streets, and that isn't even counting the ones who go to the morgue. Yet while I can treat someone for drugs, I can't treat someone with a .357 magnum bullet in his head. There's hope for a drug addict, but not for a dead man."

JUST SAY WHOA!

. . . to George Bush's race-based war on drugs, and to legalizers, too. We sought bold alternatives in Amsterdam, Liverpool, and the streets of Daryl Gates' L.A.

David Beers

David Beers is senior editor of Mother Jones.

Leo Zaal, the James Woods look-alike who is chief superintendent of the Amsterdam Narcotics squad, focuses his eyes on the news clipping I've handed him, and gasps quietly. L.A. CHIEF SAYS SHOOT DRUG USERS. "You're talking about human life. You're talking about a human being," Zaal says, scanning Daryl Gates's now famous suggestion to the Senate Judiciary Committee that casual drug users "ought to be taken out and shot." Gates would execute those "who blast some pot on a casual basis" because, as he clarified later, "we're in a war," and even casual drug use "is treason."

"It could be his son or daughter. You'd like to shoot your family?" Zaal asks. We smile at the absurdity, not knowing what comes to light later, that in fact Gates's own son is a drug addict.

Our interview in Zaal's sparse office took place last fall, just as an impending war against Iraqis had begun distracting Americans from the other, already declared war at home, even as the war on drugs was already producing its own lopsided statistics. While 80 percent of drug users are white, the majority arrested are black. One quarter of black men in their twenties are either imprisoned, on probation, or on parole. Between 1985 and 1988, drug prosecutions of white juveniles dropped 15 percent while jumping 88 percent for minority youth. After doubling its prison population in the last decade, the United States now incarcerates its citizens at a higher rate than South Africa or any other nation. And yet, 75 percent of the new nearly ten-billion-dollar drug-war budget continues to go to law enforcement instead of education and treatment. The results so far: inner-city crack and heroin use is on the rise, and HIV spread via dirty needles is today the

number-one cause of AIDS among heterosexuals in the United States, hitting minority groups especially hard.

The day Zaal and I talk, Gates's words are so fresh and seemingly wild it is hard to imagine that, months later, the chief would be singled out as an exemplary drug warrior by the president of the United States. George Bush would call Daryl Gates "one of the all-American heroes," and that same day, the nation would get its first look at the video images of Gates's men beating and crippling Rodney King. Twenty-seven officers around one crouching, twisting, tortured black man; it was the crystallized video image of what the statistics tell: that the war on drugs, with its imperative of more cops, weapons, arrests, mandatory sentences, and prisons, has blurred with the war on crime and degenerated into a dirty war on certain races and classes. The fact that the Los Angeles white middle class saw the tape and then largely backed Gates confirmed its support for that war. If Rodney King did not deserve to have his face and body broken, then Desert Storm had taught Americans a new term for him: collateral damage.

Chief Superintendent Zaal is tough enough. He calls busting big coke and heroin shipments "my favorite meal," and he was for the invasion of Panama, because "Noriega is a dangerous man." What Zaal doesn't understand is our choice of metaphor: Why, he asks, must our drug policy be a *war?* "We don't use the expression." Daryl Gates, says Zaal, handing the clipping back, makes him think of the Gestapo, which once terrorized Holland. They, too, were police who "thought they could change society's behavior. The police are a very dangerous element in society if they are not limited. We know what war means," Zaal tells me, "even those of us born after World War II. We fight war against our enemies, not with our own citizens."

But drug-war logic is a hard line that

bisects political lines. While he was drug czar, William Bennett cut a virile figure in his "bully pulpit," advocating "boot camps" for drug users and declaring the beheading of dealers "morally plausible." He found a backer in Jesse Jackson, who urged that Bennett be given even more money and power to wage his war, as "if communists were infiltrating us."

In the midst of this war, of course, has come dissent: the logic of legalization. It's the drug black market, not drug use, that breeds most violence and uses up too much of law-enforcement money, goes the increasingly familiar argument. Better to legalize the stuff, regulate it and tax it, say unlikely bedfellows including archconservatives like Milton Friedman and William F. Buckley as well as Baltimore's mayor Kurt Schmoke, a few other liberal black politicians, and even a federal judge.

And yet the problem with legalization logic is the war that it creates in the country's conscience. Make crack, heroin, and other hard drugs freely available over the counter, and won't you have handed the underclass, maybe even your own child, a prescription for self-administered oblivion? Addiction rates would rise, almost everyone agrees, but by how much is a groping guess. Drug use, flatly states Jesse Jackson, is a "sin," and there the debate usually comes to a thudding stop.

It was a search for a way out of this stale standoff between Legalizers and Warriors that led me to Leo Zaal's office. I had come to the Netherlands, and also to the Merseyside area around Liverpool, England, to see how Europe as a whole increasingly thinks about and practices drug control, an approach called Harm Reduction. It could become a buzzword in the United States, as well, because harm reduction offers a third path, a logic that stops short of full legalization, while softening the toll of the war on drugs and challenging its basic premises.

If the war on drugs is waged in the

name of a "drug-free" nation, harm reduction starts with the fact that no nation ever has been, so how best to minimize the damage drugs do?

Drug-war logic: more arrests and stiffer sentences are the antidote to the permissiveness that invites drug use. Harm-reduction logic: severely criminalizing drug use just drives it underground, making health and crime problems worse.

On the drug war's front line: cops. On harm reduction's: health and social workers.

If that sounds rational enough, harm-reduction logic, played out, can produce some seemingly drug-induced scenarios. In my travels I met a doctor who treats addicts by prescribing them heroin; a reverend who lets visitors shoot up in his church; a state-built prostitution drive-thru; a taxpayer-funded union of junkies; coffee shops with eight kinds of cannabis on the menu; and the proud promoter of a vending machine that serves up syringes to the public around the clock. When such scenes turned me queasy and tumbled my ethical compass, harm-reduction believers were ready with their bottom-line calculation: their policies, they say, quite simply save more lives than ours.

The Netherlands

RENE MOL IS AGITATED, RUMMAGING around the airy old canalside offices of the Amsterdam Junkybund (Junkie Union), which he heads. While addicts chat around a big window-lit table or send the clatter of typewriters off the high ceilings, Mol is trying to dig out the news article that launched his latest battle. Here it is, see? The needle exchange in the red-light district must now close at 9:00 P.M., not midnight. The city council is "scapegoating" drug users, says Mol, so he and his union of addicts will fight back with posters and opinions in the papers, and they'll do it with tax money the city government gives them: $100,000 a year. The boyish Mol, who uses no drugs ("I am very strange, because I don't drink, I have never drunk. I quit smoking. I'm a bit dull"), seems addicted to political battle. Last year, when the city started allowing police to "get tough" on chronic druggies by kicking them out of the city center for up to two weeks, the Junkybund got the national government to slap down the order.

Such are the parameters of debate in the Netherlands, a country that pays addicts to fight for their rights, and that, more than any other nation, has made harm reduction its official policy. As controversial as Holland's stand is internationally, at home it is so well accepted that during the last national election drugs didn't make it into campaign speeches.

Field Marshal
DARYL GATES

"It's estimated that by 1970, 45 percent of the metropolitan area of Los Angeles will be Negro; if you want any protection for your home and family . . . you're going to have to get in and support a strong police department. If you don't do that, come 1970, God help you."—Former LAPD chief William H. Parker, mentor to Daryl Gates

"We may be finding that, in some blacks, when [the choke hold] is applied, the veins or arteries do not open up as fast as they do in normal people."—Daryl Gates in 1982, explaining why so many black suspects died from choke holds by his police.

George Bush called him "one of the all-American heroes." He was lauded by Democrat Joseph Biden, chair of the Senate Judiciary Committee. Indeed, before the political fallout from Rodney King's savaging, Bush and Biden competed in a love fest for Los Angeles Police Chief Daryl Gates, the embodiment, apparently, of their war on drugs.
• To rescue the U.S. hostages in Iran, Gates offered the LAPD SWAT team to the State Department.
• When Philadelphia mayor Wilson Goode approved aerial bombing of the MOVE house, which set ablaze blocks of homes, Gates called Goode "an inspiration for the nation."
• To stem cocaine from Latin America, Gates suggested, if sanctions didn't work, "a friendly invasion."
• In 1988, looking for drugs on a tip, over eighty officers with sledgehammers systematically demolished two duplex houses. The damage was so extensive that the Red Cross offered assistance to residents. Small amounts of rock cocaine and marijuana were found. Officers left behind spray-painted sign: "LAPD Rules." The victims later received a $3.5 million settlement.
• Between 1984 and 1988, Los Angeles incurred $13 million in civil police misconduct awards.
• Under Gates, the department illegally spied on Mayor Tom Bradley, members of the city council, and more than two hundred lawful groups, including the National Council of Churches.
• Gates answered L.A.'s growing problem with gangs by launching Operation Hammer, a series of indiscriminate sweeps in which over twenty-five thousand young blacks and Latinos were arrested.
• After christening with a wine bottle a fourteen-foot battering ram, the chief climbed aboard and rode shotgun, as a gaping hole was smashed into a nearby suspected crack house. Inside were two women and three small children, two of them eating ice cream. A search turned up a small amount of marijuana. The ram is still in use.

Despite Gates's paramilitary tactics, major crimes in Los Angeles rose by over 8 percent in 1989. Last year, murders were up by more than 11 percent and robberies more than 16 percent. Such a record didn't dull the admiration of Biden and Bush for their field marshal. When reformers tried to rein him in some years ago, Gates had a ready answer: Douglas MacArthur "was just trying to win his war too, but they wouldn't let him either."

By Joe Domanick

A popular misconception from afar is that Holland, uninterested in drug control, has made "anything goes" its dogma. Open the Dutch law books, however, and the disapproval of drugs is there in black and white: possession of heroin, cocaine, amphetamines, LSD, can mean four years in prison; selling may get you twelve. Pot and hash are categorized as "soft drugs," which don't pose the "unacceptable risk" of the others, but they are illegal, too. On paper, then, Holland and the United States are roughly in step; in practice they are not at all. Dutch authorities don't wink at their laws: a third of all prisoners are in for drug-related crimes. But the government, as its fact sheet explains, "tries to ensure that drug users are not caused more harm by prosecution and imprisonment than by the use of drugs themselves."

The result is what the Dutch call "flexible enforcement," which means taking a light touch to petty users and sellers. Outside the Rotterdam Central Train Station, I observe young men quite openly buying and selling heroin; they occasionally duck into a phone booth with a bit of the drug on a scrap of folded foil, lighting it and sucking the smoke through a straw, a practice known as "chasing the dragon." Across the street sits an idle police van. The flip side of flexible enforcement, the one that upsets Rene Mol, snaps into view one night in Amsterdam's red-light district, when I see police hauling away a cuffed, dark-skinned dealer, while his peers look on.

"The drug crisis is a crisis of authority," former drug czar Bennett is fond of telling audiences. Upon hearing this,

Eddy Engelsman, Holland's bespectacled drug czar in the Ministry of Welfare, Public Health, and Cultural Affairs, smiles and offers me more tea. "I think we have to stick to the drug problem. Restoration of authority has nothing to do with the drug problem." The best approach, says Engelsman, is nuanced, pragmatic, businesslike. The Dutch have a word for all three rolled into one, a word that he likes very much: *zakelijk*. As Amsterdam judge Frits Ruter, unencumbered by mandatory sentencing of drug users, tells me in his calm, *zakelijk* tone of voice: "To us the law is a means; it's not a holy thing. When the criminal law doesn't work, we look for some other means. The law may forbid something, but that is only the outer landscape of what can be done."

Exploring their inner landscape of possibility, the Dutch have navigated boldly. Amsterdam's legendary coffee shops, where "illegal" cannabis can be freely bought and smoked, are sanctioned refuges because, Engelsman explains, they "split the market," so that a pot buyer won't be urged to try anything more dangerous. Coffee shops caught purveying harder drugs, like coke or heroin, are promptly shut down.

Anyway, it's not pot smoking that worries Dutch officials; unsurprisingly, it's the AIDS virus, which is easily spread among drug injectors who share infected needles. Backed by the full weight of a well-endowed national health-care system, fifty-two Dutch cities have syringe-exchange programs. In 1984, a few dozen Junkybund members helped design the first experiment; today, Amsterdam alone swaps nearly a million syringes a year through clinics and creative outreach. Buses crisscross Amsterdam and Rotterdam, dispensing the heroin substitute methadone, clean needles, and AIDS advice, a mobile approach that reaches skittish users and defuses citizens' "not in my neighborhood" attitudes toward permanent clinics. In Rotterdam, I meet the health department's Rien Klaassen, who shows me the new kind of ATM—call it an Addict Teller Machine—that he helped bring into being for serving needle users when clinics are closed. Pop a used needle in the syringe-shaped slot, and out slides a wrapped, sterile replacement. There are several such devices sprinkled around Rotterdam and Amsterdam now. The Junkybund helped iron the bugs out of the prototype, using its expertise to figure out how needles might be ripped off. That sort of data, straight from the source, makes the union a good investment for the government, Engelsman tells me.

Sensitive to outside criticism, the Dutch obsessively collect data on their drug population, and they are eager to share it. Government figures show that the nation's addict population, smaller per capita than our own, is aging and not growing. HIV rates among injectors in the big cities leveled off at 30 percent three years ago. (In New York City, where Mayor David Dinkins closed down a needle-exchange experiment, calling it a "surrender to drug abuse," the HIV rate among junkies is around 60 percent). The Dutch say their cocaine use is rising slightly, though it's still well below U.S. levels, and crack is nowhere as prevalent as it is in the United States. Since the cannabis coffee shops opened, pot and hash consumption has declined. About 5 percent of Amsterdam's population and 15 percent of its biggest smokers (twenty-three- and twenty-four-year-olds) say that they lit up a joint in the last month; American teenagers, on average, are three times more likely to smoke than their Dutch counterparts.

The Dutch invert the U.S. drug-budget ratios, spending the bulk of their money not on law enforcement but on prevention, treatment and research, and on a curriculum that teaches kids the risks of *all* intoxicants and to take responsibility for their actions. For fear of glamorizing illegal drug taking's outlaw appeal, "We want to keep a low profile," says Engelsman. "No mass media campaigns. No policemen into the school. No fingers pointing, saying you shouldn't do this and that. Reduce the problem, control the

PUSHING THE
Pentagon

And you thought the *war on drugs* was some speech-writer's metaphor. In fact, the Pentagon now occupies a front-and-center role in U.S. drug-control policy. In the name of fighting narcotics, heavily armed troops are waging battle in cities and countrysides, and under the 1988 Anti-Drug Abuse Act, the Department of Defense is responsible for gathering and sharing intelligence about drug trafficking on U.S. soil. The DoD reports directly to the president and, unlike the FBI and CIA, its domestic activity is not subject to oversight by Congress.

• In Washington, D.C., National Guard helicopter pilots chase drug suspects with floodlights, and deploy police commanders to crack-house busts.

• On the Arizona-Mexico border, U.S. Marines engaged in a gunfight with unidentified horsemen suspected of drug smuggling.

• In Northern California, while army pilots reportedly flew gunships overhead, an infantry division in search of marijuana growers cordoned off a square mile of elk preserve and arrested everyone who trespassed.

• In Kentucky bluegrass country, the National Guard searches people's backyards, and buzzes them with helicopters.

• A DoD-inspired program called "Guard Against Drugs" orders weapon-toting Arizona guardsmen to land their helicopters at grade schools and deliver antidrug talks.

• Last year, Congress authorized $450 million to expand the DoD's drug war, a 33 percent increase over 1989. This did not include the cost of the National Guard's new antidrug law-enforcement activities.

• The Pentagon spent $130 million last year for aerostats, tethered blimps equipped with radar, on the southern border.

• Former Virginia governor Gerald Bailes authorized National Guard units to perform undercover surveillance on suspected drug dealers in rural areas. The Pentagon has approved spying by guard troops in other states.

• Secretary of Defense Dick Cheney has expressed interest in making military bases and ships available to house drug arrestees when jails and prisons are full.

• Intelligence hardware, such as secure telephone transmission lines and new computers with broad database capabilities, is being funded via the DoD budget. Every official from the FBI, the IRS, and the CIA to your local sheriff can tie into this system and share otherwise classified material, which may contain hearsay, political data, and anything else an informant, reliable or not, has to say about you. It all gets sifted, stored, and routed through the El Paso Intelligence Center, a major U.S. drug-data network. EPIC is hooked into lots of other DoD and civilian data banks and operates under the jurisdiction of the Department of Justice. One of EPIC's many sources is Operation Alliance, a center established in 1986 by then drug czar George Bush, which gathers information from border control, customs, and the Drug Enforcement Agency. Whom did Bush put in command of his Operation Alliance? The Pentagon's own Joint Chiefs of Staff.

By Matthew Reiss

The War
ON YOUR RIGHTS

You're driving around with enough marijuana for one joint in your glove compartment. Maybe your cousin Betty stashed it there, so you don't even know it exists. Oh well. Since the real war on drugs is being fought in crack houses and along borders, what's to lose?

These days, plenty — starting with your car, which is promptly seized when cops find the pot. Next you're sitting in jail, detained with no bail privilege. "What about innocent until proven guilty?" you protest. That idea is just one more civil-liberties casualty during wartime.

They never did this on "Adam 12." Throughout the Reagan-Bush era, the U.S. Supreme Court has upheld the rights of police officers to search your car and what's inside (like briefcases, trunks); to sift your trash; to fly over your house and scan your backyard; to secretly tape your phone or face-to-face conversations; to stop, detain, and question travelers who resemble "drug couriers" — all without a search warrant.

Since 1984, if customs officials find *any* amount of drugs on you or in your car, they can seize your property and keep it without a trial or conviction. And if you're facing criminal drug charges — not convicted, just facing them — officials can seize not only your car but your house, typewriter, or barn, and can freeze your bank accounts. That may prohibit you from hiring the attorney of your choice, if you can't pay the retainer fee. That's bad, since these days, losing means losing big. Possession of *any* quantity of marijuana can mean a ten-thousand-dollar fine. Possession of as little as a teaspoon of crack — same weight as two pennies — carries a mandatory jail sentence of five years, no parole.

Remember the Fourth Amendment? Police no longer need "reliable sources" to gain a search warrant; an anonymous tip is plenty. A nameless phone call has become the drug-war equivalent of "probable cause." Once that search warrant lets them through your door, *any* evidence they seize is assumed to be gotten in "good faith" — as long as the police claim later not to have violated the Constitution.

Whom can you trust? Not your own lawyer anymore. "The government is calling attorneys to testify against their own clients at the rate of one subpoena a day," says criminal attorney Kevin Zeese, counsel to the Washington, D.C.–based Drug Policy Foundation. "I have to warn my own clients that what they say to me can be used against them. So much for the attorney-client privilege."

These days, even your urine isn't yours. The Supreme Court has ruled that if you refuse to submit to a drug test, a private employer can deny you a job. Despite the well-documented inaccuracy of urine testing, several states require hospitals to report positive drug tests of pregnant women, who then can be prosecuted for drug possession and distribution.

You ain't seen nothin' yet. "The kind of moral force that freed Kuwait from abuse can free America's cities from crime," says Bush, stumping for HR 1400, his latest assault on the Constitution, now in the House. If HR 1400 passes, it will severely limit opportunities for federal death-penalty appeals, speed executions (and no one ever makes a mistake, right?), and expand capital punishment to include drug offenses that do not involve a murder. Bush says: "We need [to] ensure that evidence gathered by good cops acting in good faith is not barred by technicalities that let bad people go free." He means: HR 1400 will give police the right to enter your house *with no warrant whatsoever,* seize property, and use it as admissible evidence. Get ready for more life during wartime.

By Debi Howell

problem, and don't make a moral issue of it."

Drug policy in Holland, Engelsman explains, is a careful balance of harm reduction for society as well as drug users, a tension always between public order and public health. Rene Mol of the Junkybund believes that addicts deserve everything that Holland gives them: the methadone that allows them to stabilize their lives, and the health care, needles, and condoms that might save them. He wants even more—safe public places to do drugs and prescribed "maintenance" drugs other than methadone—but he, too, also acknowledges a balance owed society. "If there is a system that gives good care, then I think drug users owe 'social use,' meaning they don't litter, steal."

One rainy evening, I learned how the city of Utrecht has struck a *zakelijk* balance with the dangerous nexus of drugs, sex, and AIDS risk. Utrecht's street hookers, many of them addicts, are allowed to ply their trade, but only after shops close. On a road where drive-by

business is especially brisk, the government pays Carmen, a former hooker who prefers to give only her first name, to run a prostitute contact center, a trailer where the women can get out of the weather, shower, and meet with a doctor.

"Prostitutes are the real AIDS workers," believes Carmen, so she hands out "fun packs" of condoms to educate, and sells thousands more. The venereal-disease rate among her group, she claims, is lower than for the population at large. Prostitutes are drawn to the center by its services (which include physical therapy for work-related injuries) and by its social web. Carmen shows me one scrapbook of past Christmas parties, and another in which the women are invited to write feelings, thoughts, jokes: "You know what's worse than AIDS? If you're allergic to rubber." The women are drawn by the promise of protection, too. Police rush to the scene if the center reports that someone is threatened; otherwise they leave the hookers alone.

Recently, a new attraction was added.

A two-minute drive around the corner from the trailer is a parking lot with eight stalls partitioned for privacy, cleanly designed in a Dutch sort of way. At night, the stalls are filled with jouncing cars, creating a safe spot where, as Engelsman puts it, "prostitutes can do their business." In keeping with Dutch egalitarianism, there are two smaller stalls for bicyclists, and trash receptacles for all. As I peer into one, counting the used rubbers, the police roar up, taking me for a customer who's here too early. No sex allowed here for another forty-five minutes, city regulations.

A few hours later, I'm sitting in the trailer, watching a skinny young blond woman named Marian smear on makeup as she tells me a common prostitute story, about the time a john drove her "somewhere in the back of Utrecht, stabbed me with a screwdriver, and left me for dead." Why does she risk it? Drugs, and fear of withdrawal pains. "I'm not coming here because I want to get high; it's because I don't want to get sick."

Above her, on the television, a tuxedoed Dixieland band is playing with idiotic gusto and I'm struck by the banal, sad absurdity. For Marian and the others, this trailer is a refuge from some of the danger, disease, and degradation of the streets, and so it can be termed a harm-reduction success. Marian, though, knows that more harm will likely come her way unless she can summon the will to escape it. The state regulates her hell, and lessens it some, but she makes it. "I think I can get out of it," she says with irony, not conviction. "I'm going to go on a vacation to kick my habit. I'm going to kick it into the Mediterranean."

THE DAY I VISIT AMSTERDAM CHIEF SUPERintendent Zaal, he tells me about the FBI course he attended in the United States with American cops, and recalls the position a classmate voiced on how to stem cocaine from Colombia: "We oughta bomb the goddamn place."

Zaal ventures the difference between his police and ours: "My colleagues in the U.S. are more convinced that *they* can solve the drug problem. They are prideful about their job and want to show it. Here we are not prideful. It's our job, nothing more and nothing less. Authority, power—we need it in our society, but it's not our favorite thing." As far as Zaal is concerned, factors out of his hands—"employment, social programs, education"—are the real keys to limiting drug abuse. In the meantime, he spends most of his effort going after major shipments of coke and heroin. Some years he nabs more than others, but he's not a headline seeker ("If we publicize a big take, the public says we have good police, or else they get afraid") and the large hauls tell him little ("Is there more cocaine now or are we just better cops?"). Above all, Zaal believes in flexible enforcement. Addicts "are patients, and we can't help them by putting them in jail." When he recently busted a house supplying ninety junkies, "We didn't solve the problem; we just moved it."

BOB MARTINEZ:
A Czar Is Born

After Bill Bennett's bombast, Bob Martinez gives the impression he wants to be a kinder, gentler drug czar. Within hours of his Senate confirmation on March 21, Martinez even told a roomful of drug- and alcohol-abuse officials that he values education and treatment. Will he make good on the rhetoric? So far, all the evidence is to the contrary.

Between 1986 and 1990, when Martinez was governor of Florida, the state spent more than any other to incarcerate drug users and dealers, but ranked twenty-first in funding treatment programs and thirty-second in spending on drug prevention.

Only one in four Floridians who needed drug treatment was able to get it, according to state government figures. And the U.S. Office for Treatment Improvement found that by 1990, those Floridians who did get into treatment facilities had to wait more than two months for an opening.

While they waited, it was harder than ever for them to stay out of jail. When Martinez took office, the state already had a mandatory three-year prison term for anyone convicted of using, buying, or selling drugs within one thousand feet of a school. Martinez fought successfully to extend that penalty to similar drug activity near public parks and college campuses. He also pushed through a law establishing a mandatory one-year jail term for anyone using, buying, or selling drugs near housing projects.

The result: a nonstop parade of Floridians are being marched off to prison. A study prepared by Martinez's Criminal Justice Estimating Conference last year projected that prison admissions for drug offenses will zoom by nearly 60 percent between 1990 and 1995.

Many of those will be for first-time offenders: According to Martinez's own office, 27.5 percent of those arrested for first-time drug possession in 1989 went to jail. Two Florida State University professors who studied Martinez's drug strategy found that the vast majority of these arrestees had no prior criminal record. Senate aides say that the growth in Florida's prison population will be exacerbated by the fact that more and more addicts will be coming out of prison with a criminal record and thus have difficulty finding work, making it all the more probable they'll run afoul of the law again.

Martinez's crackdown may have made life miserable for a lot of petty drug users and dealers, but it didn't change business as usual for the kingpins. Between 1985 and 1990, the number of Floridians jailed for possessing drugs jumped 580 percent, and the number sent to prison for the "purchase/sale" of drugs, a catchall Florida statute that covers a range of low-level drug activity, rose by 700 percent. Meanwhile, the number of drug *traffickers* imprisoned didn't budge a bit: about a thousand in 1985 and about a thousand in 1990.

And when jails became full-to-overflowing with first-time drug offenders serving mandatory sentences, something had to give—so hardened criminals were let out on the street through a variety of sentence-reduction and early-release programs designed to ease the sudden prison crowding problem. During the Martinez years, the average Florida murder sentence decreased by 40 percent, the average robbery sentence went down by 42 percent, and the overall average sentence declined by 38 percent. When Martinez was voted out of office in 1990, Florida inmates were serving, on average, 32.5 percent of their sentences, the lowest percentage in the nation.

The bottom line makes clear where Martinez's priorities lay: funding for treatment in Florida increased from $35 million to $42 million, and received a special one-year, $18 million boost from a tax on rental cars, between 1988 and 1991. During that same period, state spending on prisons and jails skyrocketed from $514 million to $859 million, a $345 million increase. Martinez's office boasts that more prisons were built during his four years as governor than during the previous two decades.

In his Senate confirmation hearing, Martinez signaled no break with his past—nor with his predecessor. The restaurant owner-turned-politician refused to make even the mildest criticism of the budget he inherited from Bennett. The 1992 budget proposes $8.8 billion for drug interdiction, prison construction, and other "law and order" programs, and only $1.6 billion for treating drug abusers. That is a 10 percent rise over current treatment funding, but a huge chunk of the proposed increase—$99 million to expand community treatment programs—will not be awarded unless states can match the federal contribution level. It's a dubious proposition, given that a decade of federal domestic-spending cuts has left more than thirty states fighting deficits.

So what does Bob Martinez really mean when he talks of more drug education and treatment, and how will he fight for the resources needed? Your guess is as good as ours. So far he's given more spin than specifics, and Martinez refused to be interviewed for this article, even though *Mother Jones* provided him with a draft of the accompanying text and offered to submit a list of questions in advance.

By Richard Keil

While Zaal and his forces are serious about their jobs, Amsterdam's reputation as a place where you can get any kind of drug, at a good price and relatively pure, is well warranted. As criminologist Hans Korff gives me a tour of inner Amsterdam one afternoon, he points out the canal bridges where this or that drug is peddled, stopping from time to time to peel off the pavement burned foil dropped by dragon-chasers. We talk in a café, and along comes one of Korff's research subjects, just back from Spain on what was probably a drug-buying trip, his two athletic bags suspiciously plump.

Dutch officials acknowledge this reality, but it simply doesn't keep them awake at night, because they put the relative harm that illegal drugs cause in sharp perspective. "Tobacco kills eighteen thousand people a year in this country. That is like a big jumbo jet crashing every week!" says Engelsman, whose job is to minimize not only drug addiction but lung cancer and alcoholism, both of which kill vastly more Dutch than illegal drugs do, mirroring the United States. "Society does not perceive alcohol as a real problem. But it is very, very destructive to society. Still, we can live with it. It is integrated into everyday society. Society can absorb *lots* of problems."

Americans who dismiss Dutch society as too homogeneous to be an apt comparison to our own may be surprised to learn about Holland's over 5 percent, and growing, minority population, made up of Surinamese blacks, Indonesians, Turks, Moroccans, and other Third World groups. In some of Amsterdam's elementary schools, more than half the children are not white Dutch. Minorities are concentrated in big cities, are poorer, and suffer more drug addiction, says University of Chicago sociologist William Julius Wilson, who found in Holland "pockets of poverty that are beginning to resemble U.S. ghettos." The jobless immigrants, invited in when there was a labor shortage, are taking the brunt of a decade of deindustrialization, and a strain of scapegoating racism is beginning to surface in Dutch politics, Wilson says. The Netherlands remains a welfare state with a gap between rich and poor far narrower than in the United States (a Dutch yuppie can surrender 65 percent of income to taxes); but even through the generous and tightly woven Dutch safety net, people do slip.

Father Hans Visser catches some in St. Paul's Church in the heart of Rotterdam. Visser, burly, gray-haired, and open-faced, is not a policy man, but he may be Holland's ultimate harm-reduction activist. He invites street people into his church, gives them food, a bed, pingpong or cards, and, if they want, religion. Some of his flock are junkies, and Visser decided it was safer and saner that they do their drugs in his church rather than on the street. The night I visit, Visser and his Surinamese aide, Nel, proudly show me the clean, bright room set aside for the purpose. In one corner stands one of Rien Klaassen's syringe-exchange machines. The police told Visser that exchanging needles was okay, but allowing addicts to shoot up on his premises—that was going too far. "They said I'm 'giving opportunity to drug users.'" So Visser and Nel built a big lavatory with roomy, comfortable stalls, and put a bucket in the corner with a sign saying DROP USED NEEDLES IN HERE. "How am I supposed to know what goes on in the bathroom? I can't intrude on their privacy, can I?" he asks with a straight face.

I ask the Reverend Visser, is drug use a sin? "I think God created the drugs for us," he says. "But if I use drugs in a wrong manner, and take risks, that may be a sin." He thinks a bit. "Heroin and cocaine are hard drugs and you have to be careful. They can make you a slave. I can also imagine a prostitute girl who was abused by her father; she may use heroin as a medicine against stress." He thinks some more, and his voice remains

---

A new drug-war strategy, coming soon to a neighborhood near you: Send in the marines!

---

free of judgment. "They say cocaine causes explosions of gladness. It is better to look for other explosions of gladness."

Liverpool

THE NAGGING THING ABOUT HOLLAND IS that it works too smoothly. The culture is so reasonable that it bicycles everywhere, so cozy that it gives a cookie with every cup of coffee. One can squint at Amsterdam, a city slightly bigger than Boston, and see what one wishes Boston could become, but little of what Boston, Chicago, New York, or any hard-hit U.S. city is today. To find a better match, one needs to visit Liverpool, a once muscular port swamped in the last decade by unemployment. And by heroin: "You use some, the day goes," is how veteran drug worker Alan Matthews sums up the appeal.

Matthews remembers, back in 1986, asking a thriving dealer where his buyers got their needles. "He answered, 'Oh, I've got big boxes of them in the house, had 'em two years. Customer comes in, buys the heroin, rummages through the box, finds the cleanest-looking, shoots up, and throws it back in the box.' So we said, 'This is unbelievable.'"

Unbelievably dangerous, but opportune, too, since this dealer was just the sort of collaborator Matthews and local health workers had been seeking. "We said, 'Bring all those needles into our new syringe-exchange scheme, and we'll give you boxes of clean ones.' And he brought in a bag of them about two foot by three foot high." Four years later, the dealer, joined by many others, is still exchanging hundreds of used "rigs" a week at the Maryland Center, transporting them not in paper sacks but in plastic safety boxes. In essence, I point out, you are supplying a pusher with his business equipment. "Oh, sure," Matthews shrugs.

Indeed, one needle-exchange worker tells me anonymously that he regularly hauls boxes of new "sharps" straight to the doorstep of a certain major dealer. The worker argues that without clean needles, drug users will use infected ones; he believes that if the dealer is fingered, another, less accessible one would take his place; his purpose, free of "moral judgments," is to establish and keep contact with injectors, and so reduce the greatest harm that can befall them —AIDS. It jars me, after seeing so many smack dealers personifying predatory evil nightly on American TV cop shows, that Matthews speaks of his pioneering pusher appreciatively: "We'd give him clean ones and he'd go on his way. It was basically an extension of what we were supposed to do. He was probably seeing a few more people than we were seeing."

Seeing drug-using people, as many as possible, is key to harm-reduction philosophy, and is the goal of Liverpool's Maryland Center. As Allan Parry, another founder, puts it: "Drug services in this country have been aimed at people who want to stop. Now, because of AIDS, we have to reach drug users who want to carry on. And that means we have to change our services to suit their lifestyle." So the clinic sends savvy workers out to find drug users and not only swap needles and hand out condoms, but teach them less dangerous ways of injecting. The Maryland Center, which draws in most addicts first because it offers syringes, ends up treating abscesses and other conditions that plague junkies unwilling to expose themselves to the regular health-care system. A companion drug-dependency clinic prescribes methadone to hundreds of aboveground, "registered" addicts, and the Merseyside Drug Training and Information Center counsels users and their families.

Liverpool's drug workers say that their approach enables them to reach up to half of the local hard-drug users. Yes, drug use is high, they argue, but the real reason that Merseyside has many more officially recognized addicts than any other region—1,718 —is that it has made the effort to find them. A few hours north in Scotland's Edinburgh, where needle exchange has just started, the HIV rate among injectors is around 50 percent. In Liverpool, the rate is 1.6 percent. Derek O'Connell, superintendent of the

Liverpool police's drug squad tells me that he considers AIDS a far greater threat than drugs, so when his forces bust a user and find a needle, they confiscate it—and issue a receipt for a new one at the needle-exchange clinic, to which they refer the arrestee. Though it's tempting for police to snoop around the clinics for leads in drug cases, they keep away for fear of undermining the program's credibility. O'Connell isn't worried that he's being too soft: drug-related crime in his city, he tells me, has steadily dropped for three straight years.

ON A DRIZZLY AFTERNOON, ALAN MATthews drives me to the chemical-company town of Widnes, just outside of Liverpool, to introduce me to John Marks, a psychiatrist who has followed harm-reduction logic to startling ends. Marks has decided that the best way to see the most heroin addicts is to give them exactly what they want: substantial doses of pure heroin on a regular basis. From his innocuous office, wedged between shops on a sleepy street, he writes out prescriptions for dozens of clients, redeemable at a pharmacy and paid for by the government health-care system. To get on this list, you have to convince Marks you're a local, regular user—and haven't the slightest intention of quitting.

A tall, freckled man with a droll impassivity that borders on jadedness, Marks is accustomed to defending against the charge that he is a mad doctor. Actually it has been British policy since 1924 that the best way to treat addicts is to wean them off drugs, but if that can't be done, to prescribe whatever the doctor thinks they need. Marks is one of the few doctors with the stomach to prescribe hard stuff, though. He says he's helping his patients, and society. He points out that heroin addicts finance their habits by buying extra drugs, cutting them with "something nice and heavy, like brick dust," pushing that to new recruits, thus expanding the industry. Marks asserts that his prescriptions have undermined that criminal pyramid scheme: "Nobody's going to pay a fortune to gangsters to get rubbish and perhaps be threatened, when they can get pure, excellent stuff from me for free."

Given a way out of the black-market hustle, his clients might now be able to imagine a future beyond the next fix. If that leads them to decide that they do want to kick, Marks is there to guide them into one of many free rehab programs. Until then, Marks simply requires clients to participate in a weekly rap session, but he's not one to proselytize the straight life: "If you knew that every time you went to a bar you'd have to endure a homily on the evils of drinking, would you frequent the place?" In fact, Marks is one psychiatrist skeptical of his profession's power to sway addiction. His modest aim is

to keep his clients alive as long as possible, and he is adamant that heroin taken safely in a pure form causes far less direct physical damage to the body than alcohol. "Studies from around the world show there's really nothing you can do to make an addict stop if he doesn't want to. But after ten years, there is a 50 percent chance they will have decided to quit." I ask how he would treat addicts more prevalent in America: crack heads, speed freaks. "Just as I already do. To a small number of patients I prescribe cocaine and heroin in smokable form, and amphetamines, as well."

Hanging around after his rap group breaks up, elaborately tattooed Dave tells me what the drug chase, before the doctor's fixes, had been like. "I've walked in my house, unplugged my own color television while my family was watching it, thrown it in the car, and swapped it for a ten-pound bag of speed." Knowing laughter floats over from Bob, a twitchy, red-haired wisp, who says: "You've got more time to think now. You're not a robot, y'know what I mean? Y'don't have one thing on your mind. Y'can see more to life."

I ask Dave, Do you think the doctor wants you off drugs? "I don't know." He laughs. "If everybody was off drugs, they wouldn't have a job, would they?" Bob tells me that when he started the program eight months before, he was angry with Marks, distrustful, but after a battle of wills, the doctor upped his dose and now he is getting "enough."

The natural question arises: Who, really, is in control here, Bob or his doctor? Marks says he uses his own supply of drugs as a way to bind addicts to his universe, and keep them from doing themselves and society more damage. To the drug-dependent who are now Marks-dependent, "I'm a patronizing, shithead quack, who controls their lives," the doctor says, smiling. But he draws boundaries within the relationship, refusing to let himself or his staff become complicit in drug crimes. When a grandmotherly clinic nurse named (yes) Betty Ford discovered stolen, falsified prescriptions on a home visit to a client, she had the man arrested. The day I'm there, the man shows up to say he's served six months in jail and is out; with warmth he greets Ford as "Mom." This cooperation with police, and the fact that heroin street sales and drug-related crime have dropped in the Widnes area, has the powers that be on his side, says Marks.

Until recently, Marks ran his experiment on a bigger scale in Liverpool. Depending on whom you talk to, Marks preferred to return to his original practice in Widnes, or he was pushed out by Liverpool politicians who didn't like the idea of a doctor prescribing narcotics. Still, the Merseyside area, with its needle exchanges, treatment programs,

abundant methadone, cooperative police, and Marks's drug prescriptions, would be an oasis of harm reduction anywhere in the United States. Indeed, it is an anomaly even in England, allowed to exist as long as crime and HIV rates stay down.

Alan Matthews has no illusions. "Liverpool is an experiment in a glass jar," he says. "If it's unsuccessful, they'll say, outside, in London, 'Well, it's just Liverpool.'"

TO WASHINGTON, D.C.—BASED DR. ARnold Trebach, the Dutch and Liverpool harm-reduction proponents I've met are heroes, and he considers it his mission to build support for their "fragile" position against war-on-drugs logic. In fact, his privately funded Drug Policy Foundation gave Liverpool needle-exchange workers and Eddy Engelsman awards last fall. Trebach, sometimes called the "Shadow Drug Czar" because so many drug workers and officials take his courses in the Criminology Department of American University, has written a couple of drug-myth-debunking books, the latest titled *The Great Drug War* (1987).

Trebach, a silver-haired, vigorously optimistic man, tells me that the Europeans can guide us out of our morass: "The key lessons start with a basic attitude. I just think they're a lot cooler about the drug problem than we are. What the English and the Dutch taught me was that you can disapprove of drug use, but you don't have to hate users."

Trebach wants our own government-funded junkybunds to press addict interests, and send the signal that addicts are "basically decent people. That would take some of the venom out of the drug war." He would immediately establish needle-exchange health clinics, modeled on Liverpool's, in the most drug-infested areas (needle exchange is publicly funded in only five states now). It's too difficult for U.S. addicts to get methadone now, Trebach argues, and also less-potent drug substitutes: "The madness of the American drug policy is illustrated by the fact that an addict to a weak narcotic generally can only get a more powerful narcotic, methadone, if that person wants to be legal, and be maintained by a doctor." He'd allow doctors to prescribe codeine, for example.

For whatever reason—culture, market forces, or perhaps, as Trebach thinks, "irrational" fashion—crack and cocaine aren't nearly as popular in Europe, and haven't fueled the gangster violence that now grips many U.S. cities. Here, "cocaine is a threat, but it's not a greater threat than bullets," says Trebach, pointing to a recent study of 434 New York City homicides. One hundred thirty-one were "related to crack," he says. "But virtually all of them were in the crack *trade*. You read that, well, the reason we get all this crime is that people have been

driven crazy by crack and they go out and rape, loot, rob, and murder. They don't. There were at most three homicides in the entire group brought about by crack intoxication and disorientation."

When Trebach looks at our predicament and applies harm-reduction logic, he goes further than his European colleagues. "Down the line," he says, cocaine, heroin, and all drugs must be legalized and sold through pharmacies or in some other heavily regulated way. "Cocaine and crack is perhaps the most destructive contraband trade we've ever had in our history. So I want to cut the guts out of that trade at any price."

Trebach acknowledges that while murders would drop, addiction might well rise, so he proposes shifting freed-up police and prison money to massive treatment. The bill would go higher: In poverty-hit areas, he says, drugs are merely a symptom, not the cause of the "destruction of whole communities, where normal social controls are gone." With "a combination of government and private initiatives," he argues, "we've got to build up the social defense against all kinds of things. Against teen pregnancy, against crime and violence in general, spousal abuse—and in the process, we will have erected barriers to drug abuse."

Legalization is as easy as rewriting a law, but are Americans willing to invest in this social reconstruction that Trebach describes? That is the question weighing on anyone truly serious about reducing harm to this nation's drug- and crime-ravaged communities. Places like Los Angeles's South Central district, for instance, home to the Bloods, the Crips, their warred-over turf, and the black and Latino communities that bear the brunt of Daryl Gates's paramilitary police style.

Los Angeles

ON AN APRIL AFTERNOON, SIX WEEKS AFTER the Rodney King beating, I talk to Mark Ridley-Thomas, a Gates-bashing, savvy black progressive who honed his community-based politics through the Southern Christian Leadership Conference, and who the day before won the primary for the South Central district city-council seat handily enough to be favored in the coming runoff. In his storefront campaign headquarters, wearing a red hooded sweatshirt and horn-rimmed glasses, Ridley-Thomas gives his verdict on the idea of drug legalization: "Nonsensical."

In his tough corner of L.A., the abuse of legal alcohol "has a far more devastating impact on the quality of life than the abuse of crack cocaine in its current state," he reasons, so why invite more misery? And Ridley-Thomas is, after all, a politician. Campaigning among constituents, he says,

"I can recall only one example of someone calling for legalization." (His skepticism reminds me of Sam Foster, a black treatment-program founder I visited in Washington's crack-ridden Southeast section, who told me that he suspects the worst of would-be legalizers: "All they know is there is a lot of money being passed through and they're not getting their share of the taxes"—taxes he'd never expect to see spent in his neighborhood. "They can do that now. They don't have to legalize drugs to invest in here.")

What gains thirty-six-year-old Ridley-Thomas local support is his self-styled "progressive attack" on drugs. He helped snare a federal grant to train teams of community organizers, who have begun fanning throughout South Central, searching for homegrown solutions to addiction and the drug trade. The next night I attend a meeting of fifty such organizers and local leaders, who are working the bugs out of a self-administered survey of their own community. "Each time we hear about the severity of our drug problem, the numbers come from downtown," community organizer and substance-abuse counselor Michael Wynn tells me. "So every time we hear a solution, it's always more jails, cutting treatment, giving prevention funds to the LAPD and sheriff."

Ridley-Thomas advocates treatment on demand for addicts. When I point out that treatment success rates are quite low, he shrugs in agreement. Talking treatment is popular in his district, and at least it communicates "that these are persons who are not criminals; they are sick, so treat them." In short order, Ridley-Thomas arrives at the true harm-reduction prescription for the South Central district: "You need to have a job agenda." The flight of rubber, steel, and auto factories has sucked the blue-collar guts out of the area's economy, and when he lists off the growing local woes—". . . dropouts and teen pregnancies intolerably high, venereal disease up 400 percent . . ."—Ridley-Thomas trails off and tells me without a smile, "*You* run for city council."

A job agenda. A drug policy obviously sensible enough that Dr. Charles Schuster, director of the National Institute on Drug Abuse, has said, "The best predictor of [treatment] success is whether the addict has a job." A drug policy that also somehow seems utterly radical in a country clinging so tightly and blindly to its yawning class division, and asking the Daryl Gateses to enforce it. The Europeans saw it clearly enough. At the end of our discussions about the nuances of harm reduction, they would often say, with a tone of wonder, something like: "Of course, we do not have your ghettos. We can't imagine having so many poor, abandoned people in our cities."

Given that most of Los Angeles and the rest of this country doesn't seem serious about closing that gap any time soon, European-style harm reduction still offers a range of approaches that deserve honest study and experimentation here. Depending on how you want to apply it, harm-reduction logic brings its own unnerving images: dragon-chasers in phone booths; a physician feeding his patient's heroin addiction; even, as in Zurich, the shocking tableaux of addicts jabbing their arms openly, and legally, in a park. But against those stark pictures we can increasingly juxtapose worse ones from our own failed war: New York children wearing bulletproof vests to school, the raining batons cracking Rodney King's skull. And, for me the most lasting, a binder full of pictures collected by Los Angeles lawyers Robert Mann and Donald Cook.

Page after page holds photographs of persons holding out an arm or a leg, or turning to show a part of their torso, the better to let the camera capture their red, raw wound, skin and muscle torn out by the jaws of a police dog. Since 1984, say Mann and Cook, Los Angeles cops have allowed their dogs to gnaw over a thousand arrestees, many of them suspected of petty drug-related crimes, some of them quite innocent of any wrongdoing, the vast majority unarmed. About 98 percent of those bitten are minorities. The Los Angeles County Sheriff's Department has a similarly skewed record. "Many of these bites are totally unnecessary," Cook says, showing me a chewed-up fifteen-year-old Latino who was caught joyriding in a hot car. "They're bites that occur *after* the person has surrendered."

The LAPD's Lieutenant Pete Durham, officer in charge of the metropolitan division's canine platoon, says: "We don't use dogs in routine patrol work. The dogs are used to search and find people who we believe are felons or armed misdemeanors, and they've run away from the police. A suspect who conceals himself and refuses our commands to surrender, I expect him to get bit. We don't keep track of bites by race. I don't see a reason to."

The lawyers say bite rates are so high that Los Angeles police must be using the dogs not as a law-enforcement safety tool, but as instruments of terror. "Someone will be apprehended in a location that is known for a lot of drug usage, and they'll just let the dog rip him apart," says Mann, flipping through the binder. He speaks of the "primal fear" that a snarling German shepherd can arouse in a person, and reminds me that dogs were used to track slaves, to repress civil-rights activists, and (as Amsterdam's Chief Superintendent Leo Zaal also knows) by an occupying police force called the Gestapo.

LEGALLY BOMBED

G E O R G E   J O N A S

My great-uncle in Vienna used cocaine. The family thought him a fool, but that didn't prevent them from fobbing off nephews and nieces on him for holidays. In addition to being a cocaine user and a bit of a rake, great-uncle Erwin was a shrewd businessman and a kindly soul. He made his money, then gave a lot of it away to people who asked for it. He never abused his wife, ran no-one over with his Packard (mind you, he always kept a chauffeur), and when he eventually committed suicide it had nothing to do with his drug habit. He killed himself because Hitler marched into Austria in 1938.

I'm not telling this story to make a point about cocaine use, which I consider moronic. I'm telling the story a) because it happened, b) because it happened half a century ago (indicating that there's nothing very new about cocaine), and c) because my great-uncle, whatever his failings, was an ordinary middle-class citizen. He was neither a criminal nor a menace and he certainly required no social support. On the contrary, he supported other people. He had good reasons to fear Hitler (he was a Jew), but I dare say he'd have been surprised to hear a president of the United States declaring war on him.

President George Bush's celebrated declaration of war on drugs permits us to look at the question in military terms. In a war it's useful to have an answer to the following question: who is the enemy and what are we fighting for? In this case the answer seems to be that the enemy is us, or at least many of us. What we are fighting for is to be different from what we are.

As human beings, we're drug users. Few societies, ancient or modern, have been without mind-altering substances. Their earliest use, as the Toronto psychiatrist Dr. A.I. Malcolm pointed out in his 1971 book, *The Pursuit of Intoxication*, was probably ritual. Chewing or sniffing certain leaves and roots seemed to put us in touch with the great beyond.

Soon we started chewing or sniffing them for conviviality and fun. The recreational use of many drugs became intertwined with their medicinal, religious, or ceremonial use — as it still is, to a vestigial extent, in our society. We toast the queen with a glass of wine (we'd consider it unseemly to do so with a can of 7-Up), and some of us firmly believe that a hot toddy is an excellent cure for the common cold.

A "drug problem" exists because many of us take drugs. A few of us become dependent on drugs and permit them to rule and ruin our lives. Also, at times, the lives of our families or neighbours.

While taking drugs is universal, the drugs that are dearest to our minds and hearts — or stomachs, lungs, and veins — vary with the culture in which we live. Even within the same culture they vary among social classes or historical periods. Different drugs have different pharmacologies. This means that their use is likely to have different social consequences. Smoking a few cigarettes and knocking back a few glasses of port are both enjoyable (and unhealthy) to the user, but they have vastly different effects on his ability to make reasoned decisions, touch his own nose, or walk a straight line.

> "MANY RESPECTABLE THINKERS NOW BELIEVE THAT A SOCIETY HOOKED ON DRUGS SHOULD SIMPLY LEGALIZE THEM. WE WOULD HAVE A LOWER CRIME RATE IN EXCHANGE FOR WIDER DRUG ABUSE. MAYBE NORTH AMERICANS REALLY DO WANT TO PROTECT THEIR VCRs AT THE EXPENSE OF MILLIONS OF PARALYSED MINDS"

Even the same drug may differ in its influence on different individuals and, perhaps, on different groups. Societies develop different ways of coping or failing to cope with drugs. All

From *Saturday Night*, September 1990, pp. 34-39, 42-43. Copyright © 1990 by George Jonas.

these variables are liable to create confusion in the minds of U.S. presidents, to say nothing of legislators, talk-show hosts, drug users, and drug-enforcement officials. In recent years it has become difficult to comment on the subject without sorting out a few things first.

When we say "drugs" we're obviously not talking about aspirin. Aspirin reduces physical pain; the drugs we're talking about reduce the pain of everyday perception. They're mood-altering or psychoactive substances such as alcohol, marijuana, cocaine, nicotine, or caffeine—in other words, stimulants or depressants people take primarily for pleasure. Why is it a pleasure to take them?

The chief reasons are that 1) many of these drugs create a feeling of wellbeing or euphoria, and 2) they tend to reduce tension and existential anxiety in human beings.

All recreational drugs are addictive. Though addictiveness varies with the chemical properties of specific drugs, anything that's strong enough to give you a high (or even to take away your pain) is likely to be strong enough to hook you. Still, it's common knowledge that some individuals become dependent on the same drug in worse ways than others. Seventy-eight per cent of the population of Canada drinks alcohol, but only about ten per cent of the drinkers end up as alcoholics. Why?

"MOST DRUG USERS AREN'T CRIMINALS, LIBERALS SAY. PUNISHING THEM FOR MERE USE IS LIKE PUNISHING SOMEONE FOR BUYING A CAR. NO DOUBT IT CAN BE A HAZARD, BUT WE ONLY PENALIZE THE UNSAFE OPERATION OF A CAR, NOT ITS SALE AND POSSESSION"

Here the answers are more complex. One harsh view is that abusers are losers. Their ambitions outstrip their abilities, so they turn to the bottle. Alternatively — or maybe in addition — they suffer from an unusual degree of existential anxiety, which needs continual relief.

Some are craven in their yearning for acceptance and can be swayed by fashions of drug use and abuse that crop up in some cultures or subcultures from time to time. In certain settings — corporate, social, or artistic — a drug may become a symbol of reliability: gin and tonic for the country-club set, marijuana for peaceniks, vodka for members of the Politburo. If you fail to imbibe or shoot up with the boys, you're just not one of them.

A drug taken in such circumstances may become part of a person's cultural identity. Any attempt to dissuade him may be resented as a rejection of his entire system of values. Conversely, a stubborn individualist may resist social pressure to give up his habit as an attack on his sovereignty. Of course, people also become addicted simply because many drugs create a physical dependency. If a person stops taking them, he feels sick.

While culture and personality seem to define the addict, recent studies tend to confirm some age-old suspicions, namely that biological and genetic dispositions for dependency also vary, perhaps not just among individuals but among sexual, ethnic, and racial groups. One study suggests that females have about thirty per cent fewer enzymes for breaking down alcohol in their systems than males. In some Oriental groups a percentage of people "produce" their own Antabuse, as it were, by a different enzyme reaction. They soon feel sick when they drink, so they learn not to drink too much. Anyone can become an alcoholic, but your chances may be less if you're Chinese or Jewish and greater if you're an Irishman or a native American.

Not all of these facts are undisputed. However, even the facts we know beyond a doubt fail to lead us to a consensus. We still try to control the social use of drugs with strategies that fly in the face of what we know.

If all drugs that are currently illicit were to be legalized tomorrow, there's little doubt (none in my mind) that two things would happen.

The number of users would double, maybe even triple. That's the bad news. Since it's estimated that about 30-million people use illicit drugs in the U.S. (compared with about 140-million users of alcohol and about 50-million users of nicotine), legalizing substances like marijuana, heroin, and cocaine would probably result in 30- to 60-million additional users. This is just a guess, but it's a reasonable one: it's extrapolated from the 350-per-cent increase in the use of alcohol that reportedly followed Prohibition. (Canada's figures are similar when expressed in percentages. According to a 1987 Gallup Poll, seventy-eight per cent of adult Canadians use alcohol [in the U.S. it's eighty per cent], thirty-four per cent use tobacco [U.S. thirty per cent], and about fifteen per cent use all other drugs combined [U.S. sixteen per cent]—though the last number may include legal prescription drugs here, according to Manuella Adrian of the Addiction Research Foundation of Ontario.)

If about ten to fifteen per cent of users become abusers, this should result in an increase of 3- to 9-million abusers in the U.S. Translate this dry figure into an additional 3- to 9-million sick human beings who would suffer like dogs and die before their time. Even worse, translate it into 3- to 9-million unpredictable zombies who would not only require social support but might annoy and assault the rest of us, shunt our trains on the wrong track, or run us down in their cars.

Now for the good news. With legalization, the criminal activities associated with illegal drug traffic would drastically diminish. Fewer citizens would be mugged, burgled, or murdered in their beds by addicts seeking to support their habit. Dealers would no longer shoot it out on street corners to protect their turf. In fact, dealers and drug barons would be out of business. The public expense of fighting drug traffickers would be replaced by a public revenue from the controlled sale of drugs.

8. FIGHTING THE DRUG WAR

Taxpayers, instead of wasting money on other people's cocaine habit, would be *making* money on it. Professor Ethan A. Nadelmann, of Princeton University, estimates that the net upside, after combining the savings on law enforcement with the expected tax revenues, would amount to some $10-billion annually in the U.S.

Less tangibly but just as importantly, the private conduct of peaceable citizens would no longer be criminalized by the authorities. Those who commit crimes under the influence of drugs would still be penalized, but only for their actual breach of the queen's peace. People who endanger no-one with their temperate, civilized enjoyment of drugs would no longer be hounded and punished.

Measures that are distasteful to a liberal society but that any "war" on drugs inevitably entails—drug-testing employees, say, or body-searching high-school students—could be happily shelved. Wiretaps and other police-state methods, now used against activities no more inherently criminal than selling or buying a case of beer, could be reserved for genuine threats like terrorism or espionage. Our civil liberties would not be devalued by a false sense of emergency.

To me, the increase in drug abuse and the decrease in criminal activity are both predictable consequences of legalization – but many serious and thoughtful people disagree. Those who detest the idea of legalized drugs tend to dispute the good news, i.e. that, if drug prohibition ended, fewer citizens would be hurt by crimes engendered solely by our desire to keep certain drugs illegal. Those who'd like to see drugs legalized dispute the first consequence, i.e. that drugs, if legally available, would hurt many more people.

Princeton's Nadelmann, whose 1988 essay in the U.S. quarterly *Foreign Policy* did much to spark the current debate, points to the fact that cocaine, opium, and cannabis were more or less legal in North America throughout the late nineteenth and early twentieth centuries. The earliest U.S. federal legislation to restrict the sale of cocaine and the opiates was the 1914 Harrison Act. Canada's first narcotics-control act is a little older: it received royal assent in 1908. According to Nadelmann, before the passage of the Harrison Act, the U.S. "had a drug abuse problem of roughly similar magnitude to today's problem."

So, to paraphrase Nadelmann's argument – and the arguments of those who, like the Berkeley criminologist Rosann Greenspan, agree with him – the rate of addiction is more or less constant in a given society, no matter what that society's laws or enforcement policies may be. The main variables are cultural and personal. "There is good reason to assume," Nadelmann writes, "that even if all the illegal drugs were made legally available, the same cultural restraints that now keep most Americans from becoming drug abusers would persist and perhaps even strengthen. . . . In this respect, most Americans differ from monkeys, who have demonstrated in tests that they will starve themselves to death if provided with unlimited cocaine." In support of this view, Nadelmann cites the experience of the Netherlands, *inter alia,* where marijuana abuse stayed level or even diminished after the relaxation of legal controls.

The Princeton professor also takes the view that forbidden drugs are no more inherently harmful or addictive than legal drugs. In other words, cocaine, heroin, the hallucinogens, and marijuana are capable of being enjoyed as moderately and harmlessly as wine or Scotch are at present by most social drinkers. And more harmlessly than tobacco in terms of the user's health.

Nadelmann relies on a 1986 study by the National Institute on Drug Abuse to show that cocaine put only three per cent of the people who tried it at risk of becoming abusers. Even among those who used it *monthly,* only ten per cent were at risk—much the same as the figure for alcohol. As for heroin, it *is* very addictive, though no more so than nicotine. Since Nadelmann sees the dangers as roughly equivalent, he concludes: "The 'moral' condemnation of some substances and not others is revealed as little more than a prejudice in favor of some drugs and against others."

Utter rubbish, opponents say. For one thing, the population at risk is simply a percentage of the population exposed. If in a given culture 30-million people experiment with drugs that are illegal, significantly more can be expected to experiment with them when they're legal. And if users increase, so will abusers. In Dr. Malcolm's words, "The number of people injured by a drug will, in general, vary directly with the overall consumption of that drug."

The U.S. criminologist James Q. Wilson, appointed in 1972

> **"IF ALL ILLICIT DRUGS WERE LEGALIZED TOMORROW, THE NUMBER OF USERS WOULD DOUBLE, MAYBE TRIPLE. LEGALIZING SUBSTANCES LIKE MARIJUANA, HEROIN, AND COCAINE IN THE U.S. WOULD PROBABLY RESULT IN 30- TO 60-MILLION ADDITIONAL USERS"**

as chairman of the National Advisory Council on Drug Abuse Prevention, and today one of the most eloquent opponents of legalization, feels that Professor Nadelmann's argument is based on "a logical fallacy and a factual error." Writing in the February, 1990, issue of *Commentary* magazine, Wilson points out the fallacy: "The percentage of occasional cocaine users who become binge users *when the drug is illegal* (and thus expensive and hard to find) tells us nothing about the percentage who will become dependent when the drug is legal (and thus cheap and abundant)." As for Nadelmann's factual error, Wilson says that his conclusions are based on a 1985 study done

"before crack had become common. Thus the probability of becoming dependent on cocaine was derived from the responses of users who snorted the drug. The speed and potency of cocaine's action increases dramatically when it is smoked."

Dr. Malcolm has a similar view. He feels that there's "no justification for cocaine whatsoever. It can be taken in ever more dramatic fashions. It's vicious. It has no utility, has not been acculturated, and can still be controlled."

This is at the core of the disagreement: bad as legal drugs are, say prohibitionists, the drugs that are now illegal are worse. As Dr. Malcolm points out, crack, hash, LSD, ice (the new smokable form of speed), or heroin are almost invariably used to get stoned, bombed out of one's mind, while alcohol is being used by most people not to get roaring drunk but as a pleasant accompaniment to a meal or a genial get-together.

It's nonsense to talk about only 3,562 people dying in the U.S. in a given year (1985) from all illegal drugs combined, as opposed to nearly 500,000 dying as the direct or indirect result of alcohol and tobacco use. There's no evidence that this has been due to the benign properties of illicit drugs and all sorts of evidence that it has been due to their illegality. If they were legalized, cocaine, heroin, marijuana, or hallucinogens would also kill at least 500,000 people. "Suppose that in the 1920s we had made heroin and cocaine legal and alcohol illegal," says Wilson. "Can anyone doubt that Nadelmann would now be writing that it is folly to continue our ban on alcohol because cocaine and heroin are so much more harmful?"

As for legalization putting drug barons out of business, prohibitionists dismiss the idea. They say that racketeers will simply find another racket, and burglars another reason to burgle. Nor are prohibitionists impressed by the reduced costs of law enforcement or by potential profits from the controlled sale of legalized drugs. Any profits, they say, would be eaten up by the social services that new addicts would require. Anyway, as Wilson writes, if taxes on legalized drugs were high, addicts would still have to commit crimes to feed their habits; and if taxes weren't high, drugs wouldn't be very profitable to the treasury.

The calls for legalization aren't new, of course. Still, there *is* something new about them: some of the lines, and some of the players reading them.

Old lines are rarely being heard these days. Conspicuously absent are the arguments of those carefree years that culminated in the 1973 recommendations of Gerald LeDain's commission on the nonmedical use of drugs, which urged Canadians to decriminalize cannabis. In those heady days, many who favoured legalization tended to talk in terms of a benign drug culture. Their arguments were infused with the climate of the Greening of America, the Age of Aquarius, the gentle dawn of a new enlightenment.

For people caught up in that trend, the "high" heralded a coming age of creativity and love. Drugs, particularly the "soft" drugs marijuana and hashish but also the psychedelic LSD, served as leitmotivs in the triumphant symphony of a more youthful and humane culture. Even those who doubted the miraculous somatic society—LeDain himself, in all likelihood—felt obliged to give it the benefit of their doubts. People who spoke out against the hazards of drug use (whether or not they dared to employ such phrases as "the killer weed") were

regarded as antediluvian. A cautionary tone about drugs in media circles—a tone that's almost *de rigueur* in the daily press today—fifteen to twenty years ago would have exposed one to the risk of losing one's intellectual licence.

A cautionary tone wasn't safe even in scientific circles. In 1973, Barbara Amiel wrote an article in *Saturday Night* about Dr. Malcolm, who had been dismissed from the Addiction Research Foundation of Ontario. Malcolm, in Amiel's words, "ran afoul of what was emerging as the dominant cult of the ARF. He disagreed with the concept of 'wise personal choice.'" This concept suggested that scientists should make no value judgments, only describe what they knew about the properties of certain chemicals so that people could make wise personal choices about their use. That included, presumably, people with little demonstrated wisdom.

Malcolm disagreed. Nor did he go along with another concept of some ARF people, namely that it wasn't scientific to say that drug dependence in itself was "an adverse effect." As a clinician who had worked with and observed addicts, Malcolm felt that "he had a responsibility to say that 'drug dependence' was an 'adverse effect' in any form."

The ARF's dismissal didn't disrupt Malcolm's career. His books, notably *The Case Against the Drugged Mind* and *The Tyranny of the Group*, had some influence both in Canada and in the U.S. Today he's a prominent forensic psychiatrist. However, the dismissal, whether literal or figurative, of people like Malcolm twenty years ago may have disrupted our society in

"REFERRING TO NICOTINE IN THE SAME BREATH WITH COCAINE CROSSES A LINE THAT SEPARATES LEGITIMATE CONCERN FROM ECO-FASCISM. NICOTINE, WHATEVER ELSE IT MAY DO, CANNOT ALTER COGNITION. USERS DON'T GO OUT OF THEIR MINDS"

significant ways. Arguably, it was our intellectual elite's quest for enlightenment, combined with our establishment's abject surrender to what the poet Schiller called "the sword of fashion," that helped spread the deadly malaise of drugs into our inner cities and suburbs.

By now, of course, the climate of the debate has changed. No-one argues that a "turned-on" society will lead to higher plateaus of enlightenment. Those who call for legalization in 1990 have no such illusions. Most consider drugs stupid and

potentially harmful. They only think that avoidable government should be avoided; and that, while crack is the pits, invoking the genie of the state to save us from ourselves can be even more dangerous.

As a result many who favour legalization today, far from being associated with the youth culture or the "left," would be identified as being on the "right" of the sociopolitical spectrum. In the U.S. they include the economist Milton Friedman, the criminologist Ernest van den Haag, writers Lewis H. Lapham and William F. Buckley, Jr., and lately even former secretary of state George Shultz. In Britain it is the editorial position of *The Economist*.

This is, of course, by no means the position of everyone who might be described in the media as "right-wing." Prominent conservatives James Q. Wilson and George F. Will are among the most outspoken opponents of legalizing drugs, especially cocaine and heroin. At the same time, staunch civil-rights activists such as Canada's Alan Borovoy and Edward L. Greenspan help swell the ranks of those who support decriminalization. The drug debate is cutting across traditional left-right divisions today.

My problem with the entire debate is that I'm a somewhat callous and cussed person. Being callous, I have no interest in saving people from themselves; being cussed, I hate it when people try to save me from myself.

There's merit in the arguments of both sides. I find it incontestable that legalization will increase consumption; increased consumption will increase abuse; and a lot of zombies can't help but lower the resilience and moral tone of society. I also feel — though it may not be *comme il faut* to say so — that drugs are more harmful for today's mass than for yesterday's class society. The perfect individual liberty I cherish may be a luxury mass societies can't quite afford.

Some of the drugs now spreading through our egalitarian culture were once confined mainly to the leisure or bohemian classes in the West. The damage that could be done by a Sherlock Holmes smoking his opium pipe or my great-uncle Erwin sniffing his cocaine was mitigated by their income and maybe even by their sense of noblesse oblige. No such restraints operate on kids smoking crack in the slums of Washington or in Toronto's Jane-Finch corridor today.

At the same time I agree with Eddie Greenspan when he points out that popular support for a presidential drug war comes mainly from citizens tired of not finding their stereos when they get home. Those who fear drugs really fear crime — and crime could better be reduced by legalizing drugs. "People feel sorry about 'junkies' wasting their lives," says Greenspan, "but what really upsets them is that addicts or pushers waste citizens' lives when they mug or shoot them." If this is the trade-off, it may not be so immoral to suggest that it's better for more voluntary abusers to overdose than for more involuntary passers-by to be shot.

Unfortunately, much of the debate is hypocritical. Everybody wants to crap on the other guy's drug while defending his own. Sentimental ex-hippies, for instance, have been among the first to jump on the anti-nicotine bandwagon. "If we can't smoke our grass," they seem to say, "then by golly you aren't going to smoke your cigarettes."

Cigarettes, of course, are unhealthy to users. They're also a nuisance to some bystanders. But nicotine, whatever else it may do, cannot alter cognition. It doesn't impair motor skills. It doesn't make users go out of their minds.

Referring to nicotine in the same breath with cocaine is crossing a line: the line that separates legitimate social concern from eco-fascism. Curiously (or perhaps not) this line is crossed most often by those who call for lifting all bans on illicit drugs. *They* keep stressing the social harm of nicotine. It is James Q. Wilson, the ostensible regulator, who emphasizes the difference: "Tobacco shortens one's life, cocaine debases it. Nicotine alters one's habits, cocaine alters one's soul. . . . To say, as does Nadelmann, that distinguishing morally between tobacco and cocaine is 'little more than a transient prejudice' is close to saying that morality itself is but a prejudice."

Having quoted this, I suppose I should add one thing. I'm a smoker and I don't intend to quit.

Another problem with the debate is that it keeps harping on the nebulous concept of "social cost." Prohibitionists justify the state's interest in private habits by pointing to taxpayers' expenditures and by talking about hospital bills and early deaths. But book-keeping is a complex matter. The true economic effects of a social problem cannot be assessed only by adding up amounts spent on its cure and control.

If an abuser gets sick and dies before his time, it's a human tragedy — that's easy — but it's not necessarily a social cost. At least, not until the cost of geriatric services and pensions paid to people who linger beyond their productive years is deducted from it. No-one has calculated what it would "cost" if every year another 500,000 people lived to be ninety. Perhaps if someone did, fiscal responsibility would compel him to recommend that we force people to abstain from everything until retirement — and then oblige them to take up drinking, smoking, hang-gliding, and unsafe sex.

My final problem is that drug wars concentrate on Mr. Big, but Mr. Big is a small problem. The big problem is Mr. Small. Mr. Big supplies, but it's Mr. Small who demands drugs. A traffic for which there's a demand can't be eradicated by attacking its supply alone, not even with tanks and helicopters. As long as there's a demand, there will always be someone to supply it. If you make it tough for one guy, the next one will supply it at a higher price.

Can demand be attacked? Yes, by socioeconomic and cultural changes, which are slow, or with draconian measures, which are, well, draconian. Death for pushers, as in Malaysia, and seven-year minimums for first-time users might reduce a demand for drugs quite speedily. They could also turn a society into a rather nasty police state. So if we find the tempo of social change too glacial and have no stomach for getting tough, legalization may be a better option. Going after Mr. Big alone, at home or abroad, is a waste of money. Also of innocent lives, as in the case of Panama.

Perhaps luckily, Canada can't launch any invasions. Even beyond that, our problems may be different — or at least delayed. Ancient and universal as addiction is, a special concern today is that illicit drugs have invaded groups that are the least equipped to cope with their effects; it's within these groups that drug use is most likely to turn into drug abuse and can lead most readily to crime and disintegration. The young constitute one such group, obviously; some minority

subcultures form another. In black ghettos, for instance, crime is a necessity for users to support their habit. There are huge economic incentives — for slum dwellers, often the only incentives — to deal in illicit drugs.

Canada has proportionately the same number of young people as the U.S., but most of our minority subcultures are relatively much smaller. If drugs have been less of a problem here than in America, this is one of the reasons. But things are changing. We've had new concentrations of black and Asian immigrants since the 1960s. And, like the Americans, we're seeing pushers targeting the young of all groups and classes.

"Drug use is increasing and users are getting younger," says Herb Stephen, president of the Canadian Association of Chiefs of Police and police chief of Winnipeg. "Crack is just starting here. Toronto and Vancouver have had it longer, but there was none in Winnipeg until just before Christmas. There is now. Probably the next thing will be ice."

If this still sounds tame by U.S. standards, it has an interesting side effect. Legalization used to be a counsel of hope. By now it has become a counsel of despair, but, while drugs are a problem in Canada, we are not yet despairing. In Canada there are fewer calls for legalization. Most people feel that things can still be nipped in the bud.

Chief Stephen and his fellow police chiefs stress enforcement as usual, coupled with education and rehabilitation. They oppose legalization, sure, but: "We're not even bothering to develop a position paper on it," Chief Stephen comments. "There's no real debate in this country yet."

Drug Policy: Striking the Right Balance

Drug policy should strike the right balance between reducing the harm done by psychoactive drugs and reducing the harm that results from strict legal prohibitions and their enforcement. It is concluded, from a cost-benefit analysis based on pharmacologic, toxicologic, sociologic, and historical facts, that radical steps to repeal the prohibitions on presently illicit drugs would be likely, on balance, to make matters worse rather than better. Specific recommendations are offered for ameliorating the dangers to users and to society that are posed by each addictive drug.

Avram Goldstein and Harold Kalant

A. Goldstein is professor of pharmacology, emeritus, at Stanford University, Stanford, CA 94305 and former director of the Addiction Research Foundation at Palo Alto. H. Kalant is professor of pharmacology at the University of Toronto, Toronto, Canada M5S 1A8 and formerly associate research director of the Addiction Research Foundation of Ontario.

P SYCHOACTIVE DRUGS OBVIOUSLY PROVIDE PLEASURE OR relief to millions of users, but also can do enormous individual and social harm. The recurring debate about legalizing illicit drugs arises from different perceptions of the degree of harm caused by their prohibition, relative to the harm caused by the drugs themselves (*1*). At one extreme are libertarians who advocate removal of criminal sanctions from all drugs. At the other extreme are governments that apply the death penalty for even minor levels of trafficking. The status quo in most of the world consists of different degrees of regulation for different psychoactive drugs, only caffeine being available without restriction. Accordingly, the debate is not about the oversimplified dichotomy, legalization versus prohibition, but rather about the specifics of regulatory policies for each drug.

An ideal policy for each drug would strike the best balance among all the costs and benefits (*2*). The right to enjoy the pleasurable effects of drugs and freedom from state interference in citizens' private lives must be weighed against the benefits of governmental measures to protect the well-being of drug users, people around them, and society at large. The harm produced by excessive drug use must be weighed against the costs, both monetary and social, of enforcing whatever degree of regulation is imposed. Every cost-benefit analysis carries an implicit bias, which reflects the ethical, social, religious, and political views of those doing the analysis. Our bias is toward a humane and democratic society that provides maximum individual freedom, but the exercise of such freedom must be consistent with the rights of others and the harmonious functioning of the community. All laws have potentially harmful effects, but policy recommendations based only on considering harm caused by the law would be just as unbalanced as those based only on considering harm caused by the drugs themselves.

All drugs can be dangerous; even when they are pure and are used on prescription to treat disease, they often have adverse effects. Most governments are required, by public consensus and demand, to protect citizens against numerous avoidable hazards and not merely to warn them of possible dangers. The U.S. Pure Food and Drug Laws, enacted in 1906, set up the technical machinery, the Food and Drug Administration (FDA), for assessing drug hazards, forbidding over-the-counter sale of the more dangerous drugs, requiring manufacturers to report on unanticipated adverse reactions, and exercising legal control over drug distribution. This legislation grew out of the recognition that innocent people, without the technical expertise needed to assess the risks, were being hurt by drugs with unacceptably high risk-to-benefit ratios (*3*).

The use of drugs for nonmedical purposes carries risks not only for the user, but for society as well. A compassionate society ultimately pays the costs, not only of injury to nonusers, but even of self-inflicted injuries to users themselves. Society pays the costs of all acute and chronic toxicity through loss of productivity and by subsidizing medical care, providing welfare assistance to users' families and dealing with the special educational needs of children whose brains were damaged in utero (*4, 5*). Thus, drug abuse is rarely a victimless crime. We think that society has a right to take the costs into account in formulating its drug policies.

We shall argue here that (i) psychoactive drugs are, to varying degrees, dangerous to users and to society, (ii) drug consumption is strongly influenced by availability, (iii) availability can be modified, not only by outright prohibition, but in many ways short of prohibition, (iv) although supply reduction is a desirable goal, demand reduction is the real key to lasting amelioration of the drug problem, and (v) rational drug policy ought to be tailored to the dangers presented by each psychoactive drug to users and to society.

Psychoactive Drugs Are Dangerous

Legalizing and regulating drugs that are now illicit would, through quality control measures, eliminate harmful effects due to unknown and variable potencies, adulterants (such as particulates responsible for embolism after intravenous injection), toxic byproducts of illicit manufacture, and bacterial or viral contamination. All other adverse effects, however, are due to intrinsic properties of each drug (Table 1) and thus are independent of legal status. Harm to the user may occur immediately or only after chronic use and may be due to behavioral effects of the drug or to toxic actions on organ systems (6–8).

An example of a significant threat to both the user and society is the paranoid psychosis, sometimes accompanied by violence, that can result from repeated use of amphetamines or cocaine (9). In classic experiments (for example, 10) administration of amphetamine or cocaine to normal human volunteers on a regular dosage schedule produced paranoid psychotic behavior. Such studies showed that no previous psychopathology was required and that paranoid reactions to drugs of this class by addicts cannot be attributed to fear of law enforcement but are due to direct drug effects on the brain. Another example is the possibility of lasting brain damage from alcohol, volatile solvents, cocaine, phencyclidine (PCP), marijuana, and 3,4-methylenedioxy-methamphetamine (MDMA, which is also known as ecstasy) (11).

The addicting drugs have two special characteristics with policy implications. First, repeated long-term administration produces a state of physical dependence (12), so that neurochemical brain function is disturbed (withdrawal syndrome) if the drug is suddenly discontinued. This dependence occurs in animals as well as in humans. The pattern of dependence and the intensity of the withdrawal syndrome differ among drugs and among users. Dependence accounts, in part, for the compulsion to continue use of an addicting drug, and it complicates the treatment of addicts. However, there are effective medical procedures for ameliorating withdrawal distress during detoxification (6, 13, 14).

The second special characteristic, tolerance (12), which is typically associated with the development of physical dependence, is manifested by a tendency to escalate dosage because the same dose is no longer as effective as it was before. As with physical dependence, the degree of tolerance differs among drugs and among users. An extreme form of dosage escalation is seen with heroin and cocaine under both experimental and real-life conditions (15). Dosage escalation complicates schemes for providing addicts with their favorite drugs free or at low prices; when this was tried in the British clinics for heroin addicts, the black market was resorted to for supplemental supplies when the dosage ceiling (high though it was) had been reached (16).

Many people are able to use addictive drugs in moderation. There are coffee drinkers who take only a cup or two a day, occasional smokers who use only a few cigarettes a day, social drinkers who consume no more than a couple of drinks a day, and marijuana users

Table 1. Toxic effects and addiction risk of the major psychoactive drugs. Listed here are effects due to the drugs themselves. The effects are dose-related and subject to individual variation in sensitivity, so not all are expected to be seen in every user. Approximate rankings for relative risk of addiction are on a 5-point scale, where 1 is most severe.

Drug category	Acute toxicity	Chronic toxicity	Relative risk of addiction
Alcohol and related drugs (benzodiazepines, barbiturates)	Psychomotor impairment, impaired thinking and judgment, reckless or violent behavior. Lowering of body temperature, respiratory depression.	Hypertension, stroke, hepatitis, cirrhosis, gastritis, pancreatitis.* Organic brain damage, cognitive deficits. Fetal alcohol syndrome.* Withdrawal effects: shakes, seizures, delirium tremens.	3
Cocaine, amphetamines	Sympathetic overactivity: hypertension, cardiac arrhythmias, hyperthermia. Acute toxic psychosis: delusions, hallucinations, paranoia, violence. Anorexia.	Paresthesias. Stereotypy. Seizures, withdrawal depression. Chronic rhinitis, perforation of nasal septum.	1
Caffeine	Cardiac arrhythmias. Insomnia, restlessness, excitement. Muscle tension, jitteriness. Gastric discomfort.	Hypertension. Anxiety, depression. Withdrawal headaches.	5
Cannabis (marijuana, hashish)	Psychomotor impairment. Synergism with alcohol and sedatives.	Apathy and mental slowing, impaired memory and learning (brain damage?). Impaired immune response?†	4
Nicotine	Nausea, tremor, tachycardia. High doses: hypertension, bradycardia, diarrhea, muscle twitching, respiratory paralysis.	Coronary, cerebral and peripheral vascular disease, gangrene. Gastric acidity, peptic ulcer. Withdrawal irritability, impaired attention and concentration. Retarded fetal growth, spontaneous abortion.†	2
Opiates	Sedation, analgesia, emotional blunting, dream state. Nausea, vomiting, spasm of ureter and bile duct. Respiratory depression, coma, synergism with alcohol and sedatives. Impaired thermoregulation. Suppression of sex hormones.	Disorders of hypothalamic and pituitary hormone secretion. Constipation. Withdrawal cramps, diarrhea, vomiting, gooseflesh, lacrimation, and rhinorrhea.	2
Hallucinogens (LSD, PCP)	Sympathetic overactivity. Visual and auditory illusions, hallucinations, depersonalization. PCP only: muscle rigidity, hyperpyrexia, ataxia, agitation, violence, stereotypy, convulsions.	Flashbacks. Depression, prolonged psychotic episodes.	5

*These effects result only from alcohol, not benzodiazepines or barbiturates.   †Bronchitis, emphysema, precancerous changes, lung cancer, pulmonary hypertension, and cardiovascular damage by carbon monoxide are consequences of smoking tobacco or marijuana, not due to the respective psychoactive drugs. Inhalation of smoke by nonsmokers is also a significant hazard (5). With equivalent smoking, these chronic toxic effects occur sooner with marijuana than with tobacco.

who smoke a "joint" once in a while. Some people (at least for some period of time) can restrict their use of heroin to weekends, or of cocaine to an occasional party (17). Others, in contrast, are vulnerable to becoming compulsive heavy users, then stopping only with great difficulty if at all, and relapsing readily. There is no sharp separation between so-called social users and addicted users, but rather a continuum of increasing levels of use and increasing levels of risk (18).

The compulsive quality of drug addiction presents a special danger because for most drugs there is no way to predict who is at greatest risk (19). People who become addicted usually believe, at the outset, that they will be able to maintain control. After the compulsion takes control, addicts persist in using high doses, often by dangerous routes of administration. As the heavy users constitute the heart of the drug problem, there is an urgent need for more research to explain why they doggedly persist in a self-destructive activity despite full knowledge of its consequences.

A part of the explanation is in the pharmacology of the drugs themselves. Despite the acknowledged importance of peer group pressures, fads, personal and social stresses, price, and numerous other factors that affect drug use by humans, one cannot ignore the psychoactive drug actions, which are sought by the users. Experiments with rats, monkeys, and other species have shown that an animal fitted with an indwelling venous cannula, through which it can obtain an injection by pressing a lever, will establish a regular rhythm of lever-pressing if (and only if) the injection contains one of the known addicting drugs (20). One measure of the addictiveness of a drug is how hard the animal will work (that is, how many lever-presses it will make) for each injection. Another measure is the extent to which the animal engages in drug self-administration to the exclusion of normal activities such as eating, drinking, exploratory behavior, grooming, or sex. Yet another measure is the rapidity of relapse after a period of enforced abstinence. By these criteria cocaine is the most addictive drug known. Monkeys with unrestricted access in this laboratory procedure will actually kill themselves with cocaine by cardiovascular collapse, starvation, dehydration, or skin infections due to self-mutilation (21).

Cognitive factors have a role in moderating the behavior of humans who try psychoactive drugs but do not become addicted. Nevertheless, single-minded preoccupation of many cocaine, heroin, nicotine, and alcohol addicts with obtaining and using their respective drugs is disturbingly reminiscent of the animal experiments and reflects a major role of direct drug effects in driving addictive behavior. Research has begun to reveal where the addicting drugs act in the brain to produce the rewarding effects that give rise to self-administration behavior (22). We are far from understanding fully how and where each psychoactive drug acts on these reward pathways, but the emerging picture suggests the following. Reward systems have developed over the course of evolution to reinforce useful behaviors and extinguish harmful ones and to maintain and adaptively regulate a fine-tuned set of drives related to pleasure and pain, emotional and sexual satisfaction, hunger, thirst, and satiety. Addicting drugs act on these same systems by substituting for the natural neurotransmitters that act at different points in the circuitry, thus producing an artificial state of reward (euphoria), a powerful compulsion to sustain that state, and possibly irreversible (or long persistent) dysfunctions of the reward mechanisms.

Availability Affects Consumption

As would be expected, the ease of obtaining a drug affects its consumption. Contrary to the prevalent view that prohibition failed, there is substantial evidence that it reduced alcohol consumption substantially, albeit at the price of bootlegging, gangsterism, violence, and disrespect for the law among some segments of society. De facto prohibition of alcohol was introduced in the United States around 1916 (23) and continued as a wartime restriction, at a time when the temperance movement (and then the war effort) enjoyed a wide public support. A prompt fall occurred in the death rate from liver cirrhosis, which is a good index of the prevalence of alcoholism in the population and which correlates well with the mean per capita consumption of alcohol. The decrease in cirrhosis deaths from about 12 per 100,000 in 1916 to less than 7 in 1920 corresponds to a 50% fall in alcohol use (24, 25).

Conversely, lowering of the legal drinking age in a number of states and provinces led to an immediate increase in alcohol-related driving accidents contributed by those under 21 (26). Thus, although drinking by those under 21 had, no doubt, gone on previously, it increased sharply when the law permitted it. The potential effectiveness of legal restraints is also indicated by the ending of the Japanese methamphetamine epidemic through stringent enforcement by the police, backed by an anti-drug consensus among the general population (27).

An example of how availability affects drug use is provided by the experience of physicians, dentists, and nurses, who have easy (though illegal) personal access to psychoactive drugs that are forbidden to the general public. Despite the risk of heavy sanctions, such as loss of professional license and possible criminal prosecution, the per capita prevalence of addiction to opiates and other drugs was found to be much higher than in a matched control population (28, 29).

Injudicious prescribing practices may allow diversion of a medically approved drug into the illicit market. In New York State, the simple step of imposing a triplicate prescription system for benzodiazepines, to permit accurate record keeping by the authorities, produced a dramatic drop in consumption (especially of Valium) and a steep increase in the street price of these widely abused drugs (30).

From the standpoint of the consumer, a rise in price is tantamount to decreased availability and vice versa. Thus, price affects drug use. The mean per capita consumption of alcohol in Ontario between 1928 and 1974 varied inversely with the unit price of alcohol in constant dollars, in almost perfect mirror-image fashion, and a similar relationship has been shown for several European countries. The cirrhosis death rate also varied inversely with price, indicating that alcoholics as well as social drinkers are affected by price changes. This price elasticity of alcohol use by alcoholics has even been demonstrated experimentally (Babor et al., 31). Similarly, smoking has varied inversely with the level of taxation on cigarettes. The sudden large increase in the use of cocaine in North American cities following the introduction of crack, a crude form of cocaine free base, has been attributed to the lower price of crack than of cocaine salt preparations, as well as to the easier and more effective method of administration by smoking. These data suggest that anything making drugs less expensive, such as legal sale at lower prices, would result in substantial increases in use and in the harmful consequences of heavy use (31).

Finally, education, fashion, and social consensus contribute to the shaping of public attitudes and practices with respect to drugs. Alcohol in western societies, cannabis in the Moslem world, and hallucinogens in Native American religions illustrate how socially accepted psychoactive drugs are incorporated into the traditions, values, and practices of a society (32). Social incorporation of a drug

rests on a consensus with respect to the circumstances, amounts, and patterns of use that are considered acceptable. There is therefore an important difference between behaviors with respect to a long-acculturated drug and a newly introduced one, especially in a society undergoing rapid change (*33*). Illustrative are the current difficulties with cocaine in some American and Canadian cities in contrast to the stable or even declining use of longer established drugs in both countries (*34, 35*).

Policy Options: The Polar Extremes

The pharmacologic, toxicologic, social, and historical factors noted above provide a basis for predicting the consequences of various options for reducing drug availability. One option would be an even more Draconian enforcement of current drug prohibition laws. However, greater expenditure on measures of the kind now being used seems unlikely; political difficulties would arise if funds were diverted massively from other high-priority programs. Consequently, a more militant antidrug policy might well take the form of new measures that do not cost more but increase police powers by infringement of civil liberties, such as search without warrant, prolonged detention for interrogation without formal charges, or further dramatic increases in the severity of penalties.

Stern measures have, indeed, been credited with ending major drug problems. It is claimed that the serious opium problem in China was ended by stern measures, including the death penalty, after the Communists came to power (*36*). The Japanese methamphetamine epidemic was stamped out by less brutal but nonetheless forceful measures (*27*). However, the cost, if democratic governments were to adopt similar measures, would be a significant change in the character of the society. In addition, the explicit constitutional guarantees of the U.S. Bill of Rights and Canadian Charter of Rights would pose formidable obstacles to such a drastic course.

The antithesis of this approach, the legalization of psychoactive drugs, has been proposed as a possible way to reduce the high costs of enforcing existing prohibitions. Not only would the police, courts, and prisons no longer have to deal with the huge load of drug cases with which they are now burdened, but also the legal sale of drugs of known purity at moderate prices would, it is argued, drive the illicit traffic out of existence. In addition, licit businesses and governments would allegedly earn huge revenues that now find their way into drug traffickers' bank accounts (*37*).

On the cost side, however, would be the consequences of increased use and abuse of the drugs themselves. Even the proponents of legalization acknowledge some risk of increased drug use with its attendant problems, but they argue that the extent of such increase would be small. However, as an editorial in *The New York Times* remarked, " . . . there is little evidence to support so stupendous a contradiction of common sense" (*38*); indeed, past experience suggests that the increase in use would be very large.

This common-sense expectation is generally confirmed by historical evidence. Alcohol and tobacco, which are now so freely available, are also the most widely abused drugs, but—as noted earlier—alcohol consumption was much lower when the drug was less readily available. Social custom made cigarettes effectively unavailable to women until after World War I; then consumption increased steadily as it became more acceptable for women to smoke, and the lung cancer rate for females eventually matched that for males. Opiates and cocaine were legal and freely available before passage of the Harrison Act in 1914 (*39*). Despite the absence of sound nationwide surveys, there is evidence to suggest that this availability

had given rise to widespread and serious misuse. According to an epidemiologic study conducted in 1913 (*40*), the percentage of adults addicted to these drugs appears to have been not very different from the percentage addicted to alcohol in present-day North America.

The history of alcohol provides some basis for predicting what might be expected from the removal of all drug prohibitions (*41*). The key question is whether legalization of opiates and cocaine would result in levels of addiction comparable to those seen currently among the users of alcohol and tobacco. Opiates and cocaine are certainly not less addictive than alcohol or nicotine by any criterion. And although the intravenous route might never become widely popular, smoking (especially of crack) would be the route of choice for the millions. There is no reason to doubt that the increased costs to society would rival those now attributable to alcohol. In that case the economic savings that might be achieved, even if it were possible to eliminate all the costs of drug law enforcement, might well be offset by the additional costs resulting from the consequences of increased drug use.

If the government were to attempt to prevent large increases in consumption by raising the prices for drugs sold through licit outlets, as suggested by some proponents of legalization, prices of illicit drugs could then be competitive, and drug traffickers could continue in business. Government would be in the unhappy position of having to choose between raising prices to discourage excessive use, thus allowing the illicit traffic to continue, and lowering prices enough to drive out the illicit trade, thus increasing consumption (*42*).

It has been argued that legalizing and taxing drugs would provide financial resources for treatment of those who become addicted, but in Canada in 1984 the total social costs of alcohol were double the revenues generated from alcohol at all levels of government. In the United States in 1983 this ratio exceeded 10 to 1 (*43*).

A further inevitable consequence of legalization would be the impact on public attitudes toward psychoactive drugs. The recent decline in drug use among high school students in the United States and Canada (*34*) probably reflects a gradual acceptance of medical evidence that has been part of the justification for the continued illegal status of some drugs. Removal of the legal restrictions would risk conveying the message that drug use is not really as harmful as the students had come to believe and thus would weaken an important influence tending to keep consumption levels low.

The right balance, we believe, lies somewhere between these policy extremes. The specific recommendations offered in the next section embody a variety of intermediate options based on two goals: (i) to reduce the recruitment of new addicts by making it more difficult and more expensive to obtain psychoactive drugs and by strengthening an anti-drug consensus through education; and (ii) to ameliorate the circumstances of those already addicted by regarding them as victims of a life-threatening disease (as indeed they are) requiring compassionate treatment.

Current Extent of the Problem

The "War on Drugs" may be a useful metaphor, in the sense that war mobilizes social forces, sets priorities, marshals extraordinary resources, and embodies shared societal goals. But, as with so many medical and social dysfunctions, total victory is an illusory goal. Psychoactive drugs have always been with us and probably always will be. The practical aim of drug policy should be to minimize the extent of use, and thus to minimize the harm. How best to do this is

often uncertain, so budgets established in drug legislation should routinely mandate sufficient funds for evaluation. And inasmuch as behavior change comes slowly, it is important, as the elements of an improved drug policy are put in place, to be patient and give them time to work; this may well prove the most difficult of our recommendations to implement.

The first step toward a more rational and more effective drug policy is for the media, the public, and governments to see the drug problem in correct perspective. The current degree of concern about illicit drug use, bordering on hysteria, is at variance with the actual data on the magnitude of the problem. As to how this distorted perception came about, one is reminded of Lincoln Steffens's description of how newspapers, in his day, created "crime waves" (44).

What is the magnitude of the problem? Regular sources of national U.S. data are the National Household Survey and the High School Seniors Survey (34), DAWN [the Drug Abuse Warning Network for emergency room drug mentions (45)], and surveys of military personnel (46). These are supplemented by ad hoc (47) and local epidemiologic studies. In Ontario, surveys of students in grades 7 through 13 and of the adult general population have been carried out biennially since 1972 (43). The most recent estimates [Table 2 (48)] show that our most serious problem drugs by far are alcohol and nicotine (tobacco), whether assessed by damage to users, harm to society, or numbers of addicts (49).

The data in Table 2 (48–50), which indicate use in the past month

Table 2. The magnitude of the drug problem. Data are numbers of users, in millions (48). The population base sampled for this survey consisted of 198 million people aged 12 and over, living in households. Tobacco use includes smokeless tobacco, cocaine use includes cocaine free base (crack). U, unknown.

Drug	Frequency of drug use	
	In the past month	Once or more weekly
Caffeine	178	178*
Alcohol	106	47†
Tobacco (nicotine)	57	57*†
smokeless‡	7.1	7.1*
Marijuana	12	6.0
Nonmedical use of any psychotherapeutic drug	3.4	U
Cocaine	2.9	0.9–2.2§
crack‡	0.5	0.3‖
Inhalants	1.2	U
Hallucinogens	0.8	U
Heroin	1.9¶	0.6‖

*These are our estimates, based on the fact that virtually all users of these two drugs, if they use monthly, also use at least weekly (and usually daily). See text for daily use of other drugs. †Including 12 to 17 million functionally impaired alcoholics who use daily (the precise number depends on one's definition); virtually all tobacco users smoke or chew more than once daily. ‡These values are included in the immediately preceding amounts. §The lower number, from the Household Survey (48) is acknowledged to be an underestimate, as it excludes those living outside households. The higher number (50), could be an overestimate, biased by the fact that it is based on urine tests of arrestees (including those arrested for cocaine use), not on direct or indirect evidence of use once or more weekly. ‖This estimate is for daily use. ¶This estimate is for people who have ever used heroin, not just in the last month.

or week, obviously overestimate the size of the hard core of addicts who use drugs several times daily. On the other hand, all data sources tend to underestimate drug use in populations of low socioeconomic status (for example, homeless and transients). However, it is a fact (though not sensationalized by the media) that drug use, overall, has been declining—in all sections of the population, all

parts of North America, and for all psychoactive drugs whether licit or illicit (34). The exception to this encouraging trend has been the recent increase in the number of people who use crack daily. This number is still relatively small, but it is of concern because of the peculiarly seductive quality of this form of cocaine (51) and because of the concentration of sales and associated violence in the inner cities (52).

Recommendations

Concerning supply reduction and the appropriate degrees of regulation. Ideally, one would wish to match the degree of regulation and the effort expended in enforcement to the real dangers posed by each drug to the user and to society. This would respond effectively to the criticism that our present laws are hypocritical, in that dangerous addicting drugs like alcohol and nicotine are freely available and even advertised, whereas marijuana, which is less dangerous than cocaine or heroin (but by no means harmless), is under stringent legal controls (53, 54).

One way to use technical expertise instead of politics to formulate more rational policies would be to apply the model of the FDA, whose mission, with respect to therapeutic agents, is to match the degree of regulation to the actual danger each presents. Congress could delegate regulation of the nonmedical use of psychoactive drugs to the existing Alcohol, Drug Abuse, and Mental Health Administration (ADAMHA) with its three component institutes, the National Institute on Drug Abuse (NIDA), the National Institute on Alcohol Abuse and Alcoholism (NIAAA), and the National Institute on Mental Health (NIMH), much as it has delegated the regulation of therapeutic agents to the FDA. Under such a system, law enforcement responsibilities would remain with the Department of Justice. If removing the drug problem from politics is not yet feasible, the legislature should at least be guided, on a routine ongoing basis, by the best factual information from nongovernmental experts on psychoactive self-administered drugs, representing such fields as pharmacology, toxicology, medicine, psychology, psychiatry, criminology, law enforcement, and education.

Whatever degree of regulation is deemed, on balance, to be desirable for each drug, enforcement is essential for credibility and as a concrete expression of social disapproval. Enforcement has the desirable consequence of raising the black-market price of illicit drugs and making such drugs more difficult to obtain. The present situation, in which drug bazaars operate in full view of the police (55), seems intolerable in a society that claims to be ruled by law. It is unclear in such cases whether the police are corrupt or only demoralized, but it is noteworthy that corruption cuts through all strata of our governmental and private sectors, as numerous recent scandals have revealed. Thus, dealing effectively with the drug problem has broad implications for the rule of law in a democratic society.

Enforcement should be directed primarily at the higher levels of the distribution chain, but grandiose attempts to achieve a total interdiction of drug entry from abroad are a relatively poor investment. Advances in pharmaceutical chemistry are such that highly potent psychoactive drugs of every kind can be synthesized readily in clandestine laboratories, so the illicit market would adjust quickly even to a complete sealing of our borders, were that possible. A modest level of highly visible interdiction activities should probably be continued, if only for their symbolic value. But a massive shift of available funds is called for, from supply reduction to demand reduction (prevention education, treatment, and research). The

federal drug war budget would be more cost-effective if the presently proposed ratio of of supply reduction to demand reduction—71% to 29%—were reversed (56).

Enforcement will be most effective if coupled to community action, originating locally but supported by adequate governmental funding and other forms of assistance. Especially in some inner-city, ethnic minority communities, enforcement is presently weakened by a widespread perception that the police apparatus behaves as a hostile, alien, and often racist force invading the community (57).

We advise retaining, for the present—and enforcing—the legal prohibitions on the importation, manufacture, distribution, and sale of opiates, amphetamines, cocaine, marijuana, and dangerous hallucinogens like PCP. At the same time we suggest reducing the penalties for possession of small amounts of these drugs for personal use. Other differential enforcement options should be explored; without rewriting the laws, some laws could be enforced more strictly than others, according to the dangers of the particular drugs and the individual circumstances, as has been done for marijuana in some jurisdictions (58). Unfortunately, recent U.S. legislation (59) compels judges to inflict minimum 5-year sentences even for small-time users who sell or share small amounts of drugs. We believe that criminalizing drug use per se is not productive, and we recommend that humane and constructive sentencing options be restored in drug cases.

It is sometimes argued that as marijuana seems to be the least harmful of the psychoactive drugs (excepting only caffeine), it could be legalized safely. However, the scientific evidence is still insufficient as to the potential magnitude of long-term harm (54), whereas the acute disturbance of psychomotor behavior is clearly dangerous under certain circumstances. It is not possible to predict with confidence what the result would be of vast expansion of the user pool, especially of heavy users. If prevention education achieves its goals, and public attitudes and other nonlegal controls over cannabis use become strong enough, it might eventually be possible to loosen the regulatory controls without risk of a major increase in use and the likely attendant problems. The experience of states like Oregon and Alaska, which have experimented with relaxing total prohibition, should be studied carefully with a view to understanding the effects on consumption. The much-vaunted Dutch system deserves study; however, it was not a sweeping drug legalization, but rather a specific reduction of penalties for use of cannabis, while penalties on trafficking in other drugs were made more severe (58, 60).

We advise increased taxation on tobacco and alcohol—as is already being done in some jurisdictions—inasmuch as this is known to be an effective means of discouraging consumption (31). However, the resulting price increases must not be so great as to make an illicit market profitable. Uniformity of taxation across the country will be essential to avoid providing an incentive for interstate smuggling (42). One problem is preventing tax revenues from becoming incentives for government agencies to promote increased consumption. In the government monopoly retail sales model (another means of discouraging consumption), sales revenues themselves have this potential. Therefore, tax revenues (or sales profits) should go only to drug-related research, education, and treatment, not into the general treasury.

The degree of regulation on tobacco should be increased. Social pressures are reducing consumption, especially in the adult middle-class population, but sales to minors are still a problem. Federal and state laws abolishing cigarette vending machines would have a significant beneficial impact; with such machines accessible, laws forbidding sale to minors are completely ineffective, as shown in a recent study in the Washington, D.C., metropolitan area (61).

Regulation on alcohol should also be increased. As with tobacco, there are many options short of total prohibition that would decrease consumption without stimulating a black market and associated criminal activities (62).

In principle, routine or random drug testing is justifiable for people in sensitive jobs, whose use of psychoactive drugs (whether licit or illicit) could endanger public safety. As the role of alcohol and other drugs in highway accidents is well documented (8), we believe that on-the-highway testing of drivers for alcohol on a nondiscriminatory basis at road blocks is justified as a protection for the innocent, and the U.S. Supreme Court has ruled that such tests are not unreasonable searches as specified in the U.S. Constitution (63). Moreover, lowering of the permissible legal limit (currently 0.10% in many jurisdictions) to 0.08% or 0.06% could have significant beneficial effects on highway safety (8, 64). However, although urine testing for other drugs has improved greatly in accuracy (65), a significant problem in inferring psychomotor impairment from test results is that whereas breath or blood tests give a real-time result, urine tests provide only a record of past use and therefore cannot determine whether a person is under the influence of a drug at the time the sample is obtained. Further research is needed for the development of noninvasive analytical methods for estimating concentrations of psychoactive drugs in blood.

The North American demand for drugs is the driving force that creates major socioeconomic and political stress for the producer countries, especially in Latin America. The United States and Canada should assist these countries in reducing their economic dependence on drug exports. We should recognize and acknowledge that U.S. export of tobacco (especially to developing countries) undercuts any principled opposition to coca or opium export by other countries. A trade deficit does not justify our continuing in the role of major world supplier of a highly toxic and addictive substance.

Concerning demand reduction through prevention education, treatment, and research. All kinds of prevention efforts should be expanded as part of a broad strategy of demand reduction. Perhaps the most effective single factor in achieving this goal would be a social consensus on the appropriate circumstances and amounts of drug use. To change attitudes, beliefs, and values at all levels of a society in order to achieve the desired consensus requires carefully planned, internally consistent, and sustained long-term programs of education aimed at different ages, cultures, and socioeconomic groups (66).

The time is long overdue to recognize officially, publicize, and incorporate into common speech and legislation the fact that tobacco (nicotine) and alcohol are potentially hazardous addicting drugs. We need to expunge from the language the phrases "alcohol and drugs" and "tobacco and drugs." This is not mere semantic nit-picking; language influences the way we think.

The ban on TV advertising of cigarettes should be strengthened to prevent its circumvention by the prominent, supposedly incidental, display of cigarette product names during TV coverage of sports and other public events. Current U.S. and Canadian policies forbidding advertisements for distilled spirits on television were a useful first step, but there is not yet a well-founded policy on alcohol advertising in either country. A flood of beer advertisements has appeared, appealing primarily to youth, and linking beer to sports and sexual interests; and international comparisons show that alcoholism can occur just as readily in predominantly beer- or wine-drinking as in spirit-drinking countries (31). To date, scientific studies have failed either to prove or to exclude a short-term effect of

alcohol advertising on consumption (64). This is not surprising, given the ubiquity of drinking in films, TV, and print media, which probably have a greater impact on attitudes and behavioral norms than commercial advertising does. Nevertheless, we regard a progressive restriction of the right to advertise addictive drugs as an important and desirable first step in a long-term process of altering the present public perception of these substances as ordinary consumer products.

Ideally, classroom programs should not be drug-specific but should deal more broadly with the hazards of using psychoactive drugs. Integrated prevention efforts involving both the schools and the community are desirable. Finally, effective education is honest education; the educational message has to be the real dangers of each drug to the user and to society. It is useless to merely warn of the dangers of being caught, and health personnel (not law officers) should carry the drug message into the classrooms.

For specific populations with exceptionally severe drug problems, such as American Indian communities, or low-income African-American or Hispanic groups in major urban centers, effective prevention may be impossible without creating opportunities for economic advancement within a licit social framework and for enhanced self-respect through reinforcement of traditional social and cultural values.

Treatment should be available to all who desire it; long waiting lists are counterproductive. Having enough clinics to meet the demand will require very large investments, but these could be cost-effective in the long run. Adequate funding should be furnished for treatment research to test innovative therapeutic approaches, provided the research design will permit rigorous evaluation. Programs should be developed for making humane contact with addicts as a first step to treatment; needle exchanges may serve a useful purpose in this regard (67).

We should consider developing and testing treatment programs that incorporate an initial phase in which the addict's drug of choice is made available. This approach might serve as a lure to bring some alienated users of heroin or cocaine into contact with health personnel, but it must be in the context of a genuine treatment and rehabilitation program. Many formidable practical difficulties would have to be overcome, not the least of which is to work out reliable methods of preventing the clinic itself from becoming a recruiting ground for new addicts (68).

A different medical approach is illustrated by methadone maintenance, in which opiate addicts are stabilized on a long-lasting, orally administered opiate (69). Many methadone programs—provided they employ adequate dosages—have achieved the successful social rehabilitation of a considerable fraction of addicts (about one-half to two-thirds), some of them continuing to take methadone, some eventually becoming opiate-free. Reduction of street crime by addicts enrolled in methadone programs is well documented. Experts agree that methadone maintenance should not be the sole treatment for heroin addicts, but this treatment modality is well enough established to warrant expansion to meet the need (70–72).

Some heroin addicts unquestionably benefit from drug-free residential environments (halfway houses). Extensive follow-up data show that some treatment is better than no treatment, but that a variety of therapeutic modalities is probably required to meet the needs of all heroin addicts (71). Although treatment programs of all types have achieved beneficial and humane results, there have also been practical difficulties, not the least of which is the relatively small proportion of addicts (especially to drugs other than opiates) who are treated during any given year (73). In addition, although some lessons can undoubtedly be learned from treatment experiences with heroin addicts, there is no agreement yet on appropriate treatment strategies for cocaine addicts (74).

The funding should be increased for basic and applied research on all aspects of the drug problem. We predict that neurochemical and neurobiologic research will yield new understandings about the mechanisms of the drug addictions. In the future, as in the past, such knowledge can be counted on to produce novel diagnostic, predictive, and therapeutic interventions. Specifically, learning more about the neurobiology and pharmacology of reward will lay a sounder basis for therapy. Testing for genetic vulnerability might permit better targeting of prevention efforts to those who are most vulnerable. Novel pharmacologic treatments that need to be developed include a long-acting agonist to supplant cocaine (analogous to methadone in opiate addiction), long-acting antagonists or immunization procedures, and drugs to facilitate detoxification and suppress craving. Finally, we need the patience to fund and carry out very long-term studies on the effectiveness of prevention education strategies; to do these studies well will be very expensive (75).

Concluding Remarks

An atmosphere of desperation, which seems to prevail today in the War on Drugs, is not conducive to sound policy decisions or effective legislation. Until calm and reason can prevail, it may be better to do nothing than to take actions rashly that will make matters worse. If we strike the right balance in drug policies, as we have suggested here, it should be possible to bring about a reduction in the demand for psychoactive drugs. A reduced demand for drugs offers the only real hope of eventually achieving, not a drug-free society, but one with substantially less drug abuse.

REFERENCES AND NOTES

1. E. A. Nadelmann, *Foreign Policy* 70, 83 (1988); *Science* 245, 939 (1989); *ibid.* 246, 1104 (1989); S. Meisler, "Drug legalization: Interest rises in prestigious circles," *Los Angeles Times*, 20 November 1989, p. 1; M. Friedman, "An open letter to Bill Bennett," *The Wall Street Journal*, 7 September 1989, p. A16; R. W. Sweet, speech at Commonwealth Club, New York, reported in *New York Times*, 13 December 1989, p. 1; K. L. Schmoke, *Omni* 11, (no. 7), 8 (1989); W. F. Buckley, *Natl. Rev.* 41, 70 (29 September 1989).
2. H. Kalant and O. J. Kalant, *Drugs, Society and Personal Choice* (Addiction Research Foundation, Toronto, 1971).
3. Examples of long-established legislation that protects as well as informs are laws requiring motorcycle helmets and automobile safety belts, pasteurization of milk, fluoridation of municipal drinking water supplies, and immunizations of school children. The history of drug regulation in the United States is recounted by P. Temin [*Taking Your Medicine* (Harvard Univ. Press, Cambridge, MA, 1980)].
4. Fetal damage associated with use of an illicit drug (L. P. Finnegan, *Ann. N.Y. Acad. Sci.* 362, 136 (1981); D. E. Hutchings, ed., *ibid.* 562 (1989) is complicated by adulterants, malnutrition, and concurrent infections, making it difficult to implicate the drug itself with certainty. Even in the absence of these confounding factors, however, low birth weight and prematurity are associated with maternal smoking (5) and alcohol use [C. L. Randall and E. P. Noble, in *Advances in Substance Abuse: Behavioral and Biological Research*, N. K. Mello, Ed. (JAI, Greenwich, CT, 1980), vol. 1, pp. 327–367]. The fetal alcohol syndrome, characterized by abnormal facial features and mental retardation, is now recognized as a direct teratogenic effect of alcohol consumption during pregnancy [S. K. Clarren and D. W. Smith, *N. Engl. J. Med.* 298, 1063 (1978); N. A. Brown *et al.*, *Science* 206, 573 (1979); R. E. Little and A. P. Streissguth, *Can. Med. Assoc. J.* 125, 159 (1981); K. R. Warren and R. J. Bast, *Public Health Rep.* 103, 638 (1988)].
5. Office of Smoking and Health, Public Health Service, *The Health Consequences of Smoking: Nicotine Addiction: A Report of the Surgeon General* [Department of Health and Human Services (DHHS) publ. CDC 88-8406, 1988].
6. A. G. Gilman, L. S. Goodman, T. W. Rall, F. Murad, Eds. *Goodman and Gilman's The Pharmacological Basis of Therapeutics* (Macmillan, New York, ed. 7, 1985). Drug toxicity, in general, is dose-related, and toxic dose thresholds vary widely among people. Only a small proportion of users will experience the most serious toxic effects listed in the table, but the larger the user pool, the greater the absolute number of people who are harmed. As with diets high in saturated fats, which lead to atherosclerosis in only a small percentage of consumers, the absolute numbers can be great enough to constitute a major medical problem with high health care costs.

7. D. B. Goldstein, *Pharmacology of Alcohol* (Oxford Univ. Press, New York, 1983); H. Wallgren and H. Barry, *Actions of Alcohol* (Elsevier, New York, 1970) vols. 1 and 2; C. S. Lieber, *Medical Disorders of Alcoholism: Pathogenesis and Treatment* (Saunders, Philadelphia, 1982); Institute of Medicine, *Alcoholism, Alcohol Abuse, and Related Problems* (National Academy Press, Washington, DC, 1980); *Alcohol and the Brain: Chronic Effects*, R. E. Tarter and D. H. Van Thiel, Eds. (Plenum, New York, 1985); *The Health Consequences of Smoking: A Report of the Surgeon General* [Department of Health, Education, and Welfare (DHEW) *Publ. HSM 73–8704*, 1973]; Office of Smoking and Health, Public Health Service, *The Health Consequences of Smoking: Cancer: A Report of the Surgeon General* (*DHHS Publ. PHS 82–50179*, 1982); *The Health Consequences of Smoking: Chronic Obstructive Lung Disease: A Report of the Surgeon General* (*DHHS Publ. PHS 84–50205*, 1984); *The Health Consequences of Smoking: Cardiovascular Disease: A Report of the Surgeon General* (*DHHS Publ. PHS 84–50204*, 1984).

8. A drug that delays reaction time or clouds judgment can endanger the lives of others if the user operates complex machinery or vehicles. A drug that causes violent paranoid behavior can endanger all who come in contact with the user. Behavioral effects, even at the moderate intensity sought by the average user, can present a major threat to society. For example, moderate doses of alcohol imbibed in ordinary social drinking are sufficient to cause a measurable decrement of performance in tests of reaction time, vigilance, or judgment, making for dangerous driving and hazardous operation of complex equipment [H. Moskowitz and C. D. Robinson, *Effects of Low Doses of Ethanol on Driving-Related Skills: A Review of the Evidence* (Department of Commerce, National Technical Information Service, Washington, DC, 1988]. Similar findings apply to marijuana [J. A. Yesavage, V. O. Leirer, M. Denari, L. E. Hollister, *Am. J. Psychiatry* 142, 1325 (1985)]. In general, any drug taken for the purpose of altering mood and behavior can, in some circumstances, endanger other people.

9. O. J. Kalant, *The Amphetamines: Toxicity and Addiction* (Univ. of Toronto Press, Toronto, ed. 2, 1973); P. H. Connell, *Amphetamine Psychosis* (Chapman and Hall, London, 1958); A. Arif, Ed. *Adverse Health Consequences of Cocaine Abuse* (World Health Organization, Geneva, 1987).

10. J. D. Griffith *et al.*, *Arch. Gen. Psychiatry*. 26, 97 (1972).

11. O. D. Escalante and E. H. Ellinwood, Jr., *Brain Res.* 21, 151 (1970); R. C. Peterson and R. C. Stillman, Eds., *Phencyclidine (PCP) Abuse: An Appraisal* [National Institute on Drug Abuse (NIDA) *Res. Monogr. 21* (1978)]; W. Schmidt, *J. Public Health Policy* 1, 25 (1980); R. G. Heath, A. T. Fitzjarrell, C. J. Fontana, R. E. Garey, *Biol. Psychiatry* 15, 657 (1980); R. E. Popham, W. Schmidt, S. Israelstam, *Res. Adv. Alcohol Drug Probl.* 8, 149 (1984); J. W. Olney, J. Labruyere, M. T. Price, *Science* 244, 1360 (1989); D. J. McKenna and S. J. Peroutka, *J. Neurochem.* 54, 14 (1990).

12. J. H. Jaffe, in (6), chap. 23; H. Kalant *et al.*, *Pharmacol. Rev.* 23, 135 (1971); D. B. Goldstein, *Res. Adv. Alcohol Drug Probl.* 4, 77 (1978); C. W. Sharp, Ed., *Mechanisms of Tolerance and Dependence* (NIDA *Res. Monogr. 54*, 1984).

13. M. S. Gold and C. A. Dackis, *Clin. Ther.* 7, 6 (1984); K. L. Preston and G. E. Bigelow, *Int. J. Addict.* 20, 845 (1985); R. L. Dupont, A. Goldstein, J. O'Donnell, Eds., *Handbook on Drug Abuse* (National Institute on Drug Abuse, Government Printing Office, Washington, DC, 1979).

14. Defense attorneys often claim that physical dependence exculpates crimes committed to obtain drugs. This argument is invalid if treatment is readily available as an alternative to criminal activity.

15. R. E. Meyer and S. M. Mirin, *The Heroin Stimulus: Implications for a Theory of Addiction* (Plenum, New York, 1979); S. Fisher, A. Raskin, E. H. Uhlenhuth, Eds., *Cocaine: Clinical and Biobehavioral Aspects* (Oxford Univ. Press, New York, 1987); A. M. Washton and M. S. Gold, Eds., *Cocaine: A Clinician's Handbook* (Guilford, New York, 1987).

16. R. L. Hartnoll *et al.*, *Arch. Gen. Psychiatry* 37, 877 (1980).

17. N. J. Kozel and E. H. Adams, Eds., *Cocaine Use in America: Epidemiologic and Clinical Perspectives* (NIDA *Res. Monogr. 61*, 1985); N. E. Zinberg and R. C. Jacobson, *Am. J. Psychiatry* 133, 37 (1976).

18. W. Schmidt and R. E. Popham, *J. Stud. Alcohol* 39, 400 (1978); R. G. Smart and P. C. Whitehead, *Bull. Narc.* 24, 39 (1972); K. Mäkelä, *Res. Adv. Alcohol Drug Probl.* 4, 303 (1978).

19. We do not know to what extent predisposition is conditioned by experience, caused by endogenous depression or other psychiatric disorders, molded by drug-induced changes in brain chemistry, or genetically predetermined. We do not know whether, for a given person, the predisposition applies to all addicting drugs or is drug-specific; in alcoholism, it seems to be drug-specific. Attempts are being made to identify genetic markers of predisposition to addiction (especially to alcohol) [R. H. Pickens and D. S. Svikis, Eds., *Biological Vulnerability to Drug Abuse* (NIDA *Res. Monogr. 89*, 1988), pp. 1–180; J. B. Martin, in *Molecular and Cellular Aspects of the Drug Addictions*, A. Goldstein, Ed. (Springer-Verlag, New York, 1989), p. 198; K. Blum *et al.*, *J. Am. Med. Assoc.* 263, 2055 (1990)].

20. Animal experiments have the virtue that they permit direct study of the inherent reinforcing properties of the drugs themselves, uncomplicated by social factors [C. R. Schuster and C. E. Johanson, *Res. Adv. Alcohol Drug Problems* 1, 1 (1974); A. J. Karoly, G. Winger, F. Ikomi, J. H. Woods, *Psychopharmacology* 58, 19 (1978); J. V. Brady and S. E. Lukas, Eds., *Testing Drugs for Physical Dependence Potential and Abuse Liability* (NIDA *Res. Monogr. 52*, 1984); D. H. Clouet, K. Asghar, R. M. Brown, Eds., *Mechanisms of Cocaine Abuse and Toxicity* (NIDA *Res. Monogr. 88*, 1988).

21. T. G. Aigner and R. L. Balster, *Science* 201, 534 (1978); M. W. Fischman, *J. Clin. Psychiatry Suppl.* 49, 7 (1988).

22. Microinjections directly into the brain have permitted the identification of a few specific sites and pathways that mediate the drug-induced positive reinforcement. One site is a cluster of dopaminergic neurons in the ventral tegmental area that project to the nucleus accumbens in the forebrain. Cocaine and and amphetamines appear to stimulate this so-called reward pathway directly, whereas opiates evidently free the pathway from inhibitory controls [A. Goldstein, Ed., *Molecular and Cellular Aspects of the Drug Addictions* (Springer-Verlag, New York, 1989); R. A. Wise, P. P. Rompre, *Annu. Rev. Psychol.* 40, 191 (1989); G. F. Koob and F. E. Bloom, *Science* 242, 715 (1988); C. Kornetsky, G. T. Bain, E. M. Unterwald, M. J. Lewis, *Alcoholism* 12, 609 (1988).

23. Although the 18th Amendment was not enacted until 1920, a variety of federal, state, and local measures were applied strongly and effectively, beginning in 1916. Measures included the strict regulation of interstate commerce in alcohol, prohibition of sale to persons under 21 years of age, local prohibition, and other restrictive measures. These measures constituted de facto prohibition, which was later formalized by the slower process of constitutional amendment [N. H. Clark, *Deliver Us From Evil: An Interpretation of American Prohibition* (Norton, New York, 1976)].

24. G. Klatskin, *Gastroenterology* 41, 443 (1961); R. E. Popham, in *Alcohol and Alcoholism*, R. E. Popham, Ed. (Univ. of Toronto Press, Toronto, 1970), pp. 294–306; W. Schmidt, in *Alcohol and the Liver*, M. M. Fisher and J. G. Rankin, Eds. (Plenum, New York, 1977), pp. 1–26; *Alcohol and Public Policy: Beyond the Shadow of Prohibition*, M. H. Moore and D. Gerstein, Eds. (National Academy Press, Washington, DC, 1981).

25. This decline also means that even alcoholics drank less when drinking became illegal, because the fall in cirrhosis death rate is due exclusively to the change in consumption by the very heavy drinkers.

26. P. C. Whitehead *et al.*, *J. Stud. Alcohol* 36, 1208 (1975); A. C. Wagenaar, *Alcohol, Young Drivers, and Traffic Accidents: Effects of Minimum-Age Laws* (Lexington Books, Lexington, MA, 1983); H. Wechsler, Ed., *Minimum-Drinking-Age Laws: An Evaluation* (Lexington Books, Lexington, MA, 1980); P. C. Whitehead, *Alcohol and Young Drivers: Impact and Implications of Lowering the Drinking Age* (National Health and Welfare, Ottawa, 1977).

27. H. Brill and T. Hirose, *Semin. Psychiatry* 1, 179 (1969).

28. G. E. Vaillant, J. R. Brighton, C. McArthur, *N. Engl. J. Med.* 282, 365 (1970); Council on Mental Health, American Medical Association, *J. Am. Med. Assoc.* 223, 684 (1973); W. E. McAuliffe *et al.*, *N. Engl. J. Med.* 315, 805 (1986); J. M. Brewster, *J. Am. Med. Assoc.* 255, 1913 (1986).

29. A few other examples of availability affecting consumption are pub closing hours in Britain [R. G. Smart, *Br. J. Addict.* 69, 109 (1974)], cigarette vending machines in the United States [D. G. Altman, V. Foster, L. Rasenick-Douss, J. B. Tye, *J. Am. Med. Assoc.* 261, 80 (1989)], the change from clerk-service to self-service in Ontario liquor stores [R. G. Smart, *Q. J. Stud. Alcohol* 35, 1397 (1974)], and proximity to opium production areas in Laos [J. Westermeyer, *Am. J. Epidemiol.* 109, 550 (1979)]. Court decisions holding establishments responsible, both in criminal and in civil law, for the consequences of serving liquor to someone already intoxicated (Insurance Law Reports 89-631,O, Hague *vs.* Billings, 27 April 1989, Supreme Court of Ontario, Grainger J.) exemplify yet another mechanism for reducing excessive consumption and ameliorating some adverse effects on society.

30. "Benzodiazepines: Prescribing declines under triplicate program," *Epidemiology Notes, New York State Department of Health*, 4 (no. 12) (December 1989); "Benzodiazepines: Additional effects of the triplicate program," *ibid.*, 5 (no. 1) (January 1990).

31. R. E. Popham, W. Schmidt, J. deLint, *Br. J. Addict.* 70, 125 (1975); P. Davies, in *Economics and Alcohol: Consumption and Controls*, M. Grant, M. Plant, A. Williams, Eds. (Gardner, New York, 1983), pp. 140–158; T. F. Babor, J. H. Mendelson, I. Greenberg, J. Kuehnle, *Psychopharmacology* 58, 35 (1978); special issue on The Economics of Addiction, *Br. J. Addict.* 84 (10) (1989), see especially M. Grossman, pp. 1193–1204 and E. M. Lewit, pp. 1217–1234; M. A. H. Russell, *Br. J. Prev. Soc. Med.* 27, 1 (1973).

32. D. H. Efron, B. Holmstedt, N. S. Kline, *Ethnopharmacologic Search for Psychoactive Drugs* (Raven, New York, 1979); W. La Barre, *The Peyote Cult* (Archon Books, Hamden, CT, ed. 4, 1975); B. Roueché, *The Neutral Spirit: A Portrait of Alcohol* (Little, Brown, Boston, 1960); V. Rubin, Ed., *Cannabis and Culture* (Mouton, The Hague, 1975).

33. Britain, in the 18th century, had successfully evolved a pattern of moderate use of ale, but suffered disaster with the introduction of gin at the time of the Industrial Revolution [M. M. Glatt, *Br. J. Addict.* 55, 51 (1958)]. Japan, which had long handled sake without major difficulties, experienced a serious epidemic of medical and social problems when huge military stocks of methamphetamine were dumped on the civilian market after World War II (27).

34. L. D. Johnston, P. M. O'Malley, J. G. Bachman, *Drug Use, Drinking, and Smoking: National Survey Results from High School, College, and Young Adults Populations, 1975–1988* (DHHS Publ. ADM 89–1638, 1989); L. D. Johnston, "Monitoring the future," 1989 data, tables, and figures (press release, Univ. of Michigan, 9 February 1990); *Statistics on Alcohol and Drug Use in Canada and Other Countries*, vol. 2, *Statistics on Drug Use, Data Available by 1988*, compiled by A. Adrian, P. Jull, R. Williams (Addiction Research Foundation, Toronto, 1989); *Drug Abuse and Drug Abuse Research, Second Triennial Report to Congress from the Secretary, Department of Health and Human Services* (National Institute on Drug Abuse, Rockville, MD, 1987); H. I. Abelson and J. D. Miller, *NIDA Res. Monogr. 61* (1985), p. 35; R. A. Crider, *NIDA Res. Monogr. 57* (1985), p. 125; P. M. O'Malley, J. G. Bachman, L. D. Johnston, *Am. J. Public Health* 78, 1315 (1988); J. G. Bachman, L. D. Johnston, P. M. O'Malley, R. H. Humphrey, *J. Health Soc. Behav.* 29, 92 (1988).

35. The rapid growth of cocaine use over the past decade has been attributed, at least in part, to the glamorization of cocaine in the mass media and its use by sports and entertainment celebrities [A. Crittenden and M. Ruby, *Addictions* 21, 62 (1974)].

36. Y. L. Yao, *Bull. Narc.* 10 (no. 1), 1 (1958).

37. Likely consequences of legalizing heroin in the United States were discussed by one

of us over a decade ago during a previous war on drugs [A. Goldstein, *J. Drug Issues* **9**, 341 (1979)].

38. Editorial, "Why rush to surrender on drugs," *New York Times*, 14 December 1989.

39. D. F. Musto, *The American Disease: Origins of Narcotic Control* (Yale Univ. Press, New Haven, CT, 1973).

40. C. E. Terry, Health Officer for Jacksonville, FL, persuaded the city council to set up a clinic at which known addicts could receive free prescriptions for the drugs they desired, in any amounts they wished [C. E. Terry and M. Pellens, *The Opium Problem*, reprinted with foreword by J. C. Ball and preface by C. Winick (Patterson Smith, Montclair, NJ, 1970)]. The prescriptions, of which duplicates were sent to Terry's office, bore the names and addresses of the recipients, so that he was able to compile a detailed list of the individual users and the types and amounts of the drugs they habitually used. The results showed, remarkably, that almost 1% of the entire population of Jacksonville were habitual users. As Terry noted, this figure was a gross underestimate; at least half the population were children under the age of 15, who did not use drugs. Not included were over-the-counter purchases from pharmacists (still legal at that time) or direct provision of drugs to affluent patients by their own physicians (the clinic served primarily indigent or low-income users). Moreover, it was considered likely that the level of drug use in large urban centers was much higher than in Jacksonville (1913 population: 67,209) (*39*).

41. The immediate post-repeal increase in consumption in the United States was 43%, which led to a near doubling of the cirrhosis death rate. In addition, reflecting the inverse relation between real price and consumption, a 50% reduction in the price of alcohol in Ontario led to a 100% increase in consumption (*24*). Similarly, in California, a 50% increase in real income between 1953 and 1975 was associated with a 50% rise in per capita alcohol consumption [R. Bunce, *Alcoholic Beverage Consumption, Beverage Prices and Income in California 1952–1975*, report no. 6, June 1976 (State Office of Alcoholism, Sacramento, CA)]. Thus, simultaneous removal of legal constraints on currently illicit drugs, and lowering of drug prices, would probably lead to at least a tripling of consumption, and this in turn would result in proportionately larger increases in all the health and social costs arising from heavy use.

42. D. T. Courtwright, "Drug legalization and drug trafficking in historical and economic perspective," paper presented at Banbury Center conference on addictions, Banbury Center of the Cold Spring Harbor Laboratory, Cold Spring Harbor, NY, 25 to 27 January 1990.

43. Canadian health care costs due to alcohol-related diseases were calculated at some $6.0 billion (Canadian), reduced labor productivity costs due to alcohol amounted to $2.5 billion, social welfare costs caused by alcohol totalled about $1.5 billion, and alcohol-related motor vehicle accidents were estimated to cost $0.3 billion. The total of these estimates comes to $10.3 billion. Revenue generated for all levels of government by the sale of alcohol in the same year was only $5.1 billion [*Statistics on Alcohol and Drug Use in Canada and Other Countries*, vol. 1, *Statistics on Alcohol Use, Data Available by 1988*, compiled by M. Adrian, P. Jull, R. Williams (Addiction Research Foundation, Toronto, 1989) Table 23]. Comparable U.S. data for a population about ten times greater were about $117 billion in social and health costs, compared to an estimated alcohol revenue of $10.3 billion [*Alcohol and Health, Sixth Special Report to the U.S. Congress* (Department of Health and Human Services, National Institute on Alcohol Abuse and Alcoholism, Rockville, MD, 1987, Table 13); *Annual Statistical Review 1983/84* (Distilled Spirits Council of the United States, Washington, DC, 1984, Table 42); *Brewers Almanac 1987* (Beer Institute, Washington, DC, 1987, Tables 59, 60, 65)]. The Canadian estimates of alcohol-related revenue include not only excise taxes and duties and licensing fees but also corporate income taxes and real estate taxes paid by the alcohol beverage industry, profits earned by the provincial government alcohol sales monopolies, and other indirect revenue. In contrast, the U.S. figures refer only to direct taxes on alcohol and therefore underestimate the total benefits to federal, state, and municipal governments.

44. J. L. Steffens, *The Autobiography of Lincoln Steffens* (Harcourt Brace, New York, 1931).

45. J. D. Swisher and T. W. Hu, *Int. J. Addict.* **19**, 57 (1984).

46. M. R. Burt, *Am. J. Drug Alcohol Abuse* **82**, 419 (1981).

47. I. Leveson, Ed. *Quantitative Explorations in Drug Abuse Policy* (Spectrum, Jamaica, NY, 1980).

48. Data from *NIDA Household Survey on Drug Abuse, Population Estimates, 1988*, and supplemental data quoted in *HHS News* (Department of Health and Human Services, Washington, DC, 31 July 1989). For this population, daily users of heroin probably do not exceed a few hundred thousand, but heroin users are known to be underrepresented in the household population. Regular users of caffeine (as coffee, tea, chocolate, and soft drinks) are estimated conservatively at 90% of the population [R. M. Gilbert, *Prog. Clin. Biol. Res.* **158**, 185 (1984)].

49. Caffeine, although it is the most widely used psychoactive drug, appears to be relatively benign although not without dangers to users at high dosages [P. W. Curatolo, *Ann. Intern. Med.* **98**, 641 (1983); this refers to our Table 1].

50. *Hard-Core Cocaine Addicts: Measuring—and Fighting—the Epidemic*, draft staff report prepared for the use of the Committee on the Judiciary, U.S. Senate, 10 May 1990 (supervised by M. A. R. Kleiman).

51. The smoking route delivers a drug to the blood flowing through the lungs. This blood, carrying a high concentration of cocaine, reaches the brain within a few seconds and without dilution. The chemical properties of crack (cocaine free base) suit it for efficient delivery by this convenient route. In this respect crack is much like nicotine.

52. However, the enormous sums of money being generated by the drug traffic imply that cocaine use (as distinct from trafficking) has a major middle- and upper-class component.

53. A strictly rational approach is impractical because public acceptance and political feasibility of legislation depends not only on scientific evidence but also on long-established values and practices. It is extremely unlikely, for example, that present-day North American society would agree to put alcohol under stricter control than marijuana, even if currently available scientific evidence were to suggest that this is warranted. Polls show that the great majority, including those who were themselves users of marijuana, did not favor its legalization [Gallup Poll (Canada), 2 September 1985; see also R. C. Peterson (*54*)].

54. R. C. Peterson, Ed., *Marijuana Research Findings: 1980* (NIDA Res. Monogr. 31, 1980); K. O. Fahr and H. Kalant, Eds., *Cannabis and Health Hazards: Proceedings of an ARF/WHO Scientific Meeting* (Addiction Research Foundation, Toronto, 1983).

55. M. Marriott, "New York's worst drug sites: persistent markets of death," *New York Times*, 1 June 1989, p. 1.

56. In President Bush's fiscal 1991 budget request for the "National Drug Control Strategy," 29% is for interdiction and other offshore activities and 42% is for law enforcement, for a total 71% for supply reduction. Demand reduction totals 29%. Data from Office of National Drug Control Policy.

57. A. Hamid, paper presented at Banbury Center conference on addictions, Banbury Center of the Cold Spring Harbor Laboratory, Cold Spring Harbor, NY, 25 to 27 January 1990.

58. In Canada the legal status of cannabis has not been changed, but prosecutors do not oppose the use of discretionary powers by judges in sentencing, so as to grant absolute or conditional discharges, or impose only a modest fine, in cases of possession of small amounts for personal use. As pointed out by Single [*J. Public Health Policy* **10**, 456 (1989)], decriminalization is not an appropriate term for the lessening of penalties for marijuana possession. Consequently, the fact that substantial increases in use did not occur in certain states does not indicate what would happen over a period of years if the possession and use of this drug were actually decriminalized. Very little solid data have yet been published in support of the frequent journalistic assertions that the relaxed Dutch policy has produced no increase in the use of cannabis or other psychoactive drugs (G. F. van de Wijngaart, *J. Drug. Issues* **18**, 481 (1988); E. L. Engelsman, *Br. J. Addict.* **84**, 211 (1989); N. Dorn *et al.*, *ibid.*, p. 989].

59. *U.S. Sentencing Commission Guidelines*, pursuant to Sec. 994(a) of Title 28, U.S. Code, as amended November 1, 1989; S. Taylor, Jr., *American Lawyer* **12**, 65 (1990).

60. M. A. R. Kleiman, *Marijuana: Costs of Abuse, Costs of Control* (Greenwood, New York, 1989).

61. R. M. Davis and A. Lyman, Hearings before the Subcommittee on transportation and hazardous materials of the committee on energy and commerce, House of Representatives (Serial no. 101–85, Government Printing Office, Washington, DC, 1989). A possibly useful step would be to restrict sale of tobacco to liquor stores, because they are accustomed to excluding minors as customers, and they are monitored as to their compliance with requiring proof of age.

62. Happy hours and other devices to promote increased consumption could be forbidden. A system like the British "pub closing hours" could be instituted. Tougher enforcement and tougher penalties on drunk driving (or, for that matter, driving in an impaired condition due to any drug) could be implemented. Sale of distilled liquors, wine, and beer by the package could be restricted to licensed liquor stores or even to state-operated retail outlets as in some states now and to a major extent in the Canadian provinces.

63. "Court approves sobriety checks along the road" *The New York Times*, 15 June 1990, p. 1.

64. J. M. Moskowitz, *J. Stud. Alcohol* **50**, 54 (1989); L. T. Kozlowski, R. B. Coambs, R. G. Ferrence, E. M. Adlaf, *Can. J. Public Health* **80**, 452 (1989).

65. R. L. Foltz, A. F. Fentiman, R. B. Foltz, *GC/MS Assays for Abused Drugs in Body Fluids* (NIDA Res. Monogr. 32, 1980), pp. 1–198; R. L. Hawks and C. N. Chia, Eds., *Urine Testing for Drugs of Abuse* (*NIDA Res Monogr.* 73, 1986).

66. It is now recognized that neither mere drug information nor stern warnings about the dangers are effective. Recent programs, such as that developed by National Institute on Alcohol Abuse and Alcoholism (*Helping Your Students Say No to Alcohol and Other Drugs*, Dept. of Health and Human Services, Alcohol, Drug Abuse, and Mental Health Administration, 1989) are aimed at the lower grades, which do not yet present drug abuse problems. They have tried to teach children to make value judgments on all matters (including but not limited to drug use), to have confidence in their own ability to do so, to resist peer pressure that goes against their own judgments, and to find alternative drug-free outlets for their drives and curiosity. Disappointingly, evaluation has not shown these elements to be effective in changing attitudes and behaviors; only an honest, calm, health-based message has proved to be effective (*64*). Total expenditures on prevention education directed toward alcohol and other drugs by all federal and state departments and agencies in the United States in the current year is about $0.75 billion, 7.5% of the proposed budget for the war on drugs. (Information from Office of the Director, NIAAA.)

67. As the addict group is now a major infectious focus of the acquired immunodeficiency syndrome (AIDS) epidemic in the United States, it is essential to educate them in how to stop the spread of AIDS. Means of education include informational programs about human immunodeficiency virus (HIV) transmission by blood and unsafe sexual practices, distribution of free condoms to men and women, free contraceptive advice and supplies for women, as well as access to sterilization and early abortion for HIV-positive women. Needle exchanges may be helpful, primarily when used to bring intravenous drug users into a comprehensive treatment program [G. J. Hart *et al.*, *AIDS* **3**, 261 (1989)]. However, before the AIDS epidemic a British experiment that provided sterile equipment and pure heroin to registered addicts did not reduce the incidence of blood-borne infections (*16*); addicts shared their "sterile" equipment. Ironically, HIV is a fragile virus, easy to kill with brief heating or exposure to a disinfectant. Thus, simple means of

sterilizing equipment are readily available to addicts, just as are condoms for preventing sexual transmission. But addicts do not necessarily govern their impulsive behavior according to rational guidelines, and persistent educational efforts are required. See *AIDS and Intravenous Drug Use: Future Directions for Community-Based Prevention Research*, C. G. Leukefeld, R. J. Battjes, Z. Amsel, Eds. (*NIDA Res. Monogr. 93*, 1990).

68. A. S. Trebach, *The Heroin Solution* (Yale Univ. Press, New Haven, CT, 1982); A. Goldstein, *Arch. Gen. Psychiatry* **33**, 353 (1976)]. A similar medical model was tried in England for heroin addicts, but is now largely superseded by oral methadone maintenance. Heroin was not legalized; the drug remained illegal, but registered addicts were provided with it and with sterile syringes and needles [H. F. Judson, *Heroin Addiction in Britain: What Americans Can Learn from the English Experience* (Harcourt Brace Jovanovich, New York, 1974)]. The objective was to establish therapeutic contact and reduce the social harm caused by crimes committed by addicts in order to purchase drugs at high prices on the black market. Few of the expected favorable results were observed, however, probably because multiple intravenous injections of heroin every day represented a continuation rather than a change in addict lifestyle [J. Kaplan, *The Hardest Drug: Heroin and Public Policy* (Univ. of Chicago Press, Chicago, 1983); G. D. Wiepert, P. T. d'Orban, T. H. Bewley, *Br. J. Psychiatry* **134**, 14 (1979). No attempts have been made to apply this methodology to cocaine addicts.

69. V. P. Dole and M. E. Nyswander, *Arch. Intern. Med.* **120**, 19 (1967); V. P. Dole, *J. Am. Med. Assoc.* **260**, 3025 (1988).

70. S. S. Wilmarth and A. Goldstein, *Therapeutic Effectiveness of Methadone Maintenance Programs in the Management of Drug Dependence of Morphine Type in the United States* (World Health Organization, Offset Publication no. 3, Geneva, 1974); J. Holmstrand, E. Abgaard, L.-M. Gunne, *Clin. Pharmacol. Ther.* **23**, 175 (1978); B. A. Judson and A. Goldstein, *Drug Alcohol Depend.* **10**, 383 (1982); D. N. Nurco, T. E. Hanlon, T. W. Kinlock, K. R. Duszynski, *Compr. Psychiatry* **30**, 391 (1989).

71. S. B. Sells and D. D. Simpson, *Br. J. Addict.* **75**, 117 (1980); *Studies of the Effectiveness of Treatments for Drug Abuse*, S. B. Sells, Ed. (Ballinger, Cambridge, 1974–1976), vols. 1 to 5.

72. Methadone programs must be under the control of medical authorities so that adequate dosages can be used; political and moralistic concerns have often interfered with treatment efficacy by mandating dosage ceilings that are too low and too short a limit on the duration of treatment (*69*). An urgent need is to make widely available to physicians the long-acting methadone congener LAAM (levo-alphaacetylmethadol), which is in several respects superior to methadone itself (J. D. Blaine and P. F. Renault, Eds., *Rx: 3x/week LAAM Alternative to Methadone* (NIDA Res. Monogr. 8, 1976); B. A. Judson and A. Goldstein, *Drug Alcohol Depend.* **10**, 269 (1982).

73. R. Hartnoll, R. Lewis, M. Mitcheson, S. Bryer, *Lancet* i, 203 (1985); B. L. Levin, J. H. Glasser, C. L. Jaffee, *Am. J. Public Health* **78**, 1222 (1988).

74. The medical approach cannot be used in preventing recruitment of new addicts, except possibly to deglamorize addiction. Whenever a clinic offers psychoactive drugs as part of a treatment plan, methods have to be developed for excluding young experimenters who are not yet addicted but seek a convenient source of drugs.

75. M. A. Pentz *et al.*, *Ann. Med.* **21**, 219 (1989); M. A. Pentz *et al.*, *J. Am. Med. Assoc.* **261**, 3259 (1989); C. S. Bell and R. Battjes, Eds., *Prevention Research: Deterring Drug Abuse Among Children and Adolescents* (NIDA Res. Monogr. 63, 1985). Educational efforts achieve their effects relatively slowly as compared with changes in the law or in the price of drugs, so it is essential to support education programs long enough to give them a chance to achieve whatever results they are capable of, and to permit scientific evaluation of their efficacy.

76. We thank R. G. Ferrence, D. B. Goldstein, and O. J. Kalant for helpful comments. The views expressed in this paper are those of the authors and do not necessarily represent the policy of the Addiction Research Foundation of Ontario.

The Dutch Model

Eddy Engelsman

The Netherlands is the only country to have decriminalized drugs such as marijuana and hashish, although its punishment for traffickers is severe. Eddy Engelsman is the Dutch drug czar, in charge of drug policy in the ministry of Welfare, Public Health and Cultural Affairs. We talked to him recently about the Dutch model.

In 1982, the Netherlands amended the 1928 Opium Act and gave the new drug policy the name "normalization." Under this policy, drug use, even heroin and cocaine use, is not prohibited by law. Only possession is prohibited.

Drug normalization should not be misinterpreted as a lenient policy. It is, on the contrary, a well-considered and very practical policy that neither hides the drug problems of our society nor allows them to get out of control.

We never use the words "hard" and "soft" drugs in our legislation. Instead, we refer to Schedule One drugs – cocaine, heroin, amphetamines, LSD – as those with an "unacceptable risk." The other schedule refers only to what we call "traditional cannabis products," including marijuana and hashish.

Possession of these drugs, both Schedule One and the cannabis products, is prohibited, but possession of up to 30 grams of the cannabis products is only a misdemeanor – it is punishable by law, but our pragmatic prosecution policy allows for discretion.

Every country has this kind of prioritized drug policy, though probably not as overt as in the Netherlands. Indeed, if one asks a policeman in any American city what he would do, whether he would choose to catch the dealer of one

> Normalization is a well-considered and very practical policy that neither hides the drug problems of Dutch society nor allows them to get out of control.

kilogram of heroin or cocaine, or the dealer of 10 kilograms of marijuana, he would inevitably choose to put his energy into catching the cocaine or heroin dealer. In the Netherlands, this process is just more formalized.

Normalization does not mean everything is legal. If someone traffics in drugs, or if they steal for drugs, they will be punished. In the Netherlands, 30 percent of the prison population is incarcerated for drug-related reasons. In Amsterdam and Rotterdam, the number is 50 percent.

Avoiding A Cure Worse Than Disease | The Dutch drug policy of *de facto* decriminalization of cannabis products has not encouraged more drug use. In fact, the prevalence of cannabis use in the Netherlands is low. In the age bracket between 10 and 18 years, 4.2 percent has ever used cannabis in their lifetime. Among this group, less than two percent are still using occasionally. The number of daily cannabis users appears to be one in 1,000.

The Dutch have been pragmatic and have tried to avoid a situation in which consumers of cannabis products suffer more damage from criminal proceedings than from the use of the drug itself. This same principle accounts for the sale of limited quantities of hashish in youth centers and coffee shops, a policy that aims at separating markets in which hard drugs and soft drugs circulate. According to the Minister of Justice, this policy has succeeded in keeping the sale of hashish out of the realm of hard crime.

Compound Drug-Related Problems | Due to the mind-altering effect of drugs, most governments have tried to discourage their use through law enforcement and health education.

Today, however, we see that in addition to

By Eddy Engelsman. From *New Perspectives Quarterly*, Summer 1989, pp. 44-45. Reprinted by permission.

the mind-altering component of drug use, addicts are also affected by secondary problems – ones that are perhaps more serious than the original medical and social problems caused by addiction.

For the most part, initial medical problems have been compounded by risks of infectious disease, violence and social ostracism – complications that inevitably arise when drugs are pushed into the illegal sphere. On the societal level, additional problems have arisen from an intensified approach toward drug traffickers and the adoption of new, far-reaching legal measures that have led to an increasing corruption of the police, judiciary and government authorities.

These additional consequences – increased criminality and health problems – are the secondary problems, the unintended side-effects of conventional drug policy.

Harm Reduction Policy | The Dutch drug treatment philosophy addresses the socially backward position of most addicts and attempts to focus policy on the primary problems involved in drug abuse. The government encourages forms of treatment that are not intended to end addiction as such, but to improve addicts' physical and social well-being, and to help them function in society.

This kind of assistance may be defined as harm-reduction, or, more traditionally, secondary and tertiary prevention. The effort takes the form of fieldwork in the street, hospitals, jails and open door clinics for prostitutes.

This treatment effort also supplies medically prescribed methadone, material support and social rehabilitation opportunities. In Amsterdam, the conditions for participation in methadone treatment are regular contact with a medical doctor, registration with the methadone clinic, and a prohibition on take-home dosages of methadone.

In spite of the wide availability of medically prescribed methadone, there have never been so many addicts asking for detoxification and drug-free treatment. In Amsterdam, such requests doubled between 1981 and 1986.

The fact that the government has this policy toward addicts who are not able or do not, at least for the time being, want to establish a drug-free lifestyle is indicative of the realistic and pragmatic Dutch approach. It also shows the

The Dutch have been pragmatic and have tried to avoid a situation in which consumers of cannabis products suffer more damage from criminal proceedings than from the use of the drug itself.

determination not to leave drug addicts in the lurch. Failure to provide care of this type would simply increase the risk to the individual and to our society.

The result of Dutch health policy is that it is able to reach a very large segment of the total population of drug addicts. In Amsterdam, about 60-80 percent are being reached by some kind of assistance.

Needle exchange programs have also been instituted, since it is an established fact that many drug users are using intravenously and share needles. The effects of this approach: Only eight percent of the 605 Dutch AIDS patients are intravenous drug users, whereas this figure in Europe generally is 23 percent and is 26 percent in the United States. We have seen no negative side-effects, such as an increasing number of intravenous drug users, nor have we seen reduced interest in drug-free treatment.

Some other data: Reliable estimates on the number of drug addicts in the Netherlands, with a population of 14.5 million, vary between 15,000 and 20,000. Drug use appears to be stabilizing, even decreasing in some cities. Estimates on the number of addicts in Amsterdam, the largest city, vary from 4,000 to 7,000. The prevalence of heroin use in Amsterdam is estimated at 0.4 percent. The use of cocaine has stabilized at 0.6 percent, while crack use is still a virtual rarity. Finally, and perhaps most importantly, between 1981 and 1987 the average age of heroin and cocaine users in Amsterdam rose from 26 to 36 years.

The Dutch drug policy, which is administered by the Minister of Welfare, Health and Cultural Affairs, should not be seen as different from policies toward other areas of our society. Dutch measures for controlling drug abuse can only be understood in the context of history, and, perhaps, geography: The most striking feature of the Netherlands has always been the abundance of water – water that has historically constituted both a threat and a means of livelihood. The Dutch have never conquered the sea, but have succeeded in controlling this enemy. That sort of realistic relationship with the natural world has provided an important stimulus for a realistic and pragmatic approach to life in general for the Dutch, and has now come to typify our national drug policy approach.

215

Drug Prevention and Treatment

How do we convince nonusers not to become involved with drugs in the first place? How do we get abusers who are involved off drugs—and convince them to stay off drugs? Regardless of the legal question, we are still faced with the twin problems of prevention and treatment.

What is the best way of making sure that young people do not experiment with and become seriously involved with illegal drugs? In the 1980s, the then-first lady Nancy Reagan's "Just Say No" slogan became the most well-known statement on the drug scene. But did it work? Did the slogan deter many, or any, young people from the path of drug abuse? This issue is still being debated. Ads appear on television and in magazines and local newspapers claiming that one's brain on drugs is roughly the same as an egg frying in a hot skillet. Does this campaign—its truth value aside—actually dissuade youngsters from using drugs? Again, the evidence is not conclusive. Celebrities appear regularly in the media denouncing drug use and urging that young people not try any drug. Again, is this effort effective? And, once again, the answer has to be, it is not clear. Nonetheless, the issue of prevention is a much-discussed, hotly debated question.

Once someone does become ensnared in a compulsive, destructive pattern of drug abuse, what is to be done? What works? What treatment is most successful—or successful at all—in getting abusers off drugs—permanently?

Some treatment programs entail the addict living in a community, a *therapeutic community* (or TC), for a period of time, usually with strict supervision by ex-addict supervisors, eventually emerging back into society a changed person, purged of the impulses that caused him or her to abuse drugs in the first place. Therapeutic communities are a controversial mode of treatment, since they require a sizable investment of resources, the "split" rate—addicts leaving the program prematurely, against the advice of the staff, to return to the streets—tends to be very high, and proponents often develop a dogmatic, sectarian attitude toward other treatment modalities. Still, for a minority of drug abusers, the therapeutic community clearly works.

Some experts believe that programs based on the Alcoholics Anonymous (AA) model will work for most, or some, drug abusers. Here, addicts living in the community meet on a regular basis, sharing testimony about their lives with one another. Still other observers believe that drug abusers need to be threatened with a jail or prison term in order to force them into a mandatory treatment program. Others argue that, at least for the long-term, hard-core heroin addict, methadone maintenance is the only viable program. Some insist that the environment in which abusers live—including friends, family, and employment—has to be changed before their drug use can be addressed. Others opt for a multimodality approach; they feel that abusers of each drug or drug type, as well as different kinds of drug abusers, are sufficiently distinct as to require a variety of programs, each tailored to each drug and drug abuser.

Regardless of which approach to drug abuse treatment is correct, three facts remain widely agreed-upon. First, there are not enough spaces in treatment programs to handle all the drug abusers who wish treatment. Second, there are not enough financial resources currently allocated to drug treatment to make a serious dent in the problem of abuse and addiction. And third, not enough is known about the outcome of the various treatment programs that are used to say definitively which one works best, or even which one works best for which type of drug abuser.

Looking Ahead: Challenge Questions

What is the best drug treatment? Is there any such thing as a single "best" treatment program?

Will an AA-type program work for drug addicts?

Does the threat of incarceration work as a way of motivating addicts to enter—and profit from—treatment?

Why hasn't the government allocated sufficient resources to drug treatment programs?

Why are so many addicts on the street reluctant or unwilling to enter treatment? What can we do to get them to get help?

Unit 9

In Making Drug Strategy, No Accord on Treatment

Andrew H. Malcolm

Even though drug experts cannot agree on how to define "treatment on demand" for addicts, there are widespread complaints that neither President Bush's proposed program nor any existing state approach provides nearly enough capacity to treat drug addicts who want to break the habit.

But how much more treatment, and, indeed, what kind of treatment should be provided are issues that bring no consensus.

Nor is there anything near unanimity over calls for required treatment or civil commitment that would force addicts who do not want treatment to get it. Forcing treatment is now illegal in a majority of states unless the addict has been convicted of a criminal charge.

There does appear to be agreement on the urgent need for a system of local coordination to steer those of the nation's estimated four million addicts who seek treatment into the 5,000 existing treatment centers.

Recent Federal and academic reports and interviews with Federal and state officials and private experts, reveal stark differences between those in hard-hit drug cities like New York who urge large-scale treatment expansion immediately, and others in the Bush Administration who advocate a more measured growth in treatment coupled with more thorough evaluation.

"There's a fire going on right now killing people and our communities," said Dr. Robert G. Newman, president of Beth Israel Medical Center in Manhattan, which runs the country's largest methadone program for heroin addicts. "Sure, I agree we need eval-

uation. But what are we going to do immediately for hundreds of thousands who need help this minute?"

Dr. Herbert Kleber, a Yale University professor who ran his own drug treatment clinic until becoming deputy director in the Bush Administration's Office of National Drug Control Policy last summer, replies: "Unless we improve the treatment system, simply increasing capacity will only increase the speed of the revolving door. We need to increase and improve at the same time."

Actually, no one knows precisely how many American drug addicts exist, there being no standard definition of addiction and no accurate census. Nor does anyone know how many addicts might actually benefit from treatment.

But President Bush's September speech announcing his anti-drug plan used a National Institute on Drug Abuse estimate of four million addicts, based on a 1988 household survey defining serious drug users as those who used drugs at least 200 times in the preceding 12 months.

50 Percent Need Treatment

The President's report estimated that 25 percent of those addicts could stop drug use with support from friends, family and clergy; that another 25 percent were hardcore users unable or unwilling to stop, and that two million users would benefit from well-designed professional treatment.

But there is not enough such treatment to go around. According to Salvatore di Menza, special assistant to

the director of the National Institute on Drug Abuse, statistics for 1987, the latest available, showed 338,365 drug treatment slots in the United States—60 percent in private nonprofit centers, 25 percent state and local, about 11 percent in profit-making centers and approximately 3 percent in Federal centers like Veterans Administration hospitals.

With graduates, dropouts and repeaters, that means there are centers where about 800,000 addicts can undergo treatment each year. That suggests that more than a million addicts want treatment that is not available.

To reduce that gap, the Bush Administration and Congress have agreed to spend nearly $700 million on drug treatment in fiscal 1990. States and local governments plan additional appropriations, and the Senate has approved a measure introduced by Senator Daniel Patrick Moynihan, Democrat of New York, to allow Medicaid to reimburse states for the cost of substance abuse treatment.

House and Senate negotiators proposed 1990 Federal drug treatment spending at a level 77 percent higher than the 1989 figure. But no national plans exist about how to spend the money or how to evaluate the results.

One stumbling block is disagreement over the advisability, affordability or efficiency of treatment on demand, that is, creating enough surplus treatment slots to have beds always available for walk-ins.

New York, which probably has the nation's most serious urban drug problems, is in the forefront of those

demanding dramatic, immediate action. "Drug addiction is the greatest threat to our civilization and Government since the Civil War," said Stan Lundine, Lieutenant Governor of New York. "We believe in treatment for every addicted person who asks for help. We will have a very ambitious strategy and move every quickly."

Few centers treat the most urgent need: cocaine addiction.

He said the state soon plans to announce proposals for two massive drug treatment compounds or campuses on state or Federal land, each treating perhaps 1,000 addicts, where a variety of strategies would be implemented and simultaneously evaluated.

Treatment on Demand

Bush Administration officials said treatment on demand implies that somehow there should always be a vacancy available at every center, a system they said would be overwhelmingly expensive and inefficient. It also implies, Dr. Kleber said, "that people should get treatment from behind the same door they happen to knock on. But that treatment may not match their needs best."

The very existence of waiting lists can be an emotional issue. "Busy emergency rooms don't tell the seriously ill to come back another time," said Hector Maldonado, a Beth Israel drug counselor. "So how can we tell addicts looking for help to come back in a few weeks?"

Dr. Newman said that methadone treatment could be rapidly expanded, and that his center's five-month waiting list of 800 patients could be quickly reduced, simply by altering Government regulations to allow staff members to treat more patients.

"It's a scandal," he said. "Waiting lists are grossly understated because many programs are so full they don't even bother keeping a list and addicts, knowing this, don't even bother to apply."

Others disagree. "I'm always suspicious of walk-ins," said Bob Gilhooly, director of substance abuse technical services for the Roanoke Valley Mental Health Services. "I could

use 50 more residential beds tomorrow. But very few walk-ins want residential drug treatment. They're just looking to get detoxed for a couple days and go back out."

"Waiting lists are soft," says Dr. Mitchell S. Rosenthal, head of Phoenix House, which has 1,500 residential patients in New York and California and a 21-day waiting list. You've got one guy on four lists for two weeks and he's not waiting anymore anyway. Addicts by nature call for help one moment, and an hour later they're far away, emotionally or geographically. It's a motivation built on sand."

And even when accepted, many patients quit. Fully half the patients in therapeutic communities drop out. In Phoenix House's 18-month program, for instance, the average stay is only 11 months. "Yes, absolutely, we need more treatment slots," Dr. Rosenthal added. "And we know enough to expand and evaluate at the same time. Treatment on demand? Sure, but we also need demanding treatment, which requires learning another mode of behavior so when life gets tough, they don't mindlessly go off and take drugs again."

Not Enough Cocaine Treatment

A majority of the spaces for drug-addiction treatment in the United States are still designed for treating heroin users, who are now far outnumbered by cocaine addicts.

Cocaine addicts, who typically abuse several substances simultaneously, are treated differently from heroin addicts.

One result is that many of the available treatment slots do not match the addiction needing treatment. On any given day, according to the President's report, 20 percent of total treatment spaces in this country may be empty while many centers have waiting lists months long.

This is why most experts maintain that major metropolitan areas, at least, must get better information and referral services. One example is a drug counseling office in Kansas City, Mo.

Cecile van Thullenar, who is coordinator of the Assessment and Referral Center there, said it receives about a thousand calls a month from addicts seeking help. The center provides initial evaluations and steers addicts toward appropriate treatment; in many

cases, professional services are donated—$1 million worth in the past two years, she said.

Involuntary Programs

In recent years, an individual's decision to seek drug treatment in the United States has generally been voluntary. But that is expected to change as treatment programs expand to meet toughened sanctions. And treatment on demand may come to mean treatment on the demand of someone other than the addict.

Should addicts be able to get treatment upon demand?

"There's going to be a long, hard debate next year about civil commitment," said Dr. Joseph Autry, associate administrator for policy coordination in the Federal Government's Alcohol, Drug Abuse and Mental Health division, the Department of Health and Human Services.

Now courts can mandate drug treatment as part of punishment, although enforcement of treatment for convicts is often lax.

Nineteen states including California already have civil commitment laws, Dr. Autry said. These enable parents, for example, to commit troubled children for mandatory drug treatment. But in other states, including New York, this is illegal before a conviction.

"It's going to be a hot potato," Dr. Rosenthal said. "But the nature of addiction and its denial requires some method of humane coercion."

"There's no doubt," Mr. Lundine agreed, "we are moving toward the reality of coerced treatment. The problem is too serious. And the early evaluation of shock incarceration, for instance, is surprisingly positive."

Mr. di Menza foresees central urban treatment registries and a variety of drug treatment programs evolving in coming years as research shows which work best for which kinds of addicts. Research also continues on chemicals to block cocaine's high, as methadone does for heroin; buprenorphine, for example, has shown some preliminary effectiveness in blocking cocaine craving.

9. DRUG PREVENTION AND TREATMENT

"It may be more satisfying to think mainly of residential programs," Mr. di Menza said, "because the addict is put away somewhere safe. But we're going to need a range of strategies. For many addicts, for instance, it's not rehabilitation; it's habilitation. They don't know how to read or look for work, let alone beat their addiction."

Research has shown, for example, no difference in effectiveness in similar cases between expensive inpatient programs, which can cost $1,000 or more a day, and less expensive outpatient treatment, increasingly popular with insurers, which allow addicts to remain at work while practicing recovery and staying under daily supervision including urine testing.

"Instead of making inpatient the first line of defense," Dr. Arnold Washton said, "let's reserve expensive residential treatment for those addicts with serious psychiatric problems who really need it."

Dr. Washton's New York City institute, which bears his name, handles 450 outpatients a year, charging $4,800 for an 18-week daily course of treatment. "It's no panacea," Dr. Washton said, "but outpatient care is grossly underutilized."

"There's no question," Mr. Lundine added, "that the country, and especially New York, has a colossal drug problem. We need five times the existing 50,000 treatment slots in this state alone. And we're just in the infancy of finding a solution."

Out in the Open

Changing attitudes and new research give fresh hope to alcoholics

Just before the Betty Ford Center opened in the affluent desert town of Rancho Mirage, Calif., in 1982, neighbors ventured out across their well-manicured lawns to ask the staff a few questions. "Will there be bars on the windows?" they wanted to know. "Will they get out and go drinking in the neighborhood?" The answer in each case was of course no, but the questions reveal a familiar attitude toward alcoholics: many people thought of them as hardly better than criminals or at the very least disturbed and bothersome people. But at the same time the fact that a sanatorium for alcoholics had been started by a former First Lady who openly admitted to a drinking problem signaled that a hopeful change was in the air. Since then, a stream of recovering alcoholics, among them such celebrities as Elizabeth Taylor, Jason Robards and Liza Minnelli, have stepped forward to tell their stories with bracing candor—of being caught in the vortex of alcoholism, of taking the strenuous route to sobriety offered in therapy and of regaining their health and self-respect. The long process of recovering from alcohol abuse, which experts insist never ends, suddenly began to get favorable notices.

Today, in treatment centers nationwide, patients are getting a message of openness and hope. In his therapy sessions, John Wallace, director of treatment at Edgehill Newport, a center in Newport, R.I., explains that alcoholism is a disease with a genetic basis, and nothing to be ashamed of. "I ask how many had a close alcoholic relative," he says, "and 95% raise their hands. That astonishes them." He describes the latest theories about neurochemical imbalances that make an alcoholic incapable of drinking normally. "They are really fascinated," he says. "It takes away a lot of their guilt and makes them less defensive."

In ways unimagined ten years ago, the shadow that has obscured the truth about alcohol has begun to lift. There is encouraging news, and it is substantial. "Silence is each day giving way to courage," Otis Bowen, Secretary of Health and Human Services, said recently, "and shame to strength." Evident all around is a busy sense of awakening. Children are learning about the perils of alcohol in school through slogans like "Get Smart, Don't Start—Just Say No." The accumulated sci-entific findings of the past decade are having a major impact on the public. Recently a Gallup poll found that a great majority of American adults are convinced that alcoholism is indeed an illness rather than a sign of moral backsliding. In that, they have the support of the American Medical Association, which 21 years ago formally declared alcoholism a disease. At that time, only a handful of programs, such as Hazelden in Minnesota, offered treatment for alcoholics. Since then medical centers and treatment programs have proliferated across the country. There are more than 7,000 treatment programs, a 65% increase in the past six years alone. Partly because of the new spotlight on the dangers of alcohol, Americans are beginning to moderate their drinking habits: consumption of alcohol peaked in 1981 and has since declined by 5%. In many social circles today, the big drinker stands out like W.C. Fields at a temperance meeting.

The most exciting developments in the battle against alcoholism are taking place in the nation's laboratories, where scientists and medical researchers are probing its neurochemical roots and hunting for genes that may influence its development. Next month researchers from six national laboratories will meet in New York City to coordinate their search through human DNA for the genes that may underlie alcoholism. If they are successful, doctors may one day be able to test young people for certain genetic markers, the chromosomal quirks that predispose some individuals to alcoholism, and warn those who are at risk of developing the disease. Says Henri Begleiter, professor of psychiatry at the State University of New York Health Science Center and president of the Research Society on Alcoholism: "Never in the history of alcoholism have we made as much progress as we have in recent years."

For the 18 million Americans with serious drinking problems, life is a runaway roller coaster that, left untended, inevitably leads to disaster. "It ruins everything that matters to you," says *New York Times* Reporter Nan Robertson, a recovered alcoholic. "In the end, the bottle is your only friend. Alcoholics would rather do anything than stop drinking." For the vast majority of Americans, the occasional social drink is a harmless affair. For the afflicted, however-er, the most innocent gathering of family or friends—a wedding at a suburban country club, a casual gathering on an urban sidewalk—can turn into a nightmare of temptation, indulgence and worse. Recalls a youthful recovering alcoholic: "My biggest fear was getting through life without a drink. Today it is that I might pick up that one sucker drink."

The stakes are high. Alcoholism claims tens of thousands of lives each year, ruins untold numbers of families and costs $117 billion a year in everything from medical bills to lost workdays. The magnitude of the problem has been overshadowed in recent years by the national preoccupation with the new threat of AIDS and the widespread use of drugs such as heroin, cocaine, marijuana and crack. "Take the deaths from every other abused drug," says Loran Archer, deputy director of the National Institute on Alcohol Abuse and Alcoholism (NIAAA) in Washington. "Add them together, and they still don't equal the deaths or the cost to society of alcohol alone."

Alcoholism's toll is frightening. Cirrhosis of the liver kills at least 14,000 alcoholics a year. Drunk drivers were responsible for approximately half the 46,000 driving fatalities in the U.S. in 1986. Alcohol was implicated in up to 70% of the 4,000 drowning deaths last year and in about 30% of the nearly 30,000 suicides. A Department of Justice survey estimates that nearly a third of the nation's 523,000 state-prison inmates drank heavily before committing rapes, burglaries and assaults. As many as 45% of the country's more than 250,000 homeless are alcoholics.

Despite all the advances in knowledge and attitudes, plus the deluge of books, movies and television programs on alcoholism, the cartoon image of the cross-eyed drunk slumped in the gutter or staggering through the front door still lingers in the minds of some Americans. Not long ago many believed, as two researchers put it in the 1950s, that "alcoholism is no more a disease than thieving or lynching." Such attitudes are fading fast, to be sure, but not without leaving a residue of ambivalence. Says LeClair Bissell, 59, a recovered alcoholic and physician: "At the same time we say through our lips that alcoholism is a chronic disease, many of us feel in our guts that it's a moral or self-inflicted problem."

From *Time*, November 30, 1987, pp. 42-50. Copyright 1987, The Time Inc. Magazine Company. Reprinted by permission.

Yet it is a disease, and it can be a ruinously expensive one. A four-week drying-out regimen can cost anywhere from $4,000 to $20,000 for in-patient care; today medical insurance covers the tab for 70% of American workers in companies with more than 100 employees. In the early 1970s, the Kemper Group of Long Grove, Ill., was the first national insurance company to include coverage for alcoholism in all its group policies. The firm's hunch: the bill for helping an alcoholic quit today would be cheaper than nursing him through afflictions like cirrhosis of the liver and strokes later in life. The logic of acting sooner rather than later has since spread throughout corporate America. Some 10,000 firms and public agencies, including 70% of the FORTUNE 500 companies, now have employee-assistance programs to help alcohol and drug abusers pull their lives together and get back to work. "Before this," says William Durkin, employee assistant manager at ARCO, "the normal handling was to tolerate the alcoholic employee until he became intolerable and then to fire him."

Progress in the actual treatment of alcoholism is disappointing. Most facilities still rely on basic therapies worked out in the 1940s. Though some centers advertise grossly exaggerated success rates of 70% after four years, the best estimates are that only 12% to 25% of patients manage to stay on the wagon for three years. Alcoholics Anonymous, the tremendously popular association of an estimated 1 million recovering alcoholics, remains the single biggest source of support for chronic drinkers. But its record is hard to assess because of members' anonymity. Even so, only 15% to 20% of alcoholics get any treatment at all. Says Enoch Gordis, director of the NIAAA: "Something very important is still missing here."

Simultaneously, another shadowy fact of life about alcoholics has been dragged into the light: the severe emotional scars they leave on their spouses and especially on their children. "Years ago the focus fell solely on the alcoholic," says Carol, a mother of four and wife of an alcoholic. "Nobody identified the needs of the family." Indeed, alcohol abuse accounts for more family troubles than any other single factor. A Gallup poll this year found that one in four families reported a problem with liquor at home, the highest reported rate since 1950 and twice the 1974 rate. According to Health Secretary Bowen, alcohol is the culprit in 40% of family-court cases and accounts for between 25% and 50% of violence between spouses and a third of child-molestation incidents.

Though awareness of alcoholism's destructiveness is growing, the sheer number of alcoholics shows no sign of abating. Young people are especially vulnerable. Bowen states that nearly 5 million adolescents, or three in every ten, have drinking problems. Several studies show that children are beginning to drink earlier than ever before, and a *Weekly Reader* study earlier this year reported that 36% of fourth-graders were pressured by peers to drink. "Kids are making decisions about alcohol and drugs when they are 12 to 14, whereas in the preceding generation they made those decisions at ages 16 to 18," says Lee Dogoloff, executive director of the American Council for Drug Education. "The younger a person starts drinking, the more likely he is to develop problems later in life."

Who, exactly, is an alcoholic? The question is a tricky one: symptoms are not always clear cut, and even doctors do not agree on a definition of the disease. The extreme cases are obvious. A person in the grip of alcoholism blacks out from drinking too much, suffers memory loss, and wakes up trembling with craving for another drink. But most cases show fewer dramatic symptoms. Also, the behavior of alcoholics fluctuates wildly. Some drink heavily every day, while others can stop for brief periods, only to go off on binges. This past year the American Psychiatric Association settled on three basic criteria to define and diagnose alcoholism: physiological symptoms, such as hand tremors and blackouts; psychological difficulties, which include an obsessive desire to drink; and behavioral problems that disrupt social or work life.

The search for alcoholism's genetic underpinnings began in earnest in the early 1970s with a simple question: Why does the disease seem to run in families? Dr. Donald Goodwin, chairman of the psychiatry department at the University of Kansas School of Medicine, set about seeking an answer by studying 133 Danish men who were all adopted as small children and raised by nonalcoholics. Goodwin divided his subjects into two categories: those with nonalcoholic biological parents and those with at least one alcoholic parent. Then he interviewed each of the adopted men in depth and examined health records to see which of them developed alcoholism in adulthood. If the disease had a genetic basis, Goodwin reasoned, then the children who had an alcoholic biological parent would wind up with drinking problems more often than the others.

His findings were startling. The sons of alcoholics turned up with drinking problems four times as often as the sons of nonalcoholics. That result helped put to rest the popular assumption that alcoholics took up drinking simply because they learned it at home or turned to it because of abuse suffered at the hands of an alcoholic parent. The study, however, did not rule out environmental factors. Indeed, scientists now estimate that fully 30% of alcoholics have no family history of the disease. But Goodwin showed that some inherited attribute was involved. "What we learned from the adoption studies," says Dr. C. Robert Cloninger, a professor of psychiatry at Washington University in St. Louis, "is not that nature was important or nurture was important but that both are important."

But it was still far from clear how hereditary and environmental factors combine to create an alcoholic. In the early 1980s, Cloninger joined a team of Swedish investigators led by Michael Bohman, a psychiatrist at the University of Umeå, to study an even larger group of adoptees. Since Sweden's extensive welfare system keeps thorough records on each citizen, Bohman was able to compile detailed sketches of 1,775 adopted men and women, more than a third of whom had an alcoholic biological parent. As Cloninger studied the health, insurance, work and police records of his subjects, two distinct categories seemed to emerge—and with them new evidence that alcoholism may have more than one form.

Cloninger's first group of alcoholics, about 25% of the total, tended to drink heavily before the age of 25, had bad work and police records and met with little success in treatment programs. Drinking was a habit they seemed to pick up on their own, with little encouragement from friends or other influences. When Cloninger checked how often alcoholism appeared in the sons of men who fit this description, he found it surfaced nine times as often as in the general population. This variation of the disease, Cloninger concludes, is heavily influenced by heredity. Because it appears primarily in men, he calls this form "male limited" alcoholism.

The second type included both men and women and made up about 75% of the study's alcoholics. They started chronic drinking usually well after the age of 25, rarely had trouble with the law, and often successfully kicked the habit. Their children were only twice as likely to have trouble with alcohol compared with the general population. Cloninger labeled this category of alcoholism "milieu limited," indicating a genetic predisposition to the disease that is triggered by extended heavy drinking.

Cloninger's work added key pieces to the puzzle of alcoholism by suggesting traits that certain types of alcoholics have in common. For example, Cloninger found that his male-limited alcoholics tended to be aggressive, even violent types. He hypothesizes that the nervous system underlying such behavior may react to alcohol in a way that quickly leads to dependence. "It's not proved," says Cloninger. "It's testable." Says Boris Tabakoff of the NIAAA: "For those of us looking for biological markers, Dr. Cloninger's work gives us a road map we can follow to link genetic traits to behavior."

If researchers could develop medical tests that identify biochemical signposts indicating a predisposition to alcoholism, they could warn potential alcoholics before trouble started. SUNY's Begleiter found just such a potential marker in the brain. By using an electroencephalograph to measure the brain waves on nondrinking sons of alcoholic fathers, Begleiter discovered that a particular

brain wave called the P_3 showed a dampened response. In each instance the sons' brain waves closely duplicated those of their fathers, while other subjects with no family history of alcoholism showed strong P_3 waves. In addition, Dr. Marc Schuckit, a researcher at the San Diego Veterans Administration, has found that after several drinks some men whose fathers are alcoholics show fewer changes in the levels of two hormones, prolactin and cortisol, than men whose fathers are nonalcoholics. Eventually, such findings may provide important clues in the search for the genes involved in alcoholism.

Scientists acknowledge that work on the effects of alcohol on individual brain cells is still in its infancy. Part of the problem is that ethanol, the active ingredient in alcoholic drinks, easily penetrates the membranes of all cells and disrupts their normal function. Unlike other psychoactive drugs, ethanol does not target specific parts of nerve cells, or neurons, but seems to enter cell membranes and sabotage the nervous system indiscriminately.

Steven Paul, chief of the clinical neuroscience branch at the National Institute of Mental Health, is studying how ethanol affects certain cells in the brain to induce sedative effects. He is looking at a group of receptors, sites on the membranes of brain cells, that link with a molecule called gamma-aminobutyric acid (GABA), a neurotransmitter that moves across the synapses between neurons. GABA homes in on a complex known as the GABA-benzodiazepine receptor. If there are a sufficient number of GABA molecules present in certain areas of the brain, anxiety diminishes. Tranquilizers such as Valium and Librium work by attaching themselves to the receptor and increasing GABA's effectiveness.

Paul believes ethanol also reduces anxiety by acting on those GABA-sensitive neurons. Altering the amount of GABA in the brain could theoretically neutralize the effects of intoxication. To that end, Paul is currently experimenting with a drug, Ro15-4513, that blocks ethanol's ability to activate the GABA receptor, thus sharply reducing alcohol's sedative effects in rats. Although the drug is toxic to humans, variants could one day be useful in treatment. Other scientists are studying a new class of drugs that seem to block the alcoholic's craving for a drink. These compounds boost the amount of another neurotransmitter, serotonin, in the brain, thus encouraging a sense of well-being— and bolstering abstinence.

Ethanol has a harmful effect on nearly every organ in the body. Chronic heavy drinking increases the risk of myocardial disease and high blood pressure. Alcohol eats away at the stomach and intestines, causing bleeding in some drinkers. Alcoholic males may experience shrunken testes, reduced testosterone levels, and even impotence. Sustained drinking sometimes disrupts women's menstrual cycles and can render them infertile. Among expectant mothers, drinking can produce birth defects and is a major cause of mental retardation in American children. Even the immune system's efficiency is reduced by alcohol. Studies are under way to determine whether heavy drinking might cause AIDS to surface more quickly in infected carriers.

But alcohol takes the worst toll on the liver, where most of the ethanol in the bloodstream is broken down. Because alcohol is so high in calories (there are 110 calories per jigger of 90-proof liquor), the liver metabolizes it instead of important nutrients, a phenomenon that can lead to severe malnutrition. The high caloric content of ethanol also causes fat to build up in the liver, one of the earliest stages of alcoholic liver disease. This is frequently followed by scarring of the liver tissue, which interferes with the organ's task of filtering toxins from the blood. The slow poisoning leads to other complications, including cirrhosis, an often fatal degeneration of the liver that affects at least 10% of all alcoholics and is especially hard on women. "They die of cirrhosis earlier than men, even though they consume less alcohol," says Judith Gavaler, an epidemiologist at the University of Pittsburgh Medical School.

This year studies at the Harvard Medical School and the National Cancer Institute reported that even women who drink moderately may have a 30% to 50% greater chance than nondrinkers of developing breast cancer. Heavy drinking among men and women alike has been linked to cancer of the liver, lung, pancreas, colon and rectum. In October a team led by Dr. Charles Lieber, a leading alcoholism researcher at the Bronx Veterans Administration Medical Center in New York City, reported that it had isolated a possible link between alcohol and cancer in humans. The culprit appears to be a member of the family of enzymes called cytochrome P-450s. In the presence of alcohol, the cytochrome can turn certain chemicals in the body into carcinogens.

Despite the medical recognition of alcoholism as a disease 21 years ago, there is still uncertainty over its legal status as an illness. Michael Deaver, the former aide to President Reagan who is on trial for lying to a grand jury about his lobbying activities, is arguing that he was not responsible because he is an alcoholic and his drinking at the time impaired his memory of events and facts. In the past the so-called alcoholism defense generally has not been very successful, but it has worked on occasion in perjury cases.

Next month the Supreme Court will hear a case that is likely to hinge on the Justices' decision as to whether alcoholism is a disease. Two former soldiers, now recovered alcoholics, are seeking to overturn a 56-year-old Veterans Administration policy that classifies alcoholism as "willful misconduct" rather than a sickness. The VA's definition prevents alcoholics from receiving benefit extensions awarded to veterans with illnesses. In seeking to make their case, the plaintiffs' lawyers are expected to bring up the new evidence that alcoholism may have a genetic basis. Says Kirk Johnson, general counsel for the A.M.A., which filed an amicus brief in the case: "We want a medical judgment, not a ruling based on fear, misunderstanding and prejudice."

For alcoholics, the only way to stop the havoc alcohol causes is, of course, to quit drinking. That is easier said than done. The main barrier to ending the torment is the alcoholic's characteristic, and usually adamant, denial that any problem exists. Mary, 61, who has not taken a drink for 14 years, remembers blacking out and waking up with her hands trembling so badly that she could not hold a cup of coffee. "I had reasons for all those things happening to me," she says, "and none of them had to do with my drinking."

How, then, to break the psychological impasse? One way is to follow a strategy called intervention, which was pioneered in the early 1960s by Vernon Johnson, an Episcopal priest in a Minneapolis suburb. In intervention, family members, friends and co-workers directly confront the alcoholic to shatter his carefully nurtured self-delusions. Beforehand they meet with a specially trained counselor (the fee: $500 to $750) to rehearse. In the actual confrontation, the alcoholic is presented with a tough but sympathetic portrayal of the mess he is in and is urged to accept prearranged admission to a treatment center, often on the same day. Says Carol Remboldt, publications director at Johnson's institute in Minnesota: "Intervention allows a tiny aperture to be poked in the wall of an alcoholic."

The process can be painful. A 31-year-old daughter read her alcoholic parents a letter in which she described how she had seen her mother change "from the best friend I ever had" to an unhappy and unreliable woman. "The good parts of your character," she said, "are being stolen away by alcohol. Don't let the bottle overtake your life." Indeed, children often provide the most persuasive statements. One alcoholic's resistance crumbled when his son said, "Daddy, when you read me the funnies on Sunday morning, you smell." Peggi, a former schoolteacher and recovered alcoholic, remembers the day seven years ago when she was faced down by her husband, sister and three sons. "It was awful," she recalls. "But it was crucial for me to see how my drinking affected their lives."

As Poet Robert Bly, the son of an alcoholic, puts it in a book called *Family Secrets,* edited by Rachel V. (Harper & Row, 1987): "Every child of an alcoholic receives the knowledge that the bottle is more important to the parent than he or she is." To mend the damage from those year-in, year-out trau-

mas, hundreds of thousands of Americans have turned to Al-Anon and other family-therapy organizations. An offshoot of A.A. that was formed in 1951 for relatives and friends of alcoholics, Al-Anon has more than doubled in size since 1975 and now boasts some 26,000 regional groups. But the real comer is the children-of-alcoholics movement, aimed at the nearly 30 million offspring of chronic drinkers in the U.S. Made up of a variety of organizations, the movement took off four years ago with the best-selling book *Adult Children of Alcoholics,* a guide to the dilemmas C.O.A.s face, by Janet Geringer Woititz, a human-relations counselor in Verona, N.J.

At a typical C.O.A. meeting, participants sit in a circle and offer reflections on their own experiences, from a paralyzing fear of intimacy to acute conditions like bulimia, a disorder marked by episodes of excessive eating. At the heart of their pain and confusion is a childhood fraught with anxiety. "When we were kids and our parents were drunk, it was our problem," a 21-year-old daughter of an alcoholic told TIME's Scott Brown. "Somehow it seemed that we should be super people and make our family healthy." Reliving painful childhood experiences among sympathetic listeners enables the C.O.A.s to feel emotions they had suppressed. Recalls Rokelle Lerner, a pioneer in the movement: "I had to learn to re-parent myself, to comfort the little girl inside."

For both family members and chronic drinkers, the greatest frustration is the absence of a surefire treatment for alcoholism. The truth is that success rates often depend more on the individual makeup of the alcoholic than on the treatment. Alcoholics fitting Cloninger's male-limited type are less likely to remain sober after treatment, along with those with unstable work and family backgrounds. "The best predictor of patient outcome is the patient," says Thomas Seessel, executive director of the National Council on Alcoholism. "Those who are steadily employed, married and in the upper middle class are more likely to succeed." In response to allegations that some centers have exaggerated how well their patients do after treatment, Congress has ordered the NIAAA to investigate treatment programs.

Today about 95% of in-patient treatment centers in the U.S. use a 28-day drying-out program developed in 1949 at Hazelden. For the first few days, staff help patients through the tremors and anxiety of withdrawal. From that point on, the emphasis is on counseling. The aims: dispel the alcoholic's self-delusions about drinking, drive home an understanding of alcohol's destructive properties, and make it clear that the only reasonable course is to stop drinking—permanently. Some centers use Antabuse, a drug that induces vomiting and other symptoms if the patient has a drink. Schick Shadel, a program with hospitals in California, Texas and Washington, employs aversion therapy to condition alcoholics to recoil at the smell, taste and even sight of a drink. Most programs, however, rely on A.A. or other counseling programs to help reinforce the message of abstinence.

"Everyone knows how to get sober," says Michael Baar, an Albany, Calif., psychologist. "The problem is keeping them in that state." Relapse prevention is the latest attempt to help reduce the number of recovering alcoholics who fall off the wagon. Terence Gorski, president of the Center for Applied Sciences in Hazel Crest, Ill., has studied thousands of relapse cases and found that on their way to recovery, alcoholics go through specific stages, each with its dangerous temptation to return to drinking. Early on, it may be hard to cope with withdrawal. Later, the patient may falter in developing a normal family and social life. Finally, there is a period of complacency, when the recovering alcoholic no longer fears drinking as he once did. At each point, says Gorski, "the person is out of control before he actually starts to drink." His solution: counselors who meet regularly with recovering alcoholics to help them identify and face problems before they get out of hand. Says Gorski: "It is compatible with A.A. and self-help groups. The only difference is that we go beyond what A.A. has to offer."

Will there ever be a simple cure for alcoholism? Probably not. Even so, the next decade or so holds dramatic promise for advances in understanding and effectively treating the disease. Researchers hope eventually to sort out alcoholics according to the neurochemical bases of their addiction and treat them accordingly. "We are still trying to map out these neurochemical systems," says Edgehill Newport's Wallace. "If we succeed, then it is likely that we will be able to design treatments." A.A. and other groups may always be necessary to help alcoholics assess the psychological and emotional damage of chronic drinking, but there is hope that medicine may make the course to sobriety less perilous.

Medical and scientific promise, however, should not eclipse the importance of public policy efforts to curb heavy drinking among adults—and stop it altogether among youngsters and adolescents. Education is one approach. The Government's "Be Smart" campaign, aimed at eight-to-twelve-year-olds, has had some success. Mothers Against Drunk Driving has been a primary factor in the fight that has raised drinking ages from 18 to 21 in 34 states plus the District of Columbia since 1982. Despite strong opposition from the alcohol industry, which lobbies vigorously against higher excise taxes for alcohol and warning labels on beer, wine and liquor bottles, groups like MADD and the National Council on Alcoholism continue to push initiatives that will further discourage consumption of alcohol.

In his speech two weeks ago, Health Secretary Bowen complained that brewers and beer distributors spend $15 million to $20 million a year marketing their products on college campuses, encouraging heavy drinking and "contributing to poor grades, excessive vandalism, many injuries, and not so infrequently, death." Bowen asked Education Secretary William Bennett to encourage university presidents to restrict alcohol promotions on campus. Spuds MacKenzie, the canine star of Anheuser-Busch's advertising campaign for Bud Light beer, is also in the doghouse. This fall the National Association of State Alcohol and Drug Abuse Directors filed complaints with several federal agencies charging that the campaign encouraged kids to drink.

For those who know what British Novelist Malcolm Lowry described as the alcoholic's "fine balance between the shakes of too little and the abyss of too much," sobriety cannot come too soon. That is the challenge for medical researchers. But just as much energy should go into the job of preventing the disease. That means not only finding genetic markers to warn those susceptible but also changing attitudes in a society that still glorifies drinking. As Bowen remarked recently, "To do anything less than all this would be a disservice to ourselves, our society and to the many future generations whose lives and livelihoods are at stake." For millions of American alcoholics, there is no time to lose.   —*By Edward W. Desmond. Reported by Barbara Dolan/St. Louis, Andrea Dorfman/New York and Melissa Ludtke/Boston*

The Changing World of ALCOHOLICS ANONYMOUS

Nan Robertson

Nan Robertson is a reporter for The Times's culture department. She is a Pulitzer Prize-winner and a longtime member of Alcoholics Anonymous.

ONLY BILL WILSON COULD HAVE imagined A.A. as it is today, because only Bill, among the old-timers of Alcoholics Anonymous, had such grandiose, improbable dreams. In the summer of 1935, there were only two A.A. members — Wilson, a failed Wall Street stockbroker, and Dr. Bob Smith, a practicing surgeon — sitting in the Smith kitchen in Akron, Ohio, through half the night, chain-smoking and gulping coffee and trying to figure out how they could sober up other drunks like themselves. The society they had founded would attract only 100 members over the next four years; it would not even have a name until 1939. Now there are more than a million and a half of us around the world — members of the most successful, imitated, yet often misunderstood self-help movement of the 20th century.

About half of all A.A.'s are in the United States, the rest are scattered among 114 other countries. Many additional millions have passed through the movement and been made whole by its program, but A.A. periodically counts only those who are regularly attending meetings.

For those in the know, there are clues to A.A.'s presence everywhere: the sign on a jeep's hood in a Mexican town that says the "Grupo Bill Wilson" will meet that night; a West Virginia bumper sticker advising "Keep It Simple." The Serenity Prayer, attributed to the theologian Reinhold Niebuhr and recited at the end of A.A. meetings, appears framed on the wall in a South African living room or embroidered on a pillow in a chic Madison Avenue shop.

A.A.'s meet in Pagopago, American Samoa, on Wednesday nights, in McMurdo Sound, Antarctica, on Saturdays, and in Lilongwe, Malawi, on Mondays and Fridays. They find one another just to sit and chat between meetings in a doughnut and coffee shop on the main street of Peterborough, N.H., a town of 5,200 that has four A.A. groups. One of them is called Our Town in honor of Thornton Wilder, who took Peterborough as the model for his nostalgic play about American small-town life. The belfry of a Roman Catholic church near Covent Garden in London and a bank's board room in Marin County, Calif., are reserved for A.A. meetings once each week. Some groups meet on ships, at sea or in port. To these exotic settings must be added the thousands of prosaic basements and halls in churches, community centers and hospitals where most A.A.'s inch their way back to a life of quality.

In the last decade or so, large numbers of Americans, mainly entertainers, have gone public to say they are recovered alcoholics. Almost all said their motivation, and their hope, was, by their example, to inspire still-drinking alcoholics to recovery. But the great mass of the membership everywhere is composed of more or less ordinary people. They are neither movie stars nor skid row bums; the great drama of their lives has not been played out in the spotlight or in squalid flophouses. These alcoholics have suffered, increasingly isolated, in bars, in their own bedrooms, or in the living rooms of friends who have become estranged by their drunken behavior. Their recovery has been worked out in private.

Over the last 50 years, the substance of A.A. — its core literature, its program of recovery and its ways of looking at life — has changed very little. But in terms of the numbers and diversity of its members, A.A. today would be unrecognizable to its pioneers. In the early years, A.A. members were almost exclusively male, white, middle-class, middle-aged and of Western European extraction. They were men who had fallen very far, often from

From *The New York Times Magazine*, February 21, 1988, pp. 40, 42-44, 47, 92. Adapted from *Getting Better: Inside Alcoholics Anonymous* by Nan Robertson. Copyright © 1991, William Morrow & Company, Inc.

the top of their businesses and professions.

The A.A. of 1988 is huge, increasingly international, multiethnic, multiracial, cutting across social classes, less rigidly religious than it was in the beginning, more accepting of gay people, and of women, who now form one-third of the total North American membership and about half of the A.A. membership in big cities. Increasingly, many turn to A.A. for help in earlier stages of their disease.

A much more abrupt and spectacular trend is that young people have streamed into A.A. in the last 10 years, most of them addicted to other drugs as well as to alcohol. Dr. LeClair Bissell, the founding director of the Smithers alcoholism center, in Manhattan, expresses the consensus of the alcoholism research and treatment world when she says: "There are almost no 'pure' alcoholics among young people anymore. They are hooked on booze and other drugs, or only on other drugs."

It is common now at A.A. meetings to hear a young speaker say, "My name is Joe, and I'm a drug addict and an alcoholic."

The dually addicted anger some A.A. members. One with 20 years of sobriety says: "This fellowship was formed to help suffering alcoholics, and alcoholics only. That's why it has been so successful — we don't monkey around with other problems."

In a few communities, A.A. members have formed groups billed for those "over 30." The message is clear: No druggies wanted. This development infuriates John T. Schwarzlose, executive director of the Betty Ford Center for substance abusers in Rancho Mirage, Calif.: "A.A. is the epitome of tolerance, flexibility and inclusiveness, but some drug addicts have told me about being turned away from A.A. meetings in the Midwest and South when they said they were just addicted to drugs. Now I tell them to say they are both alcoholics and drug abusers." In the big cities and at A.A. headquarters, attitudes toward the dually addicted are much more welcoming.

FOR A LONG TIME, ALCOHOLICS ANONymous was believed to be a purely North American phenomenon. It was thought that its themes of self-help and volunteerism would not transfer to more relaxed cultures. A.A.'s Ecuador-born coordinator for Hispanic groups voiced the early point of view among his Latin friends: "A.A. is O.K. for gringos, but not for us. In Latin America ... if a man doesn't drink, he's not a macho." To his surprise, A.A. began to boom among Hispanics in the 1970's. Mexico's membership of 250,000 is now second only to that of the United States. Brazil, with 78,000 members, and Guatemala, with 43,000, are next-highest in Latin America.

Until recently, A.A. had been unable to gain a toehold in the Soviet Union or in Eastern Europe. The movement had been regarded there as possibly threatening, because of its precepts of anonymity and confidentiality, its religious overtones and the fact that it operates outside any government control. Then last summer, the Soviet Union sent to the United States four doctors specializing in addiction. They visited alcoholism-treatment centers, the Summer School of Alcohol Studies at Rutgers University and numerous A.A. meetings. When they returned home, they took back quantities of A.A. pamphlets translated for them into Russian. Still, the only Eastern European nation to embrace A.A. has been Poland. Its Government finally recognized what it called the "psychotherapeutic" value of A.A.

In the United States, those long familiar with A.A. meetings notice that there seem to be disproportionately high numbers from certain ethnic groups. "Alcoholism goes with certain cultures, such as the Celtic or the Scandinavian, that approve of drinking, or at least are ambivalent about it," says Dr. Bissell. "But in some environments or religions, people don't drink on principle. These abstinent cultures in the United States include Baptists, some other Southern Protestant sects and Mormons."

For a long time, there was a widely held belief that Jews did not become alcoholics. The work of JACS — Jewish Alcoholics, Chemically Dependent Persons and Significant Others — is helping to dispel that myth. Jews are present in large numbers, JACS says, at A.A. meetings in many cities where there is a significant Jewish population. But rarely do A.A. meetings take place in synagogues or Jewish community centers.

Sheldon B., an alcoholism counselor in New York, told of how, a few years ago, he approached his own rabbi with the idea of opening their temple to an A.A. group. He thought that Jewish members in any A.A. group might be more comfortable about accepting help in a synagogue setting rather than in a church. The rabbi informed him that there was no need: "There are no Jewish alcoholics." When Sheldon B. said, "But I am an alcoholic," the rabbi thought for a moment and then replied, "Are you sure you know who your real father was?"

Although there are black A.A. groups and mixed racial groups in large Northern cities, the number of blacks in A.A. does not appear to reflect the race's proportion in the nation — 29 million, or 12 percent of the population.

"There is a great stigma in being black and being drunk, even recovered," a black Philadelphia teacher declared at a meeting devoted to the subject. "I made the mistake of telling my principal that I had a problem. I checked myself into a treatment center. She used a hatchet on me."

As a black Milwaukee social worker explained: "The black community is afraid that if blacks admit their alcoholism, it will reinforce the white stereotype that they are shiftless. ... The black community likes to think that oppression causes their alcoholism. ... Other oppressed minorities use the same argument. 'Who wouldn't drink?' they say. 'Our lives are so goddamned awful. ... Oblivion is the only way out of our pain.'"

Homosexuals are coming into A.A., and in sophisticated communities are welcomed. Some recovered alcoholics have formed all-gay groups, just as there are special groups for women, doctors, agnostics, lawyers, airline pilots and others.

"Growing up in Alabama, I was taught to hate myself," one gay member told an A.A. meeting. "I was a nigger sissy. In A.A., I learned that God loves us all. My business in A.A. is to stay sober and help you if you want it."

A.A. surveys do not inquire whether members attend religious services or if they believe in God. There are no questions about ethnic or racial origins, sexual preference or whether alcoholism runs in the family. But a family predisposition to alcoholism is reflected strikingly within A.A. Often, speakers at meetings begin: "My name is Mary, and I am an alcoholic . . . and my father [or mother] was an alcoholic."

Longtime A.A. members believe that it is hopeless to drag another into sobriety if the alcoholic is determined not to be helped or refuses to believe he is ill. Even so, the courts in some states are sending thousands of offenders to A.A. meetings instead of to jail. But the A.A. program sometimes catches on even with unwilling alcoholics.

THERE ARE MANY THINGS OUTSIDers believe A.A. to be that it is not.

It is not a temperance organization or Prohibitionist society. A.A. does not want to save the world from gin. Nobody invites you to join A.A. You are a member if you say you are, or if you walk into an A.A. meeting with the thought that you have a drinking problem and you want to stop. There are no papers to sign, no pledges to take, no obligation to speak up, no arms twisted. The attitude of members toward those outside who drink moderately is "I wish I could drink as you do, but I can't."

A.A. is not a religious cult. Some members are agnostics or atheists. Many choose to believe that their "higher power" is their A.A. group. Most members prefer to call A.A.'s program "spiritual." Yet God is mentioned directly or indirectly in five of the Twelve Steps, which A.A. uses to help heal individuals, and this sometimes repels outsiders who might otherwise be attracted. (Boiled down to six instantly understandable principles, the Twelve Step program might read: We admit we are licked and cannot get well on our own. We get honest with ourselves. We talk it out with somebody else. We try to make amends to people we have harmed. We pray to whatever greater Power we think there is. We try to give of ourselves for our own sake and without stint to other alcoholics, with no thought of reward.)

A.A. DOES NOT WORK FOR EVERYBODY. BUT THEN, nothing does. About 60 percent of those coming to A.A. for the first time remain in A.A. after going to meetings and assiduously "working the program" for months or even years. Usually, they stay sober for good. But about 40 percent drop out. These statistics refute a widely held notion that A.A. is always successful or an "instant fix." Even so, its success rate is phenomenally high.

Freudian analysis and religious faith, for example, may be two great ways to heal the human spirit, but they do not work *on their own* for alcoholics. The vast majority of doctors, psychologists and members of the clergy who are familiar with A.A., as well as almost all experts in alcoholism, make A.A. their No. 1 choice for a long-term program of recovery. A.A. precepts are built into the programs of every respected intensive alcoholism treatment center in the country, including

those of Hazelden in Minnesota, Smithers in New York and the Betty Ford Center. John Schwarzlose of the Betty Ford Center expresses a typical opinion: "Patients ask how important it is that they go to A.A. after they're through here. I say, 'I can give you a guarantee. When you leave here, if you *don't* go to A.A., you won't make it.' "

A.A. has no ties with political parties, foundations, charities or causes, nor does it sponsor research into alcoholism.

And unlike most tax-exempt organizations, A.A., whose current annual budget is $11.5 million, does no fund-raising. Nor does A.A. accept money from outsiders. The funds supporting headquarters services comes mainly from A.A.'s huge publishing empire, which distributes authorized literature to members.

Each group is self-supporting, passing a basket at every meeting to help pay for coffee, snacks, literature and rent for the meeting space. Those present often give a dollar. Others may just drop a coin into the basket. Some cannot give anything.

No member may donate more than $1,000 a year to A.A. Nor may a member bequeath more than $1,000, or leave property to A.A., which has never owned any real estate.

"The reason we discourage gifts and bequests," says Dennis Manders, a nonalcoholic who served for 35 years as the controller at A.A. headquarters, "is that we don't ever want some person dropping a million bucks in the A.A. hopper and saying, 'Now, *I'm* going to call the tune.' "

About half of the groups contribute nothing at all for headquarters services. Many members feel that carrying the expenses of their "home group" is enough. This kind of autonomy and decentralization typifies Alcoholics Anonymous.

The average A.A. member, according to surveys, attends four meetings a week. After about five years of regular attendance, some A.A.'s go to fewer and fewer meetings. They may stop altogether when they feel they are able to function comfortably without alcohol. However, some speakers at meetings are full of cautionary tales about how they drifted away from A.A. and drank again, sometimes disastrously and for long periods of time, before returning to the fold.

The movement works in quiet and simple ways. Members usually give of themselves without reservation; exchange telephone numbers with newcomers; come to help at any hour when a fellow member is in crisis; are free with tips on how to avoid that first drink. Most people in A.A. are flexible, tolerant of eccentrics, suspicious of rules and "musts." The lack of ritual can be a surprise to beginners. So is the absence of confrontation, finger-pointing, blame-laying, angry debate and chronic whining.

The essence of A.A. can only be guessed at in big, showy gatherings, such as its international conventions every five years. It is in the intimacy of neighborhood meetings that the truth, the flavor and an inkling of the reasons for A.A.'s success can be grasped. The members may meet in groups as small as 2 or 3, or as large as 200, but the usual attendance is somewhere between a dozen and 40 people. In New York City, the most active single A.A. spot anywhere, there is a choice of 1,826 listed meetings held by 724 groups every week.

As A.A. grew and diversified, the stigma of alcoholism gradually faded. There were many stages along A.A.'s road to respectability, beginning in the 1940's,

that gradually transformed the public's perception of the society of recovered drunks from a butt of disbelief and even ridicule to that of an accepted and admired organization. None was more significant than the action taken by the American Medical Association. In 1956, the A.M.A.'s trustees and its House of Delegates declared that alcoholism was a disease, thereby validating a central belief of A.A., from its co-founders on, that it is a sickness, not a sin.

Now the Supreme Court of the United States is debating the legality of the issue. [On] Dec. 7, [1988,] the court heard a challenge by two Vietnam War veterans against the Veterans Administration for excluding "primary alcoholism" (in which drinking itself is the root disorder) from the list of illnesses and disabilities that allow veterans more time to claim education benefits. Extensions can be granted to veterans hindered by physical or mental problems "not the result of their own willful misconduct." The justices are expected to hand down an opinion before the Court's term ends in June.

THE STRUCTURE OF A.A. IS A LITTLE HARDER TO grasp than the disease theory of alcoholism. It is close to the truth to say that A.A. consists of a million Indians and no chiefs. And that it is less an organization than an organism that keeps splitting, amoebalike, into ever more groups. If a member doesn't like how things are run in his group, he can start another one with people he finds more compatible. This has given rise to an A.A. saying: "All you need to start a new group is two drunks, a coffee pot and some resentment."

There *is* a structure in Alcoholics Anonymous, but it would set any conventional notion of how to run a business on its head. Basically, the local groups are boss, and the board of trustees and the staff at the General Service Office are supposed to carry out their orders. The board of trustees is made up of 14 A.A. members and 7 nonalcoholics.

Although alcoholics hold all the top administrative jobs, they never handle money. A.A.'s financial operation is run by nonalcoholics. The reason is that Bill Wilson and the early A.A.'s were afraid that if anybody running A.A. fell off the wagon, that would be bad enough, but if he were handling finances as well, the results could be disastrous. The philosophy has endured.

The manner in which A.A. directs its collective affairs and sets policy can be seen most clearly—or in all its democratic confusion—at its yearly General Service Conference, the closest approximation to a governing body of A.A. About 135 people attend, including 91 delegates elected at regional A.A. assemblies in the United States and Canada. Also on hand are the trustees of the board and representatives of the headquarters staff.

The day-to-day business of Alcoholics Anonymous has been carried on since 1970 in a brick building at 468 Park Avenue South, in midtown Manhattan. Whatever policies are decided at the conference are carried out by the headquarters staff. Their jobs are divided into specialties, such as literature, treatment centers, prisons, public information and cooperation with professionals—doctors, counselors, social workers and teachers, for example—in the alcoholism field. And just in case someone should become overly fond of a specialty, all the top staff members, except the general

manager and the Hispanic coordinator, regularly rotate jobs every two years. The same frequent rotation occurs at every level in A.A. Officers in local groups usually step down after six months.

The seven nonalcoholic trustees, who are often experts in some profession, such as medicine, law, banking or social work, serve a special need. Joan K. Jackson, a sociologist with long experience among alcoholics, explains: "We can use our full names in public. We are not perceived by outsiders as having any vested interest. Privately within A.A., our greatest function is as gadflies and questioners."

What makes A.A. headquarters run is the A.A. World Services publishing empire. It now brings in $8.8 million annually, or 76 percent of A.A.'s yearly corporate revenues. It is the cause of some trepidation among those who have taken what amounts to a vow of poverty. Each year, A.A. distributes 7 million copies of more than 40 pamphlets (mostly gratis for members), and almost a million and a half copies of 6 books and 2 booklets. Seven million copies of the Big Book (A.A.'s central text, published in 1939, whose formal title is "Alcoholics Anonymous") have been sold. Last year alone, about a million Big Books were purchased, virtually all of them at A.A. meetings, alcoholic rehabilitation centers or through mail orders.

At the time of his death, early in 1971, Bill Wilson was earning about $65,000 a year in royalties from the Big Book and three other books he wrote for A.A. Last year, his widow, Lois, received $912,500 in royalties. Under the terms of an agreement Bill concluded with A.A. headquarters in 1963, she was allocated 13.5 percent of Wilson's royalties. Another 1.5 percent went to his last mistress, who died a few years after Bill.

THERE HAS BEEN ALMOST NO NEGATIVE PUBLICITY about Alcoholics Anonymous over the five decades of its history. Extensive research turns up only a handful of critical views in the press. Writing in The Nation in 1964, Jerome Ellison charged that A.A.'s conservative top councils had lost touch with the ever more diverse rank-and-file. The same year, Arthur H. Cain, a New York psychologist, in a book and articles for various magazines, called A.A. a "cult" that enslaved its members to self-righteous sobriety. Bill Wilson's reaction was typical of the man's tolerance. The co-founder, trying to calm the ensuing fuss at headquarters, said: "In all the years, this is the first thorough-going criticism our fellowship ever had. So the practice of absorbing stuff like that in good humor should be of value." It was the first public criticism, and it proved to be one of the last.

Privately within A.A., there has been growing dissatisfaction with headquarters. Some members say staff members are becoming frozen in bureaucracy and are overly sensitive to pressure from the most rigid and narrow-minded members, particularly old-timers, who regard the Big Book and other authorized A.A. literature almost as Holy Writ.

"If anything is going to destroy A.A.," says Dr. John Norris, a nonalcoholic physician, friend of Bill Wilson's and for many years chairman of A.A.'s board of trustees, "it will be what I call the 'tradition lawyers.' They find it easier to live with black and white than they do with gray. These 'bleeding deacons'—these fundamentalists—are afraid of and fight any change."

Rx FOR ADDICTION

Probing the mysteries of drug addiction is revealing basic knowledge about the brain and may yield a new generation of pharmaceuticals.

Marguerite Holloway

Staff writer

Patches over both eyes, his scalp studded with electrodes to record brain waves, a cocaine addict from Baltimore describes how it feels to be high on cocaine—in real time. For half an hour, while the drug produces feelings of intense pleasure, researcher Edythe D. London asks him whether he agrees or disagrees with a series of statements: I would be happy all the time if I felt as I do now? I feel more clear-headed than dreamy?

The addict's brain activity is later recorded by a positron emission tomographic (PET) scanner. It creates images from the stream of high-energy particles released during the decay of short-lived radioactive isotopes that were injected into the drug user at the outset of the session. Because the brain absorbs more of the isotope in areas where levels of glucose metabolism are high, the images show active regions in bright red; slower areas light up as yellow or blue.

When London, chief of the neuropharmacology laboratory at the Addiction Research Center of the National Institute on Drug Abuse (NIDA), correlates what she sees with what the addict has said, she can create one of the most complete pictures yet obtained of the way cocaine acts in the living brain. Using formulas and readings of the blood levels of isotopes, London can retrospectively develop PET images for the 30 minutes of the experiment. "It is very exciting—you can watch what is happening chemically at the same time that someone talks about his or her subjective state," says London, a pioneer in the use of PET scans to study the acute effects of drugs of abuse.

London's research puts her at the forefront of a small group of investigators who are beginning to make headway against the intractable and devastating problem of addiction. Some 5.5 million people in the U.S. are addicted to illegal drugs, according to the Institute of Medicine—that figure does not include people addicted to legal substances such as barbiturates or amphetamines. Another 59 million or more are dependent on alcohol and nicotine, according to the National Institute on Alcohol Abuse and Alcoholism and the American Lung Association. Drug abuse remains disproportionately more prevalent among minorities, who often have less access to health care. The toll in terms of lives, health cost, crime and productivity cannot be measured.

Ironically, these often destructive, and illegal, substances provide valuable scientific information. And addiction researchers are using these insights to pioneer a frontier in pharmacology. In the past, drug developers randomly screened for chemicals that had therapeutic benefits—relying in large part on serendipity. Indeed, vacationing employees of some drug companies still return with bags of soil that are analyzed for microbial substances with biological activity. The way these drugs worked was usually uncovered years later, often yielding important clues about the systems in which they intervened. Now that process also works in reverse. The advent of modern biology has begun to make the understanding of how an organism functions an important source of potential therapeutic opportunities.

The promise of this approach is especially bright in the pharmacology of the central nervous system (CNS). Over the past decade scientists armed with molecular biology and powerful imaging technologies such as PET have gleaned new knowledge of the brain. Those discoveries have begun to illuminate how abused substances affect neurochemistry. Scientists are beginning to design highly targeted drugs that may soon be used to treat addiction on a chemical and even a genetic level.

The research being conducted in the most recent, and controversial, pharmacological offensive in "the war on drugs" may have wide application. Scientists searching for the biological foundation of addiction are making important contributions to the understanding of the basic machinery of the most protected and mysterious organ, the brain. At the same time, they are illuminating aspects of mental illness and neurological disorders. Clinicians testing medications already on the market—including those for depression, anxiety and schizophrenia—are observ-

ing that a few of them seem surprisingly helpful in treating addiction.

Eventually, if the overlap between mental illness and drug addiction becomes more clear, medications developed to treat addiction may be used to combat aspects of mental illnesses. In biological terms, drugs that are abused can create states that are very similar to some mental disorders. "The diseases of brain cells, or the perturbations of brain cells, that are associated with drug, alcohol and probably tobacco use and with mental illness may involve similar brain processes," says William E. Bunney, professor of psychiatry at the University of California at Irvine, one of the first scientists to probe the connections between mental disease and addiction.

PET Probes

Developing drugs to treat drug addiction has recently become a major research focus at NIDA, amounting to some $36 million in 1990, partly because of the risk of spreading AIDS through intravenous drug use. Although that amount is hardly impressive, especially when compared with the estimated $6.5 billion the U.S. government spent on drug law enforcement and criminal justice last year, NIDA is hop-

ing to catalyze joint research efforts with pharmaceutical companies. Many drugmakers have steered away from developing drugs for the CNS because they believe that neuroscience is too young—and too complex—to translate into products. The CNS field, particularly in the U.S., has been largely the province of venture capitalists, who over the past decade funded several neuroscience start-up companies, including Nova Pharmaceuticals, Athena Neurosciences and Alkermes, Inc.

Now, however, some major drug companies, including Glaxo, Du Pont and Bristol-Myers Squibb, are becoming more interested as NIDA courts them—and as London and others report a wave of findings. "Fifteen years ago we couldn't see any of this," whispered Michael J. Kuhar, chief of neuroscience at NIDA's Addiction Research Center (ARC), during London's presentation at a December 1990 meeting of the American College of Neuropsychopharmacology in San Juan, Puerto Rico.

What London showed with her brightly colored slides was that cocaine caused glucose metabolism to plummet in the cortex (the outer region of the brain) in 16 male cocaine addicts. She also observed that this metabolism fell in the amygdala, which lies in

the mesolimbic system, an inner brain region governing emotion and such drives as hunger, thirst and sex. The lower the metabolic activity, the more the addicts felt the effects of cocaine, London noted. This observation held true for amphetamines, barbituates, benzodiazepines and morphine, she added, but not for marijuana, which caused a surge of glucose metabolism.

On a molecular level, the activity shown in London's PET scans reflects the complex interplay of chemical messengers, called neurotransmitters, that carry nerve impulses from one cell to another. Neurotransmitters travel across a synapse, the junction between two nerve cells, where they bind to proteins—receptors—on the other side, triggering activity in the next cell. Scientists have found that most drugs of abuse interfere with this normal transmission. They have also hypothesized that forms of mental illness, such as schizophrenia and major depression, could be characterized by abnormalities in the neurotransmitter systems.

The discovery of some of these neurotransmitters gave neuroscience a big push in the early 1970s. A team led by Solomon H. Snyder, a neurobiologist at Johns Hopkins University, explored the way narcotics bind to receptors in the brain and discovered an opiate receptor. Snyder, who later founded Nova Pharmaceuticals, presumed that receptors existed to bind with some biologically important chemical. He and two other scientists—John Hughes of Parke-Davis in England and Hans W. Kosterlitz of the University of Aberdeen—discovered within a few months of one another that the body does make its own opiatelike compounds. These neurotransmitters, called endorphins, bind to opioid receptors, producing sensations of pleasure as well as serving to kill pain.

By the mid-1980s a number of other opioid receptors had been identified, and the number of receptors that accept drugs continues to proliferate. For instance, a receptor for marijuana was recently discovered by researchers at the National Institute of Mental Health (NIMH).

The existence of this cannabinoid receptor may mean that there is another, as yet undiscovered, neurotransmitter that normally binds to it. Nicotine also has receptors, which may be identical to those for the neurotransmitter acetylcholine. Alcohol, however, has not been found to bind to any one identified receptor, although it appears to influence many of them.

Cocaine may work differently. Kuhar,

Cocaine and Heroin Use

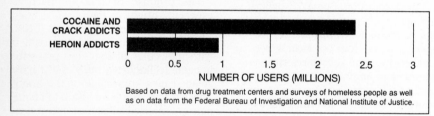

Based on data from drug treatment centers and surveys of homeless people as well as on data from the Federal Bureau of Investigation and National Institute of Justice.

Other Drug Use

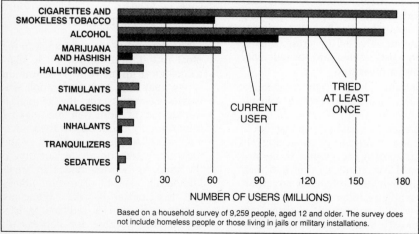

Based on a household survey of 9,259 people, aged 12 and older. The survey does not include homeless people or those living in jails or military installations.

SOURCE: *Senate Judiciary Committee, 1990* (top); *National Institute on Drug Abuse, 1990* (bottom).

Courting the Industry

Drugs to treat addiction are not popular in the pharmaceutical industry. In addition to the challenge and high cost of developing medications for the central nervous system (CNS), many companies worry about what they consider the stigma of addiction. They insist, for example, that buyers of a well-known drug for depression would no longer want to take it if they learned that it was being used to treat cocaine addiction. "It would be the kiss of death," says Salvatore Enna, senior vice president of research at Nova Pharmaceuticals.

As a result, some drugmakers have thwarted investigators seeking treatments for addiction. In one such case, according to a researcher who wished to remain unnamed, a drug was available in Europe. But the European company refused to make animal data available to U.S. researchers, stalling efforts to obtain permission from the Food and Drug Administration to investigate the product as treatment for addiction. Companies "will do everything in their power to stop us from playing with their compounds," comments Thomas R. Kosten, an associate professor of psychiatry and acting co-director of the Substance Abuse Treatment Unit at Yale University.

Stigma is not the only concern. Because addicts are often not paragons of health, companies fear that addicts might develop side effects that would delay approval from the FDA or lead to liability claims. Any "nasty adverse effects in addicts are going to be a problem," concedes Frank J. Vocci, chief of developmental therapeutics in the medications development program at the National Institute on Drug Abuse (NIDA). Says one drug industry executive: "It sounds cruel, but companies are out to make a profit, and society hasn't accepted that addiction is a disease."

Vocci and other government officials hope to change that attitude. In 1988 Congress authorized $10 million to create NIDA's medications development program. To entice the manufacturers, NIDA offered research secrecy agreements and access to the government's medication-screening capabilities and to clinical beds. The FDA has pitched in by promising special attention to medications for drug addiction.

The NIDA approach is based on the successful model of the National Cancer Institute, which many years ago found itself short of cancer treatments and encouraged industry to come in and help. And the effort may be paying off. Last winter NIDA's efforts received a boost from the Pharmaceutical Manufacturers Association (PMA)—representing 100 member companies—which created a commission to encourage members to pursue treatments for addiction. "There is a lot of movement all of a sudden," Vocci notes, adding that NIDA is now working with some 15 companies.

Even so, many industry executives believe Congress will have to become involved before drugmakers devote resources to fighting addiction. Despite NIDA estimates, precise numbers of addicts are difficult to quantify, as is the question of who would seek treatment. "Without legislative incentives, many companies are not going to get involved," admitted an industry executive, who spoke anonymously.

One way to ensure drug companies could cover their development costs would be to give drugs for addiction the same protection granted to orphan drugs, medications developed for rare diseases or small markets. Last year Senator Joseph R. Biden, Jr., of Delaware proposed such legislative incentives, including seven-year marketing exclusivity, but the measures were not enacted into law.

Meanwhile some researchers see European drug manufacturers as a rich source of drugs to test. They say these companies have devoted more money to developing CNS drugs than have those in the U.S. For instance, clozapine, a "new" drug for the treatment of schizophrenia, has been on the market in Europe for at least a decade, according to Donald F. Klein, director of research at the New York State Psychiatric Institute. In a recent survey of 50 European compounds, Klein found 20 of immediate interest for drug abuse and mental illness treatment.

Even if the FDA, NIDA and PMA do their utmost to propel development of CNS medications, drug addiction is clouded with ethical and practical concerns. "If you had the cure today, who would pay for it? How would it be used? It is my understanding that we don't even have enough methadone clinics," comments John W. Kebabian, senior project leader of the pharmaceutical products division at Abbott Laboratories. "It is easier to look at the neurochemical aspects of drug addiction; social issues are more difficult to deal with."

who is using PET to study cocaine addiction, has found that this stimulant interferes with the neurotransmitter dopamine (although it also affects other neurotransmitters and opioid-producing neurons). Cocaine, it turns out, hooks up with a protein called the dopamine reuptake transporter.

The intricacies of dopamine's actions remain unclear, but the neurotransmitter seems to work in part by turning a neuron on and leaving it on, causing feelings of pleasure. It does this until the transporter shuttles it back to its home neuron for storage. Dopamine acts much like a light switch, as Kuhar energetically demonstrates in his ARC office, where a yellow and red PET scan of dopamine receptors, the first of its kind, is proudly displayed. To produce these images, Kuhar and others inject experimental animals with radioactive compounds that bind to the dopamine receptors. When those compounds bind, areas with large numbers of dopamine receptors appear red or yellow. Areas without dopamine receptors appear blue.

Cocaine throws a wrench into the works, according to Kuhar. It hops on board the shuttle, leaving no room for dopamine, which continues to bombard its receptors, causing heightened feelings of pleasure in the drug user. (John D. Elsworth and his colleagues at Yale University reported last year that a new and potentially lethal drug—cocaethylene—formed by cocaine and alcohol together also binds to the transporter.) Kuhar and several other laboratories competing with his are rushing to characterize the transporter.

The Reward Pathway

Understanding the dopamine transporter may provide clues about dopamine itself and, like good counterintelligence, allow researchers to run interference on cocaine's meddling. Such knowledge could also help resolve a controversy over whether dopamine is the critical neurotransmitter responsible for the enjoyable effects of many illicit drugs. Most drugs of abuse are thought to produce good feelings by ultimately acting on the mesolimbic system, which may be one theoretical "reward pathway."

One group of scientists believes that in the end all pleasure comes down to dopamine or the cells with which dopamine communicates. Indeed, the neurotransmitter has been shown to bind to many receptors in the mesolimbic system; neurons producing dopamine make up a significant part of this sys-

tem. Dopamine may also play a role in mental illnesses such as schizophrenia, which has been hypothesized to involve the overactivity of dopamine-producing neurons, and in Parkinson's disease, which is partly the result of a loss of dopamine-producing neurons.

Proposed by Roy A. Wise, a professor of psychiatry at Concordia University, the dopamine theory holds that strongly habit-forming drugs ultimately cause the release of dopamine in a part of the mesolimbic system called the nucleus accumbens. "Behind those opposite effects [of amphetamines and opiates] were very subtle effects that were common," Wise says.

A leading proponent of this dopamine hypothesis is Gaetano Di Chiara of the Institute of Experimental Pharmacology and Toxicology at the University of Cagliari in Italy. Three years ago Di Chiara reported that opiates, alcohol, nicotine, amphetamines and cocaine caused an accumulation of dopamine in the nucleus accumbens. At the recent San Juan meeting, Di Chiara found himself face to face with his nemesis, George F. Koob, a critic of the hypothesis. When Di Chiara made his presentation, some researchers anticipated "blood on the floor."

There was no bloodshed, but no agreement either. Koob, an associate member of the Research Institute of Scripps Clinic in La Jolla, Calif., says he remains committed to his own theory. He holds that dopamine is important but not primary—that many other neurotransmitters are involved. Indeed, "it would be a great oversimplification and disservice to the elegance of the brain to postulate one system," agrees Edward A. Sellers, a professor of pharmacology at the University of Toronto who has tested many compounds for the treatment of alcoholism.

Koob does think, however, that the first step in the pleasure route may involve the nucleus accumbens. But given the elusive nature of the brain, even pinning down the functions of different regions can be hard. Hans C. Fibiger, a neurobiologist at the University of British Columbia in Vancouver, pointed out that participants at the Society for Neuroscience meeting in St. Louis last year said they did not know where the nucleus accumbens started or ended. Nor, for that matter, did they know if it existed at all, Fibiger added with a hint of rascality in his voice.

Even without precise knowledge about a pleasure pathway, or pathways, drug developers know enough about neurotransmitters and receptors to create and evaluate compounds. In-

deed, most medications for the brain on drugstore shelves today operate by modulating one or the other, or both.

Treatments for addiction often seek to block the effects of a drug or the craving for it. Generally, drug-abuse medications take two approaches: agonism or antagonism. In the first strategy the medication binds with the receptor to produce a feeling of satisfaction but with less potential for abuse. Antagonism, in contrast, causes the compound to bind to a receptor blocking the usual neurotransmitter, preventing feelings of pleasure. Some agonists and antagonists being tested in clinical trials and laboratory animals are already on the market [see box on next page].

Methadone, made by Eli Lilly, is the most famous agonist. Addicts can stay on it indefinitely, but if they stop treatment they must weather a withdrawal that lasts twice as long as that from heroin, albeit a milder one. Methadone, unlike heroin, does not disrupt normal hormonal functioning or the body's response to stress, says Mary Jeanne Kreek, an associate professor at the Rockefeller University.

Naltrexone, which is marketed as Trexan by Du Pont, is an antagonist. Because it binds to opioid receptors and can outcompete heroin for these receptors, it is used to counteract heroin overdoses. But as a treatment for overcoming addiction, some researchers think naltrexone is not very effective.

Unmotivated Addicts

"Just blocking the euphoria is not the panacea that some naive individuals think it is," says Frank H. Gawin, an associate professor of clinical psychiatry at the University of California at Los Angeles. Roy W. Pickens, acting director of the ARC, agrees. "People may switch to another drug that is not blocked by these antagonists," he says. Many drug abusers are multiple-drug users, which makes rehabilitation even more complicated.

As a treatment for addiction, naltrexone may be effective only in people who are highly motivated to stay drug free. "It is most successful in those who have a lot to lose because of their addiction," says James W. Cornish, a clinical assistant professor of psychiatry at the University of Pennsylvania. Cornish just completed a study of federal probationers taking naltrexone and found them highly compliant. The reason, he says, is that the results of their weekly urine tests determined the length of their probation.

For those with less incentive, another

approach could improve compliance. A naltrexone implant is being developed, says Frank J. Vocci, chief of developmental therapeutics at NIDA. Both Cornish's results and the potential use of an implant raise the possibility that some successful drug treatment programs could be coercive, says Donald F. Klein, director of research at the New York State Psychiatric Institute. "We have to face that bluntly," he observes.

Naltrexone recently revealed yet another side. In a finding that illustrates the complex interactions among neurotransmitters and reward pathways in the brain, a clinician reported at the San Juan meeting that naltrexone also blocks the craving for alcohol. Charles P. O'Brien, chief of psychiatry at the Veteran's Administration Medical Center in Philadelphia and a professor of psychiatry at the University of Pennsylvania, presented the initial data from a trial he and his colleagues are conducting at the university. Of 52 alcoholics taking naltrexone, the relapse rate was remarkably low—only 8 percent as compared with 48 percent of those taking a placebo. The findings were replicated at Yale University, O'Brien added.

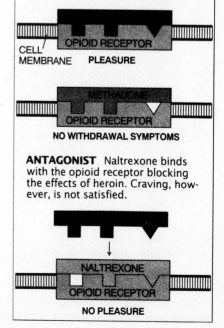

Two Strategies for Drug Design

AGONIST When a narcotic like heroin binds with an opioid receptor, it causes feelings of pleasure—mimicking the natural opioids, the endorphins. Agonists like methadone also bind with the receptor to satisfy craving for an opioid. Methadone prevents withdrawal symptoms.

CELL MEMBRANE | OPIOID RECEPTOR | PLEASURE

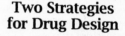

OPIOID RECEPTOR — NO WITHDRAWAL SYMPTOMS

ANTAGONIST Naltrexone binds with the opioid receptor blocking the effects of heroin. Craving, however, is not satisfied.

NALTREXONE / OPIOID RECEPTOR — NO PLEASURE

The naltrexone data compelled E. Leong Way, a professor of pharmacology and toxicology at the University of California at San Francisco, to comment that "if it can be confirmed, this is the most exciting stuff I've heard at the meeting." The source of his incredulity was that the craving for alcohol, for which no specific receptor has been identified, seems to be reduced by an opioid antagonist.

Joseph R. Volpicelli, program director at the University of Pennsylvania's Treatment Research Center, may have an explanation. The common link between alcohol and opiates, he thinks, is that alcohol may cause the release of endogenous opioids like endorphins, and so blocking opioid receptors could block craving.

Stress may also be involved. The body's usual response to stress is fight or flight—which causes the release of opioids. By the time stress has subsided, the body is accustomed to these excess painkillers and wants more. Alcohol therefore could provide a perfect way to medicate oneself. Volpicelli first tested his hypothesis in rats in 1987. But he explains that the connection was historically recognized: morphine was used in the U.S. at the turn of the century to treat alcoholism.

Among the drugs being tested against addiction is one that combines agonism and antagonism. Called buprenorphine, this pain-killing drug was developed by the British company Reckitt and Coleman Products Ltd. and licensed in the U.S. by Norwich Eaton. At low doses it works as an agonist, satisfying the craving for cocaine and heroin. At very high doses, however, it blocks the effects of opiates. "The bad news is that at higher doses it may enhance self-administration of cocaine," says Jack H. Mendelson, a professor of psychiatry and co-director of the Alcohol and Drug Abuse Research Center at McLean Hospital near Boston, who recently completed a study of 12 heroin and cocaine users taking buprenorphine.

In addition to testing these available medications, researchers hope to develop more specific receptor-based therapies for drug addiction. Armed with a growing knowledge of receptors, scientists from industry, academia and the government are working to design ones that have fewer side effects and greater specificity. In particular, such specificity could help treat women and children—the most visible victims of drug scourges—who are often not included in clinical trials. Compounds are being screened that bind with an opioid receptor called delta, says Richard L. Hawks in NIDA's research technology branch. Because fetuses do not have a well-developed delta-receptor system, any medication that could treat the mother by acting on the delta receptors may not endanger the fetus, Hawks explains.

Because of the stigma attached to drug abuse, few companies will discuss their efforts [*see box on page 231*]. But several, including Abbott Laboratories and Schering-Plough, are developing dopamine-receptor blockers that could be effective in treating cocaine addic-

---

Some Medications Being Tested to Treat Addiction

ABBOTT 69024 is a dopamine antagonist that selectively binds with the D1 subclass of receptors. D1 antagonists have been reported to be effective in preventing animals from taking doses of cocaine.

AMANTIDINE, a treatment for Parkinson's disease, has been tested on cocaine abusers. In animals, it seems to cause a release of dopamine; in humans, it is unclear how it works. Results have not been striking.

BUPROPION is an antidepressant that appears to inhibit the uptake of dopamine. In tests at Yale University, it is proving to be fairly effective against the depression that follows cocaine use and addiction.

BUPRENORPHINE, an analgesic, binds to one of the subclasses of opioid receptors called mu receptors. At very high doses it blocks the effects of heroin but may increase craving for cocaine. Low doses may be an effective treatment for both heroin and cocaine craving. It is also being tested in combination with naltrexone for heroin addiction.

BROMOCRIPTINE binds with dopamine receptors and may suppress craving for cocaine. Clinical trials using bromocriptine as a treatment for cocaine addicts who are receiving methadone are planned. Earlier trials found no positive results.

BUSPIRONE, an antianxiety medication, apparently binds with serotonin—another neurotransmitter—receptors and may affect dopamine receptors as well. It has been reported to block cocaine self-administration in animals. It is also being used to treat alcoholics.

CARBAMAZEPINE (Tegretol) is an anticonvulsant that has been shown in animals to prevent "kindling"—the development of seizures that can result from repeated cocaine use. Human trials are under way.

FLUOXETINE (Prozac), an antidepressant, apparently blocks the reuptake of serotonin but not of norepinephrine—another neurotransmitter. It is currently being tested for its usefulness in treating cocaine and alcohol addiction. So far results are not impressive.

FLUPENTHIXOL is a tranquilizer that seems to be a dopamine-receptor blocker. It works primarily on the D2 receptors, with some effects on the D1 receptors. Craving in some cocaine addicts becomes manageable but is not eliminated.

GEPIRONE, an antidepressant, acts on serotonin and dopamine levels—and is very similar to buspirone. It is being tested for its potential in changing drug-seeking behavior as well as for depression and anxiety in cocaine addicts.

LAAM (levo-alpha acetylmethadol) is an experimental treatment for heroin addiction that was developed by German scientists around 1948 as an analgesic. Like methadone, it binds with opioid receptors, but it is longer acting. The drug has not been produced by a company, because it is no longer patentable.

MAZINDOL, an appetite suppressant, seems to act on the limbic system in a manner similar to amphetamines. Because it binds to the dopamine transporter more tightly than cocaine, it has shown some encouraging results in a few cocaine addicts.

NALTREXONE is an opioid antagonist used for the treatment of heroin addiction. It appears to be beneficial in addicts motivated to stay drug free. Recently researchers have found that it is also effective in blocking the effects of alcohol.

SCHERING 23390 is a D1-receptor antagonist being developed for the treatment of schizophrenia. Some researchers are testing it as a way of curtailing cocaine abuse in animals.

tion. (A spokeswoman for Schering-Plough says their compound currently is being developed solely for the treatment of schizophrenia.)

These experimental drugs are aimed at a subclass of dopamine receptors—called D1 receptors—that may be critical in the process by which cocaine becomes addicting. Most medications, such as clozapine, an antipsychotic being used to treat schizophrenics, work on a combination of D1 and another group known as D2 receptors simultaneously, or just on D2s. Abbott has developed an experimental D1-receptor antagonist called A69024, and Schering-Plough has developed another designated 23390.

Those compounds could prove important. Last year William L. Woolverton, an associate professor of pharmacological and physiological sciences and of psychiatry at the University of Chicago, reported that D1 antagonists could prevent monkeys from taking cocaine. "To the best of our knowledge, the pharmacology of cocaine is identical in humans and monkeys," Woolverton notes. Observes Koob: "If you could get a long-acting D1 drug, it would be like methadone for cocaine."

The current focus on neurotransmitters and receptors may turn out to be just a starting point for drug development. "Most people realize that if you just look at the synapse, you are missing a whole world of other signals that act in the brain," says Bruce M. Cohen, a psychiatrist and molecular geneticist at McLean Hospital.

Second Messengers

When a neurotransmitter binds with a receptor, it is like the first domino falling in a series. Only recently have scientists started to understand the intricate details of this cellular response. So-called second messengers, like the second runners in a relay race, pick up where the receptor left off.

One group of second messengers is known as G proteins. Discovered in the past decade by Alfred G. Gilman, a professor of pharmacology at the University of Texas at Dallas, G proteins lie embedded in the cell membrane. They issue instructions when a neurotransmitter binds to a cell-surface receptor. Several G proteins have been found; they are named according to their inhibitory, excitatory or other abilities.

When a narcotic such as morphine binds with a receptor, the shape of the receptor is changed. That change allows the receptor to bind to a G protein. In turn, G proteins can alter the polarity of neurons, triggering the electric impulse that travels along a nerve cell by regulating the passage of ions through the cell membranes. They can also play an indirect role in the expression of genes in the cell by causing proteins to bind with DNA.

Although all medications that act on receptors indirectly affect second messengers, they have been studied in a hit-or-miss fashion, says Steven E. Hyman, a molecular neurobiologist at the Massachusetts General Hospital. That is, they have never been designed to intervene after the receptor-based reaction, although some, like lithium, act only on second messengers. "Drugs could be developed that interfere in this area rather than at the receptor site," says Way, whose work on narcotics elucidated some of the second-messenger changes.

David C. U'Prichard, vice president for biomedical research at ICI Pharmaceuticals Group, and others speculate that modulating the second messengers may offer scientists a way to fine-tune the effects they want to induce in a neuron. Medications could be designed specifically to target receptors that interact with different subclasses of G proteins, offering greater control of the drug's effects. Other treatments could work on autoreceptors—receptors, located on the first neuron, that serve as a thermostat to regulate the release of a neurotransmitter.

Simply intervening in receptor and neurotransmitter systems—even with second messengers—gets at only part of the problem, however. "Something slow happens in the brain. It changes how it responds to a drug," Cohen says, citing the example of antidepressants, which often take several weeks to have an effect.

Using PET to study radioactively labeled dopamine receptors, Nora D. Volcow, associate chief of staff in the medical department at Brookhaven National Laboratory, has documented some of these changes. She found fewer dopamine receptors in cocaine addicts as compared with normal controls. Whether this change is permanent is unclear, but at this point "it is not obvious that the number of receptors goes back to normal," Volcow says.

Volcow's PET findings reflect what clinicians report. When they are not high, cocaine addicts can feel depressed or cannot feel any pleasure (anhedonic). Feeling less pleasure could be the result of there being fewer receptors to receive normal amounts of dopamine. (This idea supports the "self-medication" theory of drug abuse: people take drugs to restore neurochemical abnormalities.) Medications that increase the number of dopamine receptors may therefore be effective in treating anhedonia—and treating anhedonia could keep people from craving cocaine.

Gawin, one of a handful of young researchers working on drug addiction, has tested several antidepressants already on the market to see if they could help cocaine addicts. One compound, flupenthixol, was not available in the U.S., so Gawin set sail for the Bahamas to test a first round of patients several years ago.

The drug, which the addicts nicknamed Fixall, works to make craving manageable but does not eliminate it. "One addict described craving as being two hands grabbing him by the back of the neck and pushing him into the gutter," Gawin relates. After taking flupenthixol, the subject said the craving was "like one hand that is not pushing him so hard." Gawin is now testing flupenthixol in a double-blind trial.

Also hoping to combat craving in addicts, London is ready to study images of glucose metabolism during opiate and cocaine withdrawal. She found that rats going through withdrawal have frenzied glucose activity—as if stopping opiates causes the brain to work overtime. Since some aspect of pleasure seems to be associated with decreased metabolism, the misery of withdrawal may be associated with excess activity. If this proves true in humans, London will test buprenorphine and clonidine, a drug for high blood pressure that binds with opioid receptors, to see if they decrease metabolism. Another researcher, Anna Rose Childress of the University of Pennsylvania, will use PET to examine environmentally induced craving.

To get to the roots of these changes, some investigators believe they must intervene on the genetic level. Recent research by Eric J. Nestler, a molecular psychiatrist at Yale, Hyman at Massachusetts General and Cohen at McLean, among others, has shown that even though genes are not altered, they can be turned on or off by drugs of abuse as well as by medications that work in the brain. Finding out how to turn them on or off could be the key to new treatments. "The technology to look at this has only been available for the past few years," Cohen points out.

Understanding how drugs affect genes may also unlock the secrets of addiction. Scientists still do not know what neurochemical changes lead to tolerance or addiction. Cohen, for one, believes that watching changes in gene

expression can yield a better understanding of reward systems. He views those pathways as based on circuits extending through different brain regions rather than confined to one region. By tracing which genes are turned on by, say, cocaine, he and his colleagues hope to use the drug as a probe. If they can see which genes are activated in which nerve cells, it would highlight the brain circuit where cocaine has its effects.

Changes in a pathway that occur over time—caused by repeated drug use—may underlie addiction. Because of this wiring, "there may be some overlap between the craving, the need for drugs and a shared reward system," Cohen explains. With regard to treatment, finding this circuit could lead to a medication that could combat craving for opioids, cocaine and alcohol—something pharmaceutical companies are ever vigilant for because it could have application for more acceptable cravings as well, including those for nicotine and food. "If we could find the aspirin of the abuse system, we would be in great shape," related Michael Williams, acting area head for neuroscience research at Abbott, to a group of researchers at a recent conference on developing drugs to treat drug addiction.

New evidence indicates that the genes that underlie the dopamine system might be a good starting point. At the meeting in San Juan, Cohen and others presented their findings on gene expression and drug use. Cohen reported that drugs that acted on the rat brain—including cocaine and two for the treatment of schizophrenia—

caused an increase in the production of certain types of messenger RNA (mRNA), a likely sign that genes had been activated.

Cohen determined that in the case of the antipsychotic drugs, the mRNAs led to the synthesis of dopamine receptors and to the activation of two immediate early genes—genes that respond to a stimulus, such as a drug, right away. As is often true, these genes activate other groups of genes. The changes in gene expression varied in both their extent and their location in the brain depending on which drug was used, Cohen observed.

Although scientists have known that drugs could alter the number of dopamine receptors—as Volcow of Brookhaven found in her PET scans—they were not sure how. "But now we know new receptors are being made," Cohen notes, referring to the antipsychotic findings. "We are able to look directly at the gene product, the RNA right off the gene."

Viral Shuttle

The next step, and one that could take years, will be finding ways to alter gene expression or undo the effects of abused drugs on genes. One possibility is to flood cells with RNA that is a mirror image of that produced by the cells. This "antisense" RNA would bind with the cells' mRNA, rendering it unable to transcribe proteins.

Using vectors, or carriers, such as carefully tailored viruses that travel only to neurons, researchers could get

the antisense strands to the right cell. For example, workers at the University of Pittsburgh and Harvard Medical School are using herpes simplex as a shuttle to implant genes into neurons. Such vectors might also introduce regulatory sequences: segments of the DNA that control the transcription of certain genes and proteins.

Such gene regulation is very far off, but "the possibilities are mind-boggling," Cohen asserts. "At some point it becomes like going to the moon. The technology is now beginning to look so powerful that it becomes reasonable to talk about these things." Indeed, several pharmaceutical companies have approached Hyman, who works on regulatory sequences. "Companies are looking for drugs that act on transcription factors," Hyman declares. And they want to "look at changes in gene expression as a biological readout of the neurons that are affected by a compound." That would provide drugmakers with a new way to screen potential drugs for activity in the CNS, he notes.

Still very undecided is the debate over whether genes do in fact contribute to addiction and other mental illnesses. Few question the striking similarities between some mental illnesses and drug abuse—both of which may be characterized by imbalances in neurotransmitters. These alterations can be observed neurochemically as well as behaviorally.

None of these connections, however, has been made genetically, only epidemiologically. A recent study coordinated by Darrel A. Regier, director of

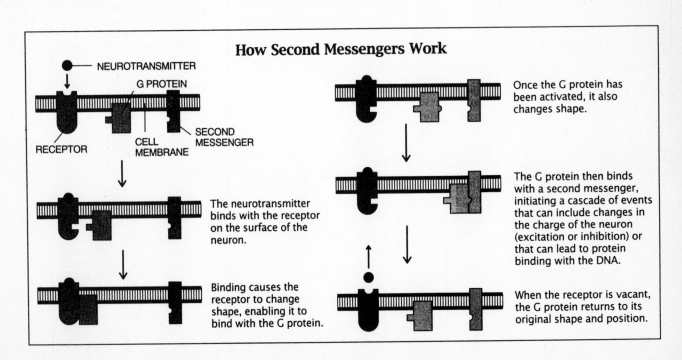

How Second Messengers Work

NEUROTRANSMITTER
G PROTEIN
RECEPTOR
CELL MEMBRANE
SECOND MESSENGER

The neurotransmitter binds with the receptor on the surface of the neuron.

Binding causes the receptor to change shape, enabling it to bind with the G protein.

Once the G protein has been activated, it also changes shape.

The G protein then binds with a second messenger, initiating a cascade of events that can include changes in the charge of the neuron (excitation or inhibition) or that can lead to protein binding with the DNA.

When the receptor is vacant, the G protein returns to its original shape and position.

the division of clinical research at NIMH, looked at 20,291 people from the general community, from mental hospitals and from nursing homes and prisons and found that 53 percent of those who abused drugs had a mental health disorder such as schizophrenia, anxiety or major depression. (The prison population, when taken alone, had nearly a 90 percent overlap.) The study "suggests that one disorder may cause the other or that an underlying biologic vulnerability to these disorders exists in affected individuals," Regier reported.

The effort to locate genes for specific mental illnesses, such as manic depression and schizophrenia, has not yet born fruit, says Elliot S. Gershon, chief of the clinical neurogenetics branch at NIMH, who has been screening chromosomes to find genes that could underlie these disorders for many years. In studies of twins conducted in the early 1980s, Gershon documented a response to amphetamine that was genetically based. He believes that genetics may predispose individuals to drug addiction.

One effort to determine a genetic component to drug abuse has focused on alcoholics. The research remains highly controversial. A team led by Kenneth Blum of the University of Texas Health Sciences Center at San Antonio reported last year an association between alcoholism and a gene that encoded a dopamine receptor. Later that year David Goldman, chief of genetic studies at the National Institute on Alcohol Abuse and Alcoholism reported finding no such association. But Blum was looking at cadavers while Goldman was studying living alcoholics, so the issue is far from resolved.

Although most researchers agree that alcoholism has some hereditary component, linking it to a specific gene is difficult. In an as yet unpublished study of twins, Pickens of the ARC concluded that heredity was responsible for between 20 and 30 percent of the risk for alcoholism (although the genetic influence was greater in certain subtypes of alcoholism). "The literature is so murky, and this is the first study that uses a standard genetic approach," comments George Uhl, a molecular geneticist at the ARC who is working to clone the dopamine transporter.

While they wait for the laboratories to produce medications based on receptors, second messengers or even gene expression, clinicians are struggling to treat the myriad problems of addicts. By easing some side effects of addiction—or some associated mental disorders—they can relieve pain. "It is simplistic to think of these drugs as being curative," points out O'Brien of the University of Pennsylvania, whose sentiments are echoed by nearly every researcher in the field. Treatment must work in concert with counseling, changes in daily activities and help with housing and employment. "Our best hope is to find medications that will treat the biological changes produced by abusing drugs," he adds.

But shortages of treatment programs as well as staff impair clinicians' ability to provide good care to everyone who needs and wants it. Compounding the shortage is the fact that no one is clamoring for a methadone clinic or its equivalent to be set up in his or her neighborhood. Few pharmaceutical companies are pushing back the frontiers of science in order to lock up the addict market. "Despite the hype—and that's what it has been, hype—of the

war on drugs, the addict on the street is getting less treatment money than he was in 1971," O'Brien notes.

Perhaps the loudest objection is philosophical: drugs to treat addiction just perpetuate dependency, an emotional weakness. "We have the simple notion that we can solve drug addiction by fixing bad chemistry with better chemistry," says Lester Grinspoon, an associate professor of psychiatry at Harvard Medical School.

Some drug abusers also worry about becoming addicted to another substance, even if it is a medication. Margaret Catrambone, a middle-aged administrator who started drinking when she was a teenager, only reluctantly entered the naltrexone clinical trial at the University of Pennsylvania. "I thought, 'This can't work, this pill can't take away the craving,' " Catrambone remembers. But after three months, she says she did not feel the craving. "It enabled me to see how I could be sober and change my life." Catrambone now takes the medication only if a difficult time is approaching—like the holidays. "I do not feel dependent on naltrexone, and I was very much afraid of that."

Clearly, many clinicians agree that medications may be able to help addicts get their lives in order. "I don't fully understand the philosophical objections," says Stephen Magura, deputy director of research at Narcotic and Drug Research, Inc., in New York City. "Drug abuse is an illness. If a medication would help an addict, why would you withhold it? For your own benefit or for the addict's benefit?" But until the drugs are developed—and until all the addicts that wish to be treated can be accommodated—that question is moot.

Glossary

This glossary of 185 drug terms is included to provide you with a convenient and ready reference as you encounter general terms in your study of drugs and drug and alcohol abuse that are unfamiliar, technical, or require a review. It is not intended to be comprehensive, but, taken together with the many definitions included in the articles themselves, it should prove to be useful.

Absorption   The passage of chemical compounds, such as drugs or nutrients, into the bloodstream through the skin, intestinal lining, or other bodily membranes.

Acetylcholine   A cholinergic transmitter that forms salts used to lower blood pressure and increases peristalsis, and thought to be involved in the inhibition of behavior.

Addiction   Chronic, compulsive, or uncontrollable behavior.

Adrenergic System   The group of transmitters, including epinephrine, norepinephrine, and dopamine, that activates the sympathetic nervous system.

Alcohol Abuse   *See* Alcoholism.

Alcoholics Anonymous (AA)   A voluntary fellowship founded in 1935 and concerned with the recovery and continued sobriety of the alcoholic members who turn to the organization for help. The AA program consists basically of "Twelve Suggested Steps" designed for the personal recovery from alcoholism, and AA is the major proponent of the disease model of alcoholism.

Alcoholism   Any use of alcoholic beverages that causes damage to the individual or to society. *See also* Disease Model.

Amphetamines   A class of drugs, similar in some ways to the body's own adrenaline (epinephrine), that act as stimulants to the central nervous system.

Analgesics   Drugs that relieve pain.

Anesthetics   Drugs that abolish the sensation of pain, often used during surgery.

Angel Dust   Slang term for phencyclidine.

Anorectic   A drug that decreases appetite.

Antagonist Programs   Drug treatment programs that use antagonist agents, like naltrexone (antagonist of heroin) or antabuse (used in treating alcoholism), to block the effect of drugs on the body.

Antianxiety Tranquilizers   Tranquilizers, like Valium and Librium, used to relieve anxiety and tension, sometimes called minor tranquilizers.

Anticholinergics   Drugs that block the transmission of impulses in the parasympathetic nerves.

Antidepressants   Drugs that relieve mental depression. *See also* Depression, Mental

Antihistamines   Drugs that relieve allergy or cold symptoms by blocking the effects of histamine production.

Antipsychotic Tranquilizers   Drugs used to treat psychosis; include Thorazine (chlorpromazine). Also called major tranquilizers or neuroleptics. *See also* Tranquilizers.

Atropine   An alkaloid derivative of the belladonna and related plants that blocks responses to parasympathetic stimulation.

Autonomic Nervous System (ANS)   That part of the nervous system that regulates involuntary action, such as heartbeat; consists of the sympathetic and parasympathetic nervous systems.

Axon   The core of the nerve fiber that conducts impulses away from the nerve cell to the neurons and other tissue.

Barbiturates   Drugs used for sedation and to relieve tension and anxiety.

Binding   The attachment of a transmitter to its appropriate receptor site.

Blood Level   The concentration of alcohol in the blood, usually expressed in percent by weight.

Caffeine   An alkaloid found in coffee, tea, and kola nuts, that acts as a stimulant.

Caffeinism   Dependence on caffeine.

Cannabis   *See* Marijuana.

Capsule   A container, usually of gelatin, that encloses a dose of an oral medicine.

Central Nervous System (CNS)   The brain and spinal cord.

Chewing Tobacco   A form of tobacco leaves, sometimes mixed with molasses, that is chewed.

Chlorpromazine   An antianxiety tranquilizer, manufactured under the name of Thorazine, used for treating severe psychoses. Also used as an antagonist to LSD panic reactions.

Choline   A transmitter, part of the cholinergic system.

Cholinergic System   Group of transmitters that activate the parasympathetic nervous system.

Cocaine   A white crystaline narcotic alkaloid derived from the coca plant and used as a surface anesthetic and a stimulant.

Codeine   A narcotic alkaloid found in opium, most often used as an analgesic or cough suppressant.

Coke   Slang term for cocaine.

Cold Turkey   Slang expression for abrupt and complete withdrawal from drugs or alcohol without medication.

Compulsive Drug Use   Drug use that is frequent, with intensive levels of long duration, producing physiological or psychological dependence.

Constriction   Narrowing or shrinking.

Contraindication   A condition that makes it inadvisable or hazardous to use a particular drug or medicine.

Controlled Drinking   Moderate drinking by recovered alcoholics, discouraged by AA.

Controlled Drug Use   Use of drugs over a period of time without abusing them.

Controlled Substances   All psychoactive substances covered by laws regulating their sale and possession.

Controlled Substances Act of 1970   Federal act that classifies controlled substances into five categories and regulates their use. Schedule I drugs are those most strictly controlled, and include heroin, marijuana, LSD, and other drugs believed to have high abuse potential. Schedule II drugs are also strictly controlled but have some medicinal uses. These drugs include morphine, methadone, and amphetamines. Schedule III, IV, and V substances include drugs that have increasingly less abuse potential. Over-the-counter medicines not subject to any refill regulations fall into Schedule V.

Craving   Refers to both physical and psychological dependence; a strong desire or need for a substance.

Crisis Intervention   The process of diagnosing a drug crisis situation and acting immediately to arrest the condition.

Decriminalization   The legal process by which the possession of a certain drug would become a civil penalty instead of a criminal penalty. *See also* Legalization.

Deliriants   Substances, like some inhalants, that produce delirium.

Delirium   State of temporary mental confusion and diminished consciousness, characterized by anxiety, hallucinations, and delusions.

Dendrite   The part of the nerve cell that transmits impulses to the cell body.

Dependence, Drug   A physical or psychological dependence on a particular drug resulting from continued use of that drug.

Dependence, Physical   The physical need of the body for a particular substance such that abstinence from the substance leads to physical withdrawal symptoms. *See also* Addiction; Withdrawal Syndrome.

Dependence, Psychological   A psychological or emotional reliance on a particular substance; a strong and continued craving.

Depression, Mental   The state of mind that ranges from mild sadness to deep despair, often accompanied by a general feeling of hopelessness.

Detoxification   Removal of a poisonous substance, such as a drug or alcohol, from the body.

Dilation   Widening or enlargement.

Disease Model   A theory of alcoholism, endorsed by AA, in which the alcoholism is seen as a disease rather than a psychological or social problem.

DMT   Dimethyltryptamine, a psychedelic drug.

DNA   Deoxyribonucleic acid, the carrier of chromosomes in the cell.

Dopamine   An indoleaminergic transmitter necessary for normal nerve activity.

Downers   Slang term for drugs that act to depress the central nervous system.

Drug   Any substance that alters the structure or function of a living organism.

Drug Abuse   Use of a drug to the extent that it is excessive, hazardous, or undesirable to the individual or the community.

Drug Misuse   Use of a drug for any purpose other than that for which it is medically prescribed.

Drug Paraphernalia   Materials, like hypodermic syringes, that are used for the preparation or administration of illicit drugs.

Drunkenness   The state of being under the influence of alcohol such that mental and physical faculties are impaired; severe intoxication.

DWI   Driving while intoxicated.

Dysphoria   Emotional state characterized by anxiety, depression, and restlessness, as opposed to euphoria.

Ecstasy   A derivative of nutmeg or sassafras, causing euphoria and sometimes hallucinations; also known as XTC, Adam, or MDMA.

Endorphins   Any group of hormones released by the brain that have painkilling and tranquilizing abilities.

Epinephrine   An adrenal hormone that acts as a transmitter and stimulates autonomic nerve action.

Ethical Drugs   Drugs dispensed by prescription only.

Euphoria   Exaggerated sense of happiness or well-being.

Experimental Drug Use   According to the U.S. National Commission on Marijuana and Drug Abuse, the short-term non-patterned trial of one or more drugs, either concurrently or consecutively, with variable intensity but maximum frequency of ten times per drug.

Fetal Alcohol Syndrome (FAS)   A pattern of birth defects, cardiac abnormalities, and developmental retardation seen in babies of alcoholic mothers.

Flashback   A spontaneous and involuntary recurrence of psychedelic drug effects after the initial drug experience.

Food and Drug Administration (FDA)   Agency of the U.S. Department of Health and Human Services that administers federal laws regarding the purity of food, the safety and effectiveness of drugs, and the safety of cosmetics.

Habituation   Chronic or continuous use of a drug, with an attachment less severe than addiction.

Hallucination   A sensory perception without external stimuli.

Hallucinogen   Or, hallucinogenic drugs. Drugs that cause hallucinations. Also known as psychedelic drugs.

Harrison Narcotics Act   Federal act passed in 1914 that controlled the sale and possession of prescription drugs, heroin, opium, and cocaine.

Hash Oil   An oily extract of the marijuana plant, containing high levels of THC.

Hashish   The dried resin of the marijuana plant, often smoked in water pipes.

Herb   Commonly, any one of various aromatic plants used for medical or other purposes.

Heroin   Diacetylmorphine hydrochloride, an opiate derivative of morphine.

High   Intoxicated by a drug or alcohol; the state of being high.

Illicit Drugs   Drugs whose use, possession, or sale is illegal.

Illusion   A distorted or mistaken perception.

Indole   An indoleaminergic transmitter.

Indoleaminergic System   A system of neurotransmitters, including indole and serotonin.

Inebriation   The state of being drunk or habitually drunk.

Intoxication   Medically, the state of being poisoned. Usually refers to the state of being drunk, falling between drunkenness and a mild high.

Involuntary Smoking   Involuntary inhalation of the cigarette smoke of others.

Ketamin   A general anesthetic, also used as a deliriant.

Legalization   The movement to have the sale or possession of certain illicit drugs made legal.

LSD   Lysergic acid diethylamide-25, a hallucinogen.

Maintenance Treatment   Treatment of drug dependence by a small dosage of the drug or another drug, such as methadone, that will prevent withdrawal symptoms.

Marijuana   The dried leaves of the cannabis plant, usually smoked and resulting in feelings of well-being, relaxation, or euphoria. Also spelled: Marihuana.

MDMA   *See* Ecstasy.

Medical Model   A theory of drug abuse or addiction in which the addiction is seen as a medical, rather than a social, problem.

Medicine   A drug used to treat disease or injury; medication.

Mescaline   A hallucinogenic alkaloid drug, either derived from the peyote plant or made synthetically.

Metabolism   The set of physical and chemical processes involved in the maintenance of life; or, the functioning of a particular substance in the body.

Methadone   A synthetic opiate sometimes used to treat heroin or morphine addiction. *See also* Maintenance Treatment.

Methaqualone   A non-barbiturate sedative/hypnotic drug, used to bring on feelings of muscular relaxation, contentment, and passivity. Also known as Quaaludes.

Morphine   An organic compound extracted from opium, a light anesthetic or sedative.

Multimodality Programs   Programs for the treatment of drug abuse or alcoholism involving several simultaneous treatment methods.

Multiprescribing The situation in which a person is taking more than one prescription or over-the-counter drug simultaneously.

Narcotic Any drug that dulls a person's senses and produces a sense of well-being in smaller doses, and insensibility, sometimes even death, in larger doses.

Nervous System In human beings, the brain, spinal cord, and nerves. *See also* Somatic Nervous System; Autonomic Nervous System.

Neuroleptic Any major, or antipsychotic, tranquilizer.

Neuron The basic element responsible for the reception, transmission, and processing of sensory, motor, and other information of physiological or psychological importance to the individual.

Neurotransmitter *See* Transmitter.

Nicotine The main active ingredient of tobacco, extremely toxic and causing irritation of lung tissues, constriction of blood vessels, increased blood pressure and heart rate, and, in general, central nervous system stimulation.

Norepinephrine Hormone found in the sympathetic nerve endings that acts as an adrenergic transmitter and is a vasoconstrictor.

Opiate Narcotics A major subclass of drugs that act as pain relievers as well as central nervous system depressants; includes opium, morphine, codeine, and methadone.

Opiates The drugs derived from opium—morphine and codeine—as well as those derived from them, such as heroin.

Opium Narcotic derivative of the poppy plant that acts as an analgesic.

Opoids The group of synthetic drugs, including Demerol and Darvon, that resemble the opiates in action and effect.

Overmedication The prescription and use of more medication than necessary to treat a specific illness or condition.

Over-the-Counter Drugs Drugs legally sold without a prescription.

Parasympathetic Nervous System The part of the autonomic nervous system that inhibits or opposes the actions of the sympathetic nerves.

Parasympathomimetics Drugs that produce effects similar to those of the parasympathetic nervous system.

Parkinson's Disease A progressive disease of the nervous system characterized by muscular tremor, slowing of movement, partial facial paralysis, and general weakness.

Patent Medicines Drugs or other medications protected by a patent and sold over the counter.

Peristalsis Wave-like muscular contractions that help move matter through the tubular organs (e.g., intestines).

Phencyclidine (PCP) A synthetic depressant drug used as a veterinary anesthetic and illegally as a hallucinogen. Also known as angel dust.

Placebo An inactive substance used as a control in an experiment.

Placenta The membranous organ that develops in the uterus of a pregnant female mammal to nourish the fetus. Though the fetus and mother are thus separated, drugs and alcohol are often still able to reach the developing fetus.

Polyabuse Abuse of various drugs simultaneously.

Pot Slang term for marijuana.

Potency Term used to compare the relative strength of two or more drugs used to produce a given effect.

Prescription Drugs Drugs dispensed only by a physician's prescription.

Primary Prevention Efforts designed to prevent a person from starting to use drugs.

Proprietary Drugs Patent medicines.

Psilocybin A hallucinogenic alkaloid, found in various types of mushrooms, chemically related to LSD.

Psychedelic Drugs Hallucinogens.

Psychoactive Any drug that can cause alterations in the user's mood or behavior.

Psychopharmacology The study of the effects of drugs on mood, sensation, or consciousness, or other psychological or behavioral functions.

Psychosis Severe mental disorder, characterized by withdrawal from reality and deterioration of normal intellectual and social functioning.

Psychotherapeutic Drugs Drugs that are used as medicines to alleviate psychological disorders.

Psychotomimetics Drugs that produce psychosis-like effects.

Receptors The input organs for the nervous system.

Recidivism Return to former behavior.

Recombinant DNA DNA prepared in the laboratory by the transfer or exchange of individual genes from one organism to another.

Recreational Drug Use Drug use that takes place in social settings among friends who want to share a pleasant experience; characterized by less frequency and intensity than addictive drug use. Also called social-recreational drug use.

Rehabilitation Restoration of a person's ability to function normally.

Reinforcement A stimulus that increases the probability that a desired response will occur.

Rush Slang term for an immediate feeling of physical well-being and euphoria after the administration of a drug.

Schedules Categories of drugs as defined in the Controlled Substances Act of 1970.

Schizophrenia A psychosis characterized by withdrawal from reality accompanied by affective, behavioral, and intellectual disturbances.

Scopolamine Poisonous alkaloid found in the roots of various plants, used as a truth serum or with morphine as a sedative.

Secondary Prevention Early treatment of drug abuse to prevent it from becoming more severe.

Sedative/Hypnotics Class of non-narcotic depressant drugs that calm, sedate, or induce hypnosis or sleep. Sedative/hypnotics are divided into four categories: barbiturates, alcohol, antianxiety tranquilizers (minor tranquilizers), and nonbarbiturate proprietary drugs.

Serotonin An indoleaminergic transmitter found in the blood serum, cells, and central nervous system, that acts as a vasoconstrictor.

Set The combination of physical, mental, and emotional characteristics of an individual at the time a drug is administered.

Setting The external environment of an individual at the time a drug is administered.

Side Effects Secondary effects, usually undesirable, of a drug or therapy.

Snuff A preparation of pulverized tobacco that is inhaled into the nostrils.

Sobriety The quality of being free from alcohol intoxication.

Social-Recreational Drug Use *See* Recreational Drug Use.

Socioeconomic Both social and economic.

Somatic Nervous System That part of the nervous system that deals with the senses and voluntary muscles.

Somatic Nervous System That part of the nervous system that deals with the senses and voluntary muscles.

Speed Slang term for methamphetamine, a central nervous system stimulant.

Stereospecificity The matching of both electrical and chemical characteristics of the transmitter and receptor site so that binding can take place.

Stimulants A major class of drugs that stimulate the central nervous system, causing mood elevation, increased mental and physical activity, alertness, and appetite suppression. Primary stimulants include the amphetamines and cocaine. Secondary stimulants include nicotine and caffeine.

STP Early slang term for phencyclidine.

Subcutaneous Beneath the skin.

Substance Abuse Refers to overeating, cigarette smoking, alcohol abuse, or drug abuse.

Sympathetic Nervous System That part of the autonomic nervous system that acts to release sugars from the liver, slow digestion, and increase heart and breathing rates.

Sympathomimetic Any drug that produces effects like those resulting from stimulation of the sympathetic nervous system.

Synapse The space, or gap, between two neurons.

Tars The dark, oily, viscid substances created by burning tobacco, known to contain carcinogenic agents.

Temperance The practice of moderation, especially with regard to alcohol consumption. The Temperance Movement was a popular movement in the nineteenth and twentieth centuries to restrict or prohibit the use of alcoholic beverages.

Tertiary Prevention Treatment to prevent the permanent disability or death of a drug abuser.

THC Tetrahydrocannabinol, a psychoactive derivative of the cannabis plant.

Therapeutic Community Setting in which persons with similar problems meet and provide mutual support to help overcome those problems.

Titration The ability to determine desired drug dosage.

Tolerance The capacity to absorb a drug continuously or in large doses with no adverse effect.

Trance Dazed or hypnotic state.

Tranquilizers Drugs that depress the central nervous system, thus relieving anxiety and tension and sometimes relaxing the muscles, divided into the major tranquilizers, or antipsychotics, and minor tranquilizers, or antianxiety tranquilizers. *See also* Antianxiety Tranquilizers; Antipsychotic Tranquilizers.

Transmitters Also known as neurotransmitters. Any substance that aids in transmitting impulses between a nerve and a muscle. Three known categories of transmitters are the cholinergic system, adrenergic system, and indoleaminergic system.

Treatment Drug treatment programs can be drug-free or maintenance, residential or ambulatory, medical or nonmedical, voluntary or involuntary, or some combination of these.

Uppers Slang term for amphetamines, and, sometimes, cocaine.

Withdrawal Syndrome The group of reactions or behavior that follows abrupt cessation of the use of a drug upon which the body has become dependent. May include anxiety, insomnia, perspiration, hot flashes, nausea, dehydration, tremor, weakness, dizziness, convulsions, and psychotic behavior.

Credits/ Acknowledgments

Cover design by Charles Vitelli

1. Thinking About Drugs
Facing overview—EPA Documerica. 13—Yale Medical School Library. 15—American Institute of Pharmacy, University of Wisconsin-Madison. 17—Randy Santos, Randolph Photographer. 18—Time Warner, Inc. © 1981, 1986.

2. Use, Addiction, and Dependence
Facing overview—United Nations photo by John Isaac.

3. Why Drugs?
Facing overview—WHO photo by E. Mandelmann and S. Bojar.

4. Patterns and Trends in Drug Use
Facing overview—United Nations photo.

5. Major Drugs of Use and Abuse
Facing overview—United Nations photo by John Robaton.

6. Impact of Drug Use on Society
Facing overview—United Nations photo by P. S. Sudhakaran. 140-141, 143—Courtesy Children of Alcoholics Foundation.

7. Economy of Drug Use
Facing overview—The Dushkin Publishing Group photo by Pamela Carley Petersen.

8. Fighting the Drug War
Facing overview—United Nations photo by Y. Nagata.

9. Drug Prevention and Treatment
Facing overview—WHO photo by Jean Mohr.

ANNUAL EDITIONS ARTICLE REVIEW FORM

■ NAME: _____ DATE: _____

■ TITLE AND NUMBER OF ARTICLE: _____

■ BRIEFLY STATE THE MAIN IDEA OF THIS ARTICLE: _____

_____

_____

_____

_____

■ LIST THREE IMPORTANT FACTS THAT THE AUTHOR USES TO SUPPORT THE MAIN IDEA:

_____

_____

_____

_____

_____

_____

■ WHAT INFORMATION OR IDEAS DISCUSSED IN THIS ARTICLE ARE ALSO DISCUSSED IN YOUR
TEXTBOOK OR OTHER READING YOU HAVE DONE? LIST THE TEXTBOOK CHAPTERS AND PAGE
NUMBERS:

_____

_____

_____

_____

_____

_____

_____

■ LIST ANY EXAMPLES OF BIAS OR FAULTY REASONING THAT YOU FOUND IN THE ARTICLE:

_____

_____

_____

_____

_____

■ LIST ANY NEW TERMS/CONCEPTS THAT WERE DISCUSSED IN THE ARTICLE AND WRITE A
SHORT DEFINITION:

_____

_____

_____

_____

_____

*Your instructor may require you to use this Annual Editions Article Review Form in any number of ways:
for articles that are assigned, for extra credit, as a tool to assist in developing assigned papers, or simply
for your own reference. Even if it is not required, we encourage you to photocopy and use this page;
you'll find that reflecting on the articles will greatly enhance the information from your text.

Unit 8

Fighting the Drug War

Six articles in this section examine the current state of
the war on drug usage. Topics include today's drug
scene, new programs to combat drugs, and drug
legalization.

Unit 6

The Impact of Drug Use on Society

Five selections in this section discuss how drugs have devastated some portions of our society.

Unit 7

The Economy of Drug Use

Six selections in this section discuss the enormous driving economic force behind the marketing of both legal and illegal drugs.

Unit 5

The Major Drugs of Use and Abuse

Eight articles in this section examine some of the major drugs in use today. The drugs discussed include cocaine, crack, methamphetamine (speed, crank, or "ice"), marijuana, prescription drugs, alcohol, and heroin.

The concepts in bold italics are developed in the article. For further expansion please refer to the Topic Guide, the Index, and the Glossary.

Unit 4

Patterns and Trends in Drug Use

Four articles in this section discuss the divergent patterns in the use of drugs as they lose and gain popularity.

Unit 3

Why Drugs?

Six articles in this section discuss how and why individuals get "hooked" on drugs.

The concepts in bold italics are developed in the article. For further expansion please refer to the Topic Guide, the Index, and the Glossary.

Contents

Unit 1

Thinking About Drugs

Six articles in this section examine how drugs are defined today. The history of drugs in our culture is also discussed.

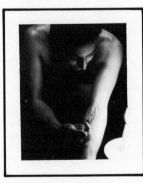

Unit 2

Use, Addiction, and Dependence

Six selections in this section discuss what is meant by drug addiction. Topics examined include physical dependency and drugs such as crack, alcohol, and nicotine.

The concepts in bold italics are developed in the article. For further expansion please refer to the Topic Guide, the Index, and the Glossary.

To the Reader

In publishing ANNUAL EDITIONS we recognize the enormous role played by the magazines, newspapers, and journals of the *public press* in providing current, first-rate educational information in a broad spectrum of interest areas. Within the articles, the best scientists, practitioners, researchers, and commentators draw issues into new perspective as accepted theories and viewpoints are called into account by new events, recent discoveries change old facts, and fresh debate breaks out over important controversies.

Many of the articles resulting from this enormous editorial effort are appropriate for students, researchers, and professionals seeking accurate, current material to help bridge the gap between principles and theories and the real world. These articles, however, become more useful for study when those of lasting value are carefully *collected, organized, indexed,* and *reproduced* in a *low-cost format*, which provides easy and permanent access when the material is needed. That is the role played by *Annual Editions.* Under the direction of each volume's *Editor,* who is an expert in the subject area, and with the guidance of an *Advisory Board,* we seek each year to provide in each *ANNUAL EDITION* a current, well-balanced, carefully selected collection of the best of the public press for your study and enjoyment. We think you'll find this volume useful, and we hope you'll take a moment to let us know what you think.

Interest in and concern about drug use comes in cycles. In some decades, there is relatively little concern about the issue; people rarely talk about drugs, few articles are written about their use in newspapers and magazines, little drug activity is reported in the broadcast media, and hardly anyone considers drug abuse the most important social problem facing the country. In other decades, drug use emerges as a central social issue; it provides a major topic of conversation, the newspapers, magazines, and broadcast media are filled with news and commentary on the subject, and a substantial proportion of the population regards drug abuse the number-one problem that the country faces.

In the mid-1980s, public concern over drug abuse fairly exploded. While this concern declined as a result of the Gulf crisis and war, and later the economic recession, it remains, relative to many pressing issues, fairly high. In many quarters, our society is intensely concerned about the problem of drug use and abuse, and among some, this concern borders on being a kind of hysteria or panic. Is this panic justified? Are drugs as central a problem as much of the public believes? What are drugs in the first place? What short-term effects do they have? How do they affect the individual and the society over the long run? How should we deal with drugs and drug abuse? The articles included in *Annual Editions: Drugs, Society, and Behavior 92/93* represent a sampling of current thinking on the subject of drug use. The selections are intended to be thought-provoking and informative. I hope that reading them will help the student meet the challenge that drug use poses and permit him or her to reach reasonable, well-informed conclusions on this troubling issue.

Unit 1 is designed to provide the student with a general framework toward drugs; it makes four basic points. First, our society tolerates certain (legal) drugs, and is concerned about other (that is, illegal) drugs. Second, drug use has a long history, both around the world generally and in this society specifically. Third, illegal drug use generates a worldwide structure or network of sellers that makes use extremely difficult to eradicate, but it is the consumer, ultimately, on which this enterprise is based. And fourth, all drug use is a sociological or anthropological phenomenon that has to be understood before the problem can be attacked. Unit 2 emphasizes the fact that drug use and abuse—or physical dependence—form a continuum or spectrum. Too often, many of us assume that if someone is a user of a given (usually illegal) drug, he or she is chemically dependent, indeed, high nearly all the time. Unit 2 shows that users come in all degrees of involvement, from experimenters to heavy, chronic, dependent abusers. Unit 3 explores a variety of explanations for drug use: Why do people use and abuse drugs? Why do *some* people use certain drugs—while the rest of us do not? In short, *why drugs?* Unit 4 demonstrates that drug use is highly patterned and variable over time and according to social characteristics. Who uses? Who does not? What are some basic recent *trends* in drug use?

Unit 5 emphasizes the fact that drugs are not unitary phenomena, but can be classified according to type. Too often we refer to drugs—illegal drugs, that is—in a generic fashion, as if they all had identical or extremely similar effects. This is false; in fact, certain drugs do certain things to us, others do very different things. Unit 6 looks at the impact of drugs on the society over the long run. Unit 7 focuses on an extremely crucial aspect of drug use: buying and selling. Drug consumption is an economic enterprise, and that fact influences many features of the drug scene. Why? How? In what specific ways? Unit 8 looks at how our society is attacking the problem of drug abuse, what is wrong with what we are doing, and what should be done about it. Is legalization a viable option? Several observers support this option, while others do not. And finally, Unit 9 deals with how drug abusers and the people they hurt can be treated, and what educational programs are effective in convincing young people to avoid becoming involved in the first place.

Erich Goode
Editor

Editors/ Advisory Board

The Annual Editions Series

Annual Editions is a series of over 55 volumes designed to provide the reader with convenient, low-cost access to a wide range of current, carefully selected articles from some of the most important magazines, newspapers, and journals published today. Annual Editions are updated on an annual basis through a continuous monitoring of over 300 periodical sources. All Annual Editions have a number of features designed to make them particularly useful, including topic guides, annotated tables of contents, unit overviews, and indexes. For the teacher using Annual Editions in the classroom, an Instructor's Resource Guide with test questions is available for each volume.

VOLUMES AVAILABLE

Africa
Aging
American Government
American History, Pre-Civil War
American History, Post-Civil War
Anthropology
Biology
Business and Management
Business Ethics
Canadian Politics
China
Commonwealth of Independent States and Central/Eastern Europe (Soviet Union)
Comparative Politics
Computers in Education
Computers in Business
Computers in Society
Criminal Justice
Drugs, Society, and Behavior
Early Childhood Education
Economics
Educating Exceptional Children
Education
Educational Psychology
Environment
Geography
Global Issues
Health
Human Development
Human Resources
Human Sexuality

International Business
Japan
Latin America
Life Management
Macroeconomics
Management
Marketing
Marriage and Family
Microeconomics
Middle East and the Islamic World
Money and Banking
Nutrition
Personal Growth and Behavior
Physical Anthropology
Psychology
Public Administration
Race and Ethnic Relations
Social Problems
Sociology
State and Local Government
Third World
Urban Society
Violence and Terrorism
Western Civilization, Pre-Reformation
Western Civilization, Post-Reformation
Western Europe
World History, Pre-Modern
World History, Modern
World Politics

Library of Congress Cataloging in Publication Data
Main entry under title: Annual Editions: Drugs, Society, and Behavior. 1992/93.
    1. Drugs—Periodicals. 2. Drug abuse—United States—Periodicals. 3. Alcohol—Periodicals. 4. Drunk driving—Periodicals. I. Goode, Erich, comp. II. Title: Drugs, Society, and Behavior.
ISBN 1-56134-083-9   362.2′92′0973′05

Seventh Edition

Manufactured by The Banta Company, Harrisonburg, Virginia 22801

DRUGS, SOCIETY, AND BEHAVIOR 92/93

Seventh Edition

Editor

Erich Goode
State University of New York at Stony Brook

Erich Goode received his undergraduate degree from Oberlin College and his Ph.D. in sociology from Columbia University. He is currently professor of sociology at the State University of New York at Stony Brook; he has also taught courses at Columbia, New York University, Florida Atlantic University, and the University of North Carolina, Chapel Hill. He is the author of a number of books, articles, and chapters on drug use and abuse, including *The Marijuana Smokers* (Basic Books, 1970), *The Drug Phenomenon* (Bobbs-Merrill, 1973), and *Drugs in American Society* (3rd edition, McGraw-Hill, 1989). Professor Goode has taught several courses on alcoholism and drug abuse.

Annual Editions
A Library of Information from the Public Press

Cover illustration by Mike Eagle

The Dushkin Publishing Group, Inc.
Sluice Dock, Guilford, Connecticut 06437